AN INTRODUCTION TO HUMAN RESOURCE MANAGEMENT

An Introduction to Human Resource Management is an ideal text for those studying human resource management for the first time. This straightforward and accessible book takes the reader through both theoretical and practical aspects of the subject and is designed to be used concurrently with semester-based teaching. The range and nature of HR work is illustrated by a combination of real-life case studies and examples of current research that will heighten awareness of the key issues involved in HR today.

All fundamental issues within contemporary HRM are covered in this text including: employee relations, performance management, equal opportunities, learning and development, health and safety, with an entire chapter devoted to international HRM.

This updated third edition is an indispensable resource for students looking for a solid foundation in the principles of HRM. To help with revision, understanding and application, there are additional online resources including extra case studies and quizzes.

New to this edition:

- New activities throughout to reflect on chapter learning
- Contemporary case studies to help put theory into practice
- Extra online testing material to aid revision of HRM principles
- Online annotated further reading guide to help students read around the text and further their research.

John Stredwick is a writer and consultant in human resources, specialising in reward and flexible working practices. He spent 25 years as an HR practitioner, including experience in publishing, shipbuilding and building services with 11 years as Head of HR at Everest Double Glazing. From 1992 to 2010, he was Senior Lecturer and Head of CIPD studies at Bedfordshire University. He has taught in Singapore and Dubai, and was Visiting Professor at the London campus of Websters University.

'This textbook provides a current and refreshing insight into key HR topics and examines current developments in policy and practice. As an HR professional I would recommend the book as it assists with understanding and interpretation of the CIPD professional standards.'

Kym Drady, Sunderland University

'This book provides a comprehensive introduction to the changing world of human resource management. It nicely balances conceptual models of HRM with their practical application. This book will be particularly well received by undergraduates studying on specialist HR courses as well as HR streams within business studies courses.'

Dr Bob Mason, University of Ulster

'A well written HRM text introducing key concepts through the use of numerous case studies. The clear structure followed makes the reader's journey through the areas of employee resourcing, rewards, relations and learning an easy one to follow. This text also emphasises some key contemporary HRM issues, such as diversity and wellbeing at the workplace, often neglected from other introductory texts.'

Dr Rea Prouska, Middlesex University

AN INTRODUCTION TO HUMAN RESOURCE MANAGEMENT

THIRD EDITION

John Stredwick

 Routledge
Taylor & Francis Group

LONDON AND NEW YORK

First published 2000
by Butterworth

Second edition published 2005
by Elsevier

Third edition published 2014
by Routledge

Simultaneously published in the USA and Canada
by Routledge
711 Third Avenue, New York, NY 10017

Routledge is an imprint of the Taylor & Francis Group, an informa business

British Library Cataloguing in Publication Data
A catalogue record for this book is available from the British Library

Library of Congress Cataloging in Publication Data
Stredwick, John.
An introduction to human resource management / John Stredwick. – Third edition.
   pages cm
Includes bibliographical references and index.
1. Personnel management.   I. Title.
HF5549.S77 2014
658.3–dc23

2013000533

ISBN: 978–0–415–62226–4 (hbk)
ISBN: 978–0–415–62229–5 (pbk)
ISBN: 978–0–203–75945–5 (ebk)

Typeset in Berthold Akzidenz Grotesk
by RefineCatch Limited, Bungay, Suffolk

Printed and bound in Great Britain by
TJ International Ltd, Padstow, Cornwall

CONTENTS

List of illustrations   ix
Preface to the third edition   xiii
Visual tour of An Introduction to Human Resource Management   xvi

1 Introduction   1

Introduction   3
The economic and business context   4
Origins of human resource management   8
The role of human resources today   9
Best practice or best fit?   29
Current concepts in human resourcing   35

2 Recruitment, employer branding and employer of choice *'*   41

Introduction   42
Employer branding   43
Difficulties with employer branding   45
Identifying talent   45
Drafting a recruitment policy   46
Does a vacancy exist?   46
Defining the details of the vacancy   49
Attracting the applicants   63
Integrated approach to recruitment   80
Who carries out the recruitment and selection processes?   82

3 Selection   88

Introduction   89
Talent management   89
Short-listing   92
Selection testing   94
Activity 3.1   96

Activity 3.2   101
Interviewing the candidates   103
Assessment centres   114
Choosing the successful candidate   116
Technology in selection   116
Using a variety of approaches   117
Obtaining references   118
Offering the position   120
Evaluating the selection process   121

4   Relationships with employees   127

Introduction   128
Workplace negotiating   128
Activity 4.1   137
Involvement and participation   137
Employee engagement   145
Dealing with individual sources of conflict – grievance,
   discipline and dismissal   151
Redundancy and its implications   163
Activity 4.2   165
Activity 4.3   169

5   Performance management   177

Introduction   178
The purpose of performance management   179
What should the process be called?   182
Stages in the performance management framework   182
Operational issues   214
Activity 5.1   215
Conclusion   215
Extended activity/case study – balanced scorecard   216

6   Rewarding employees   221

Introduction   222
Strategic elements of reward   222
Activity 6.1   227
Component parts of the reward package   232
Designing basic pay structures   234
Paying for performance   249
Using technology in reward   265

7   Flexible working   272

Introduction   273
Flexible working practices   273
The flexible firm   273
Temporal flexibility   276
Activity 7.1.   278
Numerical flexibility   281
Geographical flexibility   282
Activity 7.2   282
Activity 7.3   289
Occupational flexibility   290
Policies that support flexibility   292
Summing up flexibility   295
Talent management   296
Technology and flexibility   299

8   Learning and talent development: theory and practice   304

Introduction   305
How people learn   306
Talent management   313
Tailored approach to learning   313
Training aims and objectives   314
Specialist learning and talent programmes and initiatives   329
Activity 8.1   329
National government and non-governmental schemes and initiatives   342
Legal considerations in learning and development activities   351
The role and responsibilities of learning and
      talent development practitioners   352
Is the role changing?   352

9   Equal opportunities and managing diversity   357

Introduction   358
The business case for equal opportunities   359
Equal opportunities legislation   362
Discrimination as it applies to specific groups   365
Regulating equality and human rights   377
Remedies for the employee   378
Approaches to equal opportunities policy   381
Implications for equal opportunities (EO) practice   384
Criticism of the equality industry   396

10	Health, safety and employee well-being	401
	Introduction	402
	Legal interventions	404
	Enforcing the law	415
	Risk assessment	418
	Welfare issues and policies	419
	Challenges to management and the role of human resources	425
	Activity 10.1	427

11	An international perspective	435
	Introduction	436
	National culture – Hofstede's studies	437
	Globe study – culture and leadership effectiveness	439
	Convergence and divergence	443
	Global comparisons	446
	HRM models and international strategies for overseas subsidiaries	456
	Labour standards and social responsibility	460

12	Human resource planning	467
	Introduction	468
	Reasons for lack of planning	469
	Purpose of human resource planning	470
	Planning for specific purposes	471
	Carrying out human resource planning	474
	Producing the human resource plan	491
	Technology	494
	Conclusion	494

Subject index	*501*
Author index	*509*

ILLUSTRATIONS

We are indebted to the people and institutions below for permission to reproduce figures and tables. Every effort has been made to trace copyright holders, but in a few cases this has not been possible. Any omissions brought to our attention will be remedied in future editions.

FIGURES

1.1	Human resource interventions	11
1.2	Role of human resources	13
2.1	Employer branding	43
2.2	Task-oriented job description	52
2.3	Accountability-oriented job description	53
2.4	An example of a job statement at a UK building society	55
2.5	Selection of unusual headlines	68
2.6	Example of an eye-catching advertisement	69
2.7	Application form for Wine Rack	73
3.1	Accuracy of recruitment methods	89
3.2	Examples of ability/aptitude questions	96
3.3	A situational or hypothetical question	109
4.1	Briefing group operation	140
4.2	Essential features of a disciplinary procedure	154
4.3	Process of redundancy	165
5.1	Performance management input model	179
5.2	The performance management framework	183
5.3	Example of technical objective, Dartford Council	188
5.4	Balanced Scorecard at Sainsbury's	189
5.5	'The customer comes first' measurement grid	190
5.6	Competency rating scales at a clearing bank (detail)	198
5.7	Job chat summary form	199
5.8	360-degree appraisal – sources of feedback	206
5.9	Example of competencies at Eastern Group with 360-degree feedback	207

6.1	Model of the psychological contract	229
6.2	Maslow's Hierarchy of Needs	230
6.3	Components of the reward package	233
6.4	Example of paired comparison job evaluation scheme	237
6.5	Example of job classification job evaluation scheme	238
6.6	Overlapping and non-overlapping salary grades	245
6.7	Broad-banded salary structure	247
7.1	Core and peripheral workforces	274
8.1	Bennett and Leduchowicz model	305
8.2	The learning cycle	307
8.3	The training cycle	316
8.4	Learning Framework	316
8.5	Identification of training needs	317
9.1	Action on equal opportunities	385
10.1	Fatal injuries to workers in the UK, 1980–2011	402
10.2	External monitoring process	416
12.1	The process of human resource planning	475
12.2	Employers' responses to labour shortages	479

TABLES

1.1	Roles of HR practitioners	9
1.2	HR practices associated with high-performance organisations	29
1.3	Barriers to high performance	35
2.1	Person specification – Branch Manager, Employment Agency	59
2.2	Magistrates' Court clerk competencies	60
2.3	Court clerk competency 1	60
2.4	Example of competencies at a brewer	61
2.5	Example of competencies in detail	62
2.6	Use of third parties	66
2.7	Alternatives or additions to newspaper/magazine advertising	74
2.8	Most effective initiatives used in overcoming difficulties in recruitment	75
3.1	Use of selection tests	95
3.2	16PF traits	98
3.3	Techniques to test for various competencies	115
4.1	Union membership in 2012	129
4.2	Guest model of approaches to industrial relations and HRM	133
4.3	Perspectives on partnership agreements	145
4.4	Misdemeanours and gross misconduct	155

4.5	Grievance and disciplinary procedure stages	156
4.6	Example of performance measurement system relating to redundancy selection	167
5.1	Performance target examples used in an Australian university	188
5.2	Example of BARS: teamwork dimension	195
5.3	Cultural approaches to performance management	205
6.1	Changing nature of pay and rewards	223
6.2	Expectations of employers and employees from each other	227
6.3	Herzberg's two-factor theory	230
6.4	Job evaluation factor point grid	240
6.5	Job evaluated salary structure	244
6.6	Conversion of ratings into a pay increase	252
6.7	Conversion of ratings into a pay increase in a complex scheme	253
7.1	Types of flexible working	275
7.2	Part-time employees 1951 to 2010 ('000s)	277
7.3	Flexibility requirements	295
8.1	Bloom's taxonomy	309
8.2	Comparing and contrasting talent management/learning with training, learning and development	315
8.3	Generations	318
8.4	Techniques of training	323
8.5	E-learning	325
8.6	Induction programme	330
9.1	Statistics on formal industrial tribunal claims concerning equal opportunities in 2009/10	379
9.2	Equality targets	381
9.3	Cultural change v equality programme	382
9.4	Equal opportunities and managing diversity	383
9.5	Aspects of discrimination in pay systems	393
10.1	Cost of work-based injuries and ill-health in the UK, 2011 (£millions)	403
10.2	Making risk assessments by rating hazards	419
10.3	Causes of workplace stress	421
11.1	Power distance index	438
11.2	Uncertainty avoidance index	438
11.3	Individuality index	439
11.4	Masculinity index	439
11.5	GLOBE cultural dimensions and country clusters	440
11.6	GLOBE societal clusters and leader styles	440
11.7	International comparison of women on boards	448
12.1	Current staff	477

12.2	Demand for nurses	478
12.3	Causes of absenteeism	482
12.4	Internal supply of nurses	491
12.5	Meteor Gantt chart	497

PREFACE TO THE THIRD EDITION

The main purpose of this book is to give a balanced introduction to the complex world of human resource management (HRM). Essentially, it is intended for first degree students studying the subject as part of a modular degree course or for students on a foundation degree in Business Studies. It may also be used as a prime text for Masters courses in HRM or for MBA courses, especially where students have little or no experience in the subject area.

The book combines the main theoretical underpinning for the subject area with a large number of practical examples and cases to assist the learning process. It is divided into 12 chapters to provide one topic a week on a modular course, but many of the chapters have sufficient material to allow work to be extended into two semesters if this is required.

The third edition has been influenced by a number of recent developments. Firstly, by the financial crisis and the accompanying economic recession, which began in 2008 and, at the time of writing, shows little sign of ending, with forecasters predicting continuation in the UK until at least 2015. The recession has simplified the recruitment and retention process, and assisted the decline in UK union membership. However, the influence on most other HR areas, such as performance management, reward or equal opportunities, has been felt much less strongly. Although there may be fewer employees in place in many (although not all) organisations, they still need to be trained, motivated and rewarded successfully, and the increased competitive pressures that the recession has brought has made the HR contribution increasingly valuable.

A second influence has been the greater emphasis in recent years on talent management – the concept that embraces recruitment, selection, training, developing, motivating, rewarding and retaining the best talent available.

A further influence has been the growing importance of the concept of employee engagement – the belief that employees do not just need to be developed and retained but they also need to be genuinely concerned and involved with the aims and culture of the organisation and to present an enthusiastic and positive view of their organisation to the outside world.

This edition has updated a large number of areas of legislation, especially in the field of equal opportunities, employee rights (particularly in flexible working and discrimination) and employee relations generally. Many new cases and examples of research have been added. Chapter 1 has been revised to place a greater emphasis on the role of human resources in improving organisational and employee performance and introduces concepts that will be examined in detail in later chapters.

The chapters have been reordered since the last edition in response to helpful suggestions from colleagues and reviewers for which I am very grateful. The chapter on International HRM has been extensively altered to take advantage of the swiftly changing and rich sources of cases and research in the international field.

Chapter 1 introduces the reader to the main roles and responsibilities of staff working in the HRM field, starting with the economic and social context, summarising the developments of HR roles and looking in detail at a number of models and theories relating to the operation of human resources.

Chapters 2 and 3 examine *recruitment* and *selection*, where the key roles and activities are in defining vacancies, advertising, short-listing, interviewing, testing, selecting and appointing staff with the appropriate terms and conditions. Setting out the policy is also an important function to ensure the best and appropriate practices are in place, especially in terms of equal opportunities.

Chapter 4 is concerned with the changing environment of *employee relations*. The areas involved here include building relationships with employees on a collective and individual basis, dealing with the collective functions of bargaining and negotiating, reaching agreements on terms and conditions of employment and handling major initiatives, such as improved flexibility, site relocation and redundancy. A major aim in recent years has been to improve levels of *employee engagement*, which is dealt with at length. The person will also deal either directly, or through line management, with individual issues that relate to grievances, discipline and dismissal.

Chapters 5 and 6 deal with the closely related areas of *performance management* and *reward*. The principal concern here is the establishment of a system of measuring organisational and employee performance and subsequently relating this to a fair system of pay and rewards that meets the needs of both the organisation and the bulk of the employees. This will involve establishing a basic pay structure and individual rates, systems of rewarding performance and generating a selection of benefits across the organisation appropriate to the circumstances.

Chapter 7 is dedicated to the vital area of *employee flexibility* where the benefits and difficulties associated with the many types of flexibility are compared and analysed from the viewpoint of both the employee and the organisation.

Chapter 8 contains a detailed analysis of the many facets of *learning and development*. This involves the analysis of training needs to identify where training is required and what form it is to take, setting up internal and external training facilities with the necessary resources and evaluating how successful the training has been. Training areas include initial induction, specialist skills training, supervisory and management training and any other areas that help the organisation achieve success in the initiatives it plans. Investors in

People, learning organisations and the various UK government initiatives in L&D are examined.

Chapters 9 and 10 deal with two subject areas that cut across all other HR activity, namely *equal opportunities* and *health and safety*. Both deal with the legislative framework, the business case for using advanced approaches and techniques, and the role of human resources in devising strategy, policy, training and communicating with staff, carrying out investigations and dealing with high-profile cases.

Chapter 11 examines the context and operation of *human resources in an international setting*. The context of globalisation, the varieties of cultural differences and their effect on human resources and the human resource issues that apply to international organisations, such as the employment of expatriate staff, are considered, supported by a variety of individual cases and research reports.

Chapter 12 draws a number of strands together to look at the way organisations operate *human resource strategy and planning* systems in practice, including detailed sections on the influence of retention and absence management strategies and practice.

HOW TO GET THE BEST OUT OF THE BOOK

At the start of each chapter, there is a short list of objectives and you should keep these in mind as you read through the chapter so that, by the end, you are confident of reaching those objectives. The summary at the end of each chapter should also help to reinforce the main issues, theories and body of knowledge discussed within the chapter. Also at the end of each chapter is a set of activities for you to carry out that will help you to bolster your learning.

A further intention is to encourage you to read up on research, so each chapter has one or more summaries of important research articles or publications, called 'focus on research', and some of the activities are related to these articles. The case studies are of two kinds. The majority are real-life cases from published sources or from the author's experience. There is also a linked case study around a fictitious company called 'Meteor Telecoms', which is intended to demonstrate some of the experiences that occur within a human resources department. Again, some of the student activities are related to these episodes.

At the end of each chapter, you will find activities for students, chapter questions and additional reading sections. You will also be guided to the dedicated website throughout the book for further cases, and other areas to help tutors and students.

VISUAL TOUR OF *AN INTRODUCTION TO HUMAN RESOURCE MANAGEMENT*

PEDAGOGICAL FEATURES

An Introduction to Human Resource Management offers a number of features to engage students with current issues in human resource management, bridging the gap between theory and practice. In addition, at the end of each chapter you will find a website logo indicating that further resources are available on the companion website at www.routledge.com/cw/stredwick.

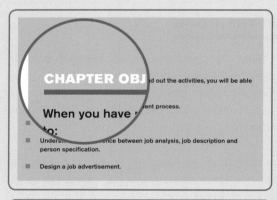

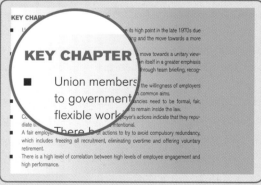

CHAPTER OBJECTIVES AND KEY CHAPTER SUMMARY POINTS

At the beginning of each chapter, a number of learning objectives are set out so that the student understands clearly what is to be covered in the forthcoming chapter. Closing each chapter is a box of key summary points which underline and revise the main issues that have been covered.

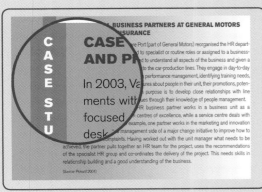

CASE STUDY BOXES

These case studies provide 'real-life' examples to illustrate practical applications of the theoretical points under discussion.

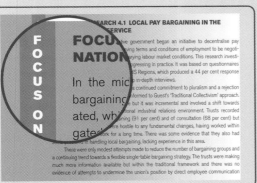

'FOCUS ON RESEARCH' BOXES

These boxes examine research done in the HR field to heighten awareness of the current issues and hot topics within human resources. These boxes also give an insight into the kind of research that can be embarked upon in HR and the practical ways that such research can be used in the work environment.

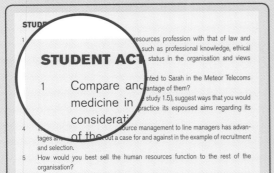

STUDENT ACTIVITY SECTIONS

Each chapter concludes with a list of activities that students can undertake individually or in groups; inside or outside the classroom. These include discussion or potential essay questions to help the revision of the previous chapter and engage with topics.

1 INTRODUCTION

CHAPTER OBJECTIVES

By the end of this chapter, you will be able to:

- Understand some of the influences on the business environment that have changed the approaches to employing people.

- Explain the origins of human resources (HR) and their development over the last 100 years.

- Evaluate a selection of HR models and appreciate their inherent contradictions.

- Identify the roles and purpose of human resources in today's environment.

- Comprehend the links between human resource management (HRM) practices and high performance.

- Understand the importance of current HR issues, including the drive for talent management, the development of engagement strategies and the uses and difficulties involved in shared services.

Sarah was waiting anxiously in the reception area of the head office of Meteor Telecoms. It was her first day with the organisation as a trainee HR officer and she was not sure what to expect. Her 2:1 degree in Business Studies had pleased her with an especially good mark for her final-year dissertation on the 'learning organisation'.

She had enjoyed the selection process three months earlier, which had involved an assessment centre spread over a very long day, and had been overjoyed when she was offered the position. This had sounded exciting with considerable opportunities for personal development and promotion in a quickly growing organisation, although the actual job description seemed a little vague. She had been told that her workload would have considerable variety, and she would be joining a number of project groups as well as getting involved in head office recruitment and training. She was to work for David Martin, Personnel Director, who had joined the company six months earlier and had a department of six staff.

After a wait of 20 minutes or so, David's secretary came down to meet her, apologised for the delay and took her into David's office. David explained that he had to make a presentation to the board on future strategy and this meeting had been brought forward so he had been making last-minute preparations. He went on to say that he had obtained agreement from the chief executive that Sarah could sit in on this presentation, which would give her a good introduction to the organisation.

Sarah had been doing her homework on Meteor Telecoms since her offer of employment. She knew that this company, set up 15 years ago, initially manufactured and installed telecommunication equipment but it had moved on to other associated businesses, such as helping companies set up call centres. It had around 2,000 employees, spread over a number of sites around the UK. It went public five years ago with the two founding directors retaining a minority stake. City reports indicated that it was well respected and had kept to its growth forecasts, although the profits were taking longer to realise than had been expected initially.

An hour later, she was sitting in the board room and David had started his presentation. He began by going over the background to the company, its rapid growth, some of the difficulties this had produced and the current issues involved in recruiting, retaining, motivating and managing employees. He explained that the company had now reached a turning point in the way that people resources were managed. In its first 15 years, the growth rate had been such that there was a heavy concentration of recruitment and selection at all levels to get enough skilled employees on board. More recently, training and pay systems had had a higher profile but the activities were disjointed and reactive to the immediate circumstances. Given the tightening of the labour market, the highly competitive market for specific skills and a turnover rate higher than expected, it was time to put together an overall strategy in the people-management area.

The proposal he put forward dealt with the change from a tactical and reactive approach to one that puts people management at the heart of all business initiatives. He gave a number of examples of how this would lead to higher performance of employees and help the company achieve its corporate objectives. The introduction of a competence framework would encourage all employees to focus on the key skills and competencies that lead to business success. The framework would be at the heart of the talent-management initiative to ensure the best people would be recruited, trained and developed in the organisation.

Linking these skills and competencies with a performance-management programme would lead to the identification of training and development needs and the rewarding of high-performing employees. Although trade unions had made little inroads into the business, David warned against complacency and advised a programme of greater employee involvement in planning, decision-making and innovation. There would be a substantial drive to increase the engagement level of all staff, which should reduce the worrying increase in the turnover rate. He continued with further examples and some detailed proposals on each of the major proposals, emphasising that these were HR 'best practices' and would have a strong impact on improving performance in the organisation.

The structure of the HR department needed to be re-examined. Although big changes had been made eight years earlier with the introduction of the three-legged Ulrich model, he knew that there were some doubts over the operation of the model, especially the distinction between the three groups of HR staff and the effectiveness of the 'business partnering' in some parts of the organisation. He wanted a small focus group to investigate the realities of the situation and bring forward ideas on how it should be changed. He especially wanted well-researched ideas on outsourcing of the function and whether introducing any shared-service operations could be feasible.

After the presentation, discussion ranged between David and some directors who remained unconvinced, outlining the major uncertainties inherent in the business and the inability to plan too far ahead, certainly in terms of employment. David pointed out that, no matter which way the business turned, there would still need to be a sizeable core of skilled, flexible and committed employees and, without them, the business would flounder. At the end of the meeting, the chief executive asked David to head up a small team to put up a fully detailed proposal for two months' time, together with an action plan. Sarah left the meeting excited by the opportunities evident in influencing the course of the business.

M E T E O R   T E L E C O M S   C A S E   S T U D Y

INTRODUCTION

The opening scenario has taken place in board rooms up and down the country ever since the term 'human resource management' was popularised in the mid-1980s. In this chapter, we will first examine the economic and business context that has stimulated so much discussion on the role of employees in the organisation; this will be followed by a brief history of the personnel profession and then an analysis of the various models that have been put forward regarding the role and nature of human resource management. The chapter will end with some examples of human resource strategy in theory and practice, including an analysis of recent developments, including talent management, engagement, outsourcing and shared services, and the technology that can support these initiatives.

THE ECONOMIC AND BUSINESS CONTEXT

For the 15 years up until 2008, there was an unprecedented boom in most of the world's economies with consistent expansions in growth rates, benign inflation and low levels of unemployment. This came to a crashing halt with the world banking and financial crisis leading to a succession of sovereign debt crises in the Western world. Whereas human resource practitioners had spent much of the boom years dealing with a shortage of labour, especially skilled labour (referred to as a 'talent crisis'), this process was rapidly reversed with the onset of recession, growing unemployment and the need to downsize in most sectors. What appeared to be an unending period of growth, rising living standards and certainty changed abruptly into a period of retrenchment, reducing confidence and considerable uncertainty.

That is not to say that the UK business environment has not changed over the last two decades. Although actual unemployment has been low, employment itself has shown a high degree of variability. Levels of redundancy have been high throughout the period, brought about through structural changes, mainly through the growth of manufacturing and services in the developing world, especially China and India. The number of employees in manufacturing in the UK has reduced by almost a half since 1980. Although the numbers of jobs in the service industries have increased substantially to more than make up the shortfall in manufacturing, many of these jobs are poorly paid, part-time and temporary.

Over a considerable period, the finance sector was one of the great creators of jobs, as London retained its position as one of the top major world financial centres. It provided the base for major hedge fund and private equity activity and still remains a major player in all forms of investment banking, including mergers and takeovers. However, the extended banking and financial crisis, which commenced in 2007, has dented this reputation and numbers employed have contracted sharply.

At the same time, advances in technology have replaced face-to-face contact with automated, Internet and telephone services, which have occurred throughout organisations. Programmes of de-layering (reducing the levels of management and supervision), business process engineering (making processes more efficient and usually reducing administrative and other associated staff) and decentralisation have all created waves of doubt, fear and mistrust among the mass of employees involved. Add to this the constant flux through takeovers, mergers, buy-ins, buy-outs and float-offs, and it is not surprising that being employed is regarded as an insecure occupation.

Even in the public sector, uncertainty has been created with the massive privatisation programmes in the 1980s and 1990s covering the coal, gas, electricity, water, rail, airports and telecommunication industries, together with British Airways, British Aerospace and BP. Furthermore, direct government employment in the Civil Service, local authorities, education and health has been fundamentally altered by outsourcing, the creation of semi-autonomous 'agencies', and the complex workings of compulsory competitive tendering and 'best value' programmes. The government austerity programmes arising from the need to reduce the public indebtedness have also contributed to the reduction in numbers, estimated at around 400,000, and created a considerable sense of unease among public sector employees unused to insecurity of employment.

Change, therefore, has been the only constant. A number of commentators have analysed the changes in the economic, business and cultural context that are common to almost every organisation and which will have a major influence on employment policies in the foreseeable future:

Rapidly changing technologies

This has probably had the biggest impact. In a few short years, the computer has fundamentally changed jobs. The spreadsheet alone has eliminated huge numbers of jobs. The work that had previously been carried out by roomfuls of mid-level analysts in finance, sales and marketing can now be handled by one clerical person on a personal computer. Information Technology (IT) goes further than just making offices more productive. Organisational charts and rules are ignored by the cable that links employees, and information now flows more freely than ever before. Employees are linked in buildings, around countrywide units and around the world. Networking has moved beyond a technical definition to a way of employees working together, often in different locations and many from a home base.

Technology also leads to shorter and shorter cycle times, and the reduction in costs has been substantial. Cars that used to take seven years from design to mass production now take only three to four years. The release date on computer games is crucial to a week or less, so lead times are often brought forward to steal a march on competitors. The demands created by just-in-time logistics operations have meant that gaps or delays cannot be tolerated, so urgency, time-directed performance and unmoveable deadlines are part and parcel of employees' normal working environment. The need for employees to work flexibly is crucial in this respect. They need to be able to move quickly from one task to another, to be able to service their own areas and to change their working hours and practices. Technology has been changed in a generation from large mainframe computers, via PCs and laptops, to eventually finish up with inexpensive hand-held and pocket-sized devices, primarily smartphones.

Before 2020, it is estimated that more than 5 billion people will become connected on the world stage (Gratton 2011). This will take place in the megacities of the world and will extend to rural areas. The extent of this connectivity will create the possibility of a 'global consciousness' that has not been seen before (except possibly in Greek and Roman times). As Gratton explains:

The extent of this global consciousness will be shaped by 'the cloud' becoming ubiquitous, creating a global infrastructure upon which services will become available – applications and resources. It will allow anyone with a computer or hand-held device to rent services on a minute-to-minute basis, and this has enormous potential to bring sophisticated technology to every corner of the world.

(2011: 32)

Changing role of the customer

Technology makes it happen but it is the *ever-demanding customer* that drives the process. Today's customers are better educated, more informed and have less time to want to wait about either for the service that isn't good enough or the new products that they can afford now and want today. This is partly because women, who have always taken more purchasing decisions, spend more time working now. A faster response, higher quality and a heightened, more personalised sensitivity to their needs are other customer demands, along with retaining accessibility, functionality and reliability. They want it their own way, not the way it has been presented to them in the past without a choice. To be successful, businesses and their employees have to make sure that they meet these demands in full or they will lose their client base. No excuses ('someone in head office will deal with that for you', 'they don't deliver after 3.30', 'we are short of staff today') are acceptable.

This puts additional pressure on frontline employees who need to be able to solve or, better still, prevent customer problems by working closely together with employees who provide an internal service to them. Organisations need to learn how to use technology effectively to assist the consumer (call centres, voice-recognition, etc.) without putting off customers through the impersonality and glitches that such systems produce.

Globalisation

A poor product or service will not survive today because of the nature of *globalisation*. Markets have been liberalised throughout the world. The European communist bloc has imploded, providing vast new potential markets. Trading agreements through the World Trade Association have allowed goods to be marketed in most countries with tariffs and barriers eliminated or vastly reduced. The Asia-Pacific region has grown at an extraordinary pace, especially China, providing a vast range of competitive or alternative goods for the world market at lower prices. China and India have a domestic market of over 2 billion consumers and the capacity to be the factory and back office of the world. Moreover, through their educational advancement, they are creating a new and very valuable 'talent pool' not just for cheap labour but also for highly skilled engineers, scientists and technology staff. Brazil is the fourth of the BRIC (Brazil, Russia, India and China) countries that are having such a substantial effect upon world markets.

The competition provided by the globalisation of production and services has led to organisations taking far more care of their labour costs by either increasing productivity, eliminating wasteful bureaucracies and jobs, which add no value, or outsourcing to cheaper suppliers. All of these actions affect the way people are employed. Charles Handy (1994) created a new equation for success: success = ½ workforce, paid twice as much, producing three times as much.

With increased competition, organisations are finding that a good product or service alone does not ensure success. Instead, as Flannery *et al.* as long ago as 1996 put it:

> [T]hey must distinguish themselves by focusing on fundamental competencies and capabilities that will set them aside from the pack. To achieve this, organisations must maximise . . . competencies – those underlying attributes or characteristics that can predict superior performance. These range from tangible attributes, such as skills and knowledge – technical know-how, for example, or the ability to operate a sophisticated computer – to intangible attitudes and values . . . such as teamwork and flexibility. These competencies will become a part of the organisation's foundation and will be the focus of everything from hiring and training to marketing.
>
> (1996: 11)

The changing employee role

The sixth major change has been alluded to already and is a consequence of the other five, *namely what is required from employees.* Organisations no longer want robots, performing their job mechanically, working fixed hours. What is wanted is an intellectualised workforce, with employees making their own informed decisions, using good judgement and assuming more responsibility for the organisation's performance. Such a dramatic change requires that people accept new values, behave differently, learn new skills and competencies, and be prepared to take risks. This was made clear in another influential publication by Hamel and Prahalad: 'Delegation and empowerment are not just buzzwords, they are desperately needed antidotes to the elitism that robs so many companies of so much brainpower' (1994: 131).

Two major categories of employees that are likely to grow in Western economies have been identified by Reich (2004):

■ Knowledge workers who identify and solve new problems, analysing, manipulating and communicating, often working in small teams or alone; and
■ Personal service workers doing jobs that computers cannot yet do (not even robots) because they require human beings with their value coming from human touch, care and attentiveness.

Coyle has explained this as:

The economy is becoming increasingly weightless: what is valuable is not the material stuff that goes into making goods … we pay for the characteristics of the people providing the services. The burgeoning professional and managerial classes are spending their time acquiring information and presenting it in a performance for co-workers or customers. The more the economy is made up of services, the more of us will be performing.

(1997: 13)

The need to initiate changes in employee practices represents a major challenge for the human resources department. For employees in the service industry, the specific competencies and behaviours they exhibit are vital to the success of the business. For human resources departments, the way they recruit, select, train and develop employees is the way they make their major contribution to the organisation. We will look again at these changes in respect of the models of human resource management that have been put forward in recent years in various chapters in the book that relate to selection, motivation, training, performance management and reward.

ORIGINS OF HUMAN RESOURCE MANAGEMENT

Modern-day requirements of the human resources department are a far cry from the origins of the profession, which began in the mid-nineteenth century through the early interventions of high-profile social reformers such as Lord Shaftesbury and Robert Owen. They became concerned at the exploitation of the factory workers, where the emphasis had been strongly on discipline and cost control, at the expense of the employees' health, welfare and personal living standards. Concentrating at first on the appalling working conditions, especially for women and young children, enlightened employers started to believe that, if employees were treated humanely and rewarded fairly, they may work better and become more productive.

Their influence, plus the interests of public health and order, helped to bring in a number of statutes relating to hours and conditions of work, which were policed by factory inspectors. Alongside such regulation, a small number of paternalist employers, motivated by Christian beliefs (especially Quakers), appointed welfare officers to provide individual and group support for employees' health, accommodation, financial and personal situations. In 1913, the Welfare Workers' Association (WWA) was formed with thirty-four members, supported by six companies and sponsored by Seebohm Rowntree of the chocolate factory fame. It is a matter of interest that the Scottish Society of Welfare Supervisors, which was set up shortly afterwards, refused to join with the WWA because 'they did not wish to join with the ladies, whose problems are very different from the men's'. How times and attitudes have changed!

Five name changes followed over the next 90 years before it became the Chartered Institute of Personnel and Development (CIPD) in 2000. By 2011, the Institute had over

Table 1.1 Roles of HR practitioners

Humane bureaucrat	Setting up formal systems of recruitment, selection, appraisal, discipline and grievance
Consensus negotiator	Bargaining with unions, creating systems of involvement and participation
Manpower analyst	Providing a longer-term plan for employment numbers, together with programmes for skills, competence and career development
Organisation man	Working strategically with top management to create organisation structures and management development systems

Source: Adapted from Torrington *et al.* (2004) *Human Resource Management.* Financial Times/Prentice Hall.

135,000 members and had become the largest institute concerning the management of people in the world.

The roles of practitioners have varied over this period as identified by Torrington *et al.* (2004) in Table 1.1.

THE ROLE OF HUMAN RESOURCES TODAY

Introduction

There has been much dispute in recent years as to what human resource management departments should actually do. For example, the earliest role, welfare, took a back seat in the 1960s and 1970s as management decided this was too 'soft' an activity and away from the mainstream corporate objectives. Personnel professionals saw their role as tough, masculine negotiators, dealing with hard-nosed unions. This has now been generally recognised as a bad mistake. The unions stepped into the breach and raised their profile and their membership by taking time to look after their members' personal, financial and occupational concerns. In return, through this period of confrontation, employees chose to follow the union leadership and oppose much of the management's agenda, which led, inevitably, to poor productivity and lack of competitiveness. Although regarded as distant history now, the period of the late 1970s was as close as Britain ever came to a form of revolutionary shift of power.

Welfare, albeit perhaps in a different guise, returned in the 1990s through concern for such areas as family-friendly and flexible benefits – with some evidence from *The 1998 Workplace Employee Relations Survey* (Cully *et al.* 1999) and elsewhere – that this concern from employers provides an increase in commitment and job satisfaction among employees.

By the end of the 1980s, it became important to differentiate between the established 'personnel' thinking and that of the *new concept of 'human resource management'*. This was set out persuasively by Guest (1989) who outlined four main areas where HRM can be identified and analysed, which makes it a different beast:

■ *The policy goals of HRM.* These consist of a package of four main areas. Firstly, to encourage the commitment of employees to high performance and loyalty to the organisation as a whole. Secondly, an emphasis on quality of staff which, in turn, will produce quality goods and services. Thirdly, a concern to ensure that flexibility plays an important part in the way staff are organised, so that they are adaptive and receptive to all forms of changes – in their jobs, in the hours they work and their methods of working. Finally, and most importantly, that these goals are integrated into strategic planning so that HRM policies 'cohere both across policy areas and across hierarchies' (Guest 1989: 49). They also need to be accepted and used by line managers as part of their everyday work.

■ *The HRM policies.* While using conventional personnel practices, such as selection and training, it is important that these practices are of high quality and that they go towards meeting the organisational goals. Employees need to be trained, for example, to be flexible and to respect high-quality work. Communication should be goal-directed, i.e. achieving results, rather than simply concerned with getting out a monthly magazine on time.

■ *The cement.* To make these policies work, there needs to be support from key leadership from the top, a strong culture that can drive through the policies consistently and fairly with no sudden change of direction, and there must also be a willingness throughout the organisation to value the success that can come through the effective utilisation of human resources.

■ *The organisational outcomes.* These include a low level of staff turnover, absence and grievances (individual or collective), together with a high-level change, problem-solving and innovation.

The operation of HRM in practice

Since HRM systems and practices replaced Personnel in the 1990s, there have been a number of examples of models illustrating the varying roles and styles for the operation of HR departments and practitioners.

An early model was produced by Storey (1992), who designed a grid that contrasts, on one axis, how far the work undertaken is strategic or merely tactical and, on the other axis, the degree to which the human resources manager intervenes in the management process. This is shown in Figure 1.1.

Working clockwise, human resource specialists who fall into the *adviser* category are those who focus on strategic issues but are not themselves responsible for carrying out the actions they recommend. *Handmaidens* are those who also have little part in implementing policy but they only operate at a tactical level, dealing with administration and the provision of welfare, training and basic recruitment. *Regulators* are, again, involved only in tactical issues but they are more interventionary, trying to ensure that the human resources policy is carried out properly in co-operation with line managers. The *changemakers*, on the other hand, are both strategic and interventionary, concerned less with administration and more with the broader view of people management in their organisations. A changemaker is expected to assess the organisation's needs, reach appropriate conclusions and then drive the required changes to completion. This is regarded, Storey indicates, as the proper role for an effective and senior human resource specialist.

Purcell and Ahlstrand (1994) concentrated on setting out the core activities that HRM departments should engage in to become fully influential in an organisation. They assumed that the HR department would be centralised and that the following activities would be applicable to most, but not all, medium to large organisations:

	STRATEGIC		
I N T E R V E N T I O N A R Y	CHANGEMAKERS	ADVISERS	N O N - I N T E R V E N T I O N I S T
	REGULATORS	HANDMAIDENS	
	TACTICAL		

Figure 1.1
Human resource interventions

Source: Adapted from Storey, J. (1992) *Developments in the Management of Human Resources.* Blackwell.

Corporate culture and communications. Organisations are bound together internally not just by common ownership or by everything being included on the balance sheet. Culture – 'the ways we do things around here' – is difficult to define but easy to identify, especially when it is articulated well and often. It is normally up to the chief executive to set out or redefine the principal aspects, the philosophy, the set of values and the essential style of management, but it is human resources that must be responsible for championing and disseminating these cultural aspects around the organisation in an effective fashion.

Human resource planning in strategic management. Developing a human resource plan that emerges from the strategic plan is the second core activity. This is clearly a core activity but one where the link is not always made as tightly as it should be.

Essential policy formulation and monitoring. Established policies and procedures remain an essential feature of an effective organisation and policies regarding the way people should act and be treated are no exception. Standards need to be set and monitored for compliance. The recognised difficulty here is striking the happy medium between a rigid bureaucratic set of procedures that deal with every eventuality but restrict innovation and empowerment and a set of vague guidelines that have many interpretations and are largely ignored.

'Cabinet office' services. This is a more unusual observation and based on the need for the chief executive to have advice from a trusted senior subordinate, one that is not linked to a major department, such as finance or sales, which would be liable to defend their own territory and not be regarded as independent. The advice would be principally concerning the implications for staff in general, and succession planning for senior executives, but would also include the cultural development issues and some specific investigations set in place through issues raised by non-executive directors. This is a considerable source of power and influence for human resources and emerged from their personal relationship, not from their specific position.

Senior management development and career planning. This is another undisputed, important role, even when longer-term planning is more difficult to undertake. It is linked with the succession planning process and with the need to develop managers with wide experience so there is flexibility in place for strategic moves into new or existing marketplaces.

External advocacy – internal advice. As human resources develop a close relationship with the chief executive, their 'cabinet' responsibilities may stretch to representing the organisation in the corridors of power. This is not just on local matters such as trade association committees, but also involves some political lobbying on crucial issues such as government legislation or interpretation of European directives. The internal advice is feeding matters such as this back to the executives in the organisation.

Information co-ordination. This involves helping large organisations to co-ordinate necessary information across the group on pay, bargaining and general personnel statistics, such as headcount, turnover and absenteeism.

Internal consultancy and mediation services. Included in this role are aspects of organisational design and learning. The introduction of competencies would be an example here.

Human resources for small units. An extension of the internal consultancy to part of the larger group that have little or no human resource presence.

Purcell and Ahlstrand recognise that this list does not indicate a comprehensive attention to all human resource matters. Training, health and safety, recruitment and pay issues do not come to the fore on their own. In fact:

> Our research shows that the role and authority of corporate personnel departments is becoming more ambiguous and uncertain. . . . Much of the activity identified . . . places

a premium on political and interpersonal skills and 'corridor power'. In this situation, the authority of corporate human resources staff comes more from their own expertise and style than from a clearly defined role and function. It has often been noted that human resources managers need to be adept at handling ambiguity.

(Purcell and Ahlstrand 1994: 113)

Strategic partnering – Ulrich's concepts of HR roles and structure

The most influential ideas in recent years have come from David Ulrich and his colleagues (Pritchard 2010). They combined models that both defined HR roles and integrated them into a new non-centralised structure. These models have been adapted since their original formation in 1998. We will examine the revised roles first, then see how the new structures can operate.

Human resource roles

Following a similar tack to Storey, Ulrich and Brockbank (2005) developed the model substantially so that the *x*-axis measures the degree to which the HR practitioner manages the process and, on the other hand, manages the people involved, as shown in Figure 1.2.

The four quadrants are as follows:

Functional expert. Previously called the *administrative expert*, this role manages the processes on a day-to-day basis, ensuring that policies on grievances, discipline, equal opportunities and incentive arrangements work effectively. This is not a role to be derided because it is generally vital to the organisation's smooth running. Recognition, however, does not come easily or this role as it is only really noticed when things go wrong.

As a profession, HR possesses a body of knowledge. With the body of knowledge, HR functional experts improve decisions and deliver results. This role can be divided into two categories: foundational and emerging HR practices. Foundational HR practices are those practices for which most HR departments have direct responsibility.

	STRATEGIC	
MANAGEMENT OF PROCESSES	STRATEGIC PARTNER	HUMAN CAPITAL DEVELOPER
	FUNCTIONAL EXPERT	EMPLOYEE ADVOCATE
	TACTICAL	

(with MANAGEMENT OF PEOPLE along the right-hand axis)

Figure 1.2
Role of human resources

Source: Ulrich, D. and Brockbank, W. (2005) The HR Value Proposition. *People Management*, 15 June, Personnel Publications.

They include recruitment, promotions, transfers, outplacement, measurement, rewards, training and development. Emerging HR practices have substantial influence on the human side of the business but are usually not under the direct influence of most HR professionals. They include work process design, internal communications, organisational structures, design of physical setting, dissemination of external information throughout the firm and executive leadership development.

By mastering the concepts and research for these foundational and emerging HR practices and ensuring their alignment with key business priorities, HR professionals will optimise their impact on business performance.

Functional expertise also operates at multiple levels. Tier one involves creating solutions to routine HR problems. This includes placing HR solutions online through a company intranet or secure Internet site. In Tier-two work, HR specialists create menus of choices, drawing on theory, research and best practices in other companies. Tier three involves HR specialists consulting with businesses and adapting their programmes to unique business needs. Tier four sets overall policy and direction for HR practices within a speciality. This calls for understanding of strategy and the ability to adapt to a strategic context. While requirements for functional experts may vary across these tiers of work, some general principles apply to all functional specialists.

Employee advocate. Previously the *employee champion*, this role acts as a voice for employees on a day-to-day basis, working for an improvement in their position, their contribution and their engagement with the organisation.

Caring for, listening to and responding to employees remains a centrepiece of HR work. This role emphasises that HR professionals need to see the world through employees' eyes – to listen to them, understand their concerns and empathise with them – while at the same time looking through customers', shareholders' and managers' eyes and communicating to employees what is required for them to be successful in creating value.

An example that Ulrich and Brockbank give is:

> [W]hen the management team discusses the strategy for closing a plant, expanding a product line or exploring a new geographic market, your job is to represent employees. What will this strategy do to them? What abilities will help or hinder the execution of this strategy? How will employees respond to this strategy? Are mechanisms in place through which they have a forum to express their needs, concerns and suggestions?
>
> (2005: 24)

A corporate reputation for fairness and equity requires policies that treat employees fairly. The HR advocacy role includes proposing fair policies for equal opportunities, health and safety, terms and conditions of work, reward and discipline, as well as implementing these policies corporate-wide. It also includes the difficulties of announcing the realities of a competitive world including bad news – site closures and redundancies.

Human capital developer. This could also be titled as '*talent developer*'. Increasingly, people are recognised as critical assets and HR professionals as managing human capital: developing the workforce, emphasising individual employees more than organisation processes. As human capital developers, HR professionals focus on the future, often one employee at a time, developing plans that offer each employee opportunities to develop future abilities, matching desires with opportunities. The role also includes helping employees, as individual and as teams, forget old skills and master new ones through coaching and working to competencies and behaviours.

Strategic partner. This was originally called *business partner* and many practitioners still use that title. HR professionals bring know-how about business, change, consulting and learning to their relationships with line managers. They partner with line managers to help them reach their goals through strategy formulation and execution.

As strategy formulators, HR professionals play at least three distinct roles. Firstly, they act as reactive devil's advocates, asking tough questions about the accuracy of the strategy and about the company's ability to make it happen. Secondly, they play an active role in crafting strategies based on knowledge of current and future customers and exploring how corporate resources may be aligned to those demands. Third, they play a developmental role in helping to raise the standards of strategic thinking for the management team.

As strategy implementers and change agents, they align HR systems to help accomplish the organisation's vision and mission. They diagnose organisation problems, separate symptoms from causes, help to set an agenda for the future, and create plans for making things happen. They help to make change happen fast by being not only thought leaders, but also masters of practice who turn what they know into what they do. They serve as coaches, shaping points of view and offering feedback on progress.

As facilitators, they work with knowledge and skill to help both individual managers and management teams get things done. As integrators, they disseminate learning across the organisation – generating and generalising ideas with impact.

Ulrich – human resource structure

Linked very closely to Ulrich's roles is his analysis of the structure of the HR department, his so-called 'three-legged stool'. Here, the HR department moves from a monolithic, centralised (and often isolated) whole to one that is separated, yet integrated with the business organisation. There are many versions of the three legs but the most common takes the following form:

CENTRES OF EXPERTISE

This is a central service where small teams of professionals with expertise in strategy and specific functional areas provide advice to the rest of the organisation in the following ways:

- Devising strategy and policies in areas such as reward, relations, talent management and career development.
- Researching these areas, including theory and current practice, consulting with line management and reaching agreements on implementation.
- They are likely to be owners of mandated areas, such as legislative requirements in equal opportunities and employment law.
- Understanding and educating the business, with special responsibilities for communication, pushing and coaching line managers in strategic aims.
- They are likely to own developments to increase employee involvement and engagement.
- Setting up innovative practices and monitoring experiments.

SHARED SERVICES

This is the 'transactional' area where routine work takes place and policies are applied consistently. The burden of routine is taken away from line management and the shared-service team provides services not just to the company concerned but may provide a number of services for a set of subsidiaries under the same holding company.

Areas covered include:

- Recruitment advertising, dealing with applicant response, routine testing
- Advice on details of reward policies, especially benefits, including pensions
- Advice on employment law and its application to specific routine situations
- Updating of all employee records – absence, salaries, performance management, training
- Advice on health and safety issues.

The shared services usually operate as a call centre with more serious issues referred to the centre of expertise. The service can be provided in-house or, in a minority of cases, entirely outsourced to an external provider (4 per cent of organisations, according to Reilly 2006).

Royal Mail set up a shared-service operation in 2003, which was accompanied by a 70 per cent reduction in the regional HR teams. In recent years, the staff have adopted a more proactive approach, offering specific help over problems triggered by data coming into the centre, such as absence or increased grievances. This replaced a passive approach, when the centre simply responded to a call and provided information and advice.

Whether to create some form of shared services, whether outsourced or not, would appear to be more of a financial question rather than a strategic one. However, because the creation of such a unit affects the structure of the department and the provision of all HR services, the decision has to be essentially a strategic one. As with much of outsourcing, the saving in costs through grouping together similar routine functions can be substantial. Processing job applications, handling advertisements, recording absence and performance management outcomes, and keeping training records are all examples of jobs that can be carried out much more efficiently in a central location rather than in each HR outpost. Hopefully, they can provide a quicker service to the internal customer.

Being in charge of such a centre can be a substantial responsibility. BHP Billiton advertised in 2010 for a 'Shared Services Leader' to provide HR and payroll services to employees in Malaysia and Chile at a salary of $650,000 plus ex-pat benefits.

However, the system is not without its critics. Pickard (2009) reported the following difficulties:

- Shared services often have gaps in their provision and problems in communicating and defining the boundary with other parts of HR.
- Customers are not always happy at the generality of the advice. For example, dismissal questions have a very strong contextual element, which needs careful consideration. Simply quoting the law or ACAS procedural advice is not always sufficient, especially where the unit being advised is small.
- Customers can get confused by the multiple contact points and staff may simply not have the organisational or HR experience to give the level of advice needed.
- HR staff can get bored and their careers are often limited in this setting.

In addition, the cost savings are not always achieved. Liverpool Victoria saved £3 million by bringing the HR function back in-house in 2008. David Smith, HR Director, saw the HR department as a key driver to support business growth and not a function to be run by someone else (*People Management* 2009).

STRATEGIC (OR BUSINESS) PARTNERS

HR generalists are allocated to, and report to, business units and act as internal consultants, giving advice and support to line management. They are generally responsible for the day-to-day human resource activities (although some have a more strategic role – see later discussion) and make use of both centres of excellence and shared services as appropriate. They have immediate responsibility to recruit and manage talent in their unit, to organise learning and development, and for career planning up to junior management level, together with other local issues, such as reward and relations. Ulrich and Beatty have summed up their role as a 'player' whose aim is to add value through acting as a 'coach, architect, builder, facilitator, leader and conscience' (2001: 294).

EXAMPLES OF BUSINESS PARTNERING

The concept of the business partner has found many supporters in recent years. It is interpreted in different ways but there is a central precept of the close relationships with business units, helping to solve practical problems and delivering real value to the organisation. Two examples are shown in case study 1.1.

CASE STUDY 1.1 BUSINESS PARTNERS AT GENERAL MOTORS AND PRUDENTIAL INSURANCE

In 2003, Vauxhall Motors at Ellesmere Port (part of General Motors) reorganised the HR departments with HR staff either outsourced to specialist or routine roles or assigned to a business-focused role. The latter staff were trained to understand all aspects of the business and given a desk in the unit's open-plan offices next to the car-production lines. They engage in day-to-day operations, such as assisting managers in performance management, identifying training needs, coaching and discussing the facts and figures about people in their unit, their promotions, potential, disabilities and concerns. The main purpose is to develop close relationships with line managers, helping to solve business issues through their knowledge of people management.

At Prudential Insurance, the HR business partner works in a business unit as a consultant, drawing down help from centres of excellence, while a service centre deals with HR administration issues. As an example, one partner works in the marketing and innovation function, running the people management side of a major change initiative to improve how to deal with customer complaints. Having worked out with the unit manager what needs to be achieved, the partner pulls together an HR team for the project, uses the recommendations of the specialist HR group and co-ordinates the delivery of the project. This needs skills in relationship building and a good understanding of the business.

(Source: Pickard 2004)

Critique of the 'three-legged stool' structure

Ulrich's suggested structure can be seen to have a number of advantages:

- It places the 'ownership' of much day-to-day HR operations in the hands of line managers, where it should belong – areas such as selecting staff, training and developing them, managing their performance and rewarding them. They need help and advice to do these jobs well and the business partner is there to provide this.
- Removing the transactional side to service centres should be much more efficient, gathering together all the data and necessary expertise. By providing these services to a wider clientele, more efficiencies are achieved.
- Having centres of expertise means that HR knowledge and skills are concentrated, rather than spread thinly round the organisation. Research and innovation can be planned, executed, communicated and monitored far more efficiently.
- It provides a clear career opportunity for HR staff, moving around the structure, usually from transactional to business partner, then to centre of excellence, then back to strategic partnering.

However, a number of drawbacks have been found in practice. Holbeche (2007) detailed the following problem areas identified in a CIPD survey:

- The lack of clarity as to what a 'strategic partner' is actually supposed to do. How strategic should they be? Isn't strategy handled by the centres of expertise, rather than in the operating areas?
- Business partners had difficulty in identifying how they 'added value' and too much time was taken up by trying to 'measure' this value.
- Partners were supposed to be able to diagnose problems, prescribe solutions, ensure effective implementation and move out of the 'hamster wheel' of activity to create strategic approaches to organisational challenges. Often, however, they reverted to what they knew best and simply became a generalist working for their line management team.
- Insufficient training has been given to business partners in consultancy, relationship management and third-party management skills.
- Similarly, line managers have not received enough training to develop expertise in day-to-day HR activities (so business partners carried on doing this part of their job).
- The cost of service centres has been greater than anticipated.
- The loss of 'generalist' activity has been regretted by HR staff who had regarded this area as their heartland.

Reilly has also identified the confusion over roles:

> One consequence of the division [of HR into three legs] is that lines of responsibility are not always clearly defined. Take, for example, responsibility for delivery against internal service-level agreements. The shared-service centre may contribute the most to the success of these agreements, but the main customer interface is between business partners and line managers. Yet business partners may not have been involved in making the agreements and have little or no control over their outcomes. Are they accountable for HR's performance in this regard? It's not always clear.
>
> (2006: 37)

Reilly also points out that the shared services can appear very remote and not much value in helping with immediate problems, such as absenteeism.

In practice, organisations have adopted their own versions of Ulrich's three-legged stool. The Ministry of Defence, for example, has three types of business partner – single job holders covering a whole business area and giving support to its leadership team; people providing support at a similar level but in specialisms such as learning and development; and those that supply transactional support but cannot be swept into a shared-service unit. The Ministry has found that, as it is such a large, diverse organisation, a single model does not appear to work well. Reuters' HR structure has added a fourth, separate HR component structured along geographic lines, although the line between this component and their global business partners can be blurred (Arkin 2007).

HR practitioners have mixed views on the success of the model. In a Roffey Park (2009) survey of 171 organisations, 55 per cent reported that the structure was 'quite successful', 32 per cent were unsure and 10 per cent said it was not successful. Only 3 per cent reported it to be 'very successful'. Line managers were even less sanguine, with 27 per cent reporting it as unsuccessful, although 26 per cent agreed it was 'very successful'.

The CIPD report (2007) concludes that 'best practice' in the setting of business partnering does not seem to exist – it is best fit that applies. In Cisco, for example, business partners are very involved in a cultural stewardship role – being the conscience of the person you are business partner to – although they have found that there is a fine line between cultural stewardship and reducing autonomy by imposing centralised diktats (Smedley 2011).

Some of these difficulties were found in focus on research 1.1 at a London investment bank.

FOCUS ON RESEARCH 1.1 NEW HR STRUCTURE AT A LONDON INVESTMENT BANK

During 2004, the 200-strong HR department was reorganised around key roles and processes reflecting the three-legged stool model. This change was presented as necessary to integrate HR operations after recent mergers and further justified as a means of improving efficiency, effectiveness and client service. Partners (who were previously generalists) were allocated to one of eight business-facing teams, with a strategic partner leading each team. The research project investigated closely the role of strategic partner and the job holder's perception of the challenges and success of the new structure.

The strategic partners all welcomed the changing role, enjoying the emphasis on strategy and the 'strategic dialogue' with line managers. They were enthusiastic about losing the 'day-to-day grind' and concentration on work that 'adds value'.

However, a number did acknowledge that they could not be certain that they actually added value in practice. The nature of their clients (egotistical, opinionated, prima donna-ish) often led to difficulties in accepting their advice or making real progress in developing a strategic approach. They found it difficult to step back from the 'transactional' side and leave this to the functional teams because their clients often wanted functional information and advice from them. Sometimes they simply found it easier to do the functional work themselves, especially as a way to build trust with their clients.

The clash between the partners and the functional teams led to a number of meetings with senior HR managers. Complaints were made that strategic partners were bypassing new procedures, and they, in turn, complained that the transactional work was not being carried out effectively. Another clash occurred when the service centre staff claimed that they had a feel for the mood of the organisation and were a valuable source of strategic knowledge as this was firmly rejected by the strategic partners.

(Source: Pritchard 2010)

HR – adding value to the organisation?

So what does adding value to the organisation really mean? Rucci (1997) has set out six key requirements for HR departments to add value to the organisation and ensure its own survival:

Create change – HR should move away from the control, standardisation and compliance model, and encourage the development of an organisational capability of flexibility, speed and risk-taking. This will mean eliminating unnecessary rules and giving greater emphasis to individual judgement and accountability for line managers.

Develop principled leaders – top executives who ground themselves in a base of moral or ethical principles are few and far between, but they are the people that lead organisations to sustained long-term success. HR needs to set in motion systems to develop such talent, especially leaders who have the courage of their conviction and an unwillingness to compromise on ethical issues. Written ten years before the banking crisis, this could be an important point for the HR directors and non-executives of banks and other financial services to consider carefully.

Promote economic literacy – too much specialisation has led to many managers not having the breadth of outlook to understand the 'big picture' within the organisation. HR should give more emphasis to ensuring managers learn all the skills and knowledge so they can contribute advice on big policy decisions.

Centre on the customer – HR should help to create boundary-less organisations where the customers' viewpoint seriously influences policy decisions and ensure that customer-directed activity is central in performance reviews, promotion criteria and reward decisions.

Maximise services/minimise staff – HR needs to focus on its internal customers, identifying where it adds value and driving down its costs.

Steward the values – HR's role should not just be the organisation's conscience or the 'values police'. It should ensure that the values are understood and that the progress is monitored and measured by embedding them in all HR activities – selection, training, performance management and reward.

These prescriptions reflect the nature of HR programmes entered into by progressive and successful companies. An example in practice is set out in case study 1.2.

CASE STUDY 1.2 HUMAN RESOURCE STRATEGIES AND ACTIONS AT AEHN

In the late 1990s, AEHN, an American acute care hospital, was faced by what it regarded as a tumultuous and unpredictable period in its history and the new CEO undertook to transform it from an organisation that was largely stable and complacent to one that was 'nimble, agile and change-hardy' or it may not have survived. Alongside a number of strategic changes in direction, five key HR initiatives were set in motion:

Achieving contextual clarity. AEHN went to great lengths to be quite sure that employees at all levels understood the CEO's new vision for the organisation, the progress towards achieving that vision and the links between their individual and collective actions to raise organisational performance. Although using conventional methods, the messages were delivered in a fairly intense way with bulletin boards refurbished with a constant flow of relevant stories and reports; banners saying 'Are you ready for change? Are your skills ahead of the game?'; and a steady flow of short courses and meetings to illuminate the organisation's progress for all to understand. Workshops included subjects such as 'survival tactics in times of change'.

Embedding core values. Central to the culture change process, embedding and sustaining the set of core values became the fundamental driving force for the HR initiatives. Taken up by the top team after a year's debate, they were cascaded through the organisation with references weaved into all forms of communication and into HR practices. For example, the selection process was revised to add an assessment of applicants' core values by means of situational interviewing and the performance management scheme was heavily revamped to focus on behavioural manifestations of the values.

Enriching work. A number of work redesign experiments were started to encourage much greater flexibility and empowerment. A position called patient care associate was created to administer tests, take blood and do other duties that previously had been carried out by specialists; staff moved much more around units to fill gaps and to broaden perspectives and encourage social networks; self-managed teams were created to provide 'seamless, patient-focused care'.

Promoting personal growth. Employees were encouraged to take responsibility for their personal growth to help them perform better and be prepared for promotions. This was helped by the introduction of 360-degree feedback which generated more convincing reasons for personal development and change. Alongside this, there was an agreed policy of zero tolerance of employees who failed to pursue and eventually succeed in needed development.

Providing commensurate returns. Not a great deal could be done on substantially improving salaries so the programme concentrated on non-financial benefits. The work enrichment was one important step and the 'Recognise, Appreciate, Celebrate' initiative was another. Staff received 'pat on the back notices' and a 'celebration of a risk taken award' (given for a good effort irrespective of result).

These initiatives were business-based and fitted together well so employees were both able to understand why the changes were necessary and also to see them as a coherent set, which would benefit the patients, the staff and the organisation.

(Source: Shafer *et al.* 2001)

The role of human resources in raising performance

Although there may be considerable doubt concerning the actual role HR should perform and how it should be done, human resources had established a place at the senior management table by the early 1990s through their ability to identify and solve practical problems in fields such as recruitment, employee relations and training. HR professionals and researchers then turned their attention to interpreting and reinforcing the maxim that '*people make the difference*'. This has been approached in three different ways:

■ Firstly, researchers have attempted to identify whether adopting HR practices can make an observable difference in practice to organisational performance in measurable terms. This has often been referred to as '*opening the Black box*'.

■ Secondly, a number of projects have been set up to examine what makes up a truly exceptional collection of HR practices, often called '*bundles*', that raises performance in the organisation.

■ Thirdly, there has been a considerable debate – one that is still very much alive – as to whether such a collection of practices (called '*best practices*') will work in every situation, or whether the context and nature of the organisation puts different demands upon the practices to be operated (called '*best fit*').

Opening the 'Black box'

In attempting to examine the impact of HR practices on organisational performance, a number of researchers have discovered some impressive and direct impacts and influences. This is referred to by Ramsey *et al.* as 'the "high road" approach to management, in which organisations choose to compete primarily on quality and rely especially on human resource development and employee contributions to succeed in this' (2000: 502).

Much of this research has been carried out in America, with the best known being Mark Huselid (1995). He carried out in-depth surveys in top companies, measuring the nature of the HR practices against performance measures, such as growth, productivity and profits. Using market value as the key indicator, he found that organisations with significantly above-average scores on using HR practices provided an extra market value per employee of between £10,000 and £40,000. He also found that the introduction of such practices led to an immediate impact (Guest 1998).

In the UK, a CIPD-financed project by the University of Sheffield's Institute of Work Psychology (West and Patterson 1998) concluded that HR practices are not only critical to business performance but also have a greater importance than an emphasis on quality, technology and research and development (R&D) in terms of influence on bottom-line profits. For example, effective HR practices were found to account for 19 per cent of the variation in profitability and 18 per cent in productivity while R&D accounted for only 8 per cent. This led them to conclude that, if managers wish to influence performance of their companies, the most important area they should emphasise is the management of people.

Patterson and his colleagues studied a group of small and medium-sized companies, and an example of the type of practices implemented in the most successful company of the group (Zotefoams) is shown in case study 1.3.

Some of these findings have arisen from broad surveys across sectors and others from selected industries. Thompson (2000), for example, investigated 400 UK aerospace companies and concluded that high-performing organisations, as measured by value added per employee, tend to use a wider range of innovative HR practices covering a higher proportion of employees. The greatest differentials between higher- and lower-performing organisations (as measured by value added per employee) was in the use of two-way communication systems, broader job gradings and employees being responsible for their own quality.

CASE STUDY

CASE STUDY 1.3 ZOTEFOAMS' HR PRACTICES

Zotefoams achieved the highest profits and productivity of all the companies taking part in the University of Sheffield research, resulting from a heavy investment in unlocking the employee potential, especially on the shop floor. Their HR practices included empowering the employees to determine work priorities, deal with quality issues and solve day-to-day problems. To support these changes, 75 per cent of employees have received problem-solving training; flexibility is achieved through the extensive use of NVQs; and developing skills are rewarded through skills-based pay. Team ethos has been promoted through a benefits harmonisation programme together with employee share options and profit-sharing schemes.

(Source: West and Patterson 1998)

'Bundles' of HR practices

At the same time that researchers were attempting to prove conclusively that successful and effective HR practices improved the bottom-line performance, it became clear that a differentiation needed to be made between such practices: in effect, that some worked better than others, and, more critically, that, although individual practices may be relatively unsuccessful, when brought together in a 'bundle', their combined outcome was much greater than their individual contribution. A number of writers have formulated these bundles into what they call a system of 'high performance' or 'high commitment', indicating that using the full set will inevitably lead to improved organisational improvement. All the researchers emphasised that these bundles have to be coherent and integrated to have their full effect, with Wood explaining that 'it is through the combined effects of such practices that management can most hope to elicit high levels of commitment' (1995: 52).

The *level of commitment* shown by employees is seen as key to high performance. Without such a commitment, employees will not be prepared to develop their skills and competencies, take on board the enhanced responsibilities for quality, work organisation and problem-solving, and 'go the extra mile' to come up with improvements and innovations or improve the customer's experience. That is why a number of researchers use the level of commitment as a key reflection of organisational success from a people management viewpoint.

For Purcell *et al.* (2003), a committed employee will use discretionary behaviour in that the employee can give co-operation, effort and initiative because they want to, arising out of the fact that they like their job and feel motivated by the systems in place, especially the HR ones.

By the middle of the 2000s, the similar concept of 'employee engagement' had mostly replaced 'commitment' as a measure of the positive view of the employee towards the organisation. (See later in the chapter for a further analysis of engagement.)

Researchers have found that a high level of commitment/engagement comes about from the implementation of the following HR practices:

EMPLOYEE INVOLVEMENT

The importance of involvement is explained more fully in Chapter 4, but the basic thinking is that it is impossible to gain the employees' trust if they do not have the essential business information available to management and unless they have at least the opportunity to be consulted on important issues that may affect their jobs and the way they are carried out. This passes the message that employees are treated as mature, intelligent beings, not just 'hands' or 'labour' who leave their brains in their lockers. There is a willingness, in fact, a concerted effort, to involve employees in resolving work-based problems. The process of involvement can include briefing groups, staff surveys, focus groups or more sophisticated systems such as quality circles or recognition schemes. It can also extend to financial involvement through employee share-ownership. Marchington (2001) points out from his research that these practices are very popular with employees (80–85 per cent of employees involved in such practices want them to continue), although he adds the disillusioning caveat that some employees enjoy working with them because it is 'better than working' or 'gives me a half-hour off work'!

EMPLOYEE VOICE

Millward *et al.* (2000), using the data from *The 1998 Workplace Employee Relations Survey*, have shown the close association between positive responses in attitude surveys and direct voice arrangement. A 'voice' for the employees does not have to be through a formal trade union and it is certainly not just ensuring there is a formal grievance procedure. It can be through a works council or a staff representative committee working in a non-union environment. The importance of this practice is that the employer recognises the importance of employee group viewpoints and suggestions and that the employee does not feel isolated, so important issues can be raised in a formal (or informal) setting without the employees themselves having to, in effect, raise their heads above the parapet.

HARMONISATION OF TERMS AND CONDITIONS

'Everybody works for the same team' is a common form of encouragement from senior management but falls on deaf ears if there is a clear manifestation of differing benefits at varying levels in the organisation. When Japanese companies began setting up satellite operations in the UK in the late 1970s and early 1980s, one of the surprises to commentators was the degree of egalitarian symbols on display. In Nissan in Sunderland, for example, there was one canteen serving everybody and it was frequented by all staff including senior management; everybody was on the same level of holiday entitlement and wore the same overalls. Of the expected managerial hierarchy, there were few overt signs, although they were inevitable within the background culture. Employees, however, respected the equality and it fed the belief in the 'one company' ethos, leading, in turn, to effective team-working at all levels (Wickens 1987).

EMPLOYMENT SECURITY

The 'jobs for life' culture evident some 30 to 40 years ago no longer exists. Rather, it never really existed in the first place, except in pockets of the public services, such as prisons and the Post Office. Even in the large banks and multinational corporations, employees may have had a clear, well-trodden career pathway set out, but the precise directions, both geographically and occupationally, may have worked out very differently to expectations and preferences. In the last 20 years, the global and business environmental changes have caused such changes in employment that the pathway has become one made up of crazy paving and employees have to lay it themselves!

So how can any business promise employment security? The theorists indicate that the security is of a different dimension. There may be short-term guarantees of employment, such as 12 months or for the life of a large-scale contract, or, more usually, it is the cultural imperative of the organisation that redundancies will only take place as a very last resort. Internal transfers, skills retraining and short-time working are all alternatives to try to extend the employee's contract as long as possible to get over difficult times. It is, in effect, the opposite of the tough employer's 'high and fire' short-term employment policy. It keeps to the HRM thinking that the employee is a critical asset, not a cost to be reduced.

Alongside these practices to encourage commitment, there are a group of practices that integrate with the *organisation's business strategy*:

SOPHISTICATED RECRUITMENT AND SELECTION

The essence of what 'sophisticated' means in this context will be explained in Chapters 2, 3 and 12. It is essentially the combination of recognising the importance of bringing into the organisation the right people with the right skills and personality (having a strategic approach to human resource planning) and carrying out careful and detailed recruitment and selection procedures. These procedures especially refer to using psychological tests and structured interviews that match people effectively to the organisational culture, the job and the team requirements. It is also associated with using the latest technology such as online recruitment.

EXTENSIVE TRAINING AND DEVELOPMENT (TALENT MANAGEMENT)

It is clearly not enough to select the right people, as will be set out in Chapter 8. In the swiftly changing world, employees need to constantly learn new jobs, which involves developing their skills and knowledge. They must also be prepared for enlargement of their jobs and to be ready for promotion opportunities. The emphasis switches in a subtle way from the organisation organising training courses to the organisation encouraging employees (individually or in groups) to undertake learning experiences, which can take many forms. As employees take greater control over their own learning, their level of commitment is likely to rise. The 'ideal' form of this item in the bundle is of employees undertaking self-directed lifelong learning with the framework of a 'learning organisation' as explained in Chapter 8.

SELF-MANAGED TEAMS

The practice of allowing teams to have greater control over their work is a relatively recent one, although theorists, such as Mayo and his colleagues at the Hawthorne production plant in America in the 1930s, have been advocating it throughout the twentieth century. It is linked closely to involvement and, in a fully fledged system, team members are involved in decisions concerning work rotas, breaks, changes in production processes, leave and sickness arrangements. Moreover, they are encouraged to think about and promote local improvements on an individual and team basis. It is quite an adventurous concept because it involves reducing the power and day-to-day authority of local management, but, at the same time, retains their accountability. It requires very careful training and monitoring for all parties concerned but the research has shown that, when it works well, it is closely associated with high productivity and overall performance. Geary and Dobbins's study of a pharmaceutical company found that: 'For some employees who had enjoyed little autonomy (previously), the extension in their discretion made a substantial positive impression in their sense of achievement and job satisfaction' (2001: 17).

EXTENSIVE SYSTEMS OF FLEXIBILITY

If constant and rapid change is the norm, then successful organisations need a workforce that is flexible enough to respond quickly to the required changes. They need to be multi-skilled, willing to work hours that suit the customer (such as over a 24-hour cycle in supermarket retailing) and willing to switch jobs and locations when necessary. The organisation also needs to have in place facilities to increase and reduce the employee numbers when required through systems of annualised hours or use of temporary and short-term contracts or by outsourcing work. More details are given of these systems in Chapter 7, which shows examples of how such practices can lead to improved performance.

PERFORMANCE PAY

The emphasis on high-performance outcomes inevitably has meant that pay systems are geared to reflect the level of performance. Employees' pay at all levels is contingent; in other words, it has an element that varies depending on the success of the outcomes. Examples of these systems can include bonus schemes for production employees and call-centre staff, performance-related pay for managers and administrative staff, incentive systems for sales and service staff, and executive bonuses for directors. Commitment should be encouraged by aligning the pay of employees with organisational performance, through share options, profit-sharing and gainsharing. Details of all these systems, and the associated performance management processes that must support them, are set out in Chapters 5 and 6.

Table 1.2 summarises the identification of high-performance HR practices as reported by a number of researchers.

Each of the research studies indicate additional practices that they regard as 'high performance'. For example, in the EEF/CIPD study (2003), the list includes comprehensive induction, coherent performance management systems with wide coverage, job variety and responsibility, use of quality improvement teams, market competitive pay and policies to achieve an appropriate work–life balance. The 1998 US Department of Labor study adds a focus on

Table 1.2 HR practices associated with high-performance organisations

	Pfeffer 1998	US Dept of Labor 1998	West and Patterson 1998	EEF/CIPD 2003	Wood and Albanese 1995
Employee involvement	x		x		x
Employee voice	x				
Harmonisation	x		x	x	x
Security of employment	x				x
Sophisticated selection	x		x	x	x
Extensive training/ development	x	x	x	x	x
Self-managed teams	x	x	x	x	x
Extensive flexibility			x	x	x
Performance pay	x			x	x

the customer and developing measures of success, while West and Patterson (1998) stress the need for 'favourable' reward systems and job systems that promote problem-solving.

Given that a bundle of HR practices leads to improved performance, it follows that using this bundle is the best thing to do. In theory, it becomes a set of 'best practices' which can be universally applied.

BEST PRACTICE OR BEST FIT?

When reading the previous section and looking at Table 1.2 it may have occurred to you that there does not appear to be much consensus as to what HR practices make up the full set. Each item of research comes up with a different set of best practices, some of which overlap with other research, but each has a special leaning. In America, Boselie and Dietz (2003) have reviewed ten years of research in this area and have found little that recommends a common approach, with the practices reported more extensively being training and development, participation and empowerment, performance pay and information sharing through involvement.

Because the extensive research reveals such a varied set of bundles, considerable doubt has been shed on whether the application of the set of bundles or best practices will lead inevitably to improved performance. Many writers, therefore, have taken an alternative view that there is no 'holy grail' of practices that will magically improve organisational performance. What works well in one organisation may fail dismally in another where the context may be totally different. In a private sector organisation (a manufacturing company, for example), you may well expect performance pay to be widespread and to form the bulwark of performance management and motivation systems; however, in the voluntary sector (a hospice charity, for example), it is highly unlikely that any of the staff would work under a performance pay scheme. The context, the vision, the values can all be very different.

Huselid himself comes down firmly on the side of a range of possible bundles, based on the reasoning that sustained competitive advantage depends partly on being able to develop arrangements that are hard to imitate. If the 'holy grail' was quite distinctive, then every organisation would immediately adopt it and the competitive advantage would be lost. He terms the practices that would work for the organisation in question a set of 'idio-syncratic contingencies', those that happen to fit well into the specific strategy and culture of the organisation (Guest 1998).

Thompson, similarly, is reticent in recommending wholesale adoption of the innovative HR practices associated with high-performing aerospace companies: 'That is probably too simplistic a message. . . . There is certainly a risk in encouraging businesses to adopt partic-ular sets of working practices if they are not ready for them or if they do not fit with existing strategies' (2000: 19).

Purcell is even more dismissive, claiming that:

> The search for bundles of high commitment work practices is important, but so too is the search for understanding of the circumstances of where and when it is applied, why some organisations do and others do not adopt HRM, and how some firms seem to have more appropriate HR systems for their current and future needs than others. . . . Our concern should be less about the precise policy mix in the bundle and more on how and when organisations manage the HR side of change.
>
> (1999: 36–37)

Marchington and Grugulis adopt the same viewpoint:

> Best practice, it seems, is problematic. When unpacked, the practices are much less 'best' than they might be hoped, there are times when they appear to be contradictory messages, they are not universally applicable and they tend to ignore any active input from employees.
>
> (2000: 1121)

How do you know which HR practices an organisation should adopt? Only by a com-bination of knowing and understanding the true nature and strengths of the organisation, so you can eliminate those practices that have little chance of success, and then by experiment.

For Claridge's, the luxury hotel, the bundle of HR practices that supported their turnaround strategy was quite specific to their unique context, as shown in case study 1.4.

CASE STUDY 1.4 INITIATIVES SUPPORTING CLARIDGE'S' TURNAROUND

In 1998, Claridge's, the luxury hotel group, was battling to maintain its place in the market with occupancy down, complaints up and 73 per cent staff turnover rate. The staff satisfaction survey was returned by only 47 per cent of staff, indicating widespread distrust of management, and only 67 per cent said they felt proud to work for the hotel. The response by senior management was to create a transformation strategy, putting employees' attitudes and performance with customers at the top of the list. This was encapsulated in the new core values:

Passion, team spirit, service perfection, responsibility for actions, communication, interpersonal relations and maximising resources.

The aim was to embed these new values, through lively, participative and sometimes amusing training, involving acting out sketches indicating the working of the new core values which became memorable 'events'.

The main elements of the HR initiatives included a new *reward and recognition scheme*, where staff who demonstrated excellence in implementing the new values would have the chance to win prizes ranging from a limo home to an overnight stay in the penthouse (worth up to £4,000). The new *performance management (PM) scheme* was based on measuring the employees' contribution to the new values with individual and general training based on the gaps that the PM scheme identifies. Sideways experience is encouraged, with staff receiving *training in a collection of different skills. Internal promotion* is now much more common with a natural progression from kitchen porter up to waiter and beyond. The *quarterly newsletter* and staff surveys attempt to enhance the communication quality and draw the teams together.

Within three years, the staff turnover had dropped to 27 per cent and pride in working for the organisation increased to 99 per cent, as shown by the 100 per cent staff return on the survey, a sure indication that trust in management had returned.

(Source: Edwards 2004)

In knowledge-intensive firms, the best fit of practices has been found to be the kind that develops intellectual and social capital needed in order to acquire business and manager customer relationships. Here, the crucial aspect is the development of knowledge-sharing processes, not just the knowledge and skills of the workforce (Swart *et al.* 2003).

Purcell's (1999) distinct preference for 'best fit' has led him to urge a much greater emphasis on sharing employee knowledge throughout the organisation. If organisations have unique circumstances that require unique sets of HRM practices, then it is vital that the knowledge and understanding of both circumstances and practices are held in common by all employees:

> The key point about those firms which adopt high commitment management success-
> fully and adapt it to their unique circumstances is that this codified knowledge, this
> ability in the passing game, has to be shared among core members of the organisa-
> tion. If the organisation is to . . . keep on managing the transition from the current to
> the future state and avoid sharp punctuated change, then roles become diffuse and
> 'belonging' becomes important.
>
> (Purcell 1999: 37)

Although there appears to be extensive evidence of HR practices adding to organisational improvement, there are a number of critics who doubt the close association. The greatest is Legge (2001) whose scepticism has been consistent and vociferous for many years. She points out the vagueness of the definition of the 'best practice', such as performance pay, and the appropriateness of the measures used for organisational success. She also doubts whether the use of the practices actually influences the performance (the lack of causality).

There have also been studies that demonstrate that HRM practices can lead to a deterioration in working life. Danford *et al.* (2004) researched the high-performance HR practices introduced in an aerospace company and found some major negative impacts on the employees, such as substantial downsizing, a superficial implementation of empowerment and a lack of trust between the parties.

A final word on this debate goes to Storey (2007), who attempts to square the circle by suggesting that the two approaches are reconcilable. He suggests that best practice (he calls it 'good practice') can be used as the foundation of a set of universal human resource practices and then each organisation needs to explore what special factors necessitate specific adjustments that need to be made to human resource practice so that alignment with organisational strategy can be achieved. Such practices may be a specific set of exceptionally customer-focused competencies for certain service-facing companies (hospitality, caring) or highly trained and developed team-working made up of disparate skills for fast-moving IT technological companies.

Resource-based view of the organisation

Alongside these investigations, theories have been developed regarding the nature of human resources, whereby they can be regarded as uniquely valuable to the organisation because they are a collection of assets (skills, competencies, experience) that are much more difficult to imitate or replicate, unlike other conventional assets such as land or capital. This is associated with the 'resource-based view' (RBV) of the organisation where competitive advantage is associated with four key attributes – value, rarity, a lack of substitutes and difficulty to imitate.

- ■ Human resources are seen to be *valuable*; looking at employees of football teams, for example, the very skilled ones are certainly seen to be extremely valuable and some senior executives transfer to new organisations with an upfront payment. The cost of replacing employees who leave organisations is often high, especially if they are experienced and are seen by customers as important. As explained by Boxall and Purcell:

> [organisations] can never entirely capture what individual [employees] know. Some of what we know – including many of our best skills – cannot be reduced to writing or to formulas. When we leave the firm, we take this knowledge with us. When whole teams leave . . . the effects can be devastating.
>
> (2003: 83)

■ *Rarity* is associated with the value as there will always be a labour group that is in short supply: IT staff in the 1980s and 1990s, nurses and teachers in the early 2000s, plumbers most of the time. Organisations that have a steady supply of skills in short supply will have a competitive advantage.

■ It is possible to *substitute for labour*, through automated call centres and production lines, but those organisations that possess skilled employees where such substitution is impossible (most service organisations, consultancies, etc.) should be able to gain an advantage. It has been argued that the UK's competitive advantage has been maintained because of the country's very large service sector, whereas Germany's large manufacturing sector has been constantly chipped away by international competition and automation.

■ Similarly, it is *difficult to imitate* the skilled work of employees. Cheaper versions of services can be available (self-service in restaurants) but the market for high-quality service by skilled employees is normally in a state of constant growth.

Having recognised the importance of people as a resource, it provides encouragement to employers to identify and then improve the quality of their 'human capital'. In terms of identification, the CIPD (Brown 2003) put forward a proposal in the form of a framework so that organisations could report on the way they:

■ Acquire and retain staff, explaining how the firm sources its supply, the composition of the workforce in terms of diversity and employment relationships, and its retention policies

■ Develop staff, including details of skills levels and development strategies

■ Motivate, involve and communicate with employees

■ Account for the value created by employees, including how they manage the bank of employee knowledge and the methods of determining team and individual performance.

An example of treating employees as a valuable resource is shown in case study 1.5, which deals with Google's people policy.

CASE STUDY 1.5 GOOGLE'S APPROACH TO THE VALUE OF EMPLOYEES

The growth of Google is staggering. From 5,700 employees in 2005, it has grown to 20,000 in 2008*, over half employed outside America. Despite the rush to bring talent into the company, it still approaches it in a slow and measured way. To get a job, you need to attend four or five interviews, down from around eight a few years back, and you will be interviewed by at least two would-be colleagues and, for management positions, some of your existing staff. If any of the interviewers have any doubts about a candidate, they are not taken on.

Many of the senior managers take around 25 per cent of their time in recruitment and selection activities. This is justified by Liane Hornsey, Director of People: 'Of course, it's a huge investment of time but we do not measure it or put a cost on it. If we concentrate our efforts on getting the right people ... then we won't have trouble downstream.'

Their HR policies are unusual. They have no specific 'talent' programmes and don't measure absence, preferring to treat everyone as an individual where possible. The company has a very flat management structure so promotion opportunities are rare and managers generally have large numbers of staff who report to them.

The most innovative concept is the 70–20–10 policy for engineers, which insists that each programmer should spend only 70 per cent of their time doing their core job, and 20 per cent should be spent on related activity or a project that will help them do their core job better. The remaining 10 per cent can be spent on 'blue-sky thinking' perhaps on new products or services.

Google employees' benefits in Mountain View California include free food all day, on-site gym, doctor and masseur. Moreover, the company does all it can to fit in with individual requests for flexible working – 'we hire great people and we really want to keep them, so let's work out what is right for them in their work–life balance,' says Hornsey.

(Source: Brockett 2008)
*Note: In September 2011, Google employed over 30,000 staff worldwide.
(See Chapter 2 for another Google case.)

Barriers to high performance

Finally in this section, a quick look at research that identifies how HR practices are not easily implemented. Kim and Mauborgne (2003) from the Boston Consulting Group, in a study of 125 US companies, have identified four main hurdles that consistently prevent HR professionals from effecting high performance, as shown in Table 1.3. Although the prescription applies to any change process, the perceived lack of natural influence of HR practitioners makes the prognosis more compelling in terms of HR processes improving overall performance.

Table 1.3 Barriers to high performance

Barrier	How to overcome barrier
Cognitive hurdle – managers cannot see that radical change is required	Pointing out the numbers is insufficient. Managers need to be put face to face with the problems – with dissatisfied employees or customers
Resource hurdle – insufficient resources available to implement the practice successfully	Reduce HR resources that are not adding value (cold spots) and transfer resources to those practices which have a high potential performance gain (hot spots)
Motivational hurdle – that discourages and demoralises staff	Work on the major influencers, the champions of change. Bring problems out into the open and ensure everybody follows the improving story line
Political hurdle – that brings internal and external resistance to change	Identify and silence internal opponents by building alliances with natural allies. Isolate external opponents

Source: Kim, W. and Mauborgne, R. (2003) Tipped for the Top. *People Management*, 24 July, Personnel Publications.

CURRENT CONCEPTS IN HUMAN RESOURCING

This chapter finishes with a brief examination of two concepts in human resources which have been the subject of considerable interest among both academics and practitioners towards the end of the 2000s: 'talent management' and 'engagement', and how they can be implemented in the workplace.

Talent and talent management

The CIPD give the following useful definitions:

■ *Talent* consists of those individuals who can make a difference to organisational performance either through their immediate contribution or, in the longer term, by demonstrating the highest levels of potential.

■ *Talent management* is the systematic attraction, identification, development, engagement, retention and deployment of those individuals who are of particular value to an organisation, either in view of their 'high potential' for the future or because they are fulfilling business/operation-critical roles.

The usefulness of this concept is that it provides a universal approach to the management of people in an organisation. In order for organisations to gain competitive advantage, they need to develop a strategic approach to talent management that suits their business and gets the best from their people. The value of a tailored, organisation-wide talent management strategy is that it provides a focus for investment in human capital and places the subject high on the corporate agenda. In recent years, the concept of talent management has evolved into a common and essential management practice and what was once solely associated with recruitment now covers a multitude of areas including organisational capability, individual development, performance enhancement, workforce planning and succession planning (CIPD 2012).

Talent management covers the following areas:

- Attracting talent – ensuring that high-quality applicants with the appropriate skills, competencies, qualifications and experience are attracted to the organisation. Also that a good proportion of promotions take place from within. This is covered in more detail in Chapters 2 and 3.
- Retaining talent – ensuring that there is an engaged workforce that has high levels of job satisfaction and stays with the organisation for an extended period. This is covered in Chapters 4 and 5.
- Developing and managing talent – ensuring that employees reach their potential through well-focused learning development and career planning and that there is a strong cadre of potential leaders coming through the organisation. More details in this area in Chapter 8.
- Rewarding talent – ensuring that effective performance management and reward schemes are in place so that talent is rewarded appropriately. Coverage of this area is in Chapters 5 and 6.

When a talent management programme works well, it can also contribute to other strategic objectives, including:

- Building a high-performance workplace
- Encouraging a learning organisation (details in Chapter 8)
- Adding value to the 'employer of choice' and branding agenda (details in Chapter 2)
- Contributing to diversity management (details in Chapter 9).

Talent management can be approached in two ways. There can be an 'exclusive' approach where resources are focused on a relatively small cadre of outstanding employees who will be developed into future leaders in the organisation. This was the original concept at a time, in the late 1990s and early 2000s, when such talent was in very high demand in buoyant economies around the world. The second approach is a more 'inclusive' one, which covers the whole workforce. Here the aim is to identify and achieve the potential of every employee at all levels and this is strongly linked to the concept of having an 'engaged' workforce.

Employee engagement

The concept of engagement is a development from the earlier idea of employee involvement and commitment. However, although both involvement and commitment indicate a willingness of employees to readily contribute towards organisational goals, engagement indicates a higher level of non-contractual effort by the employee, often referred to as 'going the extra mile'. At the same time, this willingness to contribute by the employee is linked to a genuine belief that the job is worthwhile, that it satisfies and often inspires them, and that they buy into the underlying culture of the organisation. They feel that they play an important part in organisational success and that they are recognised and rewarded for so doing.

It has been found that building engagement in an organisation requires considerable time, energy and a thoroughly consistent and fair approach to people management. The level of engagement can be reduced very easily by management actions such as redundancies and closures or by eliminating some attractive benefits or bonuses. It is known to fall sharply after takeovers and mergers where swift cost-cutting actions often take place amid considerable uncertainty. Similarly, recessions place considerable stress on an engaged workforce (Arkin 2011).

There are now accepted measures that indicate levels of engagement and these are explained in detail in Chapter 4, together with examples of how organisations are working towards raising engagement levels.

Throughout this book, you will see a number of references to both subject areas.

KEY CHAPTER SUMMARY POINTS

■   Recent worldwide economic and social developments have brought closer the impact of the global economy, dependent largely on the skills, initiatives and abilities of employees.

■   Human resources have had many different roles in the past but the major role today is to initiate change in employment practices that support the successful operations of the organisation.

■   There is a major role for human resources in improving organisational performance through identifying ways that bring out the best performance in individuals and teams.

■   There is considerable debate as to whether there are a set of 'best practices' that can be applied universally or whether it requires a different set of practices which 'fit' the organisation's culture and context.

STUDENT ACTIVITIES

1   Compare and contrast the human resources profession with that of law and medicine in respect of characteristics such as professional knowledge, ethical considerations, local expertise required, status in the organisation and views of the general public.

2   Set out some of the opportunities presented to Sarah in the Meteor Telecoms case study. How would she best take advantage of them?

3   If you were an employee of Google (case study 1.5), suggest ways that you would expect the organisation to put into practice its espoused aims regarding its employees.

4   The move to devolve human resource management to line managers has advantages and difficulties. Set out a case for and against in the example of recruitment and selection.

5   How would you best sell the human resources function to the rest of the organisation?

REFERENCES

Arkin, A. (2007) Street Smart. *People Management*, 5 April, 24–28.

—(2011) Live Issue – Employee Engagement, November, 22–27.

Boselie, P. and Dietz, G. (2003) Commonalities and Contradictions in Research on Human Resource Management and Performance. Paper presented at the Academy of Management Seattle.

Boxall, P. and Purcell, J. (2003) *Strategy and Human Resource Management*. Palgrave.

Brockett, J. (2008) Finders Keepers. *People Management*, 18 September, 28–31.

Brown, D. (2003) A Capital Idea. *People Management*, 26 June, 42–46.

CIPD (2007) *The Changing HR Function*. CIPD.

—(2012) Talent Management – An Overview. Factsheet, accessed at www.cipd.co.uk/hr-resources/factsheets.

Coyle, D. (1997) *The Weightless World – Strategies for Managing the Digital Economy*. MIT Press.

Cully, M., O'Reilly, A., Millward, N., Forth, J., Woodland, S., Dix, G. and Bryson, A. (1999) *The 1998 Workplace Employee Relations Survey – First Findings*. DTI.

Danford, A., Richardson, M., Stewart, P., Tailby, S. and Upchurch, M. (2004) High Performance Work Systems and Workplace Partnership: A Case Study of Aerospace Workers. *New Technology, Work and Employment*, 19(1): 14–29.

Edwards, C. (2004) Five-Star Strategy. *People Management*, 8 April, 34–35.

EEF/CIPD (2003) *Maximising Employee Potential and Business Performance: The Role of High Performance Working*. EEF/CIPD.

Flannery, T., Hofrichter, D. and Platten, P. (1996) *People, Performance and Pay*. The Free Press.

Geary, J. and Dobbins, A. (2001) Teamworking: A New Dynamic in the Pursuit of Management Control. *Human Resource Management Journal*, 11(1): 2–23.

Gratton, L. (2011) Work the Shift: The Changing Shape of Jobs. *People Management*, May, 32–34.

Guest, D. (1989) Personnel and HRM: Can You Tell the Difference? *Personnel Management*, January, 48–51.

—(1998) Combine Harvest. *People Management*, 29 October, 64–66.

Hamel, G. and Prahalad, C. (1994) *Competing for the Future*. Harvard Business School Press.

Handy, C. (1994) *The Age of Paradox*. Harvard Business School Press.

Holbeche, L. (2007) HR Transformation – High Road or Rocky Road? *Impact*, November, 21: 14–15.

Huselid, M. (1995) The Impact of Human Resource Management Practices on Turnover, Productivity and Corporate Financial Performance. *Academy of Management Journal*, 38: 400–422.

Kim, W. and Mauborgne, R. (2003) Tipped for the Top. *People Management*, 24 July, 26–31.

Legge, K. (2001) Silver Bullet or Spent Round? Assessing the Meaning of the 'High Commitment/Performance Relationship', in J. Storey (ed) *Human Resource Management: A Critical Text*, 2nd ed. Thomson Learning.

Marchington, M. (2001) Employee Involvement at Work, in J. Storey (ed.) *Human Resource Management: A Critical Text*, 2nd ed. Thomson Learning.

Marchington, M. and Grugulis, I. (2000) 'Best Practice' Human Resource Management: Perfect Opportunity or Dangerous Illusion? *International Journal of Human Resource Management*, 11(6): 1104–1124.

Millward, N., Bryson, A. and Forth, J. (2000) *All Change at Work: British Employment Relations 1980 to 1998 as portrayed by the Workplace Industrial Relations Survey Series*. Routledge.

People Management (2009) In-House HR Saves £3million for Insurance Group, 24 September, 10.

Pfeffer, J. (1998) *The Human Equation*. Harvard Business School Press.

Pickard, J. (2004) One Step Beyond. *People Management*, 30 June, 27–31.

—(2009) Calling the Shots. *People Management*, 2 July, 20–23.

Pritchard, K. (2010) Becoming an HR Strategic Partner: Tales of Transition. *Human Resource Management Journal*, 20(2): 175–188.

Purcell, J. (1999) Best Practice and Best Fit: Chimera or Cul-de-sac? *Human Resource Management Journal*, 9(3): 26–41.

Purcell, J. and Ahlstrand, B. (1994) *Human Resource Management in the Multi-Divisional Company*. Oxford University Press.

Purcell, J., Kinnie, N. and Hutchinson, S. (2003) Open Minded. *People Management*, 15 May, 30–33.

Ramsey, H., Scholarios, D. and Harley, B. (2000) Employees and High Performance Work Systems: Testing Inside the Black Box. *British Journal of Industrial Relations*, 38(4): 501–531.

Reich, R. (2004) *Reason: Why Liberals Will Win the Battle for America*. Knopf.

Reilly, P. (2006) Falling Between Stools. *People Management*, 23 November, 36–37.

Roffey Park (2009) *Maximising the Value of HR Partnering*. Roffey Park.

Rucci, A. (1997) Should HR Survive? A Profession at the Crossroads. *Human Resource Management*, 36(1): 169–173.

Shafer, R., Dyer, L., Kilty, J., Amos, J. and Ericksen, J. (2001) Crafting a Human Resource Strategy to Foster Organisational Agility. *Human Resource Management*, 40(3): 197–211.

Smedley, T. (2011) On My Agenda. *People Management*, April, 31–33.

Storey, J. (1992) *Developments in the Management of Human Resources*. Blackwell.

—(ed.) (2007) *Human Resource Management*, 3rd ed. Thomson.

Swart, J., Kinnie, N. and Purcell, J. (2003) *People and Performance in Knowledge-intensive Firms*. CIPD.

Thompson, M. (2000) *The Competitiveness Challenge: Final Report: The Bottom Line Benefits of Strategic Human Resource Management*. Society of British Aerospace Companies.

Torrington, D., Hall, L. and Taylor, S. (2004) *Human Resource Management*. Financial Times/Prentice Hall.

Ulrich, D. and Beatty, D. (2001) From Partners to Players: Extending the HR Playing Field. *Human Resource Management*, 40(4): 293–307.

Ulrich, D. and Brockbank, W. (2005) The HR Value Proposition. *People Management*, 15 June.

US Department of Labor (1998) *Government as a High-Performance Employer*. SCANS Report for America 2000.

West, M. and Patterson, M. (1998) Profitable Personnel. *People Management*, 8 January, 28–31.

Wickens, P. (1987) *The Road to Nissan: Flexibility, Quality, Teamwork*. Macmillan.

Wood, S. (1995) The Four Pillars of Human Resource Management: Are They Connected? *Human Resource Management Journal*, 5(5): 49–59.

Wood, S. and Albanese, M. (1995) Can we Speak of a High Commitment Management on the Shop Floor? *Journal of Management*, 32(2): 1–33.

ADDITIONAL FEATURES

 Please visit the companion website at: www.routledge.com/cw/stredwick where you will find additional case studies and reading material together with short self-tests and other resources for both students and lecturers.

2 RECRUITMENT, EMPLOYER BRANDING AND EMPLOYER OF CHOICE

CHAPTER OBJECTIVES

When you have read this chapter and carried out the activities, you will be able to:

■ Identify the key aims of the recruitment process.

■ Plan a recruitment campaign.

■ Understand the difference between job analysis, job description and person specification.

■ Design a job advertisement.

■ Identify the various ways that technology can enhance a recruiting exercise.

■ Set out the main benefits and difficulties in the concept of Employer Branding.

INTRODUCTION

In Chapter 1, we saw that recruitment, effectively renamed '*resourcing talent*', remains one of the most crucial activities of human resource specialists in the organisation with the central purpose of attracting the best applicants for vacant posts. It was explained that 'talent' consists of those individuals who can make a difference to organisational performance either through their immediate contribution or, in the longer term, by demonstrating the highest levels of potential. Resourcing talent is the systematic attraction, identification, selection and deployment of individuals who are of particular value to the organisation either immediately or because of their potential.

Increasingly, however, resourcing talent is also seen as very much a public relations exercise, giving the opportunity to sell the organisation to the public and to present a desirable public image to successful and unsuccessful candidates alike. This process, variously called 'becoming an *employer of choice*' or '*employer branding*', has always been in the background, especially when applied to advertisements and subsequent interviews but, over the last ten years, it has been converted into a company strategy to recruit and keep the best talent available. The concept of employee branding, which, hopefully, will lead to the organisation becoming an 'employer of choice' will be covered at the start of this chapter. Next, the stages and mechanics of recruitment will be discussed in detail. Finally, as the field of recruitment and selection has been one of the most fruitful for adopting new technology, the many options, benefits and difficulties in this field will be covered.

It should be borne in mind that equal opportunities legislation, which will be covered in Chapter 9, has a strong effect on each of these stages and practitioners need to remind themselves at each stage (advertising, short-listing, etc.) how legislation affects best practice in each area.

One of the biggest drivers for the changing world of recruitment is the growing costs involved. The current estimate of the average cost of replacing an employee has risen to close to £4,000, with the cost of recruiting managers as much as £10,000 (CIPD 2010) so the bottom line is immediately affected if recruitment is not handled well.

In this chapter, therefore, the main stages in the recruitment process will be examined:

■ *Determining how the employer brand can enhance the recruitment process.*
■ *Determining whether a vacancy exists*, or whether the apparent gap can be filled in another way.
■ *Defining the details of the vacancy*, including the job description and person specification.
■ *Attracting the applicants* through advertising and other methods, including employer branding.
■ *Using technology to improve the recruitment outcomes.*

EMPLOYER BRANDING

The application of branding to the employment situation has emerged in the last dozen years. The principal driver towards branding is to ensure that existing employees buy into the organisation's culture, which is often associated with the product itself, and

	HIGH *LEVEL OF REWARDS* LOW	**EMPLOYER OF CASH**	**EMPLOYER OF CHOICE (QUALITY EMPLOYER BRAND)**
		EMPLOYER OF CHURN	**EMPLOYER OF VALUES**
		LOW *IMPORTANCE OF CULTURE* HIGH	

Figure 2.1
Employer branding

Source: Adapted from Higgs, M. (2004) Future Trends in HRM, in D. Rees and R. McBain (eds) *People Management Challenges and Opportunities.* Palgrave Macmillan.

that potential employees see the company as one they really want to work for. This is usually due to the combination of the quality of the organisation's work values and the attraction of the level of pay. This is set out in the model by Higgs (2004) in Figure 2.1.

From this model, you can see that an employer that has little by way of organisational culture and poor pay awards usually is faced by a high employee churn (turnover) rate. At the other end of the quadrant, high scores in both values and satisfaction with financial return will produce the outcome of becoming an employer of choice. In practice, it has generally been found that a third element is required to raise the brand level; this is a sense of 'fun' in the job which makes working in the organisation not just worthy and well paid but also highly enjoyable and fulfilling. A highly rated employer brand can be used to compete effectively in the labour market by making themselves distinctly different (just think 'Google') and drive employee loyalty through effective recruitment, engagement and retention policies.

Case studies 2.1 and 2.2, Beaverbrooks and Adidas, are examples of organisations that have successfully developed their employer brand.

The Beaverbrook and Adidas case studies demonstrate a number of facets for employer brand:

■ *The propositions put forward by the brand must be attractive to employees.* They can appeal because they carry a prestige, such as Microsoft or Shell, so the work experience is valuable in the employee's career development; alternatively, they may provide a substantial potential for excitement and career development, such as in a small but growing high-tech or service organisation, such as Beaverbrooks; the brand may align closely with the employee's deeply felt values, such as working in the voluntary sector, having strong and effective equal opportunities practices, always promoting from within or an organisation closely allied to environmental issues; increasingly, the brand may be associated with a 'fun' or 'cool' culture, such as Virgin, Adidas or an organisation in the entertainment or media sector; finally, the brand may specifically offer working conditions that are currently very attractive – such as encouraging flexible working or involving foreign travel. If a brand can appeal in a number of these areas, then it becomes more valuable.

- *There must be meaningful and realistic company values.* It is vital that the employees see the values as relevant and real. As with many aspects of the consumer society, it does not take long for consumers (employees) to tire or become cynical about the supposed values of a product (company) if it does not 'do what it says on the tin'. Where values are too general, such as 'emphasis on team-working' or 'reward for high performance', the employee may need considerably more convincing that the values really work in practice.

- *The link between company brand and employer brand must be very clear and integrated.* As explained by Glyn House of Wagamama:

> In a branded organisation, the consistency between the customer and employee experience is so important. And that's where I feel that HR and marketing should come together. The Wagamama brand is food-driven but it is also service driven. So it is vital to build an understanding of what the customer wants and how to deliver that.

> (Roberts 2006: 32)

Adidas's emphasis on 'mind, body and soul' attempts to strengthen this link.

C A S E   S T U D Y

CASE STUDY 2.1 BEAVERBROOKS THE JEWELLERS – AN EMPLOYER OF CHOICE

The company's main ethos is focused on providing 'memorable customer service'. This might be a free lunch for a customer while a ring is being altered, or a gift of flowers for a newly engaged couple. Ninety-seven per cent of staff recognise that the company has strong principles for treating customers well and buy into that concept. This is matched by the way the organisation treats its 600 staff in 75 outlets. All promotions to branch manager are made from within and the company invests a considerable amount in training, including a sector award. Those who pass this award receive a bonus, a trip to London and dinner with the managing director. Staff have reported that they have considerable faith in their managers and believe they talk honestly to them and express appreciation of their work.

The company encourages staff to have fun at work, which has been added to the mission statement, while pay and benefits are above the retail average. This led to the company gaining first place in the *Sunday Times* 100 best companies to work for in 2009.

(Source: *Sunday Times* 2009)

CASE STUDY 2.2 ADIDAS – MIND, BODY AND SOUL

Adidas developed a new take on employer branding in 2011 with an underlying theme of 'mind, body and soul' as the basis of its employee value proposition. This messaging was used to help frame all of its recruitment activities and communication. The term 'mind' covered areas such as innovation, employee development and training summed up as 'developing the mind of a winning athlete'. 'Body' covered the way the company looked after the health and well-being of its employees by providing on-site gyms as well as environmentally friendly offices. 'Soul' covered the company's aim to work with honesty and integrity and to be socially and environmentally responsible. The idea of the employer branding launch was to deliver something original in 2010 that would chime in with the consumer brand image as a fresh, innovative company.

(Source: IDS 2011a)

DIFFICULTIES WITH EMPLOYER BRANDING

Not all commentators support this concept. Jenner suggests that companies encouraging employees to 'live the brand' are, at best, controlling, rather creepy and possibly unethical. At their worst, they could exacerbate the problems of talent management that they have been designed to solve:

> Employer branding represents a shift from a traditional psychological contract that embodies mutual obligation and reciprocity. By viewing employment as a consumer good, we reduce a person's sense of responsibility to their employer and encourage a self-absorbed career trajectory.
>
> (Jenner, quoted in Carrington 2007: 38)

Other critics worry that branding is too much of a 'black art' associated with spin and does not encourage the degree of honesty and trust that should be associated with human resource practices. Taylor (2010) suggests that organisations should call the practice of branding 'reputation management' to improve the image of the exercise.

IDENTIFYING TALENT

As set out in Chapter 1, talent management is increasingly becoming an inclusive concept, not just dealing with a cadre of highly qualified applicants with board-room potential. As applied to the whole workforce, it can have the effect of boosting internal mobility, countering perceptions of elitism and supporting a wider cultural change, helping staff to feel more confident about voicing their ambitions and to identify ways of pursuing them (IDS 2008).

Identifying talent will therefore include all the normal recruitment aspects, such as defining the job, working out the person specification, deciding on how it can be filled, advertising the vacancy, using third parties and deciding on the required technology to assist the process. At the same time, it needs to be linked to a built-in process of successful induction, career planning and performance management for the successful applicant.

DRAFTING A RECRUITMENT POLICY

From an ethical viewpoint, a recruitment policy represents the organisation's code of conduct, including the rules to be followed and the standards to be reached. It should include the following areas:

- The importance of considering internal applications and developing existing employees to enable them to be considered for promotion.
- Handling and processing applications with due speed, diligence and courtesy.
- Ensuring the successful applicants will be chosen without regard to sex, race, age, disability, marital status, religion or any other factor unconnected with their ability to carry out the job.
- Making sure that no false or exaggerated claims are made in recruitment literature or job advertisements.

DOES A VACANCY EXIST?

Vacancies can occur either through an existing occupant leaving the organisation or through the creation of a new post through expansion or reorganisation. In either case, it is all too easy to opt for recruitment without first thinking through all the alternatives that could be considered, especially as substantial savings can be made by not recruiting or replacing. Here are some alternatives:

Doing away with the work altogether

Although less likely in these competitive times, there are still some positions where the work carried out adds insufficient value to the organisation to justify a replacement. This may come about through the changing nature of the business, a reduction in the activity that this position services or simply because the job was created in the first place without sufficient thought or justification. The arrival of business process reorganisation has often, through a thorough and detailed examination of each business process, weeded out jobs where the main function may be to process figures or write reports that are no longer required.

Automate the work

The number of employees working in manufacturing industries has drastically reduced over the last 30 years as their work has been replaced with new technology. The latest industrial revolution is in the offices where computer developments have rapidly changed the face of communications and information processing. Although it is seldom possible to replace one employee through mechanisation, the arrival of a vacancy can present the opportunity for a rethink of the work structure.

Contract out/in-source the work

Sub-contracting (or outsourcing, as it is more commonly called today) is becoming more frequent at all levels. Employers are seeing the advantages of avoiding employment costs and making overall savings, especially where the work is put out to competitive tender. It is very common in the building industry and in IT but can equally well apply to work done in or outside the organisation's premises. However, there are potential hazards of having much less control, as well as, in some cases, the complexities of TUPE legislation, which deals with the legal aspects of transferring employees from one business to another as the work is outsourced. The work can be contracted to a specialist organisation, such as a facilities maintenance company, or to an agency, which will deal with a large number of unskilled or semi-skilled operations and which will recruit, train and supervise the staff itself. An example of the latter is at the Xerox Corporation plant in the Forest of Dean where much of the production operations were outsourced to Manpower PLC (Stredwick and Ellis 2005).

In-sourcing the work means hiring temporary employees to carry out the work. There are two reasons for using this form of labour:

1   Specialist, skilled labour is required for specific jobs which are for a limited period. It may prove more expensive to use such labour (as it often carries a highly skilled premium) but employing such labour on a permanent basis cannot be justified. IT staff often come into this category.

2   It is seen as cheaper to employ temporary workers as they have much fewer benefits and can often be on lower rates. However, the Agency Worker Regulations 2010 (effective from 1 October 2011) have essentially put a stop to this practice. After 12 weeks' employment, agency workers have the right to the same pay and conditions as permanent staff, as well as rights from day one to access to the end-users' collective facilities, such as canteens and childcare facilities. It is possible to insist that agency staff have an employment contract with the agency (the so-called Swedish derogation model – SDM) so the regulations do not apply to them. However, SDM-employed workers are entitled to up to four weeks' pay in between assignments and it is likely that agency fees will need to be increased to cover the agencies' increased costs (Chynoweth 2011).

Reorganising the work

This can take the form of replacing the post by separating different parts of the work, eliminating those that are unnecessary and farming out the rest within the department or even to other departments. It can also take the form of *job enrichment*, which is to extend the work of existing employees to cover more responsibility and decision-making. For example, W. Gore encourage their employees to take an interest in a wide variety of job areas or projects. They can stretch and build on their roles to suit their interests, aspirations and business needs (CIPD 2008). Another example is that of multi-skilling of nurses at Nottingham City Hospital (Stredwick and Ellis 2005).

Reorganising the hours

It may be possible for other members of staff to work overtime to carry out the work, especially if it can be shown that it does not justify a full-time post. This has the advantages of avoiding the recruitment exercise and providing additional salary for those staff willing to work the overtime. It is not, though, a recommended viable long-term alternative as overtime costs are high and it can help to create an overtime culture where work is extended simply to justify working overtime. A second alternative is to rejig the shift system to partly increase the overall hours or to spread out the work in a more even way. Finally, the post can be converted into a part-time position that should bring cost savings and also allow a degree of flexibility should the volume of work increase in the future.

Use an intern – get the work done for free!

At their best, internships can offer structured, well-planned short-term placements that can help the intern (usually a new graduate or a person on a gap year) to learn about particular careers while, at the same time, providing a useful view for the employer of the potential of the 'recruit' before making any costly investment.

On the other hand, many internships are an effective way for unscrupulous employers to get unpaid labour doing unpopular work from young people who are desperate to get their foot in the door in a challenging job market. For example, a report by the National Union of Journalists (NUJ) found that 70 per cent of media industry interns did not even receive expenses when sent out on reporting jobs, let alone a minimum wage (Chynoweth 2012).

The legal position is that, if the intern is classed as a 'worker', they are entitled to the National Minimum Wage (NMW) rates. Simply being a 'volunteer' cuts no ice with the law if the intern is contributing to the company, has a list of duties and is working set hours as shown in spotlight on the law 2.1. The only exceptions are for students undertaking short-term experience as part of a university course or if the intern is not obliged, or expected, to actually carry out meaningful work.

SPOTLIGHT ON THE LAW 2.1 INTERN WINS RIGHT TO PAY

Keri Hudson, 21, was successful at a Central London employment tribunal in May 2011 in proving she had a right to be paid for work carried out over several weeks at the My Village Website in late 2010.

The tribunal heard that, despite the fact that she worked each day from 10am to 6pm and had been personally responsible for and in charge of a team of writers, for training and delegating tasks, collecting briefs, scheduling articles and even for hiring new interns, the company had told her she was not eligible for any pay because they considered her an intern.

In her evidence, Keri Hudson said she had been asked when the site was taken over by TPG Web Publishing Ltd if she would stay on and work for the new company. She was assured her pay would be fixed.

After five more weeks, she was informed she would not now be receiving a payment for the work she carried out – she resigned and took out a grievance. With the support of the NUJ, she began proceedings. The tribunal found she was a worker in law even though she didn't have a written contract and was therefore entitled to be paid at least the National Minimum Wage and holiday pay, totalling around £1500.

(Source: Malik 2011)

Most high-profile organisations that use internships to identify potential pay a salary to the intern. Allianz, for example, pay £18,500 pro rata with meaningful, planned projects, resulting in 20 per cent of the interns joining the organisation after graduation (Chynoweth 2012).

DEFINING THE DETAILS OF THE VACANCY

When it has been decided that a vacancy exists, the specific details of the position need to be agreed. This is carried out in three stages which will be looked at separately:

- Investigating the nature of the work and its key features. This is carried out through *job analysis.*
- Agreeing a summary of the job and the nature of the person who will best fit the post. This means drawing up a *job description* (or, in some cases, a *job profile*) and a *person specification.* Alternatively, a competency profile can be drawn up which will define the nature of the job and the competencies required to carry out that job efficiently. If competencies are used, they will be part of a wider competency framework in use in the organisation.
- Deciding on the terms and conditions of the post, including hours of work, salary and benefits. This is known as an *employment package.*

Job analysis

PURPOSE OF JOB ANALYSIS

Analysing jobs is central to the people management process. Establishing and defining jobs correctly is the starting point not just for the recruitment process; it also plays a major part in the way employees are managed and motivated, becoming the basis for the performance management process (see Chapter 5); it helps to establish how employees' training needs are analysed (see Chapter 8) and has a major input into the design of pay systems, especially the comparison of one employee's pay with another (see Chapter 6).

Job analysis can take place in a number of situations, all of which are associated with organisational change. In the event of a merger or takeover, it is not uncommon for an analysis of some of the critical jobs to be commissioned to see if changes need to be made in the light of the new business imperatives. This may result in the work being redesigned, often with fewer employees. When a major expansion takes place and many more staff are required for one or two posts, job analysis may take place to correctly define the posts for recruitment purposes or to redesign them so there is greater efficiency. In a third situation, when redundancies are necessary, jobs may be analysed in terms of workload and purpose. Business process engineering – where organisations closely examined every activity and process within the process, taking out those which did not add value – was very common in the late 1980s and early 1990s and used job analysis extensively but its importance as an analytical process has declined since 2000.

The size of the organisation can influence the process of job analysis. In large organisations, where hundreds of recruits are sought each year, such as in defence or banking, it is worth undertaking rigorous job analyses, as the consequences of selection mistakes can be very costly to the organisation. For example, employing an unsuitable candidate in a control room of a nuclear power station could result in millions of pounds' worth of damage. Similarly, as recruiting and training a police officer can cost £100,000, it is vital to get the job design right and match this with the recruitment processes and methods so fewer trainees leave before their training is completed (Cooper *et al.* 2003).

An important element to remember, although it gets very blurred in practice, is that the aim of job analysis is to analyse *the job*, not the performance of the employee carrying out the job.

HOW TO CARRY OUT JOB ANALYSIS

The analysis starts with a *definition of what information needs to be gathered*. This can include the instructions given as to how to carry out the work, the processes that lead to the job holder's actions (communications, flow of work, etc.), the nature of the mental and physical processes required, the degree of flexibility in the work itself and in the employee's thought patterns, the targets and required outcomes, the relationships with other employees

– superiors, peers and subordinates – and the general terms and conditions attached to the work.

The next stage is to decide on the format for collecting the information required. For a full description of this topic, see Taylor (2010, chapter 6) but here is a summary of a number of ways that this can be done:

Ask employees to complete a questionnaire. This can be designed by the organisation, with or without the help of specialist consultancy services, or there are a number of standard questionnaires available on the market. The questionnaire needs to be able to be easily computerised from which job descriptions and person specifications can be readily drawn. The advantage of using this system is that the questions are standard and, if tested properly, will be user-friendly. The difficulty is that filling in questionnaires about their job is not always a favourite pastime of employees and they may choose to exaggerate the importance of some aspects of their work.

Ask employees to keep work diaries. This method, if carried out properly, will get a very accurate picture of what actually happens over an extended period, say a week or month. However, many employees will be generally reluctant to carry out such a demand and those that do it properly may not be typical. Again, it is possible to build up the job beyond its actual importance.

Observe the employee. A realistic picture can certainly be drawn up using this method. However, a one-to-one observation is very expensive and time-consuming and may need to be spread over a period of time for it to be representative. It would not be very appropriate for work in accounting offices, where there is a monthly cycle and an annual cycle and often a quarterly cycle as well. It may well be that employees behave differently when they know they are being observed but this may have less truth these days following so many 'fly on the wall' television programmes. Even in today's more compliant workplace, it is unlikely (and unethical) to consider using video recorders for this purpose.

Interview the employee. Sometimes carried out in groups, this provides the opportunity to get the full picture of the post by using probing, clarifying and reinforcing questions. With a group of employees, it may be possible to obtain a more consistent all-round picture, especially in the areas of responsibility and decision-taking. Through interviewing, two specific techniques can be used to produce an outcome. The first is the *Repertory Grid* technique where, through questioning, a grid is constructed of the tasks carried out and the skills and competencies required to carry out those tasks, scored from, say, one to five. This is of considerable assistance in producing an accurate person specification.

The second technique is that of drawing out a set of *critical incidents* to examine which parts of the job are crucial to its success or failure. Starting from a study of key job objectives, the employee is asked to set out anecdotal incidents that resulted in achieving or not achieving those objectives and the part they played in these incidents. This process assists in being able to draw up the skills required to be successful in the job.

Job description

Although principally drawn up for the purpose of recruitment, job descriptions are used for a number of other purposes. They are an integral part of the job evaluation process, where grading and salary decisions are taken on the basis of carefully sculpted job descriptions. They are also used as a basis for training programmes, where training is focused on the elements of a job and how employees can perform better in their job. They are also key to the performance management process where an employee is measured to a larger or smaller extent against the requirements of the job set out in the job description.

Job descriptions come in many shapes and sizes. There are simple versions that give a basic description of the main tasks (see Figure 2.2) There are more complex (and useful) versions that indicate accountabilities and standards as shown in Figure 2.3.

There are organisations, such as Deloitte and Google, who essentially delegate the job of drawing up job descriptions to the job holders themselves (Sartain 2009). This is a new concept known as 'job sculpting' where jobs are designed around individuals' needs,

---

Job Title   Secretary, Sales Office
Reports to   Sales Office Manager
Location   Head Office
Hours   Full-time

Summary of Position

To carry out secretarial duties, including word processing of letters and sales reports, telephone work, filing, essential hospitality and general assistance with meetings.

Main Activities

1 To produce sales reports from information provided by the regional sales teams.
2 To word process letters, circulars, etc. for the sales managers and supervisors.
3 To deal with essential email circulation to sales staff.
4 To handle telephone queries relating to the sales report and commission issues.
5 To file documents, letters and reports and any other items for the department.
6 To help with hospitality at times of conferences and weekly meetings.
7 To take minutes of sales meetings and help initiate any action pending from these meetings with the appropriate manager.
8 To carry out any other necessary duties associated with the sales office.

Figure 2.2
Task-oriented
job description

Job Title	Senior Library Assistant
Reports to	Senior Librarian
Location	Main Library
Hours	Total of 38 per week on shift rota basis

Main Accountability

To implement library procedures in respect of book ordering, cataloguing and loans within the appropriate time span and within costs allocated.

Key Result Areas (extracts)

1 *Book Ordering.* To place orders for books as requested, to check their arrival within the agreed time span, to complete the certificate and pass all documentation to the senior librarian to authorise payment within.
2 *Cataloguing.* To ensure that books delivered are catalogued correctly and on the shelves within eight working days.
3 *Library Loans.* To handle applications for, and safe return of, all inter-library loans within the stipulated time period. To chase up any non-returned books if more than two days overdue, recording accurately all transactions.

Figure 2.3
Accountability-oriented job description

rather than those of the organisation. The belief here is that an organisation needs to gain a capacity for flexibility and creativity above all things in order to attain competitive advantage. In order to achieve this, they need to attract creative and confident individuals who realise how they can use their skills to the advantage of the organisation and have a high degree of curiosity to develop those skills further. This is demonstrated in the Google study, case study 2.3.

The decision on which format to use will be contingent on the current size, complexity and culture of the organisation and the purpose for which the job descriptions are being drawn up. If it is only for recruitment of basic clerical employees, then a simple version will

CASE STUDY 2.3 JOB STRUCTURING '70–20–10' AT GOOGLE UK

Alongside many innovations in job design and employee development, Google lays great emphasis on the flexibility of work practices. The most notable manifestation of this is the company's '70–20–10' policy for engineers, which prescribes that each programmer should spend only around 70 per cent of their time doing their core job; 20 per cent should be spent on related activity or a project that will help them do their core job better, while the remaining 10 per cent can be spent on less focused 'blue-sky thinking', such as dreaming up new products.

(Source: Brockett 2008)

suffice. If it is for supervisory or managerial employees or if the descriptions are also being used for other purposes, then a more complex version is necessary.

The essential ingredients of every job description are:

■ Job title
■ Job location
■ The superior to whom the job holder reports
■ The staff who are responsible to the job holder
■ The overall purpose of the job
■ Whether it is or can be full-time or part-time
■ Most frequently performed duties with some indication of their importance.

Job profile

There has been much discussion in recent years on the restrictive nature of job descriptions. It has been argued that modern-day working practices serve to make descriptions outdated and superfluous. The pace of change is so great that the work that an employee actually carries out can alter within months, even days, of their starting date; so job descriptions need constant updating, which can take considerable time and effort. Furthermore, as we have seen in Chapter 1, employees are now encouraged to work beyond contract; in other words, to do anything that helps them, their unit and their organisation to achieve results quickly, efficiently and in the interests of the customers they serve. This *modus operandi* is difficult to write into a job description and limits to the description can only be tested by practice and experience. The profile, therefore, will only indicate the main tasks and accountabilities and use more generalised statements as to the nature of the work. At Abbey National Building Society (now Santander), they combined a job profile with key aspects of the specification, relevant competencies and indicators of performance and call this a *job statement*. An extract (excluding the specific competencies) is shown in Figure 2.4.

Person specification

The specification has three objectives. Firstly, to provide a focus for the organisation to agree on the traits of the person who is likely to be successful. This is an internal process to ensure that human resources and line management are reading, so to speak, from the same hymn sheet. Secondly, when incorporated into advertising material, it communicates the required information to potential applicants. This should help to reduce the number of applications that are quite unsuitable. Thirdly, the specification can be used as a selecting aid whereby a scientific and objective method can be used to select applicants for the short-list by means of measuring them for proximity to the specification.

JOB STATEMENT FOR
Administrative Assistant, Personnel

Job Purpose: To deliver a range of administration support services within Personnel

	ACCOUNTABILITIES	PERFORMANCE INDICATORS
1. Administration	Undertake broad range of administrative processes; input data onto computerised systems; check for accuracy and completeness. Provide *ad hoc* information.	Workload targets met on time
2. Communication	Initiate contact with others in order to commence/ complete processes, gather information by face to face, telephone or in writing. Feedback regularly to customers/ line managers on progress.	Accuracy of work
3. Respond to enquiries	Resolve standard queries received either face to face, by telephone or letter; refer promptly and accurately enquiries requiring additional expertise; access and annotate records.	Effectiveness at processing enquiries, accurately assessing when to refer, annotating records accurately
4. Work planning	Prioritise and plan tasks to be completed. Clearly communicate areas where you are unable to meet requirements.	Work planned effectively, customers kept well informed
5. Service standards/compliance	Ensure that procedures are in place to meet all statutory requirements so that internal and external customers are given quality service. Contribute ideas to improve service/processes.	Compliance with processes/regulatory requirements and legislative work completed to schedule

KNOWLEDGE, SKILLS AND EXPERIENCE	COMPETENCIES
1–2 years in admin. experience Good knowledge of range of systems Keyboard, WP and telephone skills Team focus Focus on customer care Numerate Problem solving Ability to work under pressure	

Distinguishing features: There is a diverse range of jobs requiring differing levels of specialist knowledge across the personnel function

(Continued overleaf)

Figure 2.4
An example of a job statement at a UK building society

JOB STATEMENT FOR
Administrative Assistant, Personnel

(This page describes differences from the CENTRAL level of the job statement and needs to be read in conjunction with the first page)

COMPREHENSIVE

ACCOUNTABILITIES	PERFORMANCE INDICATORS
Handles complex admin. work	Effectiveness at handling more complex admin. work and problems
Is autonomous in planning own work	Accuracy of completed tasks to service standards
Provides more complex management information reports and analysis	Prompt completion of accurate reports
Undertakes day-to-day supervision, more systematic coaching and development of core/central levels	Effectiveness of coaching/development support
Proposes improvements to admin. processes and local systems	Successful implementation of new processes
Covers for professional management level	
Keeps abreast of current legislation	
Technical advice	

KNOWLEDGE, SKILLS AND EXPERIENCE	COMPETENCIES
Good knowledge of systems/procedures and how they need to be applied	
Keyboard, telephone, spreadsheet and WP skills	
Thorough understanding of how software needs to be applied	
At least 2 years in admin. role	
Ability to prioritise own and others' work	
Awareness of policy/legislation information	
Numerate	
Interpersonal skills	
Problem solving	
Ability to work under pressure	

Figure 2.4
(*Continued*)

JOB STATEMENT FOR
Administrative Assistant, Personnel

(This page describes differences from the CENTRAL level of the job statement and needs to be read in conjunction with the first page)

CORE

ACCOUNTABILITIES	PERFORMANCE INDICATORS
Works on less complex and closely defined clerical admin. processes	Speed and accuracy of completed tasks to service standards
Generation of standard correspondence to customers	Adherence to standard documentation, referral where appropriate
Resolves basic information enquiries and refers where necessary	Effectiveness at resolving enquiries, accurately assessing when to refer
Input of data onto computerised systems likely to be a focus of the job	Speed and accuracy of input
Receives close supervision when processing work	Learns from instruction and supervision

KNOWLEDGE, SKILLS AND EXPERIENCE	COMPETENCIES
Ability to learn procedures and systems	
Keyboard, telephone and WP skills	
Ability to assimilate basic data and information	
Numerate	
Ability to work under pressure	

Figure 2.4
(*Continued*)

Before the era of equal opportunities legislation, person specifications followed closely the models laid down by either:

- Rodger's seven-point plan (1952) – Physical Make-up, Attainments, General Intelligence, Special Aptitudes, Interests, Disposition and Circumstances; or
- Munro-Fraser's five-fold framework (1954) – Impact on Others, Qualifications and Experience, Innate Abilities, Motivation and Emotional Adjustment.

Neither of these models remains safe or satisfactory today. General intelligence and innate ability is impossible to quantify, given the demise of the IQ test, which leaves only a vague and unworkable statement of 'a good level of intelligence'. Most practitioners accept that interests are irrelevant and likely to be discriminatory, especially if they wish, as was often the case, to draw out interests in male activities such as golf or shooting. Questions on circumstances are especially discriminatory, referring to ability to work shifts, to be geographically mobile or likelihood of length of time before the applicant starts a family. Even physical make-up has been steadily eroded as a required specification, with few occupations able to justify height, strength or even manual dexterity in their specification on grounds of equal opportunities. Even 'ability to lift heavy weights' is a doubtful requirement since the introduction of the Manual Handling Operations Regulations 1992.

This leaves qualifications, knowledge, skills and experience plus certain personal qualities that should make up the conventional person specification. Personal qualities have a more subjective element, but psychometric testing (see Chapter 3) provides a more solid objectivity as long as the qualities required are based on well-defined and justified organisational requirements rather than the personal preferences of the recruiter.

A conventional person specification will take the form of Table 2.1 with characteristics distinguished by the 'essential' and 'desirable' tags. It is important that the level of qualifications, skills and experience is not over-rated as this will have a double negative effect. It will discourage both a number of suitable applicants from applying and then the successful application when they find that their skills and experience may not be put to best use.

Using a competency framework

Up to a certain level, conventional person specification methodology can be acceptable in providing the framework for the short-list selection process, but it does have a glaring omission. It fails to focus on the elements that are likely, in the end, to provide success in the job, namely the competencies that applicants will bring to the job – not what they have done and what qualifications they bring, but how they have performed, as measured in terms of outputs and standards of performance.

Since the late 1980s, there has been a gradual growth in the number of organisations that have started creating competency frameworks. They have been established as part of the enhanced performance management process to enable the organisation to obtain,

Table 2.1 Person specification – Branch Manager, Employment Agency

Requirement	Essential	Desirable
Education and qualifications	❏ Educated to A level standard	❏ Good grades in English and Maths
Work experience	❏ 2–3 years' experience in a supervisory role within a customer service or sales environment	❏ Agency experience ❏ Sales experience ❏ Managerial experience
Abilities	❏ Good verbal communication ❏ Managerial skills ❏ Analytical skills ❏ Planning and organising skills	❏ Good written and numerical skills ❏ Computer literate ❏ Good business acumen
Motivation	❏ Self-motivated ❏ Competitive ❏ Results oriented ❏ Prepared to invest in staff development	❏ Desires career advancement ❏ Ambitious
Personality	❏ Socially confident in all situations ❏ Empathetic ❏ Persuasive ❏ Able to cope under pressure ❏ Adaptable ❏ Creative and innovative	❏ Diplomatic ❏ Able to direct and control others
Circumstances	❏ Commitment to overcome difficulties in meeting work requirements	❏ Lives within one hour's travel from the branch

manage, develop and reward people who can ensure the organisations meet their goals. Part of that process is to change the emphasis from a *job description*, which simply sets out what employees do, to a *competency profile*, which lays down the essential competencies required for effective performance in that job. To these organisations, these competencies are indivisible from the jobs.

For all jobs, the organisation will have a set of organisational or *core competencies* that will apply to all positions. These are usually linked to the organisation's core values and include such areas as customer care, flexibility, effective communications and attention to quality. There will also be *specific or technical competencies* that apply to certain jobs or occupations. For each of these competencies, there will be a series of levels setting out the degree of depth or importance as it may apply to each position (Holt and Perry 2011).

For example, Metropolitan Housing Trust turned to competencies when it wanted to broaden the criteria used for selection from technical proficiency to relevant behavioural skills for posts involving sensitive interactions with clients (Warner 2002).

Table 2.2 Magistrates' Court clerk competencies

Competency 1	Build and maintain an effective working relationship with magistrates
Competency 2	Facilitate the business of the court
Competency 3	Contribute to the aims and objectives of the court
Competency 4	Advise and work in partnership with administrative staff
Competency 5	Train and develop magistrates and staff
Competency 6	Organise and support statutory and other committees

Table 2.3 Court clerk competency 1

Competency title: Build and maintain an effect working relationship with magistrates

Outcome	Magistrates' decisions are appropriate and legally correct
What does the court clerk do?	What is the required standard?
Facilitates a structured decision-making process	*Advice to magistrates is accurate, objective and communicated in a way that is structured, clear and comprehensible *Occasions when it is appropriate to intervene are anticipated, relevant issues are identified and necessary information is obtained *Interventions address the specific issues decisively and clearly *Advice is given whether elicited or not
Liaises with magistrates	*Respective roles are clearly identified and agreed *Pre-court consultation with magistrates is carried out on every occasion *Other opportunities are taken to encourage open dialogue with magistrates, e.g. attending training sessions and bench meetings *Feedback is sought and given with magistrates regularly

Source: Lord Chancellor's Office.

Having established the framework, the final stage is to draw up a competency profile for each position, setting out the competencies applicable and the level of application.

A simple version is shown in Table 2.2, where a set of six competencies have been drawn up for magistrates' clerks, and Table 2.3, which details one of these competencies.

The set of competencies act as an effective job description and can also be used to specify the applicants required. They should either already possess the competencies detailed or be capable of being trained to achieve them. These precise definitions are used as the basis of the required training and also to assist in monitoring performance in the job.

Table 2.4 Example of competencies at a brewer

Breaking down roles into measurable, bite-sized pieces

Fingerprints are unique, as are the various management roles in the Beer Co.

A job fingerprint takes each overall competence label; for example, leadership or business awareness and sub-divides it into more specific sub-categories.

Each competence ends with a 'summary of importance' section. This is used to simplify outputs. The greater detail made possible by sub-categories is available as and when required.

Examples:

	Behavioural	Technical (e.g. sales)
LABEL	**3. PERSUADING AND INFLUENCING**	**L-NEGOTIATION**
DEFINITION	Seeks to sell ideas rather than impose them, using rational and logical argument. Adopts an appropriate style according to the situation. Argues a point in a compelling yet unemotional way and is comfortable when dealing with conflict.	Able to effectively negotiate agreements, satisfying both company interests and customer needs.
SUB-CATEGORIES	a. AUDIENCE b. STYLE c. CONFLICT d. DEPTH OF ISSUES e. RESPONSIBILITIES f. ROLE RELATIONSHIPS g. CONSULTATION h. SUMMARY OF IMPORTANCE	a. INVESTMENT AND FACT FINDING b. PLANNING AND FINANCIAL AWARENESS c. KNOWLEDGE AND APPLICATION OF TECHNIQUES d. NEGOTIATED IMPACT AND OUTCOME e. CREATIVE SOLUTIONS f. COMPLEXITY OF THE NEGOTIATIONS g. SUMMARY OF IMPORTANCE

pointing the way to continuous improvement

Table 2.4 gives a more complex example of how the overall framework was constructed for management at a brewer. Table 2.5 details how one of the competencies, Persuading and Influencing, has a sub-group category, Negotiation, which has a five-scale ranking that can be applied to every applicable position.

Table 2.5 Example of competencies in detail

Once this is done each sub-category is ranked on a scale of 1–5 in terms of **how much is required** by the role (Role Profile) or **how much is demonstrated** by the individual (Individual Profile)

Examples:

Behavioural

3. PERSUADING AND INFLUENCING

Seeks to sell ideas rather than impose them, using rational and logical argument. Adopts an appropriate style according to the situation. Argues a point in a compelling yet unemotional way and is comfortable when dealing with conflict.

a.   AUDIENCE

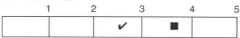

1. Interaction is mainly limited to own team and peers.
3. Interaction is often cross functional, involving other managers.
5. Interaction is mainly with Board and Senior Management or cross divisional.

b.   STYLE

1. Typically one style of influencing (selling, negotiating, telling, etc.)
3. Maybe required to vary style.
5. An ability to constantly vary style and approach.

c.   CONFLICT

1. Minimal challenge or conflict.
3. Some challenge or conflict.
5. A high degree of challenge or conflict.

Key: *Role* ■ *Individual* ✔

Technical (e.g. sales)

L-NEGOTIATION

Able to effectively negotiate agreements satisfying both company interests and customer needs.

a.   INVESTIGATION AND FACT FINDING

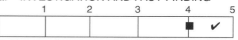

1. Has a basic understanding of the customer structure and can identify key decision makers.
3. Can identify specific customer needs and wants and understands the business context.
5. Has a detailed understanding of the customer's marketplace and strategies and is able to identify the strategic value to WBC.

b.   PLANNING AND FINANCIAL AWARENESS

1. Is able to identify low cost/high value concessions and their financial implications at a basic level.
3. Is able to identify and cost more complex sanctions and incentives which may fall outside functional guidelines.
5. Is able to identify the strategic value of the negotiation/relationship.

c.   KNOWLEDGE AND APPLICATIONS OF TECHNIQUES

1. Can identify the common ground in a straightforward negotiation.
3. Can identify how to manage more complex negotiations by summarising and testing the understanding of others, being able to make tentative proposals and identifying how to manage 'low reactors'.
5. Is able to manage very complex negotiations by identifying how to avoid 'spirals' and how to deal with hard bargainers.

 pointing the way to continuous improvement

Selecting the employment package

The position offered has to be attractive to potential applicants so the package on offer must aim to meet a number of needs. Setting the salary range can be a complex process and is dealt with in detail in Chapter 6. Briefly, it has to be in tune with the marketplace but also to be congruent with the internal pay system. Although general terms and conditions, such as holidays, pension and sick pay, are likely to be standard across positions at that level, there may be certain terms which need finalising. For example, does a company car go with the position? What are the actual hours of work, if they are defined? Is there any opportunity for flexibility associated with those hours? Are there any optional benefits that the successful candidate can sign up to, such as private health insurance?

ATTRACTING THE APPLICANTS

A number of general issues are involved at this point. Will internal candidates be encouraged to apply? Will the entire recruitment process be handled by the organisation or will third parties be brought in to assist? Will the advertising process be a traditional one involving local or national newspapers or will more innovative methods be used involving, for example, the Internet? What alternative methods of attracting applicants will be used besides newspaper advertising? How will the requirements of equal opportunities legislation, as detailed in Chapter 9, be met successfully? Who deals with the various stages of the process – human resources or line management? These issues will be dealt with in turn.

Internal candidates

There are numerous advantages in recruiting internally:

- The candidate's performance is known well, as are their attendance records and their strengths and weaknesses. Hopefully, as set out in Chapter 8, an effective career development plan will be in place that can identify employees who are ready to be promoted or who are available to take up project-style positions.
- From an employee's viewpoint, an internal promotion is normally a far more satisfying move than the risk involved in moving to another organisation when service rights are lost and a mass of cultural and technical information has to be learned in a very short time.
- A promotion generally gives a healthy signal to the individual, who will feel valued, but a signal is also given to the rest of the workforce who will be encouraged to stay, all being well, with the hope of following in the successful employee's footsteps.
- An existing employee knows the organisation, its systems and procedures and should find it easier to adjust and settle in the position.

- Internal recruitment is normally short, except in the largest public sector organisations, and it is certainly cheaper than external advertising. The vacancy can be advertised through internal advertising on notice boards and in newsletters to denote that it is open to all employees and to support a culture of transparency.

- Nothing is more demotivational than the sudden announcement of internal promotions without the position being advertised.

Given such advantages, why has external recruitment continued to grow so strongly at the comparative expense of internal promotion? There are two main reasons:

- Firstly, the pace of change has become so great that organisations are wary of creating a 'cloned' labour force that follows policies and procedures that have been successful in the past. The belief is strong that a flow of new blood, or 'talent', into organisations is essential and that external applicants will bring different experiences into play.

- Secondly, there is no conclusive proof that internal appointments are actually more successful; employees may be promoted because they do their job well but may find the new job beyond them. This is known as the Peter Principle – employees are always promoted one step above their competency. Some employees also find it difficult to achieve the necessary respect when they had started a few years back as the office junior.

A balance, then, is usually required with a careful analysis of both internal and external applications to determine whether their existing skills and experience will allow a prediction of future competent performance in the advertised position.

Using third parties

Before advertising is considered, an important decision needs to be taken whether to use third parties in any way in the recruitment process. Third parties take the following forms:

- Recruitment agencies, who will handle the entire recruitment process up to short-listing, providing candidates from their own sources or advertising on your behalf. These were used by 76 per cent of employers in 2009 (CIPD 2010), up from 64 per cent in 2002.

- Advertising agencies, who help devise a single advertisement or complete campaign and advise on the advertising media.

- Executive search agencies (sometimes known as 'head-hunters') who will search for senior staff on your behalf, approaching suitable candidates directly, often under considerable secrecy. The extent to which such agencies are used rose to 40 per cent in 2003 but dropped back to 31 per cent in 2009 due to the effect of the recession (CIPD 2010).

- Job centres can give energetic support, especially if the organisation is either moving into the area or has an expansion programme with multiple vacancies, particularly at operative or clerical and administrative level. Use of this facility has been slipping in recent years, down to 43 per cent in 2009 (CIPD 2010).

■ Educational establishments – schools, colleges, universities – can help provide a willing, if often inexperienced, source of applicants; 34 per cent of employers keep up this link (CIPD 2010).

All these sources can be valuable but have certain disadvantages as Table 2.6 shows.

Whether third parties are used or not depends entirely on the nature of the vacancy and the context of the organisation. Here are examples of situations where organisations are likely to use third parties:

■ *Example 1:* A large organisation setting up a satellite operation in an area new to them which needs a variety of semi-skilled and unskilled labour will use an advertising agency to design a series of job advertisements and the job centre where candidates will respond to the advertisements and where interviews can be held.

■ *Example 2:* An organisation recruiting a senior director will be likely to use an executive search agency to approach potential candidates on a confidential basis and to draw up a short-list.

■ *Example 3:* An organisation that has a regular need for 'year out' sandwich students to carry out project work in marketing or personnel will build up a relationship with a number of universities so suitable students can be easily recruited at minimal cost.

■ *Example 4:* An organisation with an uncertain longer-term administrative requirement will build up a relationship with a recruitment agency that will provide them with a combination of temporary staff and short-listed permanent staff on both a full-time and part-time basis.

Designing and placing newspaper and online advertisements

Advertising is a costly business. Although a single insertion for a small advertisement on a limited-circulation local newspaper may cost less than £200, this can rise to over £20,000 for a substantial, full-colour advertisement in a national quality newspaper. With an average cost moving towards the £1,000 mark, it is vital that the right results are obtained. Although situations vacant advertisements have dropped sharply in newspapers in recent years, organisations still report that they make use of them and find them effective. According to the 2010 CIPD survey, 36 per cent of organisations find local newspapers effective, with the figures for specialist trade magazines and national newspapers at 31 per cent and 16 per cent, respectively. These figures have declined substantially since the onset of the recession. Organisations' effectiveness rating of advertisements on commercial job boards rose to 33 per cent in 2010 but their ratings on social networking sites were surprising low at 3 per cent, despite their growing popularity (CIPD 2010).

Table 2.6 Use of third parties

Third party	Advantages	Disadvantages	Effectiveness rating by employers in CIPD 2010 survey
Recruitment agencies	Can provide candidates at speed using their database Save considerable time on dealing with large numbers of applications Some specialist agencies have a very good knowledge of the vacancy market. This applies to accounting and IT staff especially	Charge a fee from 10% to 20% depending on level of vacancy and competitive situation May not provide appropriate candidates especially if they have not been briefed adequately Staff recruited through agencies have a tendency to move on quicker. Although the agency that provided them cannot supply them with further job details for ethical reasons, they are almost certainly bound to be on the books of other agencies who are under no such restriction	Recruitment Agencies – 60%
Advertising agencies	Experts in copy writing, especially with eye-catching headlines, use of colour and house style Provide high-quality artwork, which the media cannot usually provide Know the media options well with up-to-date prices	Charge fees for the service, although less than may be expected as they negotiate discounts on the actual advertisement space with the media concerned May persuade you to spend more on the advertisement than you originally intended	
Executive search	When secrecy is important due to internal reasons, such as a restructuring, they are a discreet agent They know where to look in a very limited market, such as for a head of research for a pharmaceutical company They save on all the time and effort involved in responding to advertisements	They charge high fees, from 25% to 50% of the first-year salary. Some of the fees are chargeable even when the appointment is not made They can be of variable quality so it is important to use one referred to you who is of high reputation	Search Consultants – 22%

Table 2.6 (*Continued*)

Third party	Advantages	Disadvantages	Effectiveness rating by employers in CIPD 2010 survey
Job centres	A central and convenient place for applicants to use providing a high response rate They offer a venue for mass interviewing They usually do not charge a fee	No sifting takes place so much of the response can be unsuitable Response can be weighted towards the unemployed rather than a wider marketplace	Jobcentre Plus – 23% Local Employment Partnerships – 6%
Educational establishments	They provide a free service Where the demand is regular, such as in graduate trainees or trainee computer operators, colleges or universities can provide a regular supply	Applicants may not be experienced	Links with colleges/ universities – 18%

The three key objectives of a good advertisement are that it:

■ *Attracts attention* – to successfully compete with other job advertisements in that media.
■ *Creates and maintains interest* – it has to communicate accurate information about the job, the company, the rewards, the nature of the job and the type of person wanted and do all this in an interesting and attractive way.
■ *Stimulates action* – the message must be sufficiently strong for potential applicants to read it to the end and then make the time and effort to respond in the required way. It should also have a negative effect, in that unsuitable applicants will be discouraged from applying (Armstrong 2003).

One of the many common misunderstandings that occur in the field of recruitment is that the success of the advertisement is measured by the volume of the response. Quite the reverse is true in reality. It is only the *quality* of the response that matters – how many applications are received from candidates that have the necessary requirements to fit the specification. Taken to the extreme, a response of one applicant can be a perfect response if that applicant is right for the job and the company. A response from 100+ applicants, on the other hand, can be a complete failure if none has the necessary requirements.

Attracting attention can be achieved by a number of means:

■ Using bold and unusual headlines (see Figure 2.5 for examples)
■ Salary and location clearly displayed
■ An effective illustration or striking artwork (see Figure 2.6 for example)
■ Using full- or part-colour, although there are cost extras involved here
■ Agreeing with the publisher a prominent location of the advertisement, again with a supplementary cost
■ Prominent display of a high-profile corporate image, where that applies
■ Placing advertisement in unexpected places. For example, Harrods has placed an advertisement in the performing arts newspaper *The Stage* to find employees to work in its new toy department because they wanted 'people with a service style that was more theatrical' (Clegg 2012).

Figure 2.5
Selection of unusual headlines

Source: Advertisements in *People Management.*

> • If you do not raise your eyes, you will think you're at the highest point.
>   (HH Human Resources – for a selection of vacancies)
>
> • So how many jobs do you want?
>   (Gardner Merchant – HR Manager)
>
> • Work over Christmas. Travel round the world. Spread joy and happiness. Wear a red suit.
>   (Virgin Atlantic – Cabin Crew)

Increase turnover

Team Manager (Hygiene)
c.£30,000

Our name strikes terror in the hearts of roaches, rats and vermin all over London. From pest control and the mortuary service to clinical waste collection, we're one of the biggest forces in hygiene – and we want to be the best. As a professional business manager who's seen pest control 'action', you'll lead a hungry, motivated team of 35 into areas teeming with opportunities.

It's a target-driven environment, so here are yours: achieving ISO 9002, generating more income than last year's £1 m, and maintaining impressively high standards. We're not necessarily looking for a public sector background, but we do insist on customer-focused performance management experience in a large, income-driven hygiene business. This is the opportunity to expand our successful business in an environment where only skill and professionalism are allowed to thrive.

For an informal discussion call Roy Merchant on: 0181 356 4968 or write to him at Regulatory Services, London Borough of Hackney, 205 Morning Lane, London E9 6DC. Please quote ref: 7728/G3. Closing date: 29 June 1998.

One of the core values of transforming Hackney is an unequivocal commitment to the principle and operation of equality in terms of how we deliver the best service to our customers and all the people of Hackney, how we recruit and how we support our staff. We welcome applications from people who can make the principle a reality.

Transforming Hackney

Figure 2.6
Example of an eye-catching advertisement

Creating and maintaining interest has a number of important issues to consider:

Does the advertisement concentrate on *stressing the positive* or is an element of the realistic included to avoid applicant disappointment either at interview or after appointment? Given the natural sceptical tendency of the public towards advertising, there is always a danger that a quotient of realism will deter good applicants who may suspect this is the tip of the iceberg. It is useful, however, to make clear if the job is a new one and why it has been created. For example, 'We have recently initiated an empowerment programme which has given more commercial responsibilities to local managers' or 'An expansion phase has led to a further x posts being created'.

Is the image of the company matched by the tone of the advertisement? A bright, breezy advertisement that would suit an informal, opportunistic company would probably be inappropriate for a regulatory public body.

How much is said about salary? Research over the years indicates that advertisements with a salary included achieve a better response with a general consensus of increased quantity (up 20 per cent) and better quality overall. Without a salary, a number of potential applicants do not apply, thinking that they may be wasting their time, and a number of applicants whose current salary is either too high or too low, making them unsuitable, actually do apply. There is general agreement here, so why are there so many positions advertised without a salary? This can be explained in part where organisations do not have transparent salary structures and believe they run the risk of alienating current employees by showing what is on offer for the vacant position. Others may follow the unfashionable and indefensible line that they will 'see who turns up and seems suitable and then negotiate an appropriate rate'. This is scarcely a professional approach and one that may well lead to discrimination on top of a confused salary structure. The way the salary is framed can be an important factor. Public sector advertisements can be unduly complex, such as 'PO3 (pay award pending)', which is acceptable for those working in that environment but will be unlikely to attract outsiders. The most common indicator currently used is to place a guide salary in the lower headline such as 'c £28K–35K' or 'salary to £28K'. An alternative method used where bonuses are common, such as in the sales or management environment, is to state 'salary OTE £40K' where OTE stands for On Target Earnings which includes the bonus element.

How genuinely meaningful is the text? In the description of the ideal candidate, for example, how often are phrases used like 'excellent communication skills', 'computer literate', 'commercially focused', 'with an energetic, hands-on approach'? Because of their vagueness, they neither attract candidates nor put off the unqualified so it is difficult to justify their inclusion. It is better either to outline the specific qualifications required or to make it clear that applicants will need to demonstrate these competencies at an early stage of the recruitment process. For example, 'leading a team of ten engineers and analysts in the design and testing of manufacturing software'.

It is essential to include the *location of the post* in the advertisement, especially if it is a national advertisement, and any relocation package should be mentioned. Any necessity for regular travel should also be included.

Should the level of benefits be spelled out? The inclusion of benefits should be cautious, stressing only those that are essential features of the job (such as a company car), or that make a real difference to the attraction of the post (such as subsidised mortgages/loans in the financial sector, private health insurance and subsidised housing). Any family-friendly benefits, such as flexible hours, job share or subsidised childcare, can also be crucial. However, very few people have been attracted by the pension scheme in recent years, or life assurance, and one should treat with reserve those applicants attracted by the sick pay scheme or holidays.

In terms of *stimulating action*, there are a number of methods by which applications can be made, which will depend on the nature of the vacancy, the number of expected applications and the technology available. Options include:

- The applicant calls a dedicated number/person for a job pack including an application form.
- The applicant responds directly to an online address with CV/completed application form.
- The applicant is invited to an open-day interview event.
- The applicant responds by sending a CV and covering letter by post or email.
- The applicant is invited to call a specified person for an informal discussion.
- The applicant calls a dedicated number for a short-listing telephone interview (see Chapter 3 for telephone screening).

There are evenly balanced arguments for asking applicants to complete an *application form* or to send in their *CVs*.

Applicants would generally prefer to simply send in their CVs with a covering letter, believing that all the relevant information is included. They may select organisations that make an application easier rather than one that insists on the laborious process of completing a four-page application form. Applicants may prefer to direct potential employers to their 'Social Resumé', a bespoke web page (as hosted by LinkedIn) which showcases their strengths in an interactive way, perhaps with added value (*People Management* 2013).

Organisations may prefer to insist on an application form because it is simpler to select a short-list from a set of identical application forms. CVs may leave out negative areas such as no current driving licence, or the applicant's having been dismissed from previous employment. Applicants may also leave out their age or not put their experience in a chronological order, which could hide a crucial time gap. If candidates are not prepared to complete an application form, they show little commitment to the application. In general terms, public sector organisations tend to insist on a consistent approach to recruiting through an application form. It is also argued that the more common process these days of including a photograph may lead to a discriminatory approach to short-listing and should be discouraged.

A further difficulty is the truthfulness of the CV. Research by the Association of Search and Selection Consultants (ASSC) in 1998 found that a quarter of job applicants lied about their qualifications and career records or attempted to hide their previous misdemeanours (*People Management* 1998). An extreme situation was the exposure in 1997 of 16 nurses at Ashworth top-security hospital in Merseyside who were found to be practising without being properly qualified.

Providing information to applicants

An advertisement can only provide a limited amount of information. The provision of a 'job pack', in hard copy or online, is therefore important both to fill in as many gaps as possible and also to show evidence of an efficient and responsive employer. The job pack may include any of the following, depending on the level of the vacancy:

- Brochure on the organisation's activities
- Job description
- Person specification
- Organisation structure showing how the vacancy fits into this structure, especially if it is a new job
- A handbook showing the benefits of working for the organisation, such as SAYE share options or profit-sharing, private health insurance, etc.
- Application form (if applicable).

The application form

The purpose of an application form is to provide full, relevant and consistent information on which to base decisions on recruitment and selection. It should also be designed to be user-friendly, with a clear and simple layout and unambiguous questions, and should not be too lengthy. It should allow the applicant to give a full and fair account of themselves. Meeting these requirements is not always easy and there are a number of issues to consider:

WILL ONE FORM BE SUFFICIENT FOR THE ORGANISATION?

For a straightforward clerical position, the information required in general is essentially factual – personal details, education, qualifications and work experience is usually sufficient. This can be achieved in a two-page form. In more senior positions, it is usually necessary to allow the applicant to reflect on their experience to date, outline their motives and ambitions, and explain why they believe they can match the requirements of the advertised post. This usually necessitates a four-page form. Having two forms can create some confusion, however, especially when jobs are on the border of seniority. Keeping to one long form, however, means requiring all applicants to plough through the sections on motives, ambitions and justifying their applications which may well put off a number of good applicants.

WHAT QUESTIONS SHOULD YOU NOT ASK?

Equal opportunities requirements have meant a changing format where questions on whether the applicant is married and the age of their children, for example, should be avoided as this information does not have a bearing on their ability to carry out the job.

DO YOU LINK IT TO A COMPETENCY FRAMEWORK?

One of the benefits of a competency framework is that it integrates a number of human resource areas – recruitment included. Having defined a job in relation to the competencies, it makes sense to try to match applicants to those required competencies, so questions on the application form should reflect this. For example, where leadership is a required competency, the form should ask such questions as 'Can you demonstrate how you have exercised leadership skills in your current position?' The problem here, however, is that the competencies and their levels vary for different jobs and an application form that asks for a response on each competency will be very long indeed. A way round this is to use a basic form for key personal data and then a supplementary form specific to that position.

An extract from Wine Rack's lively application form that tries to reflect the company culture is shown in Figure 2.7.

STORE MANAGEMENT
APPLICATION FORM

CONFIDENTIAL

Wine Rack

Vacancy ref: *TBM/0045*

Candidate ref:

Please return to THRESHER Human Resources, Recruitment Unit,
Ellis Ashton Street, Huyton Industrial Estate, Liverpool L36 6JB.

Personal Details

Surname:	Maiden name:	First names:

Address:	Telephone (home):
	Telephone (work):
	Can we contact you at work?
	YES/NO

Age:	Date of birth:	Sex: Male/female	Marital status	Children's ages

YOUR HEALTH … Please give details of any health problems or disability and state your Reg. D.P. No. if applicable:

Have you ever held a Justices Licence?   YES/NO
If so state when and where:

Do you have any civil/criminal convictions, past/current/pending?   YES/NO
Please specify:

This information is required in order for you to obtain a Justices Licence to sell alcohol.

Do you own a vehicle? YES/NO	Do you have a current driving licence? YES/NO

Please give details of any endorsements:

Do you own your own home?   YES/NO   Rent?   YES/NO   Live with relatives?   YES/NO

Are you willing to work evenings?   YES/NO   Weekends?   YES/NO

Are you prepared to relocate?   YES/NO

Please tick the area(s) where you would be prepared to work:

☐ Scotland   ☐ South West   ☐ North East   ☐ South East

☐ North West   ☐ Greater London   ☐ Midlands   ☐ Central London

Are there any areas where you would not work? Please specify:

Figure 2.7
Application form
for Wine Rack

Table 2.7 Alternatives or additions to newspaper/magazine advertising

	Advantages	Hazards and difficulties encountered	Effectiveness rating by employers in CIPD 2010 survey
Word of mouth, including relatives	❑ Very cheap and simple ❑ Can be bolstered by offering a bonus to a member of staff who introduces a successful applicant ❑ It is likely that the applicant will have a reasonable knowledge of the organisation and the job ❑ Should fit easily into the culture and ways of the organisation ❑ No need to plough through a large response	❑ If used as a sole method of recruitment, then the staff will only come from a narrow range ❑ Outside applicants may not know about opportunities so the source is limited ❑ Can, and has, been regarded as a discriminatory approach in practice, as females (or males) and ethnic minorities can be excluded from the process in predominantly white, single-sex organisational environment	❑ Employee referral scheme – 35% ❑ Speculative applications and word of mouth – 24%
Approaching previous applicants	❑ Very cheap and simple ❑ Applicants may already have been interviewed but just missed being selected on the last occasion so an appointment can be swift	❑ The post and its conditions may have changed since the applicant applied ❑ The applicant may no longer be interested, having been suited elsewhere ❑ It is necessary to maintain an effective database of such applicants with a time cut-off point	❑ Previous applicants and employees – 5%
Local mail shot through commercial leaflet distributor	❑ Can be targeted at specific areas in the locality which are convenient for travel and have produced quality applicants in the past ❑ Relatively low cost	❑ Cannot be certain of 100% delivery rate ❑ Not necessarily thought of highly by potential applicants	
Milk round to universities and colleges and job fairs	❑ Can target quality universities and colleges	❑ High cost in time, travel and accommodation ❑ Suitable only for graduate recruitment	
Open days and hotel walk-in	❑ Good for recruiting large numbers	❑ Uncertainty of response on the day makes resourcing difficult	

Table 2.8 Most effective initiatives used in overcoming difficulties in recruitment (respondents limited to three initiatives)

	%	Initiative
1	75	Providing additional training to allow internal staff to fill posts
2	71	Appointing people who have potential to grow into job
2	71	Increasing starting salaries or increasing benefits
4	68	Providing a realistic job preview
4	68	Taking account of personal qualities rather than simply qualifications
6	65	Offering flexible working
7	60	Using employer brand as a recruiting tool
8	58	Redefining the job (i.e. regrading)
9	54	Redesigning the job (i.e. moving to team-working)
10	50	Giving payments for referring candidates
11	48	Alumni recruitment (approaches to previous staff)
12–15		Overseas recruitment (36%); targeting migrant workers (32%); golden hellos (29%); offshoring the work (29%)

Source: CIPD (2010) Resourcing and Talent Planning Survey 2010. CIPD.

Other methods of attracting applicants

The recruitment strategy may include a number of other methods used alongside or instead of newspaper or magazine advertising. They may have clear advantages at times but there are also hazards, as summarised in Table 2.7.

Effective initiatives used in overcoming difficulties in recruitment

Where employers have found difficulty in recruiting, a number of options are available to them, some of which have already been mentioned, such as redesigning the work. Research by the CIPD (2010) found that providing more training to existing employees so that they could move into senior positions was top of the list, as shown in Table 2.8.

Using technology in recruitment

Recruitment has moved a long way in the last few years. Initially the changes reflected the need to attract talent from the Generation Y group, who were early adopters of new technology, but, as the use of the Internet and 3G and later technologies become universal, companies cannot afford to depend only on the printed word for their recruitment activities. This applies especially where companies are looking to recruit from Generation Z (those born from 1990) who have never known life without the Internet. Web-based recruitment is attractive because the response can be far quicker (except possibly when filling in online application forms) and it works out far cheaper, even when using generic websites. The advance of e-recruitment has saved the NHS £100 million from 2005 to 2008 with 95 per cent of applications received online and 99 per cent of short-listing carried out online (Chubb 2008).

COMPANY WEBSITES

Practically every organisation includes a career opportunity and job vacancy section on their website, and the company website came top of the effectiveness rating in the 2010 CIPD survey at 63 per cent. Some are more sophisticated than others. Whitbread developed a dedicated recruitment website in 2004 called www.run-a-restaurant.com. In its first four months, the site was searched 100,000 times, resulting in 1,300 applications, which allowed their brands Brewsters and Brewers Fayre to recruit more than 60 per cent of their candidates directly and boosted the 90-day retention figure from 90 per cent to 95 per cent. It saved them a considerable sum of money (Carrington 2004).

Procter and Gamble has extended its web-based recruitment to devise a virtual careers fair (Stevens 2010a). This six-hour event saw 1,200 people visit the fair, to view corporate videos and presentations and network with existing employees.

GENERIC WEBSITES

Sometimes called online job boards, there are a large number of Internet recruitment companies, which can be divided into those that covers all areas, such as Monster and Totaljobs, while some sites deal with only one sector, such as NHS Jobs. The CIPD (2010) reported that 33 per cent of employees rated them as effective. All newspapers and magazines, including the CIPD, have developed their own online sites to run alongside the printed version.

CV SCANNING

Software has been developed which can scan CVs to see how closely they match the job specification in terms of experience, skills, qualifications and competencies required.

PHONE/IPHONE APPLICATION

Various systems have been devised to attract applicants through their mobile phones. Adidas has developed an iPhone application specifically to drive graduates to its recruitment site, which yielded 4,500 applications in the first year (Evans 2011). A second example LV=, an insurance and pensions company, utilises interactive media as shown in case study 2.4.

SOCIAL NETWORKING

Many employers are now using social media to directly recruit. The main serious site is LinkedIn (14 per cent of employers rated them as effective in the 2010 CIPD survey)

CASE STUDY 2.4 LV= RECRUITS VIA INTERACTIVE MEDIA

Bournemouth-based LV= has introduced a scheme based on a series of posters, each of which features a real staff member. Interested jobseekers are invited to take a photo of the poster using their mobile phone and send it to a quoted number. Image-recognition software will process the request and the person will then receive a pre-recorded phone call from the employee in the poster, in which they talk about their experiences in the company. This unusual approach is to pass the message that the organisation is highly creative and that insurance is not a stuffy or dull career and to confirm that the people in the poster are real employees.

(Source: Brockett 2010)

because most individuals who have such a site will ensure they are updated with a full review of their skills and experience, which can be easily viewed by employers. Global engineering company CH2M HILL used the website to recruit 10 per cent of its hires in 2010 and typically uses the platform as a sourcing stream for highly skilled roles commanding salaries of £50,000 plus. LinkedIn recently announced the launch of a 'recruiter tool' for employers, which includes an engine for users to refer contacts for a job and a function for recruiters and managers to exchange and give feedback on candidate profiles (Stevens 2011). Another example is KPMG, which uses social networking sites to tell students about campus events and setting up online communities for interns. It also communicates through the platform of second life (Chynoweth 2007).

A more unlikely user is CERN, the world's largest particle physics laboratory in Switzerland, as detailed in case study 2.5.

AUTOMATED TELEPHONE SCREENING

Telephone screening is another new development. Here, an applicant calls a freephone number, day or night, and keys in their unique personal identification number, which automatically sets up a file for them on the company's HR system. During the interview, typically lasting 15 minutes, the candidate answers multiple-choice questions using their telephone keypad. The computer scores and weights their answers and automatically sends them an application form or schedules a face-to-face interview if they are successful. The system then sends the HR manager an interview schedule.

INITIAL TESTING

Large, well-known employers are often faced by a huge response for specific positions, especially in a graduate intake. Many have developed forms of online initial testing to reduce

CASE STUDY 2.5 CERN – SOCIAL MEDIA CAN TRANSFORM THE QUALITY OF RECRUITMENT

CERN recruits professionals in a wide diversity of fields, not just in physics and engineering, so it advertises all job vacancies on Twitter, LinkedIn and Facebook. It goes further than this, however, because the intention is to interact with the potential audience such as candidates and with those who may know others who could wish to apply. For example, they use Facebook to host a weekly question-and-answer session led by one of the CERN recruiters, while LinkedIn provides a forum for more specialised discussions. Since starting to use social media, CERN has seen the number of applications soar from 7,000 in 2008 to 24,000 in 2011, a far greater increase than can be explained by the recession. The range of communication media helps to clarify the requirement that appointments can only be made from one of the twenty states that fund the organisation.

(Source: Cook 2012)

CASE STUDY 2.6 JOHN LEWIS'S INITIAL SITUATIONAL JUDGEMENT TEST

John Lewis received 3,500 applicants for its retail management graduate scheme in 2010 and, given the general economic situation, more were expected in subsequent years. Dealing with this in-house proved an impossible drain on HR resources and it was calculated that to manually screen each application would cost £6 each so outsourcing was an expensive option.

The company therefore devised an online test, which presents twenty scenarios all based around situations that a branch manager might typically face, each with four possible solutions. Applicants are required to rate each solution on a five-point scale ranging from 'counter-productive' to 'very effective'. The answers are then automatically scored and those with the best scores progress to the next stage of the recruitment process.

To ensure an accurate assessment, a sample group of branch managers completed the test and their responses were analysed and used as a basis for the scoring system. A further benefit of the scheme is that it gives the applicant a semblance of a 'job preview' – an opportunity to understand the nature of the likely problems/issues that are faced in retail management.

The cost of this test was £4.50 so a saving of 25 per cent was made through devising this test.

(Source: IDS 2011b)

CASE STUDY 2.7 L'ORÉAL'S VIRTUAL BUSINESS GAME

L'Oréal introduced their online virtual business game 'Reveal' in 2010 as part of their graduate recruitment programme. Players move through the Reveal platform as avatar characters working on virtual projects and solving business tasks across various departments, including finance, sales, marketing and the supply chain. Participants are then assessed against what the company considers to be the best solutions for the problems posed. It is available in ten languages as part of the firm's global graduate recruitment strategy. The game can be played anywhere and people receive very in-depth feedback as they go through the exercises and tasks.

The best players who achieve great results are invited for interview. It is a way of bypassing the more formal part of the recruitment procedure as the company has a strong indication of the candidates' strengths. It is seen as a way of attracting candidates to the organisation and gives something back to them.

(Source: Stevens 2010b)

the number of applications to numbers they can handle without having to deal with each individually. Examples of this include John Lewis's initial Situational Judgement Test, detailed in case study 2.6, and L'Oréal's virtual business game, described in case study 2.7. Developments in this area are so fast that other devices will, no doubt, have been put in place by the time you are reading this section, so you will need to keep up with your contemporary reading on this subject.

Difficulties in using technology in recruitment

Not all professionals are whole-heartedly behind these new recruitment techniques, believing that ethical and practical issues remain unanswered. These include:

■ Online applications make unreasonable demands on the time of the applicants, especially graduates who will need to make multiple applications to get their first job. Often the candidate only hears that the position has been filled when the extended form has been completed.

■ The applicants may not always want to be judged quite so quickly and mechanically. Unless they have bought in to the computer processes (and IT staff probably have), they may prefer to apply to organisations with a more human face.

■ Research by Microsoft (2010) found that 40 per cent of their sample of 1,000 employers have chosen not to hire a candidate as a result of a negative online profile. Over 60 per cent of employers found no moral hazard in searching the web as part of a final check before offering a position.

- Online psychometric tests, which are part of the application process, are used to screen out 90 per cent of the candidates, which 'smacks of organisational expediency', according to Dulewicz (2004).

- Organisations are aware that some candidates get friends to complete the form for them or try under several names for practice (Harry Potter is very common). Organisations that set tests and business games online run the risk of a team of friends (and maybe their accountant parents) working together to produce high-level solutions that will allow them all to progress their application.

- The judgements made by telephone may enter into the realms of discrimination, in terms of age particularly, and will encourage a form of stereotyping when the specification cannot be over-ridden, as it can if handled by humans.

- Applicants may not be prepared for telephone interviews with instant forced choice judgements to be made, which cannot be reversed, unlike in an interview situation where, if a question is not understood, it can be repeated or explained in another way. Ernst and Young decided to drop their phone interviews in 2008 after just one year's operation, as too many applicants were passing this stage and little was gained, while applicants and the organisation lost the face-to-face experience that built relationships.

- Sites do not keep their promises. A study by the consultancy The Driver Is (Welch 2003) found that only 9 out of 33 companies who allowed jobseekers to register for emails alerting them when new jobs were posted had actually sent out alerts within three months of the candidate registering.

- Currently, LinkedIn is only really suitable for a small group of experienced, skilled potential applicants.

The difficulties faced are demonstrated by the findings from the CIPD 2010 survey, which showed that only 3 per cent of respondents rated social networking sites as the most effective way of recruiting. Some organisations have attempted to overcome these difficulties. Marks and Spencer have eliminated competency-based tests because they take up too much time (Czerny 2004) and they clear with candidates first whether they are prepared to work shifts and weekends and be mobile and are eligible to work in the UK. Only then do candidates take the online tests in numeracy, verbal reasoning and a 'talent screener', which judges their motivation. Successful candidates then move to the final stage, which is an assessment centre. The organisation believes that the online process has improved success rate overall from 27 to 37 per cent.

INTEGRATED APPROACH TO RECRUITMENT

This chapter has indicated a wide number of possible approaches that can be made to deliver effective recruitment. Case study 2.8 shows how Hertfordshire Constabulary used an integrated approach to recruit 100 Special Constables in 2008.

CASE STUDY 2.8 HOW HERTFORDSHIRE CONSTABULARY RECRUITED 100 SPECIAL CONSTABLES (SCs)

As part of a changing nationwide approach to policing, Hertfordshire Constabulary decided to increase their Special Constables from 175 to 275 in 2008. Recruitment had been made more difficult in the south of the county as recruits to the neighbouring Metropolitan Police were provided with free travel in London. Associated with (and partly driving) the campaign was a need to gain wider diversity and to enrich the work through involving SCs in high-tech crime, rural patrols and working with traffic units, rather than simply assisting regular police on weekend city-centre hotspots.

The Constabulary worked with a creative agency who developed an integrated campaign across multiple platforms. There was a hub on the Herts Police recruitment website linked to a wide range of outdoor, digital and print elements. Key innovative aspects of the campaign were as follows:

'Ambient advertising' that integrated with urban architecture. In train stations, for example, rail users were confronted with life-size images of unsavoury characters sitting in stairwells. In each of these scenarios, viewers were asked: Where would you put yourself? In other words, what would they do to combat the problem/crime?

The team pioneered a full-page overlay on Fish4jobs where a brick appeared to be thrown through the screen.

On one of the online advertisements, moving the cursor over a mobile phone image revealed a 'happy slapping' video enactment. On another, on clicking certain key words, a hand was shown breaking through a car window and stealing a handbag.

On the totaljobs.com website, 'surround session targeting' software allowed banners to follow relevant jobseekers around the website, popping up repeatedly to strengthen the campaign's impact.

Videos were created on ATM machines, while a wide range of posters, GP surgery guides, leaflets and targeted emails were utilised.

The outcome was very successful with the targets more than met; in fact, applications were sufficient to allow a further recruitment of 121 SCs up to early 2010. It led to an increase of 19 per cent in arrests with SCs working in excess of the required hours through choice. Of those who applied, 35 per cent have been women and 14 per cent have come from ethnic minorities, far higher than in previous campaigns. There has also been a trickle of applications from those with specialised and highly valuable knowledge, such as farmers, IT specialists and accountants where they have helped make inroads into rural and high-tech crime.

(Source: Allen 2010)

Not all outcomes are as successful as those reported in case study 2.8. In 2010, G4S won the contract to recruit 2,000 security staff for the 7 weeks of the Olympic and Paralympic Games, although this figure was raised to over 10,000 by 2011. The organisation put together an integrated programme that led to 100,000 expressions of interest and 67,000 interview bookings, with 21,000 passing the interview stage. However, problems quickly arose over the necessary documentation for the successful applicants and the logistics of training, vetting and accrediting new staff. Poor decisions were taken over appointments; many applicants who were offered positions turned them down due to the vetting and accreditation process; and G4S finally admitted in June 2012 that it could not meet the contract requirements. To cover the shortfall, 3,500 soldiers were brought in and the company was required to pay compensation to the government for its failings (Brockett 2012).

WHO CARRIES OUT THE RECRUITMENT AND SELECTION PROCESSES?

The ability to recruit and select successfully is seen as a core skill by personnel professionals. Indeed, it was the failure of line management in this task that was one major influence in allowing the transition from welfare officer to personnel officer 80 or more years ago. It is generally at the heart of the human resources department and yet a number of organisations, mostly larger ones, have recently questioned why this should be so, pointing out that this activity should be a core management skill.

The main argument here is that managers have the ultimate responsibility for their staff, that it tends to be their greatest cost and that there needs to be a close bond from the outset between the manager and a new member of staff to make an effective partnership. This viewpoint is sometimes backed up by the time taken by human resources to carry out a recruitment exercise and their over-concern with paperwork and bureaucracy. This was the view adopted by Save the Children in 2006 when they passed all recruitment responsibility to the charity's 40 country directors (Czerny 2006).

An effective partnership between human resources and line management is therefore essential. This balance was best met by human resources concentrating on those areas that carried a specific skill – commissioning advertisements from a recruitment agency, negotiating rates with newspapers, psychometric testing – and allowing the generic skills of interviewing and selection to be carried out either by the line management or jointly by the two parties. Human resources would also activate the administrative tasks, such as arranging interviews and obtaining references, which will be dealt with in the next chapter.

An example of a complex recruitment exercise is shown in the Meteor case study.

A MAJOR RECRUITMENT EXERCISE

Today was the big day and Sarah had been at work since 6.30am. The first of the recruitment advertisements was out in the regional newspaper and she had to make sure the team was all prepared. It was two years after she had joined Meteor and helped set up the original factory. She now needed to fill an additional sixty positions within a six-month period with new employees joining an induction programme every two months. The 60 positions were as follows:

- 30 production operatives
- 15 service engineers and support personnel
- 8 office support staff
- 3 sales representatives
- 4 staff for a new team to advise organisations in setting up call centres. Two, as senior advisers, would act as consultants/account executives and two would be involved in actually setting up the centres, although the roles would be flexible ones.

The call-centre team was a new initiative that was being piloted at her site, run by Gary Hands, an experienced manager head-hunted from a similar organisation.

From the original recruitment exercise, Sarah had accurate job descriptions and specifications for all the jobs except the new call-centre positions. Together with Gary, she developed a set of competencies for each of the four jobs that matched their specific requirements. For the senior advisers, they centred on consultancy skills, such as persuasion, planning, and presentation; for the operational/training roles, they centred on leading, training, problem-solving and delegation.

The recruitment team

For such a large recruitment, Sarah recognised that she would normally work with a recruitment agency, selected for their knowledge of the area. This had been the process when the site was initially set up. However, she was aware that the economy of the area had been hit over the last year by a series of plant closures so recruitment itself should not be too difficult. She wanted to see if she could avoid the inevitable high costs of agency fees (in the region of £80,000 plus) and she had not been completely satisfied with the service provided on the original recruitment. However, she could not handle it all on her own. Therefore, she had put together a small team consisting of a 'year-out' Business Studies student who had been taken on for a variety of projects three months earlier and who had quickly shown a grasp of the business and its key requirements; an early-retired ex-personnel manager whom she had met through the local CIPD branch who was happy to take on a six-month part-time brief at reasonable cost; and, finally, a staff member who was returning from maternity leave and had asked for the opportunity to carry out part of her work at home. Other clerical staff would be seconded for short periods and agency staff would be used when necessary.

Sources of recruitment

Internal advertising. In the company magazine three months earlier, Sarah had informed all the staff of the site expansion, and the bulldozers were already at work. With the next magazine, she included a complete breakdown of the positions and details of how staff could apply, giving deadlines and approximate selection timings. She also gave details of the recruitment bonus scheme, whereby employees who put forward names of friends and relatives who were eventually successful in obtaining employment would receive a Marks and Spencer voucher for £60 after the employee's probationary period had been completed. It was made quite clear, however, that applications made through this route would receive no special preferential treatment in the final selection process, although they would be guaranteed an interview.

External advertising. The main gate on the site was onto a main road, so Sarah made arrangements for a large signboard to be displayed with the vacancies detailed and for information packs to be available at reception. Also detailed were the dates of the open evenings/Saturday mornings when informal discussions could take place.

Through local networking, Sarah contacted the human resources managers of the local companies who had recently shed labour, sending them information packs to pass on to any potential applicants. She arranged a meeting with the manager of the local job centre and gave her details of all of the operative, technical and clerical vacancies, together with information packs. She had trawled through previous applicants but the pace of recruitment over the past two years had drained that source dry.

Two months earlier, she had arranged a meeting with her advertising agency to draw up a series of advertisements in the regional and local presses. There were some advertisements involving all the positions and others specialising in the sales, technical or administrative ones. Sarah knew that the site was under-represented for employees from ethnic minorities, so one of the advertisements was to go into a small regional magazine produced mostly for the Indian, Pakistani and Bangladeshi communities. The advertisements were to be phased over an eight-week period in a careful programme and cost a total of £30,000, including production costs. The agency suggested that radio advertising be considered as the local companies were currently competing fiercely and fees were not unreasonable. Sarah agreed to try a pilot exercise with a limited budget.

Dealing with the response

Sarah had made special arrangements with the Telecom company to rent additional lines for the period of the advertising campaign and these lines were manned according to the strength of the expected response. Two of the lines had a direct switch to the homes of two employees. From the telephone calls, the recruitment team placed the applicants' details onto a database and the source of their response. This was down-loaded on email to the home of the employee returning from maternity leave who printed out the appropriate letter and stuffed the information packs. Twice a day, the packages were collected by courier to be posted.

For most of the vacancies, applicants were asked to complete standard two-page application forms but, for the call-centre team posts, an additional supplementary form was necessary to capture their match with the required competencies. Applicants were discouraged from simply sending in CVs, given the volume of applications that needed to be processed.

In total, 3,000 calls were taken over the campaign and 95 per cent of the information packs were sent out within two days (a case of mumps causing a short delay for the other 5 per cent!), and 900 application forms were received through the advertisements and the other sources.

When, later on, Sarah carried out the evaluation of what was essentially a very successful campaign, she found that the advertisements produced the highest response to selection ratio and the job centre and open days the lowest response. However, in cost benefit terms, without counting processing time, the reverse was true so she felt that it was worth the additional effort. The radio advertisements proved to be quite unsuccessful but she was not sure whether this was due to her rather half-hearted approach in this case. Twelve positions were filled through being referred by existing employees.

(See Activity 5 below.)

KEY CHAPTER SUMMARY POINTS

■ There are many alternatives to filling a vacancy by recruiting a replacement for the person who has left. These include reorganising the work, redesigning the job and contracting out the work.

■ Job descriptions can be task-oriented, accountability-oriented or designed as a broader profile or statement.

- Person specifications are crucial to the recruitment process but contain pitfalls, especially in the area of equal opportunities.
- Organisations are increasingly using competency frameworks that can be utilised for recruitment, among other important areas.
- Third parties are increasingly used in the recruitment process, chiefly because of their expertise and their knowledge of the market.
- Technology is developing to assist the recruitment process, especially through the Internet, although it also presents difficulties that are not easy to overcome.

STUDENT ACTIVITIES

1 In groups of two or three, select two job advertisements from a national newspaper and produce a short comparative report on how the advertisements meet Armstrong's three criteria.

2 Individually design a job specification for a university lecturer in marketing, then compare results in groups of five. Produce a final version taking the best parts of each of your efforts.

3 As a class, list the possible sources when recruiting the following: a labourer in a sawmill; a laboratory technician for a hospital; a manager for a retail shop; and a design engineer for a car-component company.

4 Compare the Building Society job statement with a conventional job description. In what ways does it differ and how valuable might it prove for the employee?

5 In the Meteor case study, identify how Sarah's traditional approach could be enhanced by using technology in the recruitment process.

6 Consider this scenario: you have a vacancy that you know can be filled internally by a suitable candidate but they may not be interested. Is it ethical to try to encourage them to apply and, if so, how would you go about doing so?

7 Read the section on technology and draw up a list of advantages and disadvantages of using social media in the recruitment process.

8 It is often said that competencies for a manufacturing environment are different to those for a service environment. Draw up a list of five differing competencies for each sector and three competencies that would apply equally well to both sectors.

REFERENCES

Allen, A. (2010) *An Arresting Proposition*. PM Guide to Recruitment Marketing, 15 July, 18–23.

Armstrong, M. (2003) *A Handbook of Human Resource Management Practice*, 8th ed. Kogan Page.

Brockett, J. (2008) Finders Keepers. *People Management*, 18 September, 28–31.

—(2010) LV= Recruits via Interactive Media. *People Management*, 17 June, 14.

—(2012) Olympian Task. *People Management*, August, 9.

Carrington, L. (2004) Laws of Attraction. *People Management*, June 17, 27–32.

—(2007) Designs on the Dotted Line. *People Management*, 18 October, 36–37.

Chubb, L. (2008) Outsourcing Recruitment Would Free Up HR to focus on Other Priorities. *People Management*, 29 May, 9.

Chynoweth, C. (2007) War Games. *People Management*, 3 October, 13.

—(2011) A Delicate Balance. *People Management*, December, 52–54.

—(2012) Work the Experience. *People Management*, May, 43–46.

CIPD (2008) Smart Working – The Impact of Work Organisation and Job Design. CIPD. August.

—(2010) Resourcing and Talent Planning Survey 2010. CIPD.

Clegg, A. (2012) Set in Great Store. *People Management*, August, 36–39.

Cook, A. (2012) Social Media Can Transform the Quality of Recruitment. *People Management*, October, 49.

Cooper, D., Robertson, I. and Tinline, G. (2003) *Recruitment and Selection: A Framework for Success*. Thomson Learning.

Czerny, A. (2004) Not So Quick and Easy. *People Management*, 26 February, 14.

—(2006) Save the Children Hands Over Recruitment to Line Managers. *People Management*, 23 March, 12.

Dulewicz, V. (2004) Give Full Details. *People Management*, 26 February, 23.

Evans, J. (2011) Wider Appeal. *People Management*, May, 47–50.

Higgs, M. (2004) Future Trends in HRM, in D. Rees and R. McBain (eds) *People Management Challenges and Opportunities*. Palgrave Macmillan.

Holt, J. and Perry, S. (2011) *A Pragmatic Guide to Competency: Tools, Frameworks and Assessments*. BCS.

IDS (2008) Tapping into Talent. *IDS HR Study 869*, May, Incomes Data Services.

—(2011a) Recruitment Adidas Group. *IDS Study 941*, May, 10–13.

—(2011b) Recruitment John Lewis Partnership. *IDS Study 941*, May, 27–28.

Malik, S. (2011) Unpaid Website Intern Celebrates Court Victory. *The Guardian*, 23 May, 14.

Microsoft (2010) HR Managers Snoop On-line. *People Management*, 11 February, 15.

Munro-Fraser, J. (1954) *A Handbook of Employment Interviewing*. Macdonald and Evans.

People Management (1998) CV Deception Warning. 25 June, 12.

People Management (2013) Social Resumé. 12 March.

Roberts, Z. (2006) Wok 'N' Bowl Brand. *People Management*, 15 June, 31–33.

Rodger, A. (1952) *The Seven-Point Plan*. National Institute of Industrial Psychology.

Sartain, L. (2009) Is the Job Description Relevant in the New World of Work?, accessed at www.Brandfortalent.com (6 November 2011).

Stevens, M. (2010a) Proctor and Gamble Goes Virtual to Lure Graduates. *People Management*, 22 April, 9.

—(2010b) L'Oréal's Recruitment Gets a Virtual Makeover. *People Management*, 3 June, 10.

—(2011) Social Media. *People Management*, July, 10–11.

Stredwick, J. and Ellis, S. (2005) *Flexible Working Practices*. IPD.

Sunday Times (2009) Jewellery Chain with a Heart of Solid Gold. Best Companies to Work For Supplement, 15.

Taylor, S. (2010) *Resourcing and Talent Management*. CIPD.

Warner, J. (2002) Metropolitan Housing Trust Balances Technical Skills and Behaviours. *Competency and Emotional Intelligence Quarterly*, Autumn, 8–10.

Welch, J. (2003) In the Hiring Line. *People Management*, 26 June, 30–31.

ADDITIONAL FEATURES

Please visit the companion website at: www.routledge.com/cw/stredwick where you will find additional case studies and reading material together with short self-tests and other resources for both students and lecturers.

3 SELECTION

INTRODUCTION

Before we move into these areas in detail, let us examine, as a snapshot, the research carried out by Mike Smith and his colleagues at UMIST into the predictive accuracy of various selection methods. This is set out in Figure 3.1.

If a method was able to predict the selection success rate perfectly (as measured by the performance of the chosen candidate in the job), then it would have a value of 1.0. If the method had no benefit at all in predicting performance in the job, then it would have a value of 0.00 (as graphology has achieved). It can be seen straight away that the traditional approach using unstructured interviews and references comes out of this research very badly. (Incidentally, early research published in 1989 showed the conventional interview at an even more lowly 0.18.) Testing in one form or another achieves much better results. Having said this, it is worth reflecting on the fact that even the best methods achieve success in only two out of three cases and that the average of all methods used is a success rate of less than one in two. We will look at each of these methods during this chapter, except astrology and graphology, which will not be mentioned again.

Figure 3.1
Accuracy of recruitment methods

Source: Robertson, I. and Smith, M. (2001) Personnel Selection. *Journal of Occupational and Organizational Psychology*, 74(4), John Wiley and Sons.

Overall Job Performance Criteria

Validity

1.0 Perfect prediction _____

0.9 _____

0.8 _____

0.7 _____

Assessment centres – promotion 0.68 _____

0.6 _____

    Work samples 0.54 Structured interviews 0.51

0.5 Ability tests 0.51 _____

    Assessment centres – performance 0.37

0.4 Personality test 0.40 _____

0.3 Unstructured interviews 0.35 _____

    Biodata 0.30 _____

0.2 References 0.26 _____

0.1 Years of experience 0.10 _____

0   Astrology 0.0 _____   Graphology 0.0 _____

TALENT MANAGEMENT

Selection is clearly a vital part of the talent management process. There may be more applicants in an economic recession but the costs of selecting wrongly do not alter. Choosing talented applicants from a crowded application pool requires both the utilisation of technology and the skills of a trained interviewer. The outcomes are vital because the person selected will only be of value to the organisation if they have the right skills and can use them to the benefit of the organisation. There continues to be debate over whether applicants should be selected because of their immediate value or whether it is their potential that is important, but identifying both correctly is crucial to effective talent management.

Having followed a structured approach to attracting a pool of applicants for a vacancy, the next step is to follow a similar approach to selecting the right person for that vacancy. The right person can be defined as someone who:

■ matches the requirements identified by qualifications, experience, skills and competencies set out in the job specification

■ has had satisfactory references, where future predictions indicate their success in the position

■ has expressed sufficient interest in the position at interview to indicate that they wished to be offered the position.

The aim of selection is to find such a person who accepts the position and who gives satisfactory service and performance in the long term.

Systems approach or processual approach?

The systems approach to selection starts from the position of a well-defined job and a clearly analysed person specification. It assumes that there is one best way to carry out a job and a more or less 'ideal' candidate whose own history and personality will predict that they will perform very well in that job. It also tends to assume that the job will not alter a great deal in the future.

An alternative approach is to put a much greater emphasis on the *process of negotiation* between the parties where there is much more flexibility in the nature of the position. As explained by Newell and Rice:

> Both of the parties have a set of expectations related to their current and future needs and values. Selection is portrayed as a series of episodes in which increasing amounts of information are exchanged to determine whether there is indeed compatibility between the organisation and the individual. Negotiation is possible because neither the organisation nor the individual is seen as having fixed characteristics, although the underlying values and needs of both sides are seen to be more stable. The outcome of this process, if successful, is that a viable psychological contract is negotiated that encapsulates congruence between the expectations of both parties. However, if the process of negotiation breaks down because the parties are unable to develop this sense of congruence, this can be construed as positive . . . [b]ecause, in this way, the organisation avoids employing someone who will not fit within the organisation and the candidate avoids taking on a new position for which they are not suited.
>
> (1999: 133)

This description portrays a form of talent management approach rather than the traditional selection method. It certainly fits, for example, most executive management selection today. Finding a chief executive for a large organisation has a strong element of adjusting the position around the ideas and strategic vision of a candidate as much as finding somebody who is able to carry out the detailed job description. Much negotiation takes place over performance targets, remuneration and other terms and conditions before both sides are happy that they have a deal that has a good chance of working. It is not so common at more junior levels, except when positions are difficult to fill, when a job can be adjusted to meet the needs and abilities of candidates who are otherwise suitable.

This chapter will concentrate on the systems approach, setting out the logical steps in the selection process. This is not as a criticism of the processual approach but because the systems approach is more commonly used and more related to the great majority of human resource initiated selection practices. However, throughout this chapter, the essential dilemma between the two processes will become apparent. For example, using a processual approach may open the doors to accusations of discrimination as the process lacks the objectivity associated with the systems approach.

Steps in the selection process

Selection is not just a question of interviewing, although this remains the most popular device in use. Selection is very much a process of de-selecting, i.e. gradually eliminating candidates until finally one is left on the list for a vacancy. Sometimes there is nobody left on the list and the process has to be started again. No one has yet identified any one single watertight process of selecting a candidate that is totally infallible. Some methods are more reliable than others but, to a large extent, selection is about trying to minimise risk and maximising the certainty of making the right decision.

Starting from the position where the recruitment process has produced a number of applicants, the important steps in selection are as follows:

- Short-listing the candidates for the next stage
- Setting up tests for the short-listed candidates, sometimes in the form of an assessment centre (although tests do not take place on every occasion)
- Interviewing the candidates (and giving them feedback on the tests) and allowing the candidates to interview the selectors
- Choosing the successful candidate
- Obtaining references (although this is sometimes carried out before interview)
- Offering the position, confirming in writing and gaining acceptance
- Organising the induction process
- Evaluating the result.

Each of these steps will be explained and analysed in this chapter.

SHORT-LISTING

Short-listing involves reducing the number of applications received down to an appropriate-sized list of candidates to be invited for interview. The process varies in time depending on the ratio of application to vacancies. In recent years, as the number of graduate traineeships has stayed static or actually declined, especially in the financial services sector, the number of graduates applying for the positions available has increased by around 50 per cent so the current ratio of applications to vacancies has increased, in some cases, to over 200:1. On the other hand, the number of vacancies for experienced IT professionals, especially those with web-related skills, has mushroomed, so the ratio of applications to vacancies can be as low as 2:1. In the former case, there is much short-listing work to be done by the human resources department; in the latter case, to the chagrin of the HR practitioner, little short-listing needs to be done – it is more a case of further calls to the IT recruitment agency.

The aim would normally be to produce a short-list of five or six candidates for interview for each vacancy.

There are two approaches in this reduction process:

- Firstly, there is the *screening* approach where unsuitable applicants are rejected until only the required number of applicants for interview is left. Applicants may be rejected for lack of experience or qualifications but it is not unknown for arbitrary decisions to be made involving the age, place of birth, handwriting or the inclusion of a photograph. Outright discrimination can also occur over the marital status, sex or ethnic background. Apart from being illegal, these methods are profoundly unfair and unreasonable as tribunals have continued to report.
- The second method is one of *inclusion*, where each applicant is compared with the requirements set out in the person specification and given a score through a preset scoring system. For example, a maximum of 10 points could be awarded for experience, 8 for qualifications, 15 for demonstration of certain key skills or competencies, and 7 for other factors, giving a total of 40 points. It would also be agreed that a minimum number of points would need to be scored in certain categories to be included on the list. The scoring would be carried out independently by two people, perhaps the line manager and the human resources manager, and results compared. Any discrepancies would be discussed. This process avoids discrimination and is much fairer to all the candidates, if taking a little longer.

Short-listing by phone is a relatively new process and has been described in outline in Chapter 2. It can take several forms. Applicants can be asked to call a dedicated number where a member of the recruitment team will ask a series of predetermined questions, the answers to which will be scored. If the target points are reached by the end of the interview, the applicant will be invited there and then to an interview on an agreed date. Alternatively, when application forms are received, the applicant will be telephoned, usually at home, with

CASE STUDY 3.1 TELEPHONE SCREENING AT MCDONALD'S

In 2008, McDonald's launched an online application system for all hourly paid positions, which incorporated a psychometric assessment that could be used as a sifting technique to replace the first face-to-face interview. Cost savings in the first year were in the order of £977,000, according to Nicky Ivory, resourcing and reputation consultant at the restaurant chain. Ivory's team have accumulated a great deal of data on employee performance that can help judge the success of the testing process. She believes that online testing cannot completely replace traditional methods but it can enhance them. Combining online and offline tests helps to overcome the risk that a candidate may ask a friend to sit the test.

(Source: Chynoweth 2009)

the same result. A final, more sophisticated process involves automated questioning. The applicant is asked a series of multiple-choice questions by a recorded message and asked to use the keypad to indicate their answer. Their choices are automatically scored and totalled and an interview offered if appropriate. Short-listing by phone is only suitable where the organisation is very sure indeed of the necessary requirements for the position and where relatively large volumes are being dealt with. For example, it has been used often when starting up a call centre and the quality of the candidates' telephone manner can be assessed along with the answers to the specified questions.

An example of telephone screening is given in case study 3.1.

A further example of automated short-listing is the use of equipment to *electronically read CVs* using OCR (Optical Character Recognition) software. The system's artificial intelligence reads the texts and, by using search criteria such as qualifications, job titles and companies where the applicant has worked, will produce a ranking list of applicants against the mandatory and optional aspects of the person specification.

This system is quicker and more consistent than if it were carried out manually but will only be as efficient as the search engine and will certainly miss many potential candidates, let alone the difficulty the technology faces in trying to understand poor handwriting.

An interesting argument in favour of telephone screening is that it can actually reduce race discrimination where interviewers cannot see the people they interview and therefore are not quite so liable to make instant decisions (see criticisms of interviewing techniques later in the chapter).

Biodata

Another technique used in short-listing, biodata, is to make a very detailed examination of the candidate's biography, comparing it with the biography of a group of successful incumbents in the position. As with all forms of selection, the technique depends upon the assumption that your past will assist in predicting your future. Candidates are asked to complete a detailed form, which examines their previous and existing work record and also includes aspects of their personal lives. Just as with selection tests (see later), the questions are often in multiple-choice form so they can be computer-analysed. When completed, it is scored and the short-list selected from the candidates who have achieved more than the agreed threshold points. A more recent development is for the questions to be asked over the phone. It is not a commonly used technique and its use has been declining due to a number of drawbacks associated with its use:

- Developing the questionnaire is a costly process involving research into the backgrounds and competence of current job holders. It will also need to be revised on a regular basis. It is only worth the investment if there are a large number of homogenous jobs with a clear understanding and agreement on the competencies required, such as in retail or in call centres, and, as such, its use is limited. Previously, it was utilised for large cohorts of insurance agents but that industry has been transferred to the call-centre world rather than the open road.
- A separate questionnaire has to be devised for each job – the biodata for successful sales employees can be very different to those of customer service employees.
- Candidates can be put off by the completion of such detailed information on top of the standard application information required.
- There has been doubt as to the underpinning statistics, especially concerning the causality. Although there may appear to be a very high correlation between, say, the applicant's number of siblings and the level of performance, it may well be the case that this does not actually cause the level of performance.

The biodata technique, then, is only used in practice where there are a large number of applications to a standard position and where there are also a large number of current employees from which to draw up the biodata criteria. It does not even figure in the CIPD 2010 Resourcing and Talent Planning Survey.

SELECTION TESTING

Recruitment and selection is essentially about accuracy in prediction. The aim is to take on board a candidate who is going to succeed and perform well. Figure 3.1 showed that several forms of selection testing had much higher predictive success than conventional recruitment methods. Internal assessment centres are top of the league, while ability tests, assessment centres for external candidates and personality tests all do better than the traditional interview. That is why so much attention has been directed in recent years into analysing and refining tests and their results.

The first advocate of selection tests was Samuel Pepys, the famous seventeenth-century diarist who, when secretary to the navy, proposed and outlined a more systematic assessment of ability than the nepotism currently rife. It was some time on from here before they began to be developed and adopted, firstly in America in the early part of the twentieth century, and then they began to be more widely utilised in the Second World War in the UK, when soldiers were people selected for officer potential. After the war, the ideas and methods were applied in the Civil Service, but Table 3.1 shows that the explosive growth in their use did not begin until the late 1980s.

Table 3.1 Use of selection tests

Year	Percentage use by large employers
1973	7
1986	21
1989	37
1991	50
1997	75
2004	82
2010	87

There are more than 1,000 tests available on the market today, which can be divided up into the categories of measuring *ability*, *aptitude*, *performance* and *personality*. Each of these will be dealt with in turn, together with common features of what makes up a good test and the correct way to use them. Then the benefits of using tests will be examined, followed by criticisms and difficulties involved in their use. Assessment centres follows the section on interviewing, as they utilise a number of techniques involved in the selection process – personality tests, exercises and interviews.

Ability tests

These are tests that measure a candidate's existing ability, both mental and physical. They can measure a variety of areas such as verbal reasoning, numerical ability, sensory or motor skills, spatial or mechanical ability. Such tests can be constructed entirely related to the job concerned, such as wiring, assembling, bricklaying, typing or even lecturing. These are sometimes called *performance tests* or, in the case of the performing arts, *auditions*; alternatively, they can be general paper and pencil tests of mental or numerical skills. According to the CIPD (2010), 43 per cent of employers use literacy and numeracy tests, while 48 per cent use tests for specific skills.

As an example, when window surveyors were recruited into Everest double glazing, a mock-up window was constructed on their branch site and the candidates were given a performance test to measure up the window, and point out any difficulties in installing the proposed replacement window, after which they had to write a short report.

Aptitude tests

Aptitude tests are also measures of ability but they also examine whether a candidate is likely to be able to *acquire* the skills and knowledge necessary to perform the job. Again, they can be set up as strictly job-related tests or a battery of published tests can be administered,

Figure 3.2
Examples of
ability/aptitude
questions

Choose the pair of words which best completes each sentence. See how many you can do in four minutes

1   The .... invoice must be paid by ....

A	B	C	D
originall	original	original	originel
instalments	installments	instalments	installments

Each star represents a missing letter. You have to find the missing letters and write them down on the lines on the right. PRINT the letters in capitals.

Here is one that has been done for you. In this one, the second word of each pair is the first word spelled backwards.

Don	nod	pit	tip	bag	gab	tub	***	<u>BUT</u>

Now do these yourself

1	me	meat	us	user	in	inch	**	once	....

2	her	there	his	whisk	***	shade			....

such as those produced by Saville and Holdsworth or The Psychological Corporation. For example, a number of computer programming aptitude tests are available. These are typically presented as multiple-choice questions or for a gap to be filled in as shown in Figure 3.2.

ACTIVITY 3.1

Discuss the advantages and difficulties of using ability, aptitude and performance tests.

Discussion of activity 3.1

You may have come up with some of the following advantages:

■   Research has shown a reasonable prediction rate in comparison with other selection methods (0.54).

■   Tests are usually not too difficult to design for specific jobs and relatively easy to judge especially on a comparison basis.

- The tests provide objective and predictive data to be followed up at the subsequent interview.
- Fair employment policies are demonstrated by introducing objective data into the proceedings.
- Using an effective test provides a professional image for the organisation.
- For off-the-shelf tests, large quantities of comparative data are available to aid judgement.
- Paper and pencil tests can be taken up at any location and are generally not too expensive.
- The test can be identified as a useful forecast for the candidate of the nature of the work.
- It gives additional confidence to successful candidates who recognise that the selection process is professional.
- The test can eliminate candidates who are not easy to train, a facet that is difficult to identify otherwise.
- Most tests have now been introduced in computer mode so that candidates simply press the appropriate key for their answer. This means that the test is assessed very quickly indeed.

Here are some of the difficulties which may be encountered

- Many tailor-made tests are amateur and untested themselves, utilised to justify personal decisions.
- Tests continue to be found to be discriminatory by tribunals, especially where understanding English is crucial to success in the test. The verbal reasoning test in Figure 3.2 would be more difficult for candidates where English is not a first language.
- It is necessary for the assessor to be trained in the use of off-the-peg tests.
- Feedback to poor performers is not easy.
- There is some evidence that candidates can improve their test performance by practice. Research is mixed here but veers towards a marginal improvement through practice. This has been believed for some time. as the author remembers the many days at school at age 11 in the early 1950s when endless intelligence tests were practised before the 11+ examination and the subsequent high results in our year.

Personality tests

Personality tests are a type of psychological questionnaire that are designed to measure the more permanent emotional tendencies people have that make up their personality. According to the CIPD (2010), 44 per cent of employers use some form of personality or attitude questionnaire in the selection process. Their prediction rates are surprising low at 0.38 per cent but this may reflect to a large extent the way they are used (or misused) as much as the inherent defects of the tests themselves. Taylor (2010: 257) sets out the basic assumptions on which the validity of personality testing ultimately rests:

- Human personality is measurable or 'mappable'.
- Our underlying human personality remains stable over time and across different situations.
- Individual jobs can be usefully analysed in terms of their personality traits that would be most desirable for the job holder to possess.
- A personality questionnaire, completed in 30 to 60 minutes, provides sufficient information about an individual's personality to make meaningful inferences about their suitability for a job.

These requirements are tough and many practitioners use personality tests without understanding the assumptions that are required.

A selection of the most well-known tests are Saville and Holdsworth's OPQ series, the Personal Profile Analysis, the California Psychological Inventory and the Myers-Briggs Type Indicator. Cattell's 16PF (primary factors) has been in use for nearly fifty years; it has been revised four times and this test has been chosen in this publication to give a more detailed explanation (see Table 3.2). It sets out to describe personality in terms of 16 primary source traits (factors) or dimensions. These source traits are functionally different underlying characteristics and each is associated with not just one single piece of behaviour but rather is the source of a relatively broad range of behaviours. Proponents of the test argue that the

Table 3.2 16PF traits

Low score description	1	2	3	4	5	6	7	High score description
Reserved, detached, critical								Outgoing, warm-hearted
Less intelligent, concrete thinking								More intelligent, abstract thinking
Affected by feelings, easily upset								Emotionally stable, faces reality
Humble, mild, accommodating								Assertive, aggressive, stubborn
Sober, prudent, serious								Happy-go-lucky, impulsive, lively
Expedient, disregards rules								Conscientious, persevering
Shy, restrained, timid								Venturesome, socially bold
Tough-minded, self-reliant								Tender-minded, clinging
Trusting, adaptable								Suspicious, self-opinionated
Practical, careful								Imaginative
Forthright, natural								Shrewd, calculating
Self-assured, confident								Apprehensive, self-reproaching
Conservative								Experimenting, liberal
Group dependent								Self-sufficient
Undisciplined, self-conflict								Controlled, socially precise
Relaxed, tranquil								Tense, frustrated

advantage of measuring source traits is that you end up with a much richer understanding of the person because you are not just describing what can be seen but also the characteristics underlying what can be seen. It analyses how a person is likely to behave generally, including, for example, contributions likely to be made to particular work contexts, aspects of the work environment to which the person is likely to be more or less suited, and how best to manage the person.

There have been criticisms of traditional personality tests (and recent syntheses of these tests, such as the 'big five model' – emotionality, extroversion, openness, agreeableness and conscientiousness) (Iles 2001) by psychologists who have pointed out that one-dimensional exactness is a Western approach based on Cartesian logic (Trompenaars and Woolliams 2002). They suggest that tests should include options to reconcile opposites that position people on bipolar scales. For example, rather than people being forced to choose between:

■ A job that is part of a team and the organisation, where everyone works together without bothering about individual credit; and
■ A job that allows everyone to work independently and where credit is given for individual performance without restrictions

there should be the opportunity to reconcile these two positions through additional options:

■ A job where everyone works together in teams to help the organisation as a whole, but where teams encourage, stimulate, reward and celebrate individual contribution; or
■ A job which allows everyone to work independently for personal recognition, but where credit and acclaim come from the team and the organisation.

The most important element in personality tests is the interpretation of the results. Candidates are not differentiated by whether they have scored highly or 'passed' the test. They are differentiated by how closely their test profile meets the requirements of the tested job profile. An example of how such tests can change the entire nature of the selection process is set out in case study 3.2.

Tests need to be interpreted against the 'norm' and the results are expressed in the form of variation from the norm. A raw score tends to be fairly meaningless, although psychologists are sometimes asked to make a general interpretation of a random test on a candidate for a client company.

TEST FORMAT

There are three main formats of the tests. One is the Ipsative or forced-choice question where the candidate has to choose between a number of statements or adjectives that describe themselves. For example, they may be asked:

CASE STUDY 3.2 SELECTION TESTING FOR MANAGED PUBS

Some years ago, a well-known brewer became dissatisfied with the performance of their managed pubs. There were contrasting profits from pubs in comparable areas and both the staff turnover and level of fraud was unacceptably high. They entered into an exercise to try to improve their recruitment and selection. Firstly, they set out to profile the high-performers and a group of 100 or so landlords (and their partners, if applicable) were given a battery of tests including Cattell's 16PF. The results were a surprise to them. They had expected that a successful publican would have strong features on traits such as outgoing, warm-hearted, lively, relaxed and socially bold. This was not the case. Their strongest features were being practical, careful, controlled, socially precise, tense, conscientious, persevering, restrained, sober, prudent and reserved. Just the sort of profile you would expect from an accountant!

From these surprising results, they carried out a careful job analysis and profit investigation. They found that the high profits were made through efficiently serving a capacity house at the key times of the week – Friday, Saturday evening and Sundays. To be efficient, they needed to be good at planning and organising, so nothing ran out, there was a ready supply of clean glasses and they motivated and controlled their temporary staff so nothing disturbed the correct takings. Availability of food was also crucial so teamwork between the partners was essential. When talking to the customers of the successful houses, the personality of the landlord came some way down the list below the general ambience and convenience of the pub, its quality of beer, cleanliness and food. The landlord needed to be efficient and friendly but not too friendly. Reserved and prudent certainly matched their ideal profile. He or she also needed to be good at preventing trouble or sorting it out quickly.

Following this exercise, the company completely altered the person specification. Each of the short-listed candidates (and they looked for couples) completed PF16 and the test results were used to confirm (or, at times, to decide against) the appointment. By choosing candidates, many of whom did not actually drink, who closely matched the profile of their successful landlords, the company increased their profits by 40 per cent over the next three years, reduced staff turnover by 60 per cent and made a substantial reduction in cases of fraud.

(Source: Author's case study)

Would you like to be regarded by your colleagues as agreeable . . . Or well-organised?

These are questions that are not liked by candidates as they find it difficult to distinguish between those choices. The results can show contradictions and confusion unless they are carefully interpreted.

A second format is to give a third alternative in answer to a question. For example:

I would prefer to go out with friends to the cinema in the evening rather than stay in and read a book.
Agree . . . Uncertain . . . Disagree . . .

This format allows candidates a greater choice and can measure the candidate's degree of indecision.

A third format is to use the Likert scale where candidates have more than three choices:

Once I make up my mind, it is important not to change.
Strongly agree . . . Agree . . . Uncertain . . . Disagree . . . Strongly disagree . . .

ADVANTAGES OF PERSONALITY TESTS

■ They add an objective measure to the selection process in areas where interviewing alone may not tease out the salient features. A candidate may say that they are a good organiser, forthright, focused, caring, relaxed and a great entertainer but the test should give you a much clearer picture of which are the strongest traits.

■ Many of them have been around for a long time and have very well-established norms for certain occupations so comparisons can be straightforward to operate.

■ There are usually advisers/consultants who will help in the administration and interpretation or provide you with the training to carry this out yourself.

■ Candidates, in general, regard the selection process as more rigorous if selection tests are involved.

ACTIVITY 3.2

Do you consider that there any difficulties involved in using personality tests?

Discussion of activity 3.2

You may have thought of some of the following difficulties:

■ The good tests have a commercial price to pay, either through an annual licence to use them or to pay for the interpretation or both. The cost of giving a test to ten candidates works can be over £400.

■ There are tests on the market that appear cheap but they do not have the validity and reliability required. Steve Blinkhorn, Chairman of Psychometric Research and Development, calls this the 'great underworld of psychometrics: shoddy personality tests and 10-minute quickies that tell you "everything you need to know"' (Smethurst 2003).

■ The risk of stereotyping candidates is all too easy. With the belief that personality is set in stone at the age of 30, some candidates may be labelled as unsuitable because they ticked a few wrong boxes. David Leeds, Head of Human Resources at Investac, avoids personality tests for fear of stifling variety. 'We are anxious not to stereotype or characterise people by putting them into different personality labels' (Butcher 2004).

■ Tests are sometimes regarded as the clinching factor in selection. However, test providers from an early date warn against this and all marketed tests provide a clear statement that selection should not be made on the basis of the test result alone.

■ Tests are often used wrongly, attempting to measure the unmeasurable or drawing inferences from results which are not justified. Of the 'big five' personality factors, most experts point to conscientiousness and emotional stability for the best predictors of high management performance, but this is disputed by Ivan Robertson (2001), who has pointed out that the correlations between these two factors and high performance is weak and should not be relied upon.

■ Candidates gain experience the more tests they take and can guess the kind of profile that the employers are looking for, ticking the appropriate boxes.

What makes a good test?

There are a number of essential features that make a test worth using. Firstly, it must be *valid*. This means it must measure the characteristic that the test is intended to measure. If it sets out to measure the aptitude for, say, bricklaying, then it must be tested to show that it actually does do so. Secondly, it must also be *reliable* in that the results are the same if the tests are given under identical conditions. Robust tests have themselves been tested effectively over a period of time before they are put on the market, usually with the help of volunteers. Details of validity and reliability are normally given in the test handbook. Thirdly, there must be *norms* available that have arisen from standardised interpretation. Fourthly, the tests must be *free of discrimination*. Care should be taken that a norm is not established from testing predominantly Caucasian males, as pointed out by the Commission for Racial Equality in their booklet 'Psychometric Tests and Racial Equality'. Finally, tests should be *adapted for disabled candidates*.

Other essential requirements are that:

■ Proper consideration is given to the appropriateness of using tests.

■ Tests are used in a professional manner, which is relevant to the employment context.

■ Equality of opportunity is ensured throughout the process.

■ Test results are scored, interpreted and communicated by appropriately trained individuals.

■ Individuals taking tests are informed of the reasons for the test and the conditions under which it will be used, how the information will be used and stored, and are given the opportunity to receive feedback on the test results.

INTERVIEWING THE CANDIDATES

An interview has been the traditional method of selection for decades and yet research studies have shown, as indicated at the start of the chapter, that they are a poor predictor of future performance (Robertson and Smith 2001). This is due to a number of factors, all centring around the faults of the interviewer. In earlier research, Graves and Karren (1992) found that 29 interviewers from the same company used 13 different criteria weightings to make their decisions, which often led to different conclusions.

Problems associated with interviewing

The ability to arrive at a consistent and objective decision on a candidate is hampered by a long list of irrational but understandable tendencies by interviewers who:

Have different views on the person they are looking for. The person specification may be too vague or ambiguous so interviewers have different ideas on what would be the success factors in the position. One interviewer may place great importance on the candidate's previous experience, while another may be influenced by a candidate's perceived inflexible ideas. In one research programme, a group of interviewers who were aware of the person specification and were in possession of the application forms were shown a group of videoed interviews and yet there was still a variation in the recommended candidate for the position. This was despite having identical information.

Decide intuitively. Despite repeated calls for interviewers to base their decisions on the objective evidence which they have collected, there remains a constant temptation to make overall judgements based on intuition. The 'I have a gut-feel' school of interviewing still has a number of ardent supporters, who usually also subscribe to the 'I can spot them as soon as they come in the door' association!

Make decisions before the interview takes place or early on in the interview. Studies show that the average length of time between a candidate entering the interview room and a decision being made is just under four minutes. This 'expectancy effect' arises from a study of the CV or application before the interview. All the subsequent information is recorded but adjusted to fit into the decision that the interviewer has already made.

Prefer candidates like themselves. The so-called 'clone factor' indicates that interviewers give higher ratings on some traits to candidates who are similar to themselves, rather than matching the candidates against the person specification.

Continue to stereotype candidates. Despite the illegality of judging candidates on the basis of their sex, ethnic origin, disability or marital status, interviewers, often unknowingly, will allow such considerations to cloud their judgements. This can extend to areas such as age, geographical origin, accent, height and even their attire.

Cannot take on board all the information provided. The brain can only assimilate a certain amount of information. Each candidate provides a wealth of data and even 30 minutes of interview time can be transcribed into more than 10 pages of written text. A recommended interview period therefore should not extend beyond one hour individually or four hours in a day and certainly not beyond five or six candidates. Notes need to be compiled during the interview and compared and agreed after each one.

Influence candidates' behaviour. How an applicant behaves is partly dependent on how the interviewer behaves. Particular interest has been focused on non-verbal behaviours (signals such as nodding, smiling and eye contact) during the interview. In one study, it was found that, where interviewers had already decided to reject the applicants, they talked less and were more cold and critical; the candidates in this trial reported that they were more uncomfortable and became more hesitant in their replies. However, where interviewers were warm, had good eye contact and nodded their head more frequently, candidates became more relaxed, acted in a more friendly way themselves, became more talkative and generally were found to be more effective in creating a good impression.

Raise their ratings if they feel pressurised to select. After all the time, effort and cost involved in recruitment, there is considerable pressure on the interviewers to come up with a successful candidate. Knowing the delay that would be incurred if the position needed to be advertised again, interviewers may panic and allow the pressure to influence their decision. Candidates that are close to meeting the specification may be upgraded and candidates rejected for good reasons may be wrongly reconsidered.

Believe that they are good at interviewing. Interviewing is not regarded in some circles as a skill that can be learned and developed. Many line managers see it as an inherent managerial trait that they possess, chiefly because it is never pointed out to them that evidence indicates the contrary is true.

Influence candidates' responses to the offer. The interviewer represents the organisation. The candidate will judge that organisation on how they are treated and how the interviewer has behaved to them. It has been shown that up to 50 per cent of candidates change their minds about their likely acceptance of a potential job offer as a result of their experience in the interview, irrespective of the benefits and attractiveness of the post.

These are pretty serious criticisms of the interview process. They indicate that the whole process is so flawed that it ought not to be operated at all in such an important area as selection. There is an alternative view, however, which goes some way in explaining why the interview is still the most popular aid to selection decision-making. This view is that, partially flawed as it is, it has some distinct advantages and serious attempts can be made to over-come the flaws through training and specifically through utilising the more systematic and objective method of structured interviews, which will be dealt with shortly.

The general *advantages* put forward in favour of interviews are:

- It is a relatively low-cost exercise, with additional expenses limited to the time of the participants and any travelling and accommodation expenses.
- No decision on selection should be taken without an interview of some sort being carried out. At the basic level, it is a pure courtesy, an introduction both to the organi-sation and the people involved.
- Used properly, valid judgements can be made on a number of items of behaviour, espe-cially interpersonal behaviour. Sociability, verbal fluency and social confidence can all be competencies detailed in the job specification and measured effectively in the interview process. The interview can be viewed as a type of 'work sample' of these behaviours and should give some degree of prediction about future behaviour and performance.
- The interview is important in selling the job to the applicants and this is vital in certain high-demand, low-supply occupations, such as information technology or accounting. If the interview is handled positively and carefully, disappointed candidates will still feel good about the experience and the organisation.
- A degree of negotiation can and often should take place before an agreement is reached between the organisation and the selected candidate. The interview allows informal negotiation to take place on the nature of the job together with the terms and conditions.

Who carries out the interview?

There are three options for the interview format: *one-to-one interviews*, *paired interviews* or *panel interviews*. Each should be used in specific situations and avoided in others. The decision as to the appropriate format is made by reaching a balance between two contrasting objectives. Firstly, the need for informality which gives the opportunity for a frank exchange of views and information and, secondly, the need to include as many stakeholders involved as possible and work to a structured and objective agenda.

In a professionally handled *one-to-one interview*, the candidate is more likely to open up, respond to careful probing and give all the required information regarding their skills, expe-rience, competencies and viewpoints. However, the interviewer will be unlikely to be able to deal with all the information successfully. (Have you tried listening to the answers, taking notes and thinking of the next question at the same time?) Another problem arising is that the decisions made will be based on one person's views, which can be biased or wrongly based. Thirdly, there are serious questions to be answered in the area of equal opportunities where having only one interviewer greatly increases the chances of a discriminating viewpoint. In fact, it can be quite dangerous. A number of organisations have faced tribunals by unsuc-cessful applicants who have claimed that interviewers have made statements or asked questions which can be regarded as discriminatory in the fields of sex, race or disablement and, with only one interviewer, it becomes more difficult to refute.

One-to-one interviews, therefore, are appropriate in only a limited number of situations. For example, a candidate for a senior position can be invited to meet a number of potential peers who will each talk to the person separately and informally, comparing overall notes afterwards. This may result in a degree of fatigue for the applicant as the same questions are repeated but this may be regarded as part of the selection process – to see how the candidate handles the situation. Another situation involves a candidate having a preliminary interview with, say, the human resources manager, as part of a wider short-listing process. The human resources manager will be entrusted to select a number of possible candidates who will progress to the final stage.

At the other extreme, a *panel interview*, which can consist of up to ten interviewers, presents its own problems. Pure logistics is one, where simply finding a convenient time for all the participants can be difficult enough. If a candidate cannot make the required date, it is not uncommon for them to be ruled out of the equation as another date for the panel cannot be arranged. Another difficulty is the inevitable formality of a number of interviewers appearing to interrogate the applicant, moving rapidly from one questioner to another ('Sorry, Counsellor Jones, but we must move on') and from one topic to another. Question slots have to be agreed beforehand, which makes it difficult to enter into probing mode. The applicant will find it difficult to read the body language of all the interviewers, or to gauge how well the answers were received. It may also need some time after each interview for the panel to compare notes and reach a decision on each candidate, which prolongs the exercise.

So panel interviews are only used where it is considered essential for a number of stakeholders to be present and for a decision to be taken on the day when the interviews have been held. This is currently the chosen mantra within the public sector, especially in local authorities. For many such jobs, a head of department, one or more line managers, a member of human resources and a counsellor may be present. There may also be a clerk to take notes and an equal opportunities adviser to ensure procedures are followed. Internal equity and consultation is carried out and justice is seen to be done, despite the difficulties of getting agreement from a number of staff on who will be the successful candidate. Many of the applicants spend their lives in such an environment so they know what happens and are prepared for it. There is some evidence that the actual numbers are being reduced due to the continuing cutback of staff in the public domain. In certain departments of Beds County Council, for example, it has been agreed as policy that three people (no more, no less) will be present at each interview.

Given the difficulties with the other two forms, it is no surprise that the most common interviewing format is *a paired interview*, where the line manager is supported by a member of the human resources department. They agree on the nature of the interview and who will take the lead at particular points, and they will normally share in the note-taking role. A second interviewer allows probing to take place and for a merging of combined views of the outcome of the questioning.

Interviewing technique

Although interviewing is still seen generally as an art form, there are a number of essential ingredients which make up a successful interview. These can be divided into *preparation, operation* and *summation*.

Preparation includes the following elements:

■ All the relevant documents, especially the application form and candidate's accompanying letter, should be read thoroughly.

■ It should be firmly agreed between the interviewers the nature of the measurement of the candidate. It may be carried out by a points system based on how closely they meet the person specification or by an agreed system of elimination.

■ The division of the interview should be agreed, with time divided between telling the candidate a little more about the organisation and the position, the questioning of the candidate and giving the candidate the opportunity to ask questions.

■ The room allocated for the interview should be prepared. It is better for it to be informally set out, rather than interviewers on one side of the desk and the candidate on the other. There should be no interruptions of any kind.

■ The nature of the data recording must be agreed, the stationary printed and the recording roles assigned.

Operation covers a wide area and can be divided into a number of areas:

■ Opening the interview
■ Listening
■ Asking the right questions
■ Structured interviews.

Opening the interview is important as it sets the tone of the interview process. Some informal questions concerning travel arrangements or knowledge of the organisation or area are often used to break the ice. It is important at an early stage to introduce the interviewers and to make it quite clear what will be happening during the interview and after it is over. It is normal for the lead interviewer to say a few words about the position, referring to documents already sent to the candidate. This allows the candidate to relax into the interview and a chance to observe the interviewers.

For the interviewers, one of the most important techniques is *listening*. It is easy to spot the inexperienced interviewer; they believe they should dominate the proceeding and do most of the talking. The reality is that, apart from words at the start to allow the candidate to relax into the interview, the vast majority of the interview should consist of the candidate talking. The more the candidate talks, the more complete the picture the interviewer can draw.

A sign of effective listening is that the interviewer asks relevant questions, which can probe the candidate, especially any implied points that are made. For example, a slight hesitation in answer to a question as to the relationship with a certain manager would be followed up carefully. Maintaining eye contact and summarising what the candidate has said from time to time demonstrates to the candidate that what they are saying is being followed carefully and sympathetically.

Asking *the right questions* in the right way is a large subject area. There are a number of different styles and techniques that can be used. All of them depend on the nature of the information that you want to draw out from the candidate. They can take a number of forms:

(1) If you want to find out some clear factual information or to check points, then *closed* questions are appropriate, those to which the answer is either yes or no:

■   Have you a clean driving licence?
■   Were you dismissed from that employment?
■   Have you a level A BPS qualification?

(2) If you want candidates to expand on information they have given and generally open up more, then you ask *open* questions:

■   Why did you want to leave that employment?
■   What do you enjoy about customer service work?
■   Which do you consider to be your major strengths in managing people?
■   Tell me about the difficulties you faced when you became a supervisor.
■   How did you cope with moving from a local authority to working in the private sector?
■   When did you really discover that your career should be in training?

The more experienced you become in interviewing, the more is learned about how to mix the majority of open questions with the occasional closed question. For example, when interviewing for a supervisory position, you would ask a number of open questions relating to the candidate's experience of supervision and their views on how it should be done well; you would intersperse these questions with some closed questions relating to how long they acted as a supervisor or whether they had disciplined an employee for poor workmanship/ attitude/timekeeping.

(3) If you want to get into fine detail about a candidate's work history, behaviours or attitude, you would ask *probing* questions. For example, you have been sensed a slight discrepancy between the starting date of one job and the leaving date of the previous job and that the manner of leaving may not have been too happy. You would probe this situation with questions such as:

■   You seem to indicate that you were not entirely happy working at xxx. For how long were you looking to leave the employment?

- Did you have any indication that your manager found your work unsatisfactory? I should add that we may want to take up a reference with her.
- Did you finally leave the employment voluntarily?
- Was there any gap between leaving xxx and starting at yyyy?

Experienced interviewers often probe simply by asking candidates, when they pause at the end of explanation, to 'go on' or 'tell me more' or ask them 'was there a another reason?', leaving a pause for the candidate, which often results in either the fundamental truth of the situation or the candidate getting themselves caught up in the knots of their own deception.

(4) If you want to find out how a candidate may behave in a given situation, then you would ask a *situational* or *hypothetical* question. Here you would set out a specific scenario, usually related to the work situation and ask the candidate what the options would be and how they would act. An example of this is set out in Figure 3.3.

An interview has been fixed for the position of campaigns manager for a small charity at a salary of £13,000. It is possible that a young graduate will be appointed to the position.

The situation agreed by the panel is as follows:

You have agreed to telephone round to the regional officers between 10am and 11am to discuss the agenda for a critical meeting in order to decide the response to a government initiative. They all work on a voluntary basis and have full-time jobs and this time for communication was arranged a fortnight ago. You have an appraisal meeting with the charity director at 11am that has been put off a couple of times and is very important to you. Just before 10am, you get a call from the news desk of a national newspaper asking you to ring a particular journalist. This journalist has wasted your time on a couple of occasions in the past and is not a very pleasant character. The next moment, the charity director's secretary comes in to say that the director has to go out at 11am, and asks if the appraisal meeting could take place now. What do you do?

The panel have decided that candidates will be judged by their views on the best course of action as matched against the panel's concerted view of the best course of action, that is:

Explain to the director's secretary that you need to call the journalist and do not know how long this will take. Try to arrange another time for the appraisal. Call the journalist and deal with the issues raised. No matter how much difficulty there is with such people, keeping a good relationship with them is crucial and they can give you the publicity that can be vital to your organisation's development. As soon as that call is over, start ringing round to the regional officers, explaining the issues with the national newspaper and fixing alternative times to talk if possible. (Get somebody else to help if they are available.) Use email where appropriate. Your own appraisal will need to wait.

A scoring system has been devised against this answer with a maximum of 10, with marks deducted for a different set of priorities or communication faults.

Figure 3.3
A situational or hypothetical question

CASE STUDY 3.3 CRITERION-BASED INTERVIEW TECHNIQUE – MINISTRY OF DEFENCE

This is an extract from the interviewer's guide book to help determine the level of competency of an applicant in the area of *working effectively with others*.

Firstly, here is a list of *indicators* against the competency:

Evidence For	Evidence Against
– Builds rapport with others and tries to resolve conflict with tact	Poor relationships with others
– Remains calm and courteous when handling differences with others	Easily ruffled or abrasive when handling differences with others
– Helps others with their work	Little knowledge of colleagues' work
– Sensitive to others' needs	Insensitive to others' needs
– Willing to cover for others	
– Shares information with people	Keeps information to self
– Follows managers' instructions willingly	Does not inform manager of problems/ progress
– Knows when to tackle directly or ask someone else	Poor judgement on when to ask for someone else's advice
– Puts forward ideas	Puts forward few (if any) ideas

Here are the questions that will help you to judge the candidate's competency:

Opening question:

On your application form, you wrote about a time when you had to work in a group or team and what you did to keep up good relationships within the group. Can you tell me about another time when you had to work in a group or team? (If candidates cannot think of another example, probe on the one they gave on the application form.)

– What did you do to keep up co-operation and good relationships?
– What problems or difficulties did you face?
– How did you overcome these?

Follow-up questions:

Can you tell me about the occasion when you have had to help resolve conflict between people who were not co-operating with each other?

– What action did you take?
– What did you say?

- How did you react/respond?
- What was the outcome?

Give me an example of an occasion when you helped a colleague at work.

- What led up to the situation?
- What did they need?
- How could you tell?
- What help did you give?

Give me an example of a situation where you referred a work issue to your supervisor/manager.

- What did you refer to him/her?
- What did you do?
- What was the response?
- What was the result?

(Source: Ministry of Defence internal documentation)

The problem here is deciding what you are trying to find out. You may want to know the candidate's knowledge of how to deal with that specific situation. However, you may simply find out how quick thinking they are and their ability to come up with the 'right answer'. How they will act in practice may be entirely different. There is also the difficulty in deciding what is the 'right' answer, and this needs to be clarified before the interview and the candidate's answers measured against this answer.

An alternative version to this type of questioning is to describe the situation as in Figure 3.3 and then ask the candidate how they reacted in a similar situation that they faced in the past. This is called a *Patterned Behaviour Description Interview* (PBDI). The advantage here is that that you will be talking about a real situation. The problem, however, is that the candidate may not have faced such a situation or the situation they describe may not have the main elements you want to examine.

Criterion-based Interview Technique (CIT) is a similar version, where candidates are asked to produce evidence of how they acted in situations where a specific competency is required. An example of its usage at the Ministry of Defence is shown in case study 3.3.

(5) Some interviewers use *stress questions* as part of an interview. The intention here is to examine how candidates react to an aggressive or disparaging interviewer or to particularly critical remarks. This is a controversial and risky strategy as the candidate, although dealing with the situation well, may be put off the organisation by being treated in this way. Only if the job is highly specialised, such as intelligence work or direct selling

where selection methods tend to be somewhat unpredictable and this is recognised by candidates, could such a method be held to be acceptable.

Structured interviews

To be successful in the whole operation of interviewing, a planned structure is necessary. To refer again to the table of predictive success in Figure 3.1, *structured interviews* come high on the table with a predictive rating of 0.51, but, interestingly, this is a fall from 0.63 in earlier research they have carried out. However, in a wide range of research into interviewing over the last 50 years, few conclusions have been more widely supported than the idea that structuring the interview enhances reliability and validity with results generally twice as effective (Brittain 2012), and 61 per cent of employers claim to use them for selection purposes (CIPD 2010).

Structured interviews take many forms but the essential features include:

- A sense of direction and purpose – a clear agreement on what the interview is trying to elicit.
- The interviewing process attempts to predict how candidates will perform in the work situation.
- The question format is laid down and agreed beforehand, which is job analysis based.
- Controlled prompting and follow-up questions.
- Generally no questions from candidates are allowed during the interview.
- A thorough and consistent approach used with all the candidates in the same way.
- Interviewers are trained in the process to be used.
- Candidates are evaluated using the same scale.

Although it has proved to be highly successful, this approach has a number of criticisms:

- The strict following of a pre-planned process allows little chance to deviate or to follow up any areas that may be of interest to both the candidate and the interviewer.
- Occasionally, it can appear stilted and artificial.
- Following general guides too rigidly and not giving candidates opportunities to share relevant information raise the possibility of the organisation being exposed to claims of unfair discrimination.
- As candidates all have differing backgrounds and experience, putting exactly the same questions to all of them can lead to receiving many spurious results.
- Where mass recruitment takes place, interviewers may become weary and bored by having to follow an identical format.

An example of structured interviews is given in focus on research 3.1.

FOCUS ON RESEARCH 3.1 STRUCTURED INTERVIEWS

This article analyses the development of the selection process of Beyer for sales representatives in Russia and Eastern Europe. The organisation had encountered a very high turnover rate for sales staff in these areas, which had not improved with increased training or improved management. The conclusion was reached that there was a fundamental fault in the selection process. The organisation moved firstly into a greater use of assessment centres, but it became clear that the cultural differences between countries was so great that mixing candidates at one centre was not effective. Nor could they be set up at the speed and flexibility that was required.

Structured interviews were then developed for each location, using teams of experienced local managers. A detailed job analysis and associated competencies were constructed and a four-part interview structure built up, consisting of questions on job experience and background, question sets focused on the required competencies, behavioural event discussion (past oriented) and situational role-play (future oriented). Standard evaluation forms were produced alongside this structure. The structured interviews take place for those candidates who pass the telephone and base-line interview screening process.

Under this setting, structured interviews took over two hours with a panel of three interviewers who have predetermined roles, either in question asking, observation or note-taking. A detailed description of each part of the interview is set out in the article. The outcome for the organisation is not clear but early responses were very positive, especially from staff involved in the selection process.

(Source: Engle 1998)

Conversational interviews

Where organisations want to adopt a more subtle approach without a number of the formal and rigid aspects of structured interviews, a conversational interview technique can be adopted. This technique still focuses on key criteria but it also tries to put the candidate at ease and reinforce a positive employer brand. The interviewer adopts the style of a peer who is taking an interest in the candidate's role and aspirations, attempting to empower the candidate and allow the conversation to flow in a more natural way but, at the same time, ensuring that all aspects of the key criteria are investigated in a thorough and comprehensive way (Brittain 2012).

Summation

Summation is the final stage of the interviewing process. This involves recording all the necessary data and closing the interview. Before an interview is closed, it is important that candidates have the opportunity *to ask questions*. Indeed, some interview processes allow candidates to ask questions at the start. In any case, it encourages the interview to be a two-way process, it indicates how interested the candidate is in the position and how much research they have carried out, and allows a judgement to be made on how well organised the candidate is.

When questions from both sides are over, the interview is normally *closed* by a word of thanks for attending and a reiteration of the next stage in the process. Sometimes, especially for manufacturing environments, a short tour of the premises is arranged.

Recording the interview data is vital. Not only is this essential so that decisions can be taken on the basis of objective measures but also such information may be necessary as a defence against an action for discrimination in selection, which may be taken against the organisation at some time. A final use is for giving feedback to unsuccessful candidates.

ASSESSMENT CENTRES

Assessment centres are not just used for selection, although this is their main purpose in practice. They can also be used for diagnosing the training and development needs of individuals, especially those in positions of authority; as a general tool to improve team-working within a department; and to assess the special needs of those employees who can be identified as potential high-performers. According to the CIPD (2010), 42 per cent of larger organisations use some form of assessment centre. Their use has been growing for a number of reasons:

- In today's flatter organisations, mistakes made in management selection decisions are far more costly, so it is vital to get them right at the start.
- Candidates that have taken part in them are more motivated, recognising the high level of time, effort and cost put into them.
- There is a benefit for the assessors who take part. In the 1990s, for example, ICI found that training managers as assessors made them far better at the day-to-day management process.

Essentially, an assessment centre brings together a number of selection methods into a concentrated period which lasts one or two days. A programme can be made up of group exercises, presentations, role-playing, personality tests, structured interviews and in-tray exercises, all of which are scored by trained assessors.

Roberts (2005) has suggested the grid in Table 3.3 for using various tests at an assessment centre to probe for certain competencies.

The assessors are usually made up of experienced managers in the organisation, usually one or two ranks above the candidates involved in the centre, plus some external assessors who are usually consultants. According to Suff and Ward (2011), internal staff are used by 81 per cent of organisations. The internal assessors need to be thoroughly trained in the nature of the tests and how to assess the candidates. For example,

Table 3.3 Techniques to test for various competencies

Competency	Screen	Test	Interview	Exercise
Achievement	X			
Leadership				X
Creativity		X		
Resilience		X		
Flexibility			X	
Technical knowledge	X			
Judgement		X		
Decision-making		X	X	
Planning				X
Financial acumen				X

Source: Adapted from Roberts, G. (2005) *Recruitment and Selection.* CIPD.

observation of team-working will involve an assessment of positive and negative contribu-tions, idea generation and leadership, all of which need to be objectively scored. Skills of assessing are made up of observing, recording, classifying, summarising and rating. The ratio of assessors to candidates at a centre is in the order of 1:2 so the staff utilisation costs are quite high.

The aim of the activity tests is to create situations that are as realistic as possible to the workplace or where the candidate behaviour has an important bearing on the expected behaviour in the workplace. The way that candidates interact with each other and persuade, negotiate and lead each other can actually be seen, rather than discussed from a theoretical viewpoint. The centres put considerable pressure on the candidates; they are stressful occasions, especially as the outcome is perceived as success or failure with little in between. Experienced assessment centre planners try to ensure that the candidates consider the selection process is carried out *with* them, and not *done to* them. Detailed feedback to the candidates is another essential requirement. Research has indicated that candidates react well to assessment centres, and see them as a very positive event. According to Suff (2011), over 90 per cent react in this way.

Development centres are less pressurised. Some are set up with complete confiden-tiality for the participants who play a major part in planning and running the centre them-selves. The outcome is a programme of training and development for each participant to help them to achieve agreed goals.

Centres are expensive to set up and run. The costs include accommodation and travel, the tests and their interpretation, consultant fees and operating managers' time. In 2011, the average cost was calculated as £311 per candidate, although some employers quoted over £1,000 (Suff 2011). They certainly cannot be taken on lightly. An example of an assessment centre is detailed in the Meteor case study.

CHOOSING THE SUCCESSFUL CANDIDATE

The final decision on selecting the preferred candidate should follow the same process that applies to short-listing. Only the candidates who match the 'essential' aspects of the person specification should be considered. It is a poor decision to select 'the best on the day' when this person only reaches half of the necessary criteria. It is far better to start the process again than take a serious risk in a potentially hazardous investment. If there is more than one candidate who meets all the criteria, the final decision can be made by a number of ways. Generally, the decision is given to the line manager who will have to motivate, develop and manage the person concerned. Much is talked about the necessary 'personal chemistry' that needs to exist between the line manager and the successful applicant but one must be wary of the potential discrimination aspects. The manager should justify the decision in terms of as many objective criteria as possible.

Sometimes other parties are brought into the decision-making process. At The Body Shop and at Pret A Manger (see case study 3.4), the existing unit staff are consulted about the candidates and have a serious input into the equation. For senior university posts, candidates are often asked to give a formal presentation to staff in the appropriate department or faculty who are then consulted, especially on the technical elements.

TECHNOLOGY IN SELECTION

In this chapter, we have discussed details of the use of technology in selection such as automated telephone screening and online psychometric testing. Other examples include:

■ *Social media* – Reckitt Benckiser launched a Facebook-based game in 2010 to give graduate applicants a better understanding of the company's culture.
■ *Simulations* – A clearing bank has created, as part of its numerical reasoning test, a simulation that looks like the Bloomberg business TV channel, with information that applicants have to respond to on the bottom of the screen.
■ *Creative* – Ikea has developed a 'cultural fit' online questionnaire where candidates fill in multiple-choice questions, and, as they answer them, the room fills with Ikea furniture (Paton 2010).
■ *Video-conferencing* – This is commonly used in international recruitment (Sedgwick and Spiers 2009). For example, the University of Bedfordshire carries out short-list interviews through video-conferencing when academic applicants are based overseas.

CASE STUDY 3.4 THE PRET A MANGER ACADEMY

An unusual approach to selection has been adopted by Pret A Manger, the ethical and rapidly expanding sandwich chain with 118 shops and 2,400 staff. Despite a staff turnover far less than their competitors' average (90 per cent against 150 per cent), it still leaves a great deal of recruitment to carry out each year – 55,000 applications for 1,500 jobs were received in 2001.

To ensure it gets people with the right qualities, Pret uses what is perhaps the ultimate assessment centre – a job experience day. But, unlike the conventional assessment centre, would-be team members are assessed by their working colleagues who vote on whether a job is offered or not. When the team buys into a recruit, they take responsibility for getting them team-oriented and up to speed.

Before their working day, candidates have to get through a competency-based interview, which aims to discover those that have an outgoing, positive attitude to life. Candidates passing this stage are then thrown in at the deep end, working as a paid employee in the shop from 6.30am until 2.30pm. A team member will be assigned to act as guide and mentor with the idea that candidates carry out as many different tasks as possible, working with all the shop staff. The shop manager carries out an informal interview but does not have a vote, although their view can have some sway. At 2.30pm, the manager gathers the team members' votes and informs the applicant. Unsuccessful candidates go away with £30, a free lunch and feedback on their performance.

All the team take a lot of pride in their role in the Pret experience and they appreciate how important their responsibility is in taking the decision. Because it is their decision, they will want it to work out, so the team provides a great deal of help and encouragement to the new starter giving them a good induction into the organisation.

(Source: Carrington 2002)

USING A VARIETY OF APPROACHES

Most organisations will use a collection of approaches in their selection systems. They may use traditional approaches, such as a conventional interview, but also make use of testing and assessment processes, often with new technology. LexisNexis is an example of an organisation which has changed its approach in this way, as shown in case study 3.5.

C
A
S
E

S
T
U
D
Y

CASE STUDY 3.5 SELECTING SALES STAFF AT LEXISNEXIS

LexisNexis, a company that integrates information and technology in providing services in branding, web technologies and premium information sources in the legal and tax sectors, adopted a new approach to selection, which had a dramatic impact on business results with sales of new products and services doubling over a two-year period and the number of multi-year deals increasing by 70 per cent. The change was to move from a selection emphasis based primarily on knowledge and experience to one which placed a high premium on skills and behaviour. This came about because the organisation wanted to create high-performing teams to strengthen relationships with customers and respond to rising expectations.

The skills and behaviours identified included curiosity about customers' businesses, a high degree of motivation and the ability to influence others. Behavioural profiling, structured interviews and role-play were introduced to assess candidates against these attributes, while psychometric tests measured their intellectual ability. The new methods improved all the selection outcomes, for, as well as better business results, more recruits passed their probationary period and showed a more rapid sales increase. As a result of the consistent use of the new selection criteria, there was an interesting by-product. The process assisted equal opportunities as 52 per cent of the recruits were women, a far higher proportion than is usual in such a sales environment.

(Source: Arkin 2010)

OBTAINING REFERENCES

The offer of employment should not be made, even informally, until references have been obtained. Once a decision is reached on the chosen candidate, it is normal to make approaches to past employers to check the accuracy of information provided by the applicant and to ensure that there is no 'skeleton' lurking in the applicant's past that has not been revealed.

References are one of the most unsatisfactory aspects of human resources in practice. Most organisations make attempts to obtain them but the actual results are woefully inadequate. Either the requested reference never arrives, or it provides a set of platitudes that can be unconvincing or it is incomplete, leaving out some key information that may affect the decision to offer employment. In certain circumstances, effective references are vital, such as in jobs involving a high degree of security or where the work is with vulnerable people. (Details on the Vetting and Barring schemes are to be found on the CIPD website.)

Cowan and Cowan (1989) set out many of the pitfalls in obtaining references, including hidden meanings (*a sociable and gregarious individual* means the candidate drinks too much). Although written over 20 years again, little has changed in the dilemmas faced in the difficulties in referencing.

The legal situation is that there is no obligation for the employer to provide a reference where requested. However, if one is given, the House of Lords has stipulated that an employer has a duty to take reasonable care in compiling a reference by ensuring the accuracy of the information on which it is based. The duty is to provide a reference which is in substance true, accurate and fair, and this will usually involve making a reasonable enquiry into the factual basis of any statements made (*Spring v Guardian Assurance plc, 1994 IRLR 460*).

A case which demonstrates the application of this judgment is shown in spotlight on the law 3.1.

For jobs where the security or personal risks are small, a simplified reference system is to obtain at interview the names and telephone numbers of the managers that the applicant worked for in previous employment (interestingly, telling the applicant that these people will be approached for a reference sometimes prompts the applicant to tell more details about why they left their employment). The reliability of certain crucial pieces of information can be verified by one short phone call and it is not wise to make an offer until such information is received. It is sufficient to ask the following information:

- Did (John Smith) work for you from x to x as a (job)?
- Would you re-employ them if they applied again?

SPOTLIGHT ON THE LAW 3.1

Jackson had taken up a position with Sefton Council, having received a good reference from Liverpool Council, his former employer. He then applied to transfer to a position within Sefton's Youth Offending Team and it was legally necessary for Sefton to take up a reference again from Liverpool Council. On this occasion, the Council referred to concerns about Jackson's recordkeeping, although praising his timekeeping and general work ability. However, they pointed out that these concerns had not been fully investigated. An HR manager from Sefton Council telephoned Liverpool but could not obtain any further information as the manager at Liverpool explained she couldn't answer questions about the issues 'in either a positive or a negative manner'.

Jackson did not get the job within Sefton Council and was unemployed for a year so he sued Liverpool for damages. The Court of Appeal, although having sympathy with Jackson, decided that a reference was 'fair', even though it noted concerns about an ex-employee's record keeping that they had not investigated. However, the Council had made it clear that the allegations had not been tested so the reference was true and accurate. No damages were awarded.

(Source: *Jackson v Liverpool Council, 2011 EWCA Civ 1068*)

SPOTLIGHT ON THE LAW

If there is any hesitancy in answering the second question, then quick supplementary questions can be added. In most cases, although not every one, the recipient of the call will be prepared to talk in confidence, although they will not put anything down in writing.

Despite recommendations about making offers of employment 'subject to satisfactory references', it is a very unpleasant process to actually withdraw an offer when a poor reference is received. The applicant may have already handed in their notice to their existing employer and the reference received may just be vindictive or out of date. It is far better to ensure the reference is obtained before the offer is actually made. Finally, except for school leavers, it is not worth considering references from the applicant's friends or colleagues, who are unlikely to be able to make an unbiased judgement.

Having said all this, references should be treated as just one part of the jigsaw. Just as with selection tests, a decision should not be based on the reference alone; a reference will always be a subjective and incomplete item, representing a period in time. Individuals change over time and younger ones will often blossom given a supportive, encouraging and developmental environment.

OFFERING THE POSITION

Once satisfactory references have been obtained, the offer of employment can be made to the successful candidate. Of course, this needs to be confirmed in writing but, because of the need to inform the candidate as soon as possible, especially if the employer is aware that they are in the market for other positions, a telephone call with the main details usually takes place as soon as possible. Should the candidate wish to negotiate any of the details, this call allows such negotiations to proceed quickly.

The offer of employment should contain the following details:

■ Job title
■ Starting date
■ Starting salary and any agreed details on salary progression and how it is determined, especially during the first year
■ Any help with relocation if appropriate
■ Company car level and arrangements for petrol, if appropriate
■ Details of confirmation of the offer (the candidate is usually asked to sign their agreement on one copy of the letter, and return it to the company in the envelope supplied)
■ Details may also be supplied of other company benefits if not given beforehand. These can include medical and life assurance, staff discounts, parking arrangements and pension scheme
■ The candidate may be asked to bring with them on the first day their driving licence and any qualifications they have claimed for which the organisation has not yet obtained confirmation.

This offer will, when accepted, need to be followed up with a formal 'contract of employment', which needs to be given to the employee within two months of their starting employment.

Unsuccessful candidates need to be informed at this stage, usually by letter, although the candidate who is 'first reserve' should also be telephoned to be told of the decision. They will be informed that they are waiting for confirmation but, if the chosen candidate declines, they will be offered the position. This is more than just a courtesy as it keeps this candidate interested and positive towards the organisation. A further position may arise in the near future in any case.

Organisations are increasingly giving feedback to unsuccessful applicants. This is certainly carried out with internal applicants for whom the decision may be a difficult one to take. Some form of supportive counselling can be of considerable help here because they need to face their colleagues who will know they have not succeeded. An action plan can be drawn up with their line manager to allow them to work towards filling those gaps that caused them to be unsuccessful.

For external candidates, the issue is more difficult. It would be a logistical nightmare to give personal feedback to 200 or so applicants who may apply for one or more positions. However, it is not good practice to fob off an enquiry from a disappointed candidate who politely requests areas where they went wrong. For this reason, in recent years, a number of high-profile companies have instituted a policy of giving detailed feedback to all candidates at short-list and to any others that make a positive enquiry. The feedback is constructed from the assessment process that is used in the selection process, is explained very carefully and truthfully, and attempts to be as positive as possible. It is usually given verbally, which emphasises the belief by the organisation that each candidate should be treated in a fair and individual way.

EVALUATING THE SELECTION PROCESS

Evaluation takes two forms:

- Judging how successful the selection process has been
- Examining the process to judge the effectiveness of each stage.

When can you tell that you have made the right selection decision? That depends on the position. For a post-room clerk or receptionist, you may be fairly sure within a few weeks. For a factory manager, you should have a good idea after a year is up and objectives are reached. At the extreme end, for the research director of a pharmaceutical company, it may be a question of five to ten years before one or two successfully marketed drugs indicate a good level of success. However, a successfully completed recruitment exercise one minute can change into a failure the next when the employee concerned abruptly decides to leave. It is impossible to distinguish between those factors that you can influence, such as the job design, the selection process and the way the successful candidate is managed and motivated, and the external factors over which you have no control, such as the way the economy moves, the market changes and changes in the personal circumstances of the successful candidate. So recruitment is a long-term process where constant evaluation is necessary.

There are some hard facts that will give some indication of success:

■ How quickly the position was filled, measured from the date of the request to the starting date of the successful candidate.
■ The average length of tenure of the person recruited.
■ The proportion of employees recruited that were promoted within five years.
■ The response cost per candidate in terms of advertising (i.e. cost of advertising divided by number of responses).
■ The proportion of candidates who met the minimum requirements specified.

None of these, on their own, will give a complete answer. As with many management statistics, it is the comparison against previous years and similar companies that will be a better indicator of selection performance. An effective guide to the efficiency and candidate-friendly nature of recruitment can be gauged by carrying out an attitude survey of unsuccessful candidates.

METEOR CASE STUDY

THE ASSESSMENT CENTRE

Sarah stood up to introduce the assessment centre. In the room were nine candidates for the two call-centre senior adviser posts, together with Gary Hands, the manager of the call-centre team, and Helen Roads, a consultant psychologist that Sarah had brought in to design and run the assessment centre. The 9 had been chosen from 120 applicants by having the required level of experience and through matching the preferred competencies mapped out by Gary and Sarah.

She knew it was going to be a hard two days for all the participants. The programme was as follows:

Day 1

9.00	Assemble and introductions
9.30	Work simulation test 1. Call-centre activity
11.00	Warm-up exercise
12.00	Battery of ability tests – verbal reasoning and analytical ability
13.00	Lunch
14.00	Teamwork exercise – outdoors
16.00	Review and feedback on exercises
17.00	Interview/Personality questionnaire

| 19.00 | Break |
| 20.00 | Interview/Personality questionnaire feedback |

Day 2

9.00	Negotiation exercise and feedback
11.00	Work simulation test 2. In-tray exercise and feedback
13.00	Lunch and finish

The programme had been designed by Helen, who had carried out similar work for three other call-centre operators. The ability and verbal reasoning tests were of Helen's own construction, while the personality test used was the Myers-Briggs Type Indicator and the ideal candidates were those who came out strongly on 'thinking and judging'. The work simulation tests consisted of a short call-centre activity simulation and an in-tray exercise. The simulation was set up to ensure that the candidates had a basic knowledge and understanding of call-centre operator competencies and candidates only needed to pass this activity. The in-tray exercises were specifically adapted for Meteor-style call-centre management situations and marks were awarded for skills in planning, time management, initiative, judgement and realism. The negotiating test had also been designed by Helen and involved negotiations with employee representatives in changing work patterns, with candidates playing roles on different sides of the table.

The outdoor activity, involving the construction of a bridge over a stream with a limited assortment of materials and tools, was designed to test team-working, leader-ship and completion skills. Sarah had brought in three additional managers to help with the interviews, which would be videoed along with a number of other exercises to help in the final decision-taking process.

The introductions went well and the early tests went smoothly and to schedule. The problems started after lunch when the outdoor activity began amid a torrential downpour. Not all the candidates had brought appropriate clothes and the protective garments provided were not totally proof against the extreme conditions. At one point, Sarah was going to announce the abandonment of the exercise, but the weather imme-diately abated and it was decided to complete it. However, extra time was allowed and all the candidates and observers needed more time than planned to shower and gener-ally recover from the ordeal. This led to the programme being delayed by more than an hour and the evening sessions stretched almost to midnight. Of the three teams taking part, only one produced a reasonable result and, although this allowed interesting assessments of working under stress, the assessors realised that judgements had to be moderated in view of the harsh conditions.

Most of the candidates were clearly weary by the second day and one was close to exhaustion. Extra time was allowed for the exercises so, again, the programme became delayed and did not finish until around 3pm.

Having wound up the assessment centre and thanked all the candidates for their contribution, Sarah, Helen and the assessors met up to examine the test results. They agreed to eliminate five of the candidates whose scores overall were the lowest either on the practical tests or because their personality test indicated a profile that did not match the specification. They then spent the remainder of the afternoon and much of the early evening watching videos of the remaining four candidates in their interviews and performing in the group tests.

One candidate emerged as an agreed clear favourite but the second choice was more difficult. One of the female candidates, who scored highly on most of the tests, acted poorly on the outdoor activity and was not particularly strong on the negotiations. There were varying views as to her performance in the interview, some regarding her as unnecessarily critical and others regarding her personality as one that is very determined.

The other four came close to each other in the overall scoring but had weaknesses on certain tests (as shown on the scorecard). Sarah watched the discussion go backwards and forwards, knowing that the candidates had been promised a quick decision and the difficulties involved in getting the selection group together again. By 8pm, she knew time was rapidly running out.

Candidate	Max score	1	2	3	4	5	6	7	8	9
Work simulation 1 – call centre	40	20	30	30	20	20	30	20	30	40
Ability tests	30	0	15	30	0	15	35	0	15	30
Team-working exercise	50	20	40	40	20	30	15	15	15	30
Personality test match	50	30	40	50	20	40	40	20	20	50
Negotiation exercise	40	30	20	30	20	30	25	20	30	10
Work simulation 2 – in-tray	40	20	25	30	20	30	40	25	30	20
Total	250	120	170	210	100	165	185	100	140	180

KEY CHAPTER SUMMARY POINTS

■ Approaches to selection can be made either on the basis of a clearly defined predetermined system or it can concentrate on the process, whereby the job is less clearly defined and can be moulded around the person selected.

■ Short-listing can be carried out through exclusion or inclusion. Telephone and automatic screening are becoming much more common in recent years.

■ Selection tests can be divided into ability, aptitude and personality and, to be effective, they must be valid and reliable. Strict guidelines have been produced on their correct use.

■ The traditional interview has been shown to be unreliable and subjective. Structured interviews have a better record and numerous techniques have been developed to strengthen the process.

■ Assessment centres involve a collection of tests and have a high validity as a selection process. However, they put pressure on the candidates and can be costly.

STUDENT ACTIVITIES

1   Consider the Pret A Manger case and decide whether the organisation operates 'best practice' in its recruitment method.

2   Taking the Meteor case study, do you think an assessment centre is a fair method of making the final selection? What are the successes and problems associated in this particular case? Make your decision as to which candidates should be selected, justifying your decision.

3   Automatic telephone screening (case study 3.1) helps to reduce the exclusion of those over 50. Has it any other advantages for minority groups?

4   Using the example of the testing for pub landlords in case study 3.2, draw up a list of specialist positions where the use of tests may produce some interesting personality profiles.

5   Construct a structured interview for the position of student counsellor, using situational questions, patterned behavioural descriptions and criterion based questions (see case study 3.3).

6   Debate whether employment references are worth the paper they are written on.

7   How objective is an interview? What makes is *more* objective? What makes it *less* objective? Should it be regarded as the first part of a programme to socialise an applicant into the organisation? Or should it concentrate simply on fitting the right person to the job vacancy?

REFERENCES

Arkin, A. (2010) In the Mix. *PM Guide to Assessment*, October, 8–11.

Brittain, S. (2012) Interviewing Skills: Building a Solid Structure. *People Management*, April, 30–33.

Butcher, S. (2004) Be Tough and Outgoing at the Top. *EFinancial Careers*, 7 April.

Carrington, L. (2002) At the Cutting Edge. *People Management*, 16 May, 31.

Chynoweth, C. (2009) Time is of the Essence. *PM Guide to Assessment*, 8 October, 10.

CIPD (2010) Resourcing and Talent Planning Survey 2010. CIPD, Thomson Learning.

Cowan, N. and Cowan, R (1989) Are References Worth the Paper they Are Written on? *Personnel Management*, December, 38–42.

Engle, R. (1998) Multi-step, Structured Interviews to Select Sales Representatives in Russia and Eastern Europe. *European Management Journal*, 16(4): 476–484.

Graves, L. and Karren, R. (1992) Reconsidering the Employment Interview. *Personnel Psychology*, 45: 313–340.

Iles, P. (2001) Employee Resourcing, in J. Storey (ed.) *Human Resource Management: A Critical Text*, 2nd ed. Thomson Learning.

Newell, S. and Rice, C. (1999) Assessment, Selection and Evaluation, pp. 129–165, in J. Leopold, L. Harris and T. Watson (eds) *Strategic Human Resourcing: Principles, Perspectives and Practices*. Financial Times/Prentice Hall.

Paton, N. (2010) University Challenge. *PM Guide to Assessment*, 14 October, 12–15

Roberts, G. (2005) *Recruitment and Selection*. CIPD.

Robertson, I. (2001) Undue Diligence. *People Management*, 22 November, 42–43.

Robertson, I. and Smith, M. (2001) Personnel Selection. *Journal of Occupational and Organizational Psychology*, 74(4): 443.

Sedgwick, M. and Spiers, J. (2009) The Use of Videoconferencing as a Medium for the Qualitative Interview. *International Journal of Quantitative Methods*, 8(1): 245–252.

Smethurst, S. (2003) The Road to Sedition. *People Management*, 7 August, 30–31.

Suff, R. (2011) Assessment Centres 2011 Survey, Evaluation and Feedback. *IRS Employment Review*, 14 September.

Suff, R. and Ward, K. (2011) Assessment Centres 2011 Survey, Process and Employer Practice. *IRS Employment Review*, 14 September.

Taylor, S. (2010) *Resourcing and Talent Management*. CIPD.

Trompenaars, F. and Woolliams, P. (2002) Model Behaviour. *People Management*, 5 December, 31–34.

ADDITIONAL FEATURES

 Please visit the companion website at: www.routledge.com/cw/stredwick where you will find additional case studies and reading material together with short self-tests and other resources for both students and lecturers.

4 RELATIONSHIPS WITH EMPLOYEES

CHAPTER OBJECTIVES

When you have read this chapter and carried out the activities, you will be able to:

- Identify the issues involved in the choices that organisations make in their relationships with their employees.

- Explain what is meant by the terms 'unitarism' and 'pluralism'.

- Describe the various actions that employers can take to encourage participation and involvement, which will encourage high rates of employee engagement.

- Outline the essential features of a grievance, disciplinary and redundancy procedure.

- Appreciate the role of human resources in effectively handling procedures.

- Analyse the concept of 'engagement' and explain how organisations can increase their employees' engagement levels.

vill not operate effectively unless it has a stable and relatively harmonious
ts employees. Conflict and disaffection will lead, almost inevitably, to high
or attendance, lack of involvement and other indicators of poor perfor-
a relatively new item of management data, a low level of employee

In this chapter, we will be looking at the employment relationship from a number of viewpoints: firstly, from a *workplace negotiating* viewpoint. Here, the relationship is determined by an agreement on terms and conditions reached through a formal process of negotiations by representatives of management and the workforce. Secondly, from an *involvement, participation and engagement* viewpoint. This examines how the relationship is affected by the effectiveness and influence of the 'employee voice'. Finally, from a *legal and procedural* viewpoint specifically related to grievance, discipline, dismissal and redundancy, where an examination will be made of the approaches to individual sources of conflict.

These three approaches are not mutually exclusive. A heavily unionised environment has as much opportunity to make considerable progress towards involving employees and working towards partnerships as does a small family-controlled company with a history of enlightened paternalism. Both workplace negotiating and involvement/engagement operate within a legal framework. Whatever system of bargaining is in place, even where none exists, the edicts of the law remain extremely influential in the nature of relationships.

WORKPLACE NEGOTIATING

Trade unions

In Chapter 1, we saw that the post-war development of the human resources function up until the early 1980s was centred around the role of negotiator and facilitator in a growing union environment. Trade union membership grew from around 6 million in the early post-war years to a peak of over 12 million in 1979. However, for the next 20 years, there was a consistent and precipitate decline to a figure of around 7.8 million in 1998, although that decline has been more gentle in recent years and stood at 7.3 million in 2010. At that date, only 27 per cent of the labour force were union members compared with 46 per cent in 1979. Union membership is heavily skewed towards the public sector, where 56 per cent of employees belong to unions, compared with only 14 per cent in the private sector, a figure which has declined during the recession.

The reduction in what is called *union penetration* was caused by the combination of 18 years of hostile Conservative Party legislation and major changes in the labour market away from manufacturing and public service (which are the main areas of union membership) to the service sector, which has generally smaller working units, more female and part-time employees. There has also been a growth in self-employment. These changes produced a more difficult environment in which to recruit members, despite what was, until the onset of the major recession in 2008, a generally buoyant economy accompanied by a rise in the numbers employed.

Because of this large fall in trade union membership and a consequent decline in the power of trade unions, a number of human resources commentators, especially many practitioners, regard a study of trade unions to be tantamount to a 'history lesson' and irrelevant to the study of critical human resource strategy and practice. However, trade unions still remain a considerable presence, looking after the work-based interests of more than a quarter of the workforce and with considerable power in a number of sectors, especially the railways. In 2011, for example, the RMT rail union won a four-year deal for Tube drivers which gave them 5 per cent in year one and inflation plus 0.5 per cent in the next three years at a time when the average UK pay increase was running at 2.3 per cent, with many public sector workers' wages being frozen for the second year.

In 2012 there were 154 trade unions in the UK, a fall of 50 in the last 10 years, mostly through mergers. Union membership is not spread evenly across the unions. The membership of the eight largest unions represented nearly 80 per cent of all union members (see Table 4.1). Unite and GMB represent, to a large extent, employees in the private sectors (principally manufacturing and logistics), while UNISON represents employees working in the public sector. These three unions and a further seven, with more than 100,000 members, dominate the Trade Union Congress (TUC), which acts as the collective voice of the trade union movement. The TUC is very much a political body that acts as a pressure group to influence government policy and legislation and to work towards improving public opinion of trade unions. There are also a number of smaller and specialist trade unions in areas such as the fire service and the railways and very small unions in employment areas that have substantially declined, such as the coal industry, or in unions restricted to one organisation (known as staff associations). Highly specialist unions include, for example, the Prison Governors Association and the National Association of Stable Lads.

Table 4.1 Union membership in 2012

	Members ('000s)
Unite	1,515
UNISON: the Public Service Union	1,374
GMB (the General, Municipal and Boilermakers Union)	602
Total of 5 other unions with 250,000-plus members	1,809
Total of all other 151 unions	1,955
Total of all unions	7,255

Source: Certification Officer Annual Report 2012.

The decline in union penetration has been accompanied by a large reduction in days lost through strikes. In 1979, at the height of union power, over 30 million days were lost through strikes. By the end of the 1980s, this figure had fallen dramatically and it has generally remained subdued since, with only 365,000 days lost in 2010, less than 2 per cent of the 1979 figure. The figure rose in 2011 due to a number of national days of protest by public sector unions, which raised the figure to 1.4 million.

Within the workplace, trade unions are represented by two groups of officials: shop stewards and full-time union officials. Shop stewards are elected by the members in that workplace to look after their interests. In most organisations, the shop stewards spend only part of their time on union business, carrying out their normal work for the rest of their time. In a handful of large organisations where union membership is high, however, an agreement may be reached with management that the chair of the shop stewards of one union may act in a full-time capacity, being provided with an office and even secretarial help. Full-time union officials are employed by the union to look after all the members in their locality. They come into the workplace rarely and only by invitation but their presence can be vital at crucial times during major negotiations or to head off disputes that are simmering.

The role of management

In the post-war years, national bargaining was an important feature of industrial relations where agreements reached between employers' organisations and trade unions set the pattern for subsequent deals made locally. Since the 1960s, there has been a strong move towards negotiations being decentralised to each individual unit or local groups of units (Carr 1999).

The main driving force behind this change is to place pay and conditions in its localised context, just as each unit has responsibility for other operating issues such as investment and marketing.

There are a number of *strategies* for management to consider in the field of the employment relationship:

■ *Should they adopt a unitary or pluralist approach?* A *unitary* approach emphasises that the organisation and its employees have a common goal and that all employees benefit from the successes the organisation can achieve. The outlook is that higher productivity produces increased profits, which allows increased pay and investment to yield more jobs, all of which is a virtuous circle. Therefore, there is a stress on harmonious relationships and team-working. Where conflict takes place, it is based on misunderstanding rather than differing interests and it is up to management to communicate and persuade more effectively. A *pluralist* approach, on the other hand recognises that:

> organisations contain a variety of sectional groups who legitimately seek to express divergent views. The resulting conflict is inevitable and the task of

managers is to establish a series of structures and procedures in which conflict is institutionalised and a negotiated order is established.

(Redman and Wilkinson 2001: 194)

Employees, for example, want increased pay and shorter hours but management will regard this as a way to erode profits. Supervisors will want their earnings to be higher than the employees they supervise but large amounts of overtime for these employees could erode this differential.

■ *Should unions be recognised?* There are two influences here. Firstly, the decision may reflect the positioning on the unitarist–pluralist spectrum. A pluralist approach will understand the genuine need for groups to have representation in the form of unions and will see them as a way to carry out disciplined bargaining over the inevitable conflicts. A unitary approach, however, will veer towards the view that unions may be irrelevant, that they interfere with the broad process of management, confuse the joint goals and produce exaggerated employee expectations that cannot be met. There are also a number of practical considerations that influence the decision, especially the wishes of the employees. Industrial or public organisations in large units find it difficult to fend off union penetration for ever.

The second influence is legislation. In 1999, the Employment Relations Act gave unions the right to apply to the Central Arbitration Committee (CAC) to organise recognition ballots when their membership has reached at least 10 per cent in the proposed bargaining unit. The CAC has a key role in guiding the two parties to reach an agreement within tight deadlines and, if this is not possible, taking decisions on the size and nature of the bargaining unit and whether a ballot should take place. If there is clear evidence that union membership is greater than 50 per cent, the employer must accept recognition. If it is less than 50 per cent, a ballot must take place and, if the result shows that the union is supported by a majority of those voting and at least 40 per cent of those in the bargaining unit, the CAC will declare the union recognised.

In the 10 years after the union recognition clauses in the 1999 Employment Relations Act came into effect, there were 742 applications for recognition, of which employers recognised the union in 104 cases, 421 were subsequently withdrawn and 196 went to ballot. In these ballots, 121 resulted in unions being recognised and employees voted against recognition in 75 cases. The number of recognition claims has reduced considerably in recent years with only 28 received in 2010–11 from which 10 ballots were held, 6 of which were successful. An example of a successful application was that of Unite union at King and Fowler, a small Liverpool metal finisher, where the ballot resulted in 26 employees voting in favour of recognition and 4 voting against (CAC 2011).

However, the legislation did have a further effect in that it encouraged many cases of recognition outside of the formal legislative process. From 1999 to 2002, there were 1,100 union recognition agreements, which brought 200,000 more union members into the negotiating process. Only about 20 per cent of such agreements went through the statutory route. Most were voluntary agreements influenced by the impending recognition legislation where employers wanted to be certain that the agreements reached were with a single union of their choosing. Those employers who tried to fight off recognition found this approach fraught with difficulty. This was mostly because the Central Arbitration Committee has tended to side with the union applicants on issues such as size of bargaining units (Younson 2002). However, the effects of the legislation can be viewed at best as marginal, mainly because the number of cases handled by CAC has been comparatively small, covering relatively low numbers of employees and these have been concentrated in sectors of the economy where unions have a presence (Wood *et al.* 2002).

For these reasons, the continuing apparent successful operation of the recognition procedures has not led, as we have seen, to a general increase in union membership. This is still 'treading water' and showing signs of suffering declines in the recession, while unions have had little success, with certain notable exceptions, in gaining members in sectors of the economy in which they have traditionally been weak, namely services, retailing and hospitality, where employment has grown substantially in recent years (Stevens 2003).

■ *What form of bargaining should take place?* Once unions have been recognised, there are a number of forms of bargaining that can take place. There is *sole recognition rights*, which is granted to one union to represent all the employees on the site. For example, most Japanese car companies have awarded the sole rights to negotiate on behalf of employees to a single union, which is common in Japan and Germany. This makes the negotiation process easy to organise and avoids the possibility of inter-union conflict but it also means that some employees who decide to join a different union will not be fully represented. An alternative is to have *single-table negotiations*, where unions sit on a joint committee and management will negotiate only with that committee. This encourages co-operation between the unions and presents a relatively single negotiating process but often needs facilitation and mediation to keep the differing union groups together.

Although constructed some years ago, Guest's (1995) analysis of four approaches that management can adopt shows resonance in the employee relations scene in the twenty-first century (see Table 4.2).

New realism – In this option, management attempts to take forward major transformational initiatives to improve productivity, quality or customer relations, but, at the same time, to forge a new relationship with the unions. This will help to bring them to the party and get them to be wholly committed to the initiatives, and to persuade their members to come along with them. In the 1990s, Guest found only a small number of examples, mostly connected to entrenched unions in industries where changes were vital for survival, such as in vehicle manufacture. Most of these have survived in the industrial setting, such as the car

Table 4.2 Guest model of approaches to industrial relations and HRM

Industrial relations	Human resource management	Description
High	High	New realism
High	Low	Traditional collectivism
Low	High	Individualised HRM
Low	Low	Black hole – no group relationships

Source: Guest, D. (1995) Human Resource Management, Trade Unions and Industrial Relations, in J. Storey (ed.) *Human Resource Management A Critical Text*. Routledge.

industry, but there are far fewer examples in smaller organisations and practically none in the service industry, big or small.

Traditional collectivism – Here, management accepts wholly the pluralist approach and does its best to live within this situation, helped by the recent more restrictive legislation. Guest found this approach prevailed within the public sector and in non-competitive or declining industries, such as steel and coal. Today, with the huge decline in traditional industries, these have more or less disappeared, with the one exception of the railways and London Underground.

An example of union organisation in the National Health Service, which retains some aspects of traditional collectivism, is shown in focus on research 4.1.

Individualised HRM – A more radical approach is taken here with a clearly unitary approach, where the policy may extend to derecognition and encouraging employees to accept individual contracts, whose terms will emphasise individual performance. Bargaining is abandoned but communication and involvement is supported and encouraged. Evidence is strong here in American-controlled organisations and a number of new start-ups. Research into the nature of such approaches, as demonstrated in the move to personalised contracts, is shown in focus on research 4.2.

Black hole – Guest found evidence in much of the quickly growing or changing service industries that industrial relations was not considered of any importance. Their competitive advantage was based on cost and flexibility and many employees (and much of the work) would be temporary or outsourced. In their strong unitary approach, unions were totally ignored. An example of the 'black hole' that employees can find themselves is demonstrated in focus on research 4.2.

Third parties

ACAS (Advisory, Conciliation and Arbitration Service) is an unusual body in that it is entirely funded by the government but acts as an independent agency with the sole purpose of promoting and improving industrial relations. If it is invited by both parties, it

FOCUS ON RESEARCH 4.1 LOCAL PAY BARGAINING IN THE NATIONAL HEALTH SERVICE

In the mid-1990s, the Conservative government began an initiative to decentralise pay bargaining in the NHS and allow varying terms and conditions of employment to be negotiated, which would aim to reflect the varying labour market conditions. This research investigated how this local bargaining was progressing in practice. It was based on questionnaires sent to over 100 NHS Trusts in two NHS Regions, which produced a 44 per cent response rate, together with a number of follow-up in-depth interviews.

The findings were that there was a continued commitment to pluralism and a rejection of the unitarist HRM approach. This conformed to Guest's 'Traditional Collectivism' approach. There was some change taking place but it was incremental and involved a shift towards greater consultation within a traditional industrial relations environment. Trusts recorded increases in the degree of bargaining (91 per cent) and of consultation (68 per cent) but many local representatives were hostile to any fundamental changes, having worked within the national pay framework for a long time. There was some evidence that they also had some problems in handling local bargaining, lacking experience in this area.

There were only modest attempts made to reduce the number of bargaining groups and a continuing trend towards a flexible single-table bargaining strategy. The trusts were making much more information available but within the traditional framework and there was no evidence of attempts to undermine the union's position by direct employee communication approaches. Most trusts (70 per cent) were aiming to move towards a simplified grading system and harmonisation of terms and conditions, but only a handful were considering going for personal contracts.

(Source: Carr 1999)

will attempt to solve a difficult situation through conciliation, mediation or arbitration, which are known collectively as 'alternative dispute resolution'. Although mostly widely known in the context of employment tribunal claims, they are also used to help solve collective issues.

Conciliation is where ACAS will keep the two sides talking and assist them to reach their own agreement. An example of how their intervention through the conciliation process can help solve problems is shown in case study 4.1.

In *mediation*, an official from ACAS (or from some other source) will listen to the arguments from both sides and then make recommendations as to how the difference may be resolved. The parties are free to accept or reject these recommendations. *Arbitration* is where both sides agree in advance to abide by the recommendations of the arbiter who will take a decision after hearing both sides. The subjects may include

FOCUS ON RESEARCH 4.2 VULNERABILITY OF EMPLOYEES UNDER PERSONAL CONTRACTS

The researchers interviewed 4,000 people who had been in work for the previous two years and identified examples of employees who had faced problems relating to their rights at work, discrimination and harassment. Although they did not find that the lack of union recognition was the main factor in adverse treatment taking place, it was one of the contributing factors.

Adverse treatment was found to be more commonly experienced, all other things being equal, by those without a written contract of employment, those without colleagues with whom they can discuss work-related problems, those working in organisations with a poor climate of employment relations and those who consider that their employer discriminates in favour of certain types of worker. Adverse treatment was also found to be more common among younger workers, among those with long-standing health problems and those with some/deep financial difficulties. On some indicators, adverse treatment was also more common among employees in industries where labour's share of value-added has been squeezed over the past decade. The absence of a threat of unionisation, and a lack of awareness of ACAS were also found to be important in some of the analyses, but not all.

(Source: Bewley and Forth 2010)

F O C U S   O N   R E S E A R C H

CASE STUDY 4.1 ACAS CONCILIATION

In the summer of 2010, ACAS was requested to conciliate in a dispute over pay at BAA, with three unions involved, Unite, PCS and Prospect. They had moved to the balloting stage in July, and Unite and Prospect had obtained sufficient support to call for industrial action, although PCS had not. Against a backdrop of possible strike action by Unite at the heart of the holiday season and intense media coverage, the parties met at ACAS on 16 August. Discussion continued long into the evening before agreement was reached. Under the deal struck, the company offered a 2 per cent increase, backdated to 1 January 2010, plus lump-sum payments linked to the earnings performance of each airport. The unions recommended that the offer was accepted and industrial action was called off the following day.

(Source: ACAS 2011)

C A S E   S T U D Y

pay increases, shift working or allowances. For some years, a development called 'pendulum arbitration' operated in organisations where the 'new realism' existed. Under this system, the arbiter is bound to accept the arguments in full of one side or the other and cannot decide on a compromise between the two sides. The intention behind this system (which is often associated with no-strike bargaining) is to encourage realistic negotiation from both sides who will be fearful of losing a decision where compromise is not possible. However, with the decline of union power and, to a certain extent, the loss of power and degree of risk that this system brings, it is rarely used today.

Role of the government

From the early days of the nineteenth century, government legislation has been in place, principally taking the side of the employer and making it difficult for unions to operate effectively. Determined action for their just cause over the years has currently produced a legal framework that gives unions immunity, in most circumstances, from damage they may cause by taking concerted action, as long as they follow certain procedures. They need to have ballots before action is implemented, action must only be in their place of work (secondary action is illegal), picketing is strictly limited and there can be no attempts to stop employers from using non-union suppliers. Other legislative controls include the outlawing of the closed shop (employees can join, or not join, any union of their choice) and the requirement for full-time officials to be re-elected periodically. Most of the legislation governing these controls over trade union activity was brought in by the Conservative government between 1979 and 1992, following a decade of disruptive industrial warfare, where days lost through strike action reached 30 million by 1979. The legislation could be judged to be very successful in that days lost have reduced to an average of around 500,000 per annum in recent years, a rate that is one of the lowest in Europe. Most of the disputes are in the public sector, especially in the transport and postal sectors (Lynch 2011).

The arrival of the Labour government in 1997 brought some change of direction with – alongside the recognition procedures already mentioned – the introduction of the National Minimum Wage in 1999, an initiative that has been in place in parts of Europe for two decades or more. (See Chapter 6 for details of the National Minimum Wage.)

Negotiating and bargaining

Negotiations are defined as: 'The coming together of two parties to confer with a view to making a jointly acceptable agreement' (Gennard and Judge 2002: 297).

Negotiating is not synonymous with bargaining. Negotiations can take place in grievances and discipline situations relating to single employees, but bargaining normally involves the exchanging of 'shopping lists' between the parties and trading in items in order to reach agreement. Formal bargaining normally takes place only once a year over the annual pay review but separate bargaining can occur over issues that arise during the year or over longer-term changes in working patterns or processes.

ACTIVITY 4.1

Consider what subjects could be included in the bargaining process.

Response to activity 4.1

You may have included in your list any of the following issues:

- Basic pay, including differentials between skilled and non-skilled employees
- Allowances for the exercise of skills or relating to special working situations, such as travelling or working under difficult or dangerous circumstances (confined space, heights, etc.)
- Bonus rates and the operation of the bonus scheme
- Sick pay and pension schemes
- Overtime rates and allocation
- Issues of equal treatment for pay, conditions, promotion and relationships
- Redundancy arrangements
- Performance management schemes
- Flexibility issues, including between jobs and locations
- Rights to maternity and paternity pay
- Improved benefits for holidays, paid time off, career breaks and other family-friendly areas.

Much of bargaining is associated with ritual, including the presentation of claims and counter-claims and much debate over historical circumstances, promises and half-promises. However, successful bargaining arises from a well-planned and executed management campaign where the union side is supported and encouraged to work within the agreed systems and procedures. Clear establishment of aims, carrying out extensive research into the market-place, competitors' rates and the external labour environment, welding a tightly controlled negotiating team, each with specific responsibilities and handling the informal contacts with the other side are all aspects considered important by experienced negotiators.

INVOLVEMENT AND PARTICIPATION

There are few who would dispute the fact that employees who are *involved* (in the broader sense of the word) in their work, in their department goals and in the organisation's long-term aims are more likely to be committed to that organisation and to working well and effectively. A further step is to say that the involvement is linked to the degree that the employee (singly or as part of a group) *participates* in the decision-making processes of the organisation. Research by Millward *et al.* (2000) found that employee perceptions of the extent to which they are provided with information by their managers and the degree to which the manager provides the chance to comment and respond are closely associated with levels of job satisfaction, organisational commitment and performance.

Involvement and participation can take many successful forms. Encouragement towards involvement and participation can take place *individually* through the introduction of certain techniques and mechanisms, such as attitude surveys, team briefings and employee recognition schemes, or through *collective* approaches, such as works councils or a more innovative initiative demonstrated in the recent growth of 'partnership deals'. The process of effective communication underpins both systems.

In April 2005, the Information and Consultation of Employees (ICE) Regulations came into effect, arising out of the EU Directive on the subject. This requires employers with more than 50 employees to inform and consult employee representatives about employment prospects and decisions likely to lead to substantial changes in work organisation or contractual relations. Too often, employees get to learn of such major changes affecting them through the press or television, and the aim is to avoid this situation and to improve employee consultation in general.

Individual approaches

Attitude surveys are increasingly used today to seek the views of employees. They can be annual events, such as those operated by British Telecom, where a questionnaire is sent to an employee's home and returned to an external body, such as MORI. Alternatively, they can be used to gauge the degree of employee support for ideas such as flexible benefits before the organisation commits itself. *Focus groups*, which are a representative sample of employees, can also be set up to provide a balanced opinion on new or existing issues. Carrying out a survey every year will indicate the trend in morale and employee satisfaction.

Whichever system is used, it is essential that a report on the findings is published to the employees with a considered action plan, where employees have indicated that action is necessary. An additional benefit of attitude surveys is that employees involved in these processes believe that the organisation has taken some effort to gauge employee views and this, in itself, can go some way to raising the general level of satisfaction. They provide the information as to the level of employee engagement (see later in the chapter). One difficulty that has been found is 'survey fatigue', where an organisation surveys employees each year and employees simply get tired of completing the surveys. A bigger problem comes about if insufficient action is taken to remedy the problems or complaints highlighted and employees will become disillusioned and cynical.

Employee recognition schemes. In the past, these were called 'suggestion schemes' and had a somewhat dowdy image with little real support or enthusiasm from employees. The success of major Japanese manufacturing companies in world markets in the 1970s and 1980s, however, forced their competitors to examine carefully their system of 'Kaizen', especially in the light of a report in the early 1990s that Japanese employees produced 100 times as many suggestions as their American counterparts. 'Kaizen', and the various Western alternatives such as quality circles and QED, place obligations on each employee to get involved in their local area at work and to come up with proposals for improvement. Employees are trained in how to analyse and solve problems and how to present them to management. When proposals are accepted and implemented (and the small, incremental proposals are as welcome as the grand design), employees receive a proportion of the cost savings. In Vauxhall Motors' scheme, for example, a number of proposals have led to employees receiving in excess of £3,000 (Stredwick 2008).

Recognition schemes need to be constantly reinvented as their shelf life is generally very short – two to four years at most. Although they can provide interest and a degree of excitement, this quickly pales if the same employees are recognised or the rewards are not seen as sufficient or appropriate.

Briefing groups (sometimes called team briefing) are a form of communication that attempts to provide information in a systematic and timely way to all employees, so that they have the opportunity to remain involved with the progress of the organisation. Information is cascaded through the levels of the structure over a short period (half a day if possible) from a prepared script but with opportunities provided for questions to be asked and replies given. With briefing size groups of 6 to 20 (average of 12), a unit of 1,248 could, in theory, cascade the information very quickly as shown in Figure 4.1. The main difficulty faced with this initiative is the time needed to prepare and carry out the briefing. If there is insufficient news to impart, the process is seen as repetitive and meaningless. As briefings should be two-way, with questions and requests passed up the line, it is vital that answers are given to employees' questions.

Financial involvement. A number of companies encourage their employees to identify with the organisation's success through share savings and option schemes by providing shares at discounted prices and through profit-sharing and profit-related pay schemes. This policy stems from the unitarist approach, presented in a positive-sum terms, in which both employees and the enterprise seek to enhance company wealth from which both parties benefit (Hyman 2000). Around 1,500 such schemes were operating, involving 1.3 million employees, in 2010. By their nature, they can only operate in the private sector, although attempts have been made to create 'notional' shares as a means of delivering bonuses to more senior staff in some public sector enterprises.

Success in practice has been mixed. A detailed study of Irish company Eircom (see focus on research 4.3) has shown that such a scheme can be seen as a good investment by employees but fails to improve the involvement of employees. The schemes tend to be

Figure 4.1
Briefing group
operation

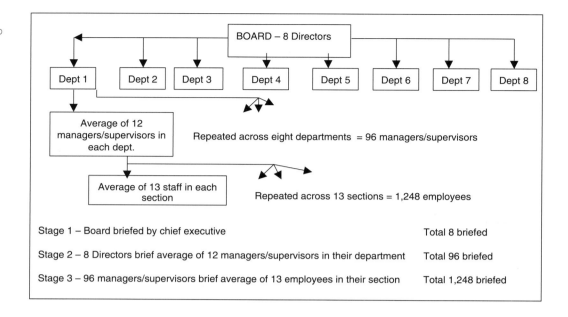

Stage 1 – Board briefed by chief executive   Total 8 briefed

Stage 2 – 8 Directors brief average of 12 managers/supervisors in their department   Total 96 briefed

Stage 3 – 96 managers/supervisors brief average of 13 employees in their section   Total 1,248 briefed

highly regarded when share prices are rising but fall into disrepute at times when the stock market drops, such as the period between 1999 and 2003 and from 2007 to 2011. In fact, some senior commentators question the wisdom of such schemes: 'Should we really be encouraging lower-paid employees to have a large amount of their investments in shares, because the equities market is so volatile' (Vicky Wright, partner in Ernst and Young, quoted in Smethurst 2003: 33).

Certainly the share-owning employees of Marconi, Telewest and Premier Foods, who saw their shares become worthless in the early 2000s, agree with these sentiments.

A more long-term sustainable system operates at the John Lewis Partnership, which is wholly owned by the employees, its partners, and where the financial outcomes are not controlled by the variations in the stock market. They operate the most innovative of financial participation schemes with substantial annual bonuses being paid to all partners, dependent upon the level of profits, linked closely to other types of employee participation (Stredwick 2008).

A relatively new arrival on the financial participation scene is called *prediction market democracy*, which, in effect, runs an internal market for employees to trade in. About 60 of the largest and most technically advanced companies ran such schemes in 2012 (Thompson 2012).

An example of how it works is that an aircraft manufacturer who wants to know whether a new plane will be delivered on time can set up a market for employees and contractors to invest in the question: 'Will the test flight take place on 15 October?' There will be a price for the correct answer (the answer will only be known in October) and the current price will

FOCUS ON RESEARCH 4.3 EMPLOYEE SHARE-OWNERSHIP AT EIRCOM

In this article, the authors outline the complex history of Eircom, Ireland's former national communications company, taking us through its rapid commercialisation in the 1980s; part then full privatisation from 1996 to 1999; the rise, fall and subsequent rise in its debt; re-flotation and further, highly leveraged buyouts; and the headcount reduction in the workforce. Alongside this, the authors track the rise of the ESOP, which started in 1998 with 14.9 per cent of shareholding and rose to 35 per cent by influencing and benefiting from the various buyouts.

This is a substantial example of employee ownership. For individuals with a full share allocation, the ESOP has paid out over €80,000 from 2002 to 2010. Yet its impact on employee productivity is mixed.

In their analysis, the authors first consider the rise in Eircom's productivity from eight years before to eight years after the ESOP was introduced. They conclude that there are too many potentially intervening factors to attribute this rise directly to the ESOP.

They then look at the survey data for evidence that the ESOP achieved its official aim 'to incentivise and motivate employees through giving them a shareholding in their company leading to improved productivity'. On the basis that the clear majority of employees feel that their influence has actually decreased since the ESOP was introduced, they reject this hypothesis.

However, it is clear from the history that the ESOP was successful in another objective of the scheme, namely as a bargaining chip to 'reduce opposition to privatisation and firm restructuring'.

The authors argue that, in practice, the drive among employees to make a profit has taken priority in Eircom's ESOP. In short, the evidence suggests that employees have viewed the scheme mainly as an investment. Crucially, it has not run alongside a general increase in employee involvement in decision-making and, because of this, it has failed to bring about the motivation–commitment–productivity impact that it promised.

(Source: McCarthy and Palcic 2012)

indicate its likelihood to be yes. If the price for 'yes' is £10, the opinion among investors (employees) is likely to be a resounding 'no' if the stock is trading at £2 because it means investors believe there is only a 20 per cent chance of success. If this is the case, management have clearly got a problem they need to address. If the price is £8, they can be a little more confident. The delay in the delivery of the Boeing 787 Dreamliner was predicted in this way, before the CEO was told of it.

Alternate schemes allow employees to invest in a number of technical innovations currently under review for the company's internal development funding, including the likely sales and profit figures in a certain period. These predictions will be priced like a futures market and, if other employees agree with the predictions, the price of the investment will rise.

The main advantage of such schemes, apart from the interest they stimulate around employees and contractors, is that they also aid management decision-making in terms of allocating resources. There is an argument that employees know far more about the reality of the organisation than the board room or outside investors. If a technical innovation has little or no employee support, as measured by the price of the innovation's 'stock', it may have its resources reduced or it may be cancelled altogether.

There are disadvantages, however. It may be regarded as a trivial pursuit by employees who will waste their time by idle 'betting' or wild trading. It could be seen as giving too much power to employees, many of whom will have little contact with the product or innovation in a large organisation.

Collective approaches

COMPANY COUNCILS AND COMMITTEES

An encouragement for employees to participate in decision-making processes through their representatives was the European Works Council Directive, which was issued by the European Union in 1994 and which became law in the UK in December 1999, covering around 300 organisations in practice. Organisations with more than 1,000 employees in any one EU member state or more than 150 employees in each of two or more states are obliged to set up a pan-European works council, which will include employee representatives.

The EU Directive on Information and Consultation of Employees came into force in 2005 as the Information and Consultation of Employees (ICE) Regulations, which has covered all establishments with more than 59 employees from 2008. Management must provide information and be consulted on the organisation's progress and prospects in a number of laid-down areas including employment, economic and financial performance. A request from 10 per cent of the workforce triggers the obligation for management to set up some formal mechanism for the provision of information and consultation.

PARTNERSHIP AGREEMENTS

Partnership agreements can be seen as representing the progressive thinking on collective relationships. In return for formal recognition and bargaining rights, together with elements of job security, unions agree to a commitment to work together to make the business more successful and to encourage their members to take a full part in the involvement processes. The attraction to the unions is that it is one of the few viable paths to a position where they might be valued by employers, while retaining an independent workers' voice (Guest 2001). Joint initiatives on quality and productivity improvements, staff skills developments, flexibility, all supported by an effective communication and representation process, are important aspects of a successful partnership deal. They can also be part of the process of saving the company from bankruptcy. There was evidence a number of years ago that employers are taking a less overall hostile view of unions and moving towards agreements of this type. Bacon and Samuel (2007) found that, of the 248 signed partnerships between 1990 and 2007, 81 per cent had, in fact, survived. Their findings suggest that partnership agreements are a lot more durable then had been previously predicted.

An example of a partnership agreement at Legal & General is shown in case study 4.2. Not all partnership agreements work out successfully. A celebrated case was that of Bausch & Lomb in Waterford, Ireland, which began a partnership agreement in 1996 (Teague and Hann 2010). Although the early years of this partnership were relatively stable, increasing difficulties arose over the issue of separating the partnership agreement from the structure of collective bargaining. Neither management nor trade unions felt able to give up their 'normal' negotiating roles in the plant and so the boundaries between the two became blurred, leading to confusion and suspicion. For example, a company initiative on internal conflict procedure in the partnership forum was rejected by the unions as they believed it was an issue for collective bargaining. One union left the partnership over a disputed gain-sharing scheme and the other left after a succession of disputes where a third party was needed before settlement was reached. The hoped-for devolving of power to the partnership council rarely took place.

In an earlier case, Centrica's retail division entered into an agreement with UNISON to share information, involve the union and 'maximise employment security'. The aim was to help to stem the large losses in that division and staff co-operated even to the extent of accepting pay cuts. However, just four months later, the decision was taken to close all of the former gas retail showrooms with the loss of 1,500 jobs (Overell 1999). There is also the risk that partnership becomes a device for management to incorporate unions, a new form of flexibility deal where 'responsible' trade unionism means that unions can never endorse industrial action.

The differing perspectives of employers and employees towards partnership agreements, shown in Table 4.3, have been a major factor in their decline in recent years.

CASE STUDY 4.2 PARTNERSHIP AGREEMENT AT LEGAL & GENERAL

Legal & General and Unite celebrated ten years of a partnership agreement in 2008. It has worked for both sides. According to their chief executive, Tim Breedon, 'It has become second nature, enabling Legal & General to embrace change in a fast-moving marketplace.' From the trade union perspective, Andy Case, national secretary, finance sector, at Unite, was initially sceptical, accustomed to seeing spin rather than substance in alleged partnership deals. Despite the inevitable difficulties that would come with any partnership, he says that there is a commitment from both parties to work at it through 'dialogue and an understanding that we can still work together even though our interests are sometimes different'. Case reported that partnership delivers access to management and an 'ability to shape discussions', as well as providing fertile ground for recruiting members. Both parties see advantages. According to Case, management hears the 'unvarnished' views of staff, while Sir Rob Margetts, Legal & General's chairman, sees that 'both sides benefit' because, as he said at last year's AGM, 'staff interests are properly represented in our business decisions'.

At the core of the Legal & General partnership agreement is a commitment to joint working in a spirit of confidence and trust that facilitates flexibility, growth and change. Each side seeks to recognise the other's unique interests and roles, alongside ones that they share. This leaves intact both managerial prerogative and union rights to collectively and individually represent members. The overarching commitment is to avoid conflict that might damage the business.

The company holds regular meetings at senior level with Unite that cover business strategy, company results, HR policy and practice. There are also separate monthly meetings on equality/diversity and remuneration; frequent ones on health and safety; a biannual discussion on CSR; plus an annual joint equal pay review. Managers are also encouraged to meet relevant representatives to discuss any local issues. Regular joint training on partnership working is available for managers, trade union representatives and HR.

In reviewing research to mark the tenth anniversary of the Legal & General agreement, there is a sense that the mixed picture of evidence results from the ill-defined nature of partnership. Mutual trust and gains, rather than the presence or absence of a written agreement, seems to be the key predictor of collaborative working between managers, employees and their representatives. This is not to say that partnership agreements are unhelpful but that they exist within, and gain strength from, a wider employment relations context. The nature of the relationship between managers and unions that underpins partnership working surely tells us more than the piece of partnership paper.

The endurance of the Legal & General agreement – long after partnership in Britain stopped being an attention-grabbing panacea – is testament to the ability of some partnerships to survive through the inevitable challenges.

(Source: Reilly and Denvira 2008)

Table 4.3 Perspectives on partnership agreements

From a management perspective	From a union perspective
Concerns over partnership agreements are due to:	Concerns over partnership agreements are due to:
Concerns of slowing down the decision-making process and having to make pragmatic decisions rather than through desire	Partnerships being regarded as 'Trojan Horses' and in reality having limited influence in management decision-making
The belief in a partnership agreement incurring extra costs	Being seen to be too involved with managers and potentially being involved in unpopular decisions
Concerns about having union influence in the strategic decision-making of large, diverse organisations	A concern that, ultimately, the balance of gain is in favour of employers than employees
The decreased attractiveness of declining union strength and effectiveness	
Promotes trade unionism by the back door: unions are perhaps only interested because of current weakness	
Forces disclosure of more information. Hindrance to swift managerial decision-taking	

Source: Adapted from Pass, S. (2008) *Working in Partnership*. Department of Health.

EMPLOYEE ENGAGEMENT

As detailed in Chapter 1, there has been considerable emphasis in recent years on improving the level of employee engagement in organisations. To a large extent, this is attempted by using various combinations of the initiatives detailed above, such as partnerships and recognition schemes. The main objective of using such initiatives is to increase the degree to which employees 'buy into' the company culture, strategy and values. Few people would disagree that engaged employees are far more likely to be productive and to employ the correct competencies to help achieve organisational success. The clearest example we have all faced is when we, as a customer, have faced employees who could not care much about our needs or expectations and provide us with appalling service. They are therefore not engaged in their jobs.

There is evidence in practice of the link between engagement and performance. Ernst & Young found that there was a very strong correlation between local engagement levels and the brand favourability index, the scores given to the organisation by clients (Smedley 2012).

The subject was considered so important by the UK government that a substantial report on the subject was commissioned in 2009 (Macleod Report). This confirmed the association of engagement with performance and the fact that:

Engagement, going to the heart of the workplace relationship between employer and employee, can be a key to unlocking productivity and transforming the working lives of many people for whom Monday morning is an especially low part of the week.

(Macleod and Clarke 2009: 2)

Measuring engagement

Earlier in the chapter, it was explained that attitude surveys are a way of helping to involve employees in the organisation and they can provide the data to analyse the level of engagement. The nature of the questions asked can be varied but will usually cover the following subject areas:

- Understanding of organisational purpose
- Commitment to key competencies, such as customer satisfaction, quality improvement, etc.
- Satisfaction in the job they carry out
- Satisfaction with the rewards
- Plans on staying or leaving the organisation
- Willingness to go the extra mile
- Willingness to put forward new ideas and to accept changes in their job and the organisation
- Proud to work for the organisation
- Agreeing to promote their organisation to their friends and recommend people to work for the organisation
- Views on 'fairness' within the organisation
- Degree of trust in senior management and their own manager
- Belief that the organisation is a 'happy' or 'fun' place to work
- Belief that the organisation cares about its employees
- Belief that the organisation is serious about equal opportunities and diversity.

For some organisations, these surveys are complex and detailed because management believe the results to be critical to the success of the organisation. Nationwide Building Society, for example, describe the survey as 'their genome project, mapping the DNA of the organisation'. Two data modellers, the 'insight team', are dedicated to the outcomes, searching for correlations. Their research has found that, if employees are 2 per cent more satisfied, that translates into customers being more satisfied and buying more – and vice versa with dissatisfied employees. Nationwide customers like staff with longevity so it is important for the organisation to find out what it is that makes staff stay and why they leave. One of the key outcomes of the surveys is that staff that strongly share the values are more likely to stay (Syedain 2009). In Marks and Spencer, survey results show that stores with high engagement scores have high mystery shopper and sales against target scores and lower absence (Arkin 2011).

FOCUS ON RESEARCH 4.4 MANAGERS AND ENGAGEMENT

The Institute for Employment Studies has studied aspects of engagement for some years and their 2009 report examined how managers who inspire and engage their teams to perform well behave in their dealings with staff. Twenty-five managers, found to rate highly on engagement, were chosen from seven organisations and these managers were interviewed, together with their teams. They had varied responsibilities from 4 to 5,000 staff.

The research discovered that engaging managers had many characteristics in common, but personality was not one of them. Some were energetic extroverts, others were quiet, even shy – some were intensely practical, while others were creative and innovative, or liked intellectual challenge. Most had been with their organisations for some time, but others were more recent recruits. Their behaviour towards their teams, however, was very consistent. The interest they took in people as individuals, and in developing and nurturing their teams, did not prevent them from tackling difficult issues like breaking bad news and managing poor performance. The consensus was that honesty and openness was important, along with empathy and a demonstration that the manager had an understanding of their possible impact on staff.

Something else they shared was a focus on performance and an expectation that their teams would deliver to a high standard. The recession was biting when we carried out our research, and some of the private sector companies we visited were suffering, but our engaging managers recognised the need to maintain their engaging behaviours in bad times as well as good. The general feeling among engaged teams was that they were happy and enjoyed their work and there was a good atmosphere, compared to other teams.

(Source: Robinson and Hayday 2009)

Most research into retaining staff demonstrates that the employee's relationship with their immediate manager is one of the most important predictors of their length of service. The features of 'engaging' managers has been set out by the Institute for Employment Studies (IES), summarised in focus on research 4.4, while an example of an organisation carrying out initiatives to improve engagement is shown in case study 4.3.

Enhancing engagement – actions by human resource practitioners

As explained in Chapter 1, engagement is so fundamental to the employment relationship that most 'best practice' employment processes have an effect upon employee opinions. So, essential features, such as providing an attractive employment contract in terms of pay and conditions, ensuring the psychological contract is working well, ensuring employees

CASE STUDY 4.3 IMPROVING EMPLOYEE ENGAGEMENT AT NEWCOUNTY AUTHORITY

Shortly after the appointment of a new chief executive at NewCounty Authority, the results of the annual staff survey were published, which showed a third year in succession of reduced staff satisfaction. The areas which recorded the *lowest* scores were:

- The workload for the department is managed efficiently and fairly by my manager.
- Communication with staff by senior management is regular, efficient and honest.
- Changes take place smoothly with full consultation.
- The performance management system works well and acts as a strong motivator.
- Staff development plans are produced in co-operation with each member of staff and monitored regularly.
- I would recommend working for the Authority to my friends.

These findings were discussed with staff representatives and management and agreement was reached that the problem was of such magnitude that it was justified to bring in a consultancy, GLN partners, which specialised in improving employee relations to improve the situation.

The agreed aim

The overall aim was to improve the level of employee engagement. This meant developing individual and team capability, improving consistency in management approach and behaviours, and encouraging staff at all levels of the business to take personal responsibility for meeting and exceeding targets.

Investigations

GLN partners began their programme with a set of organisation-wide focus groups to gain more depth on employee attitudes. Among the key findings were the following:

- Staff did not like the way changes were carried out. In fact, they were reluctant to make any changes.
- They were not impressed with the way that many decisions were sprung on staff – and that many of the decisions were reversed later.
- The budgeting process was considered to be not transparent – it seemed geared only to cost-cutting.
- Insufficient attention was given to customer service issues.

It was clear to the consultancy team that management approaches and their overall competence was lacking. A great deal of action was required to equip the management so that they could bring about a strategic behavioural, cultural and systems change.

Actions taken by consultants

Branding

Although mission statements and sets of values already existed in the Authority, they had been largely forgotten. GLN worked together with senior management to create a rebranded organisation dedicated to improved service to the community and efficient operations.

Training

GLN designed and implemented a series of training courses for management and staff including:

1   Equipping managers with the skills to coach and develop their people to improve their levels of motivation. These included specific units to build trust with their staff.
2   A training unit on planning, forecasting and decision-making, specifically geared towards departmental workloads.
3   Providing managers with a practical coaching process on performance management and a number of tools such as 'Difficult conversations' to enable them to identify, evidence, discuss and resolve performance issues. Management/staff workshops that included reverse role-play in performance management processes and grievance/discipline.
4   Joint sessions with management and staff on how to deal with change.
5   Improving communication skills, both written and oral backed up by a revamped intranet system.

Outcomes

By the end of the second year of operation, the following data were collected by an independent review which included staff survey returns:

■   All staff had development plans and met for formal one-to-ones on a three-monthly basis. All staff reported that they speak with their managers about business issues every day.
■   The senior management team was far more visible and staff felt a higher degree of involvement.
■   Staff felt that performance was managed consistently and that poor performance is effectively tackled.
■   There was an improvement in the data for staff recommending working for the Authority and there was a lower absence rate.
■   An average increase in performance of 20 per cent both for team and individual performance.
■   Managers increasing interaction with their staff by 63 per cent.

■ Staff and management reported increased confidence and ability to have difficult conversations at all levels.

■ A satisfactory level of financial savings had been achieved, matching the budgeted amount without recourse to redundancies or service cuts.

Although these outcomes reflected a general improvement in engagement ratings, there were still areas which had shown little or no improvement:

■ The planning and operation of major changes was heavily criticised by staff with ratings showing no improvement.

■ Staff still complained of major decisions being taken without sufficient consultation and a number being reversed at a later date.

■ Criticisms emerged of the reward system, which was regarded as being hierarchical and inflexible, being separated from the improved performance management system.

■ The branding exercise was generally regarded as having only a minor impact by staff.

■ The level of customer satisfaction with Authority services had not reached the targeted improvement levels. Feedback had indicated improved satisfaction with Authority staff contacts but not a great deal of improvement with outcomes.

have a development plan and providing a safe and fair environment are all likely to contribute to a high engagement rating. Further specific actions can include:

■ Communicate to senior management the crucial nature of engagement

■ Get agreement on regular surveying of the engagement levels and identify where they are succeeding and where they are failing

■ Set up training for all management to understand the key features of engagement and to identify ways they can improve their own engagement ratings, which often means moving from command and control methods to the softer 'facilitate and empower' mode

■ Ensure that employees get feedback on engagement data, together with a sufficient level of autonomy in their work.

There still remains considerable scepticism regarding the emphasis on achieving a high level of engagement. Some still regard it as a self-serving, corporate activity – something the organisation, its leaders and its hierarchies are doing to get more out of staff. Other practitioners, who see fairness and trust as cornerstones of any decent workplace, see it as an end in itself with boundless positive prospects on offer to staff (Holbeche and Matthews 2012).

DEALING WITH INDIVIDUAL SOURCES OF CONFLICT – GRIEVANCE, DISCIPLINE AND DISMISSAL

Just as a procedure for conflict resolution between management and the workforce is essential, every organisation also needs to have a system in place to deal with areas of disagreement that arise between the individual and the organisation. Where the individual is aggrieved due to an action, or a lack of action, by management, this can lead to a formal *grievance* process. Where the organisation is dissatisfied with the actions, or lack of action, of an employee, this can lead to a formal *disciplinary* process and, ultimately, if serious enough, to *dismissal* taking place.

Most minor grievances and disciplinary matters can be dealt with in the day-to-day informal contact between employees and management. A small request here, a word of advice there, an informal discussion on the shop floor or in the office can solve 90 per cent of problems from both sides. However, to find a solution to the 10 per cent that cannot be settled in this way needs a formal procedure that provides an agreed system and approach within which both sides can work towards a solution. There are specific skills that relate to successfully running a grievance or disciplinary session and there is strong evidence that insufficient training for managers and supervisors takes place in this area.

In 2002, an attempt was made to regulate grievance and disciplinary procedures through statute. It was hoped that this would reduce the number of employment tribunals. In fact, they rose steeply and employers objected to the additional bureaucracy. It was soon recognised, however, that the attempt had failed and, following the Gibbons (2007) report, the regulations were repealed and were replaced with some changes to the ACAS code of conduct, which we will consider later in this chapter.

Grievances

There are numerous incidents or situations that can lead to an employee holding a grievance. They can be extremely serious, such as a sexual assault or a severe safety hazard, or they may be less serious in totality but of serious concern to the employee, such as a new shift rota, a failure to be considered for promotion, a critical appraisal report, a lack of opportunity for overtime or too much pressure of work.

A grievance is like an infection. Unless it is dealt with quickly and efficiently, it will fester and may spread quickly causing unnecessary pain and suffering (lower productivity, reduced co-operation and commitment). A procedure, then, will aim to ensure that the employee's case is heard quickly, that the employee concerned has a fair hearing with the opportunity for full discussion to take place and that a response from management will follow without too long a gap. The procedure should make clear to whom the grievance should be addressed, who should accompany the employee if they require somebody to help them in the process, and specific time limits for the meeting to be held and the decision given, plus the stages of any appeal. It is always wise for a clear record to be made of the grievance and the outcome.

Discipline

An inevitable consequence of employing people is that there must be a set of rules laid down that, to a large extent, regulates their behaviour. The original meaning of discipline was associated with learning and study – to be a disciple – but now its associations are closer to punishment and penalties. It may be regarded as the exercise of management's legitimate prerogative of control. This is unfortunate in many ways because the concept of self-discipline and working within a mutually agreed code of behaviour are essential features of an effective workplace today. Indeed, it could be regarded as a failure on management's part whenever a disciplinary session takes place. Perhaps it is a failure in selection, or to explain the rules at induction or a failure in sufficiently understanding or influencing the behaviour of the employee in their performance in the workplace. A better approach is to regard any issue of friction that may lead to discipline as that of a problem to be solved and that punishment is only one solution that should only be used as a last resort.

Up until 1972, employers had almost unlimited powers to discipline and dismiss employees as long as the required notice was given. Since the introduction of the legal concept of unfair dismissal in that year, constraints have been imposed and clear guidelines set down. If they are not followed at any time during the disciplinary procedure, the dismissed employee has the opportunity to make a claim at an industrial tribunal. If successful, the sanction against the employer is to have to pay compensation or, occasionally, to be forced to re-employ the employee.

A discussion of discipline has three parts. Firstly, the *common rules* in place, which, if broken in some way, lead to disciplinary action. Secondly, the *disciplinary procedure* and external guidance that is given on how it should be formulated. Thirdly, issues that arise as to *operating the procedure* in practice.

RULES

In the museum in Sunderland, there are old photographs of shipyards in the late nineteenth century with workers gathered under lists of rules written large onto the shipyard walls. They make interesting reading including the various financial penalties for, among other heinous crimes, spitting, lateness and losing employer's tools. Lateness is still an offence, of course, but rules in most organisations are now published in an 'employee handbook' or similar and financial penalties are far more subtle.

Rules can be categorised under a number of headings:

- *Safety rules*. These are a vital part of the employer's duty of care to protect employees. They cover the operation of plant and equipment, wearing of safety gear and limiting access to areas of work, tools and machinery unless trained or qualified.
- *Performance rules*. These relate to many aspects of an individual's performance including attendance, timekeeping, flexibility on hours, working practices and location,

levels of performance, willingness to work overtime, the requirement to take part in bonus schemes or raise suggestions for improvements.

- *Behaviour rules*. Included here are rules that concern the relationship with customers and fellow employees, from the need to be courteous and responsive to customers, to wear certain regulation uniform and to take part in team processes.

- *Rules evolved through custom and practice*. Not all rules are written down. Rulebooks would be far too long if they had to include every conceivable situation so common sense assumes that, for example, certain violent behaviour would be not allowed. Nor do written rules apply if they are not implemented by management. For example, the rules may clearly indicate that employees may not take out of the premises any materials belonging to the organisation. In practice, employees may have been taking small quantities of certain low-grade materials for their own use with the knowledge of management so the original rule is regarded, at law, as being amended to take this custom into account.

DISCIPLINARY PROCEDURE

A starting point here is the long-standing ACAS Code of Practice (latest edition 2009). A summary of the main points are set out in Figure 4.2, which also contains some additional explanatory comments.

OPERATING THE DISCIPLINARY PROCEDURE

The objectives of the procedure are three-fold. Firstly, it is to point out to the employee the error of their ways. It is important to clearly establish that a gap exists between the level of performance or behaviour required from the employee and that which has been observed and to obtain the employee's acceptance of that gap. So, if the employee is accused of poor attendance, their record has to be matched against standards that have been laid down and the records of their colleagues. The same applies with performance levels where any accusation needs to be backed up with a clear record of how the performance is below that required. The employee will have the right to question the facts put before them and, if they produce evidence that throws doubt on the original facts, further investigations need to take place. The employee should be encouraged to explain the reasons for their failings. Some may be acceptable, such as severe family illness leading to temporary poor attendance, and will indicate areas where help can be provided.

Next, the objective is to set the employee on the path of improvement. Changes in behaviour, particularly if the behaviour in question has become habitual, often requires more effort than a quiet word. Persuading the problem person invariably involves getting them to accept the need for change. Increased awareness and intellectual acceptance, while useful, are rarely enough. This is because behaviours have been acquired through practice,

Figure 4.2
Essential
features of a
disciplinary
procedure

Source: Adapted
from Guest, D.
(1995) Human
Resource
Management, Trade
Unions and
Industrial Relations,
in J. Storey (ed.)
*Human Resource
Management. A
Critical Text.*
Routledge.

Disciplinary procedures should:

1. *Be in writing.* This is to aid communication of the procedure and to ensure that it is applied consistently.

2. *Specify to whom they apply.*

3. *Indicate the disciplinary actions that may be taken.* These include warnings, dismissal and any other sanction.

4. *Specify the levels of management which have the authority to take the various forms of disciplinary action, ensuring that immediate superiors do not normally have the power to dismiss without reference to senior management.* In a small organisation which has few levels of management, this is difficult to implement in practice.

5. *Provide for individuals to be informed of the complaints against them and to be given the opportunity to state their case before decisions are reached.* This is a key aspect of natural justice. Difficulties arise over the whether the accused employee should have the right to question witnesses, as in a court of law. Internal procedures are not courts of law, there are no independent judges or juries, and witnesses may not be prepared to come forward if they have to face a form of cross-examination. Organisations take differing practical viewpoints in this area.

6. *Give individuals the right to be accompanied by a trade union representative, an official employed by the union or a fellow employee of their choice.*

7. *Ensure that, except for cases of gross misconduct, no employees are dismissed for a first breach of discipline.* Gross misconduct is explained under the section on Dismissals.

8. *Ensure that disciplinary action is not taken until the case has been carefully investigated.* The investigation should take place without delay but should not be rushed. Where possible, the person carrying out the investigation should not be the person in charge of the disciplinary hearing. This is another important aspect of natural justice and one that tribunals take very seriously. In the case of a serious offence, the employee may be suspended with pay while the investigation takes place but the period of suspension should be as brief as possible.

9. *Ensure that individuals are given an explanation for any penalty imposed.* Which clearly tells them what they have done wrong and how long any penalty, such as a warning, will apply for.

10. *Provide for the right of appeal and specify the procedure to be followed.* The appeal will need to be made to a person in higher authority who has not been involved in the earlier decision.

sometimes over many years, and further practice is required to unlearn a problem behaviour and replace it with something better.

A positive approach can involve an action plan with the employee working with their supervisor or manager to improve performance, timekeeping or any other weakness. As with any other action plan, it will need its own objectives which are time based. Solutions that arise from the employee themselves are more likely to be successful. Help from the organisation may be needed. Where performance has deteriorated, training or guided experience can be expedited; problems with caring for an aged relative can be helped through

Table 4.4 Misdemeanours and gross misconduct

Misdemeanours	Timekeeping not up to required standard
	Attendance not up to required standard
	Performance not up to required standard
	Inappropriate attitude to management, fellow employees, customers or suppliers
Gross misconduct examples	Fighting
	Working under the influence of drink or drugs
	Providing confidential information to competitors
	Theft
	Fraud, such as claiming false expenses
	Sexual harassment
	Causing a severe safety hazard, such as smoking where prohibited
	Refusing to obey a reasonable instruction

temporary changes in the hours worked; difficulties with relationships can be rectified by providing help through counselling. Where it is clear that the required standards cannot be met, there should be consideration of alternative work, although this should be set against the cost of retraining, and the likelihood of the employee being successful in the new role. An employee's length of service and general attitude can influence such a decision.

The final objective is to come to a decision on a fair sanction for the offence committed. Table 4.4 clarifies the difference between a misdemeanour and gross misconduct.

In the case of proven gross misconduct, the employee has clearly indicated that they have gone beyond the bounds of the contract and the employer has the right to instantly dismiss the employee. With misdemeanours, which are lesser offences, there is no right of dismissal for a first offence, so warnings are the appropriate penalty.

That is not to say that a warning is necessary in every case. In many cases, informal reprimands may be more appropriate. This very much depends on the nature and severity of the offence, the reasons given by the employee and their willingness to remedy the situation. Agreement about the offence, an action plan and an enthusiastic willingness to improve the situation should lead to no more than a mild rebuke and an agreement to review the situation over the next few weeks and months.

Procedures have a number of stages. An example of a typical grievance and disciplinary procedural stages is set out in Table 4.5.

Dismissal

We have already discussed some of the legal aspects of the process that leads to dismissal. In order to defend a case at a tribunal, the employer not only needs to have a good reason for dismissing the employee but also must show that they followed the correct procedure in

Table 4.5 Grievance and disciplinary procedure stages

	Grievance procedure	Disciplinary procedure
Stage 1	The employee raises grievance informally with their immediate supervisor.	The manager raises the issue informally with the employee. The issue is settled with a mild rebuke or advice or a verbal warning, the latter being recorded.
Stage 2	If the employee is not satisfied, a meeting is convened between the employee and manager with the supervisor present.	If the issue is more serious, such as persistent absenteeism, or if the less serious issue continues to arise, a meeting is convened with the employee and their representative/ colleague. The manager will normally have another member of management present, such as a human resources officer. If proven, the outcome can be a first written warning, which is recorded.
Stage 3	If the employee is still not satisfied, they can take the grievance to the level of a director who, with the manager present, will listen to the issue and take the final decision within seven working days.	If the issue is still one of a misdemeanour but no improvement has taken place since the last warning, a further meeting will be convened by the manager with the employee and their representative/colleague. If proven, the outcome can be a final written warning, which makes it clear that the employee will be dismissed if the offence is repeated.
Stage 4		If the issue is one of gross misconduct or if there has been no improvement since the final written warning was given within the agreed elapsed time, a further meeting will be convened. A senior member of management may be present together with the parties at the previous meeting. If the offence is proven, the employee may be dismissed. The employee has the right of appeal.
Stage 5		At the appeal, which will take place within three days, a director of the organisation will listen to all the evidence and decide either to uphold the dismissal or to change the nature of sanction to a further written warning, demotion and/or suspension. This decision is taken within a further two working days.

a fair and consistent way. It is only logical to do this, in any case, if they want their organisation to be regarded as a good employer and to have committed and hard-working employees.

There are a number of other elements that need to be considered. These are the *process of an employee claiming unfair dismissal*, including the operation of tribunals, the concepts of *constructive dismissal, admissible and inadmissible reasons for dismissal* and a brief examination of *common reasons for dismissal* and *recent legal developments*.

Employment law is a very complex area that is constantly changing so students are encouraged to follow regular legal reports as shown on the website.

CLAIMING UNFAIR DISMISSAL

The qualifying employment period for claiming unfair dismissal is two years (increased from one year in 2012) and applies to both full-time and part-time staff. It is only employees that can claim, but clarifying the definition of an employee has taken up much time in the courts. As with much of employment law, it is not what is written down that is conclusive, but what actually happens within the employment relationship. Sales agents, for example, whose contract shows them to be self-employed, have made successful claims to be classified as employees when they have demonstrated the extensive degree of control by the employers and their inability to refuse any work or to be able to work for any other employer while they were under contract.

Employees need to make a claim within three months of losing their jobs and they do this by completing a form ET1 setting out their case, available from ACAS or from consumer bodies such as Citizens Advice Bureaus. From 2012, employees have had to pay fees (in July 2013 between £160 and £250) to lodge tribunal claims and to proceed to the tribunal, a move made by the Coalition government to discourage vexatious claims. Employees who win the claim will have their fees refunded. A copy of this claim is then sent to the employer to respond. The next stage is that a conciliation officer from ACAS will try to get the parties to consider settling the case before it goes to the tribunal. The officer will communicate with both parties and help them to consider alternatives, including a cash settlement, reinstatement of the employee or the claim being dropped altogether. In 2010–11, of the 42,161 claims received (a small drop from 45,261 received in 2003), around one-half were settled by conciliation, around 11,000 were withdrawn, leaving approximately 8,500 actually going to the tribunal, while 1,500 had other outcomes (ACAS 2011).

If a Conciliation Officer can facilitate an agreement between the parties, then a *compromise agreement* will be drawn up where the dismissal stands but the employee receives an agreed sum of compensation in return for which the employee gives up all statutory rights. Such an agreement can be reached directly between the organisation and the employee, although it will not stand up if the employee has had excessive pressure put on them to accept (*King v Royal Bank of Canada, UKEAT 0333 2010*). There are advantages for the organisation in reaching such an agreement, including avoiding litigation and the certainty of the costs. For the employee, it avoids the possibility of a very stressful experience, and the agreement usually includes providing a fair reference, which enhances future job chances.

Tribunals, which can last for a day or as long as a month or more in the most complex cases, normally consist of three people: a legally qualified independent chair, and one representative each taken from a list of nominated individuals by employers' bodies and trade unions, all of whom have experience of industry or commerce. The tribunal therefore represents a fair balance of opinion, although the members of the tribunals act as individuals, not representing their constituency. The process of the tribunal is less formal than a normal court of law. In England and Wales, witnesses sit in for all the proceedings, whereas they are precluded from doing so in a normal court until they have given evidence.

The normal rules of evidence apply but the tribunal members take much more initiative in directing the questions, acting more as investigators than would a judge, who, as a generalisation, leaves it to the prosecution and defence to bring out all the important elements in their case. The difference is because many individuals take their own case to a tribunal and are faced by corporate lawyers, which can be very daunting. Having listened to the evidence from both sides, the tribunal will give its written decision a short time afterwards.

Another difference to a court of law is that the organisation does not have to prove their case beyond reasonable doubt, just on the balance of probabilities. Tribunals are not allowed to replace a decision with their own view. They will only interfere with the decision if it is outside of the range of reasonable decisions that could have been taken in the circumstances. For example, take the case of an employee who has been accused of fraud where the evidence is strong but not sufficient to ensure a conviction in a court of law. The organisation has investigated thoroughly, has followed all the right procedures and, having come to the conclusion that the employee actually carried out the fraud, has dismissed the employee. A tribunal would be unlikely to allow the claim for unfair dismissal to be successful as long as they are satisfied that the procedures are fair, that all the evidence was considered carefully and that management have a strong conviction of the guilt of the employee.

The decision by the tribunal will set out whether or not the employee was unfairly dismissed and, if so, the nature of the compensation, although often the tribunal will allow the sides to try to settle their own deal first, and only if they cannot do so will they work out the compensation to be paid. Very occasionally, when the dismissal is patently unfair, they will order reinstatement. If the employers refuse, additional compensation will be ordered. The maximum compensation that could be awarded in 2013 was £74,200 and this has generally been increased in line with inflation since that date, although government plans may restrict this to three times the earnings.

If either of the parties chooses to appeal against the decision, they do so to the Employment Appeal Tribunal (EAT). From there, further appeals can go to the Court of Appeal and thence to the House of Lords. Finally, an appeal can be made to the European Court of Justice (ECJ) in Luxembourg. Cases that reach that level are ones of major principle, tantamount to a change in the law. For example, Miss Marshall, who was forced to retire at age 60, took her claim all the way to the ECJ and eventually won the right to equal treatment, causing the British government to change the law and equalise retirement ages. She then went on to claim compensation for being forced to retire early but this had a limit of around £10,000 at that time. So she followed the same route all the way back to Luxembourg and, again, won her case. This meant that unlimited compensation applied to all cases relating to sex discrimination throughout Europe.

CONSTRUCTIVE DISMISSAL

An employee will sometimes face a situation where the actions of the employer make it difficult for them to continue at work. This may be because they have been insulted or bullied by the employer in front of their colleagues, sexually harassed or treated in a totally cavalier fashion, such as bonuses being withdrawn for no reason. The claim by the employee will be based on the concept that the employer has indicated by their actions that they no longer wish to be bound by the mutual contract of employment, even though it may not be intentional. Two examples are given in spotlight on the law 4.1.

SPOTLIGHT ON THE LAW 4.1 THREE CASES OF CONSTRUCTIVE DISMISSAL

Case 1

Three London bus drivers who were transferred to the new employer's depot six miles away resigned and successfully claimed that the extra one or two hours' travelling was unreasonable. The company claimed that the claimants had a mobility agreement with their previous employer that would transfer with them to the new employer (it was a TUPE transfer). However, EAT held that it was held to be a substantial and detrimental change to their working conditions and not bound by agreements with the previous employer and the depot was at a different location.

(Source: *Abellio London v Musse and others, UKEAT 0283 2011*)

Case 2

Mr Goodwin was a construction manager for CUK who were engaged in setting up a cable television network in South Wales. As part of his duties, Goodwin had to ensure that the employer's sub-contractors complied with the relevant statutory health and safety requirements. He found one sub-contractor, CC Ltd, especially lacking, which included an incident when roads were excavated without any traffic control. Goodwin recommended that no more work be given to CC Ltd. CUK disagreed with Goodwin and asked him to act in a more conciliatory fashion.

At a subsequent meeting between the parties, CC Ltd severely criticised Goodwin who felt that he had received no support from CUK at what he felt to be a humiliating and intimidating experience. A few weeks later, Goodwin was removed from all dealings with CC Ltd and transferred into the position of assistant construction manager. He resigned and claimed constructive dismissal because of the apparent demotion and lack of support over health and safety matters.

The tribunal rejected his claim, finding that Goodwin had not responded to the justified advice given to him concerning his approach on health and safety. The employer's action had not gone to the heart of the contract as the change of job title was not a demotion. Goodwin appealed to the Employment Appeal Tribune (EAT) indicating that employees with health and safety responsibilities must be afforded some protection in the way they carry out their duties and this had not been considered by the tribunal. They allowed the appeal and the case was referred to a new tribunal to consider whether the manner in which the employee approached the health and safety problems took him outside of the scope of health and safety activities.

(Source: *Goodwin v Cabletel UK Ltd, EAT 1997 IRLR 665* – Report in IDS 1998)

Case 3

In an end-of-year examination, Professor Buckland failed 18 of the 60 students and he (together with a colleague) failed 14 of the 16 that resat the examination. All the decisions were confirmed by the University Board of Examiners. However, a different programme leader, concerned with the high failure rate, reviewed the resit papers and reported this to the head of department, who ordered them to be marked again by different academics. He did not consult Buckland over this decision. The outcome was that some students were changed from a fail to a pass. Despite a successful internal appeal, Buckland resigned claiming constructive dismissal. The Court of Appeal confirmed the tribunal decision that the decision taken by the head of department in ordering remarking and the lack of consultation with Buckland was 'calculated to destroy the relationship of trust and confidence between the claimant and the University'.

(Source: *Buckland v Bournemouth University, Court of Appeal 2010 EWCA Civ 121*)

Admissible reasons for dismissal. Apart from redundancy, there are four circumstances in which dismissals may be regarded as fair at law. They are:

- *The employee's capability.* This covers the area of poor performance or the lack, or loss, of a necessary qualification.
- *An employee's misconduct.* These include the remainder of the misdemeanours and all of the acts of gross misconduct set out in Table 4.4.
- *A statutory restriction*, such as the lack of a work permit or security clearance in parts of the public sector.
- *Some other substantial reason.* This covers other areas such as pressure from a customer, or the inability to work with other members of the department or making false statements on an application form.

The first two reasons cover the vast bulk of cases, although some of the most interesting cases are to be found under some other substantial reason.

REASONS FOR DISMISSAL

Four further cases are set out which indicate some of the issues involved in dismissals. spotlight on the law 4.2 covers dismissal for long-term absence, while spotlight on the law 4.3 has three cases which examine more recent issues involving technology. In each of these cases, there are activities for you to carry out, set out at the end of the chapter.

Unfair dismissal and technology

Technology has provided additional challenges in the field of employee relations. The question of how far should the inappropriate use of technology justify dismissal has been tested in three recent cases (with somewhat surprising outcomes) as shown in spotlight on the law 4.3.

There are a number of *inadmissible reasons* that have emerged as the law has developed in the last 20 years. They include dismissals relating to pregnancy or maternity, refusing to work on a Sunday, dismissals relating to trade union membership or activity, those related to reasonable actions taken by the employee as a health and safety representative, a pension representative or a representative for consultations on redundancy or business transfer. In each of these cases, a dismissal made solely or predominantly on the basis of these reasons would be held to be automatically unfair.

SPOTLIGHT ON THE LAW 4.2 LONG-TERM ABSENCE

Wilson started working as a postman in 1995. In the Post Office, there was a lengthy procedure applying to frequent/extended absences from work due to medical conditions, which was agreed with the unions. It involved three stages; the outcome of each could be an informal warning, a formal warning and dismissal, respectively.

Wilson's employment was beset with absences and injuries. In February 1997, he received a first-stage informal warning and this was followed by a formal warning in June 1997 following an absence for one day for an upset stomach and two days' absence for a chest infection. The warning stated that if, during any six-month period in the following twelve months, he was absent on two separate occasions or had a total of ten days' absence, it could lead to dismissal. In October 1997, Wilson was absent for ten days as a result of a neck injury sustained while playing football for the Post Office team. At the subsequent third stage, his case was considered and the decision was made to terminate his employment, a decision that was upheld at appeal. The procedures had been followed carefully, including giving Wilson all the rights of union representation. Wilson subsequently applied to a tribunal for unfair dismissal.

(Source: *Post Office v Wilson, EAT 13.04.99 (762/98)* – Report in IDS 1999)

SPOTLIGHT ON THE LAW 4.3 UNFAIR DISMISSAL AND TECHNOLOGY

Case 1

In the case of *Gosden v Lifeline Project Ltd*, a tribunal decided that an employee was fairly dismissed due to forwarding an offensive chain email outside working hours and from his home computer to the home computer of a friend who worked for the employer's client. The email eventually entered the client's computer system and caused the employer's reputation with that client to be damaged. Once the client discovered the origin of the email, G was excluded from all of the client's locations. The tribunal commented that the employer had not infringed Gosden's right to privacy as the email was clearly intended for onward transmission and could not be treated as a confidential communication. Dismissal was within the range of reasonable responses, taking into account that the employer was a charity and G had received a written warning the previous year.

(Source: IDS 2011b)

Case 2

In *City of Edinburgh Council v Dickson*, the EAT held that the dismissal of an employee for watching pornography on a school computer was unfair. D was employed as a community learning and development worker based at the community wing of a school. He had type-one diabetes, which was poorly controlled, partly because he was prescribed the wrong dose of insulin. This meant that he was at risk of falling into a hypoglycaemic state, where a person can behave wholly out of character and have no recollection of what they have done. In June 2007, it was reported by a visiting youth-club organiser that D had been seen watching pornography and D was suspended. Despite evidence produced by his union representative concerning the effects of a hypoglycaemic episode, he was dismissed, the company relying partly on the advice of the HR manager's wife that D's medical condition could not explain his behaviour. The tribunal, supported by EAT, found that a proper investigation had not taken place and there was insufficient knowledge gathered as to D's medical condition. The tribunal awarded D £25,000 and ordered reinstatement. The decision is confirmation for employers that a full and thorough investigation must be followed prior to any decision to dismiss. Even where an employee's explanation seems unlikely, employers cannot reach that conclusion unless they have considered all the evidence available to them, and their decision is based on that evidence.

(Source: *Personnel Today* 2010)

Case 3

In *Crisp v Apple Retail* (2011), an Apple Store employee posted derogatory statements outside working hours on a 'private' Facebook page about Apple and its products. A colleague, who was a Facebook friend, passed the comments to the store manager and C was dismissed. The tribunal held that Apple had a clear social media policy that was fully detailed at induction. Critical comments on products were strictly prohibited. Despite the private nature of the comments, the tribunal found that there was nothing to stop employees passing the comments on so he could not rely on the right to privacy. Apple successfully argued that it was justified and proportionate to limit his right of freedom of expression in order to protect its commercial reputation against potentially damaging posts.

(Source: Hamnett 2011)

REDUNDANCY AND ITS IMPLICATIONS

One of the least pleasant activities within human resource management is handling a redundancy situation. In parts of Europe, there are tight controls on management's prerogative to declare redundancies but these limits are only lightly applied in the UK, so a redundancy situation is much more common. It is one of the almost inevitable consequences of change within the organisation and presents difficulties from the moment that rumours start circulating and has an effect for many months, sometimes years, after the actual redundancies take place. The situation is not helped by the numerous euphemisms that have arisen in recent years including 'downsizing', 'right-sizing' and 'letting employees go'. Creating redundancies is a sharp reminder of how human resources can be seen as a cost that must be reduced, rather than an asset that attracts investment. If handled badly, the motivation and trust of the workforce can be irreparably damaged, creating long-term problems in productivity and commitment. These difficulties can be ameliorated if the appropriate policies are in place and the events are handled with tact, honesty, diplomacy and sensitivity.

Redundancies can occur arising from a number of causes:

■ The organisation, or part of it, can be sold, merged or taken over. The new owners will have seen opportunities for extracting higher returns through cost saving, closing certain operating sections due to duplication or poor performance and restructuring central services (especially head offices), and generally to stamp their mark on the new organisation.

- The organisation may be part of a business that is going through a structural decline. Many UK industries declined in the period over the last 30 years as they had to face up to a declining demand and international competition, especially from Japan and developing countries. This has been exacerbated by the rise of China as a major industrial power.
- A recession, even if short-lived, can bring the chill wind of sharply reduced demand and a demonstrated over-manned situation, which will need to be remedied.
- Advances in technology can have an especially major effect on process and assembly industries where, for example, a robotised paint shop can reduce the number of employees involved by a factor of four or more.
- A major efficiency drive using techniques, such as business process re-engineering or benchmarking, can show that benefits can accrue through a reduction in manpower.

Legislation has an influence in three main areas related to redundancy: in setting out the requirement for *consultation with the workforce*; in defining the parameters for *selection for redundancy*; and in laying out the way *minimum redundancy payments* must be calculated. There is also a clear legislative definition of redundancy (Employment Rights Act, 1996 Section 139(1)), which can be summarised as a cessation or reduction or a major change in part or all of the business activities that leads to a reduction or change in the requirements for employees. This is drawn very broadly and tribunals have very rarely challenged the right of employers to declare redundancies. The process of redundancy is shown in Figure 4.3.

Consultation with the workforce has to take place in some form in every redundancy situation. However, specific timings apply where:

- 100 or more employees are to be made redundant, in which case consultation must commence at least 45 days before the first dismissal (from 2013).
- 20–99 employees are to be made redundant, in which case consultation must commence at least 30 days before the first dismissal.

Consultation takes the form of announcing the redundancies and giving the details of reasons for the redundancies, the timings, selection procedures and form of payments. Discussions are then entered into with either union or non-union representatives (or both depending on the existing arrangements) for communication and representation. If there is no formal system at that time, one must be set up to deal with this legal requirement.

It makes good business sense for as much openness as possible, once the announcement of redundancies is made. At this most difficult of times, it will not help the situation if the workforce believe that management are hiding information or are acting from other motives than those announced. DTI research (Edwards and Hall 1999) has shown that consultation very much helps to save jobs.

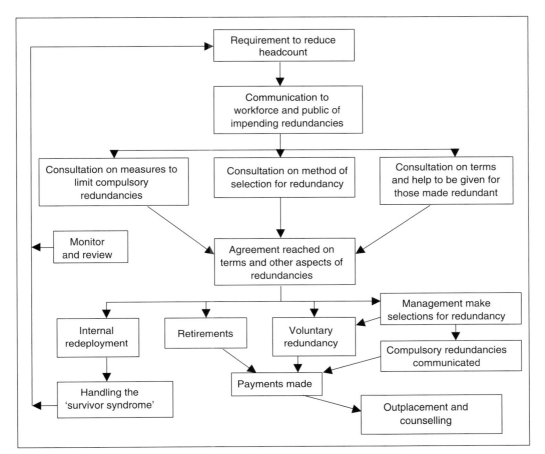

Figure 4.3
Process of
redundancy

ACTIVITY 4.2

One of the major topics of discussion in the consultation process is how to avoid compulsory redundancies. Make a list of the steps you would recommend to try to reduce compulsory redundancies.

Response to activity 4.2

You may have considered some of the following:

Immediate actions

■　　Eliminating all overtime
■　　Ceasing the use of agency staff

- Freezing recruitment
- Offering full-time employees part-time work, possibly in the form of job shares
- Offering early retirement on terms that may be attractive, especially to long-serving employees
- Accepting employees who volunteer to be made redundant.

Longer-term solutions

- Relying on natural wastage (i.e. employees leaving voluntarily) to reduce numbers
- Business solutions such as bringing back into the business work that had been sub-contracted outside and finding alternative business that potentially redundant employees could carry out
- Retraining employees who could slot into some positions that will continue but may be difficult to fill, such as in IT
- Putting employees on to short-time working, i.e. 30 hours a week instead of 37. This has been operated by a number of large manufacturers, such as Jaguar cars in 2009.

There are advantages and difficulties for each of these solutions. Short-time working, for example, is a costly solution as a form of allowance is normally payable for each normal working day that the employee is not actually working. Productivity and morale tends to fall under short-time working, as employees do not feel under pressure to produce at a high rate, as they may consider that this will simply make the redundancy situation worse. Freezing all overtime and recruitment may not be appropriate where there is a key vacancy or where an important contract has a vital delivery date. Early retirement is another costly solution if it involves adding years of service or enhancing retirement pay, although these costs may be borne by the pension fund.

Selection for redundancy

Another important aspect of the consultation process is the basis on which decisions are taken as to which employees are to be made redundant. Redundancy is covered by unfair dismissal legislation, so such decisions have to be based on procedures that are fair in themselves and are carried out fairly and transparently. A system for selection must be set out and it must be capable of being defended at a tribunal as being appropriate in the circumstances. This is far from easy and there are no simple solutions that fit all situations.

Common methods which can be used including the following:

Selecting those employees who volunteer. This would seem an obvious solution but is not always that simple. A number of employees may volunteer who consider that they can obtain an alternative position relatively easily. This may be because they are in the age group 24–36, with good experience and possessing skills in short supply. These are precisely the employees that you want to keep! The dilemma presents itself as to whether you refuse to accept such volunteers and make others compulsorily redundant, which would cause considerable unrest, or whether you accept the volunteers and lose some good employees that will affect your capacity to perform in a competitive environment. From a business view-point, you may adopt the former viewpoint, but the human resources view should veer towards the latter. The culture of equity and good employee relations is not encouraged when jobs are taken away from some employees, when others are willing to leave the organisation in their place.

Last in, first out. This used to be the standard method universally applied, especially in a unionised environment. It is certainly transparent and can be regarded as fair in that long service is rewarded. In practice, however, it means that those who are selected for redundancy are those who may be keen, enthusiastic employees who will have much to offer the organisation in the future. This may result in a stagnating, ageing workforce who lack the skills and versatility required for future business success (Foot and Hook 2011).

Performance measurement. By using comparative measures of employee performance, the organisation can make redundant those employees who it judges are not up to the mark. This can be seen as a fairer system overall and one that benefits the longer-term future of the organisation. The measures that can be used include attendance, timekeeping, speed and accuracy in their job, whether the person has been disciplined for any reason and the general attitude of the employees to their work and authority. A score sheet (such as in Table 4.6) can be produced that combines these measures and those with the lowest overall scores are made redundant.

These measures are fraught with difficulty, however. Can you give a low score to an employee whose attendance is poor due to their being treated for cancer? Should a single parent be penalised on their timekeeping because of their home responsibilities? When it

Table 4.6 Example of performance measurement system relating to redundancy selection

Measure	Description	Employee 1	Employee 2
Attendance	15 points maximum with 3 points lost for each absence	12	9
Timekeeping	10 points maximum with 2 points lost for each lateness	6	8
Quantity of work	15 points for high, 10 for average, 5 for below average	15	10
Quality of work	15 points for very accurate, 10 for average, 5 for below average	10	10
Warnings	10 points for clear, 5 lost for each warning	10	5
General attitude	Ranked on scale of 0–15	12	10
	Maximum = 80	65	52

comes to trying to judge attitude, the problems are almost insurmountable. Such decisions must be taken primarily by the employee's manager or supervisor and objectivity can always be questioned.

Skills and competencies. A final version is to score employees on the type and quality of skills or competencies that they possess. Those skills and competencies that are highly valued or are in short supply are scored highly. This system allows the organisation to retain those skills and competencies that it needs for future development. The problems of measurement also arise with this selection system. How do you distinguish between the skills and competencies acquired in the past and the way they are currently utilised?

Despite the difficulties involved, the latter two methods are growing in use and have been accepted by tribunals as long as the scheme is operated fairly and transparently and not simply put in place to construct a list of 'trouble-makers' that the organisation wants to dispense with. It was established at an early stage of the implementation of the legislation that employers do not need to prove the accuracy of the individual marks on their scoring system, only that the method of selection was fair and appeared to be applied reasonably in general. This has always seemed an unusual viewpoint to take as it limits the individual's right to question in detail the basis upon which they have lost their job. The only exception to this is where there are strong indications that discrimination has played a major role in the decision (see spotlight on the law 4.4).

SPOTLIGHT ON THE LAW 4.4 REDUNDANCY AND MATERNITY LEAVE

Eversheds needed to reduce the number of solicitors from two to one at a specialist subsidiary company. They carried out a measurement of performance with one criterion being the 'lock-up', which measured the length of time between undertaking the work and receiving payment. The male solicitor had a score of 0.5 but the female solicitor had taken one maternity leave during the period concerned so she was awarded the maximum score of 2, a policy justified by the organisation not wanting to risk disadvantaging the female. The male solicitor achieved a final score under all categories lower than the female and was made redundant.

The tribunal, supported by EAT, agreed that the female should not be disadvantaged but proportionality should be applied and giving the female a maximum score for 'lock-up' meant that she received preferential treatment, which could not be justified. Her lock-up score should have been measured on the basis of a similar period when she was last at work. The male solicitor was awarded £123,000.

(Source: *Eversheds Legal Services v De Belin*, EAT 0352/10 – Report in IDS 2011a)

Redundancy pay

The final intervention by legislation relates to the payments due under redundancy. Employees are entitled to the minimum of a week's pay for each year of service, although service over the age of 41 is paid at the rate of one and a half week's pay and service between the ages of 18 and 21 inclusive is paid at the rate of half a week's pay. A maximum figure applies to the week's pay (£430 in 2011), although this entitlement only starts when employees have completed two years' service.

These sums are not especially large and many organisations choose to enhance them by increasing (or ignoring totally) the maximum week's pay restriction or by increasing the entitlement to, say, two weeks' pay for each year of service. They take this decision both on the grounds of showing a degree of generosity towards the employees who are losing their jobs through no fault of their own and also because it may encourage a higher level of volunteers and thereby reduce the number of compulsory redundancies.

Helping employees obtain alternative employment

An important role for human resources is to help those employees who have been made redundant to obtain a suitable alternative position. This can be achieved *internally*, through matching up suitable internal vacancies (perhaps replacing key positions where the incumbent has volunteered for redundancy) with candidates selected for redundancy. This can be a complex process and needs to be handled carefully and sensitively to avoid exacerbating an already difficult situation. Employees who accept alternative positions have the right to a four-week trial period. If they take the reasonable decision that the position is not suitable for them at the end of that period, they retain the right to redundancy payments.

ACTIVITY 4.3

What help can human resources give to help employees get alternative work externally?

Response to activity 4.3

You may have listed the following actions:

■ Circulating all the major local employers telling them about the redundancies and listing the numbers and skills available. (See case study 4.4.)
■ Organising an 'open day' for local employers to attend who may be interested in taking on some of those made redundant. This may be held on site or at the local job centre.
■ Giving paid time off for employees to look for employment and attend interviews (this is a statutory right, although the maximum time has been defined only as 'reasonable').

- Helping employees to draw up CVs and preparing them for job search and interviews.
- Working with an outplacement agency that will provide professional job-search services on an individual or group basis. This will include help in coming to terms with the redundancy situation, career counselling and planning, a job-hunting strategy and office support. More importantly, the agency can provide continuing independent support for some months after the event. For supervisors and managers, the current average time to obtain an alternative position is around four to six months so such help can be particularly vital.

The role of human resources in redundancy

Firstly, policies and procedures should be in place to deal with potential redundancies. These should include the way redundancies are announced, the consultation process, commitment to ways to reduce the impact of redundancies, the selection procedures for compulsory redundancies, an appeals process and a commitment to help with obtaining alternative employment.

However, it is not enough to have procedures in place. Managers will need to be trained in the selection process so that it is carried out in a fair and consistent way. The process will need to be carefully monitored and the results communicated in an efficient but sympathetic way by human resources.

Human resources also need to ensure that the redundancy payments made are appropriate, which will involve influential discussions with the chief executive and, in a unionised environment, bargaining with the unions. Checking and communicating the actual payments is another important role. The right balance must be achieved between strategic intent, procedural fairness and humane treatment. Finally, the involvement with helping those made redundant to obtain alternative positions is vital to help diffuse some of the bitterness that many will feel against the organisation. People need to be treated as if they are valued and

CASE STUDY

CASE STUDY 4.4 HELPING REDUNDANT EMPLOYEES AT THE AA

When the AA decided to close 143 shops in 1998 and extend their call-centre operations, 900 staff were made redundant throughout the country. In a bid to support these employees, the AA published advertisements in national newspapers and *People Management*, which aimed to interest the insurance industry looking for skilled and experienced staff. There was substantial interest from all quarters, not just in insurance, and the placement level was very high, making it a very successful operation.

(Source: Prickett 1998)

handled in as humane a way as possible. They never forget the way they are treated when they are made redundant and neither do the friends and colleagues who remain behind. It is also vital that survivors experience and witness a just process and can feel comfortable in their task of taking the organisation forward. One way to improve what is a sensitive and difficult process is to use experienced *special envoys*, and a survey of their experiences is shown in an ACAS research report in focus on research 4.5.

FOCUS ON RESEARCH 4.5 USING SPECIAL ENVOYS IN REDUNDANCY SITUATIONS

Normally, it is the unhappy role of human resources to break the news to those employees chosen for redundancy. In declining organisations where this is a frequent occurrence, HR staff are often called the 'Angels of death'. Although there is a growing trend to create a team mixing HR staff with line managers to carry out mass redundancies, it remains a traumatic experience for all concerned. ACAS interviewed 50 'envoys', divided between the public and private sectors and management roles, with just over half from HR. The research found that:

■ The closer the normal working relationship with those affected, the more difficult the role became.

■ Line managers found that the envoy role had a huge impact on their workloads, because they understood how important it was, so other work became neglected while the redundancy project was under way.

■ The task was generally considered the most emotionally demanding work they had undertaken in their working lives.

■ Despite the heightened emotional burden, the envoys felt it right and proper that they should take responsibility for delivering the bad news to employees because they knew them best and wanted to provide support.

■ Line managers had less opportunity to share their experiences with colleagues and had all their other work to attend to, while HR managers could concentrate on the main task while sharing experiences with their smaller cohort of colleagues.

■ The more experience managers obtained, the better they felt they carried out the work, as they refined the process depending on the employees concerned.

■ Those working in the public sector found the whole process much more troubling as compulsory redundancies had not been prevalent in public service prior to the current recession.

■ The process was greatly improved when envoys were involved in the whole process from start to finish, including the communication, consultation and selection areas.

(Source: Ashman 2012)

MOVING HEAD OFFICE

The merger between Meteor and Landline Holdings had been announced the previous month and it had become clear quite soon that two separate head offices would not continue. Meteor's offices, however, were not large enough to accommodate further expansion and were, in any case, coming to the end of their lease. The board had decided to move to a new site 40 miles away in a state-of-the-art business park, a move that would take effect in six months' time. As soon as the announcement to staff had been made, Sarah was seconded back to head office to help David Martin prepare for the move and its consequent effect upon the employees. It was made clear that there would be no compulsory redundancies and that all Meteor and Landline staff would be invited to apply for a position in the combined head office. Details of relocation and redundancy packages would be given within one month.

The first decision David and Sarah faced was both legal and ethical. Who could be forced to relocate as part of their contract? In other words, if there was an appropriate clause in their contracts entitling the company to relocate them and they decided they did not want to move, they would not be entitled to any redundancy payment. This applied to 50 of the senior executives, managers and sales personnel, 47 of them male and 3 female. The ethical issue here, however, was that it may appear unfair if a manager feels unable to move, due to family or other constraints, and therefore receives no payment, while one of their staff in the same position receives a generous sum of redundancy. There were two further complications with this issue. Firstly, they were aware that some recent tribunal decisions had appeared to indicate that forcing a woman to relocate could be held to be discriminatory, especially where there were caring responsibilities. Secondly, the company had not actually implemented this clause previously, as relocation came up only rarely and usually took place alongside an offer and acceptance of promotion. On balance, in the interests of an equitable situation, they decided to recommend the same legal situation to all staff – the alternatives would be relocation or redundancy – despite the cost involved.

Looking at the situation from a geographical viewpoint, some staff could relocate without moving home and a special bus service would be laid on for the first year after the move. A decision, however, had to be made as to whether staff in this position should be offered the full package, including house move. There did not seem to be an imperative to do so, but the complications and apparent inequity of offering it to some staff and not others again influenced the decision to offer the full package to everybody.

The package was a generous one, covering all the costs of buying and selling, stamp duty, removal costs and a settling-in allowance of 5 per cent of the value of the property. For those who did not own houses, a package of six months' subsidised rent was offered plus a fixed settling-in sum. The generosity was based on the viewpoint that the cost of having to recruit and train key staff was very high, so it was important that as many moved as possible. Bridging loans were also offered for up to three months for staff with more than five years' service.

It was agreed that the redundancy package to be offered would be around the industry average so staff would receive the legal minimum plus a supplement of 40 per cent. Given the fact that few staff had more than ten years' service, the costs involved would not be very high.

The complete information was communicated in a series of meetings across the offices during one long day with a printed summary given to each employee. A dedicated help line was made available to give a full calculation of entitlement together with any necessary financial advice. Outplacement help was also made available through a local consultancy that specialised in this area.

In the event, far more employees chose to accept redundancy rather than move and the costs to the organisation finished up 25 per cent above those budgeted. Although the opportunity was provided to make savings in the overlapping services of the two organisations, the move became much more complex as it included a larger than expected recruitment programme, as well as all the complicated decisions arising from creating a joint head-office structure. Sarah was not sure that they had made all the right decisions.

KEY CHAPTER SUMMARY POINTS

- Union membership has declined substantially since its high point in the late 1970s due to government legislation, the decline in manufacturing and the move towards a more flexible workforce.

- There has been a growing tendency for organisations to move towards a unitary viewpoint in their relations with their employees. This has shown itself in a greater emphasis on encouraging employee involvement and participation, through team briefing, recognition schemes and works councils.

- The growing number of partnership agreements indicate the willingness of employers and trade unions to work more closely together to obtain common aims.

- Policies regarding discipline, grievances and redundancies need to be formal, fair, reasonable and communicated effectively if they are to remain inside the law.

- Constructive dismissal takes place when the employer's actions indicate that they repudiate the contract, although this may not be intentional.

- A fair employer will take a number of actions to try to avoid compulsory redundancy, which includes freezing all recruitment, eliminating overtime and offering voluntary retirement.

- There is a high level of correlation between high levels of employee engagement and high performance.

STUDENT ACTIVITIES

1   Consider spotlight on the law 4.2 and decide:
- What was the basis upon which Wilson had been dismissed out of the four admissible reasons?
- Do you think he was successful in his claim?
- What is the basis of a good attendance management scheme?

2   Consider the cases in spotlight on the law 4.3 and discuss the implications for human resource practitioners in each case.

3   Consider the redundancy scheme set out in Table 4.6. Make a list of the difficulties that could be raised by employees, the problems that could be faced in practice and how you would sell the scheme to the employees.

4   A proposal was put forward in 2012 by the Coalition government that would allow employers in small and medium-sized businesses to offer shares in the company in exchange for giving up their rights to redundancy and unfair dismissal. Debate the benefits and difficulties associated with implementing this proposal from both the employer and employee viewpoint.

5   In case study 4.3 on employee engagement, identify possible reasons why some initiatives in this case were very successful and why others appeared to fail. Put forward proposals to correct those areas which were not successful, identifying likely costs involved.

6   In the Meteor case study, how reasonable do you think were the terms of the redundancy package? Look up the tribunal cases referring to relocation and equal opportunities. Do you think that the high costs of the redundancy package outweigh the risks of a tribunal claim?

7   Set out the practical issues that may face management when working with a non-unionised workforce. For example, one issue would be how to communicate with employees.

REFERENCES

ACAS (2009) *Code of Practice on Disciplinary Practice and Procedures in Employment*. ACAS.

—(2011) *Annual Report 2010–11*. ACAS.

Arkin, A. (2011) Is Engagement Working? *People Management*, November, 22–27.

Ashman, I. (2012) *The Nature of Bad News Infects the Teller*. ACAS.

Bacon, N. and Samuel, P. (2007) *Mapping Partnership Agreements in Britain*. 8th European Congress of International Industrial Relations Association, Manchester, 3–7 September.

Bewley, H. and Forth, J. (2010) *Vulnerability and Adverse Treatment in the Workplace*. Employee Relations Research Series 112. Department for Business Innovation and Skills.

CAC (2011) Unite the Union and King and Fowler, Outcome of Ballot, accessed at www.cac.gov.uk.

Carr, F. (1999) Local Bargaining in the NHS: New Approaches to Employee Relations. *Industrial Relations Journal*, 30(3): 197–211.

Edwards, P. and Hall, M. (1999) Remission: Possible. *People Management*, 15 July, 44–46.

Foot, M. and Hook, C. (2011) *Introducing Human Resource Management*, 6th ed. Longmans.

Gennard, J. and Judge, G. (2002) *Employee Relations*. CIPD.

Gibbons, M. (2007) *Better Dispute Resolution*. Department of Trade and Industry.

Guest, D. (1995) Human Resource Management, Trade Unions and Industrial Relations, pp. 110–141, in J. Storey (ed.) *Human Resource Management: A Critical Text*. Routledge.

—(2001) Industrial Relations and Human Resource Management, in J. Storey (ed.) *Human Resource Management: A Critical Text*, 2nd ed. Thomson Learning.

Hamnett, J. (2011) Facebook Comments 'Gross Misconduct'. *People Management*, December, 21.

Holbeche, L. and Matthews, G. (2012) *Engaged: Unleashing your Organisation's Potential through Employee Engagement*. John Wiley.

Hyman, J. (2000) *Financial Participation Schemes*, in G. White and J. Drucker (eds) *Reward Management: A Critical Text*. Routledge.

IDS (1998) *IDS Brief 605*, January, 8–9.

—(1999) *IDS Brief 641*, July.

—(2011a) *Employment Brief 925*, May, 8–11.

—(2011b) Dismissal for Sending Offensive E-mail from Home was Fair. *IDS Employment Law Brief 926*, June, 12–13.

Lynch, R. (2011) Job Jitters Keep British Workers from Going on Strike. *London Evening Standard*, 18 May, 6.

McCarthy, D. and Palcic, D. (2012) The Impact of Large-Scale Ownership Plan on Labour Productivity: The Case of Eircom. *International Journal of Human Resource Management*, 23(17): 3710–3724.

Macleod, D. and Clarke, N. (2009) *Engaging for Success*. Office of Public Sector Information, accessed at http://www.bis.gov.uk/files/file52215.pdf.

Millward, N., Bryson, A. and Forth, J. (2000) *All Change at Work: British Employment Relations 1980–1998 as Portrayed by the Workplace Industrial Relations Survey Series*. Routledge.

Overell, S. (1999) An Unsocial Agreement. *Personnel Today*, 26 August, 18–19.

Pass, S. (2008) *Working in Partnership*. Department of Health.

Personnel Today (2010) City of Edinburgh Council v Dickson, 22 March, 6.

Prickett, R. (1998) The AA Puts Recruitment into Reverse. *People Management*, 17 September, 13.

Redman, T. and Wilkinson, A. (2001) *Contemporary Human Resource Management*. Financial Times/ Prentice Hall.

Reilly, P. and Denvira, A. (2008) Better Together. *People Management*, 10 January.

Robinson, D. and Hayday, S. (2009) *The Engaging Manager*, Report 470, Institute of Employment Studies, November.

Smedley, T. (2012) On My Agenda. August, 29–33.

Smethurst, S. (2003) A Slice of the Cake. *People Management*, 6 February, 32–34.

Stevens, R. (2003) Union Recognition Still Rising. Partnership @ Work website, 18 February.

Stredwick, J. (2008) *Cases in Reward Management*. Lulu.

Syedain, H. (2009) Mutual Benefit. *People Management*, 5 November, 24–26.

Teague, P. and Hann, D. (2010) Problems with Partnership at Work. *Human Resource Management Journal*, 20(1): 100–114.

Thompson, D. (2012) The Wisdom of Crowds. *People Management*, September, 37–41.

Wood, S., Moore, S. and Willman, P. (2002) Third Time Lucky for Statutory Union Recognition in the UK? *Industrial Relations Journal*, 33(3): 215–233.

Younson, F. (2002) Employers Face Scoring Own Goal. *People Management*, 7 March, 19.

ADDITIONAL FEATURES

 Please visit the companion website at: www.routledge.com/cw/stredwick where you will find additional case studies and reading material together with short self-tests and other resources for both students and lecturers.

5 PERFORMANCE MANAGEMENT

CHAPTER OBJECTIVES

When you have studied this chapter, you should be able to:

- Understand the critical nature of the performance management process and the role of human resources in influencing the associated systems and operations.

- State the meaning of performance appraisal and performance management and distinguish between the two.

- Carefully consider the appropriate measurement methods in given situations and be conscious of their shortcomings.

- Put forward reasoned proposals on how to set up and operate a basic performance management system.

INTRODUCTION

As has been discussed in the section on talent management in Chapter 1, an organisation is judged by its performance. In the private sector, performance is measured principally by its profits and the growth in value of its shares; in the public sector, measures are more controversial but sets of various performance indicators in health, education and other public services give a general overall view of how well the organisation is performing in comparison with its peers.

Organisations can perform well or poorly due to external forces, such as the state of competition in the marketplace, long-term weather patterns, legal restrictions or the level of interest rates and taxation. However, the majority of economists and commentators agree that the biggest influence on organisational performance is the quality of the labour force at all levels of the business. Teams of highly skilled, trained and motivated employees will nearly always overcome most of the difficulties created by external forces, while a poorly motivated, untrained and unskilled labour force will nearly always fail to take advantage of favourable external opportunities.

Given this situation, it could be argued that the most important role for human resources is to raise the performance of employees in the organisation. To do this, employees' performance has to be managed and this is not an easy job. As long ago as 300 AD, the Chinese philosopher Sin Yu was complaining about the unfair treatment dealt by senior mandarins in the Civil Service under their current performance management scheme: '*The Imperial Rater of nine grades seldom rates men according to their merits but always according to his likes and dislikes*' (Swan 1991: 16).

Times have changed little since then, it seems, with Peters and Waterman (1982) finding that managers would prefer to go to the dentist than carry out an appraisal of their staff. Moreover, appraisees were so generally upset by the appraisal that they took as long as six months to get over it. Many practitioners are still very wary of working to a scheme that attempts to measure the unmeasurable, communicate performance to the inattentive and make extra payments to the ungrateful.

There are strong signs in recent years, however, that a new approach is spreading, which focuses much more on the whole performance management (or 'talent management') system and much less on appraisal as a single activity. *Appraisal* can also often be regarded as a once-a-year ritual (a rain dance, it is said, where the participants intone the right phrases, make the right movements and the money will fall from the heavens), whereas *performance management* is a total company system, built into all human resources activities – recruitment, training, reward and relations. The appraisal process all too often looks backwards, looking for excuses and blame, while performance management is more concerned with looking to the future, to improvements, challenges and opportunities. And, whereas appraisal is a diaried event, performance management is a continuous process, integrated totally with the way the organisation is run.

THE PURPOSE OF PERFORMANCE MANAGEMENT

There are two main purposes driving performance management, as set out in Figure 5.1.

Firstly, the *operational reasons*, which serve to lead and control.

Control. The process is often used as a form of strict control over employees. Going back over 150 years, Robert Owen, in one of the first factory settings, used a 'silent monitor': a piece of wood mounted over a machine with one of four colours to denote the daily performance of the operator. A similar process is in place in call centres today with typical control measures including the automatic measurement of call length against prescribed time, calls waiting to be answered, the abandoned call rate, the time taken to 'wrap up' and call availability. On top of this, calls are often recorded and remote monitoring takes place where managers check that the scripts are adhered to and customers are dealt with according to the rules (Brophy 2010). Whatever the system in force, employees working under a set of published performance targets and achievements will feel the control that is exercised over them.

Communication. As organisations exist in an increasingly competitive environment, it becomes more and more important for employees to have clear guidance and direction towards the organisation's aims and objectives. The performance management system sets out to communicate that link between an organisation's mission and strategic direction and the required employee performance.

Improve effectiveness. Performance management also acts as a measure of the effectiveness or efficiency of the workforce, particularly where there are external or inter-unit comparisons. The strongest and the weaker performers can be readily identified. The strongest can be used as role models and utilised in training and development activities, while the weaker employees can be helped to improve through coaching, training or discipline.

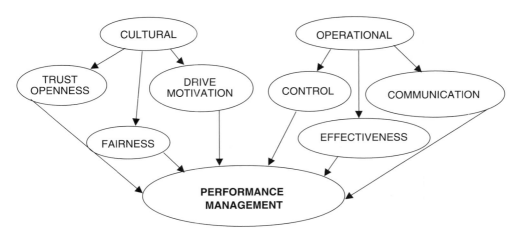

Figure 5.1
Performance management input model

Secondly, the *cultural reasons* aim to lead and influence employees' behaviour.

Trust and openness: The performance management system can feature as part of the overall drive to build a more open relationship with employees. Organisation plans can be shared, appraisal discussions can be frank within a realistic context, and means of improving performance can be encouraged and openly evaluated. Obtaining this trust is not an easy process. In an extensive US research study (Becon and Instler 2011), the researchers found that only 35 per cent of employees trusted their performance management systems. A CIPD survey found a similar lack of enthusiasm for performance management schemes, as shown in focus on research 5.1.

Drive and motivation: One of the key features of *goal theory* is that the setting and monitoring of targets can act as important motivators in themselves (see Chapter 6). Moreover, because employees always have a higher motivation towards goals with which they agree or have had some input, the performance management system provides the opportunity for employees to have a voice in the process through the individual performance plan, in whatever form it is agreed.

Fairness: Another important purpose is to produce a system that is regarded by employees as fair and equitable, especially in the rewards that emerge from the process. A well-thought-through performance management system should provide a defensible framework within which the many types of rewards can be allocated, rather than on the

FOCUS ON RESEARCH 5.1 CIPD SURVEY ON PERFORMANCE MANAGEMENT

A survey carried out by the CIPD in 2009 based on returns from 507 personnel practitioners found a surprising lack of enthusiasm for the strength of performance management to achieve results. More than 50 per cent gave a 'neutral' response to most of the propositions put forward. For example:

- Only 20 per cent agreed that performance management has a positive impact on individual performance, while 20 per cent disagreed, the rest remaining neutral.
- Only 18 per cent agreed that performance management benefited line managers in managing their employees effectively, while 37 per cent disagreed.
- Only 21 per cent agreed that performance management can help people understand the organisation's strategic priorities, while 25 per cent disagreed.

The number of organisations that operated some form of 360-degree feedback was 20 per cent, while 75 per cent utilised some form of objective setting.

(Source: CIPD 2009)

basis of personal whim or prejudice. There are many studies showing powerful links between people management practices and organisational performance, and appraisal usually comes out as a key practice in this regard. For example, in an NHS survey, West *et al.* (2006) found that a hospital that appraises around 20 per cent more staff and trains about 20 per cent more appraisers is likely to have 1,090 fewer deaths per 100,000 admissions (see focus on research 5.2).

A further objective allied with fairness relates to dealing with areas of employee performance which produce major concerns. Employees will not take kindly to criticism if they are unaware of the standards expected of them. It is certainly not possible to engage in disciplinary proceedings on performance that will be regarded as fair without having such standards in place.

All these reasons support the notion that an effective scheme embeds a culture for employees to focus on performance improvement, learning and development. An effective scheme will also add to the level of trust between employees and management as indicated by a research study summarised in focus on research 5.3.

FOCUS ON RESEARCH 5.2 THE EFFECTS OF PERFORMANCE MANAGEMENT ON PATIENT MORTALITY IN THE NHS

You will remember the research carried out by West *et al.* set out in Chapter 1, which found a strong association between HR practices and patient mortality. The extent and sophistication of appraisal systems in hospitals was particularly closely related to lower mortality rates, but there were also links with the sophistication of training and the percentage of staff working in teams.

Taking the strongest association – that between deaths following admissions for hip fractures and appraisal – the data showed that, for hospitals of equal size and local population health needs, an improvement in the extensiveness and sophistication of the appraisal system (for example, by ensuring that 25 per cent more staff who administered appraisals were trained to do so) would be associated with a drop in deaths after hip fractures equivalent to 1,090 fewer deaths per 100,000 admissions – that is, more than 1 per cent of all admissions. In other words, it could prevent 12.3 per cent of hospital deaths.

In a subsequent study, conducted between 2004 and 2006, the relationship between systems of HRM practices and the effectiveness of patient care in hospitals was examined. The findings showed that HR systems were related to the quality of healthcare and, specifically, patient mortality in hospitals. And they showed that people management systems, among other HR systems, did contribute to high-quality healthcare.

(Source: West *et al.* 2002, 2006)

F
O
C
U
S

O
N

R
E
S
E
A
R
C
H

FOCUS ON RESEARCH 5.3 PERFORMANCE MANAGEMENT AND LEVEL OF TRUST

The researchers carried out a longitudinal survey of employee views of the trust for top management and their perceptions of the performance management scheme in a small, non-union, plastics manufacturing company in the American Midwest. A base-line survey at the start of the programme was followed by two subsequent surveys between which time a new performance management scheme had been introduced. The major improvements were the inclusion of self-appraisal and an insistence that the discussions between an employee and their manager were centred on the specific behaviours and outcomes expected of the employees.

The results of the later survey showed that there was greater acceptance of the new scheme as one that was fairer and of more value. At the same time, the level of trust of senior management had risen, including the increased perception of management integrity.

(Source: Mayer and Davis 1999)

WHAT SHOULD THE PROCESS BE CALLED?

Throughout this book, the word 'appraisal' has been kept at a distance. It has a degree of distaste to the writer as being associated in the dictionary with the judging and valuing of objects, not people. It has a clear sense of being one-way with the outcome being a label 'success' or 'failure'. There are some better names available.

Sainsbury's have called their process the 'Personal Management Agenda', which sets in train the objective of performance improvement of all employees. Glaxo Wellcome encourage all their employees to develop their own 'Personal Fact File', which leads to the implementation of relevant personal development plans. Many universities, including Bedfordshire, have called their process by the more neutral name of 'Career Review'. A number of other organisations are starting to include the expression 'Employee Contribution' in the title of their scheme.

STAGES IN THE PERFORMANCE MANAGEMENT FRAMEWORK

Figure 5.2 (Armstrong 2001) shows the various stages of the performance management framework and the key HR roles have been highlighted:

1   Establishing a performance agreement with each employee/each team from which objectives and/or competency plans emerge. This agreement needs to be aligned with the business plan.

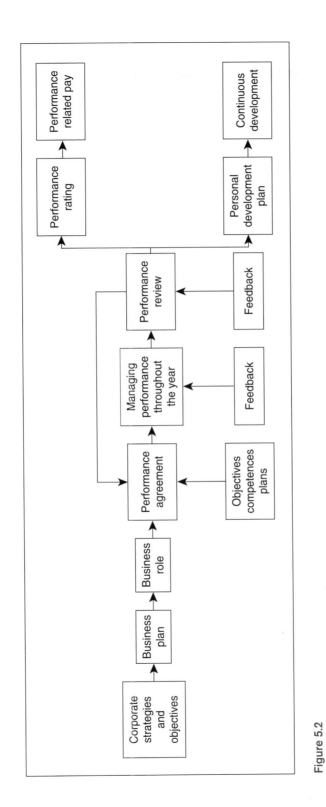

Figure 5.2

The performance management framework

Source: Armstrong, M. (2001) *Human Resource Management Practice*. Kogan Page.

2   Ensuring that the ways that performance can be measured are robust, fair and under-stood by all parties. This includes an examination of various methods of measurement, including BARS and competencies.

3   Setting up effective ways of giving feedback to employees on a regular basis both during the year and at the year end. How to carry out an appraisal interview is included here together with an examination of 360-degree appraisal.

4   Making sure that the outcomes of the process, which are normally either performance pay or personal training and development (or both), are delivered in a fair and equitable way.

The basis of this chapter will be to examine each of these important stages in turn.

Stage 1: Raising performance through performance agreements

For Armstrong, performance agreements 'Define expectations – the results to be achieved and the competences required to attain these results' (2001: 237). In other words, the manager will reach agreement with each employee on the required level of performance, and how it is to be measured. This agreement should be reached by a series of stages:

■   *Ensure corporate goals and values are shared.* An employee's performance objectives should always be aligned with those of the organisation as a whole. This is best explained in terms of the objectives for the sales department. The corporate goal will be sales of, say, £100 million made up of a defined product mix (i.e. a set of different company products) that gives optimum profitability. This will be divided into divisional targets and then cascaded down eventually to the sales targets for an individual sales employee, say £500,000. The target will then be expressed in a product mix form and may be refined in an even more precise way in terms of monthly targets, geographical targets and new/existing customers. It is very important that the sales employee knows and understands how this target was reached and how it fits in with the corporate goals. If they were to sell in excess of £500,000, this may appear to be exceeding their target and be praiseworthy; but, if this sales figure was made up of the wrong product mix, it could affect the company's ability to make sufficient profit from the sales. The same principle applies in all employees' activities. They need to know what the company is trying to achieve and the part they have to play in the whole corporate plan. The role of human resources is to ensure that the corporate goals and values (dealt with in Chapter 1) are widely disseminated and explained.

■   *Agree an individual performance plan.* The plan for each employee needs to include a number of key features:

–   It must be integrated with the plan for the department
–   It must go towards helping the individual to improve their own performance

–   It must address any areas of concern regarding past performance
–   It must clarify how the performance is to be measured.

■   *Agree on how the performance is to be monitored, measured and evaluated.* The most important part of this process is choosing the most appropriate form of measurement out of the many available, both quantitative and qualitative, which will be discussed in the next section. The role of the manager, the employee and any third parties will need to be agreed, as will the timing of meetings, both formal and informal, during the period in question.

■   *Agree on help and assistance to achieve the targets set out in the plan.* Training and development will be important here and this can include internal and external courses, mentoring and coaching, periods of secondment to another department or role, work shadowing of senior colleagues and attendance at crucial meetings. Other resources need to be agreed, including staffing and budgetary issues.

■   *Agree on the nature of the rewards available.* The plan will need to be quite clear on how the individual's pay will be influenced by the outcomes from the plan, whether promotion or any other career development issues are affected and in what way. Motivation towards achieving a successful outcome to the plan is dependent to a large extent upon how valuable are the rewards to the employee, including both extrinsic and intrinsic types of rewards.

Stage 2: Measuring performance

INPUTS OR OUTPUTS – OBJECTIVES OR COMPETENCIES?

Standards need to be developed in order to be able to measure performance. There are two main methods that are currently used for developing the standards against which the employees' performance is measured.

The first method is by *establishing targets* for employees. These can be quantified outputs or improvement targets or one-off targets relating to a particular project. They can also be standing targets dealing with the day-to-day operations of the job. The second method is *to determine the level of competency* that the individual must achieve. Competencies will be dealt with in more detail in Chapter 6 but the main link with performance is that they can be set out as required organisational behaviours for which the employee should aim.

Both methods inevitably use some form of *rating scale*. With targets, it may seem straightforward in that a target is either achieved or not achieved. In reality, there are numerous situations where targets are nearly achieved or not achieved due to certain extraneous factors. It is, therefore, normal for the outcome of the exercise to be some form of rating. With competencies, rather than measuring employees as competent or not competent, a rating scale is normally utilised ranging from 'not competent', through 'developing competence' and 'partly competent' to 'fully competent'.

There is considerable controversy concerning the benefits and difficulties arising from both of these measures. In this section, a detailed analysis will be given of each of these methods. The final part will discuss and compare their benefits and the difficulties involved.

ESTABLISHING TARGETS

There is a strong body of research that supports the theory that the setting of goals leads to the overall performance improvement of the employees concerned. Locke and Latham (1990) provided evidence that virtually any type of action that is able to be measured and controlled can be improved as long as the goal is accepted by the individual and the goal relates to the performance criteria being used. Moreover, realistic, hard, specific goals produce better performance than easy goals or no goals at all.

Goals and targets improve performance through four main mechanisms:

- They direct the attention of the employee to what needs to be achieved
- They mobilise the effort put in by the employee
- They increase the persistence of the employee in their desire to reach the goal
- They get employees to think carefully about the right strategies they need to employ to achieve the targets.

A final point from Locke and Latham's research was that commitment to a goal can be considerably improved if employees participate in the goal-setting process.

These theories were integrated into an early form of target-setting called 'Management by Objectives' (Humble 1972), which was very influential in the UK in the 1970s. Under this system, the organisational targets were cascaded down the hierarchy so each manager had a set of targets to achieve. For a period of a few years, this method of management was seen as a panacea to the ills of British industry but the system failed to produce the expected success. This was due to a number of external factors, specifically the appalling industrial relations of that period and the two oil crises of that decade, which made any form of target-setting extremely challenging.

To achieve the best results from an objectives-based system, there are a number of essential requirements:

Ensure that the targets set are in the SMART mode. This acronym helps to set out the key features of a successful set of targets.

1   Firstly, they should be *specific* and *stretching. Specific* means that they are transparent and not open to dispute. To set *stretching* targets supports further aspects of goal theory, which states that motivation and performance are higher when goals are diffi-cult but accepted, support is given to achieve them and feedback is regular and valued.
2   Secondly, targets should be *measurable* so that all sides can agree when they are achieved (or not). Measurable targets also make interim feedback so much easier.
3   Thirdly, targets should be *agreed* and *achievable*. If employees disagree with the

targets because they find them too difficult to achieve, they may well set out to prove this by determining to fail.

4   Fourthly, targets should be *realistic* and *relevant*, which makes them more attractive to all the parties.

5   Finally, they should be *time-related* so that it is clear at what point they should be achieved.

Review the targets at regular intervals. The external environment is constantly changing and the targets need to be adjusted to meet those changes. This is not to say that changes should be made each week or month, but there can be no sacrosanct target that will last for years. Organisational life is just not like that these days.

Setting the right number of targets. The right number of targets is difficult to judge. If an individual had a large number of targets, say 25 or 30, the process of monitoring and measuring these targets would be insuperably complex. If there is only one target, too much is at stake on this one target from the employee's viewpoint. Many organisations reach a compromise and provide for employees to have a minimum and maximum number of specific targets – usually from around four to ten. At Fabergé's Seacroft site, employees had three main targets, while, for AstraZeneca, employees can choose in the range of three to seven (IDS 2003).

The way that targets are set out can be in a number of forms, for example:

■   Sales employees will have a schedule that will set out the target volume of sales and the ideal breakdown between products.

■   Production employees will have a schedule of product throughput.

■   Accounts employees will have a target of invoices to be issued or payments to be processed.

The timing in a target may be of vital importance. In contracting, for example, if projects are late, penalties are often incurred. Employees responsible for some part of a major project will themselves have very important deadlines as a target because, if they are late, it can have a severe knock-on effect upon other parts of the project. A clear example here are the many contracts that were signed for the 2012 London Olympic Games where all had very clear time targets throughout their organisations, as the fate of the Games rested on whether they met the deadlines or not. The clear deadlines were a template for the performance management system for all of the managers involved in delivering the Games venues on time and to specification. On a less weighty note, the targets for a computer programmer may be to complete and test a new programme by Christmas or a human resources manager's target may be to complete the recruitment for a new site by a specific date.

Table 5.1 and Figure 5.3 present two actual forms of target-setting, showing the different approaches from two organisations in the public sector.

Table 5.1 Performance target examples used in an Australian university

	Target
1 Academic	Publish three quality research papers in a refereed journal in accordance with approved ECU research criteria by [end of year]. Demonstrate through student subject evaluation data a UTEI score of at least [minimum accepted % score] for all teaching subjects in Semester 1.
2 Managerial	Increase the number of scholarships available to Business and Law students with a minimum of $5,000 per scholarship by [end of year].
3 Marketing	Achieve attendance of at least 150 guests at national business conference in [year].
4 Administration	Organise and provide administrative support to [x] committees, including the development and distribution of agendas and minutes at least two weeks beforehand.

Source: Edith Cowan University; extracted from internal documentation, 2008.

Targets can also be set for teams. The credit control department may have a target to reduce average payment time to a certain level (say, twenty days) within six months. The design team may have a target to produce a new product design within six months. An engineering department may have a target of a new factory layout to be designed, planned and implemented to be ready for operation at the end of the summer factory closure.

A more recent development has been the concept of the 'Balanced Scorecard' and an example of how this operates at Sainsbury's is shown in case study 5.1

COMPETENCY-BASED SYSTEMS

The competency movement originated in 1973 when David McClelland, working in the educational field in the US, wrote a paper suggesting that personal competencies, which he defined as *motives* and *personality traits*, are a better means of predicting

Figure 5.3
Example of
technical
objective,
Dartford Council

Source: Internal
Dartford Council
documentation.

Target: SD4
Directorship: Development and Leisure

Target Title: Service Delivery
Target Description: CDM Regulations

1. Address requirements of Construction (Design and Management) Regulations 1994 (CDM) authority wide in liaison with Drainage and Corporate Property by 1 July.

2. Prepare draft procedure documents for discussion by 1 April.

3. Prepare draft documents for Notification to Health and Safety Executive, Safety Plan format and Procedure Notes by 1 April.

CASE STUDY 5.1 BALANCED SCORECARD AT SAINSBURY'S

Sainsbury's adopted the 'Steering Wheel' in the early 2000s as a method of measuring how well the organisation was performing and to communicate this in a direct but powerful way to employees. It was also linked to an individual's own performance. As shown in Figure 5.4, the performance measures are divided into four sectors, customers, finance, people and operations, as originally set out by Kaplan and Norton (1996). Within each sector, specific measurable objectives are defined with the outcome communicated within the organisation on a regular basis. There are two development reviews, October for the half year and March for the full year, when the organisational performance is matched up with the individual's performance and a discussion takes place with the employee. Ratings are applied against the achievement of targets and the improvements in behaviours over the period and a 'pen sketch' results, dividing employees into six categories ranging from 'top' through 'strong', 'acceptable' to 'low'.

Linking the performance management scheme to the Balanced Scorecard is seen as essential to ensure each employee understands how their actions and achievements gel into the total organisational picture.

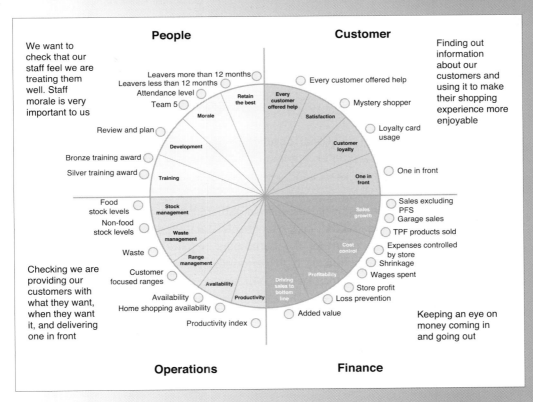

Figure 5.4
Balanced Scorecard at Sainsbury's

5	Anticipates customer requirements. Works with the customer to develop the business relationship	Sets customer expectations at a high but achievable level. Win–win situations sought between self and customer	Seen by customer as a partner	Always listens to the customer and suggests improvements to their wants	An ambassador
4	Seeks to anticipate customer requirements. Listens to customers and influences customers views	Asks customers for feedback and follows customer comments through	Sought by customers as an advisor	Performs in ways that enhance both personal and public image	
3	Reacts to customer requirements. Understands customer's viewpoint	Accepts ownership of customer problems and complaints. Adds value to the business relationship	Customers satisfied. Performs in line with reputation and image		
2	Performs own job without proper regard for customer opinion. Needs constant reminding about customer skills	Customers sometimes dissatisfied. Falls short of customer first value		Co-operation	
				Responsiveness	
				Customer relationships	
1	Limited awareness of customer needs or the effect of own actions. Adds no value to the relationship			Identifying customer needs	

Figure 5.5
'The customer comes first' measurement grid

occupational success than traditional psychometrics such as IQ and aptitude tests. McClelland's (1973) work was to be enormously influential. Of particular interest was the idea that the factors or inputs associated with individual success could be identified, and then taught to others.

Support for the competency movement has gathered strength in recent years, chiefly as a reaction to what is seen as the rigid, quantifiable, data-obsessed objectives methods. Encouraging the employee to adopt the behaviours required by the organisation and following the behaviours exhibited by high performers in the post are seen as a more coherent and broader approach to achieving improved employee performance.

In Chapter 2, an example of drawing up a person specification around the required competencies was explained. It is a natural progression to measure employees' performance against those preferred competencies. The competencies, and the preferred behaviour that measures them, need to be drawn up.

Figure 5.5 shows an extract from the competency measures used in a telecommunications company. They developed a framework centred around their set of values, namely:

- The customer comes first (measured in Figure 5.5)
- Total commitment to quality
- Teamwork makes a winning team
- Development of employee empowerment and responsibility
- Communication is open and honest.

The extract shown in Figure 5.5 relates to the value 'The customer comes first' and it shows the five levels, or ratings, that have been constructed against which employees can be judged. The judgements on the ratings are usually made by the employee's manager, although some organisations have a more sophisticated judgement process, involving a number of different sources, such as 360-degree appraisal, which will be described shortly.

TIMING OF MEASUREMENT

For each scheme, it is normal for there to be at least one main scheduled meeting when the manager will discuss the employee's performance with them in detail. Many organisations will incorporate two or more such meetings into their scheme as a year is seen to be too distant a time for discussion of such an important subject. At the Scottish Prison Service, scheduled meetings take place twice a year, while, for Microsoft, informal one-to-one meetings are encouraged much more often (IDS 2003).

WHICH SYSTEM IS BEST? TARGET-SETTING OR COMPETENCIES?

Target-setting – the pitfalls

In terms of objectivity, it would appear that the target-setting approach wins hands-down. Targets are agreed and there should be a clear system of how they can be measured so there should be no argument or need to make judgements. Either the three-monthly sales target was met or the employee failed to meet it. Either the materials were sourced by the purchasing department and in place in the factory on time or they were late. But, as indicated earlier, it is seldom this easy. Here are a few situations that can cast cloud over the objectivity accolade:

Case 1: Moving the goalposts. The annual target for sales (part of the overall company business plan) is set in the light of a poor economic situation where sales are difficult to come by. As a sales representative, you work hard and, six months into the year, you are ahead of budget. As pay is partly determined by whether you are ahead of the target, you are feeling confident and pleased. The board then announce a revised business plan on the basis that the economic situation is picking up. The sales target is then increased by 15 per cent. From a position of being ahead of target, you are now only just up to the new target. The board will argue that, if they do not increase the target, they will fall behind their competitors or give more pay to the sales force than they deserve in the light of the economic circumstances. You do not believe this is a fair move from your viewpoint.

Case 2: Taking the goalposts away. One of your major targets is to produce a revised working plan for the warehouse which will involve increasing the number of shifts and introducing annual hours. This has to be completed within six months. After three months, you have worked hard and spent a lot of time on this project, with a revised system in draft form. The company then decides to sell the warehouse as part of a general restructuring. You will get no credit at all for the work you have done.

Case 3: Changing the rules of the game. You run the credit control department and you are jointly charged with a systems analyst to introduce a new computerised system. Halfway through the period, the systems analyst leaves the company and a new one is assigned to the project. He has different views on a number of points (some of which are quite sensible) but these are not resolved in time to meet the deadline. You have failed on this target.

There are other criticisms of a system based solely on objectives/targets:

Are the objectives evenly matched?
It is all too easy for some employees to be seen as having 'soft' objectives, ones that are too easy to achieve, while others are set objectives that are too stretching. This may not occur too often in large departments, such as sales, where targets are similar (even so, difficulties can occur here when comparing sales territories, for example). When employees all have different jobs, however, such as in an administrative setting, it is almost impossible to ensure that the objectives are of equal difficulty. Some will have an easier set of objectives than others. The outcome is that some average employees with soft objectives may appear as if they are high performers and, contrary-wise, some top performers come out with only average performance.

Too narrow focused
The individual may be tempted to put all their efforts into achieving their own objectives and treat the rest of their work as less important. After all, if they are to be measured on those specific objectives, this is a strong temptation. The outcome is that their work becomes unbalanced, important routine work can be neglected and unexpected problems may not be tackled with the required enthusiasm.

Do they work against team building?
An individual employee, focused on their objectives, will also be tempted to neglect other members of the team or other teams in the organisation. It is not uncommon for the employee to indicate 'I am sorry but I cannot help – I am too busy working on my objectives – I have a

deadline.' This can have a severe effect upon both the short-term achievements, which can only happen when employees work together as a team (getting a contract completed on time, getting a complex order despatched to a customer), and upon the long-term culture of the organisation where team-working may be a required value.

Is everything measurable?

Not all jobs have easily measurable objectives. Take human resources, for example. Although examples can be given of reduced absence rates, recruitment on time, policy documents produced, training courses completed and reports that need to be completed, such as on-exit interviews or comparative pay rates, it does not take too long before one may be scratching about for further significant objectives that go to the heart of one person's job. Much of human resources activity relates to overall employee performance, attitudes, relationships and competencies, which are not too easy to measure, especially on the individual level.

In other occupations, considerable care has to be taken with what is measured. In the police force, you cannot measure on the basis of number of arrests. If you use the measure of clear-up rates, you run the risk of repeating the scandal in one force in the 2000s who were found to have colluded with burglars to get them to admit to very high numbers of burglaries that they did not commit (in return for lower charges and sentences) so that the clear-up rate improved greatly. (Incidentally, it was only when the number of identical burglaries continued and the real villains were apprehended by the police force in the next county that the fiddle came to light!) A final pause for thought. Would you like your operation to be carried out by a surgeon who is measured by the number of operations carried out?

Is setting targets self-defeating?

Setting targets may help to change and direct behaviour but it can also have a more unfortunate effect on employees who may direct energy and resources to subvert the intention of the target-setting. As Broadbent (2007), in her investigation of performance management systems in higher education indicated:

> The use of targets and measurement has long been of interest to accounting researchers who have shown the ingenuity of humankind in manipulating their successful achievement. The nature of the problem this provides was nicely encapsulated in a comment made by the BBC's economic correspondent Evan Davies who noted, in a piece on government performance, that as soon as a measure was used to monitor behaviour it became useless.
>
> (2007: 5)

Given these difficulties, should we not concentrate our energy on an effective competency framework?

There are, unfortunately, difficulties here as well.

Competencies – the main pitfall: ratings

Even when systems are in place to assist managers to rate on a consistent basis (such as set out in Figure 5.5), managers may not keep to the straight and narrow:

Halo and horns effect. Managers may rate employees on the basis of their personal relationships rather than by an objective measure of their competencies and abilities. Friendships may be regarded as too important to be spoiled by the harsh realities of a poor rating. On the other hand, a good performance can be ignored if an employee does not meet with the manager's overall approval.

Difficulty in damning people. Even without personal prejudice, a good majority of managers do find it difficult to give their employees a bad rating. Having to face employees at an appraisal interview and justify their criticisms can be an experience that managers do not want to go through. It is much easier to simply give an average rating on the scale and hope the employee will improve anyway. This problem can also lead to *rating drift* where managers are happy to raise the rating of their employees but never reduce the ratings, even when it is justified. Marshall and Wood (2000) describe a moribund system in the US Navy where a large proportion of the officers gave inflated ratings for their crew to secure promotion for their junior officers, to avoid potential conflicts with poorly performing staff and to minimise the risk of being seen as a poor manager.

Recency error. When coming to a decision on a rating on an annual appraisal, a manager may be too influenced by an event that happened a few days or weeks earlier that is fresh in their minds. Let us take the example of an employee whose performance with customers had been far from satisfactory for most of the year. In the month before the appraisal, there was a major achievement resulting in a letter of thanks from a customer. From the manager's viewpoint, it would be difficult and demotivating to dwell on their generally unsatisfactory customer-care competency and more tempting to concentrate on their recent success. However, this would result in putting the total rating out of balance.

Clone error. A manager may regard the way they act and their methods of working to be the best practice. It is all too easy for employees who take a different approach to be rated lower, despite evidence that the differing methods work just as well.

Do competencies relate to performance? There is much debate in academic circles as to the answer to this question. Is performance all about achievement of goals or can behaviour itself be regarded as a type of performance? In general, most psychologists come down on the side of a close relationship, such as Markus *et al.* who concluded that: 'Performance benefits are promised by the various definitions which include the causal or instrumental relationship of competencies and job performance and competencies and organisational performance' (2005: 118).

In practice, however, there may be occasions where the two may not operate in tandem. Take the example of a credit control administrator. One major part of the job involves chasing up old debt by telephone. One of the competencies of the job would be 'customer relations'. The administrator may have a very high rating with customer relations in that they build up a rapport with the customer, treat them with respect and understanding and have good listening skills, among other measures. But their job is to collect the overdue debt and, if their competency is too customer oriented, it runs the risk of the debt not being paid.

There are also numerous examples of athletes who are extremely competent at their chosen expertise at a world-class performance level but who never manage to produce the results on the international stage.

VARIATIONS ON RATING SYSTEMS

Because the rating element of performance management is the most difficult area to get right, a number of variations have been produced to try to ensure that the system is fair, robust and more sophisticated.

Under *Behaviourally Anchored Rating Scales (BARS)*, a scale is established that reflects the dimensions expressed by employees' behaviour. An example of a scale is set out in Table 5.2. The scale is normally drawn up in three stages. Firstly, examples of behaviour reflecting effective and ineffective job performance are obtained from people who are

Table 5.2 Example of BARS: teamwork dimension

Behavioural patterns	Points 50 max.
Consistently seeks to help others Tolerant and supportive of colleagues Contributes ideas and takes full part in group meetings	40
Listens to colleagues Willing to change own plans to fit in Keeps colleagues in the picture about own activities	30
Mixes willingly enough Is not aware of what colleagues are doing Inclined to alter arrangements to suit self	20
Always criticising others Lets everyone else do the more unpopular jobs Never goes out of the way to help or co-operate	10 0

Source: Adapted from Fletcher, C. (2008) *Appraisal Development and Feedback*, 4th ed. Routledge.

held to be expert about the job to be rated, which is then checked by a second group on the relevance of the behavioural examples within the dimension chosen (in Table 5.2, teamwork is the dimension). The experts then place each example of behaviour on to the scale. If the experts place the behaviour at different points on the scale, this example is usually deleted because a high level of clarity and consensus is required. The advantage of the scheme is that the ratings are anchored against carefully agreed observed behavioural patterns. However, it does take considerable time and effort to draw up. Getting experts to agree upon the scale can be difficult, given the ultimately subjective nature of behaviour.

With *Behavioural Observation Scales (BOS)*, the end result is the same with a series of performance dimensions linked to behavioural descriptions but each example is given a separate rating and the overall rating is an average of the ratings. Extracting three examples from Table 5.2, would give:

1   Consistently seeks to help others

Almost always   1   2   3   4   5   *Almost never*

2   Willing to change own plans to fit in

Almost always   1   2   3   4   5   *Almost never*

3   Volunteers for fair shares of unpopular work

Almost always   1   2   3   4   5   *Almost never*

DRAWING A CONCLUSION

In deciding on which system to use – objectives or competencies – organisations will be aware that both methods have clear advantages and benefits. It is no surprise then to find that organisations are deciding to incorporate both sets of measurement in their performance management framework. Individuals have their job description or profile, which sets out their day-to-day responsibilities and accountabilities; they will also agree certain objectives for the period in question; and they will also be measured against the competencies that apply to their job as part of the competency framework. By having both methods of measurement, the advantages of both are combined. On the other hand, it can lead to a performance management system that is complicated and difficult to grasp, especially for new employees.

If both methods are utilised in tandem, a great deal of communication and training is necessary for managers and employees to understand how it works. It is no coincidence that a new head of HR will often ditch the 'complex, bureaucratic scheme that nobody really understood' as one of their first actions. Some years later, their successor will probably do the same.

DOCUMENTATION

Whatever scheme is used, there has to be some type of form that will record an individual's performance as related to the way they are measured. A major drawback for many schemes is that these forms are sometimes lengthy and complicated; it is not unknown for some long-established schemes to have as many as ten pages to be completed. Although they are designed to be comprehensive and give support to the process, the parties concerned, especially the managers who may have to complete them for up to 20 employees, often baulk at having to fill them in.

Therefore, the forms should be as simple and short as is consistent with the nature of the scheme with all superfluous information or sections ruthlessly extracted. The emphasis should always be on the form being a working document, to be constantly updated and the basis of a number of informal meetings during the period concerned. It should not simply, when completed, be sent to the human resources department for filing, although they may need a copy if decisions on pay are related to the individual's performance.

An example of the documentation for one rating scale for competencies is in Figure 5.6. In this banking example, negative and positive indicators are given with clear instructions on a marking key to assist in the rating process.

A simpler version, used by a local council catering division and called a 'job chat' is shown in Figure 5.7.

Stage 3: Providing feedback

Types of feedback systems:

- Type A: Feedback can be based on the traditional method of an assessment made by the employee's manager, augmented by a degree of self-assessment, and then given in a one-to-one meeting, commonly called the *appraisal interview*.
- Type B: In recent years, however, *360-degree appraisal* has become increasingly popular, where feedback is produced by a number of sources, including colleagues, subordinates and internal and external customers, and then fed back to the employee. This normally takes place through a third party.

TYPE A: TRADITIONAL FEEDBACK SYSTEM

The performance review interview

Time is set aside for the employee and manager to have an extended discussion, which reviews the past period and agrees plans for the next period. The period in question is usually a year but some organisations have decided that the process is so important that it needs to take place twice or four times a year. It is not an easy job to carry out. Where independent research has been carried out questioning managers and employees in

Managers and Appointed Staff
Competencies Sheet 1

Name of Member of Staff:

Branch/Department:

Marking Key: (Please mark the appropriate box like this ▨)

1	**Frequently** fails to display the appropriate qualities and attitudes.
2	**Occasionally** fails to display the appropriate qualities and attitudes.
3	**Generally** displays the appropriate qualities and attitudes to a satisfactory level.
4	**Occasionally** displays above average qualities and attitudes.
5	**Frequently** displays the appropriate qualities and attitudes to a high level.
6	**Consistently** displays the appropriate qualities and attitudes to the highest level.

Voluntary Self Appraisal: The appropriate mark 1 to 6 may be inserted in each self appraisal box.

Competency	Negative indicators	Marking	Positive indicators
Strategic Awareness ...The extent to which the appraisee is aware of the Bank's competitive situation, is able to recognise business opportunities and threats and can relate these wider issues to own area of responsibility	• Out of touch with strategic events and their results • Infrequently identifies competitive opportunities and threats • Sees own work in isolation from the wider context	6 5 4 3 2 1 Self Appraisal Mark	• Clearly aware of strategic events occurring outside and inside the Group • Identifies competitive opportunities and threats • Sees how own work fits into the wider context
Initiative ...The extent to which the appraisee will promote proactively and take personal responsibility for the achievement of goals and changes which are beneficial to the Group	• Takes a rigid and narrow view of own responsibilities • Conforms to established ways of doing things without identifying improvements • Tends to resist change or gives little help to those initiating change	6 5 4 3 2 1 Self Appraisal Mark	• Expands own responsibilities to seek business opportunities • Identifies ways of improving the way work is done • Takes the action needed to ensure that changes happen
Decisiveness ...The readiness to take decisions and render judgements even though they may be difficult and/or unpopular	• Reluctant to take decisions; will disown decisions • Unable to explain or justify decisions • Gives way too easily when pressurised or dogmatically supports decisions that cannot be defended	6 5 4 3 2 1 Self Appraisal Mark	• Makes decisions and takes responsibility for their results • Easily explains and justifies decisions • Reviews a decision if new information makes this essential
Technical knowledge and experience ...The degree to which the appraisee demonstrates breadth and depth of technical knowledge and experience in the performance of his/her duties	• Shows little evidence of technical expertise in performance • Content to rely on basic knowledge, makes little effort to keep abreast of technical developments • Unable to apply technical knowledge and experience in practical situations	6 5 4 3 2 1 Self Appraisal Mark	• Possesses a high level of technical expertise and experience relevant to present duties • Keeps abreast of relevant technical development • Applies technical knowledge and experience to enhance job performance

	Initials
Reporting Manager	
Appraisee	

Figure 5.6
Competency rating scales at a clearing bank (detail)

SHIRE COUNTY CATERING

JOB CHAT SUMMARY FORM ... Example

DATE OF JOB CHAT: _____

EMPLOYEE'S NAME: Jane Smith*   SCHOOL: *ABC Primary*
JOB TITLE: *Head of Kitchen*   SCHOOL NUMBER: *40006*
LENGTH OF SERVICE: *3 years*   NAME OF INTERVIEWER: *Teresa Brown*
NO. OF HOURS PER WEEK: *25*   POSITION: *Contract Supervisor*

JOB STANDARDS:

(PLEASE TICK)	MEETS OR EXCEEDS STANDARDS	ROOM FOR IMPROVEMENT
SKILLS AND KNOWLEDGE TO ACHIEVE DUTIES		/
MANAGES WORK SCHEDULE	/	
QUALITY OF WORK	/	

COMMENTS:

Jane is a new Head of Kitchen, been in post 4 months. She lacks confidence to try out new ideas. Manages existing work schedule, but would like to develop the menu range. Very good relationship with staff.

TRAINING AND DEVELOPMENT:

DEVELOPMENT AREAS IDENTIFIED: *Requires confidence building*
                                  Needs to broaden knowledge on SCC standards

TRAINING AND DEVELOPMENT NEEDS FOR NEXT 12 MONTHS: Attend practical skills course (M)
          (INDICATE HIGH, MEDIUM OR LOW PRIORITY) *Visit 2 other school sites (H)*

CAREER PROGRESSION: *Happy at present*

COMMENTS:

Jane felt she could have had more support moving from G.A. to H. of K. position. Perhaps a weekly visit from the Contract Supervisor for the first month.

SIGNATURE OF EMPLOYEE: *Jane Smith*

SIGNATURE OF INTERVIEWER: *T. Brown*

*Not a real employee

Figure 5.7
Job chat
summary form

organisations, the participants are generally very unhappy with the interviewing process (Mathison and Vinja 2010). There is, however, a strong correlation between the satisfaction with the interview and the positive relationship between the employee and their manager carrying out the interview.

In carrying out the interview, there are many similarities with the selection interviewing guidelines set out in Chapter 3. The same principles apply of careful preparation, effective listening and questioning, together with efficient note-taking and following up. The major differences relate to dealing with areas of unsatisfactory performance and handling areas of disagreement. More important is the fact that the interview is with an employee where there is a continuing relationship and where comments, statements and decisions made can have an enduring effect upon that relationship. So it is even more important that the interview is handled well.

Before the interview

As a basis for the interview, it is customary for both parties to complete one part of the documentation. For the manager, the form will ask for an examination of the employee's performance against the agreed measures and to point out any important areas of success and failure. This will include ratings, where appropriate. The employee will be asked their views on the same subjects with an opportunity for comments on factors that may have influenced their performance over that period. The employee is usually asked to assess and rate (where appropriate) their own performance. Both parties may be asked to consider any necessary training, development and support plus consideration of general career development.

The interview itself

The purpose of the interview is often forgotten. It is sometimes seen as a combat, where the contestants, armed with their data, examples, accusations and excuses, fight to the finish to try to win their point of view. This is all too prevalent where pay increases are largely determined by the outcome of the interview. At the other extreme, it can be seen as something of an embarrassment where both sides have a tentative discussion but neither wants to risk their current placid relationship by drawing out any unpleasant truths. In the IPD research (Armstrong and Baron 2005), 31 per cent of individual employees reported that they did not get useful feedback from their interview and 38 per cent were not motivated by the meeting. Over a quarter reported dissatisfaction with the way their manager carried out the meeting. From the other side of the table, 20 per cent of managers reported they were not comfortable when conducting the meetings.

It is important from the outset to agree what the meeting is for and what will be the satisfactory outcomes. These can be summed up as:

- Agreement on the level of performance achieved
- Agreement on the factors that influenced this level of performance
- Outline agreement on the challenges/targets for the next period
- Agreement on what support needs to be arranged for the employee.

Sony's performance management scheme (IDS 2011) places great emphasis on ensuring the scheme is solidly based, as shown in case study 5.2.

CASE STUDY 5.2 PERFORMANCE MANAGEMENT SCHEME AT SONY EUROPE LTD

Sony Europe, who employed 1,400 people in the UK and 4,200 people across Europe, launched its new performance management process in 2009 called 'MyWorkstyle' in response to feedback from line managers and employees that its previous appraisal scheme was too complicated, over-structured and rigid and that it appeared to be imposed by the HR department.

In response to feedback, the organisation based the new system on five building blocks:

1   A correct mindset – present in all the parties where employees need to own and drive the process and use it to their own advantage, especially in appreciating the need to develop themselves and increase their engagement to the organisation.
2   Clear consequences arising from the PM event – so that underperformance is addressed and high performance is built into the talent management process. In addition, managers should be rewarded for developing their staff and for tackling poor performance rather than ignoring it or passing it on to another manager.
3   Ensuing the correct skills are utilised – in handling appraisals, in generating training that is fit-for-purpose for each employee and making use of online tools.
4   Making sure the system of appraisal is effective – by ensuring the forms and systems used were more flexible and controlled by the parties concerned. The parties can use a structured form or a blank sheet of paper, for example. Reviews can take place either twice a year or on a quarterly basis. Sectors of the business can also choose from a menu of rating scales.
5   Ensuring the model and processes were properly used – that employees were well prepared for the PM discussions, to be able to review their strengths and weaknesses with adult debate and guaranteed follow-up from the outcomes, whether to recognise and reward an individual for a good piece of work or plan skills development training.

Overall, the scheme was to concentrate on development and looking to the future rather than simply focusing on staff meeting immediate needs, although the eventual ratings are taken into account when determining individual rewards.

(Source: IDS 2011)

In Figure 5.6 on page 198 the diagram sets out an example in practice from a clearing bank of some of the major elements skills that can be emphasised. Here, it is vital to get the employee to recognise their own strengths and weaknesses. The self-assessment form and a review of the agreed action at the time of the last review are good starting points. However, it is the quality of the questioning and listening skills that are essential to draw out a full understanding and agreement of the difficult areas. Questions here could include:

1   'Do you think you could handle this situation any better when you face it again?'
2   'In your involvement with this project, would you have done it any differently with the benefit of hindsight?'
3   'The figures for Smith and Jones appear to be rather better than yours; are there any reasons for this?'
4   'This was clearly a difficult area for you; what help would you need for the next period?'

Where differences of opinion exist, specifically on the performance ratings, time must be given for effective feedback and discussion. The feedback from the manager must be based, first and foremost, on the facts of the situation, accurately described, not an arbitrary judgement. It should be related to specific behaviour, not impressionistic generalisations. It should be on the basis of presenting the problem and trying to ensure that this problem is solved on a joint basis. It should also be recognised by the manager that a long list of problem areas is truly demoralising for the employee, so only the major two or three difficulties should be detailed or it will result in the employee becoming over-defensive and putting up the shutters. The manager should also accept some of the reasons put forward by the employee, even if they appear doubtful, so that it is clear to the employee that their case has been listened to and not simply shot down in flames.

The interview should not be limited to areas of difficulty. Where the employee has made a substantial contribution or a major improvement, this should be fed back in congratulatory mode. To reinforce this positive feedback, suggestions should be considered as to how this could be followed up. For example, the employee may be asked to coach an inexperienced colleague in this area or to take some part in a training exercise. It is particularly helpful to express appreciation where tasks have not come easily and where the employee has put in considerable effort in their own time.

The interview should be completed by an agreed summary of the conclusions reached and an action plan for the future, which includes the major changes in the employee's responsibilities, the additional areas of help they will be given (training, time and resources) and a time span for implementation. This should be confirmed on the review form and signed by both parties with each having a copy.

This prescriptive approach is rarely followed by organisations with the result that most managers and subordinates dislike the appraisal interview, especially when it contains negative features in the feedback (Lawler 1990) and few employees concede that they gain much benefit at all from the interview (Bradley and Ashkanasy 2001). This has disappointed most human resource practitioners and researchers, who have looked for a more radical method of operating a performance management system, such as 360-degree appraisal.

Moderating process

Most organisations, while delegating the rating process to the line managers, will build in a system of moderation whereby the results are considered as a whole by the next level of management. The human resources department, as a disinterested third party, will often assist in tricky umpiring decisions. The difficulty here is that any change in the ratings may be seen by the manager as undermining their authority. This becomes even more difficult to resolve if the moderation process is taking place following an appeal by the employee.

Case study 5.3 sets out the difficulties faced by BT Operate under a traditional performance management scheme and how they have attempted to solve them.

TYPE B: 360-DEGREE APPRAISAL

Traditional appraisal schemes suffer from one major problem: if there is a difference of opinion as to the employee's performance that cannot be resolved between the manager and the employee, the basis of the whole performance management process is undermined. Let us take a simple example where a switchboard operator is rated as below average on the measure of 'co-operation'. The manager puts forward examples on which their rating is based but, despite a long discussion, the employee regards these as isolated and atypical examples. The switchboard operator is convinced that the manager's opinion is wrong because nobody has complained to them. The employee is upset by the rating and convinced that it is unfair. The rest of the interview takes place under an atmosphere of resentment and resignation.

In this example, the manager will have to make the judgement as to co-operation largely based on information that comes from third parties because the manager's own experience of the employee's co-operative behaviour may well be very limited. This is not unusual. Many employees provide a service for other departments and external customers and their managers only have a rough snapshot of how they are actually performing. They may base their opinion on anecdotal evidence, good and bad, gathered from a limited number of sources in an unsystematic way.

This is where 360-degree appraisal comes in. Through obtaining information from a variety of sources, a more all-round version of an employee's performance can be gathered together and the information, because it comes from a number of sources, is more convincing to all parties. A second influence has been more subtle. Organisations are starting to talk about being 'feedback-rich', which has been part of the cultural change from being a 'command and control' structure to one that is based on 'support and enable' concepts. Table 5.3 shows the typical skill sets required for effective performance management under the two different cultures.

CASE STUDY 5.3 PERFORMANCE MANAGEMENT AT BT OPERATE

BT Operate runs the core networks, systems and security with BT Plc, employing nearly 18,000 people. Focusing on performance standards and good performance practice has been central to its recent business transformation. The company has been applying the principles set out in the corporate review of performance management in 2010, which has meant a sharp focus on getting personal objectives aligned throughout the organisation, clarity about performance standards and a clear line of sight between individual, team and business performance. There has also been significant support and training for 'people managers' to enable them to deliver better performance management practice.

The road, however, has not been an easy one and implementing better PM practice has had its challenges. These included:

■ Some employee concerns at inconsistent and poor PM practice, as well as examples of command-and-control style from some managers.

■ The quarterly 'levelling' process of comparing and standardising performance ratings across the company was the focus for much of this concern. This was generally perceived as rigidly applying a forced distribution to deliver a targeted proportion of underperformers.

■ The process was seen to be largely driven by the HR function and this gave some managers an excuse to avoid responsibility for the final rating awarded to their people.

BT Operate is learning from these experiences and has implemented improvements as follows:

■ A common framework of five performance ratings has been introduced for all employees, which more clearly differentiates between ratings of 'unsatisfactory' and 'development needed'. There is now clarity that 'we won't force a predetermined distribution of performance'.

■ Improved communications and training are now provided for employees and their managers.

■ Quarterly assessment and levelling continues with the principles of the process now stressing that everyone should know what 'expected performance' looks like for their job and be 'supported to meet those expectations'.

■ There is a strong application of 'two-way performance deal', which sets out the responsibilities of people and their managers in the process.

(Source: Brown and Hirsh 2011)

Table 5.3 Cultural approaches to performance management

Command and control	Support and enable
Set clear targets	Agree clear targets, working parameters
Give instructions	Consult
Check work	Discuss performance
Identify deviations	Jointly identify difficulties
Correct deviations	Coach and guide to solving deviations
Give criticisms	Provide balanced feedback
Organise	Encourage self-management
Plan schedules	Create an environment where employees are motivated
Task review	People review

Source: France, S. (1997) *360-Degree Appraisal.* Industrial Society, London.

It is commonplace for organisations to carry out customer-care surveys (to see where strengths and weaknesses of the whole company operations lie from a customer's viewpoint) and Employee Attitude Surveys (to identify how well employees are managed and valued). It is just one more short step, therefore, to carry out a survey of an individual's performance as seen by a wider strand of customers.

Is this the right name? The name-tag has been fixed to this system because of the familiarity of the word 'appraisal' but organisations who dislike the association of the word 'appraisal' have changed the title to team feedback, 360-degree review or multi-level assessment.

How does it work? There are many versions currently operating and there are aspects that are much debated but the general process is as follows:

Is it carried out for all employees? Most organisations start the process at the top. Rhône-Poulenc, a French water company, centred their first system on their 60 senior managers before it was spread further down the organisation (Jacobs and Floyd 1995). By starting at the top, it sends a message to the rest of the organisation that there is serious intent behind the initiative.

Agreement on the sources of feedback. It is useful to have as many sources of feedback as possible but the cost of processing is quite high, so a balance has to be reached. Between six and nine sources is the norm (see Figure 5.8). The method of selection can vary between the employee concerned selecting their own sources and having their sources selected for them or a compromise whereby the employee selects the required number from a list of

Figure 5.8
360-degree
appraisal –
sources of
feedback

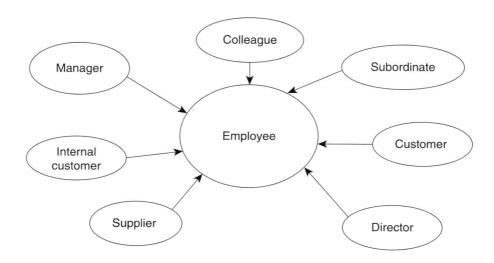

25 or so sources prepared by those organising the scheme. The list should always include the immediate manager, and representatives from subordinates, peers and customers. At Cadbury UK&I, their feedback stretches to family and friends in a form they call '720-degree feedback' for their 150 top managers. As Sarah Smith, head of the L&D Excellence Centre, explained: "'The 720 degree approach gives people a very different view of themselves as leaders and individuals". Despite being an anonymous process, she conceded that it was obvious which sections were filled in by her husband and grandmother' (*People Management* 2010: 15).

Should the scheme be voluntary or compulsory? It is generally voluntary because this accentuates the culture of openness and responsibility. In reality, it is likely that there will be internal pressures brought to bear on those who do not volunteer, especially if the scheme starts to obtain good results.

What form do the reports take? They vary only slightly from the conventional performance management documentation but, in the interests of objectivity and ease of processing, most simply ask for ratings, rather than individual comments. An exception to this, a peer assessment by Eastern Group, which asks for specific examples, is given in Figure 5.9. The forms are generally completed on an anonymous basis, although this is limited by the method of choice of the respondents.

How is the feedback given? This is an area that differs most from the conventional process. The information from the respondents needs to be processed anonymously to give some

EASTERN GROUP plc

MIDDLE MANAGEMENT COMPETENCIES

Peer
Assessment

Try to complete this form as honestly as you can. If you wish, you can use the spaces below each category to provide further evidence to support your assessment

The three columns should be interpreted as follows:

IDENTIFIED DEVELOPMENT NEED – refers to an area in which, in your view, the person is not particularly strong and needs to develop significantly.
ALREADY A STRENGTH – refers to an area in which you feel the person being assessed is already competent and has no strong development need.
NOT A PRIORITY DEVELOPMENT NEED – refers to an area which, although perhaps not a strength, is not – given the nature of his/her job or its current demands – a particular priority for development.

1. MANAGING CHANGE	ALREADY A STRENGTH	NOT A PRIORITY DEVELOPMENT NEED	IDENTIFIED DEVELOPMENT NEED
Communicates openly, clearly and often with those affected by and involved in change so that all are aware of the reasons for change, its aim and progress			
Agrees a course of action to achieve new or changed long-term goals			
Agrees intermediate goals, performance measures and contingencies			
Allocates resources effectively to achieve goals			

Can you think of any specific examples of behaviour in support of the assessment you have made within this competency area?

Figure 5.9
Example of competencies at Eastern Group with 360-degree feedback system

average scores. This processing can be carried out by the human resources department or by a third party, which is normally a specialised consultancy. Feedback is then given by that third party to the employee. Some of the information provided in this way can be quite disturbing, so it needs to be handled by a trained facilitator who will then proceed to help the employee develop their own personal development plan. A summarised version of the report may be given to the employee's manager so that an interview can be carried out after a reasonable delay to allow the employee to take on board the information and the consequent behaviour changes that may be required.

A more informal process of 360-degree feedback has been used at the Department for Environment, Food and Rural Affairs, called the 'Pairing for Performance' scheme. Here, 12 managers have been each 'paired' with a volunteer member of their staff, and the 'buddy', as they are called, provides detailed feedback on the performance of the manager at meetings and visits, and in telephone calls and emails in a candid, but constructive way. This helps them to reflect on their performance, preparation, outlook and communication skills. In the public sector, such feedback culture is not common but it has helped both sides to identify and operate better (Allen 2004). A similar scheme has operated at the Department of Health, where 80 of the department's top civil servants have been paired with administrative officers, junior and middle managers who observe their behaviour in a number of situations and then give them face-to-face feedback (Arkin 2011).

Case study 5.4 shows 360-degree feedback of teams of trainee doctors.

Advantages of 360-degree schemes

- The quality of the feedback is high, emanating from a number of sources. Those providing the information are quite likely to be part of the process and to know how crucial it is to be absolutely honest – not to be unpleasantly vindictive and not to simply give neutral responses if they are not appropriate.

- All the experience to date is that employees are more likely to change their behaviour on receiving the results from a collection of sources. They change because they cannot argue with the findings.

- Because managers find the traditional appraisal interview difficult to undertake and we have seen how difficult the process is to get right, 360-degree appraisal will allow such discussions to be carried out on a more even basis.

- It is a strong indication to employees that the performance management is being taken seriously and encourages a feedback-rich culture to develop, with employees at all levels sharing advice on 'How did I do?' or 'Tell me how to improve'.

- Even sceptical academics seem to find that it works, as shown in focus on research 5.4.

CASE STUDY 5.4 360-DEGREE FEEDBACK FOR TRAINEE DOCTORS

Background: This study was to see if the team assessment of behaviours (TAB) 360-degree assessment tool was able to identify interpersonal behaviour problems in doctors in training, to see if feedback was useful, to gauge the value of the process by those involved, and to learn lessons about implementing the process for the future.

Methods: TAB was administered to assess interpersonal behaviours of senior house officers in four hospitals in the West Midlands, UK. In addition, questionnaires were sent to all participants, some were interviewed about the whole process, and records kept of the time involved.

Results: A total of 171 trainee doctors volunteers received 1,378 assessments. The median number of ratings per trainee was 8 (mode 9); 64 per cent of trainees received 'no concern' ratings in all four behaviours (domains) assessed; 21 per cent received one 'some concern' rating; and 15 per cent received more than one 'concern' rating.

Conclusion: Assessors and trainees found the process practical, valuable and fair. Educational supervisors found it valuable, although only 23 per cent learned something new about their trainees. Clinical tutors valued the system. Administrative staff found it time-consuming. The TAB four-domain rating form with its single pass category identified specific concerns about volunteer trainees' professional behaviour. Not all trainees received skilled feedback.

(Source: Whitehouse *et al.* 2007)

Disadvantages

- If it works well and is extended to most groups of employees, the demands on the sources will be very large. A single source may have to provide as many as six or eight feedbacks, which could lead to feedback 'overload'.
- Many operators of the scheme report that it is expensive and time-consuming.
- There are some questions that the sources of feedback may find difficult to answer, especially those related to the employee's achievement of their objectives.
- It is more difficult (but not impossible) to link employees' pay to the process. The sources of the feedback may be more reticent with their information if they know that criticism can lead to a reduced pay increase.
- It is possible that it may lead to political game-playing. Just before the time of 360-degree feedback, employees may ask their manager for favours, such as pay increases or job-stretching and managers may be tempted here to court popularity (Fletcher 2008).

- Until 2003, IBM used 360-degree feedback as part of their annual performance review. This practice was halted as the reviews had become politically charged and were no longer reliable. Since IBM appreciated the value of multiple perspectives, a new employee satisfaction survey was implemented to regain the benefits found in using the survey without the pitfalls.

Research into managers' views of upward appraisal is detailed in focus on research 5.4.

A detailed study over time of the effect of 360-degree feedback (Smithers *et al.* 2005), which examined the outcomes of 24 studies and covered 7,000 managers, found that the

FOCUS ON RESEARCH 5.4 360-DEGREE FEEDBACK AT THE OPEN UNIVERSITY

During the late 1990s, the Open University initiated a 360-degree programme that was competency-based. Those managers choosing to take part received training on the aims of the programme, detailed feedback from their colleagues on their ratings on competencies, tuition on learning styles, as well as one-to-one assistance with the design and implementation of their personal development plan. Using both interviews and questionnaires, the views of the 200 managers who took part in the 360-degree systems were compared with a similar sample of managers who participated in the traditional appraisal system.

The results indicated widespread satisfaction with 360-degree feedback with significantly high mean scores from participants in areas such as:

- Appraisals help my career development
- I get regular feedback on performance
- I am satisfied with the quality and relevance of training
- The best uses are made of my skills.

Many examples were given of managers addressing weaknesses highlighted by the 360-degree process, making progress in areas of personal development and receiving positive feedback from colleagues as a result. Moreover, the positive experience from the scheme led to more favourable assessments of the organisation as a whole.

It was considered that participants appreciated the organisational commitment to developing managers, enjoyed the opportunity for careful diagnosis and tailored, more meaningful training, and heightened their awareness of the organisation's strategic intent.

(Source: Mabey 2001)

ratings of managers increased over successive feedback episodes, which reflected the perception of improved performance of those managers. This was not a huge improvement on average and there was some variability in how much change was observed. They found that, where feedback was used for developmental purposes, it resulted in greater behavioural change.

Overall, therefore, the research and case study evidence indicates that 360-degree feedback has positive outcomes in the majority of cases. This may be linked with the fact that its use is growing. According to CIPD (2009), the use of 360-degree feedback increased from 14 per cent of organisations in 2005 to 20 per cent in 2009.

360-degree feedback and culture of the organisation

Linman (2004) found that success with 360-degree feedback was closely linked with organisational culture. Schemes were operated because they supported a desire for individual growth and openness, and cultures that placed great emphasis on learning and transferring knowledge. Features included:

■ Criticisms are seen as opportunities for improvement
■ Proper framing of feedback method by management which all staff contributed to
■ 360-degree feedback operated at all levels, not just top management or office staff
■ Assurance that feedback will be kept confidential and no attempts made to identify comments from individuals
■ No link to performance pay nor overt link to promotion
■ Development of feedback tool based on organisational goals and values
■ Extensive resources utilised to train workers in appropriate methods to give and receive feedback
■ Support feedback with back-up services or customised coaching.

Stage 4: The outcomes from the performance management process

There are three major outcomes which follow from an effective performance management system: rewards, development, and discipline and redundancy.

REWARDS

We will be looking much more closely at the financial rewards that are based on an employee's performance in Chapter 6. However, the intrinsic rewards of being recognised and congratulated for the good work that has been carried out are a very powerful and effective motivator, as Herzberg (1968) first pointed out. There are also *negative* rewards in that performance data can be the basis of disciplinary proceedings or an important part of the criteria for choosing employees to be made redundant.

DEVELOPMENT

Development can take two forms. The first is career development, where performance data can influence, often decisively, promotion decisions. The second is a personal development plan (PDP) for the employee to help those areas where performance is weak. In other words, the performance management system acts as a training needs analysis. There has been a substantial increase in the use of PDPs over the last 20 years as organisations recognise the need to continually follow up the performance management process and support the employee's development on a permanent basis.

DISCIPLINE AND REDUNDANCY

During Jack Welsh's long reign as CEO of General Electric, he operated a performance management scheme where the managers who received the lowest 10 per cent of ratings were fired, or eased out of the organisation in some other way. The Coalition government announced in 2012 that they would change the system of reviewing civil servants' performance. The outline of their proposals, including the strong emphasis on the disciplinary aspects is set out in case study 5.5.

CAN THE THREE OUTCOMES BE RECONCILED?

There is considerable debate currently on the issue of whether to mix the planned outcomes of a performance management system. There is always the danger that an employee will be unwilling to admit to development needs if this could lead to a lower rating and a consequent smaller salary increase. Without an honest and open discussion, many development needs may not come out into the open and this could affect the future performance of the employee. As Hirsh (2006) has commented, appraisal schemes marked by ratings and pay linked to performance shift the discussion between manager and subordinate on to 'a more nervous and adversarial footing'. Those employees who are fearful of their job will treat the performance management process as a battle that must be won with a refusal to admit to weaknesses or fault.

On the other hand, it would be unusual, to put it mildly, if all the information gained from an effective system does not affect decisions on pay. Given that most organisations now operate a pay system that rewards higher performance in some way, it could be regarded as rather irrational to give the same pay increase to two employees, having identified that one employee performs considerably better than another, or to base pay-increase decisions on a totally different system. As Vicky Bourne of Sanofi-Aventis explained:

I think people are more comfortable with pay increases and bonuses if they can see a direct link to performance than if they feel they are group linked and rewards depend on other people. Generally we hear more requests for direct links between performance and pay. However, we are a commercial organisation and this might be different in other sectors.

(CIPD 2009: 18)

CASE STUDY 5.5 UK COALITION GOVERNMENT PROPOSALS ON PERFORMANCE MANAGEMENT FOR CIVIL SERVANTS

Civil servants consistently identify that poor performance is not tackled effectively. In the last People Survey, only 37 per cent of staff thought that poor performance was dealt with well. It is also true that good performance is often not properly recognised. To ensure that performance management is improved, departments will:

- Implement a common Civil Service *performance framework*, linked to the competency framework, for staff below the SCS during 2012/13. This will identify the top and bottom performers.
- Implement an SCS *appraisal system*, which will identify the top 25 per cent and the bottom 10 per cent. The bottom 10 per cent will need to undertake performance monitoring and improvement planning.
- Implement the new streamlined policy on *managing poor performance*, with shorter timeframes and clearer guidance. This will enable poor performance to be tackled more quickly and effectively. For all staff that remain bottom performers without improvement and are still not meeting the required standards, a decision will quickly be taken over whether they should be exited from the organisation, using this policy.
- Support all managers to implement the new performance framework and explicitly hold them to account for the management of poor performance and attendance through their objectives. Managers are too often slow to identify poor performance or do not feel confident in gathering evidence and giving early honest feedback. Currently, managers are not always supported or challenged to do so, and the obligation to act on poor performance needs to be encouraged.
- Consistently recognise and reward high performance using the new performance management approach to identify potential and develop it effectively across the Civil Service. Recognition can be as simple as a thank you, but can include financial rewards for exceptional work. Departments will develop their reward approach in line with the performance framework.

(Source: Civil Service 2012)

The importance of an effective PM system is demonstrated where an organisation has to make compulsory redundancies. As set out in Chapter 4, decisions on who to elect can only be made fairly by referring to accurate measures of an individual's performance and the PM system results are the best source of this. Unfortunately, as this tends to be well known by employees, there remains the tendency to struggle for higher ratings at every feedback session, just to avoid the possibility, however faint, of being among the chosen.

OPERATIONAL ISSUES

There are some final issues to clarify in respect of initiating and implementing a performance management scheme:

The need to consult

It is clear that performance management is central to the way an organisation and its employees operate so it is vital that all concerned understand the underpinning objectives of the scheme and how it should work in practice. Opportunities should therefore be provided for consultation with all stakeholders (managers, employees, unions and staff representatives) before a new scheme is launched. Meetings, focus groups and attitude surveys are all ways that this consultation could be carried out.

Training for participants

It is not sufficient to simply send round the organisation a printed guide to operating the scheme. Training for participants is essential. Nor is it just managers who need training, for it is a joint process between managers and their staff. Some organisations have developed joint workshops for departments who role-play appraisal interviews, often with managers and departmental staff reversing their positions.

Making use of technology in performance management processes

HR intranets are increasingly being used to provide global access to the relevant guidance materials and documentation, including allowing line managers and employees to update and exchange PM documents electronically, such as appraisal forms.

On Sony Europe's new PM website, there are a number of online training modules and external training materials linked to the operations and outcomes of PM meetings. Training modules include advice on setting SMART objectives and how to discover their own strengths and weaknesses. There are also developmental modules such as an experiential module on 'driving my career'.

At the Big Lottery Fund, the HR team are setting up a 'wiki' where managers can share information and learning materials to help keep the high-performance mentality going.

On the issue of developing performance, Reed Employment Agency has an online tool that has been developed to allow employees to benchmark their potential performance on any given day against their actual performance. By answering a set number of verbal, numerical and lateral thinking questions each day, the programme builds up a profile of the employee's capabilities. It can then assess, upon the submission of answers to different questions, whether the employee is achieving or falling behind their potential (Reed 2001).

ACTIVITY 5.1

Consider the roles that can be played by the Human Resources Department in the performance management process.

Response to activity 5.1

In your answer, you may have produced some of the following actions:

- Evaluating the current scheme and reporting on its strengths and weaknesses.
- Working with the board to identify an outline performance management framework where vital business objectives can be cascaded through the organisation and key competencies developed.
- Designing an outline scheme and carrying out a full consultation process with all of the stakeholder groups.
- Agreeing a final approved scheme including revisions arising from the consultation and producing an information pack to all involved.
- Setting up a training programme for participants.
- Designing and producing the necessary paperwork.
- Coaching management in operating the scheme effectively.
- Monitoring the scheme's progress in terms of timing and quality of outcome.
- Acting in an overall moderating role where decisions on pay are made arising out of the scheme to ensure consistency and fairness.
- Assisting in implementation of decisions on development and promotion.
- Evaluating the overall progress of the scheme.

CONCLUSION

Apart from the success of 360-degree feedback, it has been a theme of this chapter that performance management is difficult to devise, impossible to operate without severe problems, and normally received badly or, at best, indifferently, by employees. This would be too gloomy a prognosis overall. In fact, commentators such as Redman (2001) are far more optimistic, reporting from a major study in the health service (Redman *et al.* 2000) that employees value the appraisal system and would hate it to be discarded. He quotes evidence that employers who have used appraisal for longer periods report fewer problems.

However, Brown and Hirsh have reported on the difficulties experienced in practice:

> One HR director said to us 'It is expected to be part business planning, part employee and career development, part performance pay and part communication process – no wonder it is often seen to fail'. We lost count of the number of times that the process was described to us as a turgid exercise in 'box-ticking' or 'form-filling' or 'something to do to keep HR quiet'. Other complaints included the 'standardised, jargon-filled, prescriptive and overly-detailed paperwork' and 'line managers lacking the required competence and commitment for the process'.
>
> (2011: 35)

On the other hand, Brown and Hirsh did report a number of participants in their research who could give concrete examples of valuable performance discussions.

It must be emphasised that, without some system of performance management, it is highly unlikely, in all but the smallest organisations, that the performance of employees is going to improve or that employees will be given the opportunity to develop and progress. Certainly, some secure platform on which to base pay increases is vital. Although the problems are persistent and endemic, they are not completely insurmountable.

EXTENDED ACTIVITY/CASE STUDY – BALANCED SCORECARD

In this activity, we will return to the example of the Sainsbury's Balanced Scorecard set out in Figure 5.4. Here is a series of linked activities associated with this scorecard:

Activity 1 – select two segments from each of the four sectors (a total of eight segments) and design two measures for each of these segments.

Activity 2 – explain how each of the measures you have designed could be incorporated into the performance management scheme. In other words, how these measures can be converted into objectives. Note that the PM scheme can involve both individual and group/department objectives.

Activity 3 – design a scheme that sets out how the outcome of the measures can be converted into a rating, where employees are divided into six categories ranging from 'top' through 'strong' and 'acceptable' to 'low'.

Activity 4 – set out the benefits and difficulties that may arise in operating such a scheme.

It was time for Sarah's own performance review meeting. She remembered, with horror, the appraisal interview in her previous organisation, where she was faced with a completed set of subjective ratings, a fixed 30-minute slot and an old-style manager who opened up the session with the comment 'We haven't a lot of time so I hope we don't have the same old irrelevant arguments as we've had in the past'. She co-operated by withdrawing from real discussions, accepting faint praise where it was due, closing her mind to the unjust criticism and identifying her own agenda for self-improvement, part of which was to move to a new company!

The meeting had been prefaced by a series of informal discussions during the year where progress on a number of projects was reviewed and developmental issues addressed openly. So Sarah did not expect too many surprises from the review meeting nor, as it turned out, did she receive any. By agreement, the meeting with Scott took place on a Saturday morning at a local training centre they had often used, so there could be no interruptions or time restraints. Sarah had completed her self-assessment the week before and given it to David. The scheme combined a set of objectives with a focus on key competencies attached to her role and she believed that she had achieved five of the six objectives and had made progress in improving her skills and competencies with one or two exceptions.

The meeting opened with a discussion of the overall progress of the department over the year – its influence and a review of its major initiatives. Scott gave Sarah a report of the department's ratings, based on a recent internal management service survey, which indicated satisfaction in most areas, except in achieving results on time. He indicated his pleasure at the success in the recruitment and selection areas where the teams that Sarah had helped recruit appeared to be gelling well and bringing in excellent results. The introduction of assessment centres had been seen as especially successful by the managers participating. In terms of competencies, her communication skills were highly praised, both in writing reports, briefing documents and policies and also in giving presentations (David reported that her talk to senior management on the assessment centre outcomes had been highly commended). She was a valued member of the team and showed strong co-operation and innovative abilities.

Scott then raised the issue of completing projects on time, mentioning a degree of surprise and disappointment over the overrun of the project to revise the performance management system itself. Sarah herself was disappointed at this, explaining that much of this was due to the dispute in the managers' focus group between the majority who wanted to extend the 360-degree feedback and a vociferous minority who were strongly against such a move. As co-ordinator of the project, she did not feel able to over-rule the minority, so a further set of meetings was arranged over several weeks where progress was achieved, although it was slow. She realised that this did not obtain the right result.

Scott then led in to a detailed discussion on her influencing skills, getting her to talk frankly about how she dealt with opposition and dispute. She agreed that she did not find it easy to handle, taking some of it as a personal criticism and leading to a tendency to retreat into submission. Scott presented the view that some managers considered her not sufficiently tough or decisive enough on occasions. It was agreed that she needed to develop her skills in this area and she was asked to talk to training colleagues about courses in this area. He would do the same with a view to her attending an external course within the next three months plus a follow-up after a further six months. It was also fixed for her to spend a couple of days in the next few months work-shadowing a consultant (an ex-colleague of Scott) to observe the skills exercised in this area.

They went on to spend time agreeing her overall ratings and then Scott listened to her feedback on their own relationship. Sarah had not felt comfortable in this part of the session in the previous year but she had gained some confidence in the relaxed atmosphere and raised two issues that had annoyed her, namely the lack of inclusion in a crucial departmental strategy meeting and the continuous urgency attached to certain issues by Scott. The first was settled by explanation of the special circumstances of which she was unaware and the second was integrated with the issue of decisiveness discussed earlier. The review ended with a planning session for the next 12 months, a discussion of the possible future long-term promotion plans and the likely salary implications of this review. Scott made it clear that her performance and level of commitment was very strong and he was gratified to see the good progress. But future progress up the human resources ladder did require development in the areas discussed.

Sarah left the meeting feeling pleased, if rather drained by the intense, yet relaxed discussions. She realised that her good work was recognised, that she was making progress and was content that the criticisms of her were made in a constructive, positive and supportive way.

KEY CHAPTER SUMMARY POINTS

■ An organisation is judged by its performance, so setting, measuring and monitoring employee performance are substantial human resource activities.

■ A performance management scheme can be a major aid to change management, both in operating and cultural terms.

■ There are four stages to performance management, namely, entering into a performance agreement with the employee, designing robust measures of performance, ensuring effective feedback to the employee takes place and agreeing the outcomes of the process in developmental and/or reward terms.

■ Measures can be based on either objectives or competencies or a combination of both.

■ Performance normally has to be rated in some way and this presents considerable difficulties to be overcome.

- Feedback can be on the basis of top-down or 360-degrees, which is feedback from different sources. It produces extremely robust data but is expensive and time-consuming.
- There are major problems of reconciling the three outcomes of a performance management scheme, namely reward, development and discipline.

STUDENT ACTIVITIES

1   Moving the goalposts, taking the goalposts away and changing the rules of the game can all present difficulties. Take each of these situations in turn and present arguments from the viewpoint of both the organisation and the individual employee as to how they should be resolved fairly and efficiently.

2   Imagine you are a manager at Sainsbury's (case study 5.1) at the meeting where the scheme is being explained. Make a list of questions that you would want to ask to satisfy yourself that the scheme is fair and worthwhile.

3   In the Meteor case study, what were the key aspects of the meeting that left Sarah satisfied and enthusiastic?

4   Set up a debate between yourself and three other colleagues with two of you arguing in favour of your pay being affected by the performance management scheme and the other two arguing that it should only be used to help your personal development.

5   Consider the advantages and difficulties of using the bank competency form (Figure 5.6) from the viewpoint of the manager and the person being appraised.

6   Read the article on which focus on research 5.4 is based and give your views on what difficulties could be faced by introducing 360-degree feedback at a university.

REFERENCES

Allen, D. (2004) Two's Company. *People Management*, 15 January, 41–42.

Arkin, A. (2011) The Odd Couple. *People Management*, October, 44–46.

Armstrong, M. (2001) *Human Resource Management Practice*. Kogan Page.

Armstrong, M. and Baron, A. (2005) *Managing Performance*. CIPD.

Becon, A. and Instler, D. (2011) Effective Performance Management Drives High-Performing Organisations. *Workspan*, 54(2): 28–34.

Bradley, L. and Ashkanasy, N. (2001) Formal Performance Appraisal Interviews – Can They Really Be Objective and Are They Useful Anyway? *Asia Pacific Journal of Human Resources*, 39(2): 83–97.

Broadbent, J. (2007) *Performance Management Systems in Higher Education Institutions in England – Professionalism, Managerialism and Management*. Roehampton University.

Brophy, E. (2010) The Subterranean Stream – Communicative Capitalism and Call Centre Labour. *Ephemera*, 10(3): 470–483.

Brown, D. and Hirsh, W. (2011) Performance Management: Fine Intentions. *People Management*, September, 34–37.

CIPD (2009) Survey of Performance Management. CIPD

Civil Service (2012) Civil Service Reform Plan. Cabinet Office, June.

Fletcher, C. (2008) *Appraisal, Development and Feedback*, 4th ed. Routledge.

France, S. (1997) *360-Degree Appraisal*. Industrial Society.

Herzberg, F. (1968) One More Time: How Do You Motivate Your Employees? *Harvard Business Review*, January–February, 109–120.

Hirsh, W. (2006) *Improving Performance through Appraisal Dialogues*. Corporate Research Forum.

Humble, J. (1972) *Management by Objectives*. Management Publications.

IDS (2003) Performance Management. *IDS Study 748*, April.

— (2011) Performance Management. *IDS Study 938*, March.

Jacobs, R. and Floyd, M. (1995) A Bumper Crop of Insights. *People Management*, 9 February, 23–25.

Kaplan, R. and Norton, D. (1996) *The Balanced Scorecard: Translating Strategy into Action*. Harvard Business School Press.

Lawler, E. (1990) *Strategic Pay*. Jossey-Bass.

Linman, T. (2004) 360 Degree Feedback, Weighing the Pros and Cons. College of Education, accessed at http://edweb.sdsu.edu/people/arossett/pie/Interventions/360_1.htm.

Locke, E. and Latham, G. (1990) *A Theory of Goal Setting and Performance*. Prentice Hall.

Mabey, C. (2001) Closing the Circle: Participant Views of a 360 Degree Feedback Programme. *Human Resource Management Journal*, 11(1): 41–53.

McClelland, D. (1973) Testing for Competence Rather than 'Intelligence'. *American Psychologist*, 28(1): 1–14, January.

Markus, L., Cooper-Thomas, H. and Allpress, K. (2005) Confounded by Competencies? An Evaluation of the Evolution and Use of Competency Models. *New Zealand Journal of Psychology*, 34(2):117–126, July.

Marshall, V. and Wood, R. (2000) The Dynamics of Effective Performance Appraisal: An Integrated Model. *Asia Pacific Journal of Human Resources*, 38(3): 62–89.

Mathison, D. and Vinja, V. (2010) The Annual Performance Review as a Positive Source for Employee Motivation? *Journal of Business and Economic Research*, 8(12): 111–120.

Mayer, R. and Davis, J. (1999) The Effects of the Performance Appraisal System on Trust for Management. *Journal of Applied Psychology*, 84(1): 123–136.

People Management (2010) Cadbury Staff in 720-Degree Spin. 6 May, 15.

Peters, T. and Waterman, R. (1982) *In Search of Excellence*. Harper and Row.

Redman, T. (2001) Performance Appraisal, in T. Redman and A. Wilkinson (eds) *Contemporary Human Resource Management*. Financial Times.

Redman, T., Snape, E., Thompson, D. and Ka-ching Yan, F. (2000) Performance Appraisal in the National Health Service: A Trust Hospital Study. *Human Resource Management Journal*, 10(1): 1–16.

Reed, A. (2001) *Innovation in Human Resources*. CIPD.

Smithers, J., London, M. and Reilly, R. (2005) Does Performance Improve Following Multi-source Feedback? *Personnel Psychology*, 58: 33–66.

Swan, W. (1991) *How to Do a Superior Performance Appraisal*. John Wiley.

West, M.A., Borrill, C., Dawson, J., Scully, J., Carter, M., Anelay, S., Patterson, M. and Waring, J. (2002) The Link Between the Management of Employees and Patient Mortality in Acute Hospitals. *International Journal of Human Resource Management*, 13: 1299–1310.

West, M.A., Guthrie, J.P., Dawson, J.F., Borrill, C.S. and Carter, M. (2006) Reducing Patient Mortality in Hospitals: The Role of Human Resource Management. *Journal of Organizational Behavior*, 27: 983–1002.

Whitehouse, A., Hassell, A., Bullock, A, Wood, L. and Wall, D. (2007) 360 Degree Assessment (Multi-source Feedback) on UK Trainee Doctors. *Medical Teacher*, 29(23): 171–176.

ADDITIONAL FEATURES

Please visit the companion website at: www.routledge.com/cw/stredwick where you will find additional case studies and reading material together with short self-tests and other resources for both students and lecturers.

6 REWARDING EMPLOYEES

CHAPTER OBJECTIVES

When you have studied this chapter, you should be able to:

■ Understand the importance of using reward in a strategic role and the concept of Total Reward.

■ Identify the elements that make up the employee reward package.

■ Distinguish between the different types of job evaluation and how and when they should be used.

■ Appreciate the difference between conventional pay systems and broad-banded pay systems.

■ Evaluate the main methods of paying for performance in an individual and team setting.

INTRODUCTION

Payment systems have changed out of all recognition over the last 20 years. Back in the 1970s, when trade unions were at their zenith, pay itself was regarded as an outcome of the industrial relations process where a compromise was reached between the conflicting demands of the two antagonists. Today, organisations, with varying degrees of success, attempt to harness the powerful forces of pay as a motivator to encourage employees to work in ways that lead to the achievement of organisational objectives. There are many more forms of incentive payments, many varieties of recognition awards and the number of employee benefits has greatly expanded. Pay is also a vital element in the recruitment process and we have seen in Chapter 5 that it is one of the major outcomes arising from the performance management process.

In recent years, the expression 'reward' has started to replace 'pay' in the human resources vocabulary. It indicates a much broader approach, including elements of non-cash awards, and presupposes that employees need to actually achieve something to receive their wages or salaries, unlike the more mechanistic attachment that pay indicates. Most of the developments in reward come from America and it is surprising that they still refer to the subject as 'compensation' with its connotation to the belief that work is unpleasant and should be avoided.

In this chapter, we will start by examining the important components of designing a Total Reward system which is made up of the following sections:

- Determining the *strategic elements of reward* and how they link with other aspects of human resources and examining the more widely used concept of Total Reward.
- Summarising the *component parts of the reward package*.
- Designing *basic pay structures* through job evaluation systems, market tracking and competency approaches.
- Deciding which aspects of *pay for performance* schemes should be implemented and under which conditions.
- Constructing a *benefits package* that fits the needs of both the organisation and the employees.
- Considering special elements of pay practice that apply to executive pay.

The next section will look at how employees can be *motivated* to achieve the organisational objective linked to strategic reward, which includes an analysis of the *psychological contract*.

STRATEGIC ELEMENTS OF REWARD

You will recall from Chapter 1 that human resource strategy must be aligned with the business and policy objectives of the organisation. Commentators are quite clear on the part that reward strategy should play in this alignment process.

Effective Reward strategies are . . . essential in today's knowledge-driven and human capital-constrained new economy in which people really are the key to an organisation's success. Any significant mismatch between the requirements on employees to implement the business's strategic goals and the behaviours that are rewarded, can spell corporate disaster.

(Brown 2001: 22)

Table 6.1 indicates a number of areas where major changes have taken place and these can be grouped into a number of strategic areas, although many of them are interlinking.

Achieving competitive advantage. This can take a number of forms. The reward structure can be set at the top of the market range at all levels of the organisation to encourage the best people to join. This is the policy adopted by, among others, large international companies such as GlaxoSmithKline PLC (GSK) and most leading consultancies and large companies in the financial services industry. Although pay becomes a major expense, this is outweighed by the benefits obtained from employing the best talents available. This is an argument strongly advanced by organisations in respect of senior executive pay where very high levels are required to attract and retain top-quality staff in an internationally competitive market. (This is a most debatable argument, as we shall see

Table 6.1 Changing nature of pay and rewards

Past	Present
Pay regarded as an expense	Reward systems seen as an investment to achieve competitive advantage
Pay policies based on government control or national agreements	Rewards determined by the organisation to meet its global, national or local conditions
Fixed pay scales in a rigid job evaluation structure	Rewards utilised flexibly within a broad-banded salary structure
Pay seen as compensation for having to be at work	Rewards given for employees achieving the desired results
Pay to compensate for reluctant acceptance of change	Rewards to encourage positive acceptance of cultural changes
Payments made for length of service	Rewards given for performance, skills and competency
Pay differentials compressed	Wide variations in reward from board room to home improvement centre
Incentives based on narrow measures of production or sales	Performance-based systems based on broad measures of unit or organisational success
Paying for attendance	Rewarding employees for ideas, initiative and innovation
Fixed benefits without choice	Flexible benefit programmes to suit individual requirements
Equity sharing limited to directors	Share options for all employees

later in the chapter.) At a lower level, GSK have argued that, by employing very high-quality research and development staff, the flow of successful long-term pharmaceutical products is ensured. Employee retention under such a strategy generally remains high, saving on recruitment costs.

Another example is computer companies that have adopted the strategy of paying high-performance premiums to their staff for on-time project completion, leading to customer satisfaction and repeat business. Finally, schemes covering groups of employees, such as gainsharing, encourage employees to have a broad understanding of what the organisation is trying to achieve, and the associated commitment and involvement process helps the teams to work together to try to reach these objectives to the benefit of the organisation, its customers and all the employees.

Emphasise performance. The global marketplace and the increasing competition has ensured that organisations cannot rely on past performance or employees having their own performance agendas. The proportion of contingent pay (pay that depends upon the achievement of results by the individual or teams) has risen compared with automatically paid basic pay. This is to encourage employees to 'share the risks' of a business. In the John Lewis Partnership, for example, all the employees are partners and receive an annual bonus depending upon the performance of the business. This bonus is extremely variable, being as high as 24 per cent of salary (almost £5,000 on a salary of £20,000) in 1988 and as low as 13 per cent in 2009.

In many companies, the guaranteed annual increase has vanished, being replaced by an increase based on individual performance. This has been the case for most financial institutions, including the Britannia Building Society where employees are rewarded for the contribution they make in such areas as customer satisfaction (Persaud 2003).

Encourage flexibility in working practices. The increased movement towards a greater use of flexibility has led to the introduction of rewards for employees increasing their breadth of skills and competencies. SKF have introduced skills-based pay, while Triplex Safety Glass award pay increases when employees achieve an increased set of competencies that allow them to carry out a wider range of jobs.

Oil the wheels of change. Organisations that make major cultural changes use rewards to help embed those changes. For example, when GPT Telecommunications engaged in a number of human resource changes in response to the rapid marketplace, they introduced performance-related pay to support their greater emphasis on customer-related objectives and higher-quality performance. Similarly, under a 'transformation programme' at Southern focus Trust (a housing association), a broad-banded pay structure, based on a new competency framework, was introduced to reinforce the new emphasis on service and quality competency (Armstrong and Brown 2001).

Support key competencies. Rewards can be used to encourage specific competencies. Vauxhall Motors have developed an extensive recognition scheme to reward employees who demonstrate innovation and creativity. Some of these payments have exceeded £2,000 and are seen as vital to the company to compete on the level of productivity and quality in a worldwide marketplace.

Encourage local decision-taking. As part of a centrally negotiated process, pay decisions used to be made at the headquarters but the need to respond to local conditions has led to decisions on pay being delegated to localised units. Increasingly, this is being taken a stage further by delegating individual pay decisions to local managers as part of the general increase in local empowerment. Managers then have to justify such decisions in the light of their budgetary restrictions, local performance and market rate indicators.

Support engagement. Reward processes can help to promote a spirit of fairness and encourage employees to remain engaged. For example, B&Q have specified that they will:

> Provide an innovative reward package that is valued by our staff and communicated brilliantly to reinforce the benefits of working for the organisation. Reward investment will be linked to company performance so that staff share in the success they create and, by going the extra mile, receive above average reward compared to local competitors.

> (Armstrong and Brown 2006: 18)

Total Reward

The concept of Total Reward has emerged in the last decade as a way of integrating all aspects of reward into a coherent philosophy and strategy. Around 33 per cent of larger organisations have adopted its use (CIPD 2011). It links the traditional sectional approach to reward (base pay, performance pay, etc.) with the model of engagement, including areas such as work–life balance and opportunities for personal growth. A further link is to try to meet the conundrum of how to improve productivity and cut costs, while, at the same time, find ways to attract, retain and motivate staff.

A Total Reward strategy will therefore include all of the following areas:

- *Financial rewards* – such as competitive pay, benefits that are relevant and high quality, incentives that are fair, achievable and attractive
- *Non-financial rewards* – recognition of good performance, security of income and a supportive environment through provision of work–life balance opportunities
- *Future growth/opportunities* – career advancement and individual development opportunities
- *Inspirational and enabling environment* – with attractive and relevant organisational values, high-quality leadership and effective communication, together with a safe place of work with effective personal support from your manager
- *Work of value* – work that is challenging, satisfying and which provides a degree of freedom and autonomy.

> (Source: Adapted from the Hay Group 2004)

This approach recognises that reward should be tailored to the needs of the individual employee, rather than a 'one-size-fits-all' approach. Such a strategy, a unified grand theory of reward, appears very ambitious. In fact, critics have accused reward specialists of attempting to hijack the whole field of human resource management rather than keeping to their specialism. It does, however, have the advantage that a broad approach will generally find favour in some way with all applicants/employees. Those who want a high take-home pay at the start of their career will be attracted to the financial rewards, especially the incentives; those at the middle may find that the growth and inspirational areas attract them more, while those towards the end may find the work–life balance benefits more aligned to their personal needs. It is expected that companies may be offering employees a wider range of choices across the reward spectrum that can also be tailored to their individual needs (Bremen and McMullen 2010). The other advantage is that it prevents the reward specialist working in a silo, unable to link their input into the overall strategy of the human resources department.

An example of a company operating a Total Reward strategy is shown in case study 6.1.

CASE STUDY 6.1 TOTAL REWARD AT ARUP

Arup, the international engineering consultancy, adopted a Total Reward approach in 2002 and one of the key aspects was to introduce Total Reward statements throughout the organisation, first issued in 2004. They were seen as an effective way to ensure staff understood the make-up and value of their employment package and to align the values of the organisation – open, honest dealings, employee-owned – with the reward practices. Their international practices vary country by country depending upon what Arup needs to offer to compete in local markets.

The statements are tailored for each individual employee, detailing salary, profit-share payments and all the benefits to which they are entitled, so that it is possible to give a monetary value for the overall employment package. Each item carries notes as to how it is calculated. All other non-monetary benefits are also listed so that employees are aware of what is available.

The company has found a number of benefits through this open and detailed approach. Firstly, it is valuable as a recruitment aid in that applicants are impressed by the scope, size and detail of the reward package. Secondly, it has been integrated with a flexible benefits package in a number of countries so that employees have a certain choice in the format of the package, which gives them a greater degree of ownership. Thirdly, there is no doubt that the employees appreciate the alignment of the approach with the organisational values and this spills over into other aspects of human resource strategy, including competencies and communication.

(Source: Sharp 2009)

ACTIVITY 6.1

Motivating employees. The contract that employers and employees enter into in the workplace contains many subtleties relating to behavioural expectations. Consider what are some of these expectations firstly from an employee's viewpoint and then from an employer's viewpoint.

Discussion of activity 6.1

You may have thought of a number of the expectations set out in Table 6.2.

These expectations, none of which is expressed formally in the employment contract, sometimes lead to disappointments when they are not realised. Broken promises, poor communication and misunderstandings over what is expected can lead to mutual recrimination and a reduction in the degree of motivation from the employees. This, in turn, can lead to deteriorating performance and eventual termination of the employment by dismissal or mutual agreement.

The '*psychological contract*', as the group of mutual expectations has been called (Guest 2007), is crucial in helping to determine the base line for the way employees respond to the objective of working more effectively. Employers help to establish a positive contract by creating a culture where these expectations are discussed openly, where they have a strong degree of mutual agreement and where there is a genuine attempt by both sides to reach the desired goals. Although there is much discussion in the media and elsewhere that employees in the 2000s are less satisfied, feel less secure, are overworked and held in lower regard, the research evidence does not seem to support that view, as shown in focus on research 6.1.

Table 6.2 Expectations of employers and employees from each other

What employees expect from their employer	What employers expect from their employees
To be treated fairly as a human being	To work hard for the organisation
To be provided with work that suits their ability	To be committed to the organisation's values
To have opportunities for self-development and promotion	To be loyal and dependable
For employer's promises to be kept	For employees to keep their promises
To know what is expected of them	To keep to the work standards set by management
To be rewarded equitably	To be prepared for change in the job they do
To have a friendly and safe working environment	To think about how they can improve the work they do

F
O
C
U
S

O
N

R
E
S
E
A
R
C
H

FOCUS ON RESEARCH 6.1 THE STATE OF THE PSYCHOLOGICAL CONTRACT

The Chartered Institute of Personnel and Development (CIPD) have carried out an annual research project for a number of years examining employees' views of the psychological contract, defined in terms of their judgement of fairness, trust and the delivery of their employment 'deal'. The report in 2001, carried out by Guest and Conway from Kings College, London, found that 91 per cent of respondents felt secure in their jobs and the majority considered employment relations to be fair or good. Motivation levels were high, especially so in health workers and local government: 31 per cent believed that the work picture had improved in the previous year and only 24 per cent considered it had got worse. Since the previous year, private sector workers were consistently more satisfied and positive, while public sector workers were more dissatisfied and less positive, especially in respect to the work–life balance. Only a minority reported that management promises had been kept, especially in the area of involvement and consultation about change.

The report picked out the difficulties expressed by employees in the public sector in responding to all-too-frequent changes and the low levels of consultation. There was a strong viewpoint that satisfied customers will only result from having satisfied staff.

(Source: Conway and Guest 2001)

An earlier model by Guest *et al.* (1996) indicated the link between the psychological contract and motivation as shown in Figure 6.1. Here it is indicated that the consequent level of motivation is influenced firstly and immediately by the level of perceived trust and sense of fairness in the organisation and by the way the deal is delivered, and ultimately by factors such as the employee's own experience, expectations and the organisation's culture and HRM policy and practices. Motivation will join with high levels of commitment, a good feeling of satisfaction and well-being and a sense of being an important part of the organisation (organisational citizenship) to produce high levels of performance.

Some writers believe that the psychological contract contains some shared understandings that go beyond that written down in the contract (Boxall and Purcell 2008). As an example, this may be demonstrated as the expectation that employees will 'go the extra mile' to provide the highest quality of customer service or that an employer will show excessive care where an employee suffers an extreme personal difficulty, such as the death or serious illness of a partner or child.

Motivation theory

Motivation theories can be divided into three main groups: instrumentality, needs (sometimes known as content) theory and cognitive theories.

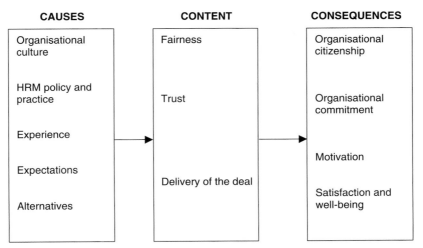

CAUSES

Organisational culture

HRM policy and practice

Experience

Expectations

Alternatives

CONTENT

Fairness

Trust

Delivery of the deal

CONSEQUENCES

Organisational citizenship

Organisational commitment

Motivation

Satisfaction and well-being

Figure 6.1
Model of the psychological contract

Source: Guest, D., Conway, N., Briner, R. and Dickman, M. (1996) The State of the Psychological Contract in Employment. *Issues in People Management*, No. 16. IPD (CPID).

Instrumentality theories emerged in the early 1900s and are based on the assumption that work has no outcomes other than economic ones. Employees, motivated only by money, need to be put in a situation where they have no choice but to work hard and efficiently. To achieve this in practice, work was grouped into large factory units, maximum specialisation was achieved through the limitation of the number of tasks an employee had to do and work was deliberately made repetitive with as limited an amount of training time as possible. Set out by Taylor (1911), and implemented throughout the Ford factories, in Detroit, where much of the labour force had migrated from their farming origins, it led to the wide application of work study techniques, incentive payments and the attitude that employees must be rigidly controlled in the most cost-effective way. This belief held sway for 50 or more years in the Western world and is still followed in some establishments today.

The difficulty arising from this theory is that it does not take into account the personal and social needs of employees or the rising level of intelligence and expectations. Subservient employees become more difficult to motivate and often take action to avoid the harsh controls. The rise of collective action (strikes, work to rule, etc.) or high levels of illness and absenteeism have been shown to be a direct result of instrumental controls.

Needs theories, on the other hand, emphasise that unsatisfied needs create tension and disequilibrium, which leads to individuals striving to achieve a goal. Maslow (1954) developed a Hierarchy of Needs (Figure 6.2) from lower-order basic needs (food and shelter) to higher-order needs (social needs, self-esteem and self-actualisation). The higher-order needs become motivators when the lower-order needs have been met. Pay has generally been regarded in this theory as a lower-order need, which rarely motivates, although the implication is that basic pay must be set high enough to provide employees with the

Figure 6.2
Maslow's
Hierarchy of
Needs

Source: Maslow,
Abraham H., Frager,
Robert and
Faidman, James
(1987) *Motivation
and Personality*,
3rd ed. Reprinted
by permission of
Pearson.

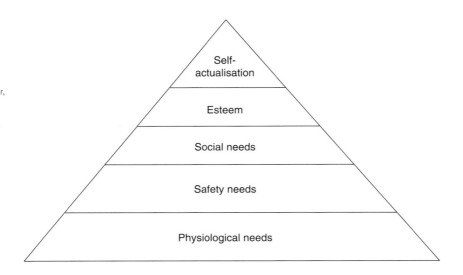

Table 6.3 Herzberg's two-factor theory

Hygiene factors	Satisfiers
Pay	Achievement
Company policy	Recognition
Working conditions	Advancement
Supervision	Responsibility
Company policy and administration	Personal growth
Security	Advancement
Relationship with subordinates	

Source: Herzberg, F. (1968) One More Time: How Do You Motivate Employees? *Harvard Business Review*, January–February, 33–62.

economic means to meet their basic living needs. It has also been argued that transparent benefits, such as the company car, can help to meet the need of self-esteem and that group incentive schemes can help to meet the need for 'love' through teams working together with mutual respect.

Herzberg's (1968) well-known two-factor theory distinguished between hygiene factors and satisfiers (see Table 6.3). Hygiene factors (or dissatisfaction avoidance factors) include pay, company policy, method of supervision and administration, all of which he called extrinsic factors. They rarely, in themselves, motivate employees to work harder or better but can cause the employee to work less hard if they are not satisfied. Satisfiers, on the other hand, which include achievement, recognition and the nature of the work itself, are the major motivating force. The implications here are clearly that reward schemes based on performance are unlikely to motivate and can be the cause of consider-able demotivation. This belief is held strongly by employees in many of the public services, including health and education, who find all their motivation from the intrinsic factors and strongly resent suggestions that they would be motivated by contingent pay. Schoolteachers, for example, have been strongly opposed to compulsory schemes where additional payments are made based on some form of individual performance measure, although they ultimately accepted performance pay as a reflection of their ability and commitment in the early 2000s.

Cognitive theories assume that individuals think their way through the situation and work out how they can benefit from particular courses of action. The leading cognitive theory is *expectancy theory* expounded by Vroom (1964). Here, motivation is the product of three variables:

- Instrumentality, which is the degree of an employee's self-belief in their ability to achieve a goal.
- Expectancy, which is the degree to which they believe that, having achieved a goal, it will lead to a secondary action, namely a reward.
- Valence, which is the value they put on that reward.

Reversing the needs theories, Vroom believed that employees respond to attempts to moti-vate them on an individual basis in their own specific situation. They may not need additional pay or they may not value the particular reward. They may not trust the organisation to come up with the rewards or they may simply consider the targets or goals unobtainable. Any of these beliefs will reduce or eliminate entirely the degree of motivation. The implication for employers is that incentive schemes will not work with everybody, that considerable care has to be taken with the rewards to ensure there is a reasonable degree of valence and that honesty and trust must prevail with both the level of targets and the application of the rewards.

Another influential theory has been put forward by Locke (1968) regarding the *effectiveness of goals*. He supports the view that goal-setting is an important part of motivation but, to retain the necessary intensity and duration of commitment, the goals must be challenging, they must be accepted by the employee, there must be an element of participation in the goal-setting process and the employee must get valued feedback on their performance.

The notion of fair play is never far away from reward considerations. *Equity theory* (Adams 1963) detailed the main pointers to maintaining motivation through the concepts of *distributive justice*, where pay is seen to be fairly distributed in line with an employee's worth and output, and *procedural justice*, where the methods of arriving at these judge-ments are seen to be fair. These methods include employee participation, accurate measure-ment, fair appraisal and appeals processes.

Summing up motivation

It is clear from many research projects that employees are motivated in different ways and that encouraging employees to work effectively is contingent upon the nature of the organisation. Knowledge workers may respond better to individual challenges for their small teams, together with freedom of action to influence the result. For manufacturing employees, motivation may arise from greater involvement in their workplace and shorter-span challenges. Communication and effective feedback is crucial to the process in all cases, as is injecting a degree of stimulation, enjoyment and excitement into the way that employees are challenged.

The influence of motivation theory

Conclusions on *motivation* are therefore difficult to reach. There is no doubt that money motivates in many ways for many people much of the time but certainly not everybody all of the time. Even more perplexing, money can motivate up to a certain level but this differs greatly between individuals. To add further confusion, much of the research basis of Herzberg and Maslow has been disputed in recent years with results leading to varying conclusions.

For this reason, the reward area remains, in practice, an area of conflicting policies. Much of the private sector has adopted the expectancy and goal-setting approach and aims to motivate the majority of its employees through pay for performance schemes based on the achievement of goals. In the public and voluntary sectors, on the other hand, the picture is very mixed, with needs theories mostly to the fore and much concentration on the intrinsic satisfaction related to the job.

COMPONENT PARTS OF THE REWARD PACKAGE

There are numerous elements in the reward package and they are illustrated in Figure 6.3.

Direct rewards consist of:

■ Basic pay, which is the hourly wage or weekly/monthly salary that is guaranteed to be paid.
■ Pay for performance, which is the pay that can vary depending on the performance of the individual, group or organisation as a whole. Adopting skills and competencies come into this group.
■ Benefits, which relate to a wide range of 'extras' from company cars, private health insurance and share options to sick pay, pensions and holidays. Most are fixed and

there is a strong movement towards harmonising most benefits throughout an organisation rather than separate schemes for different groups of employees.

■ Recognition pay, which includes special awards for employee achievement. It is less common and is associated with performance but usually operated separately. Many of the rewards take the form of non-cash.

Indirect rewards consist of:

■ Job satisfaction consisting of the intrinsic rewards of carrying out the job.
■ Cultural satisfaction, which arises from rewarding relationships with colleagues and working within an ethically satisfying organisation or sector.
■ Security, which, although not greatly evident today, still applies in a number of settings either explicitly through long-term contracts or through the nature of the psychological contract between the organisation and its staff.
■ Personal growth, including the learning of new skills.
■ Career development opportunities and the way they are developed.

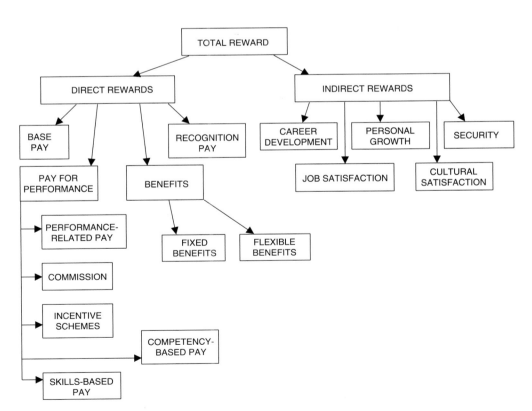

Figure 6.3
Components of the reward package

Each of these areas will be covered in this chapter. Reward, however, is not just about pay, although this is the major part, and organisations need to develop a balance between the various components. For example, there are some organisations that pay high salaries, based on performance bonuses, but still have difficulty retaining their staff, many of whom are not comfortable with the insecurity and pressure that this brings. Other organisations, perhaps still a small minority, maintain high staff performance without any form of incentive and without high base salaries. They concentrate on ensuring the indirect rewards are of high quality. Later in this chapter, we will examine different aspects of performance pay and benefits. Indirect rewards will be looked at in Chapter 8, which deals with training and development.

DESIGNING BASIC PAY STRUCTURES

The major part of most employees' reward is their basic remuneration. As Perkins and White have explained:

> Grading structures are the core building blocks of any organisation's human resource management system, not just for pay but often for conditions of service and career development as well. Small organisations (and even some bigger ones), however, may not have any formal organisational structure. As such, they may choose to pay their staff individual salaries or wage rates completely at management discretion (known as 'spot rates') based on the owner's or manager's view of each individual member of staff. But, generally, as the organisation begins to grow, the need for some sort of formal organisation, complete with job or 'grade' levels, becomes apparent . . . .
>
> Even if a formal grading structure is not acknowledged by management or communicated to staff, in reality some sort of employee 'hierarchy' will usually exist. This is because few employers have complete freedom to pay individuals simply what they wish. Pay structures are de facto created in these situations because different jobs usually attract different rates of pay according to their value in the external market because employees doing higher-level work will expect to be paid more than those doing lower-level work.

(2008: 88)

For individuals, the sense of fairness about their basic pay is related to three key facts. These are, firstly, the objective value they put on the nature of the job and the way they perform it; secondly, their perception of how this compares with other jobs in the organisation, especially those jobs and employees with which they are familiar; and, thirdly, how their pay compares with their perception of the 'market rate' for their job.

In small organisations, the salary structure is informal with the chief executive, who will know each employee, deciding the basic pay on an individual basis. The chief executive will be able to know the value of each individual's job and record it on one sheet of paper. When deciding on the pay for each employee, the chief executive will gain advice on market rates (usually from employment agencies) and then apply a 'spot rate' that appears appropriate. Consideration will be given to the rates of other comparable employees but this is not likely to be systematic.

However, when the organisation stretches beyond 60 or 80 employees, this becomes increasingly difficult. The chief executive will find the individual judgement of comparing one individual's worth against another, their comparable performance and the market rates for their jobs a complex process. Moreover, if mistakes are made, they can be costly. If remuneration is increased too much, it is almost impossible to reduce it subsequently (certainly without complaint) and, if it is not increased sufficiently, the individual may decide to look elsewhere. When the organisation expands beyond 150 or 200 employees, the task becomes practically impossible.

This is where two remuneration processes enter. *Job evaluation* attempts to ensure that the internal pay relativities are objectively set and *market tracking* compares the appropriate rates with the marketplace. When the necessary preparation has been carried out on both these processes, a remuneration structure can be put together to try to satisfy the requirements for both the organisation and the individual.

Job evaluation

The usual end result of a job evaluation exercise is to produce a hierarchy of jobs in the organisation through valuing them all against a clear set of objective criteria. Objective is the key word here because individual perception of job worth is so variable. Let us take the case of the computer programmer. Outside of people working in this skills area, there is a strong perception that it is a far from demanding position filled by people often with few qualifications, where the job holders spend much of their time sending emails to their colleagues, playing computer games and only working hard when it gets close to the deadlines. Is this correct? It depends entirely on how you value job worth. Many research scientists will look back on a number of years working on research projects that came to nothing and that appeared to add little or no value to the organisation. Yet these positions will be regarded as having a high job value.

The crucial starting point for job evaluation, therefore, is to decide on the criteria for measuring the value of jobs which can be *analytical* or *non-analytical*. Having agreed on this, the long and complex process of actually carrying out the evaluation can take place and, finally, it can be put together into a hierarchy of jobs. It has to be remembered throughout the process that it is the jobs that are being examined, not the performance of the person carrying out the job.

NON-ANALYTICAL SCHEMES

These are schemes that look at the job as a whole and do not examine their component parts. The evaluation process is normally carried out by a small group of executives working confidentially with their own knowledge of the jobs. They are only suitable for small or medium-sized organisations. It has to be said that these methods generally have a distinct lack of objectivity and are operated because they are cheap, quick and informal. They consist of the following:

- *Job ranking.* This is where jobs are simply ranked in order by the evaluation team. They may consider aspects of the jobs such as responsibility or skills but no agreed weight is given to these factors.
- *Paired comparison* takes ranking a stage further. In this process, all the jobs to be evaluated are compared on a one-by-one basis (see Figure 6.4). The job with a higher worth gets two points and, if they are considered equal, both get one point. The total points awarded under this system are added for each job to get a ranking of the jobs. This is certainly an easier process in the sense that comparing two jobs is more straightforward than trying to put a whole collection in order. However, it takes more time and there is a limit to the number of jobs that can be compared in this process. As pointed out by Armstrong *et al.* (2003), to evaluate 50 jobs involves 1,225 individual comparisons.
- *Job classification* is the process where each job is classified into a grade by reference to a prepared set of grading classifications. The number of grades is usually limited to between four and eight, and they are described in terms of factors such as experience required, quantity of non-routine tasks and elements of supervision required or that are part of the job. Each job is taken in turn and agreement reached as to which grade the job appears to fit into best. Again, this is a reasonably simple process on the surface but can lead to considerable dispute among the team making the decision because many jobs will not naturally fit into any grade, having elements of one and not the other. Decisions, in the end, will often be by compromise or due to internal political factors rather than any form of objectivity. Figure 6.5 shows an extract from a typical scheme.

ANALYTICAL SCHEMES

Analytical schemes differ from non-analytical schemes in that they aim to have a much greater transparency, objectivity and rationality if they are carried out in an open and consistent way. According to the 2011 CIPD Reward Management Survey (CIPD 2011), 31 per cent of organisations used a job evaluation database as the most important factor in determining pay rates. In previous surveys, a slightly different set of questions was asked and the figures for usage were somewhat higher – around 46 per cent in 2004 (CIPD 2004).

Job titles	Estimator	Senior Purchasing Officer	Receptionist	Finance Manager	Training Officer	Purchasing Clerk	QS	Senior Site Secretary	Marketing Manager	Administrator	Commercial Manager	Accounts Manager	Accounts Clerk	Planner	Personnel Assistant	Total score	Ranking position
Estimator		0	2	0	1	2	1	2	0	2	0	0	2	1	2	15	4
Senior Purchasing Officer	2		2	0	2	2	2	2	1	2	0	0	2	2	2	21	3
Receptionist	0	0		0	0	1	0	1	0	1	0	0	2	0	0	5	7
Finance Manager	2	2	2		2	2	2	2	1	2	1	1	2	2	2	25	1
Training Officer	1	0	2	0		2	1	2	0	2	0	0	2	1	1	14	5
Purchasing Clerk	0	0	1	0	0		0	0	0	1	0	0	1	0	0	3	9
Quantity Surveyor	1	0	2	0	1	2		2	0	2	0	0	2	1	2	15	4
Senior Site Secretary	0	0	1	0	0	1	0		0	1	0	0	1	0	0	4	8
Marketing Manager	2	1	2	1	2	2	2	2		2	1	1	2	2	2	24	2
Administrator	0	0	1	0	0	1	0	1	1		0	0	1	0	0	4	8
Commercial Manager	2	2	2	1	2	2	2	2	1	2		1	2	2	2	25	1
Accounts Manager	2	2	2	1	2	2	2	2	1	2	1		2	2	2	25	1
Accounts Clerk	0	0	1	0	0	1	0	1	0	1	0	0		0	0	4	8
Planner	1	0	2	0	1	2	1	2	0	2	0	0	2		2	15	4
Personnel Asst.	0	0	2	0	1	2	0	2	0	0	2	0	2	0		11	6

Points scored according to value.

Jobs valued   2 Points

Jobs valued   0 Points

Jobs equal value   1 Point

Figure 6.4

Example of paired comparison job evaluation scheme

Rank Descriptions

Rank 0 – Director

This rank covers all grades of Director (Chairman, Managing Director, Functional Directors, Non-Executive Directors, Vice Presidents, etc.). Entries should be made to this grade for all Directors with the legal responsibility of that title. It should not include those with the courtesy title 'Director' (e. g . Account Director) unless they have responsibilities for general company policy outside their functions, possibly as part of an executive management team, commonly found in foreign organisations without UK-based Directors.

Rank 1 – Senior Management or Senior Specialist

This rank covers the heads of major functions reporting to the Rank 0. In smaller organisations the Rank 0 appointment may well cover the duties of the Rank 1 and, consequently, there may be no incumbent in the Rank 1. The duty of these staff is the day-to-day running of an important major function in the organisation. Some policy formulation will be a normal part of their responsibilities. In addition, this rank covers very senior and highly qualified specialists who may have no function or department to manage. An example is Legal Adviser.

Rank 2 – Senior Middle Manager

The majority of entries into this rank will be for heads of main departments normally reporting to a Rank 1 Senior Manager, but in smaller organisations, or for less important departments, reporting to a Director. Alternatively, they may be the deputy to the Senior Manager. In addition, some important specialists whose effort is more directed to an individual technical or administrative skill, rather than the management of people, could be covered by this rank. Examples of such jobs are a Scientific Specialist, Pensions Manager, Consultant, etc. A Specialist Sales Manager may well be ranked at this level, although he may not control any Regional or Area Representatives.

Rank 3 – Junior Middle Management

The heads of less important departments are likely to be graded at this rank, as well as many specialists such as Senior Engineers, Project Leaders, Senior Systems Analysts. In the sales field, a Regional Manager controlling several Area Managers (Rank 4) would be graded Rank 3 unless the company equated his responsibility to other Rank 2 holders in the company. Most people at this rank will have Supervisors or Section Leaders reporting to them.

Rank 4 – Junior Management

This is the lowest level of management and is one rank above the first-line supervisory positions at Rank 5. Many holders of this rank would be managing a section and could be qualified or part-qualified professionally. Examples are Production Section Manager, Engineer, Accountant (not equated to Rank 3). Office Managers would normally be at this rank except in smaller organisations where they would be graded as Office Supervisors at Rank 5. Many Specialists would appear in this rank such as Senior Programmer, Health and Safety Officer, Buyer, Sales Area Manager (controlling a number of Representatives) or a Senior Representative.

Figure 6.5
Example of job
classification
job evaluation
scheme

Rank 5 – Supervisor and Senior Technician

This is primarily a rank for supervisory staff, either in the office or on the shop floor (e.g. Foreman). It also includes Senior Technicians or Specialists, such as Sales Representative, Programmer, Draughtsman, Work Study Officer, Nurse, Assistant (often newly joined graduates), Engineer, Senior Secretary, etc.

Rank 6 – Senior Clerical and Technician

This rank covers all those staff with minor supervisory roles (e.g. Section Leader, Chargehands, Senior Telephonist, etc.), Technicians and very junior Trainee Managers (e.g. Assistant Personnel Officer, etc.). It covers tasks in the office of a senior clerical nature which require experience and a limited degree of initiative such as Secretary, Senior Sales Clerk, etc. Technical jobs at this rank would include Computer (not VDU) Operator, Buying Assistant, Progress Chaser and Laboratory Technician.

Rank 7 – Skilled Operative and Specialist Clerical Grade

This rank includes all staff working under close supervision but classified by experience, training and ability as fully skilled. This would include Welders, Fitters, HGV Drivers, Craftsmen, Skilled Production Operatives and Shop Floor Inspectors. Within the office this rank would cover clerical duties of a specialist nature or those requiring skills above general clerical workers. This would include such activities as Sales Ledger Clerk, Credit Control Clerk, Shorthand Typist, Word Processing Operator, Shipping Clerk, Production Control Clerk, Telephone Sales, etc.

Rank 8 – Semi-skilled Grade

This rank covers all those whose skills are better than unskilled or completely inexperienced, and lower than fully skilled or very experienced. They would be doing routine tasks under supervision, using their knowledge, experience and aptitudes. This grade covers all Semi-Skilled Operatives, General Drivers, General Clerks, Telephonists, Typists, Laboratory Assistants, Handymen, etc.

Rank 9 – Unskilled Grade and Juniors

This rank covers all unskilled staff doing routine, simple tasks. It also includes all staff paid on age scales that is 16, 17 and 18 year olds whether they are working in the office, on the drawingboard, in an apprenticeship or working on the production line. The unskilled heading includes jobs like Filing Clerk, Junior Clerk, Unskilled Storeman/Packer, Labourer, Cleaner, Canteen Assistant, etc.

Figure 6.5
(*Continued*)

The basis of an analytical scheme is that each job is evaluated against a grid of factors and points, a simple example of which is set out in Table 6.4.

In designing this grid, there are three decisions that need to be taken:

■ *What factors to use.* In this example, only six factors have been selected. Armstrong and Baron (1995) list 31 factors in common use but only 5 to 10 factors are normally selected in the interest of simplicity and comprehension. It is important, therefore, that consideration is given to which factors are relevant and vital to the set of jobs being evaluated and which skills are important.

■ *How many levels.* Evaluating is an attempt to discriminate between jobs so a definition is required for each level for each factor to enable the evaluators to place the position into the right slot and attribute the correct points. The more levels, the more difficult it becomes to discern the correct level, so it is not common for the levels to exceed six.

■ *What points to allocate at each level for each factor.* Some factors are more important than others and this varies in different organisations depending on the cultural emphasis on aspects such as financial prudence, communication or team-working. There may even be an agreement, as in the example for financial accountability, that the points awarded should rise by unequal amounts.

There are more sophisticated factor-points schemes available, which have been developed by consultancies. By far the most widely used is the Hay Guide Chart-Profile, operated by over 7,000 organisations throughout the world. This has eight factors gathered into three groups – know-how, problem-solving and accountability – and is used principally for management and supervision grades. Although there are substantial purchase and training costs in utilising this scheme (and other similar proprietorial schemes), there are no design and validation costs, and information on market tracking is included in the package.

Carrying out a job evaluation

Once the nature and content of the scheme have been agreed, there are a number of stages involved in completing a full evaluation. A *job evaluation committee* may be created, which should consist of representatives of both managers and the employees who are being evaluated. It is essential that the scheme is seen as one that is fair and participative, especially when it comes to convincing the employees that the results are based on robust evidence. It is all the more convincing when the committee is made up of equal numbers from management and employee representatives and ensures that the committee needs to work very closely together to avoid intransigent split votes. Each job to be evaluated needs

Table 6.4 Job evaluation factor point grid

Factors	Levels				
	1	2	3	4	5
Experience level required	100	200	300	400	500
Complexity of post	80	160	240	320	400
Staff supervised	80	160	240	320	400
Responsibility	100	180	260	340	420
Innovation required	50	100	150	200	250
Financial accountability	60	120	180	260	400

a thorough and *comprehensive job description* on which the rating can be made. In some processes, a detailed questionnaire is sent to the manager and the job holders to elucidate areas of responsibility so the decision on rating can be made easier. In more recent years, computerised systems have been introduced where the response to a questionnaire on the nature and responsibilities of the job leads to the automatic awarding of points. When such a system is used, a job evaluation committee is less commonly used.

The first jobs to be evaluated are called '*benchmark*' *jobs* because subsequent rating decisions are made in comparison with those key jobs. They should be jobs that have the largest number of job holders. It is customary for the manager and a job holder to be interviewed regarding their views on the points to be allocated to ensure procedural justice. When the benchmark jobs have been agreed, the remainder of the jobs can be evaluated. When the process is complete (this can take six months to a year to evaluate 100 or more jobs), a '*sore-thumb*' discussion takes place to ensure that the full picture is reviewed and no job has been clearly wrongly evaluated. The final act is to *publish the results* of the evaluation, usually in the form of a straight hierarchical list of jobs and points, and provide the opportunity for employees to *appeal* if they believe the overall rating is wrong.

Factor-points evaluations, if carried out with full consultation and with a well-designed and operated scheme, are clearly superior to non-analytical schemes. They are based on more objective data and the organisation has demonstrated the importance it attaches to producing a fair salary structure. However, they are very time-consuming and a typical evaluation can take up two or three staff full-time for six months or a year. Moreover, the data can never be completely objective, needing individual judgements to be made in selecting the criteria and awarding points.

Market tracking

Before using the job evaluation scheme to produce a salary structure, the relationship of the organisation's pay compared with the marketplace needs to be examined. The level of pay in an organisation can be influenced by a number of factors:

How much the organisation can afford to pay. All too often in union negotiations the argument is used that the organisation simply cannot afford a high settlement and, one has to say, it usually cuts little ice with the world-weary union representatives who have just seen the latest executive car replacements come through the gates. However, there is always a good deal of truth in this assertion in the public sector where pay increases are mostly funded directly or indirectly by the government, so there is usually a fixed pot for pay increases. For other organisations that faced sectorial hard times, such as house building in the late 2000s or computer software companies after the collapse of the dot.com companies in the early 2000s, higher pay increases may simply serve to bring forward bankruptcy.

For other organisations, there are deeper issues to consider, not least the issue of the 'employer brand' as set out in Chapter 2. How the company positions itself on pay, called the *'pay stance'* can seriously affect the brand. If a company gets a reputation as a poor payer, it will not attract quality applications and many good employees will leave to go elsewhere. Cost saving through low pay increases may appear to be good accountancy but rarely makes good human resource practice. The question that needs to be answered is how to get higher performances from employees that will more than pay for the higher pay increases. That is another reason why many companies are moving towards extensive pay for performance schemes, often with fewer employees on board. The size of the organisation is sometimes an influence. Larger private organisations who wish to build a reputation will often pay more than small or medium-sized organisations in the same industry.

Government legislation has a part to play through the Equal Pay Act (see Chapter 9) and the National Minimum Wage (NMW). The NMW was implemented on 1 April 1999 with a minimum wage figure of £3.60 an hour. By 2012, this had increased to £6.19 per hour for employees over 21, with the rate of £4.98 for employees aged 18–21 and £3.68 for employees aged 16–17, excluding apprentices. The trade union movement had pressed for the NMW for many years and had argued that it would provide much-overdue assistance to up to 1.5 million employees in sweatshops and low-paying service outlets. Businesses initially responded with hostility to this concept, predicting that it would lead to inflationary pressures and loss of jobs. Research has indicated that neither of these predictions has been accurate and the NMW is now supported by all political parties.

An example of outcomes arising from the NMW are set out in focus on research 6.2.

FOCUS ON RESEARCH 6.2 THE EFFECT OF THE NMW IN THE APPAREL INDUSTRY

Funded by the Low Pay Commission, researchers from Templeton College Oxford found that 43 per cent of the 42 organisations in Northern Ireland and the East Midlands responding were affected by the NMW, these being mainly employers producing for the home market facing competition from overseas imports. There was concern from the researchers that the refusal of many organisations to respond to the request for pay rates may have been prompted by fears of disclosing a breach of the NMW so the results from the research that only a very small percentage of employees benefited from the scheme may have been understated. Those affected tended to have a high proportion of incentive pay (mainly piecework with an average of 25 per cent of total earnings). As a result of the NMW, employees who did not reach the production threshold were guaranteed at least the NMW and some employers responded by intensifying the work, increasing the discipline and sacking poor performers. The researchers recommended that the manufacturers move away from using piecework as a motivator towards more co-operative work systems and alternative reward systems.

(Source: Undy *et al.* 2002)

Shortage of key skills can have the effect of increasing pay rates. This applied in the housing booms of the early 2000s, which lead to very rapid pay rises occurring for plumbers, brick-layers and other building trades. The shortages of teachers and nurses by the early 2000s eventually forced the government to increase their basic rates and, in the case of teachers, introduce a system of performance pay to allow overall earnings to rise. Shortage of key web-based skills in the IT industry continues to lead to higher than expected pay to those with such skills.

Geographical location can have a strong influence with rates of pay for a secretarial position in Central London as much as 30 per cent or more higher than a comparable job in, say, Stevenage or Chelmsford. Similarly, pay in the South East tends to be higher than the North East or Scotland.

Macroeconomics, especially the state of the economy and the level of unemployment, will have an effect on both the demand and supply of labour, thereby affecting pay rates. At a time of high unemployment usually associated with low demand for labour, such as in the period 2008–12, employers are likely to offer low pay increases and there are circum-stances where it is possible to recruit new staff at lower rates. The situation is, of course, more complex than this as it is far from easy to lower union-agreed rates, nor is it seen as equitable to have staff doing the same job on different rates of pay. Another important element is the rise in the cost of living as measured in the UK by the Retail Prices Index. Employees would consider that a pay rise less than the cost of living was equivalent to a reduction in real pay.

Being aware and informed of the actual market pay rates is an essential prerequisite of formulating an effective pay policy. The sources of such information can include published national surveys, such as those by the CIPD or the Reward Group, management consul-tants, examining current job advertisements and being part of a pay club whose members exchange information. It must always be borne in mind that there are serious difficulties in precise matching of jobs and defining precise pay rates, such as whether to include bonus payments, so defining a 'market rate' for a job is almost impossible.

Equal pay

All pay structures need to be compatible with the Equal Pay Act (1970) and the Equal Value Regulations (1983), brought together under the Equality Act of 2006. This means that men and women must be paid under the same arrangements if they are carrying out like work, work that is rated the same under a job evaluation scheme or jobs that have the same value. In any job evaluation exercise, care must be taken that factors are not weighted in favour of men (such as ability to lift weights), that women are represented on the job evaluation committee and that there is not a 'sink' grade at the bottom of the structure that contains jobs that are all filled by females. More details of this Act are set out in Chapter 9.

Salary structures – traditional and broad-banded

Once a hierarchy of jobs has been obtained through a job evaluation exercise, market data on these jobs has been discerned and the market positioning aspect decided on, the last stage is to produce a salary structure.

Table 6.5 shows the outcome of a completed administrative job evaluation scheme. The division of the jobs into grades has been carried out in what is inevitably a subjective way because some jobs on the borderline could easily be on one or the other side of the grade line. These decisions are taken locally and often for political and cost-related factors linked to the individuals carrying out the job.

Under a *traditional salary structure*, based on narrow grades, employees would be appointed at or towards the bottom of the salary range for the grade and would move up the grade through *increments*, usually paid on an annual basis. According to the CIPD (2011), 12 per cent of organisations have such a structure. The number of increments related to a particular job can range from three to seven or eight. They will only move from one grade to another through promotion or if their job changes sufficiently to warrant the re-grading. The decision on re-grading is taken by a committee, which will consider the case put forward by the employee and their manager, taking into account the equity of the situation and any subsequent effects upon the salary structure. It is also possible to have pay grades that overlap but this means that one employee may be in a position that is in a higher grade but receiving lower pay than an employee in a lower grade. This is shown in Figure 6.6.

Table 6.5 Job evaluated salary structure

Grade	Minimum points	Maximum points	Minimum salary (£)	Maximum salary (£)
1	250	499	10,000	11,999
2	500	749	12,000	13,999
3	750	999	13,000	14,999
4	1,000	1,249	15,000	16,999
5	1,250	1,499	17,000	19,999
6	1,500	1,749	20,000	24,999
7	1,750	1,999	25,000	29,999
8	2,000	2,249	30,000	35,999
9	2,250	2,499	36,000	40,999
10	Over 2,500		41,000	46,000

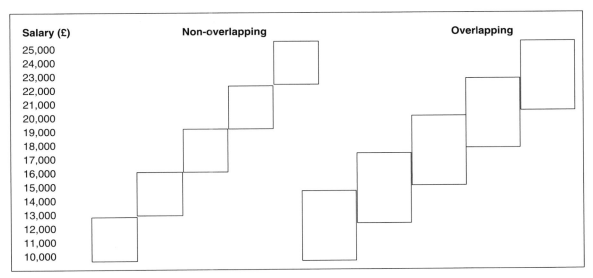

Figure 6.6
Overlapping
and non-
overlapping
salary grades

Because of a number of serious criticisms of traditional job-evaluated wage and salary structures, there has been considerable debate in recent years as to the efficiency and appropriateness of such structures. The criticisms have included:

- In the past, it has been common to create at least 5 and sometimes as many as 20 grades in a formal scheme. The aim has been to create equity by highlighting the differences between the sets of jobs and giving greater rewards to those whose jobs are rated higher than others. The structure is seen to motivate by encouraging employees to bid for promotion to a higher job through a permanent, fair and trans-parent system. A higher job, a higher grade, a bigger salary, nothing could be simpler or fairer. The first major grading system like this was set up by the US government in 1923 and operated, with some amendments, for 60 years. Today, the external environ-ment has changed considerably. The salary structure has to reflect the required culture of the organisation and the traditional job evaluation-based structure may not always be appropriate:

    > It can be bureaucratic, inflexible, time-consuming and inappropriate in today's organisations. Schemes can decay over time through use or misuse. People learn how to manipulate them to achieve a higher grade, upgradings that are not justified by a significant increase in responsibility.
    >
    > (Armstrong and Murlis 2005: 127)

- Increasingly in a business environment where organisations want to respond flexibly to global developments and customer requirements, the rigidity of a traditional scheme has too many disadvantages. Promotions are now far fewer as organisations have de-layered, reducing greatly the number of management and supervisory positions. Employees need to be far more flexible, willing to change their roles and learn more skills to meet the needs of the quickly changing national and international marketplace. The stiff, hierarchical grading structure is far less likely to match the quick-moving, responsive culture required in both manufacturing and service industries.

■ A further criticism of the multi-grade system is that it can encourage the employee to adopt a rigid approach to the job. Employees have been known to take the view that their jobs have been described closely, they have been fixed at a particular grade, therefore, that is the job they are paid for and they are not prepared to do anything new or extra outside of the job description unless they are paid more for it. In this situation, employees would apply for re-grading, which, in itself, tends to be an adversarial contest. If the employee wins, it can well upset other colleagues and lead to further claims. This can lead to grade drift, which causes salary drift and headaches for the remuneration specialist. If the employee loses, the extra work will only be carried out grudgingly, if at all. Too often, employees think of themselves, or describe others, in terms of their grades. In research the author was carrying out in a large engineering company, the question was asked what job a particular employee did. 'Oh, she's a grade 4' was the reply, as if that explained everything! In this respect, the system has a de-humanising aspect.

An alternative approach is to implement a job evaluated salary structure that is based on the *broad-banding concept*.

How broad-banding works

When the job evaluation has been completed, the artificial divisions, which normally distinguish between grades, are ignored. What normally happens is that a set of generic titles, such as manager, supervisor, operative, clerk, are gathered into one large band. This allows all of the employees in an organisation to fit into a salary structure, which may have as few as four or five broad bands.

Being broad, there is a large difference between the top of the band and the bottom (called the 'salary range'). Sometimes the top of the band can be 70 per cent higher than the bottom (i.e. a range for the 'managers' band from £30,000 to £51,000), as shown in Figure 6.7. Bands for senior managers can have a much wider range, such as over 200 per cent (i.e. from £50,000 to £150,000).

Moving up the band is the key to the whole concept. First of all, the *decision process* is in the hands of the departmental manager to act within guidelines and in line with their budget. This replaces the formalised and human resources department-controlled re-grading process. The criteria for authorising movement falls into four main areas:

- A *competency* approach where clear guidelines are laid down on the acquisition of important competencies. Measuring them is not easy and will be a mix of subjective analysis, the attainment of NVQs or equivalent, or through third-party judgements, such as in 360-degree appraisal.
- An informal system of *job development* where employees move from a probationary role through experienced employee to expert performer with guidelines on how long that should usually take. This is operated at Fabergé where employees develop from a 'competitive zone' to a 'premium zone' (IDS 2003) following the development of their skills and competency.
- *Enlarging experience* approach, where employees move between jobs and between departments, gaining extra skills and generally becoming more useful and knowledgeable employees.
- By *performance*, where the outcomes of the performance management scheme indicates a movement up the band due to enhanced and proven performance.

Other features of a broad-banded structure include the greater emphasis on external relativities (i.e. ensuring pay rates match the market rates), less concern for structure and rigid guidelines and more concern for flexibility and paying for the person rather than the job (Armstrong and Brown 2001). According to the CIPD (2011), around 25 per cent of organisations employ some form of broad-banded structures.

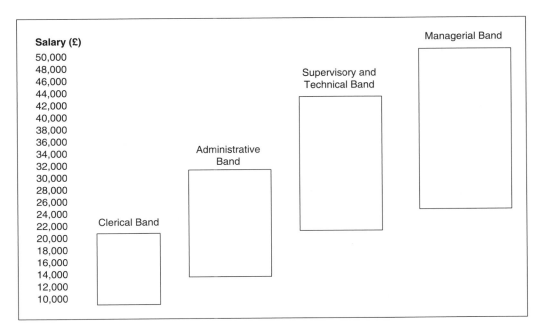

Figure 6.7
Broad-banded salary structure

Benefits and difficulties of a broad-banded structure

Advocates of the scheme put forward the following advantages:

- Employees have a much greater incentive to achieve results for the organisation. If they become more competent, have a higher performance or enlarge their skills and experience, they can be paid more. This encourages the type of values that organisations want to promote. They do not have to wait to apply for grading or a promotion.
- Giving the lack of managerial and supervisory jobs, employees can still make progress with the organisation. By employees improving and being motivated to improve, the job of the overstretched manager becomes easier.
- The system is far more flexible. New jobs and processes can be introduced easily without worrying about employees' narrowly defined jobs.
- When the decisions are put in the hands of the manager, they will act realistically and responsibly towards their staff and their total salary bill.

However, there are a number of disadvantages to such systems. It can be seen that broad-banding is not much more than the type of salary structure in a small informal organisation that has not yet found the necessity for job evaluation. In this respect, a '*spot rate*' can be applied for each job, so, in reality, broad-banding can be so flexible that there is actually no need for job evaluation at all. This informality can lead to all the accusations of subjectivity and favouritism that led to job evaluated wage structures in the first place. Unless the criteria for salary progress are robust, really understood and operated fairly, the system will not be seen as fair itself.

There can also be a tendency for it to be expensive. Under narrow grades, employees come to the top of their grade and realise they may have to stay there unless promoted. Under broad bands, most employees see an almost unlimited opportunity to make continuing progress and managers may find difficulty in holding back salary increases, particularly if employees meet the criteria. Employees may also be demotivated if they meet the criteria but the manager's budget restrictions stop the increase. Under traditional job evaluation schemes, budget restrictions could not stop a re-grading.

Making sure that managers act in a consistent fashion across the whole salary structure is not easy. Personnel's role here is crucial in acting as an auditor, an adviser, mentor and informal adjudicator. Without such fall back, the wage structure is likely to fall into chaos.

As Milkovich and Newman explain,

Flexibility is one side of the coin; chaos and favouritism is the other. Broadbanding presumes that managers will manage employees' pay to accomplish the organisation's objectives (and not their own) and treat employees fairly. Historically, this is not the first time greater flexibility has been shifted to managers and leaders. Indeed, the rationale underlying the use of grades and ranges was to reduce the former inconsistencies and favouritism that were destructive to employee relations in the 1920s and 1930s. The challenge today is to take advantage of flexibility without increasing labour costs or leaving the organisation vulnerable to charges of favouritism and inconsistency.

(1996: 285–286)

PAYING FOR PERFORMANCE

The traditional job evaluated pay system with incremental movement is based on a collectivist approach where employees are all treated the same, regardless of their performance. It is assumed that employees become increasingly knowledgeable and competent in their job as time goes by, which is why they receive increments. It is a simple scheme rewarding employees for their service and loyalty.

This picture is fading fast as society changes. As the capitalist, free-enterprise society now dominates most of the world's economies, employees have come to accept, expect and mostly approve of pay systems that differentiate between different levels of performance.

There are many forms of performance pay schemes. The original *individual piecework* systems promulgated by Taylor (1911) operated for 50 years or so and have a modicum of apparent fairness but have fallen into disrepute since the mid-1960s for a number of reasons. Constant arguments can occur over piecework rates and allowances, especially when new materials, processes or machinery are introduced; rates of pay may fluctuate through no fault of the operator due to lack of work or poor materials; individual piecework encourages the employee to only work for themselves rather than be part of a co-operating team; a costly set of rate-fixers and work study engineers is needed to maintain the system; and workers may be encouraged to cut corners in health and safety to boost their income.

Today, piecework is only in evidence in the remnant of the textiles and other traditional industries, although it still also is operated in some industries where employees work at home. It has mostly been replaced by *group incentives schemes*, which operate in a department or unit-wide environment. They can take the form of production targets only or, increasingly, a broader set of targets including quality, on-time production and accident levels. The objective is to encourage employees to understand the basis of the targets and to aim to achieve them, working co-operatively as a team. This has been taken further in America through a system called *gainsharing*, where a unit shares the cost-savings achieved through higher productivity, waste-saving and quality improvement, in the form of quarterly bonuses. One of the crucial aspects of the system is that employees have full information on the objective-setting process, are informed of the current performance on a regular basis and are encouraged to participate in problem-solving and innovation committees to aid the achievement of the objectives. An example of gainsharing is given in case study 6.2.

CASE STUDY 6.2 GAINSHARING AT CHARLOTTE COUNTY

Each year the city manager of Charlotte County Authority, North Carolina, sets a savings goal for the general fund. If the goal is met or surpassed, 50 per cent of the savings becomes available in the gainsharing pool. Only half of this pool is distributed to all employees automatically. The distribution of the other half depends on whether or not a given employee's business unit meets its key objectives for the year. These objectives are called 'incentive targets' and typically are tied to customer service, efficiency, quality, time standards and safety. If the business unit meets four out of five incentive targets, employees receive an 80 per cent share of this second component of the gainsharing pool. Employees in units meeting all their targets are eligible for a full share of both components – generally $300–$650.

(Source: Ammons and Rivenbark 2006)

In the retailing and sales environment, it is common to pay a *commission*, which is a small percentage of the price of the goods sold, to the employees concerned. In a few industries, such as double-glazing and computers, some sales staff are employed on a commission-only basis.

Another version of payments comes under the general title of *employee recognition schemes*, which have developed in recent years. An example of an innovative scheme is shown in case study 6.3.

CASE STUDY 6.3 RECOGNITION AT CLARIDGE'S HOTEL

Claridge's introduced a new employee recognition scheme in 2002 to match their changed culture, which focused on the philosophy of 'one team, one hotel' and centred on acknowledging an employee's contribution to the business.

Their 'Going for Gold' scheme referred to an actual pot of gold envelopes that sat on the HR director's desk. This symbolises the pot of gold at the end of the rainbow that is used to graphically illustrate Claridge's mission and values, set out on cards carried by every manager. If an employee successfully demonstrates one of the core values, such as service perfection, another employee can recommend that person for a lucky dip in the pot. If successful, the employee is awarded a 'going for gold' card and invited to pick out an envelope. The awards do not necessarily have a high monetary value but they do have a high perceived value to employees. They range from an extra day's leave, to a facial treatment in the hotel's beauty salon, to a ride home in the limousine. The most sought-after envelope is an all-expenses-paid night in the hotel's top suite, which would normally cost over £4,000.

The organisation has recognised the importance of an immediate response to high performance so the ritual card selection takes place on the same day.

(Source: IRS 2004)

A further example was Westminster Council's Rewarding Excellence scheme, which identified six individuals each quarter with £1,000 each for outstanding contributions to the organisation and the Council's employee of the year won £10,000.

The most common, and controversial, system of performance pay in the UK, however, is performance-related pay (PRP) and, due to its importance, a separate section is devoted to this subject.

Performance-related pay

Forms of performance-related pay (PRP), sometimes called 'merit pay', are operating in around 65 per cent of organisations surveyed (CIPD 2011). The forms vary considerably and each one is usually designed to fit the organisation, its culture and operations, and the work of the employees. The schemes can be individual or team-based, be paid monthly or annually, and be accompanied with forms of 'recognition', such as vouchers or non-financial benefits.

Despite a considerable degree of scepticism surrounding these outcomes, the majority of organisations believe that there should be pay distinctions between those individuals that perform well and those that do not. This view appears to be shared by the majority of employees, as a number of research projects found in the 1990s (Thompson 1993; Marsden and Richardson 1994). It is noteworthy that research into employees' views of PRP has been neglected in the last 20 years. There is some evidence that the introduction of PRP leads to higher productivity and performance, as shown in focus on research 6.3.

FOCUS ON RESEARCH 6.3 PERFORMANCE-RELATED PAY AT SAFELITE

Safelite, a firm installing automobile window glass, changed from a time-based system to a PRP system in the mid-1990s and this brought a productivity increase of 44 per cent. This was due not just to individual improvements in performance but also to the fact that high performers got better (the 'incentive' effect) and low performers left the organisation (the 'sorting' effect) in search of jobs with more secure pay each month. As average pay had risen because of this change, applicants wanting to work hard and raise their pay levels were encouraged to want to join the organisation. It was pointed out that the scheme worked well partly because the individual output was easily measured and team-working was not a feature.

(Source: Boxall and Purcell 2008)

FOCUS ON RESEARCH

Schemes can use the outcomes of a performance review to add a bonus payment on top of an annual increase relating to cost of living. Increasingly, however, the automatic cost of living rise is being replaced by rises linked entirely to performance.

You will recall from Chapter 5 that the process of performance management under-pins any payments arising from the employee's performance. An essential set of require-ments for any PRP scheme includes an agreed set of targets (either objectives or developing competencies or both), an effective and robust method of measuring the performance against the targets and regular feedback to the employee. The outcome of a review at the end of the period (usually a year) is normally a performance rating. This can be fairly simple, such as the rating from 1 to 5 in Table 6.6, or a more complex calculation as in Table 6.7.

The figure for the pay increase is predetermined, based on the budget available for increased labour costs.

In both of these examples, the schemes are set up as an *incentive*, to demonstrate to the workforce that there are opportunities to achieve a higher than average pay increase through working harder and smarter to meet the agreed targets. They can also act as a *reward* to those employees who perform above average.

An example of a disappointing outcome from a PRP scheme is set out in focus on research 6.4.

To sum up, the arguments in favour of PRP schemes include:

- It is fair to distinguish between the high performer and those that are only average or below average.
- Making payments to high performers reinforces the message that the organisation recognises and encourages high performance and establishes a clear culture throughout the organisation.
- The process of setting objectives clarifies what an employee needs to achieve and thereby focuses their attention and effort.

Table 6.6 Conversion of ratings into a pay increase

Performance description	Rating	Pay increase
Excellent performance, all targets greatly exceeded	5	8%
Superior performance, majority of targets met or exceeded	4	6%
Normal performance, good proportion of targets met, although a few missed	3	4%
Below-average performance with a number of key targets missed and weaknesses shown	2	2%
Very weak performance with few if any targets met and disciplinary action to be considered	1	0%

Table 6.7 Conversion of ratings into a pay increase in a complex scheme

There are six objectives for the employee to achieve with the following weightings:

Objective 1	Weighting 30%	Objective 4	Weighting 10%
Objective 2	Weighting 20%	Objective 5	Weighting 10%
Objective 3	Weighting 20%	Objective 6	Weighting 10%

At the end of the period, a decision is reached that the level of performance on the objectives is:

Objective	Achievement level	Rating	Outcome
1	80%	30%	24 points
2	100%	20%	20 points
3	90%	20%	18 points
4	50%	10%	5 points
5	100%	10%	10 points
6	60%	10%	6 points
		Total points	83 points

Conversion to salary increase

Points	Salary increase
0–50	zero
50–69	2%
70–89	4%
90–99	6%
99–100	8%

In this example, the employee would receive a pay increase of 4 per cent

FOCUS ON RESEARCH 6.4 PERFORMANCE PAY AT HEWLETT-PACKARD – A DISAPPOINTING OUTCOME

Beer and Cannon examined programmes in pay-for-performance at Hewlett-Packard (HP). Thirteen separate units of the company – at different types of sites, in different states – launched pay-for-performance plans in the early 1990s. Within three years, all had dropped them.

In the early 1990s, HP seemed a perfect setting for innovations in pay. A so-called 'built-to-last' company, it was highly decentralised and enjoyed a sense of mutual trust, high commitment and wide use of management by objectives. The workforce was salaried and the merit system was based on peer comparisons at the salaried level.

According to Beer and Cannon, managers in many companies look to pay-for-performance for good reasons. They expect that it will attract and motivate people. They expect that performance standards will outweigh the costs of whatever incentives they put in place. They also want protection against business exigencies: should the market go south, they don't want to be permanently stuck with new costs. The vast majority of employees, in general, also want pay-for-performance. While they may not think their current pay system is unfair, they do think pay-for-performance is an opportunity to make it *more* fair. They think they can outperform whatever pay they get; they usually assume they will benefit in terms of higher pay.

One HP unit that threw the matter into relief was HP's San Diego site. The experiment in pay-for-performance began naturally enough, driven by a transition to self-managed teams in production. Managers launched a programme of team goals coupled with team-based pay with three possible levels of reward. Managers reckoned that 90 per cent of teams could reach Level 1, 50 per cent could reach Level 2 and 10–15 per cent could reach Level 3.

For the first six months, everyone loved the new system. The majority of teams hit Levels 2 and 3. Because the payout was greater than expected, management adjusted the goals upward. Then the complaints began.

The teams were frustrated that factors out of their control, such as the delivery of parts, affected their work. The high-performance teams often refused to admit people whom they thought to be below their level of expertise, leading to disparities among the teams. There was reduced mobility between teams, preventing the transfer of learning across teams. Employees built their lifestyles around the higher level of pay, and were angry when they could not achieve it consistently. Managers for their part felt they were spending too much time re-engineering the pay system. They concluded that it did not motivate employees to work harder or, perhaps more importantly, to learn. It was also hard to maintain consistency of pay across the larger site. Managers also grappled with the question of sustaining pay-for-performance over time. There were clear short-term benefits but also clear longer-term costs, including the cost of constant redesign and negotiation of the system. Other HP units ran into similar difficulties. The most striking finding from these pay-for-performance experiments is the size of the gap between managers' expectations of benefits and the reality that they experienced in terms of costs.

Going forward, the researchers suggested that managers recognise pay-for-performance not just in instrumental terms – as a carrot, perhaps – but also as a larger exercise in fairness and justice within the organisation: 'Do not proceed until both sides understand what they are getting into'.

(Source: Beer and Cannon 2004)

- By being focused, employees act in a flexible way to achieve the required results rather than simply carrying out their job as defined by their job description. They become facilitators and problem-solvers and circumvent bureaucratic barriers.
- The opportunity for differential earnings is a recruitment aid, attracting ambitious, results-oriented applicants.

■   Achieving results and obtaining good pay increases is a positive force for raising morale in the organisation.

There are, however, just as many criticisms of PRP:

■   In an influential Harvard Business School article, Kohn (1993) attacked performance pay schemes for a number of reasons. He asserted that there was no hard evidence that they were effective motivators, that they discouraged employees from risk-taking as their objectives were so circumscribed, that they undermined interest and motivation in the job itself, that they punished employees when they failed, thereby demotivating them, as much as they rewarded those that succeeded, and they ruptured relationships between employees. His final criticism was that rewards took away from managers the right approach to managing:

> Managers often use incentive schemes as a substitute for giving workers what they need to do a good job. Treating workers well – providing useful feedback, social support and the room for self-determination – is the essence of good management. On the other hand, dangling a bonus in front of employees and waiting for the result requires much less effort.
>
> (Kohn 1993: 59)

■   The problems have already been set out in Chapter 5 relating to the effectiveness of the performance management process, including the danger of concentrating on just a few objectives, ignoring the needs of the team and the difficulties in actually defining meaningful objectives.

■   It is not clear how good a motivator it is. In most schemes, including the examples shown in Figures 6.6 and 6.7, the pay difference between the average performer and the high performer is only, at most, 3 or 4 per cent. On an average salary of, say £20,000, this represents an after-tax monthly difference of only £35 or so. Most evaluations find that employees do not regard PRP in financial terms as an effective motivator.

■   Managers may be tempted to pick out their favourites to award them higher PRP than the rest of the staff creating a considerable sense of cynicism and unfairness.

■   Managers, on the other hand, may not want to go through the hassle of differentiation and the difficulties it causes and may put all staff on the same level, which produces, ultimately, the same effect. Distributive justice, as it is called, has not been done or been seen to be done.

■   Individual PRP can work against team-working. If individuals are assessed entirely on their own performance, they will want to shine, to claim all achievements as their own, rather than a team's.

Making it work

A series of key criteria for the successful implementation of a PRP scheme include the following:

■ Top management 'ownership' of the concept and commitment to its introduction as an integral part of the organisation's strategy and to be personally involved with implementation 'to walk as it talks'.

■ The system to be strategically integrated with the organisational objectives and its human resource and pay strategy and policies, which include a clear and shared vision of the organisation's future.

■ A robust performance management (PM) scheme on which pay increases are based, introduced in phases from the top downwards at a pace that ensures employees understand what is happening and why.

■ The PM scheme should be integrated with the way that employees are managed, rather than an additional paper exercise, which includes regular reviews during the year and no surprises at the annual review date.

■ The review should encourage honest, positive and fair management of poor performance with time and resources to put the situation right.

■ Rewards should be capable of being 'significant' for the market sector and to be easy to understand and be publicly defensible.

■ Avoiding using PRP to compensate for recruitment problems, market pressure, inability to promote, taking on significant additional responsibilities and other issues that risk confusing the messages implicit in the system.

■ Substantial training and communication for all concerned to ensure it is thoroughly understood.

■ Regular reviews and flexible adaptation of the scheme as lessons are learned and to respond to employee feedback, reflecting the way an organisation needs to constantly develop and change.

Executive pay

Pay for top executives is similar in many ways to conventional pay. They receive a basic pay, an incentive scheme, usually a variant of PRP, and a set of benefits. However, there are key differences in each area.

On base pay, the sums have become substantially higher in recent years, with a top-100 PLC chief executive receiving a base salary close to £1 million in 2011.

Benefits tend to be generous, especially on pension, where their rate of accrual is normally much faster than a convention final salary scheme (30ths as opposed to 60ths or 80ths), which results in very high pensions on retirement.

It is in incentive schemes that the major differences occur. Although they are usually based on the measures of performance against predetermined targets, the difference is that the sums that can be earned are usually very high – often up to three times base salary. On top of this, senior executives in the private sector are usually enrolled in long-term schemes where they receive deferred bonuses in shares and share options, which they can choose to cash in, at the price when the option was granted, after between three and seven years. If the share price of the organisation has risen, the value of this reward can be very high. The most extraordinary case reported was that of Michael Eisner of Disney Corporation who received a total pay, mostly made up of bonus, of over $500 million in 1998, due to the huge increase in the company's share price while he had been CEO.

In the UK in 2010, the average pay for directors of the top 100 private companies rose by 49 per cent to average £2.7 million, compared with £24,000 for the average employee in the private sector, a rise of 3 per cent (Wachman 2011).

In addition, top executives usually have a contract with one year's notice. This means that, should they fail and need to be removed quickly, they must, at law, receive a year's pay, including bonus entitlement, which works out as a large sum of compensation. That means the organisation will sometimes pay out millions of pounds to 'reward failure'.

The high levels of executive pay have played a major part in instigating the financial crisis and subsequent recession, which started in 2008. This is because bankers and other executives in the financial and housing sectors were highly rewarded for encouraging individuals, organisations and governments to take out loans, which, in many cases, they would clearly be unable to repay. Moreover, the banking sector created and encouraged the development of complex financial instruments, such as derivatives, which were difficult to understand and had unexpected and unpleasant consequences but allowed those that created and sold them to be paid very high bonuses. This has led to much debate on the issue of whether high executive pay can be justified. Arguments put forward to support such high levels include:

Senior executives are recruited in an international labour market
A key argument has been the fact that the pool of talent for senior executive jobs is an international one as such people are generally willing to move to any country if the job and its rewards warrant such a move. To be able to persuade potential candidates from America and, to a lesser extent, other high-salary countries, such as Switzerland, for non-US senior executive positions, the job has to carry US-style levels of reward or the size of the pool will be much reduced. Once the position has been filled at US reward levels, it then becomes difficult to fill it next time round at rates that are far below this level or the next incumbent may feel undervalued.

Salary levels for executives are highly transparent in most Western countries (due to regulatory processes), so, once the decision is made (and published) to pay the new CEO highly, this process tends to trickle down the organisation. Other board members may dislike such a huge gap with their CEO and, in any case, it is not unknown for the new CEO to bring on board new colleagues paid in the same way as himself (or very occasionally 'herself'). Then executives further down the chain become aware of general reward rises and better performers will feel dismayed if they are not asked to join this attractive new culture. Within a comparatively short time, the organisation's executive pay as a whole is taken up a new notch, in line with 'international market rates'. Once there, it is very difficult to reduce.

This is good evidence to support the argument that the market for top executives is international. An example here is that of American Dick Brown, who was CEO for Cable & Wireless in 1997. He was offered a similar position at competitor AT&T at a much higher salary. Cable & Wireless managed to persuade him to stay by offering him a doubled salary and a high long-term earnings potential. Within two years, he had been head-hunted to lead another US telecoms company.

Shortage of talent

An associated argument is that the required candidates for top positions are simply not around in sufficient numbers so the price of top talent has risen sharply. Most top international companies are very large and complex, often dealing with a vast product list, such as General Electric, or operating in many countries, such as Nokia and Coca-Cola, or employing many people (Walmart employed over 1.2 million in America alone in 2009 and around double that worldwide). So, very high pay is required to find such people with the ability to take on such vast responsibilities and get them sufficiently motivated to be prepared to move anywhere and devote the whole of their time to carrying out their executive job.

The theoretical support here comes from *tournament* theory. First put forward by Lazear and Rosen (1981), the basic framework of tournament theory assumes that employees will compete in a 'knock-out' tournament to achieve promotion to the highest levels. The way to encourage huge commitment from employees at the lower levels is to make substantial prizes in the form of excessive salaries/benefits for those at the top. Employees are assumed to exert effort to increase the likelihood of securing the 'prize' and the effort expended depends on the differential in pay between the top and bottom, the number of competitors and the employees' perceived view on the possibility of their winning the prize. This theory goes some way to understand the huge pay rates for top sportspeople and celebrities in the arts and media.

In the commercial arena, however, it does not explain why more such people are not available to become top executives. In the international marketplace, where standards of business education around the world have risen substantially in the last 50 years, there should be far more, not less, available talent, especially when developing countries are taken into account. It would be expected that this rise in supply would act as a depressant on reward rates but it has not happened. The argument is that the *quantity* of supply may have increased but the *quality* is uncertain. Just as the international market for football players (or football managers) has hugely widened in the last ten years, most organisations are not prepared to take too many risks and hence go for proven talent for their top performers, with the associated reward costs, to get quick and (perhaps) guaranteed results. Sometimes it works, but not always.

Also implied in this argument is the need to take on external candidates. If an organisation needs shaking up or to set out in a new direction, external candidates with no baggage may be appropriate, but they generally cost more money, whatever the level of recruitment. At the most senior level, where they can be the most valuable in effecting change, they are very expensive indeed.

Actually, senior executives are quite cheap

An unusual argument is that the Total Reward costs for *executives that make a real difference to organisational performance* are not very high. The total pay for the eight executive board members for Tesco in 2009 was around £30–35 million (depending on what costs you count, but including most employment costs). Given that the profits in 2008–09 were over £3 billion, they cost only around 1 per cent of the profits they generated. The argument goes that they, therefore, give very good value for money. Perhaps if their salaries had been 20 per cent less, the profits may have been 50 per cent less, who knows?

Even if you add on another 100 executives below this level, this figure rises to no more than £60 million and the costs only rise to 2 per cent. The percentage in other organisations may average a little more, such as in banking or technology where employees may be more highly skilled but it is still a very small total cost.

It is difficult to combat this argument because one is dealing with uncertain scenarios. Did the skill and experience of the executives cause the high performance (however that is measured) or was this due to other factors? For example, the financial performance could have been due to a good run of benign economic performance, as in the 1990s, or high metal prices may have led to good profits all round, in the case of mining companies. Some change in government policy or legislation may have worked in their favour. And if the executives had been paid more, would performance have been even better?

High pay reflects the level of risks taken by senior executives

The risks referred to here are two-fold. Firstly, it is the ability to identify opportunities that may involve risk-taking (i.e. make substantial investments that may or may not bring a large return) and know how to deal effectively with them. This is part of a previous argument for paying for unique talent.

The second risk involved is the risk that the executive takes in working in that position. By the executive taking up such a high-profile position, the risks of failure are serious. If it does not work out as a success, the executive loses a substantial salary, which it may not be possible to recoup. Their reputation is also in the public eye, making the 'after-life' of failure quite difficult, as seems to be the case with the dismissed CEO of Royal Bank of Scotland (Fred Goodwin) and the two chief executives of BP (Brown and Hayward) who both left under a cloud and with far less wealth than they would have expected.

However, the 'high-risk' argument may apply in the case of a racing driver or even a top rugby player where death or senior injury may occur, but holds little water with executives. As long as they do not break the law, the risks they take are small. If they fail and lose their job, they will currently be paid compensation, which usually equates to at least a year's reward. This will be, of course, a sizeable sum. Moreover, a good executive will have networked effectively in their position to be able to find reasonable job alternatives should life prove unlucky in some way. So senior executives do not deserve much sympathy for the type of risks they take.

Executives' pay is heavily contingent on performance
A high proportion of executive pay is contingent upon performance, ranging from over 50 per cent for the average CEO to around 30 per cent for the executive just below board level. The argument is that the huge salaries are only paid when the organisation has performed really well. If the executive does not perform, the high rewards are not paid. This argument is supported by Kaplan (2008) whose research showed that the companies with CEOs in the top quintile of actual pay (in other words, the most highly paid, chiefly by performance pay) were the top-performing companies relative to their industry. Companies with CEOs in the bottom quintile of actual pay were the worst-performing quintile relative to their industries. In other words, CEOs were clearly paid for performance and rightly so. He even went on to indicate that there was evidence that CEOs may be underpaid.

In theory, the argument that bonuses are strongly aligned to company performance appears to be a good one but it is not watertight. There are numerous accounts of executive targets being insufficiently stretching or of targets being achieved through increased prices in limited competition areas, such as the water industry where executives received double-digit pay raises of nearly £1 million, while increasing customers' bills well above inflation (Watts 2010). However, a recent development is that some major companies, including Land Securities, are inserting a clause in executive contracts to the effect that bonuses will be clawed back if it is found that executives had acted unlawfully or with too much risk or if other reasons were determined that strongly indicated the bonuses were not deserved (Churchard 2012). For example, HSBC plans to claw back bonuses from executives, past and present, after an investigation by the US authorities revealed the bank had laundered cash for criminal organisations. The employer could recover millions of pounds in bonus awards from employees, reportedly including former chief executive Michael Geoghegan and Sandy Flockhart, a senior executive at the bank's Mexican operation (HSBC 2012).

If you publish every detail of pay, you are bound to get pay inflation
One of the factors that make executive pay different from most other pay systems is the degree of regulation that compels the full details of directors' pay to be published by the companies. This is one of the reasons that so much research is published – because the data are so readily available. It is thought that transparency provides benefits for the shareholders who can hold directors to account.

Unfortunately, too much information can be a bad thing, as explained by Dymond and Murlis: 'because executives now know what other executives earn and what they earn it for (at least in part), pay levels have increased as these highly competitive individuals demand parity' (2009: 165).

Compensation committees, when taking decisions on pay rates, will have in front of them full data on executive pay elsewhere. No self-respecting committee will want to be seen paying below the median rate and most would like to be seen paying more. An influence here is that the committee will be made up of a number of non-executive directors who are executive directors elsewhere and, therefore, cynics will say, may have a vested interest in inflationary increases.

Senior executives can move to an even more remunerative career

One of the arguments that is little discussed concerns those individuals who, in fact, never become directors, as shown in case study 6.4.

The main point made in case study 6.4 is that countries need good senior executives to run their major industrial organisations. Britain needs good (home-grown) executive talent to build and develop the country's large and medium-sized operations so they can compete in the world. If potential talented individuals decide at an early age that they can achieve wealth in an alternative way, the likelihood is that Britain as a whole is the loser. The argument, therefore, is that we must make being a senior executive attractive enough or they will choose an alternative, less vital path. Today, they are more likely to go into hedge funds or merchant banking and, given recent events, we can be less sure of the benefits those industries bring to the well-being of UK PLC.

As explained by Waples:

> In the case of at least half the FTSE100 directors, their advisers and consultants will be earning more than the directors they have to answer to. . . . The position of running one of our top 100 companies should be seen as a pinnacle of a career. . . .
>
> When you look at the amount of money that has been made out of running privately owned businesses, it has made heading a quoted company look like a mug's game. The debate about executive pay should move on, otherwise the drift of talent to private equity will continue. It is already a small gene pool from which chief executives are picked and we cannot afford it to get smaller.
>
> (2006: 4)

Summing up the arguments for high executive pay

Finding and retaining top level executives is crucial to any organisation. The quality of the leadership will determine the ability of the organisation to succeed in the long term. The job is extremely demanding and requires people with extreme talents in management, willing to take on vast responsibilities in terms of people and financial management. The market is an

CASE STUDY

CASE STUDY 6.4 HIGH PAY FOR OWNER-DIRECTORS

Back in the 1990s, I worked for a private company in the street-lighting industry. It employed 500 staff and was run by the founding chairman. In his twenties, he worked as a junior executive in the building industry but, at 27, decided to set out on his own specialising in erecting street lighting. The business was perilous for a number of years as he built it up, first locally in Hertfordshire, then spreading round the Home Counties, and he won some big contracts on the M25. In my early days as their first head of personnel, he took pleasure in telling me that any of these contracts could have brought the business to his knees if they had gone badly wrong.

His greatest innovation was in persuading a large county council, where he had carried out contract work for many years, to agree a five-year contract to maintain all the street lighting in the county. He offered terms far below those that it cost the Council to carry out the work themselves and he made it pay by driving through a series of changed labour practices among the operatives, including performance pay and self-managed teams. It proved a great success, was implemented in a number of councils over the coming years and became one of the models for Thatcher's compulsory competitive tendering system in the 1980s and 1990s.

What has this to do with executive pay? Well, when I joined, the company's turnover was around £25 million and made £2 million profit after tax. The chairman and his close family owned all the shares, reinvested at least half back into the business and generally took between £500,000 and £750,000 as their 'salary'. The business was estimated to be worth around £30 million. Yet it was a small company, important enough to the local community but did not compare in any way with a big building company such as McAlpine or Tarmac who had a turnover not far short of £1 billion at the time. However, his salary was on a par with a board director of one of these large construction companies.

The chairman was therefore a rich man, much richer than he would have been if he had achieved the position of a senior executive in the building industry. And yet, he was just the sort of person with all the right skills and experience that would be vital to some national building company. He chose not to follow this path because he could become rich in an alternative way and was therefore lost as a potential senior executive. He also told me that he found little attraction or motivation in the slow climb up the industry career path or the rewards available at the top.

international one so top talent will migrate to the highest bidder, therefore most top jobs have to pay high (US) salaries to ensure that the limited pool of top performers are persuaded to join the organisation. The pay has to be very high or executives may decide that setting up their own (relatively small) business can produce equally high rewards and they will be lost to the business. Finally, executive pay is only a very small proportion of total costs and most of it is contingent to high performance by the executive.

Sceptics will argue that the very high pay levels are excessive and create difficulties within the organisation; that they do not truly reflect the international marketplace where they are many candidates with the talent to rise to the top; that the job carries little down-side risk and the extent of responsibilities are over-stated and most are devolved; that performance pay schemes for executives are suspect and ineffective; and that the desire to run one's own business is an innate drive to be in charge and not over-influenced by the comparative wealth generation. Moreover, far too many executives get paid high rates for mediocre performance and received huge compensation when they fail.

Skills-based and competency-based pay

There has been a growing emphasis, especially in manufacturing organisations, on supporting initiatives that increase the level of skills and competencies in the workforce. Encouraging production employees to learn a variety of jobs on their team, or to learn maintenance skills, has become an essential part of the jigsaw of improving productivity and quality. This encouragement sometimes takes the form of *skills-based pay*, where the acquiring of a set of specific skills levels earns the employee a higher rate of pay. These skills can be linked to NVQs or to a specific skill set devised by the organisation. Rhône-Poulenc Agriculture employees can obtain an NVQ and a pay increase of up to £4,000 a year through their comprehensive multi-skilling scheme leading to technician status. South Caernarfon Creameries devised a skills-based scheme in 2004 to encourage employees to develop their skills and ensure that cover was available for absence (Attwood 2005).

Competency-based pay has many similarities in that employees are encouraged to develop a set of competencies, which, when obtained, leads to the opportunity of higher pay. As explained by Kessler: 'Competencies shift the focus from *what* employees do in terms of individual targets . . . to how employees meet their responsibilities. In other words, competence-based pay involves linking rewards directly to particular and desired behaviours or personal characteristics' (2001: 220).

Benefits

The final part of the reward jigsaw is the selection of benefits payable to employees. The total cost of benefits are high, making up around 30 per cent of the pay bill when pensions are included (Smith 2000), although the elimination of final salary pension schemes by most companies in the 2000s will have reduced some of the overall benefit costs. The collection of benefits in most organisations is generally haphazard, having grown without a strategic basis or direction. It is often because of the perceived need to be competitive in the market-place that they are introduced or extended. Rarely are they withdrawn, although this is not unknown, and usually some form of compensation may be offered if this occurs. The list of benefits can be divided into three main groupings:

Personal security. This is the welfare section where the employer is prepared to subsidise the employee when they have specific health or associated needs. Sick pay, life assurance, private health insurance, prolonged disability schemes and pensions all come under this heading. They operate because employers wish to be regarded as kind and generous (as they may well be). However, the generosity of a sick pay scheme may be an organisation's undoing as too many employees find that they may be just as well off on the sick as at work.

The type of pension offered had become a major issue by the early 2000s when many organisations, many extremely well known, such as Sainsbury's and British Airways found that the cost of 'defined benefits' schemes (those based on the final salary of the employee and generally involving a contribution of 12–18 per cent by the employer) had become too high (Allen 2002). This was due to the increased longevity of pensioners and the decline in the value of pension funds arising from the poor stock-market performance in the period since 2000. Investment returns in the era of low interest rates have also meant that companies have had to increase their contributions to the pension funds to ensure they meet the pension regulations. Many organisations have now switched pension schemes to 'defined contributions' where the employers' contribution has been reduced to 3–8 per cent with a subsequent reduction in the employees' pension.

Job-related benefits. Some jobs have 'perquisites' (perks), the most common being the company car. The UK has the most generous company car policy in the world with cars being issued even when the jobs are almost entirely office- or factory-based. Other benefits include relocation allowances and protective clothing allowances.

Family-friendly benefits are also developing in these times of acute awareness of the need to accommodate employees with caring responsibilities. Creches, childcare vouchers, compassionate leave, maternity and paternity leave plus special working hour arrangements are all regarded as welcome benefits to those hard-pressed by conflicting demands of home and work.

Flexible benefits describe the system that allows employees to choose their own benefit package within defined constraints. Benefits and their costs are displayed in the form of a 'cafeteria'. Each year, an employee can choose to take, for example, increased holiday but reduce their pension contribution or buy child vouchers and reduce their health insurance. These schemes are extremely popular with employees, allowing them to choose benefits to fit their lifestyle at no cost. Organisations have to pay the administrative costs but the main advantage for them is that their benefit bill is capped and the benefit brings high retention rates. Further discussion of flexible benefits is found in Chapter 7.

An example of flexible benefits is shown in case study 6.5.

CASE STUDY 6.5 INTRODUCING FLEXIBLE BENEFITS AT ASTRAZENECA

In 1999, two large pharmaceutical companies, Astra and Zeneca, merged, bringing together two financially and culturally different reward schemes. Introducing an integrated flexible benefits scheme was one of the initiatives used to integrate the culture and HR systems within the new organisation, reflecting the need to be innovative and to involve employees in the decision-making process.

Under the combined scheme, all employees had to receive a set of 'core' benefits, including annual leave, pension and healthcare, but they also had the option to choose from a large menu of additional benefits within the budget allocated to them. This included extra holidays, retail vouchers, insurance services and enhanced pension provision. Each benefit had a pricing structure and most offered benefits through corporate discounts, national insurance and tax savings. The latter have substantially reduced over recent years and AstraZeneca lost a case at the European Court of Justice in 2010 over the payment of VAT when supplying vouchers to employees. Employees could extend their benefits beyond their budget but would have to pay extra for this, usually through salary sacrifice.

The administration of the scheme was outsourced to Hewitt, Bacon & Woodrow and employees received from them a full statement of their choices, made every July, and the costs involved. The initial take-up for the scheme was very high, close to 80 per cent and the additional costs to the company worked out at around 2 per cent of total salary. Internal research indicated that the flexible benefits scheme was a major contributor in a high level of staff retention. Employees have seen that the scheme recognises the diversity among staff by allowing individuals to choose benefits according to their lifestyle.

(Source: Manocha 2002)

USING TECHNOLOGY IN REWARD

Technology has a large part to play in the recording, analysing and monitoring processes of reward:

Job evaluating/salary structures. Consultants, such as Hay, provide extensive software systems so that an online job analysis will produce a points outcome and the updating of jobs will show immediately any grading implications, producing revised salary structures. 'What if?' scenarios will help reward practitioners to decide on the correct pay structure architecture and such structures can be matched against market rates.

Market tracking. Many consultants and agencies have detailed databases of current pay rates and benefits in varied locations, plus the changes over time are monitored.

C
A
S
E

S
T
U
D
Y

CASE STUDY 6.6 EXCELLENCE THROUGH TECHNOLOGY AT UNILEVER

Following negative reactions to its revamped compensation and support package for expatriate employees, Unilever developed an employee attitude survey using social media elements and the latest data visualisation technology. As well as enabling employees to judge their position in relation to others, the company was able to use the cost-effective tool to 'crowdsource' for suggestions. Participants found the process engaging and, as a result of the findings, Unilever is planning policy changes. This innovation won the 'Excellence in Technology' CIPD award in 2011.

(Source: CIPD 2011)

Performance pay. Schemes can be computerised to show projected earnings on a group or individual basis and demonstrate earnings against targets with reasons for variations on the different target measures.

Benefits. The cost of benefits can be analysed and monitored and flexible benefits systems software can provide individualised data to show each employee the implications of their varied choices.

An example of the way an organisation can use technology in reward systems is shown in case study 6.6.

M
E
T
E
O
R

C
A
S
E

S
T
U
D
Y

DESIGNING A REWARD STRUCTURE

Another year had gone by and Sarah had achieved the promotion to the position of HR manager at head office with specific responsibility for compensation and benefits. On appointment, she had attended a three-day course on reward management run by the CIPD and had joined a small group of fellow specialists in her immediate locality who met every two months to talk informally about reward developments and market rates.

Her first major assignment was to examine the reward structure that had been in place at the corporate headquarters for over ten years. This structure served 700 employees, half of whom were management and administrative staff and the others were a mixture of sales and service staff for the telecommunications business. The base rate was set through a Hay Job Evaluation scheme and consisted of 15 grades from filing clerks on grade 1 to executive managers on grade 15. There was no performance pay scheme and the only variable element in the pay was an annual

Christmas bonus decided by the chief executive, which had given an average of 3 per cent of salary over the previous three years.

An examination was necessary for a number of reasons. Pay drift had become a matter of concern, adding nearly 2 per cent to salaries over the previous 18 months. It was difficult to see why this had accelerated recently but it was partly self-perpetuating as increases won through revised job grading by one group of employees were swiftly followed by a similar claim by a group in the next-door department. Another concern was that this grade drift had started to cause the pay rates to move beyond the median rate in the locality that they had previously occupied. To try to draw the annual salary costs back to compensate for the salary drift, the annual pay increase awarded in the previous year had been low but this had caused discontentment and a sense of unfairness among the staff. A final cause of concern was the growing unwillingness of staff to take on new duties without a major discussion arising about their grading. As many such changes had come about and were being planned for the next 12 months as the nature of the business altered, it was considered essential that a major new initiative took place.

Sarah began by talking to all of the senior management concerning the current difficulties and the possible options. She also commissioned a specific short attitude survey through MORI regarding employees' views on pay and benefits. Finally, she set up a series of focus groups with the staff to try to obtain a balance of their views.

She found that there was a clear consensus for change in most areas. Neither managers nor staff had a great commitment to the Hay scheme, recognising that it was being used for political purposes and for sectional gains. The large number of re-grading claims and the time they took to sort out merely served to divide staff rather than giving a sense of fairness on pay issues. Staff were also generally satisfied with their current pay level but there was a strong view that there should be some sort of pay arrangement that differentiated between good, average and poor employees.

Having cleared her tactics with senior management, Sarah sent out a communication briefing to staff that set out her findings on employees' current pay attitudes. Rather than come up with a new pay system to implement, Sarah offered two alternatives for staff to consider and discuss in their management teams. The first was the complete abolition of the job evaluation scheme and the introduction of a loose, broad-banded pay structure with only four bands. Movement within the band would be based entirely on the employees' performance as judged by their line manager. The second alternative retained the vestiges of the grading structure but the number of grades would be reduced to seven and the movement within those grades would occur through a combination of performance and the achievement of competencies.

After widespread debate within the teams, a majority view (although not voted on) emerged in favour of the second option. Sarah then set about designing a detailed scheme using a competency framework she had 'borrowed' from one of her colleagues in the local group who had a similar head office unit. It needed to be adapted to fit the revised mission statement and values recently issued by the board, but the overall match was good and considerable savings were made in this way by not using expensive specialist consultants. The existing jobs would need to be re-evaluated and placed in the reduced number of grades, and this would be achieved by redefining jobs against the overall competency framework. With only seven grades, there would be less opportunity for arguments at the borders.

Establishing how employees would achieve competencies was carried out through the services of a specialist who worked in the Business School at the University. The most complicated process was establishing the method of converting an individual's performance and level of competence into a rating scale. For this, she spent time with each head of department agreeing the nature of the vital performance indicators and how they could be balanced from one department to another. She knew that managers would take the decisions on both areas and that she would have to act as umpire to make sure departments were neither too generous nor too strict in their overall judgements.

After a series of short training courses for the managers and supervisors, the scheme was launched at the time of the pay increase. It had been agreed that the pay increase would be at an acceptable level and that employees who came out of the re-grading exercise as being overpaid would be 'red-circled', in other words, their pay would stay the same until annual pay increases brought their pay into line. There was general approval from staff of the overall pay increase, but Sarah knew that the real test of the scheme would come towards the end of the year when employees could see the direction that their own pay and jobs were going.

At the same time, Sarah persuaded the board, through her personnel director, to replace the arbitrary annual bonus with a gainsharing plan. A number of site targets were set, which related to overall labour costs, customer complaints, on-time delivery, employee innovation and a selection of departmental specialist targets, which added value to the organisation. Achievement of these targets would lead to a percentage bonus on a sliding scale from 1 per cent to a maximum of 10 per cent. Tying this in with profits was a challenging process as she knew that profit-sharing rarely motivated a head office environment. The final version was complicated and needed a great deal of selling. Moreover, it would be difficult to get employees involved until they saw that it actually produced the required results. A monthly meeting of a group of interested employees representing all the departments plus a monthly information sheet would be the vehicles to gain employee commitment.

KEY CHAPTER SUMMARY POINTS

- Reward strategies should be aligned to the corporate strategy to ensure that they motivate employees to achieve the required objectives and adopt the preferred skills, competencies and behaviours.
- Total Reward analyses all the areas that impact on an employee's contract, including financial and non-financial reward, career development and working environment.
- In recent years, there has been a sharp shift from paying employees according to their job and length of service to paying people for their achievements and competencies.
- Salary structures are being developed using broad-banding techniques that are beginning to replace traditional job evaluation techniques.
- There are a wide variety of performance pay systems for various employment situations. Performance-related pay, the best known, remains controversial with critics equally balanced between those who view it as subjective, divisive and too complicated to operate and those who see no alternative to a system that differentiates between those employees who perform well and those that do not.
- Payment systems should aim to be fair, equitable and cost-effective.
- Benefits make up a sizeable part of the pay bill and serve a number of functions, including personal security and supporting family-friendly policies.

STUDENT ACTIVITIES

1 As a human resources manager, you have been asked to carry out a local survey to find the 'market rate' for a marketing assistant. Detail how you would plan and implement this project; list the difficulties you would encounter and how you may overcome them.

2 Look up cases involving 'red-circling', which relates to job evaluation and equal pay claims. Examine the legal implications of the red-circling that took place in the Meteor case study.

3 In the Meteor case study, what would be the outcomes of the new pay system that would make employees very unhappy with the new system?

4 Discuss with two of your colleagues which benefits are the most important ones to offer, putting them in a league table of importance. Justify your decisions.

5 Look up the article that is the basis for focus on research 6.1. Why do you think that some of the respondents consider that their reward strategy does not operate in practice?

6   Discuss what role the government has in the area of executive pay. Ensure you update yourself on the latest developments in this area before answering this question.

7   In case study 6.2, what would happen if business turned down and the company made little or no gains over a pay period?

8   In the Hewlett-Packard research, discuss what options the company has if it moves away from the performance pay scheme it has previously operated.

9   Carry out research into how performance-related pay has worked in the UK teaching profession. (You may find the article by Marsden and Belfield (2006) useful here.) Debate whether teachers should be paid for results.

REFERENCES

Adams, J. (1963) Towards an Understanding of Inequity. *Journal of Abnormal and Social Psychology*, 67: 442–436.

Allen, A. (2002) Silver Lining? *People Management*, 29 August, 30–32.

Ammons, D. and Rivenbark, W. (2006) Gainsharing in Local Government. *Popular Government*, Spring/Summer, 31–36.

Armstrong, M. and Baron, A. (1995) *The Job Evaluation Handbook*. IPD.

Armstrong, M. and Brown, D. (2001) *New Dimensions in Pay Management*. CIPD.

—(2006) *Strategic Reward*. Kogan Page.

Armstrong, M. and Murlis, H. (2005) *Reward Management*, 5th ed. Kogan Page.

Armstrong, M., Cummins, A., Hastings, S. and Wood, W. (2003) *Job Evaluation*. Kogan Page.

Attwood, S. (2005) The Workers that Got the Cream. *IRS Employment Review*, 832, 30 September, 27–28.

Beer, M. and Cannon, M. (2004) Promise and Peril in Implementing Pay for Performance. *Human Resource Management*, Spring, 43: 3–48.

Boxall, P. and Purcell, J. (2008) *Strategy and Human Resource Management*, 2nd ed. Palgrave Macmillan.

Bremen, J. and McMullen, T. (2010) What is the Future of Total Rewards? *Workspan*, July, 57–59.

Brown, D. (2001) *Reward Strategies: From Intent to Impact*. CIPD.

Churchard, C. (2012) Bonus Clawback Proposed at Land Securities. *People Management*, 9 July.

CIPD (2004) Reward Management Survey 2004. CIPD.

—(2011) Reward Management Survey 2011. CIPD.

Conway, N. and Guest, D. (2001) *Public and Private Sector Perceptions of the Psychological Contract*. CIPD.

Dymond, J. and Murlis, H. (2009) Executive Rewards, in S. Corby, S. Palmer and E. Lindop (eds) *Re-thinking Reward*. Palgrave Macmillan.

Guest, D. (2007) HRM and the Worker: Towards a New Psychological Contract?, in J. Boxall, J. Purcell and P. Wright (eds) *The Oxford Handbook of Human Resource Management*. Oxford University Press.

Guest, D., Conway, N., Briner, R. and Dickman, M. (1996) The State of the Psychological Contract in Employment. *Issues in People Management*, No. 16. IPD (CIPD).

Hay Group (2004) Hay Group Engaged Performance Model. Hay Group.

Herzberg, F. (1968) One More Time: How Do You Motivate Employees? *Harvard Business Review*, January–February, 53–62.

HSBC (2012) HSBC Executives Set to Face Bonus Clawback. HSBC website, accessed 31 July.

IDS (2003) Performance Management. *Study 748*.

IRS (2004) Thank You Goes a Long Way. *IRS Employment Review*, 792, 23 January, 32–34.

Kaplan, S. (2008) Are US CEOs Overpaid? *Academy of Management Perspective*, May, 5–20.

Kessler, I. (2001) Reward System Choices, pp. 206–231, in J. Storey (ed) *Human Resource Management: A Critical Text*, 2nd ed. Thomson Learning.

Kohn, A. (1993) Why Incentive Plans Cannot Work. *Harvard Business Review*, September/October, 54–63.

Lazear, S. and Rosen, S. (1981) Rank Order Tournaments as Optimum Labor Contracts. *Journal of Political Economy*, 89: 841–864.

Locke, E. (1968) Towards a Theory of Task Motivation and Incentives. *Organisational Behavior and Human Performance*, 3: 157–189.

Manocha, R. (2002) Pick 'n' Mix. *People Management*, 7 November, 44–45.

Marsden, D. and Belfield, R. (2006) Pay and Performance where Output is Hard to Measure: The Case of Performance Pay for School Teachers. *Advances in Industrial and Labor Relations*, 15(1): 1–34.

Marsden, D. and Richardson, R. (1994). Performance for Pay? The Effects of Merit Pay on Motivation in a Public Service. *British Journal of Industrial Relations*, 32(2): 243–262.

Maslow, Abraham H., Frager, Robert and Faidman, James (1987) *Motivation and Personality*, 3rd ed. earson.

Milkovich, G. and Newman, J. (1996). *Compensation*. Irwin.

Perkins, S. and White, G. (2008) *Employee Reward*. CIPD.

Persaud, J. (2003) Mutual Appreciation. *People Management*, 28 August, 29–30.

Sharp, R. (2009) Total Reward at Arup. *IRS Employment Review*, 916, 19 February.

Smith, I. (2000) Benefits, pp. 152–157, in G. White and J. Drucker (eds) *Reward Management: A Critical Text*. Routledge.

Taylor, F. (1911) *Principles of Scientific Management*. Harper.

Thompson, M. (1993) *Pay and Performance – The Employee Experience*. Report No. 258. Institute of Manpower Studies.

Undy, R., Kessler, I. and Thompson, M. (2002) The Impact of the National Minimum Wage on the Apparel Industry. *Industrial Relations Journal*, 33(4): 351–364.

Vroom, V. (1964). *Work and Motivation*. Wiley.

Wachman, R. (2011) Executive Pay Consultants behind Escalating Executive Pay. *The Guardian*, 18 November, 26.

Waples, J. (2006) Why our Top Bosses Deserve to Be Well Paid. *Sunday Times*, 1 October, 4.

Watts, R. (2010) A Gush of Pay Rises for Water Chiefs while Bills Soar. *Sunday Times*, 5 September, 11.

ADDITIONAL FEATURES

Please visit the companion website at: www.routledge.com/cw/stredwick where you will find additional case studies and reading material together with short self-tests and other resources for both students and lecturers.

7 FLEXIBLE WORKING

INTRODUCTION

Chapter 1 described how the competitive nature of the global economy combined with the changing social and demographic forces has led to organisations having to adapt their shape, structure, culture and ways of working. No longer can they expect a reliable and subservient market to allow them to grow and prosper at a steady and predictable rate. One of the major responses to this situation is to place more emphasis on effective ways of working, especially those that lead to the most efficient use of human resources. An initial analysis of high-performance organisations was set out in Chapter 1 and you may wish to refresh your memory here before reading this current chapter.

FLEXIBLE WORKING PRACTICES

It was emphasised in Chapter 1 that the willingness and ability of employees to work flexibly is key to improving organisational performance. Flexible working traditionally has been described as part-time and temporary employment but, in reality, it covers a very much broader picture. As first modelled by Atkinson (1984), it includes all activities that operate to allow a quicker and more focused response to the needs of customers and clients. The subject therefore covers:

- *Temporal flexibility*, fine-tuning the total hours of the labour force through part-time working, annualised hours, job sharing and zero-hours
- *Numerical flexibility*, by extending the use of temporary employees
- *Occupational or functional flexibility*, by developing the skills and experience of employees so they can switch jobs to meet immediate needs and encouraging employees to look beyond their employment contract
- *Geographical flexibility*, through encouraging teleworking, homeworking, outsourcing work and replacing face-to-face contact by call centres.

We will look at each of these in turn, but we will start by examining the strategy employed by organisations in relation to the concept of the 'flexible firm' put forward by Atkinson and Meager (1986).

THE FLEXIBLE FIRM

Although first put forward as early as the 1980s, the model of the 'flexible firm' is still a valuable tool to analyse the overall concept of flexibility (see Figure 7.1). The starting point is that employees are divided into two main groups. Firstly, there are the '*core*' employees who tend to be full-time, permanent, career employees who carry out activities that are essential

Figure 7.1
Core and
peripheral
workforces

Source: Atkinson, J.
and Meager, N.
(1986) *New Forms
of Work
Organisation.* IMS
Report 121,
adapted by
Professor John
Purcell.

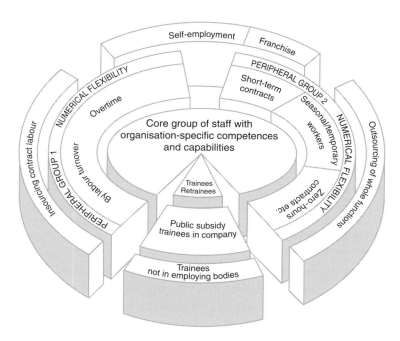

to the longer-term success of the organisation. Originally, these included managers, super-visors, plus other groups who possessed specific, relevant and vital skills in the technical, sales, production, professional and administrative areas. These groups would be well paid, investment would be made in their training and development, and they would have career paths charted for them. In return, they would be expected to be loyal and to have a full commitment to the organisation in terms of a willingness to work flexibly when necessary, such as through multi-skilling, shift working or relocating. The success of their work would ensure that their organisation was differentiated from its competitors.

The other group of employees are those on the 'periphery' of the organisation. Divided into two sections, the first group consists of employees whose skills are more general, rather than specific to the organisation's success. They may be full-time on 'perma-nent' contracts but their job security is not well defined and their work activity could be re-engineered or outsourced without causing harm to the business. These employees will be paid according to internal equity and average market rates and there will be some investment in training but not in long-term development. A high degree of flexibility is gener-ally not expected from them as their work tends to be generalised. This group, however, can be the source to fill any vacancy that occurs in the core group through a competitive process.

The second periphery group comprises of those with employees who enjoy even less security. They may be interns, working on short-term contracts or secondment, or be under some form of government traineeship. The group also includes those on part-time and job share, although it is interesting to note here that the legal situation has changed since the model was devised in that part-time and job-share employees now have identical rights as full-time employees under European law. When it is necessary to change the labour input in these areas, the tap is turned on or off through the non-renewal of short-term contracts and non-replacement of trainees or part-time staff that leave. In the work they carry out, this group would be expected to work flexibly (this would be specified in their contract) and co-operation is likely to be high because many in this group would want to be considered for permanent employment. Interns may not be paid at all but most of this group are paid at the same rates as their periphery colleagues but there is little or no investment in training.

The final labour group are not employees at all. They include agency staff, sub-contractors, self-employed and those carrying out work that has been outsourced. This group is interesting in that they may have moved from any of the above groups. A skilled group of IT staff may have moved from the core group to set up their own company and provide outsourced services. They may have been made redundant from the first periphery group and now provide occasional services on a self-employed, low-pay, high-hours basis. This last group work on a performance basis with high flexibility to complete the contract on time and within the cost. They normally receive the same pay, after 12 weeks' work as employees carrying out the same work under the Agency Workers Regulations, effective from October 2011. Some highly skilled agency workers, especially those in IT, often receive much higher rates.

There is considerable evidence that the use of flexible working practices is spreading, as shown in Table 7.1. A Demos report (Leighton and Gregory 2011) found that 91 per cent of employers offer at least one form of flexible-working arrangement to their employees. Almost 60 per cent of employees stated they currently used a form of flexible working and 83 per cent of requests for flexible working are approved.

That is not to say that the trend towards increased flexibility will inevitably continue. The effects of the recession, where the labour supply is far greater, may mean that employers may be faced with far fewer requests for flexible working and may revert to the more traditional full-time permanent employment model.

Table 7.1 Types of flexible working

	1998	2004	2011
Part-time working	46%	64%	76%
Flexible hours	19%	26%	55%
Homeworking	16%	28%	47%
Job sharing	31%	41%	46%
Term-time working	14%	28%	30%
Annualised hours	8%	13%	19%

Source: WERS (1998, 2004) Workplace Employment Relations Survey. Routledge; Leighton, D. and Gregory, T. (2011) *Re-inventing the Workplace*. Demos.

The 2011 Demos report found some evidence of that effect:

■ 81 per cent of employers did not expect that their organisation would extend flexible working in the next two years.

- Of the firms that currently do not offer any form of flexible working arrangement, 92 per cent said they were unlikely to start offering it in the next two years.
- Half of firms with fewer than 50 employees said they granted fewer than 1 in 4 flexible working requests.

However, the Family Friendly Working Hours Taskforce has found that that the recession has had the opposite effect in practice: 'The recent recession created a climate where there is an even stronger appetite for the business case for flexible working' (2010: 21).

The Taskforce pointed out that for many businesses and companies the downturn necessitated a shift towards flexible working practices in order to minimise redundancies. Companies justified continuing with developing flexible working because it was effective:

- 65 per cent of employers said flexible working had a positive effect on recruitment and retention (saving recruitment, induction and training costs)
- 70 per cent of employers noted significantly improved employee relations – suggesting greater loyalty among staff
- 58 per cent of small to medium-sized enterprises (SMEs) reported improved productivity.

In a similar vein, the CBI (2010) has observed that flexible working proved its worth during the recession and claims that, although unemployment rose, unprecedented co-operation between employers and employees helped minimise job losses.

The practicalities of implementing flexibility have been greatly assisted in the last 15 years by the lack of opposition from weakened trade unions who have traditionally opposed much of the numerical and occupational flexibility proposed. Pockets of resistance have still occurred, such as the opposition to the use of part-time labour in the Post Office or to the use of annualised hours on some of the railway networks.

Implementation by employers, however, seems to take place on an incremental basis rather than through longer-term strategy. It is part of a continuing process of change rather than a sudden volte-face from traditional employment methods. Areas such as outsourcing and use of part-time labour have shown a steady growth while others, including annualised hours and job share, have risen slowly from very low bases. Advantages and difficulties exist for each type of flexible working system and these will be dealt with later in the chapter.

TEMPORAL FLEXIBILITY

Part-time working has shown a considerable increase since the Second World War as shown in Table 7.2.

The rise for females was pronounced by the 1960s as the growing respectability of the married woman's part-time job became established and rose to the plateau of around 45 per cent by the 1990s compared with the gradual rise in men's part-time work to 8 per cent for most of this period, with a faster rise at the turn of the century up to 10 per cent. Both figures have recently been influenced by the huge growth in full-time students, most of whom need to obtain a part-time job following the abolition of student grants and high course fees.

Table 7.2 Part-time employees 1951 to 2010 ('000s)

	1951	1971	1997	2010
Male part-timers	139	584	982	1,403
% of male employees	1.9	4.4	8.3	11.1
Female part-timers	417	2,757	4,728	5,116
% of female employees	6.0	33.6	44.3	41.9
Total part-timers	556	3,341	5,710	6,519
% of all employees	2.7	15.5	25.0	26.3

Source: Labour Market Statistics (2011) November.

Part-time work can be categorised as classical, supplementary or substitution. *Classical* part-time jobs are posts where the jobs are only required for a few hours per day such as school-meals staff. *Supplementary jobs* are those used to augment and improve the efficiency of the full-time operation such as where housebuilders employ site negotiators at weekends, accounts staff may be employed for end-of-month accounting and sales staff for busy days in the week. *Substitution* part-time jobs are those where part-time employees replace full-time jobs. This has been prevalent in major retailing where part-time staff, who are easier to recruit, can be seen as just as committed and often more flexible than full-time staff. In America, United Parcel Service (UPS) implemented a policy in 1998 to replace almost all of their full-time positions with part-time ones at a lower pay rate, but a national strike by their 185,000 employees managed to achieve a reversal of this policy.

Although part-time working is rare in senior executive positions, there are a number of examples. One of these is Allen & Overy, leading solicitors, who appointed part-time directors in 2010.

This area of employment has also been augmented by *portfolio workers* (Handy 1994), who are those employees with more than one part-time job. Examples can be a person with a morning office employment who also works occasional evenings and week-ends for a banqueting company or an executive made redundant in their fifties who combines consultancy with lecturing in the UK and Eastern Europe. Some employees have found the need to *downshift*, leaving successful, if stressful employment to take up more satisfying but less remunerative part-time work. Another version of this is *V-time*, practised by a few larger organisations such as Santander, where employees are allowed to reduce their hours for a limited time period for personal, family or self-development reasons. *Job shares* are a growing form of part-time work, normally operating at a routine level but with developing examples in the managerial field. *Zero-hours* arrangements are where employees have no fixed or contractual hours of work but are called in when required. These forms of contracts exist in catering, sporting activities, film and media work and in some retailing organisations. The total number of employees on zero-hour contracts rose 25 per cent during 2012. Even the House of Commons advertises for zero-hour reporters for Hansard (Butler 2013).

ACTIVITY 7.1

Draw up a list of the advantages and difficulties from an employer's viewpoint in employing part-time employees.

Discussion of activity 7.1

You may have thought of some of the following advantages:

■ Part-time staff are usually easier to recruit than full-time staff so the quality of the applicants may be higher.

■ In the event of absence or holidays, part-time staff will normally be able to fill in by working a few extra hours, so cover is easier to obtain. This is normally the case in a job share where the parties work together to ensure the job is covered.

■ When a part-time member of staff works a few extra hours, the payment will generally not be at overtime rates as such rates are paid only when the full-time hours are exceeded.

■ Employees who are working part-time because they are bringing up a family may be available later on to switch to full-time work, which provides an efficient method of recruitment.

■ In the case of zero-hours, employees are only used when they are strictly necessary, with no waste of expensive resources.

The *difficulties* may include:

■ In the case of job shares, there will be double the amount of training, appraisal and records to maintain.

■ It is usually easy to obtain part-timers for morning jobs, not so easy to fill gaps in afternoons or evenings.

■ Managers can find part-timers more difficult to manage, especially if they depart in mid-afternoon, leaving a half-empty department.

■ As most part-timers have caring responsibilities, they may be more likely to need time off, although there is no strong evidence of this.

A further variation on temporal flexibility is *annual (or annualised) hours*. Rather than employees being contracted for a fixed number of hours per week, say 38, they are contracted to work annual hours of, say, 1,976. The actual weekly hours they will be asked to work could be seasonal, such as in food production or for the Christmas trade, where the hours may vary between 25 and 50 per week. Alternatively, they could be on a fixed rota of shifts averaging 32 hours a week, leaving a certain amount of 'reserve hours', which would be called upon in times of absence, machinery breakdown or any other difficulties. In both cases, the main aim of the system is to achieve greater flexibility in the use of available labour and to reduce or eliminate the amount of overtime that had been worked where the labour availability did not meet the business needs at that time.

An example of annualised hours in a service environment is detailed in case study 7.1. How the introduction of annualised hours changed both the formal and informal methods of working is examined in focus on research 7.1.

CASE STUDY 7.1 ANNUALISED HOURS AT THE RAC

In the late 1990s, the RAC faced very fierce competition in their marketplace. This was not just from their traditional rival, the Automobile Association, but also from a string of small players that had seen niche opportunities and who could move faster than the traditionally organised, overweight duopoly. Moreover, they had recently become a demutualised company and needed to aim for better overall performance to match the expectations of their new masters.

Their prime objective was to move away from a standard 40-hour week for their patrol teams, which did not match the seasonal variation in their work or the unpredictability of demand caused by weather and conditions. The large gaps in the service had to be supplemented by excessive (and expensive) overtime and by a network of independent garages contracted to meet unfulfilled attendance at breakdowns.

Negotiations with the TGWU produced a new system based on 1,831 annualised hours on roster (net of holidays) and an agreed level of paid reserve hours – the choice is from 92 to 368 hours, equating to average weekly hours of 42 to 48. This was accompanied by a higher basic salary. The hours for each patrol team is rostered a year in advance with hours reduced in the quieter summer months and extended during the winter with appropriate cover for weekends, keeping throughout the year within the Working Time Regulations. Patrols are notified monthly of the use of their reserve hours, based on detailed previous demand patterns, plus a day's notice of 'red alert' days when really bad weather is forecast.

The scheme was launched with substantial communication with newsletters, meetings, an audio-tape and feedback from patrols using an independent interviewer. This variety of hours did not suit every patrol team and sixty employees left within the first two months, although the majority appear very satisfied.

With productivity rising by 8 per cent, using fewer patrols than previously, and a big rise in on-the-spot completions, the scheme has proved successful, reinforced by a satisfying increase in the customer satisfaction index.

During 2000 and 2001, the scheme was extended to their three main call centres where staff had the choice of three levels of contracted hours – 991, 1,304 or 1,826 – depending on whether they wanted to work full- or part-time and the nature of the shift pattern. The shortest contract covers fixed peak periods only while the other patterns are:

- Semi-flexible – earlies or lates (1,304 or 1,826 hours)
- Nights – 1,826 hours varying between 9pm and 7am across the year
- Flexible – shift times varying during the year between 6am and 11.30pm.

Staff on 1,304- or 1,826-hour contracts also sign up for a number of 'flexible hours' which management will allocate when they are needed. In quiet periods, call-centre staff who have agreed flexible hours may be invited to leave early and half of the hours remaining not worked are then banked to be used at a busier time.

(Source: IDS 2002)

FOCUS ON RESEARCH 7.1 ANNUALISED HOURS AND THE 'KNOCK' IN A YORKSHIRE CHEMICALS PLANT

Jason Hayes spent six weeks in an old, heavily unionised chemicals plant in West Yorkshire studying the effects of the introduction of annualised hours in response to the need to improve labour utilisation. It employed 75 men working on intensive and hazardous work. An agreement with the union in 1993 introduced multi-skilling, a reduction of the working week to 36 hours, a 6-shift system and annualised hours.

Management was aware that, prior to annualised hours when an overtime culture prevailed, overtime had been systematically created through planned absenteeism – called 'knocking'. This was where one person agreed to go sick while another covered for him and received overtime with premium payments. The following week, the roles would be reversed. This meant that they both received enhanced pay for working standard hours. This reflected, in the view of Hayes, 'purposeful behaviour' rather than 'negative withdrawal'. Until the changeover, the workforce had kept it within acknowledged limits of management toleration but the external forces of the early 1990s required such indulgences to cease if the business was to be kept open.

The outcome of the annualised hours system was that labour costs were reduced by £700,000 and absenteeism dropped substantially to half its previous level with the 'knock' almost entirely eliminated. Employees were not entirely happy with the new system or the way it was operated.

(Source: Hayes 1997)

NUMERICAL FLEXIBILITY

Being able to vary the number of employees allows an organisation to respond quickly to its varying needs. This is most commonly achieved by either using *temporary staff* through an agency or by using a pool of specifically recruited temporary employees. The label 'temp' or 'casual' conveys an image of employees who are of no great importance to the organisation – unskilled, short term and low status. Because this label is often incorrect, the term '*complementary employee*' is starting to take its place. These are often key employees taken on for short-term but crucial contracts and who make a sizeable contribution to their host company. In human resources, for example, a small team of complementary managers may be employed to implement a major change programme that can involve important selection processes – for both promotion and redundancy.

An example of a partnership approach to managing temporary employees is shown in case study 7.2.

CASE STUDY 7.2 WORKING PARTNERSHIP – MANPOWER AND XEROX

In 2000, one of Xerox's strategic plans was to reduce the company's operational costs while maintaining a high level of customer service in the competitive photocopying market. To meet these objectives, Xerox wanted a strategic partner to assist in dealing with customer requests to fix faulty equipment across the UK. Xerox's key requirement was for a quality supplier of staffing solutions that could enhance their own internal capability with a fixed price, provide skilled staff and deliver a national solution with the ability to flex the workforce according to customer demand.

Manpower set up a new staffing infrastructure within Xerox, consisting of HR managers, support managers and a team of 100 skilled engineers nationwide, which had risen to 350 by 2004. Manpower managed the recruitment and training process for field engineers and schedulers, who were a mix of temporary and permanent employees. Xerox's call centre customer call-routing system was integrated with a tracking and fulfilment system to schedule engineers to deliver the required work across different customer site.

The outcome of the partnership was a reduction of between 15 and 18 per cent in staff and an improvement of 10 per cent in productivity. As Sandy Menzies, Xerox's service partner and logistics manager explained, 'By partnering with Manpower, Xerox has been able to effectively transition its highly seasonal workload to a more flexible workforce, gaining both productivity and cost per fix benefits, whilst maintaining the high quality of performance to meet our customers' demands. But the biggest benefit is for our customers, who now see an engineer more quickly.'

(Source: Stredwick and Ellis 2005)

GEOGRAPHICAL FLEXIBILITY

Teleworking and homeworking

In today's new technological world, it is no longer necessary for staff to work from a specific office location. They can operate more flexibly by being a *teleworker (tele* is the Greek word for distance) and having a home base, using the organisation's facilities only on the specific occasions when this is essential. As office space represents a considerable cost, tele-working, as well as providing location flexibility, also provides no little cost savings in terms of office costs. For some project-based jobs, especially in IT, the person concerned could live in the Outer Hebrides (some do, of course) as long as their computer and telephone links are powerful, safe and effective.

The drive to increase teleworking has various starting points. In the case of Mobil Oil, the relocation of their head office from London to Milton Keynes resulted in a situation where a number of key sales employees wanted to continue to work for the company but not to move house or travel long distances. It was also realised that proximity to the customer was probably a more important factor than proximity to the head office.

ACTIVITY 7.2

Draw up a list of the issues you need to consider when setting up a formal teleworking or homeworking operation and how you would deal with them.

Discussion of activity 7.2

You may have listed some of the following issues:

■ How is the work of the home/teleworker controlled? Day-to-day supervision becomes far more difficult when that person is not around to be supervised. A system needs to be drawn up with regular checks on objectives, targets and reviews with specific meeting dates to allow more 'normal' feedback than is possible by email.

■ How do you avoid the home/teleworker being out of touch with developments and with colleagues? Teleworkers are actually quite capable of linking up with colleagues through email and experience shows that a teleworker's grapevine can be more imaginative than most.

■ How should you pay home/teleworkers? Given the difficulty in supervision, tele-workers are much more likely to have a good proportion of their pay by way of performance reward, rather than paid for the hours they work. Crucial to this is the need for clear and robust performance criteria and targets that are realistic and agreed.

■ How can you be certain that a home/teleworker will be successful in that mode of work? You cannot be certain, of course, although psychometric tests can now give a reasonable indication of how they may respond to the special demands of isolation and self-reliance.

■ Will home/teleworkers miss out on promotion? Given that most promotions, especially into management, entail the supervision of other staff and office-based administration, then home/teleworkers may not be the natural candidates for such positions. However, lateral moves and additional technical career development are alternatives to demonstrate confidence and support.

Case studies 7.3 and 7.4 are examples of two organisations that have developed their flexibility strategies and practice in response to organisational need and employee requirements.

CASE STUDY 7.3 HOMEWORKING AT CENTRICA

Centrica, which runs the British Gas operation, has around one-third of its 36,000 employees working from home in one of the following three modes:

■ Mobile worker, who works across Centrica locations at least 60 per cent of the time

■ Homeworker, who works from home at least 60 per cent of the time

■ Office worker, who works from home some of the time but spends at least 60 per cent of their time in the office.

The strategy in recent years has been to bring about the necessary cultural change so that flexible working is considered as 'normal' as working common office hours. One of the major benefits is that it helps them to become an 'employer of choice' and widens the applicant pool.

Centrica has set up different kinds of flexibility for each of the groups detailed above. Gas engineers, for example, receive their day's working instructions direct to their laptops and begin the day from home. Parts are ordered by email and picked up from the local distribution point. They update their manager through emails and an online jobs system. Regular meetings of 25 or so engineers are held and each group has its own space on the intranet as a form of social networking to share information, solutions to common problems and to guide trainees.

For other flexible workers, Bluetooth allows most staff to access the network from a broad number of locations and the number of hot-desking arrangements has increased. Staff working from home are provided with all the technology that allows them to function outside the office.

Judy Greevy, Group Diversity Director, has pointed out that opening up wider the pool of applicants to those that want and need to work in different ways has been important for the diversity agenda. The process of increasing flexibility has been helped by the fact that the business case was made some years ago with mobile workers, such as engineers, so there have been few corporate barriers to working differently.

(Source: IRS 2004)

CASE STUDY 7.4 TELEWORKING AND HOT-DESKING AT HERTS COUNTY COUNCIL (HCC)

Workwise was an initiative in the mid-1990s by HCC to combine flexibility at work with a 'green' approach to travelling. With an increasingly congested road network, where gridlock loomed each rush hour and difficulty in recruiting staff at all levels, the Council hit on two major solutions. The first initiative was to encourage a culture of flexible working hours and locations, which was piloted with their Trading Standards Office. This department and its staff covered the whole county and originally worked from one central office. Under the new scheme, staff worked mostly from home but came into office 'Oases' to file reports and other administrative duties. The Council had over 500 individual sites, employing 26,000 staff. Within 20 of these sites, an 'Oasis' was set up which had a drop-in office with telephone, PC, email and intranet facilities. Trading Standards staff, operating mostly in their own patch of the county, use whatever Oasis is convenient. They do not even need to bring standard reference books or policies with them as they are all available on the intranet. This produced an immediate saving of 10 per cent in travelling costs, including employees' time and cost of getting into their office.

The second initiative was in the social services department where 4,500 staff worked from 5 office sites. After substantial consultation, the plan was implemented to shut and sell three of these sites and open one purpose-built one, which would include further Oasis areas with pleasant meeting rooms and coffee areas. Employees would have the choice of being home-based, mobile or office-based. Each group had the appropriate technology depending on their base. Those who were home-based would be wired up; those mobile would have laptops; and those office-based would have pedestal storage to ensure maximum advantage of storage space. This produced savings, improved the working and travelling conditions for the great majority of the department and ensured further funds were safeguarded to provide essential services to vulnerable people.

(Source: Wustermann 1997)

Difficulties with home/teleworking

Teleworking and homeworking, although having clear advantages for all parties concerned, has its critics, both in theory and practice:

Working from home lacks the drive present in the workplace. A number of women in senior positions have pronounced that it does not work for them or their colleagues. Nicola Horlick commented that 'it's the energy created by people being in the same room that drives business forward' (Chubb 2007a: 12).

A lack of 'passive face time' could affect promotion prospects, as face-to-face interaction was often key to the assessment of someone's leadership skills and dependability (Elsbach and Cable 2012). The researchers identified two types of passive face time; 'expected face time' was being seen at work during normal business hours, while 'extracurricular face time' was when employees were noted to be in the office outside their required shift. Staff seen to be working their daily hours – even if they were not performing exceptionally – were described as 'responsible' and 'dependable' in the interviews and experiments that formed the basis for the study. Furthermore, employees putting in extracurricular face time were upgraded to 'committed' and 'dedicated'. Many managers were not aware that they were making these performance evaluations based purely on face time.

Workers not involved in such arrangements may feel resentful. Those employees continuing to work full-time at the office because they had no immediate need to work at home may believe that homeworkers have an easier life with fewer pressures with the same rewards.

Receiving verbal advice from colleagues or management to solve an immediate problem is no longer possible. It requires an email or a special call, both of which can cause delays or resentment from the other party.

Working at home may bring greater demands from relatives, especially their children and their parents who do not realise that they are actually carrying out an important job and disturbance causes difficulties.

All of these issues were found in detailed research carried out by Nottingham and Sheffield Business School, as shown in focus on research 7.2.

Outsourcing

A further way that organisations can increase flexibility in the location where they carry out their work is through outsourcing, which means paying a third party to run the operations or entire function concerned. Around 1.2 million employees work under outsourced contracts in organisations turning over a total of £79 billion, around 6 per cent of GDP, an increase of 120 per cent since 1996 (Julius 2008). The outsourcing of human resource services to shared-service centres was covered in some detail in Chapter 1 and this section extends that coverage in more general terms. It has always been quite conventional for organisations to outsource their catering or security operation but developments over the last 30 years

FOCUS ON RESEARCH 7.2 HOMEWORKING AT A LOCAL AUTHORITY

The researchers investigated the effect on homeworking on seven back-office employees who had taken part in a pilot scheme. The main focus was on the expectations and experience of homeworking in practice and how it affected their views on the psychological contract. The pilot scheme was introduced at a time of staff shortages, which caused considerable stress and frustration, placing severe strains on the psychological contract. Many staff considered that managers were 'hiding' the staff shortages and that underperforming colleagues were not being brought to account by management. It was hoped that the extension of homeworking to back-office jobs would go some way towards alleviating the difficulties, including the benefit of 'escaping from the office'.

On balance, the staff who took part were very positive indeed with all participants reporting how much they had enjoyed the experience with most commenting that the benefits had exceeded their expectations. The benefits reported were:

- An improved sense of personal well-being and of feeling less stressed, by getting away from 'all that bickering and gossiping'. In fact, the occasions on which they had to return to the office for a meeting or training merely served to remind them of what a lucky escape they had.
- Homeworking enabled them to better combine their work and domestic responsibilities as they saved on travelling time and carried out tasks when they wanted and when they could fit them in.
- They all reported that they achieved a much higher rate of productivity and exceeded the targets set, clearing large backlogs and dealing with tasks that may have been left untouched for months. Many felt they were working far harder with fewer interruptions, although they did not exceed 37 hours.
- None reported a sense of social isolation, with no real feelings of missing out on the social side of work.

However, they still faced practical difficulties:

- It was far less easy to solve immediate day-to-day problems through getting advice from a colleague or their manager. A specific phone call was required, which took up more time and caused some resentment from the recipient in the office – most rang other homeworkers instead.
- Relationships with the office manager became uncertain. Homeworkers often felt that a call from the manager was to check up on them rather than genuine concern for their well-being.
- Although most reported improved personal relationships at home, some families had difficulty in this area, especially with demanding elderly relatives who assumed that, being at home, they could be contacted at any time.

For these employees, homeworking allowed the psychological contract to be redressed from their office-based employment where they had experienced low job satisfaction, inadequate managing and a culture of mistrust.

(Source: Tietze and Nadin 2011)

have stretched this concept to cover many activities that may be considered at the core of a business.

There are a number of strategic reasons why organisations go down the outsourcing route:

■ To improve business focus. Outsourcing lets a company focus on broader issues, while having operational details assumed by an outside expert. It avoids siphoning off huge amounts of management resources and attention on non-core activities.

■ To gain access to world-class capabilities. Outsourcing providers, especially in the IT field, can bring extensive worldwide knowledge and experience, giving access to new technology and career opportunities to employees who may transfer to the provider. In addition, it brings competitive advantage to the organisation, which has an expanded skills base.

■ To achieve standardising processes across a global operation through outsourcing each national operations department (say, marketing or HR) to one provider (Chynoweth 2012).

■ To benefit from accelerated re-engineering, which lets the provider, especially one that has already re-engineered to world-class standards, take over the process.

■ To share risks. A co-operative venture with a provider can halve the risks.

■ To take advantage of a cheaper alternative where wage rates can be lower and efficiency higher through economies of scale, when the operations are carried out by an organisation concentrating on providing such services to a large number of customers.

Magnet, for example, cut its average recruitment costs from £2,700 to £1,200 per head by outsourcing recruitment to an agency. This allowed it to close offices and cut the number of HR staff from 42 to 4. Staff turnover reduced from 35 per cent to 18 per cent. One of the reasons given was that HR and line managers had more time to carry out effective induction (*People Management* 2006).

■ To concentrate on their core activities and contract out their non-core areas, such as logistics and payroll.

Beginning at the end of the 1980s, the Conservative government introduced legislation to force local authorities to put their services out to tender through the process called Compulsory Competitive Tendering (CCT). Reports from the Audit Commission indicated that authorities achieved savings, sometimes in the order of 20 per cent, without a loss in quality standards. Although less than half of the contracts were won by external bodies, where the existing in-house organisation (usually called Direct Services Organisation) won the contract, it was usually at the price of fundamentally changing the way it worked. Overtime was reduced, numbers of employees reduced, incentives were introduced and more flexible operations implemented. The Labour governments from 1997 to 2010 continued to encourage a similar policy under the name of 'Best Value', although greater protection was given to employees who transferred from the public sector to the private sector.

In 2007, 14 London boroughs brokered a joint outsourcing deal for recruitment, essentially to save costs through efficiency and economies of scale. One of the councils, Sutton, expected to save £100,000 a year through this operation. Other examples are the BBC, who outsourced much of the HR to Capita, and Centrica, who transferred much of their HR organisation, including reward areas, to Hewitt Associates (Braid 2007).

A survey by the University of Sheffield (2004) into IT outsourcing found that 25 per cent of organisations had totally failed in their objectives, while only 36 per cent had achieved all or 'a lot' of their objectives. The main problems highlighted in this and similar reports were the lack of control of costs, and the problems in controlling levels of quality and service levels. Often contracts founder on the interpretation of the contracts or compensation for overruns. Communication between the parties can also prove onerous and lead to major local and national misunderstandings. Lloydspharmacy halved its staff turnover rate from 10 to 5 per cent by bringing recruitment back in-house when the company regained control of its employer brand following de-merger. Previously, the in-house recruitment team were 'CV-pushers', moving information between agencies and managers (*People Management* 2009).

An ACAS report (Huws and Podro 2011) reflected on a number of areas where outsourcing could cause difficulty in the employment relationship. Firstly, it reduced the overall security of the employee, who would be working on a contract with a limited time-span (the length of the outsourcing agreement) and which created uncertainty coming up to the time when the contract needed to be renegotiated. Secondly, it could mean that employment groups, which had a coherence, could be splintered into smaller groups by outsourcing, all managed by different organisations and working under different terms and conditions. This would present complications for management, especially in the HR field, and also may involve equal pay issues. The splintering effect would also water down a sense of the effect of an employer voice if some groups were unionised and others not. (In reality, outsourcing can be associated with de-unionisation). There have also been cases when the outsourcing of work to agencies who recruit largely foreign migrant workers can have implications for the localities' social coherence.

ACTIVITY 7.3

What are the human resource implications of outsourcing a service or operation?

Discussion of activity 7.3

You may have thought of the following points:

■ Clear communication of the impending decision to outsource, and why it is being made, needs to be made to those employees involved at an early stage to prevent rumours spreading which may demotivate staff. Paying attention to maintaining the level of engagement is crucial (Smedley 2013).

■ When a final decision on who has won the outsourcing contract has been made, employees who currently work in the operations to be outsourced need to be counselled over the choices available to them. Current legislation (Transfer of Undertakings (Protection of Employment) Regulations – a complex act stemming from European legislation) ensures the right of employees transferred to retain identical terms and conditions on transfer and for a period afterwards. They also retain all of their employment rights. Some employees may not wish to transfer and consideration has to be given to opportunities available in other departments for such staff and under what conditions.

■ Some older staff may wish to take redundancy or retire at that point and they will need to be counselled over rights and financial details.

Call centres

Linked to geographical flexibility is the establishment of call centres. More than 300,000 employees (more than 1 per cent of the working population) now work at 500 or more centres set up at locations that can be some distance from their parent company. London Electricity, for example, have their customer payment and services call centre in Sunderland, in north-east England, and many other call centres are gathered around Leeds, in Yorkshire and in Scotland. The availability of labour and the lower pay rates are the main reasons for the location decisions.

Shared-service operations, discussed in Chapter 1, often work from a call-centre environment. By their nature, most call centres operate on a mix of rigid systemisation (the fixed scripts for operators, the technology-driven call-distribution system and the need to reach predetermined call targets) and flexibly serving the customer (24-hour-a-day service, availability of all services through one operator). This systemisation can have human resource implications, such as the fact that absenteeism and sickness rates are higher than the average, as are reported stress levels. Staff turnover similarly tends to be very high with average service rarely extending beyond two years. Some of the offices resemble factory units with operators sitting in tiny pens or in long lines. Dissatisfaction can lead to industrial action. In August 2012, 6,000 members of the Public and Commercial Services Union (PCS) staged a one-day strike over what they saw as 'oppressive working conditions and unrealistic targets' in 32 call centres. The union claimed that the target-driven culture was preventing call-centre staff from answering benefit enquiries, whereas management wished to keep phone calls to a minimum. According to Mark Serwotka, general secretary of the PCS:

> These call centres provide a vital lifeline. Inquiries are often complicated, and people struggling to find their way around the benefits system are often understandably desperate and upset, but staff are being forced to end calls as quickly as possible just to meet an artificial target.
>
> (*The Guardian* 2012)

In terms of flexible working practices, call centres operate many of the features that have been detailed earlier, such as employing a good proportion of part-time and temporary employees. Multi-skilling the operators to handle all calls is an important aspect of the training. There are even a few call centres where calls are transferred to operators working at home. Some companies have outsourced a specific operation, such as sales or service, to a call-centre specialist.

An example of the difficulties involved in setting up a call centre is given in focus on research 10.1 in Chapter 10 and in the Meteor case study at the end of this chapter.

OCCUPATIONAL FLEXIBILITY

There are two main strands in the development of occupational flexibility. *Horizontal flexibility* encourages employees to develop their skills beyond their initial specialism, becoming multi-skilled and able to handle a number of different aspects of work. Traditional demarcation lines between jobs, built up over 100 years or more of union rivalries and long apprenticeship schemes, are broken down. For example, in 3M PLC's factory near Darlington, maintenance staff used to be either 'electrical' or 'mechanical' and this caused considerable inefficiency when machines needed attention as it was necessary to have one from each trade in attendance. When the two separate unions amalgamated in the 1980s, multi-skilling between the two trades began with an extensive training programme to fill all the skills and knowledge gaps. This situation has been replicated throughout modern and traditional manufacturing.

Other examples of multi-skilling are as follows:

■ An insurance company, who used to have separate administrative departments for dealing with selling policies, changing existing policies and handling claims, found that their clients (mostly insurance brokers) resented having to deal with three different groups of staff. The company then re-engineered their administration into one based on geography, and multi-skilled their staff so that they could deal with queries and action required in all three administrative areas. Customer response was very positive to this change and most staff, though being uncertain at first of the need to go through an extended learning process, found the skills acquisition challenging and satisfying.

■ A motor manufacturer found that their labour costs were too high where absence of key staff caused too much overtime to be worked. They completely reorganised the production line, developing 'cells' of workers who would all be trained in three or more jobs so that they could easily replace an absent employee. The training stretched to technical and assembly-based knowledge but was then extended further to basic maintenance and housekeeping tasks. This allowed much greater continuity of production and labour-cost reduction. It also provided greater job satisfaction for the employee, together with greater employability to counter the increased risks and insecurity within manufacturing.

The second aspect of functional flexibility is *vertical flexibility*. This refers to employees' acceptance and performance of tasks at a higher and lower level than in their existing job description and employment contract. In the motor industry case above, cleaners used to be employed to clear up the assembly areas periodically. Part of the flexibility agreement transferred the periodic cleaning and housekeeping duties to the cell. An interesting by-product of this arrangement was that the assembly employees kept their areas far cleaner in the first place, knowing that they would have to clean up for themselves! A final aspect of this case was the transfer of certain supervisory responsibilities to the cell who, together with their team leader, would decide on rest breaks, holiday rotas, overtime duties and movement within the cell. This is sometimes referred to as *empowerment*.

Other examples of empowerment programmes are:

■ In a retail company, service staff were empowered to decide whether customers would be given replacements to items they considered faulty rather than refer it to their manager.

■ In The Body Shop, employees are given the opportunity to decide on the staff that are employed at their branch.

■ Supervisors at Rank Hovis were empowered to run budgets and negotiate terms with suppliers, rather than rely on standard national arrangements.

A more informal process in this area is that of expecting employees to 'work beyond contract'. This does not just mean working longer hours than specified but also being part of a team and contributing their ideas so that planning ahead and solving problems are a natural part of every team member's brief.

POLICIES THAT SUPPORT FLEXIBILITY

Employees can be persuaded to change to work within the required flexible parameters through a number of policies. The *reward structure* can be altered to emphasise a pay for performance culture which is dealt with in Chapter 6; employees can be supported towards *self-development and learning processes* as set out in Chapter 8. A third process is to introduce or extend *family-friendly policies*.

Family-friendly policies

Demographic forecasts show that the workforce of available full-time, permanent employees may begin a secular decline in the twenty-first century as the gradual reduction in the birth rate since the 1970s comes into full effect. This could lead to a shortage of labour overall, especially in the service and public sectors, although the huge increase in migrant labour and the unexpected increase in the UK fertility rate in the 2000s make this scenario less likely. The recession starting in 2008 has also reduced overall demand for labour. Having said this, supporters of flexible working believe that the longer-term outlook may change over the next 20 years to produce conditions where labour is in short supply again.

The only internal sources of labour available comprise the increasing proportion of women who enter the workplace, the majority still on a part-time or temporary basis and, to a smaller extent, semi-retired employees also working part-time.

In April 2003, the government introduced the 'right to request flexible working'. This originally gave parents with a child aged under six (or parents of a disabled child under the age of eighteen) the right to request flexible working arrangements from their employer.

This right to request has been extended:

■ from April 2007, to the carers of certain categories of adults; and
■ from April 2009, to the parents of children aged under 17.

In April 2010, similar procedures were introduced to enable employees to request some flexibility with time off work to enable them to undertake study or training.

Employers have been generally supportive of these regulations with opposition chiefly limited to small and medium-sized organisations who believe they would suffer if too many employees took advantage of the rights. A good proportion of employers go further than the regulations and have extended these rights to all employees in the organisation, as shown in focus on research 7.3.

FOCUS ON RESEARCH 7.3 EMPLOYEE REQUESTS FOR FLEXIBILITY

IRS surveyed 162 employers in 2010 concerning their policies and practices in dealing with requests for flexibility. They found that 73 per cent would consider a request from any employee, regardless of whether or not they had a legal right to have the request considered. The number of formal requests was low at around 1 per cent of employees but many organisations dealt with such requests locally and informally without specifically recording them centrally. Over half had the policy of encouraging an informal approach. One local authority, however, recorded 200 requests from 2008–09 from its 5,000-strong workforce. The take-up covers both sexes with 32 per cent of females and 22 per cent of males working in non-traditional ways.

The *benefits* cited by employers included improved retention (73 per cent), flexibility of cover (65 per cent), improved employee engagement (63 per cent), cost savings (42 per cent), reduced absence (41 per cent) and increased productivity (31 per cent).

The *difficulties* quoted were difficulties in arranging meetings (53 per cent), complexity in scheduling working hours (48 per cent), internal communication difficulties (42 per cent), resentment from other employees (39 per cent), resentment from managers over managing flexible workers (38 per cent) and difficulties organising training (35 per cent). However, there was little (26 per cent) support for the statement 'flexible working is difficult to manage and puts pressure on other team members'.

One manufacturer commented, 'Having a workforce working smarter (this includes working anywhere/anytime with technology that allows them to do this) gives our company a competitive edge when business continuity is threatened', while a local authority reported that 'flexible working is a way of reducing sickness levels. There are times when staff are just not well enough for the journey to work, but are able to carry on their duties. Having home access allows them to stay up to date with work and also reduces the need for temps or overtime among remaining staff'.

However, difficulties remained. A charity reported that 'our major work is face-to-face with residents, customers and service users, therefore the majority of staff work rotas to ensure cover. Flexible working is very difficult in this situation'. A consulting firm have found that 'employees who work part-time or annualised hours have felt pressurised to attend meetings on days they do not usually work and feeling left out of events that take place on these days'. A large organisation reported that the main difficulty is supporting managers to manage staff who work remotely, particularly in respect of managing performance and productivity.

(Source: Wolff 2010)

Although the employer has the right to refuse the application but only for certain reasons, practice appears to indicate that refusals are relatively rare.

Employers' options on work–life balance

Employers can also demonstrate their family-friendly credentials by offering systems of work and benefits that are especially attractive to women and families under the general banner of a 'work–life balance'.

- *Flexible working hours.* Rather than forcing all employees to start and stop at the same time, employees can be offered a choice of hours, such as 10am to 6pm or 8am to 4pm, perhaps varying during the week to meet the employee's childcare or personal arrangements. Compressed working weeks into four and a half days or nine-day fortnights (operated by Texaco, among others) also has attractions to families.

- *Flexitime.* Here the employee can choose each day their starting and stopping time within the core time constraints (usually 10am to 3.30pm). Around 2.5 million employees worked under flexitime in 2002 mostly in London and other large cities where rush-hour travel presented employment difficulties. In a number of schemes, employees can work under or over their contractual weekly or monthly hours, carrying forward the surplus or making up their shortfall in later months. They can convert some of their surplus into additional holidays. The system allows employees to manage their work and home commitments far better than if they were working fixed hours. If they have to make a regular visit to an ill relative, they can make up the hours at a later date.

- *Career breaks.* Employees may wish to take an extended break from work either to extend their maternity break beyond the statutory right to return to work or because they need to look after an elderly or ill relative. Around 15 per cent of organisations have such a scheme with a small but significant (and highly grateful) take-up. In many of the schemes, contact with the employee is retained through a short period of work each year (often two to three weeks over holiday periods), which also helps to update the employee and keep them committed to the organisation. The arrangement helps to attract and retain qualified and experienced staff over a longer period of time. Most schemes have a five-year limit to the break.

- *Childcare provision.* The lack of suitable childcare is usually quoted as the largest barrier to returning to the labour force. In one recent survey, 73 per cent of women reported that it had affected their job or career prospects. Companies can make life easier for the 52 per cent of women with children under five who now work in a number of ways. They can set up an in-house nursery or creche, or get together with a group of other employers in the area to do so (this is expensive but there are some tax advantages), provide childcare vouchers or a childcare allowance, or be generally sympathetic in the workplace through time-off provisions. The latest available statistics show that developments are still slow. Only 3 per cent of employers operate a workplace nursery or jointly fund one and another 2 per cent provide child-care vouchers. Around 30 per cent have a generally sympathetic approach through formal time-off provisions.

SUMMING UP FLEXIBILITY

One way to look at flexible practices is to examine the requirements of employers and employees and to identify the areas of overlaps. This is shown in Table 7.3.

Some of the requirements match up well. Multi-skilling benefits both sides of the equation, as does the move to provide more part-time employment. Both sides are moving towards the benefits of recognising the contribution rather than simply the time spent at work.

There is a less pleasant side seen by commentators, however, where the require-ments are out of balance. Flexibility may push more employees into the periphery where insecurity is enhanced; where wages become more dependent on performance and more variable between groups; where contracts become only transactional (only for what takes place) rather than relational (based on longer-term relationships with trust and mutual obli-gations to the fore); and where the organisation has little long-term concern with most of the

Table 7.3 Flexibility requirements

Objectives for employers	Objectives for employees
Temporal flexibility	
Matching employees' time to the market needs	*Matching work to personal and family needs*
■ Complex but efficient shift systems	■ Choice of working patterns – morning, afternoon, evening
Annualised hours	
■ Eliminating hours from the contract through 'working beyond contract' and zero-hours	■ Keep hours to a level that allows family and personal responsibilities
■ Making greater use of available labour sources through temporary and part-time work	■ Greater demand for temporary and part-time/ job-share work
Geographical/occupational flexibility	
Improving operational efficiency	*Providing greater involvement and work interest*
■ Increasing value of labour through multi-skilling	■ Opportunities for broadening skills and experience
■ Teleworking – saving in office space	■ Benefits in flexible hours and reduced travel costs
■ Outsourcing functions and workloads	■ Stability in the workplace
■ Call centres to replace face-to-face contact	
General objectives	
■ Reward for contribution made, not time at work	■ Reward for contribution made, not time at work

FOCUS ON RESEARCH 7.4 FLEXIBLE WORKING AND THE GENDER PAY GAP

The researchers interviewed 50 chartered accountants on their experience of flexible working and found that women who worked flexibly or part-time to combine their work with caring arrangements damaged their career prospects and opportunities of well-paid promotions. This did not apply to men who, when they worked flexibly, did so at a much later stage when their career had progressed further and were therefore on a higher rate of pay when they worked flexibly. This has been contrary to the expected belief that the opportunity to work flexibly provides the means to reduce the gender gap, not reinforce it.

It is concluded that the attitudes to flexible working need to change in the professions so that those who work flexibly are not seen as 'time deviants' and that it is actively promoted for men to give them an opportunity to be active parents. Only then can the pay gap be reduced.

(Source: Smithson *et al.* 2004)

labour force. Research by Linklow *et al.* (2011) found that men are less likely to take up flexible working options not because of their different personal needs (looking after dependants) but mainly because they are fearful of its effect on their career opportunities. An example of the effect of flexible working on equal pay is shown in focus on research 7.4.

Employees become more vulnerable, liable to forced changes and to being asked to share in the risks of the enterprise. Outsourcing is seen as the least satisfying from an employee's viewpoint. Having taken employment with a known organisation, under agreed terms and in an agreed location, the employee is asked (often without a reasonable alternative) to transfer to an unknown organisation, with terms that may alter in the medium term and often in a changed location.

TALENT MANAGEMENT

Flexible working provides two opportunities to enhance the process of talent management. Firstly, by operating efficiency-based systems, such as annualised hours, multi-skilling and call centres, the investment in talent produces higher returns in the accounting sense. Just as important, the second opportunity is that, by offering forms of flexible working that appeal to different sections of the labour force (such as part-time work, homeworking and teleworking), new talent is encouraged to join the organisation and existing talent is encouraged to stay and continue to contribute efficiently. The presence of flexible working that provides a genuine benefit for all sides will encourage the development of a highly rated employer brand.

Evans (1998) has recommended nine key ingredients for success in managing flexible workers:

- Provide clear signposting concerning the options available on flexibility.
- Invest considerable time in getting the right fit between the needs of the organisation and the preferences of the employee.
- Be realistic about the relationship between skills, responsibilities and work patterns required and whether they can be accommodated through flexible working.
- Show respect for employees' other commitments and let them be involved in decisions that affect these commitments.
- Create a balanced team of age, experience and working patterns.
- Ensure responsibilities for service quality and delivery are shared by employees on conventional and flexible contracts.
- Be prepared to experiment with new ways of working.
- Adopt a flexible approach to training and development.
- Provide support for managers who look after flexible workers.

An example of an integrated approach to flexible working at PepsiCo is shown in case study 7.5.

CASE STUDY 7.5 CREATING A FLEXIBLE CULTURE AT PEPSICO

This case study examines how PepsiCo have taken steps to bring about real organisational change. PepsiCo know that, to recruit and retain the best and most talented people, the organisation needs to meet the employee need of greater flexibility. Aware that Europe's workforce could face a shortfall of 24 million by 2040, PepsiCo are taking steps to ensure they are viewed as an inclusive employer.

In 2006, PepsiCo undertook an Organisational Health Survey, which showed employees wanted support from PepsiCo to achieve a better work–home balance. Workload complexity and a lack of flexible working options were the two main concerns, combined with need for more recognition and greater empowerment in their work.

In 2007, PepsiCo decided to demonstrate their commitment to their staff by comprehensively addressing these issues.

Action

The first step was to create a strong permission culture, empowering employees to balance the demands of home and work. A large-scale campaign was actively sponsored and communicated by the executive team called 'The Dinner isn't in the Dog!', launching a number of commitments and initiatives. Flexible working policies under the title of FlexiCo were proactively introduced to all office-based roles and included:

- Flexibility beyond core hours
- The option to work compressed hours during June–September and December
- The option to work from home on a regular basis.

PepsiCo actively encouraged requests from their population and ensured that they took practical steps to support this, through the move to laptops for all and enhanced wireless technology. For employees in operational or shift-based roles, PepsiCo worked with managers to introduce 'everyday flexibility' through the encouragement of shift swaps and rota flexibility for those roles that do not lend themselves to homeworking or flexitime.

At the same time, the 'Fit For Life' programme was introduced, a bespoke programme designed for PepsiCo, and delivered by expert coaches. The programme helped employees identify areas in their current lifestyles that led to an imbalance and provided support to make sustainable, positive change. Positioned as 'an investment in you', this programme was made available to staff at all levels who were able to self-nominate to participate.

To address the work overload reported in the 2006 staff survey, PepsiCo also introduced the 'Less is More' initiative, encouraging employees to take control of the way they work and to adopt six simple behaviours that help them work more efficiently. A training toolkit was designed and rolled out to managers to help them and their teams develop their awareness of 'Less is More'. PepsiCo encouraged experimentation in this initiative as an enabler for learning about better ways of working, and changing behaviours to support this.

Since the initial launch of initiatives in 2007, PepsiCo have continued to evolve and sustain their commitments, and ensure visibility through regular updates to employees during 'Town Halls' and widespread communications from the executive team. In 2009, the 'One Simple Thing' initiative was launched to help employees sustain their work–home balance. As part of their annual objectives, employees are encouraged to consider and agree a work–home balance objective that supports their individual needs, such as scheduling regular exercise, doing the school run, learning a new skill or 'taking time out for me'. This annual objective is then assessed with the line manager and progress is rewarded as part of the annual performance review process.

Impact

Comparing the 2009 employer survey against the 2007 survey, PepsiCo saw a 40 per cent increase in staff seeing them as an employer that supports their efforts to balance work and personal life.

(Source: Opportunity Now awards 2011)

TECHNOLOGY AND FLEXIBILITY

Technology is at the heart of operating effective flexible working. Homeworking, teleworking and call-centre operations are totally dependent on technology, while outsourcing is strongly supported by IT systems that provide information both in the supply chain for manufacturing or in service operations and management information in other sectors.

The technology in call centres is extensive. Whereas manual dialling would allow you to make 30 calls and probably talk to 10 customers over a 4-hour period, the power dialling system will get 80 calls over the same period and the strong likelihood that you would talk to all of them. The screens allow the agent to work from guided scripts with clear instructions on how to deal with each customer response or detail of changes on the customer's contracts. There are systems to monitor agents in and out, constantly tracking agents' actual work rate with a comparison with their target work rate. The moment a discrepancy occurs within the planned tolerance, the agent's name and amount of time involved is noted and a colour-coded report shows the nature of each discrepancy. However, as with all technology-driven systems, the ultimate strength of the system depends on the quality of the supervision in their ability to interpret and act on the figures produced. A case dealing with stress in call centres is detailed focus on research 10.1 in Chapter 10.

Initial developments are taking place in bringing homeworkers into the call-centre orbit with companies such as TeleTech@Home introducing the concept. They use the same platform as in a traditional call centre but calls are directed to employees' homes during specific hours. It will allow call centres to employ staff who are unable to travel or have childcare commitments. TeleTech use an entirely telephone-based application and interview process and training takes place online to reinforce the process of working in a virtual community (Chubb 2007b).

In outsourcing recruitment and selection, economies of scale can be achieved through providers having better security clearance systems. Rather than taking weeks for the occasional recruiter, a specialist outsourcer can run Criminal Records Bureau, Financial Services Authority and County Court Judgments checks and have a clearance within a day (Stone 2007).

SETTING UP A CALL CENTRE

It had been a thoroughly dispiriting experience, Sarah admitted. Six months earlier, she had being seconded at a week's notice to work with a small team and an external consultant to set up a call centre, which needed to be up and running within three months. This was for an associated company that dealt with IT equipment and servicing. It was located within a factory site where spare office facilities were available. The initial appointee to advise on human resource issues had suddenly left the team to join a competitor. When Sarah arrived, she found that many of the basic HR decisions had been made, as had the internal call-centre layout and technology.

It had been decided that the centre would be staffed exclusively on a full-time basis with standard shifts of 7am to 3pm (day), 3pm to 11pm (back) and 11pm to 7am (night). Night shifts would be on a permanent basis with days and back shifts alternating each week. Overtime shifts would be worked during the day on Saturday and Sunday. This system was going to be used because it reflected the existing factory arrangements, as would other terms and conditions including holidays and sick pay. Employees had four weeks' intensive training to learn the basics of the business and to deal with customers. There would be 70 staff in total, based in teams in three departments, dealing with specific IT purchase areas, plus a fourth concentrating on the servicing operation. The payment system had a heavy loading on to incentives, with employees able to add up to 70 per cent to their base salary. There were also team incentives, which could add a further 10 per cent, plus some one-off team non-cash prizes, such as vouchers and celebratory 'events'.

The recruitment was far from easy as most applicants were young men whose IT experience was very limited. As time was short, the employment decision was based on an interview and short IT knowledge test with some references followed up afterwards. It was hoped to recruit a number of team leaders with experience of call centres, but there were few applications so appointments were made based on age and experience.

The first few days after opening the centre were chaotic. The refurbishment of the office environment fell behind schedule and the time to test the technology was truncated so numerous technical faults occurred. The initial call rate was very high and a number of staff left in the first fortnight, having decided that the pressure in the job was not for them. Others reported on leaving that they did not like the office arrangement with staff in long rows with little space of their own. Difficulties in recruiting the right calibre staff continued, so many were thrown into the 'hot seat' with little preparation.

The first customer survey after three months of operation revealed the depth of the problem. Customers complained that either they were pressurised to buy IT equipment that did not really meet their specification or they were passed from one member of staff to another with long waits in between. There were strong complaints about staff who could not answer the questions or gave answers that the customers could not understand. There were numerous examples of the wrong equipment being sent or of servicing staff being completely unaware of the details of the servicing required.

In discussions with some of the staff who left, Sarah heard stories of pressure from their team leaders to meet their quotas or to be top of the league table together with the difficulties between one shift and another in communicating information. She decided that the whole operation needed a complete revamp.

KEY CHAPTER SUMMARY POINTS

- High-performance workplaces require the operation of a strong psychological contract so that employees are committed, involved and motivated.

- Motivation is a complex subject where no simple theory explains the efforts that employees put into a particular work situation.

- Flexibility in the workplace has developed rapidly in recent years. It can be divided into temporal, numerical, geographical and occupational flexibility, each representing a system that attempts to utilise the skills, time and energy of the labour force to the benefit of the business.

- Recent developments include sophisticated systems, such as annualised hours and flexible rostering, a rapid rise in the operation of call centres and extension of the concept of teleworking.

- Multi-skilling has been a crucial factor in retaining the competitiveness of manufacturing and has been extended in administrative and technical areas.

STUDENT ACTIVITIES

1   Family-friendly benefits may be attractive to staff but have disadvantages to employers. Select three of the benefits detailed in this chapter, list the disadvantages that may accompany introducing the arrangement or benefit and consider how those disadvantages can be overcome.

2   In respect of the Meteor case study, put yourself in Sarah's position and carry out the following:
- Explain how you would put together a proposal for a series of changes, including how you would gather information and the objectives you would set.
- Suggest a series of proposals that may go into the report which would include the shift system, hours of work, the office lay-out, the pay system (you may want to look at Chapter 6 here) and other areas you consider relevant.

3   You have 50 points to allocate between the following aspects of a job:
- Physical working conditions
- Hours of work
- Pay
- Relationships with your boss
- Relationships with colleagues
- Opportunity for promotion
- Benefits
- Convenience of location.

Allocate those points, compare your results with your colleagues and draw conclusions on how this may affect motivation in the workplace.

4   Annualised hours (see case study 7.1 and focus on research 7.1) appear to have considerable advantages for the employer. Read the article and book chapter on which these extracts are based and discuss the advantages and disadvantages for the employee.

5   Identify the issues that arose over the call-centre strike in 2012. Put forward arguments for both the union and management sides in this issue. Discuss the proposition that the growth of call centres has led to more, rather than less flexibility.

REFERENCES

Atkinson, J. (1984) Manpower Strategies for Flexible Organisations. *Personnel Management*, August, 28–31.

Atkinson, J. and Meager, N. (1986) *New Forms of Work Organisation*. IMS Report 121.

Braid, M. (2007) Outsourcing Cuts Cost of Hiring. *Sunday Times*, 1 April, 10.

Butler, S. (2013) Signing Up To Zero Hour Contracts. *Evening Standard*, 11 April, 40.

CBI (2010) Making Britain the Place to Work. Confederation of British Industry.

Chubb, L. (2007a) Homeworking 'A Nightmare' Say Female Leaders. *People Management*, 13 December, 12.

— (2007b) Homeworking on the Way for Call Centre Staff. *People Management*, 20 September, 14.

Chynoweth, C. (2012) It's Not All About the Money. *People Management*, July, 41–44.

Elsbach, K. and Cable, D. (2012) Why Showing your Face Matters. *Sloane Management Review*, Summer, 53–57.

Evans, C. (1998) *Managing the Flexible Workforce*. Roffey Park Management Institute.

Family Friendly Working Hours Taskforce (2010) Flexible Working – Working for Families, Working for Business. CIPD

The Guardian (2012) Job Centre Staff Go on Strike. 13 August. Available at www.guardian.co.uk/society/2012/aug/13/jobcentre-staff-strike.

Handy, C. (1994) *The Empty Raincoat*. Hutchinson.

Hayes, J. (1997) Annualised Hours and the 'Knock'. The Organisation of Working Time in a Chemicals Plant. *Work, Employment and Society*, 11(1): 65–81.

Huws, V. and Podro, S. (2011) *Outsourcing and the Fragmentation of Employment Relations: The Challenges Ahead*. ACAS.

IDS (2002) *Study 721*, January.

IRS (2004) Home Is Where the Work Is. *IRS Employment Review 797*, 2 April, 18–20.

Julius, D. (2008) *Public Services Industry Review*. Department of Business Enterprise and Regulatory Reform.

Labour Market Statistics (2011) November, accessed at www.ons.gov.uk.

Leighton, D. and Gregory, T. (2011) *Re-inventing the Workplace*. Demos.

Linklow, P., Civian, J. and Lingle, K. (2011) Men and Worklife: Bridging the Perceived Gap. *Workspan*, October.

Opportunity Now Awards (2011) accessed at www.bitcdiversity.org.uk/awards.

People Management (2006) Magnet Attracts. 1 June, 18.

—(2009) Lloydspharmacy Brings Hiring In-house. 5 November, 10.

Smedley, T. (2013) Victoria's Secret. *People Management*, April, 40–42.

Smithson, J., Lewis, S., Cooper, C. and Dyer, J. (2004) Flexible Working and the Gender Pay Gap in the Accounting Profession. *Work, Employment and Society*, 18, 1, 115–131.

Stone, A. (2007) Click with Your Clients. *Sunday Times* Outsourcing Supplement, 14 January, 7.

Stredwick, J. and Ellis, S. (2005) *Flexible Working Practices*. CIPD.

Tietze, S. and Nadin, S. (2011) The Psychological Contract and the Transition from Office-based to Home-based Work. *Human Resource Management Journal*, 21(3): 318–324.

University of Sheffield (2004) *New Strategies in IT Outsourcing: Major Trends and Global Best Practice*. University of Sheffield.

WERS (1998 and 2004) *Workplace Employment Relations Survey*. Routledge

Wolff, C. (2010) IRS Flexible Working Survey. *IRS Employment Review*, March 22.

Wustermann, L. (1997) Moving Up a Gear – Workwise at Hertfordshire County Council. *Flexible Working*, September, 18–22.

ADDITIONAL FEATURES

 Please visit the companion website at: www.routledge.com/cw/stredwick where you will find additional case studies and reading material together with short self-tests and other resources for both students and lecturers.

8 LEARNING AND TALENT DEVELOPMENT

Theory and practice

John Stredwick and Robert Labe

CHAPTER OBJECTIVES

When you have read this chapter and carried out the activities, you will be able to:

- Explain a number of different approaches organisations take to learning and talent development.

- Understand the component parts of the learning cycle.

- Analyse the various techniques of training and learning.

- Identify the importance of specialised training and learning arrangements such as action learning, induction and sales training.

- Assess the role of government and other agencies in initiating development in learning and training.

- Explain the impact the economic climate is having on the way in which learning and talent development is being delivered and managed.

- Appreciate the impact of legal issues on training, learning and development.

- Consider the role and responsibilities of learning and talent development practitioners.

INTRODUCTION

As we saw in Chapter 5, there is a strong argument that the most important role in human resources is to help employees to improve their performance and, by so doing, improve the performance of the organisation. To improve, employees need a combination of the will to improve (motivation) and the encouragement to acquire job-related knowledge, skills and attitudes (KSAs). This chapter will cover how the second part can be achieved, by looking firstly at *the way people learn*, followed by an examination of a selection of *training and development techniques*. Finally, we will look at the *government initiatives* that are intended to help the learning process, including Investors in People. Throughout this chapter, you will see reference to 'talent' and this recognises that talent management is now becoming firmly established throughout human resource management and human resources development. The other underpinning theme to many parts of this chapter is the impact that the economic climate of recent years is having on how organisations manage and deliver learning and talent development and the growing importance of tailored programmes.

Storey and Sisson (1993) refer to the 'virtuous circle' of development, whereby a high investment can lead to a more effective utilisation of high technology, higher skills levels, higher wages and lower unit labour costs, leading ultimately to competitive advantage. On the other hand, a large swathe of business and industry relies on badly applied 'on-the-job' training, with little opportunity for planned personal development, which often leads to the opposite effect, namely lower wages, higher unit costs and an inferior competitive stance overall.

The Bennett and Leduchowicz (1983) model seeks to plot why organisations train and the predominant ways in which they carry out their training (see Figure 8.1).

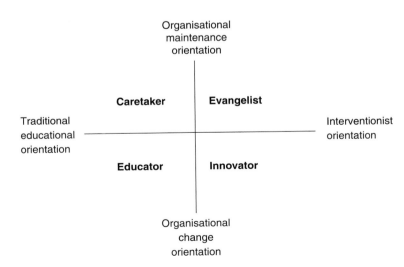

Figure 8.1
Bennett and Leduchowicz model

Source: Bennett, R. and Leduchowicz, T. (1983) What Makes for an Effective Trainer? *Journal of European Industrial Training*, 7(2): 31. © Emerald Group Publishing.

The vertical axis shows the contrast between maintaining the existing organisational and employee work patterns (as with the old apprenticeships schemes) and simply responding to situations and, at the other end of the spectrum, using training to support initiatives in fundamental changes to the organisation and its practices. The horizontal axis indicates how the training takes place from a traditional tutor-led programme to one that may be less structured but intervenes in the workplace through such methods as coaching, mentoring, action learning and team building.

- The *caretaker* approach keeps training on its traditional path to support what is in place without rocking the boat.
- The *educators* use traditional means but see their role as assisting in organisation change. This is the least likely to be successful in practice.
- *Evangelists* still want to maintain the status quo but will use all the more progressive methods of training to support this viewpoint.
- *Innovators* also use such methods but utilise them to support major organisational change.

Learning needs to take place not just at the start of employment life or on commencing a new job, but throughout a person's career right up to their retirement day, whenever that may be. Some people would argue that learning to live with retirement is one of the most difficult learning processes and many large organisations even run courses on this subject for their impending retirees! The impact of the removal of a compulsory retirement age and the economic reasons for people wanting or needing to stay in employment beyond 65 years of age also needs to feature in training and development considerations.

HOW PEOPLE LEARN

Learning has taken place, as defined by Honey and Mumford (1992), when someone: 'Knows something they did not know earlier, and can show it and is able to do something which they were not able to do before'.

We all know that people learn in different ways but models can be useful which show a comprehensive approach to the learning process. Kolb's (1984) learning cycle, also known as experiential learning (see Figure 8.2), is the most well known and is based on the concept that learning starts from having a concrete experience. The learner then moves on to review that experience by observation and reflection, draws conclusions from that experience, often with the use of abstract concepts, and finally plans the next steps by testing the concepts.

Let us take an example of a learning cycle with which you may be familiar. Mary, a student, joins with two others in sharing a flat. They make no formal arrangement at first on buying basic essentials, such as bread, milk and potatoes, leaving it to chance as to when they need them.

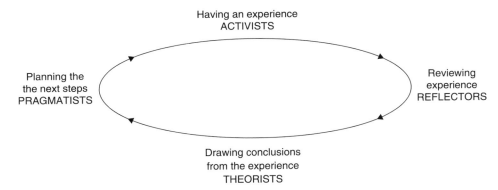

Figure 8.2
The learning cycle

Source: Kolb, D. (1984) *Experiential Learning*. Prentice Hall; Honey, P. and Mumford, A. (1992) *The Manual of Learning Styles*. Peter Honey Publications.

Stage 1 Mary experiences for the third week running that they are out of essentials and she has to go out and buy them.

Stage 2 She reflects on this situation, considering that it is not fair and equitable or an efficient way of running the flat.

Stage 3 She concludes that some formal system will need to be introduced, whereby one person is responsible and collects money from the other two on a regular basis to reimburse her.

Stage 4 She sits down with the other two students and obtains their agreement and together they plan how it is to be operated.

Kolb's original work was carried out in the 1970s and it has been adapted and developed by Honey and Mumford, who have created a Learning Style analysis based on the learning cycle. They realised that some people are stronger at one stage than another and have put titles to people who prefer each of the four stages, which can be identified by way of a learning styles questionnaire (LSQ):

■ *Activists.* Some very active people look at life as a continuous set of new experiences from which to intuitively learn. They approach each new experience with enthusiasm and tend to act first and consider the consequences later. They often lead in discussions but do not necessarily produce logically thought-out ideas or proposals.

■ *Reflectors.* Others may prefer to have fewer experiences but will reflect carefully on those experiences, collecting data and bringing in to discussions a range of other people's experiences. They are good at listening and may not take it upon themselves to lead discussions.

■ *Theorists.* A third group are those that can think through problems and create sound and logical theories to explain what they see. They prefer everything to fit together and may not be happy to proceed unless every 't' has been crossed.

■ *Pragmatists* are those that like agreements to be reached so they can be put into action. They are down to earth, can be good negotiators and realise that agreements often leave small details to be sorted out later.

An understanding of learning styles can be advantageous to the individual to assist them in fine-tuning their own style to gain the greatest advantage from it, perhaps in making it more balanced and rounded. It can also help in relationships between staff. An example here can be the greater understanding that can be achieved between an 'activist' manager and their 'theorist' subordinate when they are considering a current incentive scheme that appears to be failing. The manager will want to move quickly on from that scheme and introduce a new idea that he has just thought up, whereas the subordinate will want to take more time in trying to put the experience of the failed scheme into a theoretical context, so that the same mistakes are not made a second time. If they are aware of their learning styles, they will have a better appreciation of each other's viewpoint and be more likely to reach a compromise on a course of action.

Honey and Mumford's four groupings are not mutually exclusive. In fact, the great majority of individuals emerge from the questionnaire with a combination of two. For example, the reflector-theorist will both consider all aspects of the experience and come up with theories and explanations to give a comprehensive and well-thought-through analysis of the learning experience. On the other hand, the activist-pragmatist will be good at coming up with ideas and getting them agreed and put into practice so the learning process takes place quickly. Honey and Mumford – while noting that the 1982 80-item LSQ was still popular in 2000 and revised again in 2006 – published a streamlined 40-item LSQ.

Many respondents to the CIPD 2012 Learning and Talent Development Survey indicated that they still use the Honey and Mumford learning styles questionnaire to identify individual and team learning needs alongside Belbin Team Roles and the 'Plan–Do–Check' system.

There are a number of theories that attempt to explain the *learning process* itself, which Marchington and Wilkinson (2007) place into four groups:

1   *Learning by association.* The experiments by Pavlov and others with animals show that learning takes place through association with food and praise, and this can be applied to human learning through immediate feedback and recognition. For example, the immediate praise (and, perhaps, some criticism) of a student's presentation after the event will lead to a reinforcement of how to carry out a good presentation. Taking association a stage further, much of customer-care training will aim to build into the minds of the trainees immediate positive responses to customer needs, so that trainees will learn to give the appropriate response and even anticipate what customers want.

2   *Cognitive learning.* This is what most of us understand as conventional learning when we sit down and think our way through a situation or theory, learning in the process. An easy example here is learning a new computer program from an instruction manual

(badly written, of course!), where the combination of using logical thought with the pleasure of gaining insight acts as a powerful reinforcer of learning.

3   *Cybernetics*. This approach regards learning as an 'information-processing system in which a signal containing information is passed along a communication channel subject to interference from a variety of sources' (Collin 2001). Learning a language through programmed learning will come into this category with the interference being personal problems of the trainees that can impair their learning.

4   The final category is *social learning theory*, which used to be known as 'sitting by Nellie' or picking the job up by imitation. The advantage of this form is that the social processes are learned at the same time, but it is by no means systematic and, in practice, the trainee learns to imitate the wrong ways as well as the correct ways of the job.

Other theories and models that are relevant to this subject area include Maslow's Hierarchy of Needs and Herzberg's Motivation and Hygiene Factors, which have been discussed in Chapter 6, and Bloom's Taxonomy.

This theory set out by Benjamin Bloom (see Table 8.1) in 1956 looks at three domains that everyone can relate to. Individuals can be tested on these domains in the same way as learning styles questionnaires to determine which domain is the most prominent.

Individuals do not, of course, always fit in with one domain, and, as with learning styles, there may be two out of three domains that are prominent or even all three may be of equal importance. None of the domains is rigid and one-dimensional as all have the scope to cater for ever-increasing levels of learning, comprehension and application.

Table 8.1 Bloom's taxonomy

Cognitive domain	This domain is about a person's ability and preference for learning by acquiring knowledge and by applying thinking and analytical skills to an issue. So a practical exercise may not suit a person where this domain is prominent. (Revised by Lorin Anderson in 2001 with a change in the names of the categories and rearrangement of them.)
Affective domain	This domain recognises that an individual learns through techniques that enable the person to look at feelings and attitudes, where emotions can be discussed and analysed. Role-plays and case studies may be useful to use and the use of soft skills such as listening, reflection and empathy can be encouraged. (Revised by Bloom and others in 1973.)
Psychomotor domain	This domain is about the learning of practical skills, use of motor skills and dexterity. Practical exercises and learning by doing might be useful here but probably not either of the other domains if a person has this as their prominent domain. (Simpson in 1972 developed the categories and verbs that the original committee led by Bloom had not done.)

Learning needs to be reinforced

Reinforcement can be achieved through practising the skills obtained and using the knowledge acquired back in the workplace. If there is no immediate opportunity to do this, the skills might be lost and the knowledge fade; motivation will also suffer – so what was the point of doing the learning?

While learning formally or informally, the learner needs to receive *positive reinforcement*, such as praise from manager or peers, constructive feedback and suggestions for developing the skills or knowledge further, and success being rewarded. This encourages the learner to practise complex skills or the use of complex information and knowledge, which enables it to become embedded in the learner's way of working. Not only is the learning consolidated after its initial acquisition, but it also encourages greater willingness for future learning and change. Where tasks need to be repeated at a consistently high quality, positive reinforcement is very important in developing the confidence that this requires.

Negative reinforcement can consist of undermining the importance of the learning being undertaken or achieved, creating barriers to prevent applying the learning in practice, negative comments from managers and peers on the learning being undertaken or achieved, or even the taking away from an individual of tasks/responsibilities for which they have the relevant skills or knowledge and inferring or claiming their efforts are not of a sufficient standard. At the most extreme, negative reinforcement can lead to *learned helplessness* where, through repeated negative reinforcement, an individual becomes unable to fulfil a task.

Reinforcement can also be viewed as either *extrinsic* or *intrinsic*. Extrinsic reinforcement comes from outside the learner, such as the support of peers and managers, while intrinsic reinforcement comes from within the learner themselves and draws on their own strengths, possibly through reflection on the initial learning.

So how do these theories fit together? Maslow and Herzberg are very much about creating the right learning environment where students/trainees feel safe and that their basic needs are being met. The environment in the workplace can impact positively or negatively on learning, as can the way in which people are treated in a learning situation, which may be somewhere other than their normal workplace. Having achieved that, the structure of the learning event needs to motivate the learner to work up the levels within the Maslow and Herzberg models.

Bloom's theory relates to how learners learn – by doing, by thinking or by feeling. Identifying the prominent domain will help to design and use the right mix of methods that will enable the individual to learn effectively. Other models will identify visual, auditory or practical learners. All such models give practitioners useful information for choosing the right methods to enable learning.

Linked to Bloom's theory, it is important to identifying a participant's learning styles, using tools such as the Honey and Mumford learning styles questionnaires if you can – if not, consider asking the learner, as they may have carried out a test previously and be aware of their preferred learning style. This knowledge will enable you to adapt your training methods to meet these, although bear in mind you will not always be able to meet everyone's learning style all of the time. A good range of methods and different types of activity that allow for experiential learning (Kolb's model) should go some way to achieving this.

Recognise the importance and need for reinforcement and the benefit of social learning, whether gained in formal or informal situations, which helps learning, training and development practitioners to develop strategies for enabling learning. Further, problem-solving, which enables learners to both use their existing experience and knowledge and to learn from the exercise, is an andragogic strategy that fits well with adult learners.

By having regard for these issues, the conditions for effective learning can be achieved and the learning transferred back to the workplace both in the learner's own work and in the way they share their experience and knowledge with people around them.

Barriers to learning

When assessing learning needs and designing learning interventions, you also need to consider the barriers to learning. An individual may not want to go on to a learning activity because of a bad experience at a previous learning event, the long time period since they last undertook any form of learning or they cannot see how the learning will benefit them. The training or learning activity itself and/or the deliverer may have been poor and thereby undermines credibility by perpetuating poor practice.

From an organisational or management viewpoint, spending time and money on learning and development only for the newly qualified or knowledgeable person to leave the organisation or be poached by another one can be a disincentive.

Learning methods have changed substantially over recent years with more emphasis on e-learning at work or at home. Less classroom/training room attendance and more self-directed learning may suit some employees, but by no means all like the de-personalised approach. The assumption that everyone is comfortable with electronic systems can also be misplaced, with many workers finding difficulty coping with the technology of computers and other devices.

See the website for a more detailed analysis of the barriers.

The learning organisation

Research in the late 1980s introduced the notion of the learning organisation. This concept involves regarding the organisation as a living organism existing in its environment that needs to have good feedback mechanisms and the ability to adapt to changing circumstances by taking timely action (Moorby 1996). A definition by Wick and Leon (1995) is an organisation that 'continually improves by rapidly creating and refining the capabilities required for future successes'. A key proponent of the learning organisation was Peter Senge (1990) and later in developing the notion of innovation practice (1998).

According to Peter Senge (1990) learning organisations are:

> organizations where people continually expand their capacity to create the results they truly desire, where new and expansive patterns of thinking are nurtured, where collective aspiration is set free, and where people are continually learning to see the whole together.

In practice, it has a very broad interpretation but is generally regarded as having some or all of the following features:

- The ability to approach problem-solving in a systematic way by encouraging employees to learn statistical and questioning techniques. (The CIPD recognises the importance of this in their qualifications including a unit on researching, analysing and presenting information to managers.)
- A willingness to search for new ideas and to use them, especially when they come from employees through a 'Kaizen' scheme or similar. Originally, Kaizen was a Japanese strategy for continuous improvement and it advocates elimination of waste in systems and procedures, a gradual rather than a rapid improvement in practices, and a multi-skilled and flexible workforce.
- A desire to openly evaluate past successes and failures and to learn from both.
- To continually look outside the organisation for 'best practice' and analysing if and how it can be transferred to the organisation successfully. (HR and other practitioners through their CPD activities will be one of the resources for this aspect.)
- To establish a culture where employees can question existing rules and procedures and take part in decision-making processes from which they can learn. (For HR practitioners the CIPD's HR Profession Map includes the desired behaviour to be 'curious' and to have the 'courage to challenge'.)
- The acceptance that mistakes will be made and that this is part of the learning process.
- A recognition that learning is open to all employees, not just managers or supervisors, and that self-development is as important as development planned by management.
- To implement systems that can be accessed by a wide group of users, not just experts.

Organisations that subscribe to these tenets will aim to create a labour force that is eager to learn, to question, to experiment, to take part in decisions and to take responsibility for its actions. It can be seen at once that this conflicts with a culture that is hierarchically based, where management take decisions and where employees carry out the work as directed. Moving to a learning organisation will normally need major cultural shifts, as well as the adoption of some of the features listed above. An example of such a move is given in the Meteor case study at the end of the chapter.

In practice, the change is not an easy one to achieve. As Harrison has pointed out, it requires a 'skilful balance between formal systems and informal features . . . and presupposes a sophisticated approach to the knowledge process that does not fit easily with the lack of expertise and awareness that research indicates actually prevails in the field' (2002: 388).

Nonetheless, in the CIPD 2012 Learning and Talent Development Survey, two-fifths of respondents say creativity and innovation are critical to develop their organisations and that every level of the organisation needs to be involved. The survey concludes that such organisations can deliver faster and more efficiently to customers; and that such an approach enables organisations to find ideas that might bring in new markets and opportunities, and aids product design and improvement. Only through investment in developing talent and capability will this succeed, and the current economic climate means that companies are having to focus on what will bring added value and contribute directly to business goals being achieved and, for some, what will enable them to survive.

TALENT MANAGEMENT

Originating in the late 1990s, when McKinsey management consultancy advocated 'the war for talent', the concept of talent management has evolved into essential management practice and covers the range of human resource issues from recruitment to performance enhancement and organisational development.

> Talent management is the systematic attraction, identification, development, engage-ment, retention and deployment of those individuals who are of particular value to an organisation, either in view of their high potential for the future or because they are fulfilling business/operation-critical roles.
>
> (CIPD 2011b)

Organisations are now extending the concept across all staff groups, not just those with potential, as part of performance enhancement and looking at the talents of everyone in the organisation.

As far as learning and development goes, talent development encompasses such areas as individual development, mentoring and coaching, identifying skills to support busi-ness strategy, networking and, through succession planning, identifying and preparing future managers and leaders.

You will see from some of the case studies in this chapter how talent management now features as an integral part of learning and development.

TAILORED APPROACH TO LEARNING

Successive government reviews and several recent reports (see 'National Government and non-governmental schemes and initiatives' section) have put pressure on employers to take their share of enabling and encouraging their employees to take up lifelong learning and to develop skills, knowledge and expertise useful not only to the organisation but also to them personally in terms of mobility of skills and career development.

With an economic downturn in recent years, this has become increasingly difficult for employers to manage. Instead of a one-size-fits-all approach, increasingly organisations want tailor-made learning to focus on those target groups and skills that will make the most difference to the achievement of their business goals, as well as economic survival. Individual learning goals, therefore, have to be aligned with business-specific goals.

The ways in which development and learning is delivered to employees is also changing to match the economic climate and budget constraints and to achieve value for money. According to the 2011 CIPD Learning and Talent Development Survey (CIPD 2011a), organisations are seeing coaching in-house as the most effective way to deliver learning to the workforce, supplemented by in-house rather than external training programmes. Internal secondment and 360-degree feedback are also seen as effective learning methods, together with greater use of e-learning. When asked about the future, organisations saw the integration of coaching, organisational development and performance management to drive organisational change.

The development of leadership skills is seen as very important and external coaching is used as the main method to improve these skills. This, together with in-house coaching for other groups of employees, mentoring for apprentices or trainees and the link to performance management, shows an increasing emphasis on an individual-level approach to learning and development.

The case studies in this chapter all illustrate in a range of ways how organisations have identified different learning techniques and environments, tailored to their own needs. They also serve as an example to other organisations of what can be achieved by creative and innovative thinking and to show that learning and development can be effective and cost-effective in an era of difficult economic circumstances. A comparison of talent management with training, learning and development is shown in Table 8.2.

TRAINING AIMS AND OBJECTIVES

The fundamental aim of training is to help the organisation to meet its organisational objectives by increasing the value of its major resource, namely, its employees. Armstrong (2001) sets out three specific training objectives:

- To develop the competencies of employees and improve their performance.
- To help people grow within the organisation in order that, as far as possible, its future needs for human resources can be met from within the organisation.
- To reduce the learning time for employees starting in new jobs on appointment, transfer or promotion, and ensure that they become fully competent as quickly and economically as possible.

Table 8.2 Comparing and contrasting talent management/learning with training, learning and development

Talent management Based on CIPD Talent Management Factsheet 2012	A focus on individuals who can make a difference to organisational performance through immediate contribution or in the long term. The systematic attraction, identification of development, engagement and retention, and deployment of those individuals with high potential and who are of practical value to an organisation. It is not enough to just attract individuals with high potential but it is also necessary to have a planned strategy for managing their talent (investment in human capital, retention strategy, encouragement of innovation, creativity). Compare this approach with that of a recruitment and retention strategy of five years or more ago where the individual would not have had the same focus or direct relevance to business planning and goals.
Learning and talent development Based on CIPD Learning and Development Factsheet 2012	Developed the L&D approach into a much more systematic, strategic business-orientated one. Supports the management of talent directly by identifying individual and group capabilities, skills and competencies, and uses and develops these to ensure a sustainable and successful organisation. It underpins organisational effectiveness. It focuses on the long-term development of exceptional high performers or those with high potential, who are essential to long-term business success. Coaching and mentoring models feature highly in this respect. There is an emphasis on return on investment and value for money. Investors in people processes are often used to assess and show learning and talent development.
Learning and development Based on CIPD Change Agenda report 2005	Started to address the inadequacies of 'training'. Introduced self-directed, work-based learning processes leading to increased potential in the workplace. Developed individuals' and groups' long-term capabilities. Incorporated organisational values and vision into the learning equation. Wanted to create a supportive learning environment. Wanted to get away from separate learning activities to a joined-up approach to organisational learning. A systematic development of individuals and groups to meet organisational and business needs. As such L&D can be seen as the precursor to talent development and was an important stepping stone from the narrow focus and undefinable value of training.
Training Based on CIPD Change Agenda report 2005	A production-line interventionist approach reacting to a current situation or need rather than building up the capabilities of individuals or groups for meeting future business needs. Transferring a large amount of information rather than ensuring the knowledge was assimilated and used to build capability and competency. Detached from the reality of the business or the context of the organisation.

There needs to be a systematic approach to training, which means that training must be directed towards specific ends. It is all too common for employees to be sent on training courses as a result of an attractive brochure arriving on a manager's desk without the manager considering the real needs of the employee or the implications of the training. A systematic approach is best explained through an analysis of the training cycle.

The four-stage training cycle

The training cycle (see Figure 8.3) has similar stages to the learning cycle, to which it has more than a passing resemblance.

Figure 8.4 shows the National Training Awards' Learning Framework, which has been developed by UK Skills, which has run the awards since 1987. Although similar to the cycle

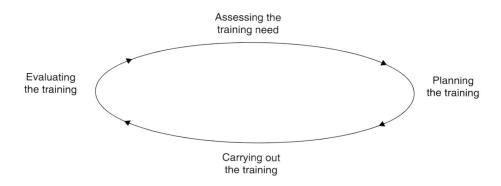

Figure 8.3
The training cycle

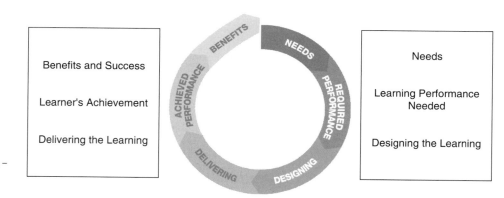

Figure 8.4
Learning Framework

Source: UK Skills – National Training Awards.

seen elsewhere, it goes into a little more detail as it distinguishes between the need for learning activity in a particular subject or topic area and the further investigation that should occur into the level at which that learning is needed. This takes account of the current level of knowledge or skill of learners and ensures the new intervention is pitched correctly to meet their needs and those of the organisation.

There is one further benefit to this diagram over the traditional, closed circle and that relates to the fact that the end of the cycle is an arrow pointing to the future. This reflects the fact that learning and development should be continuous and ongoing.

ASSESSING LEARNING AND TALENT DEVELOPMENT NEEDS

A development need arises due to the identified gap between the required knowledge, skills and experience for the individual carrying out the work and that actually possessed by the employee concerned (see Figure 8.5).

The reasons why an individual needs developing range from not fully meeting the skills specification for the job when appointed, benefiting from more support to improve confidence and proficiency to changes in the role, which mean that the demands change or added responsibility is taken on.

There are also situations, especially through performance appraisal/review processes, where opportunities to access learning and development are treated as a reward, especially in times when it is not possible to reward success in financial ways.

When reviewing an individual's needs, it may be easy to simply find them some internal or external training, but, if the individual's motivation to learn or their preferred learning styles are not taken into account, the resultant training might not be as effective as it could be. So a learning needs analysis will also help to match the right people with the right learning event, making the process cost-effective.

Involving individuals at this stage will help with their ownership of the learning or training plan compiled for them. It will also identify any obstacles or difficulties that may arise. These can then be dealt with prior to the learning taking place.

GENERATIONS AND THEIR IMPACT

A further consideration when designing learning and development and in delivering learning activities is the recent analysis that has been carried out on the differences between the generations in the workplace.

Figure 8.5

Identification of training needs

As with all aspects of learning, training and development that relate to diversity issues, generalisations do need to be treated with caution and the needs and preferences of individuals sought. Table 8.3 sets out the specific learning requirements of the generations.

This identification of the learning and development needs process can take place in a number of ways.

When an employee starts a *new job*, an analysis will be carried out that examines the job requirements (through the job description and specification or a role profile for competency-based roles – see Chapter 2) and matches that against the employee's existing profile. No candidate is ever perfect, so there will always be a number of gaps to fill, especially if it is an internal transfer or promotion or if the new employee is specifically taken on as a trainee.

Through the *annual performance review/appraisal* process (see Chapter 5) the employee and their manager sit down together and draw up a list of areas where training

Table 8.3 Generations

Baby boomers (aged 49–68)	**Born between 1946 and 1964**	May now be considering retirement options but: This generation has lobbied against age discrimination and compulsory retirement at a certain age and won. Some are keen to exercise that right for positive reasons. Consider the more recent economic situations and organisations seeking to retain these skills, while baby boomers are finding it more difficult to leave even if they want to. Have a great deal of knowledge, talent and experience. Are looking for new ways to work. Like collaborative working and working in teams. Baby boomers are considered excellent mentors.
Generation X (aged 34–48)	**Born between 1965 and 1979**	Independent, enjoy informality, entrepreneurial. Want balance in their lives. Want to build a range of skills and experiences they can take with them, and want a career path laid out. Want immediate and honest feedback.
Generation Y (aged 24–33)	**Born between 1980 and 1990**	Recently or just entering employment. Family and social life is prioritised over work. Have grown up with technology and rely on it to perform their jobs better, plugged in 24 hours a day, 7 days a week. Prefer to communicate and learn through technology rather than face to face or classrooms. Achievement-orientated and ambitious, more confident than earlier generations. Will challenge the established order. Will seek new challenges and want a solid learning curve.

Millennials/ Generation Z (aged 13–23)	Born between 1990s and 2000	As for Generation Z – those 'millennials' born in the 1990s or later, who grew up in the Internet age and will be entering the workforce in the decade ahead – they want workplace connectivity.
		According to the 2011 Cisco Connected World Technology Report, 'The desire of young professionals and college students to use technology is strong enough to influence their future job choice, sometimes more than salary does.'
		■ An extension of Generation Y.
		■ Need to see where their career is going, and what they need to get there.
		■ Must have continual challenges.
		■ Most connected generation via social and professional networking, and will find new job/career quickly or will be found by others through computer networking systems. Access to social media, mobile devices and the Internet are expected to be used more freely in the workplace.
		■ Want daily feedback, want ongoing learning and coaching. Self-assured can-do attitude, positive self-image. They believe passionately in teams.

Table 8.3 (*Continued*)

can help the employee to perform better, after agreeing on the existing job requirements and the employee's actual performance level.

A *Personal Development Plan (PDP)*, which may also form part of the process, enables opportunities to be looked at that will allow an individual's career to develop or their role options to broaden. The *CIPD Continuous Professional Development Plan* is an example of a PDP, but organisations or individuals can develop their own format to record learning needs, and how it is intended to meet the needs identified within a specified timeframe.

In addition to the structured performance appraisal/review, there will be opportunities to identify learning needs during routine situations such as supervision meetings and simply by someone else who is more knowledgeable about the task, such as a more experienced colleague or supervisor/manager, observing someone's work.

A *specific incident* may occur that demonstrates a major gap. For example, a number of customer complaints close together will indicate customer-care training is required for the employee concerned. If a member of staff takes up a grievance against a manager's attitude or actions, this could indicate that the manager concerned needs some form of training on handling staff. If there is a 'near miss' reported that lays the blame on a pilot, it is vital that retraining of that pilot takes place.

All new recruits should be going through an *induction programme*. This is an ongoing learning need but the learning styles of participants and the needs of the organisation may change over time so the induction process requires regular review to meet changing needs.

During the *probationary or review period*, issues may arise over an individual's competence or skill, and before decisions are made about the person's future a learning or improvement plan may be needed, involving learning activities to assist the person to meet the required standards. These may require shorter, more creative learning within a limited timeframe.

When someone *moves into a different job role* and working environment, there may be learning required to help the person adapt to their new role and, if a person has had a prolonged absence due, for example, to maternity, paternity or adoption leave, sickness or a sabbatical, a *reintroduction process* may be needed to help them adapt back into working life, as well as updating them on what has changed in their job role and within the organisation during their absence. This is a variation on induction. A *development centre* (see Chapter 3) will throw up a selection of needs, especially those relating to interpersonal skills, such as group problem-solving or running meetings.

Exit interviews may also show training needs, in that employees leaving the organisation may make it clear that one of the reasons they are leaving is because they were not adequately prepared for the work they were doing.

A *training needs analysis* can also be carried out for a department or a whole unit. For example, it may be identified that the level of IT skills is insufficient for a purchasing department or that a production unit has a gap in identifying quality errors and remedying them. For the organisation as a whole, an examination of the business plan and the associated human resource plan may immediately bring training needs to light. An example here was the identification by Pearl Assurance of the need for a new approach for sales training. Bringing together a collection of individual training needs may show that areas of required training can be common across many employees, sections or units. Training needs arise specifically when a major change programme occurs in the organisation.

There are some specific events that affect the organisation and in turn identify learning needs for the whole organisation or specific occupational groups within it. Further details on this can be accessed on the website.

If an organisation has to change substantially, there will need to be a carefully thought-out plan to implement the changes. This plan should include identifying the learning needs and how these might be achieved. The plan should be looking at what skills and knowledge exist in the organisation now, what will be needed in the future and how any gap will be met.

Having carried out the analysis, the next stage is to negotiate a learning and development plan. It is very rarely the case that all the training needs identified can be met within the budget, so negotiation needs to take place to decide on priorities across departments, roles and individuals. Prioritising through need is a better system than the arbitrary allocation of funds on the basis of adding, say, 5 per cent on to last year's budget for each department (Reid and Barrington 1997).

PLANNING AND CARRYING OUT THE LEARNING AND DEVELOPMENT ACTIVITIES

There is no distinct cut-off point between planning and implementing the learning and development activities. Inherent within the planning process is the decision on a number of issues:

- Should the learning take place on-the-job or off-the-job?
- Should it be held in the company or outsourced to a training provider?
- Which techniques should be used?
- Can the learning activity be afforded and what gives best value for money?

On-the-job learning and development is appropriate where immediacy and realism are essential. Its *advantages* are that it provides instant entry into the job, the trainees work, learn and develop expertise at the same time, they can see the results of their actions and they can usually be effectively supervised while they are learning. They also learn the social aspects of the job, the informal culture and the small details that are often omitted from training manuals or job descriptions.

Consider what has been said about tailoring learning and development activities and the rise of the in-house coach. There are various coaching qualifications available, including from the CIPD, and qualified coaches can be a cost-effective learning and development method.

The *disadvantages* all centre on the quality of the supervisor responsible for the trainee and the way the information is passed to the trainee. All too often, the information is passed on in a haphazard way by an overworked supervisor who is untrained in instruction techniques. Worse still, the instruction may be completely delegated to an experienced fellow-employee who may then instruct them on all the shortcuts and bad habits that have developed over the years. The environment is an important aspect here in that the trainee may be put off and distracted by the noise or apparent confusion of a totally new experience and find it difficult to cope with learning to work with new people, as well as in a new job. Trainees are bound to make mistakes and this can be expensive in an on-the-job situation; in fact, because of such potential costs, the trainees are often held back for an extended period from doing the important work.

Off-the-job training, which usually takes place in a training centre or appropriate facilities away from the immediate workplace, has the *advantage* of allowing the trainee to concentrate on learning the new job without distraction and for the training to be delivered systematically by skilled and experienced trainers. It can also help to give an immediate good first impression for a new employee. Trainees can make mistakes without the fear of an immediate cost to the organisation and tests can be set up for each stage to ensure that the job has been learned thoroughly before the trainee is released into the real working situation.

The *disadvantages* are that it is difficult to re-create a situation that is close to a real-life one without a high investment cost, such as the training carried out by airlines, who, understandably, spend millions of pounds in creating simulated flying conditions. When trainees transfer on to the job, they may come across situations not covered in training or find the work to be far more complex than it was set out in the training school. As mentioned previously, cost is now a key factor for organisations and the trend in recent years has been away from external activities.

Outsourcing learning and development is an alternative chosen when the learning or training skills required are not present within the organisation. This applies with managerial, professional and technical training where the specialist training organisation has built up a reputation for running special courses. They may run these courses in their own premises, or within the company or in convenient hired premises, such as hotels or conference centres. The *advantage* is that experts should provide high-quality training and expose employees to situations that they have not experienced. Trainees may also learn from their fellow delegates how operations are carried out differently in other organisations. Until the arrival of mobile phones, there used to be the advantage that the trainees would be able to concentrate totally on the training without fear of interruption!

The *disadvantages* include the fact that the cost is usually higher, that the specialist organisation may not be aware of the organisation's specific requirements and that they do not normally follow up the trainees to see how effective the training has been in practice.

STYLES AND TECHNIQUES OF TRAINING

Many of the styles and techniques to be described can apply only to off-the-job situations but some can also apply to on-the-job training. Another way to divide the techniques is between those that have considerably active learning ingredients, such as action-learning, computer-based learning or working with case studies, and those that are essentially passive, such as demonstrations, lectures and videos. A final division is between those techniques that can apply to individual training, such as mentoring, and those that apply to groups, large or small, such as role-play or workshops. Table 8.4 indicates which category each technique falls into.

As has been said elsewhere in this chapter, the trend to tailored learning interventions has enhanced the attention given to computerised and distance-learning packages and it is worth considering these separately and in more detail.

E-LEARNING

When e-learning started to emerge in the late 1990s, it was predicted that it would replace all other forms of learning, training and development within a comparatively short time.

Table 8.4 Techniques of training

Technique	Comments	On- or off-the-job or both	Active or passive	Individual or group
Job instruction	Trainer must be trained, have a clear plan and build up an effective and encouraging relationship with the training. Applies principally to basic jobs, such as assembly or hairdressing or some retail counter work.	Both	Passive, mostly	Individual or small groups
Computerised training	This allows the trainee to work through the programme at their own pace with immediate feedback. It can cover simple skills such as learning about spreadsheets to highly complex processes such as pilot simulations. It is particularly effective for the essential basics of language learning.	Off-the-job	Active	Individual
Planned sequence of experience (job rotation)	Often operated within a department to ensure the employees know all the department's work, the training needs to be well planned and co-ordinated with mutual support given to each other by the employees within the department. There must also be clear learning objectives.	On-the-job	Active	Individual
Lectures and demonstrations	Lectures to large numbers will need an inspired speaker and an attentive, motivated audience. That is why it mostly fails! It is theoretically efficient in passing on information but research shows that only 20 per cent or less sticks. Visual aids are important and follow-up/practice is essential for this activity to be of any value. Demonstrations can be more effective if small groups are involved, if questions are allowed and if the opportunity to repeat difficult sequences is allowed.	Off-the-job	Passive	Small or large groups
Role-play	One of the most attractive forms of training where individuals adopt a role set out for them and act out the scenario as a group. In so acting, they remember much of what they have done; it can be highly relevant and practical to the subject of the training and is generally great fun. The difficulties	Off-the-job	Active	Small groups

(Continued overleaf)

Table 8.4 *(Continued)*

Technique	Comments	On- or off-the-job or both	Active or passive	Individual or group
	arise if the end result of the role-play is not as planned or if any of the 'actors' do not take the activity seriously enough. A further version of role-reversal, which can be used, say, with appraisal training where the manager and the appraisee change roles, can be highly effective in helping with interpersonal skills.			
Group discussion	Success emerges from the way a discussion is handled, to ensure it is led well, keeps to the point, involves a wide number of participants and is effectively summarised.	Off-the-job	Active, mostly	Small groups
Video/DVD	A straight video, well produced, can be a useful vehicle for imparting knowledge and demonstrating skills but it needs to be reinforced through questions or practice.	Off-the-job	Passive	Small or large groups
Distance learning	By using specially prepared materials which involve the trainee listening to tapes, carrying out exercises and responding to questions, the trainee can work at their own pace and learn the subject in a systematic way. The only major disadvantage, if the materials are well prepared, is the isolation of the trainee where a high degree of self-motivation is required.	Off-the-job	Passive and active	Individual
Project work or case study	If the project/case study chosen is stimulating and realistic, the trainee(s) will learn in-depth the subject in question and will increase their investigative and creative skills. It can also be utilised for discussion, and advocacy skills can be developed.	Off-the-job, mostly	Active	Individual or small group

Table 8.5 E-learning

Unsupported e-learning	When e-learning started, this would have been delivered by DVD (and still is in some cases) but is now commonly made available over the web. It means that the learning is self-contained and the learner does not have the benefit of support in order to address any difficulties they may have with the content or technology.
Supported e-learning	This is a term that is used differently in a number of settings. Basically, it is the opposite of unsupported e-learning because, although the learning is delivered electronically, the learner has access to support, which may be through a help line or from a tutor being present while the learning is undertaken.
Informal e-learning	This includes any learning which takes place electronically away from a course setting. Therefore, it may be social or research and discovery methods of self-study referred to earlier.

One of the biggest problems is that there is not a universally accepted definition of e-learning. The CIPD definition of e-learning is 'Learning that is delivered, enabled or mediated using electronic technology for the explicit purpose of training in organisations' (CIPD 2009).

In such a diverse field, such a simple definition has its benefits but it is equally important for practitioners to appreciate the potential scope of e-learning (see Table 8.5).

SCOPE OF E-LEARNING

This is ever changing and has moved away from simple access to information via traditional DVD or the Internet to embrace a diverse range of methods. Some examples, though not an exhaustive list, are described below.

Virtual classroom technology allows learners to be able to follow a facilitated course that requires demonstration of techniques in remote locations to the extent that the tutor may be in a room on their own delivering the learning. The challenge this causes for tutors is that it can be difficult to assess the progress individual students are making and know when to move on in a session because, although students can see the tutor, the tutor cannot see them.

The CIPD makes use of *podcasts* for delivering resources to members. They are seen as another development in methods for delivering information, and are designed to be a time- and location-flexible way of delivering via MP3 players and iPods. As such, they are often regarded as learner friendly and inclusive, but caution and the backup of paper copy is needed because it is not normally possible to use the earphones from such devices if one wears hearing aids.

Internet-based communities. From a learning perspective, they enable people to discuss their learning with one another remotely and to develop collaboratively based projects between them away from the classroom. They are used by the Open University and a wide range of professional organisations.

MOBILE LEARNING (M-LEARNING)

One could put forward an argument that this is just another variation of e-learning but it is increasingly being commented on as a specific method of delivering learning and, as such, warrants special mention. There are various explanations of just what mobile learning is. Training Zone posted an article by Andrew Jackson (2011), which describes it as any learning interaction delivered by mobile technology and therefore available whenever and wherever the learner wants. M-learning can also be used to complement more formal learning, in between classroom-based learning or afterwards.

See the website for further details about how mobile learning can be applied.

BLENDED LEARNING

One other learning delivery strategy that you may have come across is blended learning. This is not a method in the same sense as the others that have been looked at. Rather, it refers to how a range of methods are used in order to create a comprehensive learning experience. The term is frequently heard in connection with using e-learning alongside another method such as facilitation, but can also include coaching and mentoring. It is not, however, an add-on to something already existing, but a learning event that is designed with several methods interwoven into it.

See the website for further details about this subject.

In terms of carrying out the training, it is important to ensure that the employees concerned are fully aware of the objectives before they start and that they have the necessary information regarding the training itself. Nothing puts trainees off more than poor administration, so it is vital that all the necessary preparation is made in respect of materials, exercises, workbooks, cases and technology.

Case study 8.1 gives two examples of how organisations have moved away from traditional classroom- and trainer-led learning. They show how changing learning techniques can be both effective and also makes savings. The use of new technology is a factor in both cases, and new electronic, computerised and mobile learning will continue to be developed throughout the twenty-first century.

Assessment of learners

With more in-house solutions, and the introduction of coaching and mentoring and e-learning, it is important that the assessment of learners – to ascertain whether learning has been acquired and that the learner/trainee is able to transfer this to the workplace – takes place and by those qualified to undertake the assessment. Assessment of learning is something that needs to occur whenever a learning event takes place. Whether it is a course, workshop, e-learning, work-based training or any other situation that is set up to enable someone to learn, whoever is delivering or co-ordinating the initiative will need to

CASE STUDY 8.1 MOVING AWAY FROM TRADITIONAL LEARNING METHODS

Case 1: Implementing e-learning – City of Edinburgh

The driver for change to the previous training strategy at the City of Edinburgh Council was the reduction of training costs and enhancing learner experience linked to a wider agenda of increasing quality and flexibility among the workforce.

The Council had already installed an e-based HR system that allowed employees to manage their own HR accounts, and e-learning was a logical next step. There was a sticking point over making a cultural change from traditional classroom training, and the message from those involved in the design and implementation of the e-learning system is that, when managing a change in approach and methods, it is important to achieve buy-in from the stakeholders.

When the learning needs of the workforce and the skills needed had been identified, e-learning courses were created and rolled out on a phased basis. All 12,900 staff were trained via e-learning in an 8-week period, resulting in savings of nearly half a million pounds on the training budget.

Having received a BT Innovation award, the Council formed partnerships with other councils to deliver an e-induction course, and also with other agencies to deliver child-protection training. Savings continued to be made, as more topics were added to the e-learning system, including service-specific modules, equality and diversity.

Case 2: KPMG launches a graduate assessment centre

Although primarily a recruitment and selection tool, KPMG's creation of what they call an 'immersive' assessment process has many features that are also learning techniques. For instance, the Virtual Office exercise uses software with animated 3D characters that interact with the candidates, while they are engaged in pre-assigned tasks that include telephone calls and email. In another technique, already used in some learning activities, role-plays with trained actors playing the part of managers or a client take place.

Personality and skills testing takes place but at the centre of KPMG's assessment centre is the use of advanced technology to enable candidates to be engaged in a more realistic work environment, and to test their skills application as well as attitude and aptitude. Group work is now not seen as a means of how candidates would react in reality.

KPMG say that giving assessors much more input on who the candidate really is has reduced the recruitment timescales and costs. By the time candidates reach the interview stage, they are known to be strong contenders for the jobs on offer.

Lessons to be learned by learning and development practitioners and the design and delivery techniques for traditional courses.

(Source: adapted from *People Management* 2011a, 2011b)

identify whether the intended learning is being achieved. This will happen during the learning event or at the end or, very frequently, both.

Whatever method is used, assessment should be about giving constructive and developmental feedback to the learner so that they can use the feedback to further improve their development.

EVALUATING THE TRAINING

The last part of the cycle is vital to the whole process. Unless there can be reasonable proof that the training actually added value, it becomes easy to dismiss it as a waste of time and money. There are two forms of evaluation – subjective and objective. *Subjective evaluation* can be made by the trainer, who will be aware whether or not the training went well. It will also emerge from the trainees who should be asked for their opinions at various stages throughout the programme, both verbally and in written 'happy sheets'. A final evaluation by the trainees should move towards the *objective viewpoint*, having to answer questions such as: 'How has this training benefited you in the workplace?' or 'Name a number of areas where you will put into effect improvements that have arisen from what you have learned during this training'.

Other objective measures can be involved in observing improved performance – productivity, quality and customer relations – and any measures considered robust by the organisation. These will be balanced with subjective measures from the trainee's manager and internal customers. Some training, such as graduate training programmes, take some time to bear fruit, so a final evaluation may take place a year or two after the training is completed.

Research undertaken under the umbrella of CIPD's Change Agenda (2007) reported that the percentage of robust evaluations undertaken over many years was disappointingly small. What the research found was that:

> One size fits all set of metrics (measurements of performance) to establish learning value is inappropriate. A wide ranging approach is required which involves:–
>
> ■ Aligning learning processes and investment to organisational strategic priorities
> ■ Using a range of methods to assess and evaluate the contribution of learning
> ■ Establishing the most relevant approaches to assessing and reporting on the value of learning for the organisation.

The research indicated that most organisations still have some way to go with the development of appropriate measures. However, four main approaches to measuring and reporting on value were identified:

■ Learning function efficiency measures
■ Key performance indicators and benchmark measures

- Return on investment measures
- Return on expectation measures.

SPECIALIST LEARNING AND TALENT PROGRAMMES AND INITIATIVES

Induction

Induction is often considered an early part of the training process. Once an applicant accepts a position, they can be passed on to the training department who take over from that point. Recently, induction has been seen more as the final but vital part of the selection process. The selection job is not complete until the applicant is safely introduced into the organisation and helped to overcome the difficulties and pressures of those first few days and weeks.

'Induction is that process by which new recruits are integrated into an organisation so that they become active, co-operative and productive members as soon as possible' (The Industrial Society, now the Work Foundation www.workfoundation.org.uk).

The aims of induction are:

- To assimilate the person into the organisation as quickly as possible
- To establish the organisation's culture, ethics and rules/standards
- To get the person producing effectively or meeting the norm standard as soon as possible
- To retain skilled staff once they have been recruited.

For most positions, an induction of one to two days is allowed to provide the basic information to the new recruit and to introduce them to the important aspects of working in the organisation.

ACTIVITY 8.1

Make a list of all the activities and information that you would include in an induction programme for a trainee in a small engineering company.

Discussion of activity 8.1

Some of the points you may have written down (in no particular order) are shown in Table 8.6.

This can be converted into a short programme, led by the human resources officer, but bringing in other friendly faces, including the safety officer, training officer and the works manager. It is not unknown in a small organisation for the owner or chief executive

Table 8.6 Induction programme

Activities	Information
Basic safety training, including protective clothing and emergency procedures	Safety rules and regulations
Tour of the premises, including toilets, canteen and first aid provisions	Map of premises – departments
Introduction to colleagues, management (maybe shop steward)	Up-to-date organisation chart
Brief outline of company history, mission statement, set of values, system of communication	Any relevant documents
Outline of products and what they do (including demonstration) plus brief summary of customers and suppliers	Copy of main product brochures
Introduction to company handbook, including benefits, procedures on holidays and sickness, and company rules, disciplinary procedures and payment of wages	Copy of employee handbook
Introduction to work of department and the role of trainee System of performance management	Copy of any working procedures and details of practices regarding breaks, clocking, use of materials, etc. Performance management scheme
Introduction to any social activities	Details of clubs, outings

to want to meet each new employee personally on the first day. They are, after all, a considerable investment and should represent a priority. A balance needs to be drawn between ensuring that the trainee has all the information required as soon as possible and flooding them with too much information and causing them confusion and a degree of disorientation.

The arrival of any new team member will have had an impact on the team as a whole. The loss of one person and their replacement by another, even when they have similar task-orientated skills and knowledge, may well have changed the balance within the team. Progress in 'regrouping', with the new person, as a part of the team, will occur during the induction process and is ultimately the responsibility of the line manager as team leader. Case study 8.2 describes a new approach to induction at NHS Direct.

Team building

Team building is vital in developing a more effective organisation. Teams rarely flourish naturally; like tender plants, they need constant attention and encouragement. Team-building training has many forms, but the essential feature of most is for the team to go through some testing experiences together, which then forge them into a unit with common successful experiences and a 'esprit de combat'. If that sounds like the army, that is because most team training originated from US or UK armed forces research into the subject.

CASE STUDY 8.2 NHS DIRECT INDUCTION APPROACH

NHS Direct provides 24-hour expert health advice to the public via web-based or telephone contact. A new flexible rostering system has meant the way staff were inducted had to change. The 12-week classroom-based training was changed to a more flexible blended learning, in order to allow new staff to start experiencing real-life calls as well as learning about their role and the service, to be trained across a 24-hour period and to be cost-effective.

There will still be training modules delivered at convenient times and a role for more experienced clinical staff to mentor new staff. New staff will start working alongside experienced operators right from the start, exposing new starters to situations that will test their suitability for the role.

Under development is also a virtual learning environment with podcasts, discussion forums and blogs. New starters will access this virtual tool before starting to work in a call centre so that they can familiarise themselves with policies and what they need to learn.

With a modular approach, NHS Direct hope to tailor the induction to individuals' needs and lifestyles, including learning away from the work base in their own homes, but also expecting individuals to take responsibility for their own learning.

The new induction programme should make training more accessible, relevant and be cost-effective, as well as utilising the existing workforce in a mentoring role. The exposure to experiencing real-life situations right at the start of employment requires a support network that the mentoring aspect provides new starters with.

(Source: CIPD 2011a)

The role of learning and development in supporting team development is three-fold:

1   In order for the right skills to be available within the team to the right level, learning needs may be identified which will need to be addressed. These may differ or be additional needs from those an individual would require if they did not join the team.

2   There may be specific team needs where the whole team needs learning and development in a particular area. Depending on what the need is, it may be necessary for team members to learn this one at a time, but wherever possible this should be organised on a team-wide basis or at least co-ordinated as such, so it becomes a form of team-building exercise.

3   There may well also be a need for specific team-building events. A search of the web will show a wide range of these available in the marketplace and indeed some of them are quite elaborate ... with costs to match. However, with careful thought and imagination, it is possible to organise events locally in a very cost-effective way.

One important aspect of team-building events is to hold on to the perspective that it is a learning and development exercise by stating – and restating if necessary – the aims and objectives of the exercise and also to have some de-brief at the end which allows for reflection and learning.

Before the economic downturn, *outdoor training* where teams are set challenges, often, but not always, in a competitive situation, was a popular team development activity. Having successfully completed the challenge, the teams then reflect upon the process, teasing out learning points. These centre around what makes teams successful, including effective team leadership and the ability to jointly solve problems, while under a degree of stress, and listen very carefully (especially when it is getting dark, the wind is howling, the flood water is rising and the centre is across the river!). Such training is also important in developing personal competencies, such as time management, planning, delegation and evaluation, and to retain a degree of confidence under adversity.

The experience is not always successful. Sometimes fundamental flaws in the teams rise to the surface under stressful conditions and there are some team members, even in the best teams, for whom the physical challenges are simply not appropriate. Having said this, the author's own limited experience in two organisations was that the activity was an unqualified success with the teams concerned improving their performance by more than 20 per cent over the next twelve months and still talking about it five years later.

Mentoring

Two definitions of mentoring:

> Mentoring relationships are dynamic, reciprocal, personal relationships in which a more experienced person (mentor) acts as a guide, role model, teacher, and a sponsor of a less experienced person (mentee or protégé) ... mentoring is associated with positive personal and career outcomes.
>
> (Johnson and Ridley 2008)

> Mentoring is the long term passing on of support, guidance and advice. In the workplace it has tended to describe a relationship in which a more experienced colleague uses their greater knowledge and understanding of the work or workplace to support the development of a member of staff.
>
> (CIPD 2010)

You can also see mentoring as similar to the original concept of a master–apprenticeship relationship where the master shares his skills and knowledge with someone just starting in a trade. As time goes by, there is increasing independence shown by the apprentice. So the aim was for the master to build up that independence but at the same time preserving the quality and reputation of the trade.

Transferring this model to mentoring, we can say that at the outset the mentee will have quite a strong dependence on the mentor in order to understand the role and responsibilities expected, the knowledge necessary for this, as well as the culture within which they work. Over time, the aim is for this to lessen to the point where the mentee can work successfully and independently of the mentor and, indeed, may be ready to become a mentor themselves.

The role of the mentor is to share knowledge and expertise to enable the mentee to achieve a desired standard, achieved through building rapport, showing empathy, giving support, being impartial and setting goals for the mentee to achieve. Mentees seek to achieve the goals set, seek resources to aid learning, ask for feedback and clarify issues with the mentor, drive the relationship in the areas wanted and accept and respond to constructive feedback.

So mentoring is about enabling personal and professional development through support, advice and guidance from a more experienced colleague. In particular, it supports a person's career development, internship and apprenticeship schemes, and it identifies individual talents. It also helps mentees to discover more about themselves, their potential and their capacity, and forms mutual respect and trust as the core of a successful mentoring process.

The use of mentoring also implies a benefit for the organisation as well as the individual with the mentor potentially able to influence the development of positive attitudes, encouragement of good management practice and support for team and organisational learning.

An example of a mentoring scheme is shown in case study 8.3.

Coaching

Coaching appears in many disciplines and aims to improve an employee's performance beyond their current level, perhaps where the individual has become stuck and demotivated, where the coachee needs to be given new skills and knowledge to get to a higher level or where the coachee is the highly valued potential high achiever for the organisation to meet its future business needs.

A coach may well not have the same ability in the field of activity that their coachee has. By the time a coaching relationship is appropriate, the coachee would have been expected to have learned the 'basics' from a variety of learning methods including instruction, facilitation, self-discovery, practice or maybe from having a mentor. The role of coaching is to enable the coachee to improve on their performance and achieve their potential. In a work context, such development would be targeted at enabling people to enhance their individual contribution to the achievement of their organisation's goals.

The coach is an adviser to and an assessor of the coachee, and instructs or demonstrates to the coachee what a high performer can do and motivates the coachee to achieve this level. The coachee is expected to be ready to co-operate, work towards the goals set with the coach and keep to the ground rules.

CASE STUDY 8.3 MENTORING IN CASTLE CARE NURSING HOMES

At the Castle Care Village group of nursing homes, they believe that, if it is worth investing in finding the right people, it is worth taking time to make sure they stay, which is why mentoring has been introduced. Each new member of staff is allocated a mentor from day one with the organisation, chosen from existing staff who have the attributes of patience and adaptability, as well as strengths in skills and knowledge. An attempt is made to match the 20-strong mentor team (out of 180 staff) with the new staff member in terms of personality and experience. They provide a vital support for new staff in the six-week training course, helping them to identify gaps in basic skills, answering questions and dealing with any day-to-day anxieties. They also check off regularly what has been learned and how it can be implemented in practice. If basic literacy, numeracy and IT support is required, mentors support their attendance at a twice-weekly course provided by Hull College, giving discreet guidance in what could be regarded as an embarrassing weakness.

Mentors attend a specific training course and a regular refresher conference each year at the University of Hull. Before the scheme began, many new staff did not last even the induction course (a regulatory requirement), but the support and encouragement given by mentors has meant that those who leave within the first six months are now a very small minority. The enthusiasm for the job from the mentors rubs off on the trainees and provides a firm foundation for the excellent service provided for the vulnerable clients.

(Source: Learning and Skills Council website, now the Skills Funding Agency)

See the website for further discussion about the definition and applications for coaching.

Case study 8.4 shows how two different types of organisation have utilised coaching.

Action learning

Revens (1989) developed a process of training through problem-solving, essentially for managers, and gave it a new name. He recognised that most people enjoy a continuing set of challenges that they would not face if they simply worked on the same job for long periods of time. His theories, which he tested at the National Coal Board in the period after the Second World War, were centred round the concept that we are motivated to learn *something*, not just motivated to learn, and that learning is deepest when it involves the whole person, using both mind and body. He set out to use the experience, growth and prior learning of colleagues in an active way to solve real problems. In the process, by sharing their hopes, aspirations, successes and errors, each participant learned about themselves, about working together and all about the subjects in question which broadened their whole experience.

CASE STUDY 8.4 DIFFERENT WAYS IN WHICH COACHING HAS BEEN UTILISED

Grant Thornton and Kent County Council are two different kinds of organisation, one private sector, one public sector, but both have seen the value of introducing coaching into their organisations and being prepared to put time and money into the scheme. In both cases, the importance of training up coaches to work effectively is emphasised.

Grant Thornton embarked on an innovative scheme to train up its partners as coaches, but as part of a leadership development programme and in order to achieve a coaching culture across the company. The company wants its partners to coach junior partners, directors and senior managers to support career development or when individuals start in new roles.

The company has acknowledged that it has devoted a sizeable part of its staff development budget to the coaching programme, and will expect partners to devote appropriate time to continue in a coaching role once certified.

Partners will attend a series of workshops, face-to-face or telephone coaching sessions and will carry out twelve coaching sessions in total with two assigned coaches. Coachees will also be expected to give feedback to the coaches on their coaching sessions and the benefits they have gained.

Managers at Kent County Council have been trained in coaching and mentoring since 2005 and the Council's learning and development team subsequently trained up officers from Kent Fire and Rescue Service. This led to the formation of the Kent coaching and mentoring network with members coming from a range of local authorities and other public sector organisations in the county.

The key qualification required to join the network is the ILM Level 5 Coaching and Mentoring Certificate. Member organisations have reciprocal arrangements with each other so that coaches can work across all the organisations in the network.

This 'skills swapping', as those involved in the management of the network call it, enables managers from different organisations to work in different work environments and organisational cultures. It also enables a different managerial and perhaps fresh perspective to be given. It is very much seen as part of a change in emphasis in management style and the way managers are developed.

One example given is that the coaching will enable officers in Kent Fire and Rescue service to make better, more effective and speedy decisions in adverse situations.

Serena Cunningham, the account manager with responsibility for the network, says, 'The network is the first of its kind and we feel it is an excellent, cost-effective method of passing on management skills.'

(Source: Adapted from *People Management* 2010a)

Continuous (or Continuing) Professional Development (CPD)

It is increasingly recognised that professional expertise is not simply learned at the outset of a career but needs to be constantly refined and updated. Nor should professional learning be restricted to management or supervision but to all employees who wish to journey up the ladder to one or other professional qualification.

The Chartered Institute of Personnel and Development (CIPD), along with other such bodies in professions such as accounting, law and medicine, has set up a regulatory system to encourage its members to continue to learn throughout their careers. This is to make sure that they remain up to date, are aware of the power of learning and contribute towards the high standard of the profession. The encouragement takes the form of advice of recording their learning experiences through such devices as a learning log or diary, as well as actually experiencing the learning itself through courses, conferences, action learning, mentoring and the other specialist learning systems dealt with in this chapter.

Reflective thinking is also a tool advocated by a number of professions and, adapting Kolb's experiential learning cycle, practitioners can think back on a situation or learning event to analyse what happened, what went well, what did not and why, and what lessons can be learned for the future. The practitioner will then adapt and improve their practice in future accordingly.

Sales training

This has been traditionally regarded as a specialised area, carried out by experienced sale personnel where the training is directed towards ensuring the trainees meet their specific targets. Subjects include product and technical knowledge, prospecting, handling objections and closing the sales. There are a number of reasons, however, why sales training has been the subject of wider analysis and interest in recent years.

Selling is so vital to a company's prosperity that generous resources are usually allocated to the activity. This has led to many of the post-war training innovations being developed in this area, including role-play analysis, the use of videos and telephone simulations, which have then been transferred and utilised in other training areas.

Opinion has moved from the view that salespeople are born, not made, to the view that potential, which can be identified in psychometric testing, is the key and that focused, structured training and support can lead to long-term success in the sales field. Again, the research carried out, especially in America, has been one of the elements that has encouraged the more general use of psychometric testing.

The ethical aspects of selling (or mis-selling) have come to light with major UK scandals in the 1980s and 1990s concerning pensions and endowment mortgages where the skill of the sales agent has convinced the customer to buy an expensive product that is poor value to them. Arising from a tougher regulatory environment has been the requirement for sales personnel in a number of areas to be accredited through attending approved courses, which have a more balanced ethical framework.

The increased attention by organisations on satisfying customers (internally and externally) has led to the greater adoption of sales training techniques for all staff, called 'customer care'. Employees in all parts of the organisation are encouraged to find out what the customer wants, to meet those needs and to aim to provide a continuing service – all standard features of sales training. Alongside this has been the encouragement of other sales training features such as encouraging self-belief, working towards goals and using persistence and determination to see the work through to a successful conclusion.

Case study 8.5 illustrates how talent management is integrated with dealing with an ageing workforce and utilising global talent.

CASE STUDY 8.5 THE IMPORTANCE OF GLOBAL TALENT

KCA Deutag (KCAD) is a company engaged in onshore and offshore oil drilling, and operates in a range of diverse countries. There are three key factors that influence the company's talent management and development:

- The impact on health and safety that BP suffered following the Deepwater Horizon blowout in the Gulf of Mexico
- An ageing workforce – many employees started when oil exploration and drilling started in the North Sea and elsewhere in the 1970s
- Operating in different countries, cultures and languages.

KCAD recognises the importance of developing talent in a high-risk environment and globally to ensure skilled employees are available to the company wherever it operates. The company places importance on recruiting locally as this gives it local knowledge and expertise. This is a change in past approaches that involved flying in talent and as a result creating a disconnected employee group from the local communities.

Arising from the KCAD approach is the need for local employees to learn the English language (but non-local managers particularly to also learn the local language) and communication skills, and for this the company uses a 'sheep-dip' method, while recognising the importance of self-study linked to their appraisal scheme.

A 'Safe to Lead' programme focuses on uncompromising operational safety being embedded among managers and includes how to respect cultures, interact with local people and understand how things are done.

Jeremy Townsend, Head of Training & Development, summarising the importance of learning and talent development in a global company, says, 'One of our values is "Valuing all people". It's about making sure our personnel have the capability to be safe and productive and closing the loop to ensure the impact you intended is delivered.'

(Source: CIPD 2011a, 'KCA Deutag: Drilling down into the importance of global talent')

Apprenticeships/internships/career development

More will be said under 'National government and non-governmental schemes and initiatives', but it is worth saying here that there is an interest by individuals in entering the job market and developing their skills and knowledge, and thereby their employability, through some sort of traineeship.

With an economic downturn and difficulty in recruiting the right skilled employee, there is an attraction to utilise government funding and initiatives to recruit individuals on to apprenticeships and internships. This impacts on company learning and development programmes and also enables mentoring to be used to support the trainees. The promise of career development opportunities arising from these schemes is also an incentive for the individual participant.

Case study 8.6 describes two apprenticeship schemes that show how the shortage in specialist skills is being tackled and that taking a long-term view, despite the recession, can bring benefits. The ATG scheme also illustrates the value of peer mentoring.

CASE STUDY

CASE STUDY 8.6 TACKLING THE SHORTAGE IN SPECIALIST SKILLS

Case 1: IBM apprenticeship scheme

Stephen Leonard, CEO of IBM UK and Ireland, talking about the company's new apprenticeship scheme, said, 'At IBM we like to think we always play a key part in developing the skills to succeed in today's global economy.'

While the apprenticeship scheme focuses on school leavers, the company sees this as complementing its existing graduate scheme and contributing to the development of the future leaders of the international company.

The scheme will be for school leavers across the UK and will give recruits an IT specialist level 3 qualification. The learning programme includes a range of learning methods including e-learning, on-the-job training and mentoring from buddies.

Commenting on IBM's pioneering approach, John Hayes, then Minister for Further Education, Skills and Lifelong Learning, said that apprenticeships should be about advanced technology skills as well as the more traditional skills.

The government is investing in creating more apprenticeships by 2015 as part of its *national skills strategy*, and IBM's initiative is supported by the government Sector Skills Council for Business and IT.

(Source: Adapted from *People Management* 2010b)

Case 2: Automated Technology Group Ltd apprenticeship programme

Automated Technology Group Ltd (ATG) – comprising Autotech Controls in Silsoe and the Bedford-based firms Igranic Control Systems and PSJ Fabrications – is headquartered at Wrest Park Enterprise Centre in Bedfordshire. The group designs, installs, maintains and upgrades electronic systems to control automation, supporting blue-chip brands in a number of key industries, including automotive, logistics, airports, metals and utilities. As a successful SME, demand for ATG's products and services had been increasing rapidly and the company decided to take a long-term view of the prevailing engineering skills shortage by launching a major apprenticeship programme in 2012.

'Beginning my own career as an apprentice, I know the true value of grass-roots, on-the-job training. In my view, it's the best possible platform for a career in engineering or management. ATG is a forward-thinking and ever-expanding group of companies, so we're always looking for enthusiastic and dedicated employees to continue our success.'
Andy Robinson, CEO

Wanting to grow its own talent to enable the company to meet increasing demand for its products and services, ATG worked in partnership with Semta – the government-licensed Sector Skills Council for Science, Engineering and Manufacturing Technologies – to put together a four-year apprenticeship programme starting at NVQ level 3, with opportunities to progress to NVQ levels 4 and 6 and ultimately achieve graduate entry with chartered engineer status.

Demand for the apprenticeships was high, and 21 apprentices aged between 16 and 23 years were carefully selected and assigned to a group of mentors, who were experienced employees in the company. The programme they have embarked upon enables them to enrol as either technical apprentices (specialising in computer simulation, project engineering or solution design) or craft apprentices (specialising in manufacturing technology) and to experience meaningful assignments in the three businesses that make up the group, as well as seeing how the support functions – HR, finance, marketing and administration – operate. As the apprentices gain greater understanding and confidence, it is envisaged that they will become mentors for the next cohort of apprentices.

'I am impressed by the commitment and enthusiasm of the apprentices. I'm also convinced of the merits of giving them the responsibility of becoming peer mentors for the next cohort of apprentices because I see them being able to relate well to people of their own age and confident enough to be innovative in their approach to challenges.'
Nick Rance, HR Development Manager

(Source: People Network Consultancy case studies)

Management and leadership development

Managers have special training needs arising from their specific responsibilities in respect of, among others, controlling, motivating, appraising and disciplining their staff, while planning, innovating and setting the boundaries of their department. Specialist skills required include setting targets, delegation, time management and problem-solving.

Management development is the entire, *structured* process by which managers learn and improve their skills for the benefit of their employing organisations and themselves. It applies to anyone from supervisor to chief executive. Learning methods that are effective for managers include e-learning, self-directed learning, secondments and having a mentor or coach.

See the website for further information on the importance of having a management development programme.

Case study 8.7 examines how two public sector organisations have developed schemes to develop their existing and potential managers and leaders. Using the talent management and development approach, the DWP and the NHS have created schemes to identify

CASE STUDY 8.7 DEVELOPING MANAGERS AND LEADERS

Case 1: DWP talent management tool

The Department of Work and Pensions (DWP) has around 100,000 employees and covers a diverse range of responsibilities, requiring a number of different skill sets. In addition to existing talent management programmes covering graduates, senior managers/executives and emerging talent, the DWP has added an Early Talent scheme to enable a much deeper talent pool to be created.

The talent programmes have become more important as government departments have to change and reduce employee numbers. There is also a desire by the DWP to enable candidates to experience both policymaking and operational units, in the past seen as separate entities.

The Early Talent scheme is designed to enable participants to use an online tool to introduce them to the challenges of operating at a more senior level. Having decided for themselves that they want to pursue the programme, the participants go on to a series of assessments including a psychometric tool to look at an individual's thinking and personal styles as well as capability.

The assessments are designed to test individuals around situations they may face in other roles. Once completed, the successful participants join a developmental programme that is seen as career development, not necessarily leading to promotion. A consideration for creating talent pools to draw upon is that there may not always be enough senior or career-related job roles vacant to satisfy all candidates.

The development programme includes action learning sets, master classes, skills workshops and a business-critical project.

This is certainly an in-depth talent management process, using a range of learning and developmental methods. It also requires participants who are committed, motivated and who can set effective goals and timescales to progress through each stage of the process.

Case 2: NHS Leadership Framework

The Leadership Framework was developed in 2010 in order to meet a desire by the NHS to have a single over-arching leadership framework for all staff groups, to enable individuals to see how they are progressing as a leader and to foster and develop talent in the NHS.

Central to the elements of the framework is delivery of services to patients, service users, carers and the public, who have been involved in how services are planned, delivered and evaluated. The framework also provides a consistent approach to leadership development irrespective of role, function or discipline.

The key elements in the framework cover demonstrating personal qualities, working with others, creating the vision, setting direction, delivering the strategy as well as the service delivery and improvement aspects.

The NHS is keen to share the framework concept and their website provides access to each of the elements as well as supporting tools. See www.leadershipacademy.nhs.uk/discover/leadership-framework.

(Source: Adapted from Department of Health 2011; *People Management* 2008)

potential for management and leadership, and to enable these individuals to use a range of tools to develop their skills and knowledge, as well as aptitude, for these senior roles.

So what is different about leadership? According to the NHS Leadership Framework, effective leadership involves creating a compelling vision for the future, and communicating this within and across organisations; it is about developing and agreeing strategic plans, improving services and then delivering the strategy. The NHS Framework was compiled in 2010 and contains a comprehensive leadership development structure.

Knowledge management

A more recent concept is that of 'intellectual capital', which represents the greater part of intangible assets within organisations. It is created and held by knowledge workers, i.e. those that are not involved directly in manual, sales or administration operations. The knowledge refers primarily to patents and organisational competencies but also to the corporate culture, the 'way things are done around here', how it developed and why it is successful, which can define key competitive advantage. Capturing this knowledge, disseminating it throughout the organisation, building on it and then taking incremental steps towards advancing the knowledge level and depth has been promoted as an essential feature of developing employees. It has also been recognised that losing this knowledge through large-scale redundancies, early retirement of long-service employees, or groups of employees moving to a competitor or setting up a business in competition can be disastrous in the longer term in reducing the value of those knowledge-based intangible assets.

In terms of developing employees, the challenge is in the effective dissemination of both the *explicit* knowledge, that which can be easily written down, such as company policies and procedures, but also the *tacit* knowledge, which takes the form of subjective insights, intuitions and hunches (Taylor 2002). This can include knowledge on building relationships and networks, solving real problems and developing innovatory ideas. Encouraging the exchange of tacit knowledge is a subtle process but organising secondments, exchanges and informal networking opportunities can provide effective methods.

NATIONAL GOVERNMENT AND NON-GOVERNMENTAL SCHEMES AND INITIATIVES

Government initiatives to help learning and development

There is a long history of government interventions in the UK to try to improve the level of vocational training, especially in view of the low overall investment compared with the rest of Europe. The two key problems that initiatives have aimed to address are the skills shortages, especially those that relate to high organisational performance, and high levels of unemployment, especially among young people. In the 1960s and 1970s, Industrial Training Boards were set up, which levied the payrolls of each company by between 1 and 2.5 per cent. The funds created were then distributed back to the companies if they carried out training in an approved way. The aim was to discourage companies from simply poaching their required skilled employees rather than carrying out the training themselves. Unfortunately, the system became bogged down in the bureaucracy of making claims and no real evidence emerged that there had been a measurable increase in the quantity or quality of training, especially in the smaller and medium-sized organisations. By the early 1980s, most had been abolished by the Conservative government who laid more stress on the way that a competitive marketplace would force organisations to improve their training.

Their own initiatives in the early 1980s tended towards measures that would have an immediate effect upon reducing unemployment, such as the Youth Opportunity Scheme (1980) and the Youth Training Scheme (1983), both of which provided free or subsidised young people to organisations that agreed to carry out an approved training scheme. As youth unemployment declined in the late 1980s and 1990s, chiefly due to demographic changes, the government switched their attention to a broader spectrum. A National Vocational

Education and Training framework was devised, which continues to have an over-riding vision of 'lifelong learning' for every citizen, rooted in both economic and social theory. People need to be constantly learning and developing skills and competencies to ensure they can contribute in the workplace. It is also vital that no group is socially excluded or marginalised so they cannot contribute to society, thus drifting into crime or benefit dependency.

The *National Learning and Skills Council* was set up in 2001 with responsibility for the funding, planning, delivery and quality assurance of all post-16 education and training (except higher education). With its 47 local Learning and Skills Councils, it was required to encourage all 16–19-year-olds to participate in some form of education and training and achieve at least an NVQ level 2, together with raising the standards in teaching and training, increasing the demand for learning by adults and ensuring that all such education and training is directed towards improving economic performance. It had a strong representation of employers and trade unions on its local councils and its remit covered around six million people. It aimed to achieve its goals through Modern Apprenticeships, Investors in People and the New Deal, among other initiatives.

In turn, these bodies were replaced by new organisations set up by the Department for Business, Innovation & Skills when the new Coalition government came into power in 2010.

The *UK Commission for Employment and Skills* (UKCES) is a non-departmental public body providing strategic leadership on skills and employment issues in the four nations of the UK. Commissioners comprise a social partnership that includes CEOs of large and small employers across a wide range of sectors, trade unions and representatives from the devolved administrations.

The Commission's strategic objectives include provision to businesses of labour market intelligence; developing solutions to generate greater investment in skills; enhancing the value and availability of vocational training and apprenticeships; and helping to improve job opportunities and create jobs.

'The UKCES is one of the very few truly UK-wide bodies, and is uniquely placed to bring a UK-wide perspective on skills, jobs and growth' (Vince Cable, Secretary of State for Business, Innovation and Skills).

The Commission is also committed to promoting employer investment in people. In April 2010, the Commission became the champion and guardian of Investors in People, and continues to develop Investors in People's reach and impact among employers of all types and sizes.

Sector Skills Councils (SSCs) are the other new institutions to be set up throughout the UK as the independent, employer-led organisations that ensure that the skills system is driven by employers' needs. SSCs create National Occupational Standards, develop and maintain qualifications to meet industry needs and develop apprenticeship frameworks.

The *Skills Funding Agency* is the third agency set up as part of the new government strategy and is responsible for funding and regulating further education and skills training in England and, by doing this, enabling people to do their jobs better, get new jobs and progress their careers. The agency also wants to ensure adequate provision of training to meet the needs of employers and learners is adequate.

The agency is responsible for the National Apprenticeship Service, and high standards of training and development are encouraged through skills competitions, including the National Training Awards, which identify best practice in the workplace.

Skills policy in the UK

The CIPD's perspective on why skills are important is worth considering before we look at the key aims of the UK's skills policy:

> The UK's prosperity depends on how many people are in work and how productive these people are in the workplace. Skills and how they are used are a key determinant of labour productivity. Increases in skills levels thus translate into higher productive and prosperity for the UK economy. Higher overall skills levels can also lead to greater social cohesion.

The CIPD further identifies that the focus should be not only on initial education and training but also on continuing workforce training and development, adult learning and vocational training.

When looking at the UK, we must also consider that over the recent decades there has been a gradual devolution of political and in some cases financial power to regional governments – Northern Ireland, Wales and Scotland. This has complicated the picture in that each region is allowed to have its own skills strategy. However, there are common aims and initiatives:

- The need to up-skill at basic and intermediate skills levels
- Continuing to match the skills the employers need
- Improving workplace skills and see these used better through better working practices
- Increasing the level of private sector funding as public spending has to be reduced due to the economic recession
- Providing better information and guidance to learners and improved careers advice
- Better management and leadership skills
- Better support to SMEs.

National Vocational Qualifications (NVQs)

In 1986, the National Council for Vocational Qualifications was set up to rationalise and reform vocational qualifications. Lead bodies, principally of employers and unions, have been set up for every industry who have laid down agreed performance standards against which trainees can be judged. Assessment is not by examination but by assessment in the workplace. A system of independent assessment and verification moderates and confirms the process. Five levels of the awards have been established, which reflect increasingly demanding competency requirements. These range from:

> Level 1 Occupational competency in performing a wide range of work activities that are routine and predictable.
> To:
> Level 5 Competency at a professional level with mastery of a range of relevant knowledge and the ability to apply it in situations that may be unpredictable. It is likely to be accompanied with personal autonomy together with responsibility for the work of others and the allocation of resources.

The qualification is independent of any specific course and trainees can obtain the qualification through a variety of ways including open learning. There is no restriction by age or occupation and levels do not need to be tackled in chronological order. The emphasis is on the outcome of work tackled, not on the trainee's knowledge, although it is recognised that underpinning knowledge and understanding is an essential ingredient to the learning process.

Qualifications at levels 1 and 2 have been generally agreed to be very successful. They are relevant to the trainee and their situation, they provide a clear aim for the trainee to strive for and the success in achieving the NVQ reinforces the learning process. Another pointer in their success is the way that practical achievement is accompanied by the requirement for basic literacy and numeracy skills, so the NVQ provides the medium for those skills to be developed almost without the trainee being aware of their development. A good example of a comprehensive approach is that of INA Bearing Company where all 200 operators are working towards an NVQ level 2 in performing management operations, alongside initiatives in team building and a Kaizen (idea generating) scheme (Roberts 2003).

At NVQ level 3 and beyond, the qualifications are more debatable and no more so than in the management standards. Here the problem is the way that the trainee can demonstrate their own competency. With bricklaying, assembling and hairdressing, the finished result can be observed as well as the way the trainee has gone about the task. This is not the case for management standards, such as problem-solving or time management, where observation presents organisational problems. Moreover, for the majority of cases, the trainee has to try to prove their competency through paper-based solutions, using a portfolio of support materials for each unit, some of which may be acceptable to the assessor and some not. The drop-out rate on such NVQs is very high indeed – more than 60 per cent on average – with many trainees being put off by the bureaucracy involved and disappointed by the lack of emphasis on the training that actually takes place. It becomes, it is said, a 'paper-chase'.

A further criticism of the NVQ approach is that it is a conservative process in that trainees have to demonstrate they can carry out existing methods and processes rather than using training to develop new approaches and methods. Some organisations, such as ASDA and British Home Stores, having started down the NVQ route, have abandoned them because they failed to focus on business needs.

National Training Targets

National Training Targets were set for the first time in 1991 and have been revised every few years since. Although some were based on traditional academic achievement, such as GCSEs, some of the targets were couched in NVQ terms, such as the target for 28 per cent of the workforce to have a vocational, professional, management or academic qualification at NVQ level 4 or above. They have tended, as with most government targets, to be aspirational, with few actually being reached.

Modern Apprenticeships

Traditional apprenticeships, whose origins go back hundreds of years, had developed into a very rigid and limited vehicle for training young people in practical skills by the 1960s. They had a fixed entry point at 16, were time- rather than standards-based, and had a limited content related to the specific craft skill. The skills involved were usually those of the particular union of skilled workers who jealously guarded the ownership of those skills and limited entry so the training was often narrow. For example, an electrical apprentice would not learn any mechanical skills because there were two different unions involved. This reduced the value and relevance of the training and, together with the overall reduction in numbers of employees in manufacturing, led to a major decline in traditional apprenticeships since the 1970s.

The Apprenticeships, Skills, Children and Learning Act 2009 gave a statutory basis for the apprenticeship programme and created a National Apprenticeship Service for England. From 2013, all suitably qualified young people will have a statutory entitlement to apprenticeships. At the same time, greater legal protection will be given by making the apprenticeship relationship a contract of service.

See the website for further details about the new system of apprenticeships.

National Traineeships

National Traineeships were a development of the Youth Training Scheme, which attempts to ensure that all young school leavers enter into some form of training that leads to a qualification. Under this scheme, which has similarities to Modern Apprenticeships, the trainee worked under a formal training scheme towards NVQs at levels 1 and 2, under quality standards designed by the industry. National Traineeships have now become part of the apprenticeship scheme.

Internships

An internship is non-contractual work offered to a young person to gain some experience in the workplace. The title internship now encompasses work experience schemes for young people still at school (typically a couple of weeks' experience) and work placements for those at university (these can last up to a year).

Internships also offer a route for graduates wanting to enter the labour market for a particular profession.

The link is therefore made to career development. The aim of an internship is to give interns meaningful experiences that improve their employability by enhancing personal skills and acquiring work skills.

There is currently a debate on the unpaid nature of internships and the potential for exploitation, and government action may be seen, including interns being entitled to the statutory minimum wage.

New Deal

The latest in a long string of initiatives associated with reducing unemployment is the *New Deal*, originally established in 1997 to help every person aged 18–25 to gain employment or training. The first part of the programme is the 'gateway', which is a period of intensive training to prepare the trainee for gainful employment before they actually seek work. It includes basic numeracy and literacy skills training, careers advice and how to deal with interpersonal situations, such as job interviews. The gateway length of time varies depending on the existing skills of the trainee. When employment is obtained with an employer who has signed up to the scheme (and who obtains a subsidy), training must continue either with that employer or with a third party. Due to the improved economic situation after the scheme was announced, which led to a large natural reduction in youth unemployment, the scheme was opened up to all people who had been unemployed for 12 months. Since 2009, the economic situation has taken a downturn and youth employment is high once again. The government has proposed and implemented employment and learning initiatives to enable young people to have work experience and skills development to increase their employability. The government measures are designed also to once again focus on the 18–24 age range and to give employers financial incentives to take on young people and to sponsor their ongoing learning and training within the workplace.

The New Deal – now Flexible New Deal – since 2007 has been refocused on employability and skills development not only for young people but also for those who have been unemployable because of illness and disability. A range of government-sponsored pilot programmes using the voluntary as well as statutory sector organisations (Pathways to Work) have sought to provide training, personal skills development, mentoring and work skills improvement to those with physical and mental health disability. Combined with stricter medical assessment (Skills Health Checks and Work Capability Assessment) and benefit criteria, it is expected that large numbers of those previously on long-term sick leave or incapacity will have to find employment again.

Crossrail's project on the London Underground is a good example of where talent management, implementation of a skills strategy and taking account of youth unemployment have been brought together, as shown in case study 8.8.

Investors in People

Investors in People is a national standard established in 1993 and based on the practical experiences of successful organisations in developing people to meet the business goals that have been set and communicated. The standard is based on four criteria that must be met by aspiring organisations:

1   A public commitment from the top to develop all employees with a business plan, which includes information on how employees will contribute to its success.

CASE STUDY

CASE STUDY 8.8 DEVISING AND IMPLEMENTING A SKILLS STRATEGY WITH CROSSRAIL

A subsidiary of Transport for London, Crossrail is constructing a new railway route in London, covering 21km with 37 stations to be completed by 2018, in partnership with a number of contractors and sub-contractors. In human resource terms, this is a multi-dimensional project with issues such as organisational culture, managing organisational change, performance management, working across a range of disciplines and how skills are utilised.

Crossrail has strategic and operational responsibility across the project so will be responsible for talent management and development across all the different companies involved. Following a review in 2010, a matrix management structure was implemented to support the contractors, with different key functions as the central pillars – this included one for talent and resourcing.

Different roles will be important at different times as the project progresses; the employee figures set out by Crossrail are massive – up to 70,000 people employed at one time; 15,000 roles to be filled at one period of time, with many specialist roles. This led to Claire Parry, then Head of Skills and Employment for Crossrail, creating an extensive skills strategy.

The key elements of the strategy are:

■   Identification of skills gaps – bearing in mind other major construction projects elsewhere in the area might reduce the labour market for specific skills
■   Focus on health and safety, and on inspiring future talent whether school leavers or career changers

- A Tunnelling and Underground Academy (with a mock-up of a 40m tunnel) to deliver skilled tradespeople from entry level to NVQ level 2 and up to NVQ level 4
- Reskilling trades entrants who have had no experience of underground work
- Creation of a skills network to deliver the skilled people that the academy cannot due to the high volume of skilled personnel needed in many trades and professions
- Tackling youth unemployment in the London area, including work placement opportunities.

Claire Parry undertook a major skills and labour forecasting exercise, mapping worksites across London to identify the location of skills providers and support services, what other construction work was planned or underway at the same time as the Crossrail project, and matched the availability to the demand for skills during the different phases of the Crossrail project.

With funding from a range of organisations including the Skills Funding Agency and European Social Fund, Crossrail is also targeting unemployed workers, particularly young people, for pre-employment training. While a job is not guaranteed, those completing the training will have employability and transferable skills for other employers.

One important message has been made about raising skills levels:

'Employers can't sit back and moan that the skills aren't there if they don't take some ownership of the skills agenda' (Valerie Todd, Director of Talent and Resources for Crossrail).

(Source: Adapted from *People Management* 2011c)

2   Regular reviews of the training and development needs of all employees built into a performance management system.
3   Full evidence that the training and development takes place, starting with induction and carrying on throughout their career with the organisation.
4   An evaluation system is in place to judge the success of the training against the needs of the individual and the organisation.

The scheme is administered by the Learning and Skills Councils (now the Skills Funding Agency) with national supervision from Investors in People UK. When organisations have met the standards, they receive the recognition for a period of three years, at which time they need to prepare a portfolio to demonstrate that they still meet the criteria. Research carried out by Cranfield University indicates that IiP is associated with overall benefits for the organisations concerned (see focus on research 8.1).

CASE STUDY 8.9 CRANFIELD UNIVERSITY RESEARCH INTO INVESTORS IN PEOPLE

The latest research undertaken by Cranfield University's School of Management has been into the impact of Investors in People (IiP) on managerial capabilities, management performance and business results.

The study showed that IiP enhances managerial capabilities, supports the development of an organisational learning culture and improves the effectiveness of management development practices. This, in turn, it was found, led to better financial performance, compared with companies not involved with IiP. One of the features of the organisations involved in IiP was that they had given managers greater autonomy and freedom to decide how to undertake their role.

The study showed that management had an important role in delivering company performance in terms of improved quality, service and customer satisfaction, and higher profitability. IiP supports the development of a learning culture and creates an environment that focuses on performance and goal-setting that is linked to organisational needs.

(Source: Cranfield University School of Management 2010)

Successful IiP organisations can apply for National Training Awards by showing how the organisation has benefitted from linking employees' learning needs to business needs.

Lifelong learning

Successive governments have advocated and put funding into the concept of lifelong learning – that we learn throughout life from childhood to older age (the Fourth Age). An independent inquiry into the future of lifelong learning was set up in 2007, sponsored by the National Institute of Adult Continuing Education (NIACE), and it has received submissions from the government, trade unions, academia, business, the third sector and learners themselves.

It is interesting to note that several of the outcomes from this report also reflect the *Leitch Report December 2006*, which was critical of the lack of progress being made on young people and adults' learning basic skills and skills for employability, as well as the complex nature of learning provision. Leitch recommended a shared responsibility between government, employers and individuals, that there should be a basic platform of skills for all, and that skills must provide real returns for individuals and employers. Skills should be portable to deliver mobility in the employment market, and, instead of being supply-driven, learning should be demand-led, adaptable to the changing world.

See the website for a fuller input on the outcomes from the report on the future of lifelong learning.

LEGAL CONSIDERATIONS IN LEARNING AND DEVELOPMENT ACTIVITIES

As with any element of employing people, learning and talent development is subject to legal considerations. It is important to remember that this is an area that is constantly changing and one where learning, training and development practitioners need to keep up to date with both new legislation and new court rulings, which provide guidance on how the law is to be interpreted.

Legal issues relating to learning, training and talent development fall into a number of broad categories:

Equality and diversity. This is a vast subject. It has recently been enhanced by the Equality Act 2010 and the creation of nine protected characteristics. The planning and delivery of learning and development activities, and the more individualised approach using coaching and mentoring, can give rise to several equality considerations – direct or indirect discrimination, harassment and victimisation (possibly by other learners), associative and perceived discrimination.

Health and Safety at Work is, as its name implies, concerned with people's well-being and safety in the workplace. An important point to remember is that all employers are personally responsible for health and safety and that it is not 'someone else's problem'. When planning a learning, training and development event, a risk assessment needs to be undertaken. If unforeseen circumstances arise while delivering training, the practitioner may have to assess the new situation for risk and decide on the appropriate course of action.

Copyright and intellectual rights. Here the law is recognising that work created by an individual or organisation has a value. As such, they have the right to protect their property from use by others or, where it is used, to be rewarded for this. An example is if you go to an image library on the web and want to use an image, there is likely to be a charge. Some images will be inexpensive but others that are high-quality, technical images may attract a significant fee recognising the expertise that went into their creation. The development of in-house learning and development programmes and materials will increase the need to ensure these are legally protected by the organisation.

Data protection legislation is designed to ensure that personal data are used only for the purpose for which they were provided and only by the people authorised to do so. What is regarded as appropriate action is covered by the Eight Principles of the Data Protection Act. Any personal information obtained in relation to individual learning needs or the assessment of learners will be protected.

Legal issues specific to learning and development. This is a growing area that covers a number of issues:

- *Changes to the rights of apprentices from 2013* – which ties in with the changes in law relating to the School Leaving Age, which mean from that year people under 18 will no longer be able to be employed other than on apprenticeships or approved workplace training schemes.
- Improved rights for people to request *time off from their employer to undertake relevant training.*
- *Safeguarding.* This is an area which initially applied to children and came about as a result of recommendations made following the investigation of the circumstances surrounding a tragic case of child neglect. From the perspective of workplace learning, training and development issues under *Every Child Matters* are few owing to the age range of learners but legislation has been extended to cover the *Safeguarding Vulnerable Adults.* This is relevant to all and, in addition to being aware of the reference in the workbook, it is an area where all learning training and development practitioners need to be aware of new guidelines.

Indeed there is a strong case for saying that best practice means applying the principles of Safeguarding to all learners and, at its simplest, it means being alert and sensitive to their needs and ensuring inclusion.

THE ROLE AND RESPONSIBILITIES OF LEARNING AND TALENT DEVELOPMENT PRACTITIONERS

Learning and development practitioners are often in quite a unique position because their role can bring them into contact with all areas of an organisation and all levels of management. It is not unusual for a learning and development practitioner to have a degree of access to senior managers that is well above that of people of a similar grade simply because it is a necessity of the role.

IS THE ROLE CHANGING?

In general, in recent years, the role has been described as 'learning, training and development', but, going back 10 years or more, there were references only to 'training'. The term 'learning and development' then emerged alongside 'training'. You will have noticed that the term 'learning and talent development' is now being more frequently used. We discussed talent management earlier in this chapter.

See the website for further information on the role of learning and talent development practitioners.

MOVING TOWARDS A LEARNING ORGANISATION

At Sarah's third annual performance meeting, one of the major tasks given to her for the next year was to research the concept of a learning organisation, and recommend whether a move in that direction would be appropriate for her site and what form it would take. This was to be achieved within six months. This was not one of her areas of expertise so the project was a learning experience for herself.

She researched the issue in three ways: she obtained a list of books and articles from the CIPD Library Service and delved into a selection; she booked herself on to a two-day training course with a specialist consultancy; finally, she visited three organisations that had attempted to move in this direction – one who had spoken on the training course and two through networking in her local CIPD branch.

She felt this was a thorough approach but it left her somewhat confused and perplexed. The books and articles tended to be far from clear with many varying viewpoints and muzzy objectives, while the three organisations she visited had very different approaches. Some put more emphasis on every individual being involved in drawing up a learning plan with strong support and intervention. One of the organisations, however, was happy to leave it very much up to the individual and their managers to decide how much they would 'buy into' the concept.

She found that the most impressive organisation was Mattocks, a hospitality organisation of medium-sized hotels, which had a large number of outlets and employed many staff who joined them with no qualifications. They had managed to combine the culture of rigid hygiene and quality standards with considerable unit flexibility in areas such as staffing systems, learning and development. They had moved away from centralised direction because it led to over-control and bureaucracy and did nothing to motivate staff in the outlets. They had introduced a new approach to learning after experimenting at three separate units that had been keen to take part and then comparing results. The framework agreed upon consisted of the following:

- A voluntary approach, where employees signed up to a learning contract when they felt ready to do so.
- The learning contract would involve developing a learning plan for an appropriate time period from six months to five years, supported by their line manager and a mentor working within the same unit. The employee would be expected to take part in 'innovation teams', which are small leaderless groups who meet up after hours to discuss ways the work of the unit can be improved. It is expected that at least 40 per cent of any ideas would be implemented, with members of the groups taking the initiative in putting them into effect successfully. This would help to develop a number of their analytical and interpersonal skills.
- An individual learning account of up to £1,000 to be spent at a number of specified training establishments. The employee would have the choice of both the location and the course but it would be linked to the training plan.

Sarah believed that this framework could be transferred successfully to her site but she knew there would be some difficulties. Up until now, the training had been quite prescriptive, partly due to the need to build up the skills of the labour force in order to meet the production requirements. This had been achieved successfully, led by a dynamic training manager who led from the front and had a small team of loyal and competent instructors. She was not sure how they would respond to the idea that employees had the choice on whether or not to join a training programme or that the programme would be very much self-designed.

Scott had been very supportive when she had described her enthusiasm for Mattocks' system and encouraged her to float the ideas with the training staff. As she expected, their initial response was very guarded. They appeared unconvinced that her ideas would add value to their training structure which, they believed, continued to serve the company well. A major concern, not unexpectedly, was the transfer of much of their control over the training operations and the programmes, with its budgetary implications. They also appeared dismissive of the vague concepts behind the learning organisation. Sarah knew she would have a hard job on her hands to put forward proposals that could be found acceptable, not just to the training staff but to managers as a whole.

KEY CHAPTER SUMMARY POINTS

- It is important to appreciate that people learn in different ways and have preferred learning styles in order to produce an effective learning environment.
- A learning organisation seeks to encourage employees to search for new ideas, solve problems, question existing methods and look for best practice from a variety of sources. The organisation, on its part, will accept that mistakes will be made.
- The four-part training cycle consists of assessing the training needs, planning the training, carrying it out followed by assessment and evaluation.
- Training techniques need to be chosen to meet the specific needs of the learning situation.
- Coaching, Mentoring and E-Learning are techniques which support the development process.
- Government and non-governmental initiatives to encourage training include the setting of national strategies, supporting the development of NVQs, together with starting up Modern Apprenticeships and Investors in People.
- Talent management and development are integral to all aspects of learning and development.

STUDENT ACTIVITIES

1   Obtain a copy of Honey and Mumford's Learning Style Analysis and identify which grouping indicates your preferred style. Discuss with two of your colleagues how this knowledge will influence your approach to your studies.

2   Taking Sarah's position in the Meteor case study, draw up the proposal she will need to make to convince the managers of the benefits of working towards a learning organisation.

3   Specify which techniques of training are best suited to the following:
    - Learning to drive a car
    - Students needing a basic understanding of the business cycle
    - Teaching teenagers about personal relationships
    - Getting to grips with PowerPoint (or equivalent)
    - Induction for a graduate in a large blue-chip organisation
    - A busy manager or executive.

4   Identify the benefits to management of introducing coaching and/or mentoring into your organisation.

5   Read the articles and case studies on e-learning and blended learning and suggest how these might be used in (a) a supermarket chain, (b) a bank and (c) a government department of your choice.

6   Read the Alberga (1997) article on IiP, then talk to two people who have had experience as employees of IiP and compare their views of the effectiveness of the accreditation.

REFERENCES

Alberga, T. (1997) Time for a Check-up. *People Management*, 6 February, 30–32.

Anderson, L.W. (2001) *Taxonomy for Learning, Teaching and Assessing: A Revision of Bloom's Taxonomy of Educational Objectives*. Longman.

Armstrong, M. (2001) *A Handbook of Human Resource Management Practice*, 8th ed. Kogan Page.

Bennett, R. and Leduchowicz, T. (1983) What Makes for an Effective Trainer? *Journal of European Industrial Training*, 7(2): 3–46.

Bloom, P.S. (1956) *Taxonomy of Educational Objectives, Handbook 1: The Cognitive Domain*. David McKay Co. Inc.

CIPD (2005) Change Agenda: Training to Learning.

— (2007) Change Agenda Report.

— (2009) E-learning: Progress and Prospects Factsheet, June.

— (2010) Mentoring Factsheet, February.

— (2011a) Learning and Talent Development Survey – 'Improving Standards and Making Efficiency Savings: An Innovative New Approach to Employee Induction in NHS Direct'.

— (2011b) Talent Management: An Overview Factsheet, revised June.

— (2012a) Talent Management Factsheet, August.

— (2012b) Learning & Development Strategy Factsheet, February.

Cisco (2011) Connected World Technology Report.

Collin, A. (2001) Learning and Development, in I. Beardwell and L. Holden (eds) *Human Resource Management – A Contemporary Approach*. Financial Times/Prentice Hall.

Cranfield University School of Management (2010) *Investors in People: Managerial Capabilities and Performance*. March.

Department of Health (2011) *Leadership Framework*. NHS Institute for Innovation and Improvement.

Harrison, R. (2002) *Learning and Development*. CIPD.

Honey, P. and Mumford, A. (1992) *The Manual of Learning Styles*. Peter Honey Publications.

Jackson, A. (2011) Mobile Learning. *Training Zone*, 2 February.

Johnson, W.B. and Ridley, C.R. (2008) *The Elements of Mentoring*. Palgrave Macmillan.

Kolb, D. (1984) *Experiential Learning*. Prentice Hall.

Marchington, M. and Wilkinson, A. (2007) *Human Resource Management at Work*. CIPD.

Moorby, E. (1996) *How to Succeed in Employee Development*. McGraw-Hill.

People Management (2006) Talent Management: Understanding the Dimensions. CIPD, accessed at www.cipd.co.uk/researchinsights.

— (2008) Bright and Early, 2 April.

— (2010a) Grant Thornton Trains Partners to Become Coaches, 11 February.

— (2010b) IBM Launches Apprenticeship Scheme for School Leavers, 30 November.

— (2011a) City of Edinburgh Council, Implementing Self-service and E-learning, 27 July.

— (2011b) KPMG Launches 'Immersive' Graduate Assessment Centre, 14 October.

— (2011c) Crossrail: Skills on the Line, 28 November.

Reid, M. and Barrington, H. (1997) *Training Interventions*. IPD.

Revens, R. (1989) *Action Learning*. Blond and Briggs.

Roberts, Z. (2003) Learning Leads the Way. *People Management*, 6 November, 34–35.

Senge, P. (1990) *The Fifth Discipline Field Book: Strategies and Tools for Building Learning Organisations*. Random Century Group.

— (1998) The Practice of Innovation. *Leader to Leader*, Summer, 9, accessed at www.hesselbeinwinstitute.org/knowledgecenter/journal.aspx?ArticleID=159.

Simpson, E.J (1972) *The Classification of Educational Objectives in the Psychomotor Domain*. Gryphon House.

Storey, J. and Sisson, K. (1993) *Managing Human Resources and Industrial Relations*. Open University Press.

Taylor, S. (2002) *People Resourcing*. CIPD.

University of Cranfield (2010) Investors in People: Management Capabilities and Performance, March.

Wick, C. and Leon, L. (1995) From Ideas to Action: Creating a Learning Organisation. *Human Resource Management*, 34(2): 299–311.

ADDITIONAL FEATURES

 Please visit the companion website at: www.routledge.com/cw/stredwick where you will find additional case studies and reading material together with short self-tests and other resources for both students and lecturers.

9 EQUAL OPPORTUNITIES AND MANAGING DIVERSITY

CHAPTER OBJECTIVES

When you have studied this chapter, you should be able to:

- Understand the business case for equal opportunities and be able to identify how it applies in differing organisations.

- Explain the outline of the legislation relating to equal opportunities.

- State the main differences between a policy of equal opportunities and that of managing diversity.

- Identify the signs of sexual harassment and the ways it can be countered.

- Assess the implications of putting a policy into practice and evaluating the success of initiatives in this area.

INTRODUCTION

In the 1970s, three new laws came into effect that were intended to bring about a 'sea-change' in the social, economic and cultural relationships in the workplace. There has been no doubt that the Equal Pay Act, Sex Discrimination Act and the Race Relations Act all made a massive contribution to the reduction of discrimination and the promotion of equality. Subsequent legislation covering age, disability, religion and sexual orientation have served to fill in remaining gaps in discrimination so that a comprehensive legal framework exists in the UK. The Equality Acts (2006 and 2010) created a common framework for all equal opportunities issues. Few will argue that these legal interventions have not been significant or that they have not produced an identifiable overall improvement in the attitudes and efficiency of the average organisation. Differences of opinion continue, however, as to the amount of progress that has been made. The Equality and Human Rights Commission (EHRC) expresses continuing concerns over the progress of women into senior management, the continuing of a pay gap between the sexes (although it is gradually narrowing), the lack of transparency on equal pay in most organisations and the difficulty in handling harassment in employment (EHRC 2011).

Discrimination, in itself, is not always wholly negative. To be 'discriminating' is, according to the dictionary, an adjective 'showing good taste and judgement'. We all discriminate, for example, in the food we eat, our clothes, our interests, the furniture and decorations in our houses. It is where we discriminate against people, however, that this process becomes damaging. Where this discrimination is on the grounds of race, it can lead all too easily to violence and crime, as the history of segregation and race riots in America showed. In the UK, we have had our share of race disturbances, especially in the 1950s and 1960s, which arose from deprivation and discrimination over housing and employment, and crimes of a racial nature, such as the killing of Stephen Lawrence, cast a long shadow over the way that communities regard each other and the progress towards a fairer society. Discrimination by one religious or ethnic group against another can tear nations apart, as we are reminded by the horrific events in Palestine, Northern Ireland, Yugoslavia, Rwanda, Iraq and Nigeria.

Sex, age and disability discrimination is less overt but still has an insidious and restricting effect upon society and serves to waste precious skills and abilities. We no longer have advertisements for 'bright young men' to train to become bank managers, nor do we have prohibitions on men becoming midwives or women crewing submarines. Instead, most appointments and elections have been made on merit alone and there is some satisfaction that, in recent times, we have had a blind cabinet minister, a number of female chief constables and black leaders of major trade unions. In 2004, the first woman was appointed to command a UK naval ship.

There is not universal success, however. Women still make up the vast majority of employees in many badly paid sectors such as hotels, catering, cleaning, care services and unskilled and semi-skilled assembly. Despite considerable advances since 1983 when there were only 23 female MPs, the figure for the 2010 election (143) represented only 22 per cent of MPs. The idea of 'women's work' and 'men's work' remains, with the former often regarded as an extension of domestic duties leading to its being valued less and subsequently paid less. Female earnings as a percentage of male earnings, having climbed from 71 per cent in 1975 to 79 per cent in 1993, reached only 84 or 88 per cent (depending on whether you accept the mean or the median earnings rates) by 2011. The gap between male and female pay is at its widest in professional occupations. For example, a survey examining the pay gap in financial services workers in the City of London found a gap of 55 per cent, mostly due to the high level of bonuses paid, in which most women did not participate (Fawcett Society 2011).

Women are still poorly represented on the boards of British companies. Although there has been a gradual increase of female directorships, up from 7 per cent in 2000 to 15.6 per cent in 2012 (Sealy and Vinnicombe 2012), this is still some way off the target of 25 per cent set by the Davies Committee in 2011 (Davies 2011).

The unequal nature of men and women in the workplace can still be extensive. In the study by the Collinsons, the detailed case histories of harassment do not make comfortable reading. The Equal Opportunities Commission (EOC) estimated that only 5 per cent of employees who experience sexual harassment file a formal complaint and, of that minority, only 10 per cent get as far as a tribunal hearing (EOC 2001). In a detailed investigation, Cockburn (1991) found that men's social power gives them a degree of 'social authority' in the workplace which conveys the message: 'You're only a woman . . . and at that level, you are vulnerable to me and any man' (1991: 142).

The Jimmy Savile scandal, which broke in 2012, demonstrated how a huge amount of sexual harassment had taken place in the entertainment industry for 30 or more years, carried out by men who were much-loved household names and considered themselves untouchable and above the law. Research from 20 years ago (focus on research 9.1) showed the frequency of such behaviour in business.

Legislation has been shown to be a powerful driver of social change, especially on the macro level, but it is not enough to complete the task. Other arguments have been put forward that explain why providing equal opportunities makes economic sense. In this chapter, the following areas will be examined:

- The business case for equal opportunities
- A summary of the relevant legislation
- Discussion on the alternative approaches, including managing diversity
- Implications for equal opportunities policy and practices.

THE BUSINESS CASE FOR EQUAL OPPORTUNITIES

In their attempt to influence a radical change of policy within organisations in the 1970s and 1980s, both the Equal Opportunities Commission and the Race Relations Board focused

FOCUS ON RESEARCH 9.1 SEXUAL HARASSMENT

Margaret and David Collinson carried out a study of four women who had achieved promotion to management status in an insurance company. Each of them suffered extensive discrimination and harassment both before and after promotion, and the research describes the nature of the harassment, verbal and physical, in considerable detail. It was not just their own manager at fault. Harassment also came from their peer group, their subordinates and from clients. Each of the four women coped with their treatment in different ways.

One continually fought it off, attempting to freeze it out, and became very isolated and a source of disparagement within her own team. Another swam with the tide, joining in the male-oriented humour and sexual behaviour to the extent that she was honoured at one conference by being awarded the title of an 'honorary man'. However, she knew this was a dangerous course of action and on more than one occasion she had to physically fight off men who had misread the signs of her behaviour. A third went into denial, using this as a career-centred strategy disguised to protect her personal reputation within the male managerial hierarchy. The fourth did not complain, but just handled it professionally and competently, refusing to be provoked.

(Source: Collinson and Collinson 1996)

on the individual and their rights. It was thought that, faced with the threat of legal sanctions, organisations would change their policies and practices overnight. It certainly did produce some change, of a more compliant sort, but it did little to change attitudes, especially in the areas of performance management and promotion.

In the 1990s, however, it began to be realised that substantial *demographic changes* were occurring which would inevitably lead to skills shortages over the following 30 years. The birth rate had fallen dramatically in the 1970s and there was little sign of recovery in the next 20 years, so it was known that the number of 16–25-year-olds would take a sharp fall. If the traditional sources of labour (young, white, qualified, full-time males) became much reduced, organisations realised that they would have to rethink their human resources policies and look for untapped sources of expertise. Job descriptions would need to become more flexible to accommodate part-time working; specifications would have to be altered to eliminate unnecessary requirements on height and lifting ability and broadened to envelop all sections of the community; and working conditions and benefits would have to change to allow wheelchairs, language classes, career breaks and childcare facilities.

These changes in the work patterns were taken up by many employers, with females playing a larger part in business organisations. Interestingly enough, this played its part in the birth rate recovering somewhat in the 2000s, although it was also due partly to the increase in immigration to the UK of people of child-bearing age, and to the generally prosperous period with low unemployment, which encouraged support for females to be able to retain their jobs and go back to work quickly, which became more the norm.

A second reason relates to the *changing nature of the workplace*. There was a sharp decline in industrial and manufacturing jobs in the 1980s and 1990s (over two million jobs were lost in this period) and this ran alongside a growth in the service sector. Whereas a large proportion of industrial jobs were held by men, the opposite was true for a majority of the service sector employment. One forecast is that 70 per cent of all new jobs to be created up to 2020 are expected to be taken by women. Companies in this sector have a positive incentive to encourage the best applicants by providing career opportunities and a supporting environment for all staff.

The growing emphasis on *customer relations* in a competitive economy is another reason for focusing on wider opportunities. Active diversity management can open up new opportunities and improve market share by broadening the customer base. This has been seen particularly in the financial sector where banks and building societies are focusing on diversity issues in the way they target their products and services. They are becoming much more user-friendly to women, taking on board the increasing spending power of female professionals, and they are also addressing the needs of ethnic minority businesses. As a manager of GrandMet PLC put it: 'Customers are increasingly looking through the front door of the companies they buy from. If they do not like what they see in terms of social responsibility, they will not go in' (quoted in IPD 1997).

The Halifax Bank recognised this opportunity by specifically targeting the Chinese community in Manchester, which was substantially unrepresented in the bank's employees. The business benefits of having a group of Mandarin and Cantonese speakers in the branches led to an immediate increase in mortgage business of around 40 per cent (Merrick 2001). JD Wetherspoon have deliberately spread their recruiting across all ages to reflect their customer base and now employ many staff over 70 and one over 90 (Syedain 2010). When HSBC recruited in the Birmingham area in the mid-2000s, 49 per cent of their intake were from ethnic minorities to match the local community (CIPD 2005).

Conveying an image as a '*good employer*' also has repercussions on equality issues. Companies seen to have high ethical stances, with such policies as 'dignity at work', which prevent harassment and bullying, become more attractive to both customers and potential employees. It improves the Employer Brand (see Chapter 2). On the other hand, those seen as dominated by a white, male culture may not appear to provide the environment required. Moreover, in the case of equal pay, there is no greater demotivating force in the workplace than a sense of injustice over pay by a large section of the workforce. Internal equity, including fair pay and treatment for men, women and minority groups, is a vital part of the perception of 'fairness'.

C
A
S
E

S
T
U
D
Y

CASE STUDY 9.1 TACKLING GLASS CEILINGS AND STICKY FLOORS AT HERTFORDSHIRE COUNTY COUNCIL

Hertfordshire County Council (Herts CC) is the largest employer in Hertfordshire with 28,000 employees, 70 per cent of whom are women and 55 per cent are part-time. An equal opportunities policy has been in place since the early 1980s which was reviewed in 1994 as part of a general review of HR strategy. The important question was how the organisation measured up to their public statements that 'We are an equal opportunities employer' and 'positive about disabled people'.

Their actions fell into a number of categories. On *disability*, the Council introduced awareness training, access audits and an employees' forum, and became accredited as a 'two ticks' user. They also changed the stress on their policies to 'ability'. On *race*, they instituted a black employees' group and designed a specific development programme for black employees, together with a full audit of their performance against the Commission for Racial Equality (CRE) Standards. For *women*, they were the first local authority to join Opportunity Now and developed a wide range of flexible working initiatives alongside a women's development programme.

Other initiatives included the development of staff support schemes, mentoring programmes, a workplace nursery and a reassessed harassment at work policy.

They were conscious that all of these actions needed ongoing assessment and this was carried out through an annual Disability Discrimination Act audit and a set of specially designed performance indicators. Interviews with leavers included questions on their own assessment of the value of the equal opportunities policy. Four years on, an overall assessment showed success in most areas, although there were pockets where awareness was low and where management considered that equal opportunities was a job for the personnel department, not for them.

(Source: Hertfordshire County Council internal documents)

All these reasons have encouraged organisations to raise their profile on equality issues.

An early example of a comprehensive approach using a business case is shown by Hertfordshire County Council in case study 9.1.

EQUAL OPPORTUNITIES LEGISLATION

As with much of the legislation relating to individual rights, an additional stimulus was given by Britain's entry into Europe (then the Common Market) in 1973, when Britain's signature to the Treaty of Rome required national legislation to match that of its partners relating to equal pay and discrimination on the grounds of race or sex. Firstly, the two main types of discrimination, direct and indirect, will be discussed followed by a consideration of each of the areas of discrimination, brought together under the 2006 and 2010 Equality Acts. This section will finish with an analysis of the remedies open to aggrieved employees.

Defining discrimination

Discrimination was defined in both the Sex Discrimination Act and in the Race Relations Act and can take two forms:

Direct discrimination. An instance here would be to advertise for a 'Girl Friday' or to use different criteria for selection for promotion. In the case of race discrimination, it may relate to an employer indicating to a recruitment agency that they do not want black casual workers; or an employer may turn down a deaf or partially sighted applicant specifically because of this disability. In each case, an individual or group is treated less favourably than another on the grounds of sex, race or disability. The employer has no defence even if they genuinely believe what they are doing is right. The motives are irrelevant. spotlight on the law 9.1 gives an example of direct discrimination.

Indirect discrimination. This occurs where the employer treats all applicants or employees the same, but a practice, condition or policy adversely affects one sex or race

SPOTLIGHT ON THE LAW 9.1 DIRECT DISCRIMINATION

A senior NHS manager applied in 2007 for promotion to a key role running a breast-screening service for Leeds Teaching Hospitals NHS Trust. At the interview, one of the panel said, 'I didn't realise you were so old' when the applicant revealed she was three years from retirement age. The job was then offered to a younger colleague with 35 years' less experience. The tribunal decided that the trust had acted in a 'high-handed, malicious, oppressive and insulting' manner, and she was awarded £187,000, including £29,500 for injury to feelings.

(Source: *Sturdy v Leeds Teaching Hospital, ET 1803960/07*)

S
P
O
T
L
I
G
H
T

O
N

T
H
E

L
A
W

more than another, or it affects the disabled more than the able-bodied. The way it normally adversely affects that group is because the proportion of people from a particular group able to meet the condition or policy is considerably smaller. Moreover, the employer cannot objectively justify the practice, policy or condition. If the employer cannot convince the tribunal that the defence is genuine and substantial, the employer will lose the case.

Two examples are shown in spotlights on the law 9.2 and 9.3.

Other tribunal examples have included:

- The requirement to restrict applicants geographically by residence to a specific area, which discriminated against ethnic minorities, whose representation in that area was slight.
- Recruiting only through word of mouth in an employment site dominated by white males.
- Giving too much weight to family relationships when apprenticeships were chosen.

SPOTLIGHT ON THE LAW 9.2 INDIRECT DISCRIMINATION – AGE LIMIT

The University of Manchester advertised for candidates to fill the post of careers adviser, indicating that they wanted a graduate aged 27–35 with a record of successful relevant experience. Mrs Jones, aged 44, applied for the position. She was a strong candidate and was already occupying a similar temporary post, having entered the profession at the age of 38 as a mature student, but she was not selected for interview because of her age. At the subsequent tribunal hearing, Mrs Jones argued that the age limit adversely affected mature students who would not be able to meet the requirement on experience. Most of these were women who had brought up a family so this adversely affected the female group. She used statistical evidence to support her case.

In defence, the University justified the requirement on the grounds that the department contained a high proportion of older employees and an age balance was required. The case was eventually decided at the Court of Appeal who held that the discrimination caused by such a requirement should be balanced against the benefits that the requirement should bring. In this case, they agreed with the tribunal that the hardships outweighed the potential benefits. Mrs Jones was successful and was awarded compensation.

(Source: *Jones v University of Manchester, Court of Appeal 21.12.92* – Report in IDS 1993)

SPOTLIGHT ON THE LAW 9.3 INDIRECT DISCRIMINATION – RACE

A firm of household furnishers in Liverpool stipulated that they did not want job applicants from the city centre because experience had shown that their unemployed friends tended to gather round the shop and discourage customers. As a result of this stipulation, Hussein was refused an interview and he claimed race discrimination at a subsequent tribunal. The tribunal held that the employers had unjustifiably, if unknowingly, discriminated against Hussein since 50 per cent of the city centre population was black as opposed to 2 per cent of the Merseyside population. The employer's condition therefore excluded a significantly higher proportion of black applicants than white applicants.

(Source: *Hussein v Saints Complete House Furnishers, 1979 IRLR 337, ET*)

DISCRIMINATION AS IT APPLIES TO SPECIFIC GROUPS

Sex discrimination

Legislation makes it unlawful to discriminate in employment and other areas on the basis of sex or marital status or to treat less favourably any employee on the ground of sex. There is one limited exemption to this where sex is a Genuine Occupational Qualification (GOQ), such as in the pursuit of authenticity (acting or modelling), to preserve the privacy and dignity where people may object to the presence of someone from the opposite sex or where the job is in a single-sex establishment. Even here, the application of GOQ is being narrowed each year. In *Etam plc v Rowan* (*EAT 301/88*), for example, it was held that being a woman was not a GOQ for a sales assistant's job in a women's clothing shop. A further example of sex discrimination is given in spotlight on the law 9.4.

Discrimination on the grounds of race

It is unlawful to unfairly discriminate on the grounds of race, colour, nationality or ethnic origin. Again, GOQs are allowed only in very limited cases for authenticity, such as

SPOTLIGHT ON THE LAW 9.4 SEX DISCRIMINATION

Richard W. Carr was facing a downturn in business which caused the organisation to declare redundancies. When it came to the method of selection, Earl was chosen because she had a young child and it was considered that she would, therefore, be unable to make the required overnight trips.

The tribunal held that this was direct discrimination on the basis of sex, arising from the company's traditional view of a mother's responsibilities.

(Source: *Earl v Richard W. Carr and Co., COIT 4680/92*)

SPOTLIGHT ON THE LAW 9.5 RACE DISCRIMINATION

An English applicant was turned down for a position with the NJPB, a Scottish police authority, on the grounds that he was not of Scottish origin. The subsequent tribunal held that the English and the Scots could be regarded as separate racial groups by reference to their national origins and this decision was upheld by the Employment Appeal Tribunal.

(Source: *Northern Joint Police Board v Power, EAT 27-08-97 (535/97)*)

an acting role and in the provision of personal welfare services. However, even these GOQs are declining with a successful tribunal claim in 2003 by a white Englishman who was turned down for a job as a waiter in a Chinese restaurant. The definition of 'race' is broad as shown in spotlight on the law 9.5. It also covers employees of Jewish and Irish origin.

An example of a case that covers both race and sex discrimination is shown in spotlight on the law 9.6.

In another case, an Irish lecturer working at Northumberland College of Arts and Technology was subjected to what the tribunal called 'a particularly appalling case of discrimination upon discrimination', which included being called an 'Irish prat' by a fellow lecturer. He was awarded £29,000, of which £13,000 would have to be paid by the college, £2,000 by the principal, £6,500 by his line manager and £5,000 by his colleague who made the remark. This is an example, which is becoming more common, where fellow employees, not just the organisation, are liable for committing racist acts.

SPOTLIGHT ON THE LAW 9.6 RACE AND SEX DISCRIMINATION

A consultant, who told an employment tribunal she was forced to work in a 'degrading, humiliating and hostile' environment because she was a black woman has won an out-of-court settlement. Amy Betts-Priddy alleged she was subject to racial and sexual harassment by her bosses at global construction company Turner & Townsend. She was made redundant in June 2010 after working in the firm's contract services department for nearly four years. She brought a case for unfair dismissal, racial discrimination and sex discrimination against the company.

She told the tribunal how a director in her department offended her with derogatory statements about her native Africa. She was also asked why she wasn't 'married off and at home'. She claimed she was the only person to be given extra administrative duties on top of her workload. Furthermore, Ms Betts-Priddy was selected as one of five staff being considered for redundancy, four of whom were women and all five from ethnic minorities. She was made redundant after receiving the lowest score of all five employees, including a woman who had been working as a consultant for just five months after being promoted from PA level. Ms Betts-Priddy told the hearing: 'It was no surprise that as a black female I was the one to score the lowest mark.'

Part-way through the tribunal, the company offered substantial compensation which Ms Betts-Priddy accepted.

(Source: Hinton 2010)

Disability discrimination

It is unlawful to discriminate against employees or applicants because of their disability. However, the employer needs to go a stage further concerning disablement. It is an obligation on all organisations to *make reasonable adjustments* to the workplace to accommodate the needs of a disabled person and ensure they are not disadvantaged. The legislation was introduced to help protect around three million disabled people in employment.

Tribunals decided from an early stage that the definition of a disability, which can be both mental as well as physical, is being applied in a broad-brush way, as long as it has a substantial and long-term adverse effect upon the person's ability to carry out their normal duties. They have also decided that there are limits to the adjustments that an employer is required to make. They do not always have to provide personal caring services for an employee that might need them, for example, but regulations introduced in 2004 reduce the ability of the organisation to argue that they cannot afford to make the adjustments.

Two examples of important cases are given in spotlights on the law 9.7 and 9.8.

There is a limit, however, to the requirements placed on employers to meet the needs of disabled employees. In *Cordell v Foreign and Commonwealth Office (EAT 05-10-11 case 0016/11)*, a profoundly deaf employee requested a full team of lipspeakers to help her take up a role in Kazakhstan, which would cost £249,500 a year to service. The Foreign Office turned down the request and Cordell was not successful in gaining support from the EAT.

SPOTLIGHT ON THE LAW 9.7 DISABLEMENT DISCRIMINATION

Cambridge was employed in a hospital and was off work for a long period due to ill-health. She tried coming back to work but was only able to work short hours and was adversely affected by the office conditions in which she was required to work. She was eventually dismissed on the grounds of incapacity due to ill-health. She won her tribunal claim on the grounds that the employer had not made a sufficient assessment of either her condition and prognosis or the effect of the disability on her and her ability to perform the duties, together with an assessment of what steps may have been taken to reduce the disadvantages to which she was subject.

(Source: *Mid-Staffordshire General Hospitals NHS Trust v Cambridge, 2003 IRLR 353*)

SPOTLIGHT ON THE LAW 9.8 DISABLEMENT DISCRIMINATION – REASONABLE ADJUSTMENTS

Allen had muscular dystrophy and used a wheelchair. He wanted to use counter facilities at RBS's main branch in Sheffield but there was no wheelchair access. The bank argued that phone and online banking were available and that the cost of adaption, including a new lift, would be £200,000. The Court of Appeal decided that the cost was not disproportionate for a bank of this size and that disabled customers should have a similar provision of counter services as those without a disability.

(Source: *Royal Bank of Scotland v Allen, 2009 EWCA 1213*)

One of the changes brought about by the Equality Act 2010 is the requirement that online recruitment has to be accessible to users with disabilities. The test for 'reasonable adjustments' has hence been changed to a judgement as to whether a disabled person is placed at a 'substantial disadvantage' by the adjustment not being made.

The largest award made for a disability claim was to Matt Driscoll, a reporter on the *News of the World*, who was in receipt of intense and continuous bullying from senior staff at the newspaper. He became long-term sick through stress-related depression. He was awarded compensation of £729,000 in 2009. The *News of the World* was closed in 2011 as a result of the phone-hacking scandal.

Equal pay

The legislation lays down the principle that men and women working for the same organisation are entitled to the same rate of pay if they are carrying out the same work. There must be no discrimination over pay. The nature of the comparisons is refined under three categories. Firstly, 'like work', which is work that is the same or broadly similar. Secondly, work rated as the same under a non-discriminatory job evaluation scheme operating in the organisation. Thirdly, work that is of 'equal value'.

This last refinement arises from the 1983 Equal Value Regulations, which were introduced following a judgment by the European Court of Justice that the UK had failed to properly implement Article 119 of the Treaty of Rome regarding equal pay. This amendment has attempted to close a loophole where a lower-paid woman regards the work she carries out to be of equal value as different work that a man carries out, but there is no internal mechanism (i.e. a job evaluation scheme) that serves to carry out that comparison. (Job evaluation schemes were discussed in Chapter 6.) Under the Equal Value Regulations, she has the opportunity to make the equal value claim and the tribunal will commission an independent expert to investigate the claim and produce what is in effect a brief job evaluation report. The expert will compare the jobs considering aspects such as skills, responsibility and supervision. However, this process is very complex in practice and few employees take up the challenge of putting in a claim unless they are supported by their union or the EHRC.

There are a few exceptions allowed, which relate to situations where the employer claims there is a 'genuine material defence'. This is where a difference in pay is accepted by the employer but justified by a reason which is *not related to sex*. For example, it could be because the higher-paid male has a higher performance rating than a woman doing the same job or has better qualifications.

An example of a successful equal pay claim is shown in spotlight on the law 9.9.

The Equality Act 2010 requires public authorities with more than 150 employees to publish details of their gender pay gap annually from April 2011. There are also clauses that would require all organisations employing more than 250 employees to carry out pay audits

S
P
O
T
L
I
G
H
T

O
N

T
H
E

L
A
W

SPOTLIGHT ON THE LAW 9.9 EQUAL PAY WITH PREDECESSOR

Leacock (L) began working for the association as assistant database administrator, deputising for her boss, U. When U left, she took over his job but was offered a lower salary by £2,000. At the tribunal, the company argued that U had been paid at a higher rate because he was a graduate, because of his particular skills and abilities (including the fact that he was socially adept), and because of his previous experience as a manager.

The tribunal dismissed this defence. They held that the arguments were not relevant to the job in hand. There was a lack of transparency in the pay structure, there was no evidence of a performance management scheme and decisions on pay were often subjective and unstructured judgements of individual managers.

(Source: *Leacock v Association of MBAs, 2204564/2003*)

and publish the results, but no date has been set to implement this at the time of writing, and it is likely to be abandoned during the life of the Coalition government due to opposition from business organisations. However, it was announced in July 2012 that employers found guilty of sex discrimination on pay will be forced to conduct regular gender audits.

Religion or belief discrimination

Discrimination legislation defines religion simply as 'any religion, religious belief or similar philosophical belief'. Discrimination in recruitment, selection and employment applies across the board, but exceptions to the regulations can apply to churches and other public or private organisations whose ethos is based upon religion or belief. Such organisations may be permitted to recruit and employ staff on the basis of their religion or belief as long as they can show it is a 'genuine occupational requirement'. An example would be in employing schoolteachers in a school with a religious character.

One of the most controversial cases concerns the extension of the 'philosophical belief' to encompass the belief in sustainability as in the case of *Nicholson v Grainger PLC* as set out in spotlight on the law 9.10.

On the issue of religion, an interesting case has been the ruling that involved committed Christian Duke Amachree, who was sacked from his council job after suggesting to a terminally ill woman that she 'put her faith in God'. The tribunal ruled that it was reasonable for Wandsworth Council to sack the worker for gross misconduct and found the Council had not discriminated against Amachree on the basis of his religion (*Amachree v Wandsworth Council, 2328606/2009*). A similar case was that of a Muslim security employee being refused time off for prayers on Friday on the grounds that refusal was reasonable on the grounds of business needs to provide the level of security contracted to the customer.

Age discrimination

Legislation prohibiting age discrimination took effect in October 2006 introducing the principle of equal treatment into all aspects of age. Upper age limits for unfair dismissal and redundancy were removed, while the default age of retirement at 65 was also removed in October 2011. However, forced retirement can be allowed if it is objectively justified in special cases. In *Seldon v Clarkson Wright and Jakes* (2012), the Supreme Court upheld a law firm's right to retire a director because it considered employee retention and succession planning vital for a small organisation.

The legislation allows different treatment on the ground of age if objectively and reasonably justified, setting out the following examples:

■ Maximum age limits for recruitment based on training needs of the job or the need for a reasonable period before retirement. This will apply, presumably, for jobs such as airline pilots.

SPOTLIGHT ON THE LAW 9.10 SUSTAINABILITY IS HELD TO BE A SUBJECT OF 'PHILOSOPHICAL BELIEF'

Mr Nicholson was employed by Grainger PLC, a major player in the residential property industry, as head of sustainability. He was dismissed by reason of redundancy in July 2008. Mr Nicholson claimed that his dismissal was not a genuine redundancy, was unfair and, in fact, was because of his personal belief system – against anthropogenic climate change. As such, he sought protection under the Regulations from such treatment.

Grainger PLC unsuccessfully sought to strike out his claims at the employment tribunal at a pre-hearing review on the basis that his beliefs did not amount to a philosophical belief under the Regulations. They lost. On Grainger PLC then appealing to the Employment Appeal Tribunal (the 'EAT'), the EAT did, in fact, consider and apply the approach taken by the European Courts. The EAT considered the characteristics of a belief – in order to be protected by the Regulations – to be as follows:

'A belief must be weighty and be a substantial aspect of human belief and behaviour that has attained cogency, seriousness, cohesion and importance and be worthy of respect in a democratic society and is neither incompatible with human society nor in conflict with the fundamental rights of others.'

Mr Nicholson articulated the exact details of his belief, during the course of the appeal to the EAT, as follows: 'My belief in man-made climate change is not merely an opinion but a philosophical belief, which affects how I live my life including my choice of home, how I travel, what I buy, what I eat and drink, what I do with my waste and my hopes and fears. I no longer travel by aeroplane, have eco-renovated my home, buy local produce, reduced my consumption of meat, compost my food waste and I encourage others to reduce their carbon emissions. I fear very much for the future of the human race, given the failure to reduce carbon emissions on a global scale.'

The EAT ruled against Grainger PLC, allowing Mr Nicholson to pursue his claims of unfair dismissal and unlawful discrimination on the grounds of his philosophical beliefs at the employment tribunal. Mr Nicholson's belief is the basis for his entire way of life. The key factor in this case, which has not been as widely recognised in public, is that the very nature of his belief put him arguably in direct conflict with his employer in carrying out his actual job as head of sustainability. The case enabled the EAT to expand on and effectively define what would constitute a qualifying belief for the purposes of claims under the Regulations. The EAT's approach follows the approach of the European Courts in deciding such matters.

Subsequently, Nicholson reached a compensation agreement with Grainger PLC and the action was withdrawn.

(Source: *Grainger PLC v Nicholson, IRLR 4 (EAT) 2010*)

■ Protection of young workers, such as restricting their employment on night work or on dangerous machinery.

■ Encouraging or rewarding loyalty by paying long service awards.

■ Allowing employment planning to ensure a workforce that is age-balanced to a reasonable degree.

Tribunals have been all too aware of strong hints of age discrimination, as shown in spotlight on the law 9.11.

Employment Equality (Sexual Orientation)

This regulation extended all the provisions in the Sex Discrimination Act to the treatment of people on the grounds of their orientation, such as gays or lesbians.

Victimisation

This takes place when an employer treats somebody less favourably because they have taken action in making an allegation or have brought proceedings under any of the discrimination legislation.

SPOTLIGHT ON THE LAW 9.11 'YOUNGER' CANDIDATE

Beck, 42, was made redundant as head of marketing, following a difficult relationship with his manager who was 36. The company then recruited a 'marketing team head', using agencies, and the brief for this position referred to a 'younger' candidate. The employer was unable to convince the tribunal that the dismissal was not influenced by age and the tribunal found that this was not a genuine redundancy.

(Source: *Beck v Canadian Imperial Bank of Commerce, ET 232882/08*)

SPOTLIGHT ON THE LAW

Harassment

In the Equality Act 2010, harassment is defined as 'unwanted conduct related to a relevant protected characteristic, which has the purpose or effect of violating an individual's dignity or creating an intimidating, hostile, degrading, humiliating or offensive environment for that individual'.

Bullying is not specifically defined in law, but, in their advice leaflet for employees, ACAS (2009) give the following definition:

> Bullying may be characterised as offensive, intimidating, malicious or insulting behaviour, an abuse or misuse of power through means intended to undermine, humiliate, denigrate or injure the recipient. . . . Bullying or harassment may be by an individual against an individual (perhaps by someone in a position of authority such as a manager or supervisor) or involve groups of people. It may be obvious or it may be insidious.

Harassment and bullying can range from extremes such as physical violence to less obvious forms like ignoring someone. They can be delivered in a variety of ways – with or without witnesses – and be persistent behaviour over a period of time, or a one-off act and can include:

- physical contact that is unwanted
- unwelcome remarks about a person's age, dress, appearance, race or marital status
- jokes, offensive language, gossip, slander, sectarian songs and letters
- posters, graffiti, obscene gestures, flags, bunting and emblems
- isolation or non-cooperation and exclusion from social activities
- coercion for sexual favours and intrusion by pestering, spying and stalking
- pressure to participate in political/religious groups
- failure to safeguard confidential information
- setting impossible deadlines, persistent criticism or insults, or shouting at staff.

The inevitable outcome for the victim is fear, stress, which can lead to anguish and depression, and underperformance. For the general employee environment, it can lead to an unpleasant rift between those who cause and support the harassment and those who support the victims or are victims themselves. It is an exhibition of power over those who tend towards vulnerability and has no place in an organisation that wishes the culture to be one of commitment, team-working and support.

A more recent development is that of cyber-harassment/bullying, especially through social media. A report by Coyne *et al.* (2012) shows that such bullying is now more common than conventional bullying, and can have the same effects for the recipients, although its effects may be less generally harsh for those that witness it (see focus on research 9.2).

Harassment on the basis of age, disability, gender reassignment, race, religion or belief, sex and sexual orientation is covered by the Equality Act 2010. Individuals are

FOCUS ON RESEARCH 9.2 CYBERBULLYING IN THE WORKPLACE

This study included three separate surveys among employees in several universities in Britain, asking people about their experiences of cyberbullying, according to a statement by Sheffield and Nottingham Universities. A list was given of what can be classed as bullying, such as being humiliated, ignored or gossiped about, and participants were asked if they had faced such behaviour online and how often.

Of the 320 people who responded to the survey, around eight out of ten had experienced one of the listed cyberbullying behaviours on at least one occasion in the previous six months. The results also showed that 14 to 20 per cent experienced them on at least a weekly basis – a similar rate to conventional bullying. One of the conclusions reached was that bullying using emails, texts or web-postings to abuse people is as common at the workplace as 'conventional' bullying at schools, although it is more hidden in the workplace.

Overall, those that had experienced cyberbullying tended to have higher mental strain and lower job satisfaction. In one of the surveys, this effect was shown to be worse for cyberbullying than for conventional bullying. The research team also found that the impact of witnessing cyberbullying was different from that seen for conventional bullying. Compared to the research literature, people who witness conventional bullying also show evidence of reduced well-being. However, the team found that this does not appear to be the case for the online environment. Witnesses were much less affected. This might be because of the remote nature of cyberspace – perhaps people empathise less with the victims.

(Source: Coyne *et al.* 2012)

protected from harassment both while applying for a job, during it and, in some circumstances, after the working relationship ends (for example, in terms of the provision of a verbal or written reference). There is also protection for people against harassment on the basis of their membership or non-membership of a trade union and, in Northern Ireland, against harassment on the basis of political belief.

It is important to note that harassment does not have to be directed at the individual who complains – if it creates an environment that the individual finds intimidating, hostile, degrading, humiliating or offensive.

The law also covers harassment coming from a third party (a customer, for example). The employer is liable for this if it has happened on two or more occasions, the employer knows that it has happened and the employer has done nothing to stop it.

Although bullying is not protected *per se* in equality legislation, claims can be made by victims under a number of headings. Employers are under a duty of care to provide a safe environment; they have an implied duty to maintain mutual trust and confidence; finally, employees can claim that the lack of protection was sufficient to bring about constructive dismissal. It is the lack of action by the employer that enables the claim to be made against them.

Two examples of harassment and victimisation are detailed in spotlights on the law 9.12 and 9.13.

SPOTLIGHT ON THE LAW 9.12 SEXUAL HARASSMENT AT MID-YORKSHIRE NHS TRUST

Eva Michalak was dismissed from the Trust in 2008 over allegations of bullying junior doctors and arguments with colleagues. A tribunal found that she had been dismissed for reasons associated with her pregnancy in 2003. When she returned to work, she was subjected to a campaign of harassment and false accusations from senior doctors and managers, which damaged her mental and physical health and as a result of which she will never work as a doctor again. The tribunal heard that secret meetings had taken place before she went on maternity leave and staff later put forward evidence based on lies. The Trust's medical director was found to have 'manipulated' and 'engineered' her dismissal. She had claimed that she had 'suffered years of psychological abuse' and that she was hounded because she had a baby.

She was awarded £1.1 million for loss of past and future earnings plus £600,000 for loss of pension. She was also awarded damages for injury to her feelings and exemplary damages against the Trust, which took the total compensation to £4.5 million.

(Source: Laurance 2011)

SPOTLIGHT ON THE LAW 9.13 RACIAL HARASSMENT

An Asian postman, Mahmood Siddiqui, suffered a four-year campaign of racial abuse before taking sick leave and eventually retiring through ill-health in 2002. Following his tribunal hearing in 2004, he was awarded total compensation of £180,000 made up of:

- £104,142 for loss of earnings
- £20,000 in interest
- £8,000 for legal costs
- £46,400 for personal injury and injury to feelings.

The tribunal ruled that Siddiqui was subjected to a 'vicious campaign aimed at removing him from the shift'. The abuse included offensive graffiti, threats to burn him, damage to his car and threats to his wife and children. Despite repeated complaints, management took no action and, in fact, his immediate manager gave 'tacit support' to the campaign. It was only when a hidden camera was put in place, recording specific racial abuse from colleagues, that action was taken to stop the campaign.

(Source: Martin 2004)

SPOTLIGHT ON THE LAW 9.14 EXTENDED PERIOD OF HARASSMENT

Waitresses at Munchkins Restaurant claimed that they had been subjected to persistent unwanted sexual conduct for five years from a restaurant owner, including insisting on short skirts and inappropriate conversations of a sexual nature. The EAT upheld their claim, stating that putting up with such behaviour did not make it welcome or acceptable. The claimants each received £15,000 compensation.

(Source: *Munchkins Restaurant v Karmazyn, UKEAT 0359/09*)

The issue of harassment is treated differently in one respect to other contractual situations. If an employee has acquiesced to a change in their contract (change of hours or different work, for example) for a number of months, this is taken to mean that they have agreed to this change. However, if employees have accepted harassment or bullying for a long period, it is not taken to mean acceptance as spotlight on the law 9.14 demonstrates.

REGULATING EQUALITY AND HUMAN RIGHTS

The EHRC has the following main functions:

- To monitor the implementation of the Equality Act.
- To promote equal treatment at work and to eliminate discrimination.
- To draw up codes of conduct.
- To make recommendations to government for improvements in the working of the Act and to advise on how the Act should be revised to help meet the other goals.
- To undertake investigations into organisations where high levels of discrimination appear to permeate throughout the organisation.

The EHRC and its predecessors have commissioned and published extensive research, made videos and other information and communication publications, drafted codes of practice (see later in the chapter) and supported a number of high-profile tribunal cases relating to equal pay and sex discrimination. They have also carried out a number of investigations into policy and practice in certain companies including an investigation into sexual harassment of women employees in the Royal Mail business unit in 2004 (EOC 2004).

The Commission for Racial Equality (CRE), the predecessor of the EHRC, published a number of reports, commissioned research and supported applicants in their legal actions. They also took action against a handful of organisations. They began proceedings (section 62 of the Race Relations Act) against Bradford City Council in 1991 after industrial tribunals had upheld nine complaints of race discrimination against the Council over a three-year period. Four years later, following an independent report, it was decided to drop the action when the Council agreed to implement the report's recommendations in full, including reviewing its compliance with the CRE Code of Practice, introducing a thoroughgoing corporate policy against discrimination, a commitment to discipline managers and other employees who were responsible for unlawful discrimination and to improve ethnic monitoring of employees, applicants and grievances (Equal Opportunities Review 1995). Other formal investigations undertaken by the CRE include racism in the Prison Service (2000) and in the Police Service (2004), where a high degree of institutional racism was found to exist.

REMEDIES FOR THE EMPLOYEE

Under each of the Equality Acts, applicants and employees have the right to apply to a tribunal if they believe that they have been the subject of discrimination. They need to show that they have been treated differently and less favourably because of their sex, race, etc. This can apply in the recruitment and selection process where they are unsuccessful in obtaining employment or, for employees, in any aspect of their employment. If they are successful in their claim, they are entitled to compensation which has no limit (unlike unfair dismissal compensation; see Chapter 4). The highest awards have been made to women in the armed forces who, between 1978 and 1990, were forced to resign when they became pregnant. In 1981, the MOD conceded that this policy was unlawful and in breach of the EU Equal Treatment Directive. By 1994, £22 million had been paid out in compensation to around 2,415 ex-service personnel who had suffered because of this policy (IDS 1994).

The compensation in equal pay claims is calculated in respect of the loss of earnings between the pay received and the level of pay that should have been received. In sex and race cases, a payment can be made for injury to feelings which can be as high as £21,000 where a black prison officer had been the subject of racial harassment for 18 months (*Armstrong, Marsden, HM Prison Service v Johnson*, quoted in Korn 1997).

The statistics for applications are shown in Table 9.1.

Table 9.1 Statistics on formal industrial tribunal claims concerning equal opportunities in 2009/10

	Cases received	Settled before tribunal	Withdrawn before tribunal or struck out	Tribunal cases heard	Successful	Failed withdrawn or struck out	Largest award £'000	Median award £'000
Sex discrimination	18,300	4,300	11,100	1,170	290	880	289	13
Race discrimination	5,000	1,700	1,900	1,270	150	1,120	62	12
Disability discrimination	7,200	3,100	2,610	1,080	190	890	181	14
Equal Pay Act	34,600*	3,000	20,600*	2,030	280	1,950	n/a	n/a
Grounds of religion or belief	880	290	340	210	25	185	20	8
Grounds of age	6,800	1,300	1,850	550	90	460	144	30
Grounds of sexual orientation	640	270	280	120	22	98	47	12

*Included a number of large multiple claims
Note: Discrepancies in totals are due to number of outstanding cases from previous years and cases that were pending disposal at the end of the year.
Source: Employment Tribunals and EAT Statistics (2011).

In each tribunal claim, ACAS has a statutory duty to conciliate between the parties to help them to reach a settlement before the case gets to a tribunal. This involves a conciliation officer talking to each side, ensuring they both know the realities of a tribunal, clarifying the areas of differences and attempting to get the sides to agree on a satisfactory solution. As the figures show, a solution was achieved in a good number of the cases and a further third of cases were withdrawn, often because settlement was reached directly without the intervention of ACAS. In some large multiple cases brought by trade unions, negotiations have led to a settlement before the tribunal is heard. Only a small proportion actually arrives at the tribunal and, of these, less than half are ultimately successful. Although some of the individual settlements are very large, the average settlement is more modest at just over the £10,000 mark.

Many cases take an inordinate length of time to be settled. Pam Enderby, a speech therapist, started her claim for equal pay with her chosen comparator, a clinical psychologist in the same health authority, in 1986. It was a complex case with a number of significant issues and was only successfully settled in 1997 following hearing at the House of Lords and the European Court of Justice (*Enderby v Frenchay Health Authority and Secretary of State for Health, ECJ 1993 IRLR 591*).

Many employees with claims they regard as strong are put off by the cost and inordinate effort involved in taking up a case, together with the potential threat to their ability to obtain alternative employment if it is known by a potential employer that they took up a tribunal case. The most useful help and support an applicant can receive is from a trade union or the EHRC, but their funds are not unlimited.

Claims for equal pay have proved the most difficult area for an individual claimant, due to the often complex process of proving that the job of the claimant and a comparator are of 'equal value'. Reasons given for the comparative lack of claims are reported in focus on research 9.3.

In recent years, tribunals have been given additional powers to strike out claims that they regard as vexatious and misconceived. In extreme cases, they can make cost awards against the claimant. In *Smith v Pertemps* (2011 unreported), costs of £100,000 were awarded against Ms Smith, who claimed sex discrimination, whose evidence was found to be inconsistent and who had fabricated various claims against her former employer.

FOCUS ON RESEARCH 9.3 INVESTIGATION INTO WHY EQUAL PAY RIGHTS WERE NOT WIDELY USED

The researchers carried out 150 interviews in 40 organisations regarding employers' gender policies and practices and the views of female employees, including any perceived barriers. The research found that:

- The majority of the organisations had not carried out any form of pay review so they did not know if there were gender pay gaps.
- Private sector pay structures are often opaque and lacked any clear rationale so employees found that comparisons were not visible or easily identifiable.
- There was generally a culture in the private sector of not discussing one's pay with colleagues.
- An ignorance of the law existed, for example, not knowing the right to compare pay with a predecessor in the job.
- A desire by employees to not 'rock the boat' often because the employer was flexible about the hours they worked and they were grateful for that.

(Source: Corby 2009)

APPROACHES TO EQUAL OPPORTUNITIES POLICY

The combination of legislative requirements and the arguments behind the business case detailed earlier should be sufficiently convincing for most organisations. It is not enough simply to stamp 'we are an equal opportunities employee' on advertisements or even just to adapt one of the toilets so they can be used by disabled employees. In recent years, there have been a number of debates as to the make-up of 'best practice' approaches. What form should *positive action* take and how far can *affirmative action* go to remain both legal and ethical? How much can an equal opportunities approach succeed on its own without effecting a *cultural change* approach? Should *managing diversity* take the place of a conventional *equal opportunities* approach?

The original Acts gave indications that positive action was to be encouraged under certain conditions. Section 48 of the Sex Discrimination Act and Section 37 of the Race Relations Act allowed employers to direct training and experience to under-represented groups where the number of persons of that sex or race doing that work is comparatively small. It has never stretched to preferential offers of employment, which remain a form of illegal discrimination.

In their 1996 'Guidance Notes for Employers on Setting Targets for Gender Equality', the EOC set out two types of targets, as set out in Table 9.2.

They go on to differentiate between the examples of quantitative Targets and an illegal 'quota' system (e.g. 'to promote women to 80 per cent of vacant supervisory posts'). '*Positive action*' occurs when an employer must pick between two candidates of equal qualifications. The employer will pick the candidate who is under-represented in the workplace, i.e. if the employer is choosing between two candidates who have the same qualifications and similar experience, and one candidate is white and the other black, the employer may choose the black candidate because there are very few black employees at the company.

The Equality Act 2010 states that positive action is carried out in the situation where the candidate is from a genuinely under-represented or disadvantaged group in the

Table 9.2 Equality targets

Qualitative targets	Quantitative targets
To incorporate equal opportunities objectives into management appraisal	To raise the application rate of black and ethnic minority men and women from 2% to 10% over two years
To implement a flexible working/part-time/ job-sharing policy and special leave arrangements within two years	To raise the proportion of females taking part in management development training from 40% to 60% over two years
To implement a sexual harassment policy this year	To improve the return rate of women from maternity leave from 60% to 70% within a year

Source: EOC (1996) Guidance Notes for Employers on Target Setting for Gender Equality. Equal Opportunities Commission.

workplace. If the office is predominantly female, a male candidate can be hired based on positive action.

Positive action is not compulsory, nor is it unlawful. When positive action becomes positive discrimination, however, this falls into unlawful activity. A workplace cannot employ somebody on anything other than merit, so discrimination and quotas are unlawful. Positive action is only lawful because it requires that candidates must have equal merit. In short, positive action should be carried out when enough study of the current workforce is done, and the recruitment process is transparent, as the line from positive action to positive discrimination can be easily crossed.

In the UK, the high-profile Macpherson Report into the murder of black teenager Stephen Lawrence led to the Home Secretary announcing the introduction of targets for the recruitment of ethnic minorities into the police service, followed shortly afterwards by similar targets for the fire, immigration, probation and prison services (Blackstock 1999). Positive discrimination overstepped the mark in *ACAS v Taylor (EAT 11-02-98)*, where a male employee of ACAS suffered unlawful sex discrimination during a promotion exercise because the employer practised positive discrimination in favour of female candidates.

Stand-alone campaigns to improve equal opportunities are rarely successful on their own. By definition, action needs to be taken because the cultural ethos of the organisation has remained traditionally linked to unequal opportunities, with privileged groups having preferential opportunities to jobs and promotion.

A successful strategy will need to harness the authority of those directors who have achieved success under the traditional culture and encourage a fundamental shift in their approach to the subject. Hertfordshire County Council (see case study 9.1) followed this path using the model shown in Table 9.3.

Table 9.3 Cultural change v equality programme

Cultural change approach	Equality programme approach
Perceived as a high-status project	Perceived as a low-status project
Involves all stakeholders	Responsibility rests with HR department
Success linked to business strategy	Introduced to meet legal threats
Led by top management with their continual support	Initial support from top management but involvement occasional and perfunctory
Stirs positive emotions	Stirs negative emotions
New language matching the change process	Language and reality do not match
Clear goals and standards set	Steeped in generalities or vague goals
Aims to change behaviour	Aims to protect or divert unsuitable behaviour
Communicated to all parts of the organisation	Communicated only to limited areas

Source: Hertfordshire County Council internal paper, 1999.

While traditional equal opportunities approaches rely on removing the barriers to equality for disadvantaged groups through legal sanctions and firm targets, an alternative approach is through the concept of managing diversity. This is based on the theory that people should be valued as individuals for reasons related to business interests, as well as for moral and social reasons. Kandola and Fullerton defined managing diversity as:

> The basic concept of managing diversity accepts that the workforce consists of a diverse population of people. The diversity consists of visible and non-visible differences which will include factors such as sex, age, background, race, disability, personality and workstyle. It is founded on the premise that harnessing these differences will create a productive environment in which everybody feels valued, where their talents are being fully utilised and in which organisational goals are met.
>
> (1998: 146)

Managing diversity is a much subtler process than an equal opportunities drive. Employees are not selected or promoted on the basis of ethnic or gender calculations but because of the individual and varied contribution they can make to their job and the organisation. Part of the thinking is that too much of a concentration on disadvantaged groups may eventually lead to a backlash from majority groups, so the emphasis is on inclusion, fairness and relevance to all employees.

The inherent differences between the two approaches are shown in Table 9.4, and the Meteor case study at the end of the chapter looks at the practical implication of these concepts.

A ten-year research project carried out by occupational psychologists Pearn Kandola showed that firm targets and positive action by organisations had started to drop substantially, especially in targets on sex and race. However, this was not to say that the managing diversity approach had taken over. Only 25 per cent of organisations considered that they would make progress on diversity and less than 8 per cent provided diversity training for all staff.

Further evidence that managing diversity is a complex process has come from a report (CIPD 2004), which found that impressive progress had been made in finding ways of

Table 9.4 Equal opportunities and managing diversity

Equal opportunities	Managing diversity
Seeks to remove discrimination	Seeks to provide opportunities for all employees
A major issue for disadvantaged groups	Seen as relevant to all employees
Sets clear targets	Does not rely on positive action
An issue driven by human resource activists	Inclusive of all management and employees
To meet potential and actual legislative threats	Driven by business needs

Source: Adapted from Kandola, R. and Fullerton, J. (1998) *Diversity in Action: Managing the Mosaic.* IPD.

accessing diverse talent and using different perspectives and ideas to increase creativity and innovation to gain economic advantage. However, different kinds of diversity – social and knowledge-based, for example – impact on the organisation in different ways in different contexts and can cause conflict if not handled appropriately.

The two policies are not entirely contradictory. Removing discrimination can lead to opportunities for all employees. Like a good schoolteacher, a good employer will want to encourage and develop all employees, but will realise at the same time that some will need that little bit more help. A policy initiated by human resource activists can be led by all the directors and serve to include all sections and interests. It is possible, however, that the subtleties of managing diversity may disguise a policy of inaction or that a strident equal opportunities campaign can dichotomise viewpoints into two armed camps. In the next section, the implications for necessary action in human resource areas are discussed, with recommendations based on a fusion of the two viewpoints.

IMPLICATIONS FOR EQUAL OPPORTUNITIES (EO) PRACTICE

This section will look at the following areas where action is required:

- Finding out the facts including carrying out EO audits
- Generating and communicating EO policies
- Recruitment and selection
- Working practices
- Disability requirements
- Health and safety issues
- Performance management issues
- Handling harassment
- Equal pay issues.

Note: For further reading on Codes of Practice, please see details on the website. A diagrammatic indication of action required is shown in Figure 9.1.

Finding out the facts

Policies and practices cannot be effectively constructed without a systematic analysis of where the organisation finds itself. The analysis will be based on two issues. The first is the external relationship with the community at large. How does the employment structure mirror the community in terms of age, sex, race and disability? Does it vary at different management levels or by department? It is not unknown for an organisation to have a well-balanced total workforce but for the vast majority of the management and supervisory grades to be white males. Another factor to consider is the contacts with the community,

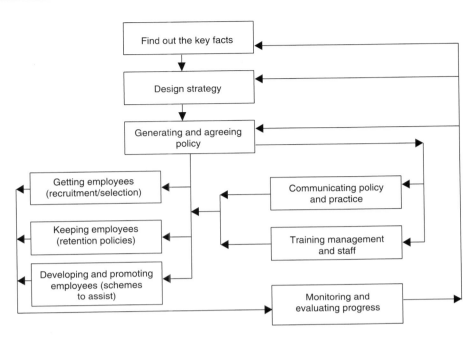

Figure 9.1
Action on equal
opportunities

especially where there is a strong ethnic presence. Does the organisation play a part in supporting community activities such as by sponsoring social or sporting events or, in larger organisations, seconding managers to work in the community for short periods as part of their personal development?

The second audit concerns the internal relationships. This should examine the number of sex, race, disability and age grievances reported and a survey of initiatives that have taken place in the period under review, such as access training, explicit policies on harassment or elimination of age criteria. Indications of a lack of success would be a lack of knowledge or indifference from employees, managers complaining of 'too much political correctness' or lack of applications from women or minority groups for promotion. Customised audits can be commissioned from specialised organisations that will find out the views of specific employee groups on the operation of EO policies.

Generating and communicating EO strategy and policies

Further decisions will have to be made on where the organisation stands in respect of the equal opportunities or managing diversity approach and whether the objectives will veer towards the quantitative or the qualitative. The policy statement should include the following features:

- Commitment to equal treatment throughout the organisation.
- Justification of why it is important for the organisation and its employees.
- Assignment of organisational responsibility (somebody with authority and ability to achieve results).
- Incorporation of EO objectives into the competency framework (if one exists) or individual performance objectives.
- Outline of the nature of training initiatives to assist the achievement of the objectives.
- Outline of recruitment, promotion and other key EO initiatives and practices.
- How grievances will be dealt with quickly and effectively.
- How monitoring is going to take place.

Not only does it need board-level commitment but it is also vital that there is a 'champion' who will take hold of the policies and ensure they are effectively implemented throughout the organisation.

It is not advisable to rely on non-verbal means of communication of this policy (and any revisions). Putting the policy on to the intranet may be necessary but will play little part in changing attitudes or culture. A series of meetings should be held (plus a corporate video from the managing director in a large organisation) so that the real message can be consistently applied across the whole organisation. Meetings should also allow questions to be asked and revealing comments to be made.

Grievances concerning equal opportunities should be dealt with through the organisation's grievance procedure, although those concerning harassment need to have especially careful consideration as we shall see later.

Recruitment and selection

This is probably the most significant area for policy and practice to ensure that all sections of the community have equal opportunities for gaining employment and that decisions are taken on merit alone.

In *advertising*, it is unlawful to publish an advertisement that may be understood to indicate an intention to discriminate. Job titles must be sexless, such as 'operator' or 'telephonist', or an indication must be given that applications from both sexes are welcomed. In *EOC v Eldridge McFarlane-Watts (COIT 17256/90)*, an advertisement for a secretary was headed 'The Secretary's Prayer' and took the form of a poem seeking a secretary 'willing to listen to her master's voice on eternal tapes'. The tribunal held that this wording gave a clear indication of an intention to discriminate against women.

A picture 'speaks a thousand words', so, if there is space, an illustration in an advertisement depicting men, women and a mix of races and disabilities clearly indicates a welcome to all applicants. Consideration should also be given as to where advertisements are placed. Choosing a magazine with predominantly male or female readership is unwise unless used as part of a balanced choice of media. Likewise, using ethnic minority media can be valuable for broadening the sources of recruits but should not be used on its own.

Sources of recruitment must be broad and not restricted simply to word of mouth, relatives, trade union sources or simply filling vacancies through unsolicited letters.

Selection processes run up against a set of potentially difficult problems:

- The job specification must not be unnecessarily restrictive or unjustifiably demanding to the extent that it may exclude large numbers of applicants in terms of sex, race or disability. Care needs to be taken here in terms of the level of skills, use of written and spoken English, mobility and years of experience required. The application form should only contain questions that are relevant to the job and working generally at the organisation. The Code of Practice on sex discrimination makes it clear that questions on marital status and number of children should not be included.
- A number of organisations use systems of ethnic monitoring that provide additional sheets for applicants to complete, which are separated from the application form.
- Short-listing should be carried out without consideration of sex, race, age or disability. This is formalised by some organisations who extract the names and ages of applicants before the short-listing process. Under the Disability 'Two Ticks' Symbol, employers give guaranteed job interviews to disabled applicants.
- Only those selection tests that are free from racial bias (some older tests were standardised on all-white groups) should be used, and sufficient additional help is given in preparation where this is required. Disabled applicants may need special assistance in taking the tests.
- Interviewing needs to be carried out in a way that all candidates are treated equally and fairly. Preparation and using a carefully worked-through structured interview system is the best protection against claims of discrimination. It is probably unwise to ask questions about domestic arrangements, even if they are asked of all candidates, except to point out positive features of the organisation's family-friendly benefits. A record of reasons for rejection must be kept in case of a subsequent claim.
- The special needs of interviewees need to be considered. When Val Milnes, a disabled HR manager who is paralysed from the waist down, attended interviews, numerous difficulties presented themselves in terms of parking, access, room suitability and interviewer reaction. Moreover, it was clear that many interviewers were just going through the motions to fulfil their requirements under the Disability 'Two Ticks' Symbol requirements (Glover 2002).

For further examples of innovative recruitment policies, see case studies 9.2 and 9.3.

CASE STUDY 9.2 ASDA'S RECRUITMENT POLICY

When Asda announced plans to set up a new store in Hulme, Manchester, which had a large ethnic population and high unemployment, it was not made welcome with open arms. Many local businesses had moved out and new ones recruited from outside the area so the area had little experience of benefits from incoming enterprises. Initially, there were fears that they would be a typical white, prejudiced employer, but Asda was determined to work with the local community and recruit locally. After an extended consultation, including a business information day, helped by the local CRE representative, they decided to advertise only in the local paper and not in the *Manchester Evening News* and also to link up with community groups and those supporting the unemployed. Help was given to the unemployed (the local figure was 70 per cent) with training provided at recruitment fairs in interview skills.

The result of the drive was that 90 per cent of the store's staff were recruited locally and that 50 per cent were of ethnic origin compared to Hulme's 32 per cent. Each new employee is given a Colleague Handbook, which outlines policy and what it means for them, including what to do if they experience unacceptable behaviour, including a confidential help line to a senior HR manager.

(Source: Equal Opportunities Review 1999)

CASE STUDY 9.3 IMPROVING RACIAL EQUALITY AT PENGUIN BOOKS

In response to a concern that Penguin, a London-based publisher, were not reflecting the overall London ethnic population, which is estimated to make up 30 per cent of the capital's population, an internal investigation indicated that people from ethnic minorities were not getting entry-level positions. It was not institutional racism, just a lack of proactive policies on recruitment. In the early 2000s, the company developed a number of initiatives. Firstly, it started to spend much more time going out to universities and working with career services to target ethnic minority students. It had particular success with its open days, to which it invited young people from 'under-represented groups'. Secondly, it started offering a number of paid internships each summer, working hard to ensure a diverse mix of people and expanded the number of unpaid work experience schemes. It was expected that these temporary staff would provide a good pool of potential permanent employees in the future. Finally, the organisation worked much closer with its agencies to ensure a representative list of potential candidates so that the proportion of ethnic candidates rose from 12 per cent to 22 per cent within two years.

(Source: Edwards 2004)

Retention and engagement policies

Family-friendly and *cultural diversity* policies have extended rapidly in recent years (see Chapter 7) and these make a real difference to the equality environment. Providing part-time or flexible hours contracts, offering job shares, creches or childcare vouchers, career and caring breaks, and out-of-school schemes all provide support and assistance to those with family responsibilities (still mostly women but a growing proportion of men) who wish to balance the demands of work and home. An example of this policy is at HSBC Bank, which has guaranteed the option of a part-time role at current title and salary grade to all staff returning from maternity leave. Jobs equivalent to at least 2.5 days a week on a pro-rata salary will be offered to returning parents to help employees balance family life with career development (Stevens 2012).

Cultural diversity includes the provision of specialised foods, choice over holidays and festivals, and freedom over dress and uniform. There is a need, however, to include all these freedoms within the requirements of health and safety and the public image for those meeting the public. Clarification was eventually reached on dress in the case of *Smith v Safeway PLC* (1996, 5 March, *The Times*). In this Court of Appeal case, Mr Smith, who worked in the delicatessen, had objected to having to cut his hair when it became shoulder length, when women were allowed to tie back their long hair. The Court rejected his claim, deciding that organisations can have different requirements of men and women, taking conventional attitudes into account. But, when viewed as a whole, it should not have a less favourable impact on one sex. In a similar case, the Employment Appeal Tribunal decided that a female nurse was required to wear a cap even though this did not apply to men who had their own uniform requirements (*Burrett, H. v West Birmingham Health Authority* – detailed in IDS 1994).

Care will have to be taken in the case of requests on the grounds of religious belief. Requests by Muslims for facilities and time off for prayers at specific times will have to be carefully considered, and balanced against business needs.

Disability requirements

By law, reasonable adjustments need to be made to employment arrangements to compensate for practical problems faced by a disabled person. Apart from wheelchair access, this can include altering the working times, accepting additional time off for treatment (disabled employees generally have excellent attendance records so this is a small burden on the employer), providing a reader or special braille equipment, and paying for specialised training where transfers to other occupations are required. The 'reasonable' nature of the adjustments relate to the cost of the adjustments in relation to the organisation's resources, the current situation in relation to the employment of disabled persons in the organisation, and the ease or difficulty and ultimate benefits of making those adjustments. The emphasis is on two situations: firstly, for existing employees faced with a developing disability or one

CASE STUDY 9.4 EMPLOYING PEOPLE WITH LEARNING DIFFICULTIES AT THE NHS IN CORNWALL

A successful pilot has resulted in a 47 per cent increase in the number of disabled people working at the NHS Cornwall and Isles of Scilly Primary Care Trust (PCT). The PCT has appointed nine people with learning difficulties as permanent staff members to work in the public health team. They check the NHS services for accessibility for people with learning difficulties and help with the training of medical practitioners. They have helped to produce easy-to-read information and a DVD for clinicians on hospital discharge for someone with learning difficulties. Each of the new staff has a 'buddy' to ease their path into employment in their job.

(Source: Higginbottom 2010)

arising from a serious accident; and, secondly, where an employer receives an application from a disabled person. In general, there is a greater onus on the employer in the case of an existing employee, but, where the organisation has a very low proportion of disabled persons, the onus on making reasonable provisions increases.

An example of a progressive approach on employing disabled people is shown in case study 9.4.

Health and safety

The issues here include the need for multi-language safety signs, documents, training and testing and necessary adjustments for disabled employees. Care should also be taken in relation to the Manual Handling Operations Regulations 1992 (see Chapter 10) to ensure warehousing and other operations can be manageable by both sexes. The effect that bullying and harassment have on stress levels and the legal implications for employers are discussed in Chapter 10.

Performance management issues

It is vital that all employees have the opportunity to carry out their work to their best ability and to share in career progression opportunities. The much-used expression 'glass ceiling' indicates that women have promotion limitations placed on them. The importance of 'role models', examples of successful women or members of ethnic minorities who show what can be achieved and are examples for others to emulate, cannot be underestimated. However, there is considerable opposition to the concept of 'tokenism', where women have been appointed to senior management positions simply so that the organisation can appear satisfied that they have carried out their equal opportunities obligations. A 'glass escalator' policy, where promotion criteria are transparent and fairly operated, should be the preferred option.

Courses limited to women, such as 'Women into Management' or 'Assertiveness Training', were popular ten years ago but have far fewer takers today. This may be a healthy sign, as more women believe that they do not need such courses and can achieve their goals without specific help. Women may also feel uncomfortable at being identified as needing such support. Mentoring has an important place here with role models providing the personal help and examples in cultivating future management and supervisory skills to aspiring trainees. A good example in the Halifax bank is shown in case study 9.5.

Within the performance management scheme itself, it is important that targets are seen to be fair and equitable across all groups, as are the resulting training and reward outcomes. Developing disabilities would need to be taken into account. For example, it would only be fair to adjust the individual targets for an employee working as a customer call-centre operator if they developed a debilitating illness.

Handling harassment and bullying

People with disabilities, gay people and young employees are the groups most at risk of workplace bullying. Staff with learning difficulties or mental ill-health are most likely to suffer badly at the hands of managers and colleagues (Fevre *et al.* 2012). So it is vital a policy should be in place to deal with such issues. The main aim of policy in this area is complete prevention. It should start with a policy statement that explains the different forms of harassment and bullying and the damage they cause to the organisation and its employees. It should stress the need for mutual respect at all levels and the need for all employees to feel valued. The way that allegations will be treated should be set out, that they will be speedy, fair and confidential and promise protection from victimisation for the complainant.

CASE STUDY 9.5 GIVING CONFIDENCE TO WOMEN TO CLIMB THE LADDER IN HALIFAX BANK

Twice a year, about 60 women gather at Halifax headquarters to take part in a 'glass ceiling' event. Since the launch of their 'Fair's Fair' diversity programme in 1998, the number of female senior managers has increased from 7 per cent to 26 per cent, while the presence of women at middle management has risen from 26 per cent to 42 per cent. The meetings are primarily to boost the confidence of the women so that they believe they can take the next step up the ladder. Encouragement is given to networking skills and the ability to display ambition and assertiveness without being aggressive.

(Source: Merrick 2001)

It should be made clear that individuals are liable to pay compensation to the victims as well as lose their jobs. This statement should be communicated to all employees in a clear and unambiguous way, giving opportunities for discussion and for questions to be asked.

In handling harassment, it is becoming more common for the organisation to provide independent counsellors to whom victims can turn for advice in the strictest confidence and without pressure. They will help the victim decide whether or not to take their complaint forward, although they will be encouraged not to ignore behaviour that makes them, and probably other members of the department, uncomfortable. They will also be encouraged to produce evidence, in the form of diary entries or notes of witnesses present. Without any action, it is not likely to stop.

Unless the incident is very serious, complaints should generally be dealt with internally and informally, so that a solution can be reached quickly and without too much embarrass-ment. What is difficult in these circumstances is the maintenance of confidentiality. The alleged harasser – having been told of their actions by a third party, often regarded as an appropriate role for a member of the human resources department, and why they cause distress – has the right to know who is making the allegation. Hopefully, once the issue has been raised, the harassment will stop and no formal punishment need be exercised. At this stage, a solution may be the agreed transfer of one of the parties.

However, if it is a one-off serious incident, or harassment continues after informal discussions, the process will need to be taken through the official grievance or disciplinary procedure. In Midland Bank, a trained investigator from another area would be appointed to carry out interviews and produce a report. On the basis of this report, the human resources department would decide if formal disciplinary proceedings were to take place. During the procedure, it is likely that neither party will want to continue to work in the same office or near locality within which most harassment occurs. In some procedures, the accused is suspended on pay, pending investigation, but this can be regarded as judgemental. Overall, it is probably better to allow both parties to take garden leave, but, because of the sensitivity of the issue, to proceed as quickly as possible.

If the complaint is upheld, the outcome depends on the severity of the offence. It can stretch from immediate dismissal to a warning and/or transfer to another position, some-times at a reduced grading. The incident should be used to examine existing arrangements and to set changes in motion, so it will, hopefully, not be repeated.

Equal pay issues

The EHRC Code of Practice on Equal Pay suggests that there are opportunities for discrim-ination on all aspects of pay as set out in Table 9.5.

When an organisation sets up pay systems or evaluates existing ones, it is important that these potential problems are open to investigation and rectification. A transparent and accessible appeal system is also essential to help women put their case before having to turn to legal redress.

Table 9.5 Aspects of discrimination in pay systems

Pay system	How discrimination could take place
Basic pay and job evaluation	Women can be on lower grades because the jobs in which they predominate have not been evaluated fairly. Women may not have been represented properly on the job evaluation committee. The factors chosen in the job evaluation scheme can favour men, such as strength required or technical skills. Women may be appointed at lower starting rates on the pay scale.
Pay progression	They move more slowly to the top of the scale if movement depends on achieving competencies or performance. This may happen because the rating system may be biased against women.
Performance pay	Women may have targets that are more demanding compared with men. Male managers may discriminate against female staff in their ratings.
Benefits	Women may have reduced access to benefits, such as allowances or company cars, because of the way their jobs are graded or because decisions are taken in a discriminatory way.

Age discrimination

The changing demography, explained in Chapter 1, will result in the over-45s dominating the workforce in the twenty-first century. By 2021, 46 per cent of the workforce will be over 45 and, taking Europe as a whole, the number of people aged 50 to 64 will have increased by 20 per cent in two decades. Despite the growing importance of this section of the workforce, ageism remains entrenched in society and the workplace.

From 2011, employers have been unable to forcibly retire employees at age 65 (except in exceptional cases as indicated earlier in the chapter). Therefore, employers will need to regularly review the performance of older employees and ensure they document their findings carefully. They will have to address poor performance in the same way for the over-65s as for other employees and set objectives that are no different for reason of age.

However, if an employee is over 65, becomes disabled and still does not want to retire, severe difficulties will be faced. Special adjustments will need to be considered, and the views of younger employees need to be considered to ensure that elderly employees are not given special treatment. Discrimination is displayed principally at recruitment when age limits are often overtly or covertly used by describing the ideal candidate in an advertisement as 'between 25 and 35' or using more indirect descriptions such as 'a recent graduate' or 'with one to three years' experience'.

The new expression 'glass precipice' indicates that older employees may be constrained from career development activities where employers see a limited investment return from training, while redundancy selection can often work against older employees, especially in non-unionised establishments where no formal selection procedure is agreed.

As with all other discrimination, it is counterproductive in that it limits the sources of available competent candidates and may result in the loss of essential skills and company operating knowledge when large numbers of older employees are encouraged or forced to leave. Having a low activity rate puts a large burden on the state through benefit payments, especially invalidity benefit and public sector early retirement pensions. It has also been one of the causes of the early twenty-first-century crisis in private pension funds, where older employees have been persuaded to accept redundancy or early retirement through generous provisions paid by the funds.

Wetherspoon are a company that has a positive policy on age as detailed in case study 9.6.

Monitoring and evaluation – the role of human resources

This final section reverts to the starting point: Where does the organisation stand in terms of its own agenda and objectives? We emphasised in Chapter 1 that two of the major strengths of human resources should be its reputation for an independent viewpoint and an ethical approach, and these areas should be fully utilised to examine and monitor what is going on and how effective initiatives have been. The central feature of an effective human resource intervention is to have an overall strategy. One of the most useful devices, apart from the statistical targets that may be utilised, is an employee attitude survey, which asks employees to give their viewpoint on equal opportunities issues, especially whether they are improving or deteriorating. Another approach is through benchmarking, in other words, to find out how the organisation is performing in relation to similar companies or those professing to operate best practice.

A further initiative is in the field of *diversity networks*, which have been set up in larger organisations over the last 20 or so years but have developed much more fully with the technical support of social networking. They are principally support groups for employees who may face discrimination but have more recently established themselves as important drivers of engagement, retention and recruitment. Examples include:

■ The National Black Crown Prosecution Association (NBCPA) carried out research into why so many ethnic minority applicants failed to make interview short-lists and visited local schools and initiated mentoring and work experience.

■ The disability network at BT organises awareness-raising for line managers to help them understand how to get the best from people living with a disability and also organises 'knowledge calls', via conference calls and desktop technology, with experts talking about subjects such as migraine and Parkinson's disease.

■ The early career network at Cisco has provided research information into the needs of Generation Y to help the organisation increase its retention rate for this group.

(Syedain 2012)

CASE STUDY 9.6 AGE POSITIVE AT WETHERSPOON

JD Wetherspoon are a pub company with more than 750 outlets throughout the UK. The company's customer base is very broad, a fact which they are keen to reflect in their work-force. Wetherspoon have taken the step of removing their retirement age, a move which ensures that they can retain valuable skills and experience and give staff the choice of working for longer.

The majority of frontline recruitment in the company is overseen by pub managers, and they have been trained to ensure that their recruitment practices do not discriminate on age. This includes the revision of all job specifications so that they are in line with good practice on age diversity and the rewriting of the company's interviewing skills course. Wetherspoon's job application forms do not ask for date of birth.

Wetherspoon have found it beneficial to attract diverse age ranges by offering flexible hours. This enables the employee to strike a balance between work and family or other commitments and the business to cover its core hours. For example, lunchtime is a particularly busy period for the company's outlets and they have found that some older workers – who might be looking to work for a few hours a week – are adaptable and happy to work at this time. The company reports that staff retention levels are well above the industry norms. Older staff are welcomed at all levels of the business, from part-time bar work to managerial posts. Feedback from pubs that employ older workers suggests they are particularly stable, with low absence, a strong work ethic and a commitment to the business. Training is also available at all levels and Wetherspoon have a number of older employees who have progressed to manager level. Turnover of pub managers at Wetherspoon is half that of the industry average.

The organisation considers that part of the success of the company is due to being innovative and progressive and this is reflected in their recruitment process. Employing a diverse workforce of men and women of all ages benefits individual pubs and the company as a whole. Pub managers are encouraged to recruit staff primarily on personality and attitude, not making age an issue.

The business benefits of Wetherspoon's age diverse approach include:

Enables the company to reflect its broad customer base.
Helps to keep pace with demographic change.
Flexible hours help to attract staff to cover busy periods.
Staff retention levels are well above the industry norms.
Frontline managers are satisfied with stability and hard work offered by older workers.
Turnover of pub managers at Wetherspoon is half that of the industry average.

(Source: DWP 2012)

Ensuring that employees responsible for recruitment, selection, performance management and health and safety are all knowledgeable is a further important role for human resources, as is the consideration of changing working practices to enable a better balance to be achieved between home and work. Human resources should also be in the best position to make fair investigations into accusations of discrimination, victimisation and harassment. They need to put procedures in place and provide advice on difficult areas such as harassment and bullying or retirement issues, which take account of the organisation's needs and current case decisions.

CRITICISM OF THE EQUALITY INDUSTRY

Although there is genuine all-party political support for the legislative framework on equality, pockets of critical comment have emerged in recent years. The first criticism is that the continuous round of legislation is self-defeating. The duties imposed on employers extend far beyond the obligation to avoid discriminating against individuals, but to a wider obligation to monitor, train and assess themselves continuously and time-consumingly as to how truly equal their outcomes are and how representative their employees are of the wider population. Marrin believes 'The duty to promote equality is almost limitless to the point of absurdity' (2011: 28). The second criticism arises from the first – that the cost of the obligations on employers is too high. This has been estimated at around £1 billion per annum – £600 million for the state sector and £400 million for the private sector (Saunders 2011).

It is not always the case that policies and procedures achieve the results that are required, as shown in the Meteor case study.

METEOR CASE STUDY

EQUAL OPPORTUNITIES IN PRACTICE

Sarah sat down to draft her Equal Opportunities Policies and Practices document ready for the management meeting the following week. She had studied the debate between the managing diversity approach and the traditional EO approach, knew the arguments from both sides and considered both had value. She was therefore determined to put in place a system that had the best of both worlds.

She knew the locality had a strong ethnic element, mostly Pakistanis, making up around 8–10 per cent of the population, and that the workforces of most factories in the area were male dominated. An objective was set in her mind to recruit at least 8 per cent from ethnic minorities and to aim to include a substantial number of females into the short-lists.

There was a thriving publication, so she included it on the list for advertising vacancies and designed an advertisement where the illustration included males and females, white and ethnic minority employees working together. However, she made no mention in the advertisements of an equal opportunities policy or any special wording to encourage it.

The recruiting team consisted of a number of line managers and she made sure that those who had not attended an EO awareness course did so before the recruitment started. She also put forward a proposal for courses to be designed to help prepare employees for promotion. Although directed at all employees, she planned to ask managers to give special consideration to minority groups. If she could ensure that a number of women and Pakistanis had the ability, aptitude and drive for promotion to team leader and made a success of it, they would act as role models. A small number of jobs on the site had been identified as possibilities for disabled employees. She planned to make contact with the Pakistani community group and arrange for a translator to be present on each of the occasions where application forms had to be completed and interviews took place. Finally, she contacted the external caterer to ensure that there was a sufficient range of meals suitable for all groups of employees.

Another set of proposals she made covered family-friendly benefits. She put forward a plan for employees to job share throughout the site. This would need to be arranged between two employees who both wanted to work part-time. They would need to work with their team leader to ensure the shifts and skills needed were covered. Given the complexities of the shift system in the factory, flexible hours and flexitime would be very difficult to organise but this would be possible in the offices.

At the management meeting, she was closely questioned by two production managers regarding the overall plan. Although not overtly racist, they indicated a small degree of hostility towards specific proposals, specifically the interpreter. They considered it essential that all applicants had a firm grasp of English so they could follow instructions, including those in health and safety. All the work was semi-skilled and skilled, requiring judgement and effective communication within the team. After considering the issues, Sarah agreed to drop that proposal.

They also could not see the point of encouraging variable hours, having the viewpoint that this would simply lead to all female employees wanting to go part-time. Sarah was not happy to concede on this issue but took Scott's advice to give way here, as it was not a key component, and made a note to raise it again in a year's time.

The recruitment process was not straightforward. Despite having a reasonable response from minority groups, there were objections from the two managers to a number of female and ethnic applicants going on to the short-list. Sarah answered most of their points by indicating that organising an interview does not mean a commitment to select. When it came to the interviews themselves, the proportion of rejections for female and ethnic applicants was particularly high from the same two managers. The reasons given were petty and illogical, and discussing the cases took up a considerable amount of time. Sarah did not want to make an appointment over their heads and it needed a round-table meeting with Scott and the site manager to reach compromise decisions where a proportion went on to the final selection stage.

Towards the end of the first batch of selections, Sarah received two letters of complaint. One was from a Pakistani who had not been selected for interview. She pointed out that her neighbour had been selected but had fewer qualifications and less experience than she had. She threatened action unless the matter was reconsidered. The second was from the husband of an applicant who claimed that his wife had been insulted by a number of questions at the interview concerning her previous experience and aspects of her personal life, such as caring responsibilities. Sarah had not been involved in either of these cases; both interviews had been carried out by the two hostile managers.

Sarah was very concerned that her ambition to introduce 'best practice' in the unit did not seem to be progressing very well.

KEY CHAPTER SUMMARY POINTS

- There are two strong cases for eliminating discrimination from the workplace. These are, firstly, the obligations from laws outlawing discrimination on the grounds of race, sex and disability and, secondly, the business case, which is based on changing demography, the need to improve relations with all customers and all communities and to be seen as a good employer.

- Indirect discrimination occurs where a condition or policy adversely affects members of one race, sex or the disabled.

- More attention is now given to cases of victimisation, bullying and harassment to ensure that vulnerable employees receive better protection.

- Organisations need to consider carefully whether an approach of managing diversity is preferable to that of a traditional equal opportunities approach.

- Champions are required to drive equal opportunities through the organisation and to ensure that it is correctly applied in recruitment, selection, retention, pay and employee development activities.

STUDENT ACTIVITIES

1   You have been asked to conduct an equal opportunities survey in an organisation of a thousand employees on one site. How would you carry this out?

    In your answer, design a questionnaire and indicate how you may use it. You may also want to explain how focus groups may provide useful information.

2   Read the research article by Collinson and Collinson (focus on research 9.1) and discuss which you believe to be the most appropriate of the four different courses of action.

3   Look up the case in spotlight on the law 9.3. Discuss how you would respond, as a tribunal member, to a claim by a citizen of Leeds that they have been discriminated against because of their location and accent.

4   Read the source of spotlight on the law 9.8 and compare their decisions over reasonable adjustment with more recent cases. Has the position changed as more decisions have been made at higher courts?

5   Role-play interviews from the two complainants in the Meteor case study. Decide on what would be Sarah's best course of action.

6   Debate the viewpoint that cyber-harassment and bullying can be just as demeaning as conventional bullying but may not receive the same degree of sympathy from witnesses.

REFERENCES

ACAS (2009) *Bullying and Harassment at Work: A Guide for Managers and Employers*. ACAS.

Blackstock, C. (1999) Straw to Set Job Targets for Minorities. *The Guardian*, 5 July.

CIPD (2004) *Diversity: Stacking up the Evidence*. Executive briefing. CIPD.

— (2005) Managing Diversity: People Make the Difference at Work – But Everyone is Different. Report 2005.

Cockburn, C. (1991) *In the Way of Women*. Macmillan.

Collinson, M. and Collinson, D. (1996) 'It's Only Dick': The Sexual Harassment of Women Managers in Insurance Sales. *Work, Employment and Society*, 10(1): 29–56.

Corby, S. (2009) Pay Equality – Gender and Age, in S. Corby, S. Palmer and E. Lindop (eds) *Rethinking Reward*. Palgrave Macmillan.

Coyne, D., Sprigg, C., Aztell, C. and Farley, S. (2012) Punched from the Screen. Paper presented at the ESRC Festival of Social Science, November.

Davies, M. (2011) Independent Review of Women on Boards. Department of Business, Innovation and Skills.

DWP (2012) Case Study JD Wetherspoon. Department of Work and Pensions, accessed at http://webarchive.nationalarchives.gov.uk/+/http://www.dwp.gov.uk/docs/case-study-jd-wetherspoons.pdf.

Edwards, C. (2004) Do the Write Thing. *People Management*, 17 June, 36–38.

EHRC (2011) Annual Report. EHRC.

Employment Tribunals and EAT Statistics (2011). HMSO.

EOC (1996). Guidance Notes for Employers on Setting Targets for Gender Equality. Equal Opportunities Commission.

— (2001) Sexual Harassment is No Joke. Equal Opportunities Commission.

— (2004) Women and Men at Work. Equal Opportunities Commission.

Equal Opportunities Review (1995) *Accord Ends CRE Three-year Court Action*. No 61, May/June, 7–8.

— (1999) *Opportunities for Ethnic Minorities*. May/June, 16–17.

Fawcett Society (2011) Equal Pay – The Facts, accessed at www.Fawcettsociety.org.uk.

Fevre, R., Lewis, D., Robinson, A. and Jones, T. (2012) Insight into Ill-treatment in the Workplace. Cardiff School of Social Sciences, July.

Glover, C. (2002) Ticked Off. *People Management*, 24 January, 38–39.

Higginbottom, K. (2010) Pilot Champions Diversity at Trust. *People Management*, 22 April, 12.

Hinton, J. (2010) Settlement in Race Discrimination Case. *Camden New Journal*, 1 April, 16.

IDS (1993) *IDS Brief 489*, March, 2–4.

— (1994) *IDS Brief 525*, September, 1.

IPD (1997) *Managing Diversity*. IPD Position Paper.

Kandola, R. and Fullerton, J. (1998) *Diversity in Action: Managing the Mosaic*. IPD.

Korn, A. (1997) EAT Rules on Pay-outs for Wounded Feelings. *Personnel Today*, 10 April, 15.

Laurance, J. (2011) £4.5m Payout for Doctor Hounded out of Job for Having Baby. *The Independent*, 17 December, 1.

Marrin, M. (2011) Beware, the Equality Zealots are Unfair and Cost Us Millions. *Sunday Times*, 27 November, 28.

Martin, N. (2004) Asian Postman Awarded £130,000 for Race Abuse. *Daily Telegraph*, 26 May, 8.

Merrick, N. (2001) Minority Interest. *People Management*, 8 November, 52–53.

Saunders, P. (2011) *The Rise of the Equalities Industry*. Civitas.

Sealy, R. and Vinnicombe, S. (2012) *The Female FTSE Board Report – Milestone or Millstone*. Cranfield School of Management.

Stevens, M. (2012) HSBC to Offer Part-time Roles to All Parents. *People Management*, March, accessed at www.peoplemanagement.co.uk/pm/articles/2012/03/hsbc-to-offer-part-time-roles-to-all-new-parents.htm.

Syedain, H. (2010) A New Era for Age. *People Management*, 14 January, 19–22.

— (2012) Premium Bonds. *People Management*, September, 23–26.

ADDITIONAL FEATURES

 Please visit the companion website at: www.routledge.com/cw/stredwick where you will find additional case studies and reading material together with short self-tests and other resources for both students and lecturers.

10 HEALTH, SAFETY AND EMPLOYEE WELL-BEING

INTRODUCTION

In 2004, Peter Pell, an industrial cleaning contractor, was sent to prison for manslaughter following the death of his employee who was driving a loading machine. Pell had removed the cage to allow the machine to get better access into a shed and, in so doing, all the safety devices were rendered inoperative. While working in the confined space, the employee was crushed to death (*Health and Safety Practitioner* 2004a). In an earlier case, Peter Kite, who ran a small outdoor activity company, was found guilty of manslaughter as a result of the death of four teenagers under his control on a canoe exercise off the Dorset coast (Whitfield 1995).

Over the last 150 years, legislation has progressively imposed greater obligations on all parties in the workplace to try to prevent unnecessary suffering arising from accidents and unsafe working conditions and to provide adequate opportunities for compensation where they do occur. The severity of the sentences in these two cases demonstrates that the courts continue to interpret the law in an increasingly strict fashion and that penalties for wrong-doing are becoming harsher.

The number of fatal accidents in the workplace has shown a steady decline in the last 25 years (see Figure 10.1), which continues the pattern during the twentieth century. Although much of this reduction has been due to improved safety operations, the sharp decline in mining and manufacturing activity in the UK has also played its part. Mining, for example, has declined from 900,000 employees in 1926 to fewer than 8,000 in 2010, although it remains a highly dangerous place to work, with 13 deaths between 2006 and 2011. It is significant that the number of deaths in service industries now make up over half the total, although, given the large number of service sector workers (over 23 million), it is a comparatively safer place to work.

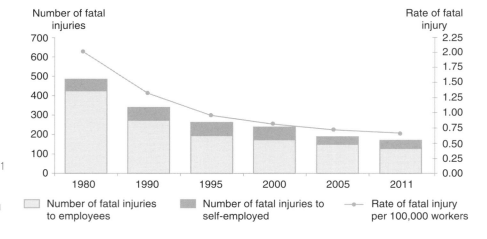

Figure 10.1
Fatal injuries to workers in the UK, 1980–2011

Source: HSE (2011a) *Annual Report.* Health and Safety Executive.

Days lost through injury at work and ill-health are substantial. The Labour Force Survey for 2010/11 reported:

- Around 26.4 million working days were lost in total, 22.1 million due to work-related illness and 4.4 million due to workplace injuries.
- On average, each person suffering took around 15 days off work. For ill-health, the average was 19 days. For accidents, the absence averaged 7.2 days.
- The number of working days lost has fallen over the past decade from 33 million in 2003.
- 10.8 million days lost were caused by stress, depression or anxiety and 7.6 million for musculoskeletal disorders, which combined accounted for the majority of days lost due to work-related ill-health, while the average absence was 27 days for the former and 15 for the latter.

A few high-profile tragedies take the headlines, such as the Piper Alpha oil rig fire in 1988 where 167 employees died, which has been the most serious accident in post-war history and led to the liquidation of Occidental Oil, the company operating the oil rig. However, most workplace deaths and serious injuries are single, avoidable accidents.

The costs involved in accidents and ill-health is extraordinary. According to the Health and Safety Executive (HSE 2012a), the total costs to employers exceeded £3 billion in 2010/11, while the government faced a bill of around the same sum, as shown in Table 10.1.

For the employers, the figure for insurance costs of £1.8 billion equates to around £60 per employee, although it is much higher in sectors where serious accidents are more likely, such as manufacturing and construction. The huge government expenditure on bene-fits is chiefly due to the rise in people claiming incapacity benefit due to various forms of long-term illnesses and injuries arising from the workplace.

In the same year, employees were awarded over £1 billion in total in compensation for work-related injury or ill-health. Employees received compensation from employers but also from some government funds set up to deal with longer-term injuries where employers may have gone out of business. An example of this is the award made by the High Court in

Table 10.1 Cost of work-based injuries and ill-health in the UK, 2011 (£millions)

Employers		Government	
Insurance	1,810	Benefits	2,425
Sick pay	1,223	Health and rehabilitation	585
Production/service disturbance	113	Administration and legal cost	40
Administration and legal costs	20		
Total	**3,166**	**Total**	**3,050**

Source: HSE (2012a) *Costs to Britain of Workplace Injuries and Work-related Ill-health 2010/11.* Health and Safety Executive.

January 1999 that totalled over £5 million to 40,000 to ex-miners who suffer from Vibration White Finger (*Health and Safety* 1999).

It was estimated that employees incurred costs including loss of income (£435 million) and rehabilitation (£122 million). An estimate was made of over £7 billion for the non-financial losses for individuals, such as the cost of pain, grief and suffering arising from injuries and ill-health. Although this figure is highly debatable, it makes clear that the compensation won by employees rarely, if ever, makes up for all of the suffering and loss of opportunities that ensues.

These payments put into the shade the court fines that are exacted where companies are found guilty of safety irregularities, which, although rising steadily, still average less than £3,000. Serious individual cases still arise, however, where the fines are large, as shown in the 'Duties on employers' section.

The format for this chapter will be as follows:

- An outline of the safety legislation currently in place.
- The parties involved in health and safety – the Health and Safety Executive, safety inspectors, safety officers and safety representatives.
- Risk assessment and safety prevention.
- Welfare issues and services, including employee assistance programmes, positive health programmes and counselling arrangements.
- The business case for having the highest standards of health, safety and employee well-being.
- The role of the human resources department, including the development of health, safety and welfare policies.

LEGAL INTERVENTIONS

Origins of legislation

Since the onset of the industrial revolution, there have been calls for a better balance of responsibility between employer and employee over health and safety issues. In medieval times, it had been assumed that those who employed staff, mostly servants of course, could be relied upon to look after these staff in their own interests so that they could get a prolonged service. This had always been, in practice, somewhat patchy and the common law had never been too clear as to their precise responsibilities. By the late eighteenth century, when industrial and mining sites of 500 employees or more began to evolve, it became clear that employees were regarded, at best, as short-term investments who could easily be replaced, when no longer productive through accident or ill-health.

Legislation, promoted by dedicated humanitarians, such as Sir Robert Peel the Elder, father of the future prime minister (who himself employed 15,000 'hands'), and Lord Shaftesbury, began to be introduced from 1833 onwards through restricting hours of work, especially for women and young people. This was accompanied by regulations setting out minimum conditions of working practices through various Factory Acts. More importantly, they were backed up through enforcement agencies. Much of this was carried through, despite considerable opposition from the industrialists. As the social historian, G.M. Trevelyan explained:

> In the earlier part of the 19th Century, state control in the interests of the working classes was not an idea congenial to the rulers of Britain. They turned a deaf ear to Robert Owen when he pointed out to them that his own New Lanark mills were a model ready to hand, to teach the world how the new industrial system could be made the instrument of standardised improvement in sanitation, welfare, hours, wages and education, raising the conditions of working-class life to an average level that could never be attained under the domestic system. . . . The great opportunity that his vision had perceived was missed, until in the slow evolution, the state had come round to his doctrine of the control of factories and the condition of life for all employed therein.
>
> (1942, 4: 47)

In the first half of the twentieth century, the attention turned from the removal of the more obvious dangers and abuses in employment to an emphasis on the 'human relations' aspects, spearheaded by the work of Elton Mayo (1945) at the Hawthorne plant of the Western Electric Company. By the company paying attention to the physical and welfare needs of employees and providing a counselling service, both productivity and morale could be raised, leading to better profits for the owners.

Today, there are over 100 separate statutes in force relating to health, safety and welfare, the oldest dating back to the Explosives Act of 1875. Much of these are now 'relevant statutory provisions' under the Health and Safety at Work Act 1974 (HASAWA) and are now enforced through the Health and Safety Executive (HSE) or local authority. There is not time or room in this publication to deal with more than a handful of the more recent Acts or regulations (many of which stem from Europe) and only the most significant will be briefly addressed. You will find advice on where to investigate further on such legislation on the website.

Health and Safety at Work Act 1974 (HASAWA)

This influential legislation, borne of general consensus between the political parties, is essentially an 'enabling' Act, with wide-ranging, if imprecise, provisions, which require interpretation by the courts or putting into effect through regulations sanctioned by Parliament. As put by Corbridge and Pilbeam:

> HASAWA represented a sea-change in the UK approach to health and safety legislation and was aimed at combating the endemic apathy towards health and safety

provision, attributed to excessive, prescriptive and unintelligible law and compounded by ineffective policing and enforcement.

(1998: 251)

Key directional changes included:

- Providing support to voluntary effort and personal responsibility for health and safety rather than simply relying on detailed regulation.
- Concentration on the protection of people, rather than buildings or machinery, and extending that protection to all people, including members of the public, and contractors on and off site, rather than just employees.
- Trying to encourage industry self-regulation through such areas as developing codes of practice, rather than imposing them by government committee.
- Providing a comprehensive cover through all industries and all employees under all conditions, building on and extending the common law provision. It has been estimated that as many as three million people came under the scope of safety legislation protection for the first time.
- Imposing criminal liability to ensure compliance with its provisions.

There are duties placed essentially on employers but the legislation also places duties on employees, designers, manufacturers, suppliers and equipment installers. We will look at each group in turn.

DUTIES ON EMPLOYERS

The Act lays down a fundamental '*duty of care*' towards the health, safety and welfare of all employees, which is the starting point of all considerations (see case study 10.1). As we shall see later, this duty has been interpreted in a much wider sense in recent years and now encompasses the duty to relieve stress where applicable.

**C
A
S
E

S
T
U
D
Y**

CASE STUDY 10.1 TWO EXAMPLES OF MANAGEMENT NOT EXERCISING THE EFFECTIVE DUTY OF CARE

Case 1: Electrocution through insufficient training

UK Power Networks was fined £300,000 and ordered to pay another £219,352 in costs after one of its engineers was fatally electrocuted. Jonathan Crosby, an employee of UK Power Networks, died instantly after being hit by 8,000 volts of electricity while working on overhead power lines in Diss, Norfolk.

The company, which owns and maintains electricity cables in the south and east of England, pleaded guilty to the charges relating to the incident in November 2007. Norwich Crown Court heard that staff at UK Power Networks – formerly EDF Energy – had not received adequate training. The Health and Safety Executive (HSE), which brought the successful prosecution, said its investigation had found that vital fuses supplying the transformer Crosby was working on had not been removed to cut the electricity supply.

HSE inspector Toni Drury said, 'A family man has lost his life in tragic circumstances, which could have been avoided if essential safety measures had been put in place by UK Power Networks.

'This tragedy illustrates how dangerous work on or near overhead power lines is, and it is imperative that employers ensure there are safe systems of work and that these are implemented and followed. There is no room for error when working with such high voltages.'

UK Power Networks said that its training programmes have since been revised.

(Source: *People Management* 2011a)

Case 2: Excess steam causes fall into open slag channel

Global steel company Tata was fined £500,000 for serious safety breaches after a worker died when he fell into a channel carrying slag waste at 1,500 degrees Celsius when covers had been removed for maintenance and not replaced. Kevin Downey, 49, was working on a night shift on the Number 4 Blast Furnace at the Port Talbot steelworks when the incident happened on 25 April 2006. At the time, the company was operating as Corus.

Swansea Crown Court heard that Mr Downey, of Port Talbot, had over 30 years' experience working on the blast furnaces when the incident happened. It was investigated by the HSE, which brought the prosecution.

The court was told that it was believed Mr Downey went to the cast house at the site to inspect the slag pool, which was due to close for maintenance work during the day shift.

While he was on a veranda area, steam from a granulator became acute, forcing him to leave. He tried to retrace his steps through the dense steam but visibility may have been as little as three feet and he fell into the open section of a channel that was running slag at 1,500 degrees Celsius. He attempted to climb out and was helped out by workers who heard his cries. Although he was conscious, he died later the same day.

HSE's investigation found that the company had a reporting system, which showed a significant number of near misses where steam had led to dangerous situations with the potential to injure workers or damage equipment.

It was also common practice to operate the furnace with sections of channels – or runners – left uncovered without taking additional precautions to prevent anyone from falling in.

(Source: HSE 2012b)

Section 2 of HASAWA sets out the general duties on employers, which cover:

1   The provision of systems of work, equipment and a workplace that are all safe.
2   Arrangements for the use, handling, storage and transport of articles and substances that are all safe.
3   Adequate and necessary information, supervision training and instruction to ensure effective employee safety.
4   Ensuring there are safe means of getting into and out of premises.
5   Adequate welfare provision.

The duties also extend to sub-contractors working on their premises (see spotlight on the law 10.1) and to members of the public. Throughout this section of the Act, the words '*as far as is reasonably practicable*' are mentioned for each clause. This limits the absolute responsibility to employers and allows them to achieve a balance between the assessed risk of an unsafe practice against the cost of avoiding that risk. Let us take an example. A factory is based alongside Heathrow Airport and there is a risk that, one day, a plane will crash into that factory. To avoid that risk, it is conceivable that the employer could build a cover to the factory that would protect the employees from the crash. Realistically, however, the cost of that cover would be colossal and could not be justified against the very low risk of the crash occurring. It would not be 'reasonably practicable'.

SPOTLIGHT ON THE LAW 10.1 RESPONSIBILITY TO SUB-CONTRACTORS

Joseph Jenkinson was a sub-contractor for construction company JDM Accord on a road maintenance contract. His main work was as a banksman, to direct the traffic on the site, but he had had no training in these duties and was directed to sweep and clear up the site. Jenkinson was struck and killed by a reversing trailer when he was involved in other work. The court found that there was no site management, no site inductions or any instructions to any of the operatives about traffic management and that drivers could make up their own system of work as they went along. JDM Accord was fined £100,000 with £32,000 costs.

(Source: *Health and Safety Practitioner* 2004b)

This is a simple case; employers each day need to consider other cases that are far more evenly balanced. Should the 20-year-old machine be replaced this year before there is an accident or should we wait until we have generated more profits to invest in the new plant? The noise levels in the assembly area are rising with increased production. Should we investigate? If the results are not good, can we afford to invest in an acoustic control system? The old offices are getting stiflingly hot in summer. With an increase in numbers, do we need to invest in air-conditioning? These may be finely judged decisions and, ultimately, should an accident or incident arise before the employer has acted, it would then be down to the courts to decide if the action was 'reasonably practicable' or not. If the court decided that the employer should have taken action as part of their 'duty of care', the employer could be punished for its failure to carry out its statutory duty.

Other duties of employers include:

- Duty to persons other than employees such as the public and contractors (Sections 3 and 4).
- The requirement to use 'best practical means' to solve safety problems. This is an ever-tightening noose trying to prevent employers from carrying out botched jobs or taking shortcuts. In industries where safety is absolutely paramount, such as nuclear power or defence, 'state of the art' safety systems are the expectation.
- The duty to prepare and update a written health and safety policy and communicate it properly to employees; to recognise the appointment of safety representatives and to form a safety committee if requested. (These duties will be examined later in the chapter.)

The duty of care extends to a degree of monitoring sickness, absence and health in the organisation. Each establishment has its own specific areas of danger and certain places are prone to a higher level of sickness if nothing is done. This includes those places where a 'sick building syndrome' occurs, through faults in the design, lighting or air-conditioning (or lack of it), and management need to show that they are responding to these problems where evidence is brought forward. Another type of establishment where high absence has been a feature in recent years is a call centre where the nature of the work pressure is likely to increase the stress levels, as shown in focus on research 10.1.

DUTIES ON EMPLOYEES

The Act recognised that responsibility for safety was not just one way. Confirming the common law implied term of the employment contract – that the employee is obliged to follow the safety instructions – Sections 7 and 8 went further by stating that the employee must co-operate with safety initiatives and the training that accompanies them, to take reasonable care of their own health and safety and not recklessly interfere with machines, plant or processes so as to make them unsafe. The clear implications are that employees have to wear the required safety gear and follow all authorised safety rules. They also risk dismissal if they refuse to follow other important health and safety instructions.

FOCUS ON RESEARCH 10.1 HEALTH, SICKNESS AND ABSENCE MANAGEMENT IN A UK CALL CENTRE

The health of employees at an energy call centre was investigated by researchers from Stirling University. They identified 17 symptoms of illness, including tiredness, stiff necks, sore eyes and backache, and found that call handlers experienced a higher number of such symptoms than non-call handlers. While many of the symptoms were insufficiently serious on their own to cause absence from work, large numbers of workers experienced them in clusters. Forty per cent of employees experienced at least three symptoms either daily or several times a week. The way in which the call handlers' tasks were structured, organised and performed produced the greatest number of complaints and the most frequently reported cause of sickness. They had to answer queuing calls and meet targets, so they spent only 4.7 per cent of time away from their station, compared with 17 per cent for non-call handlers and they had considerably less control over most aspects of their work. More than two-thirds felt pressured as a result of work on a normal day.

Also reported was a 'draconian' absence policy, which confused absence with absenteeism with a far from sympathetic employer who appeared to be uninterested in the reasons for absence.

One respondent commented, 'You get upset when you don't meet the standards expected, the targets. That's when the stress factor goes up. After training, you are put on the phones and a lot of people don't know what to do … they get into a hole they can't get out of. Then they get stressed and depressed and they are soon on tablets, then they get put on a sickness review, feel under constant pressure and feel victimised.'

Following a series of recommendations, management complied with most of the environmental issues but were less inclined to revise the absence procedures. No action was taken on the target-driven model because of competitive pressures – the level of targets determined the volume of business that they would win.

(Source: Taylor *et al.* 2003)

In one of the first prosecutions under this section in 1996, Roy Hill, a demolition worker, was sentenced to three months in prison for grossly violating asbestos regulations. Despite having instructions on safety requirements, he ignored all of them and took no precautions to prevent asbestos dust escaping from old roofing sheets and pipe lagging when demolishing a building in Bristol (*People Management* 1996).

DUTIES ON DESIGNERS, MANUFACTURERS, SUPPLIERS AND INSTALLERS

Duties here under Section 6 include incorporating safety features at the design stage, testing for risks to health and providing full safety instruction and hazard details. Again, this aspect clarified the rather unspecific common law obligations and has made a large difference in the way products are designed and marketed. Since the Act, for example, all commercial guillotines require the operator to have both hands on separate buttons for it to operate. Furthermore, one manufacturer of numerically controlled tools was successfully prosecuted because the design allowed the override of a guard while the machine was still working.

The Health and Safety Commission and Health and Safety Executive

Both the Health and Safety Commission and the Health and Safety Executive were set up under HASAWA. The Commission is a quango, with between six and nine lay members drawn from bodies representing employers, trade unions and local authorities. It is primarily an advisory body and its main responsibility is for carrying out the policy of the Act and providing advice to local authorities and others to enable them to discharge the responsibilities imposed upon them by the Act. It reports to Parliament through the Secretary of State for Education and Employment. The Commission arranges for research to be carried out, submits proposals for new regulations, produces codes of practice and generally works to reassure the public that risks are being properly controlled through information and responsiveness to public concerns.

The Health and Safety Executive is responsible for the policing and enforcement of the Act and other acts involving safety. It employs a large staff of inspectors, whose duties are covered later in the chapter.

Control of Substances Hazardous to Health Regulations (COSHH) 1988

These influential regulations came into effect in 1989. They consist of nineteen regulations and four codes of practice and are designed to protect employees who work with any substances that could be hazardous to their health unless they are handled and utilised in a properly controlled way. They apply to all workplaces, large and small, and include all substances except for those where regulations were already in force, such as lead and asbestos.

The principal requirements in these regulations are five-fold (HSE 1988).

- A *risk assessment* must be made to identify all potentially hazardous substances and to set out the precautions required. For many manufacturing employers, this list of substances can be very extensive, stretching into four figures, and much time has been taken up in producing the list. Criticisms have been made of the outcome of the regulations where lists need to include day-to-day common products such as petrol, Tipp-Ex and photo-copying fluid, but many accidents and ill-health can arise from common causes such as misuse of these products. An amendment in 1992 required employers to carry out the risk assessment every five years.
- A system must be put in place to prevent or control these risks. Consideration must be given to replace hazardous substances or to provide better-controlled working arrangements where they are used.

- Just as importantly, the employer must make sure these controls are effectively put to use and keep records of the monitoring process.
- Employers must regularly conduct health surveillance of staff engaged in work associated with these substances where there is a known identifiable risk.
- Employees must be informed of the hazards and trained in the control processes, including the precautions that they need to take.

Regulations arising from European Union Directives

It has been an objective from the early days of the European movement that laws relating to health and safety should be applied consistently across Europe. This ensures that the free market between states can operate efficiently without manufacturers and traders having to deal with different regulations in each country. The *Framework Directive*, implemented by member states in 1992, contained general safety principles and objectives, such as the prevention of occupational risks and providing balanced participation between the parties affected.

Additional regulations, known as 'daughter directives', covering specific areas have been issued within the framework of this directive and this programme will continue in the gradual move to ensure consistency across member states. They have been converted into regulations in the UK and the most important ones have been:

The *Management of Health and Safety at Work Regulations 1992*. These regulations take the requirements set out in HASAWA a stage further, making unqualified requirements on employers in areas such as carrying out risk assessments, providing training and establishing emergency procedures. Similarly, unconditional requirements have been made on employees to use equipment in the way they have been trained and to report any dangerous occurrence or gap that they see in the employer's systems.

The *Workplace (Health, Safety and Welfare) Regulations 1992* require employers to provide a good working environment with appropriate temperature, ventilation and level of lighting, provision of rest rooms and no smoking areas.

The *Manual Handling Operations Regulations 1992* make a clear requirement on the employer to reduce the risk of injuries by providing lifting gears where it is necessary and training employees on how to lift properly. The intention is to remove the 'macho lifting' culture and the operation of these regulations has helped to ensure that many more jobs involving lifting are open to women as well as men.

The *Health and Safety (Display Screen Equipment) Regulations 1992* have had a major impact on the day-to-day operations of those who spend a great deal of their time in front of display screens. There is a requirement on employers to arrange for employees to have their eyes tested regularly, ensure that the work is planned to include breaks and changes of activity, appropriate training and the location of the units to prevent damage to employees' upper limbs.

The *Working Time Regulations 1998* were implemented in the UK as a result of the Working Time Directive of November 1993. The essence of the regulations is that employees *cannot* be forced to work in excess of 48 hours a week, averaged over 17 weeks. Employees should have 11 consecutive hours of rest in any 24-hour period and a 24-hour rest in every 7-day period, plus a 20-minute break if the shift exceeds 6 hours. However, at this stage, employers and employees can agree to 'opt out' of the regulations and many employees, including most managers and, surprisingly, employees working in transport, are exempt for reasons that existing regulations are in place or that their time cannot be measured accurately.

In response to complaints concerning the extent of record keeping, revised regulations were introduced in 1999, which reduced the need to keep records for those staff who had agreed to 'opt out'. However, there is still a duty of care on the part of the employer to monitor the hours actually worked.

There have always been two areas of controversy within the Working Time Directive. The first is the arrangement where employees can *'opt out' of the regulations*. CIPD (2004) research found that long-hours culture had caused problems to develop: 47 per cent of respondents recorded strains on personal relationships, 17 per cent reported mental health problems and 69 per cent said that they missed out on leisure and hobby time, while 36 per cent believed that they performed less efficiently. Although 30 per cent claimed there was compulsion from their organisation to work long hours, up from 11 per cent when the regulations were passed, 65 per cent did not want the opt-out clause to be outlawed. Although long hours are essentially a British phenomenon, other organisations in Europe are increasing their opt-outs. This has come about because of the second controversy, namely the treatment of stand-by hours. Originally, these hours were thought to be excluded from working hours but a court ruling was made that found that these hours should be deemed to be part of working time under the regulations, a decision that led to great confusion, especially in the emergency and hospital services. Despite eight years of consultation, this problem has still not be solved, as the European Parliament has different views from the European Commission and a further set of EU consultations started in 2011 to try to resolve the issue. HR practitioners need to keep up to date on these rulings.

European regulations have also come into effect relating to the provision and use of protective equipment, the control of asbestos at work, measures to set minimum standards for the safe use of machines and equipment, and the protection of young people and pregnant women in the workplace.

Reporting of Diseases and Dangerous Occurrences Regulations (RIDDOR) 1995

All statistics on safety arise from a system of reporting by employers and this revised system was introduced to produce more accurate information and extend it to dangerous situations where nobody was hurt. All deaths and serious injuries must be immediately reported and a written report sent within ten days. For lesser accidents that cause an employee to be off work for more than three days, a completed accident form must be sent to the enforcing authorities; this also applies to some work-related diseases such as skin cancer or dermatitis. In 2010–11, 4.4 million days were lost through accidents at work, down from over 8 million in 2001–02 (HSE 2011a).

A dangerous occurrence could be a situation where a truck with a platform for mending street lights travelled down a highway with the platform extended and brought down some telephone lines. No injury followed but it could well have caused a major traffic accident and the enforcing authorities would need to know how it came to happen and to ensure it was not repeated.

Corporate Manslaughter and Corporate Homicide Act 2007 and Health and Safety Offences Act 2008

These two Acts put in place a process for employees, including senior management in an organisation, to be jailed following a conviction where it is found that that there is a 'gross failure' in the safety system that results in a person's death or serious injury. Courts are able to look at management systems across the organisation, rather than simply the actions of individuals. Offenders face up to two years in jail and an unlimited fine. Human resource practitioners can face this penalty if it is found that they have agreed to or co-operated with an offence being committed by the organisation or if the offence is attributable to their neglect (Higginbottom 2008).

The first case under this legislation came to court in 2011 as shown in spotlight on the law 10.2.

SPOTLIGHT ON THE LAW 10.2 CORPORATE MANSLAUGHTER

Geologist Alexander Wright from Cheltenham died in September 2008 when a 12.6ft-deep (3.8m) unsupported trial pit, which he was working in alone, caved in at a development site in Brimscombe Lane, near Stroud, Gloucestershire.

Cotswold Geotechnical was found guilty in November 2011 at Winchester Crown Court of corporate manslaughter relating to Mr Wright's death. The judge, Mr Justice Field, said the gross breach of the company's duty to Mr Wright was a 'grave offence'.

He said the company, which was described in court as in a parlous financial state, could pay the money back over ten years at a rate of £38,500 per annum.

He explained the fine marked the gravity of the offence and the deterrent effect it would have on companies to strongly adhere to health and safety guidance.

(Source: *Daily Telegraph* 2011)

ENFORCING THE LAW

There are two main groups who work to enforce the law:

■ The *external authorities*, made up of *inspectors* who work for the Health and Safety Executive and *local authority enforcement officers.*
■ The *internal authorities*, made up of *safety officers* and *safety representatives.*

External authorities

Local authority enforcement officers mostly deal with the service industries, such as hotels, restaurants, offices and warehouses, while inspectors deal with factories, mines, railways, schools and hospitals. Their enforcement authority consists of rights to:

■ Enter premises, with or without notice, at any reasonable time (accompanied by the police, if obstructed)
■ Take samples, measurements and photographs or recordings
■ Carry out tests
■ Direct that work be left undisturbed
■ Examine books and documents
■ Take statements from any employee concerned.

Their main enforcement activities, after persuasion has not achieved the desired results, is to issue improvement notices and prohibition notices. *Improvement notices* are issued where the inspector is satisfied there has been a contravention of a statutory provision. The improvement notice will give the employer a certain time within which that contravention must be remedied. Work can continue in the meantime. A *prohibition notice*, which means the work must immediately cease, is issued when the inspector considers that the activity involves a risk of serious personal safety or of a severe safety hazard to the employees or the public. Around 15,000 notices are issued each year and the records of such notices are on public view for up to three years, providing a deterrent to safety transgressors. A diagrammatic illustration of this process is shown in Figure 10.2.

Internal authorities

SAFETY OFFICERS AND SAFETY REPRESENTATIVES

The main authorities within an organisation are *safety officers* and *safety representatives*. There is no specific requirement for an organisation to have a safety officer but most industrial sites employing over 200 people usually have a full-time appointment. Smaller organisations may have a part-time employee or make use of consultants. The role of the safety officer is to ensure that the safety requirements imposed by legislation are met by the

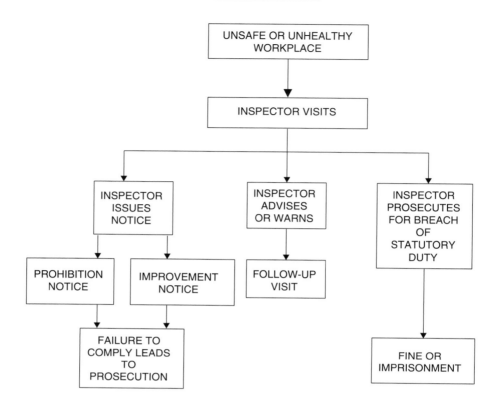

Figure 10.2
External
monitoring
process

organisation. They will set up safe systems of work, carry out risk assessments, investigate accidents and dangerous occurrences, and generally try to ensure that a 'safety culture' operates in the workplace. They are, however, employees of the organisation and their authority is limited by the position and influence they can wield.

Safety representatives are appointed or elected by the employees, either directly or through their trade union. Their rights were set down in HASAWA, and subsequently clarified by the Health and Safety (Consultation with Employees) Regulations 1996 (HSE 1996). They must be recognised by employers, involved in the consultation process through a safety committee and given reasonable paid time off to carry out their duties, together with basic facilities such as the use of a telephone and a filing cabinet. Their duties are, to a large extent, in tandem with the safety officer, with whom they will work closely in practice, in that they investigate accidents, make regular safety inspections, assess risks and bring forward employee complaints and suggestions regarding safety. Their rights extend to visiting other companies to examine their safety systems (see spotlight on the law 10.3).

SPOTLIGHT ON THE LAW 10.3 *SAFETY REPRESENTATIVES*

Healey, a safety representative at Excel, was unhappy with the entry in Excel's accident book relating to an accident that had occurred to a colleague who had been seriously injured when making a delivery to a supermarket. Healey made several visits to that supermarket and made approaches to the supermarket manager. Excel considered that the approaches Healey made to the manager amounted to gross misconduct and he was dismissed.

The tribunal agreed with Excel's version that Healey had gone on a clandestine mission to the supermarket in order to pry into the supermarket's health and safety, and his claim for unfair dismissal was dismissed. It could not be held to be a safety inspection as allowed under the Safety Representatives and Safety Committees Regulations 1977 because the supermarket was not under Excel's control.

Upon appeal, however, the Employment Appeal Tribunal (EAT) found that Healey had the right to 'inspect', 'investigate' and 'examine' in relation to safety issues concerning employees that he represented and a visit to the supermarket to look at the accident book was not an unreasonable part of such investigations. He was found to be unfairly dismissed.

(Source: IDS 1998)

SAFETY COMMITTEES

If two or more safety representatives request the formation of a safety committee, the employer must set one up. Most employers of a reasonable size do so without such a request, seeing it as an important vehicle for joint investigation and improvement. Membership usually consists of the safety representatives, the safety officer, management (in the form of the plant, maintenance or operations managers), the human resources officer and, in larger organisations, the company nurse or occupational health officer. The chair is usually a member of management who is knowledgeable on safety matters, such as the plant manager. Agenda items can include:

■ Reporting and analysis of accidents and dangerous occurrences
■ Necessary revisions to safety policy and procedures
■ Discussion of reports on specific accidents, including contacts with factory inspectors
■ Investigation into safe systems of work, including general aspects such as noise, temperature and use of protective equipment
■ Safety implications of new equipment or layouts
■ Monitoring of safety training
■ Publicity of safety issues.

RISK ASSESSMENT

Risk assessment does not apply only to materials and substances under the COSHH regulations, although these regulations stimulated interest and experience in this process. Under the 1992 Code of Practice for the Management of Health and Safety at Work, it became a legal duty for employers to assess and record health and safety risks and requires the appointment of 'competent persons' to assist in this and other safety tasks.

There are three main stages in the process of assessing and controlling risks:

■ Identifying hazards (the potential causes of harm)
■ Assessing risks (the likelihood of harm occurring and its severity) and prioritising action
■ Designing, implementing and monitoring measures to eliminate or minimise risk.

Hazard identification can be carried out in a number of ways. Observation through, say, a regular safety tour of the plant by the safety officer and safety representatives for the areas will bring to light poor housekeeping such as accumulated rubbish or blocked fire exits, safety equipment not being worn and poor lighting or ventilation. Such hazards have to be considered not only for employees, who may be aware of the dangers, but also for visitors to the site and especially new employees who could be young and be completely unaware of potential dangers.

Longer investigations by trained technicians or by external agencies may be necessary to investigate the hazards of pollution, noise or noxious fumes and their degree of danger or to decide where, if at all, smoking can be allowed on the premises. Long-term projects will be needed to identify hazards in planned changes through new equipment, machinery, materials and layouts. A proper investigation here will involve the suppliers of the equipment, machinery and the materials.

When it comes to *assessing the risks*, it is useful to attempt to identify the severity of the hazard. Fowler (1995) set out a three-part rating scale for risk assessment (see Table 10.2).

Using such a rating scale provides a consistent approach to identifying hazards and also provides help with prioritising safety action. It is not possible to eliminate every conceivable hazard. Where there are budgetary limits, the total hazard rating provides a league table of necessary action where those with the highest points are tackled first.

The final stage is to decide what can be done to *control or eliminate the risks*. Tightening up on housekeeping procedures should make the site cleaner, tidier and, therefore, safer. Supplying better protective equipment will serve to avoid the likelihood of injury to persons exposed to the risk. Replacing hazardous materials with safer alternatives will avoid or reduce the need to monitor and protect employees. Redesigning the production processes or layouts through such improvements as separating the operator from the risk by enclosing the process, using remote-control equipment, improving guarding and increasing extraction systems are all valuable investments in terms of hazard prevention.

Table 10.2 Making risk assessments by rating hazards

	Likelihood of harm	
Certain	It is certain that harm will result whenever exposure to the hazard occurs	4 points
Probable	Harm will probably result in most cases when exposure to the hazard occurs, although there may be exceptions	3 points
Possible	Harm may occur in some cases when exposure to the hazard occurs, although there are likely to be many exceptions	2 points
Slight	Unlikely that harm will occur, except in a very small minority of cases	1 point
	Severity	
Major	Death or major injury, as defined by RIDDOR, is probable	4 points
Serious	Injuries, though not necessarily formally classified as major, are likely to result in absences of more than three days	3 points
Minor	Injuries may cause some absence but probably for not more than three days	2 points
Slight	Any injuries are unlikely to result in time off work	1 point
	Extent	
Very extensive	Likely to affect the whole workforce and/or significant numbers of the public	4 points
Extensive	Likely to affect a whole work group and might affect some members of the public	3 points
Limited	Likely to affect only a small number of either employees or members of the public	2 points
Very limited	Likely to affect only single individuals	1 point

Automating lifting processes will also have a significant effect on the incidences of employees injuring their backs, although forklift trucks and other devices also provide a further source of potential danger that needs to be assessed.

Risk assessment continues to be a matter of balance. The test of 'reasonably practicable' is still used in the context of cost and difficulty balanced against likely danger. It is important, therefore, that organisations have set out policies and procedures that help them to achieve a fair balance and that will highlight actions that they have to take speedily.

WELFARE ISSUES AND POLICIES

It is no coincidence that the words 'health' and 'safety' are so closely linked. Encouraging employees to live and work in a healthy environment is as important as ensuring that the workplace is a safe environment. Recently, as safety provision has improved and the risk of physical injuries to employees has reduced, the emphasis has moved away from simply providing healthy physical working conditions, such as heating, lighting, ventilation, sufficient space per employee and noise levels. There is now a growing onus on employers to take initiatives to attempt to alleviate some of the sources of employee stress, which is estimated to be at the root cause of 60 per cent of all work absence. According to the Health and Safety Executive (HSE 2008), the number of employees experiencing ill-health as a result of work-related stress doubled between 1974 and 2008 from 820 to 1,620 per 100,000 employees.

The initiatives by companies to reduce stress can be *individual*, looking at cases where employees appear to be suffering from occupational stress, or *group*, such as promoting healthy living or introducing an employee assistance programme (EAP).

Occupational stress

The evidence is overwhelming that work-related mental ill-health is a major problem in our society with substantial economic, commercial and human costs. The incidence of work stress has been steadily increasing in the UK since 1992 at a rate of about 0.5–1.0 per cent each year with the increase particularly marked among women workers. Worryingly, during the single year 2009–2010, most measures of work stress saw an absolute increase of 4–6 per cent (Chandola 2010). The National Institute for Health and Clinical Excellence (NICE) estimated that an average firm with 1,000 employees could save £250,000 a year by tackling the causes of work-related stress (NICE 2009).

Evidence from the HSE (2012c) indicates that 13.5 million working days in 2009/10 were lost due to stress, depression and anxiety. This makes stress, depression or anxiety the largest contributor to the overall estimated annual days lost from work-related ill-health in 2009/10. GPs report that approximately one-third of all diagnoses of work-related ill-health are cases of mental ill-health, with an average length of sickness absence per certified case of 26.8 working days. According to HSE (2012c), some occupation groups have particularly high levels of work-related stress. Human health and social work activities reported 2,090 cases per 100,000, education had 1,780 cases per 100,000 people and public administration and defence had 1,810 cases. These groups report high rates of work-related mental illness, along with medical practitioners and those in public sector, security-based occupations such as police officers, prison officers and UK armed forces personnel.

Around 150,000 employees take at least one month off for ailments caused by stress at work. Employees aged between 34 and 44 suffer the most, while the problems worsen the longer they stay in the same job. Stress is the number-one cause of long-term illness for non-manual employees and stress-related absences are frequently long, averaging 21 days (Spurgeon *et al.* 2007).

The causes of occupational stress are numerous. They are associated with perceptions of job insecurity, increase in work intensity, aggressive management styles, lack of effective workplace communication, overt or insidious bullying and harassment, faulty selection for promotion or transfer, and lack of guidance and training. Employees may be exposed to situations that they find uncomfortable, such as continually dealing with customers, excessive computer work, repetitive or fragmented work or having to make regular public presentations. Probably the most common cause, however, is the constant fear of organisational change through restructuring, takeovers, mergers or business process re-engineering. A lack of control over their work, their environment or their career progression can also be stressful (CIPD 2008).

When a work environment containing these cultural aspects is added to personal problems, such as divorce or separation, ill or dying relatives, difficult housing conditions and financial problems, it is not surprising that the employer will be faced with a good proportion of employees with stress-related problems.

Stress is manifested not only in high absence levels, although fatigue, increases in infections, backache and digestive illnesses are common. Irritation, hostility, anxiety and a state of panic can arise in the workplace with knock-on effects on working practices and relationships between employees. The end result may be that the employee is 'burned out', unable to cope with pressures that previously had been regarded as challenging and stimulating. Employees may also turn to palliatives, such as alcohol or drugs.

The CIPD (2003) have summarised these causes of stress into four categories, set out in Table 10.3.

The employer who neglects the problem of occupational stress may face legal action. The first legal breakthrough for an employee was John Walker, a social work manager with Northumberland County Council, who, having had a mental breakdown arising from his occupation, returned to his job but received no positive assistance from his employer to help him to cope successfully. His case against the Council succeeded (he was awarded £175,000) because it was held by the court that his employer was negligent with regard to the 'duty of care'. The judge held that there was no logical reason why the risk of psychiatric damage should be excluded from the scope of the duty of care and the risk of a further breakdown was reasonably foreseeable. Mr Walker had been driven to despair by his employer's failure to provide him with enough resources to satisfy urgent needs for the people in his area and thereby decrease his work-load (*Walker v Northumberland County Council, 1995, IRLR 35/95*).

Successive cases have included a primary school head who won £100,000 after suffering two nervous breakdowns allegedly

Table 10.3 Causes of workplace stress

Organisational problems
- A training need
- A relationship problem
- Workload or pace
- Loss of motivation

Physical problems
- Physical illness
- Design of workstation
- Noise/lighting
- Violent attack at work

Psychological problems
- Anxiety/depression
- Phobias/panic attacks
- Anger management
- Addictive behaviours – alcoholism, gambling

Social problems
- Housing problems
- Relationship difficulties
- Financial problems
- Legal problems – divorce, custody or crime

caused by stress brought on from bullying and harassment, and an out-of-court settlement was reached in 1998 between an NHS Trust and the bereaved spouse of an employee who committed suicide. In a more recent case, Birmingham City Council admitted liability for personal injury caused by stress where they moved a 39-year-old senior draughtsman to the post of a neighbourhood housing officer without sufficient training. The nature of the work was so different and the interpersonal demands so great that she had long periods of ill-health leading to early retirement on medical grounds. She was awarded £67,000.

Greater clarification as to the employer's responsibility in the case of psychiatric injury based on exposure to unacceptable levels of stress was given by the Court of Appeal in 2002 (*Sutherland v Hatton*). The court held that an employer was entitled to assume that an employee was able to withstand the normal pressures of the job and to take what the employee said about her own health at face value. It was only if there were indications that would lead a reasonable employer to realise that there was a problem that a duty to take action would arise. In terms of whether the injury to health was foreseeable, factors that should be taken into account include whether:

- The workload was abnormally heavy
- The work was particularly intellectually or emotionally demanding
- The demands were greater compared with similar employees.

If the only way of making the employee safe was to dismiss them, there would be no breach of duty by letting the employee continue if they were willing to do so (IRS 2002). The law was further developed in *Daw v Intel Corporation (2007 EWCA Civ 70)*. Daw complained on a number of occasions about her workload and had made use of the organisation's counselling service. Eventually, she had a breakdown. Her claim for damages was successful and she received £134,000, despite the company's provision of counselling.

All of these cases show that employers need to consider carefully the way that the work demands affect their employees and ensure that they investigate each case, taking appropriate action to ameliorate potentially health-damaging situations. Employers now have a legal obligation to conduct a risk assessment for work-related stress and take action to remedy any risks identified in the same way as for physical risks (Willmott 2009). A further consideration is the level of employees' expectations on welfare provision. It is a sure sign of a sympathetic and caring employer who will make special provision for the personal and individual needs of employees. Moreover, a study by Business in the Community and Ipsos MORI (Stevens 2010) found that firms that actively promoted staff well-being and workplace health policies recorded a 10 per cent boost in their financial performance.

Management initiatives regarding stress

The CIPD (2008) recommend three levels of intervention:

- *Primary intervention.* This involves investigations regarding absence (long and short term) arising from stress and carrying out organisational research to gain employee views on processes and systems that may cause stress. This will include employee experience of areas such as bullying or heavy workloads.
- *Secondary intervention.* Arising from the results of surveys, management may run courses for managers in recognising stress and handling it effectively. Courses can also be run for employees in dealing with stress so they are not harmed. An employee assistance programme can also be set up (see later). Action can be taken at a corporate level to stamp out bullying and harassment.
- *Tertiary intervention.* This involves dealing with the impact of stress at a micro level. It includes helping individuals who are suffering from stress (changing workload, changing jobs, changing hours) and rehabilitation processes, including counselling.

Employee assistance programmes (EAPs)

EAPs were first introduced in the US in the early part of the century, mainly to combat the problem of alcoholism among employees. They have been extended substantially in recent years to deal with all aspects of health in the workplace. Usage rates by employees are in the region of 4–8 per cent and many are open to their relatives.

The types of services provided include:

- A confidential telephone help line for personal emergencies.
- Workshops to help employees who have to cope with elderly relatives, marital breakdowns or financial pressures.
- Assistance in dealing with a work-related traumatic event, such as a major fire or an armed robbery.
- Confidential referrals to specialists dealing with drugs, HIV or alcohol problems.

Such services can be offered by in-house specialists in the occupational health department, but it is much more common for the services to be outsourced. This ensures confidentiality and the opportunity to have contact with a wider set of expertise. Details of initiatives at ScottishPower and Enterprise Rent-A-Car are shown in case studies 10.2 and 10.3.

Other health initiatives can take the form of healthy food in the company canteens, assistance with membership fees for health clubs and the encouragement of outdoor exercise within a sporting and leisure club context.

CASE STUDY 10.2 DEALING WITH STRESS AT SCOTTISHPOWER

ScottishPower is one of the UK's top customer service suppliers of gas and electricity with around 5.2 million customers, employing around 9,000 staff. The company became concerned at the levels of stress in the organisation in the early 2000s, which was showing itself in increased absence levels.

The first stage was to administer an online stress survey in successive waves for each department to approximately 5,000 staff using the HSE Indicator. Absence data for each department including stress-related absence were analysed and compared with results from the staff opinion survey. Focus groups were set up to shed light on the survey results to feed into the action plan. During the roll-out programme, the director of each department provided support and commitment by being part of the steering group.

Action plans

Stress management interventions have been put in place at individual and organisational level. Additional results included the creation of better communication channels throughout the business; introduction of 360-degree feedback at all levels; more participation/visibility of senior managers at team briefs; and a wider use of occupational health services.

What worked well?

Looking back, the focus groups were a real chance for people to have an input to the business. The participation of employees and safety representatives in the steering groups was also important. And the feedback to staff on each stage of the process contributed to the worker's engagement.

'The stress project was a great initiative. It was good to see the company invest so much resources into such a valuable programme which can only improve the working lives and health of everyone at ScottishPower.'

Willie Docherty, health and safety adviser

Main challenges

During the integration of ScottishPower to the Iberdrola Group in 2007, the greatest difficulty voiced by staff in the focus group was for management to handle communication and change as employees expressed fear of redundancies. Having so many different sites and field-based staff was quite challenging as the company wanted to include all in the process.

'Embarking on such a big project was a daunting task at first. However due to the willingness and participation of so many people across the business we achieved well beyond our expectations. There were some challenges but these were quickly turned into opportunities for improvement in the future.'

> *Jennifer Hamilton, health and safety manager*

Benefits

- ScottishPower recognises that improvements will be seen in the longer term, but, since the start of implementing the management standards, there has been an 11 per cent decrease in sickness absence overall.
- Health and safety managers and health professionals involved during the three-year implementation of the approach are now fully trained to continue the work without the help of an external provider.
- A pragmatic approach has been developed on how to tackle work-related stress not only at individual but also at an organisational level to address causes of stress at source (e.g. workload, lack of control over work, etc.).
- Awareness of the sources of stress and their management has been raised within the whole organisation.
- Line managers have been made aware of the managerial behaviours (which is a recent HSE research area) that can prevent stress from occurring within their team.

(Source: HSE 2011b)

CHALLENGES TO MANAGEMENT AND THE ROLE OF HUMAN RESOURCES

In the introduction to this chapter, the huge overall costs involved to management were identified. The costs of insurance will vary depending both on the sector in which the organisation works and on how successful the organisation has been in managing the function so that accidents and work-related absence are minimised. This becomes the main challenge to management and the role of human resources is to facilitate the best possible policy and practice which helps management meet the challenge.

In the majority of organisations where separate human resources departments exist, they either have responsibility for health, safety and welfare issues in that organisation or they play a major part in those activities. The main activities consist of:

- Formulating policy statements and procedures, including the business and ethical cases for implementing the highest standards of health, safety and employee well-being.

- Monitoring safety policy and procedures.
- Advising management and employees on safety legislation.
- Designing, providing and recording health and safety training.
- Liaising with the safety inspectorate and occupational health authorities.
- Helping create a healthy working environment.

These are the activities, which will be dealt with in turn. However, there is a larger job and that is to achieve an *effective health and safety culture* in the organisation. An effective safety culture does not necessarily follow from having in place a set of detailed and costly manuals catering for every contingency, produced by knowledgeable safety engineers. What matters is the action practice followed on the ground. Although difficult to pin down, the culture can be demonstrated by the behaviour of management, employees and their representatives. An indication of this culture

CASE STUDY

CASE STUDY 10.3 INITIATIVES TO LESSEN STRESS AT ENTERPRISE RENT-A-CAR

Enterprise has a relatively young workforce as it recruits a large number of staff straight from full-time education. It is very keen to promote a supportive culture at work, helping staff through their early career, which can often be stressful. The initiatives it has introduced have included the following:

- Employee assistance programme (EAP), including access to face-to-face counselling.
- A section on the website on personal issues, such as finance, sickness and relationships.
- Training for line managers in stress management with encouragement to utilise the EAP where appropriate.
- E-newsletters including reminders on how to reduce stress – eating, exercise, sleep, health and well-being.
- Lunch and Learn events covering areas such as pensions, career development, well-being and returning to work after maternity leave. These are addressed and attended by all levels of the business, including senior management.
- Trying to reduce the stigma of stress by openly discussing it in a number of media.

The organisation has recognised that engaged employees can be more liable to stress because their character traits can include being reliable and diligent, having a strong conscience and sense of responsibility and perfectionist tendencies. It is vital, therefore, for the organisation to make a concerted effort to keep such employees on track and recognise where they may be facing unwanted stressful conditions.

(Source: IDS 2011)

operating can be seen by looking at how the parties behave in an *advanced safety culture*.

Management carry out their safety activities not, primarily, because the law directs them to do so but because it is both good business practice and because it is ethically sound. Each accident or injury is seen as regrettable and a source of information which leads to its prevention in the future, and where disciplinary procedures are used as a last resort.

Employees follow their safety instructions not just in terms of the way they carry out the work and the way they wear the required safety protective equipment; they also help to identify safety hazards, they encourage good housekeeping among themselves without being reminded and they co-operate with changing work practices where this leads to better safety provision.

Employee representatives regard their task not as an opportunity to spend time away from the job or to score points against management but as an important part of the joint determination process, a partnership to help all parties gain – fewer accidents, less cost, less disruption.

To achieve such a culture, human resources departments need to start by convincing management of the business and ethical cases.

ACTIVITY 10.1

Debate the main features of an argument to improve health and safety based on the business and ethical case.

Response to activity 10.1

You would probably have included some of the following items:

■   The business case rests essentially on the very high costs associated with poor health and safety. Accidents are expensive (a recent report by the HSE estimated that an average work-related vehicle accident is likely to cost an employer £16,000 on top of any repair costs), they cause considerable lost time by all parties – those injured, the management team in handling the aftermath and the loss of productivity by the rest of the work team.

■   A reputation as an unsafe work site can raise the cost of recruitment and can cause a workforce to become demotivated, leading to falling productivity and lower levels of engagement.

- If bad publicity occurs, it can lead to customers choosing to go elsewhere.
- Working in a poor safety environment leads to high levels of employee and manager anxiety and stress levels, which, in turn, lead to greater levels of absence and illness.
- There are additional costs that can arise, such as higher insurance, fines arising from successful prosecutions and the costs of an extended investigation.
- The ethical case stems from the need to treat employees fairly and to operate a true 'duty of care'. It is one of the saddest jobs of a human resource professional to have to visit the spouse (or widow/er) of an employee recently killed or seriously injured in the workplace and to see the massive grief that this has caused.
- Management have to take ultimate responsibility for any such tragedy, even if the cause is a mixture of employee culpability and sheer bad luck, and there is therefore a strong argument to divert resources to improve health and safety to as high a level as possible.

Formulating policies and procedures

This activity is more than a formality required by law. It is essential that new employees understand how safety works within a new organisation and the policies and procedures will set out how the safety responsibilities are structured and the requirements from each employee. Specific references to areas (such as responsibility for checking lifting gear, or guards) should be clearly spelled out. The document should give a statement of management intent as to how safety issues will be treated in the workplace. Detailed procedures should be set out for dealing with emergencies, safety training, information arising from the investigations under COSHH, and for all departments where hazards have been identified. Human resources should ensure that such documents are logical, readable and have been circulated correctly.

An example of a safety statement (which was published on notice boards around the hospital site) taken from a hospital policy document is given in case study 10.4.

Monitoring policies and procedures

At regular intervals, all procedures need examining to see if they need updating to take account of new processes, materials and layouts. By attending management and safety meetings, human resources can ensure such necessary revisions can be identified and put into place.

Advising management and employees on safety legislation

New regulations continue to emerge, especially from Europe, with different levels of importance and different implementation dates. By following regular bulletins, such as that provided by Croner, it is possible to provide an up-to-the-minute service to all

CASE STUDY 10.4 HEALTH AND SAFETY STATEMENT AT RISING HILL HOSPITAL*

1   The hospital considers that the health and safety of its staff is of the greatest importance. It is necessary for management and staff to work together to reduce personal injuries and hazards to the health of staff and others to a minimum. For this reason, the hospital aims to achieve and maintain high standards of health and safety for its staff and members of the public who use its premises or equipment.

2   The hospital will fully comply with the current health and safety legislation and expects the full support of its staff in achieving this aim.

3   To ensure this happens, the hospital will:

■   Observe in full the legislation and the hospital requirements relating to the health and safety of staff at work.

■   Ensure, as far as is possible, legislation is observed by all hospital staff and ensure adequate education and training.

■   Formulate and maintain health and safety plans by directorate that clearly set out the measures to be taken to safeguard staff and others affected by the hospital activities.

■   Produce, update and maintain for staff access, departmental health and safety policies, procedures and assessments.

■   Continually identify and eliminate or control hazards that present a risk to staff and other persons and possible damage to and loss of plant, equipment, property or service to clients.

■   Consider health and safety when planning new development, systems of work and when purchasing new equipment.

■   Keep and maintain accurate records of accidents, incidents, injuries and known exposure to health risks at work.

■   Take all practical steps to ensure adherence to this policy by all staff and other persons undertaking work on behalf of the hospital or who are on the premises.

4   Further information and details are included in the full health and safety policy document.

J. Caring, Chief Executive

*This is not the name of the actual hospital

employees, including top management, as to what actions are necessary and how these can be carried out.

Designing, providing and recording health and safety training

Systematic training is essential if procedures are to operate properly. It should start with induction training to ensure that employees who are involved in any hazardous operation have instruction in key areas before they set foot on the work site. Safety instruction should be incorporated into any new processes or where new materials are introduced on to the site. New safety representatives have the right for time off for training and this should be encouraged by the organisation so they can operate efficiently.

Liaising with the safety inspectorate

Building a relationship with the enforcing authorities is essential. Making use of their advice and extensive knowledge can be valuable, especially where new processes or production lines are being planned. A list of necessary actions arising from a late visit by the factory inspector could cause an expensive delay to a new production facility.

Helping create a healthy working environment

All the research indicates that a healthy workforce will be a successful one and a higher-performing one, so being proactive in introducing and encouraging initiatives to support health programmes can make a substantial difference to organisational performance, as shown in case studies 10.5 and 10.6.

CASE STUDY

CASE STUDY 10.5 WELL-BEING PILOT AT LEGAL & GENERAL

A well-being pilot at Legal & General that focused on stress and mental health reduced sickness absence by 15 per cent. The insurance giant staged the pilot across two of its sites – Cardiff and Hove – between November 2010 and April 2011, testing three initiatives. These were training for line managers on handling cases of stress; an online programme for staff to monitor their health and raise awareness of pressure points; and additional preventative support for those suffering from low emotional well-being.

The initiatives registered a 15 per cent improvement in absence rates compared with the same period in 2009/10 – resulting in an absence ratio of 4 per cent of days lost – saving the company an estimated £68,000 for the pilot group alone. Legal & General now intend to roll out the programme across its whole workforce.

Nicky Richards, HR consultant for Legal & General, said, 'Our own internal well-being pilot has demonstrated that early intervention and well-being programmes can have a significant impact on absence rates in businesses. Our experiences highlight the importance of early intervention before people become unwell and the appropriate support in place to help people at work when they are ill.'

Legal & General's figures show that 29 per cent of its absence is linked to mental health, the highest individual cause ahead of colds and flu (17 per cent) and musculoskeletal problems (6 per cent).

The line manager training was provided by Stand to Reason, a service-user-led organisation that aims to raise the profile and achieve equality for sufferers from mental ill-health. Topics covered included how to spot the signs of mental health problems, clarification of the manager's role and responsibilities, and an outline of the information and support available.

Meanwhile, the online health programme consisted of a 15–20-minute questionnaire, completed in work time, which provided confidential information about lifestyle and medical risks for the individual. The provider for this was GetFit Wellness.

Steve Russell, director at GetFit Wellness, said, 'Health Manager, our online health and well-being programme, provided Legal & General with tangible insight into the health needs and opportunities of the pilot group, enabling L&G to target areas of greatest need. In addition to improved workplace productivity, we saw a significant decrease in health-related absence during the pilot period, further supporting the case that well-managed ill-health prevention programmes make good business sense.'

(Source: *People Management* 2011b)

CASE STUDY 10.6 IMPROVING EMPLOYEE HEALTH AT KIMBERLY-CLARK

Kimberly-Clark, which makes products such as Kleenex and Huggies nappies, has made cost savings of £500,000 per annum and reduced long-term staff absence from 6.8 to 0.5 per cent after launching schemes in 2002 aimed at improving the health of its 174 UK staff. Under the programme, the company introduced work–life balance coaching sessions, massages for desk workers and sleep management workshops to improve employees' sleep quality. It also provided free fruit twice a week to promote healthy eating. Evidence that the scheme was getting immediate results was that, after six months, only 19 per cent admitted they suffered sleep problems, which was down from 68 per cent before the scheme started.

(Source: Watkins 2003)

SHOP STEWARDS AND SAFETY

At one of the six-monthly meetings of human resources staff in the organisation, June, who was one of Sarah's opposite numbers at another site in the south of England, explained the severe difficulties they were having with two of their shop stewards who were also safety representatives. They took a great deal of time away from the work-place dealing with what were regarded as trivial safety issues and, when challenged, pointed out their legislative rights for time off with pay. Because they were away so much, they had been moved to work that was not so essential, which only seemed to cause them to have even more time off. She recalled four specific episodes that had taken place over the last month:

- The stewards had advised their members to boycott a new piece of machinery because they were unhappy about the guarding arrangements. It was only after a visit by the factory inspector that the boycott had been lifted.
- One of the stewards had been away from his place of work for over an hour and was found in another department talking to one of his members about safety shoes. Supervisors from both departments were angry at the time that seemed to have been wasted in this case.
- A request had been made by one of the stewards to attend a union course on abrasive wheel regulations when, only the previous year, they had attended the same type of course run by the company.
- The men insisted on making a safety inspection of the site every month, even though it was pointed out to them that their rights extended only to an inspection every three months.

June knew that Sarah had become quite experienced in safety issues and asked her if she could provide some informal consulting. Sarah agreed to make a two-day visit the next month and prepared a list of questions for June to answer before she came. This included details of the safety record of the site, the safety organisation, the safety systems in place and the state of play on audits under COSHH and Display Screen Regulations.

This information arrived just before Sarah was due to visit and it made worrying reading. The accident record was poor, with the number of reportable accidents far in excess of Sarah's factory; two prosecutions had taken place over the previous five years, arising out of incidents where three serious injuries had occurred; details of the safety responsibilities were far from clear and the state of play on COSHH and Display Screens were not included.

Sarah realised that the situation may not be quite as straightforward as June indicated and knew she would have to prepare well for the visit to be able to provide the help required.

KEY CHAPTER SUMMARY POINTS

- The Health and Safety at Work Act and subsequent legislation has placed a responsibility and duty of care on employers to provide a safe place of work and on employees and sub-contractors to co-operate with all measures which reinforce this requirement.
- Important features of these duties include carrying out risk assessments, reporting accidents and dangerous occurrences and appropriate training.
- The enforcement process is shared between local authority enforcement officers and health and safety inspectors. They are able to issue improvement notices and prohibition notices. Within the organisation, employees can elect safety representatives who have rights and responsibilities supported by legislation.
- Occupational stress is increasingly being recognised as an illness and organisations are beginning to pay greater attention to their responsibilities in this area. Some are starting employee assistance programmes.
- Human resources have an important role in formulating policy, encouraging a safety culture, advising on legislation, designing training and communication, and monitoring accidents and dangerous occurrences.

STUDENT ACTIVITIES

1 (a) In respect of the Meteor case study, what additional information will Sarah need to enable her to make a balanced judgement on the situation? (b) A meeting has been fixed between Sarah, June and the shop stewards. Role-play this meeting and subsequently discuss what Sarah's next move will be.

2 Carry out a risk assessment exercise for an activity that you take part in. It might be a local amateur football or netball team, drama event or similar.

3 Look up the references on stress in the workplace and summarise the actions that human resources need to carry out in this area.

4 Health and safety legislation shows no sign of abating. Debate whether you consider that excessive legislation merely creates confusion and bureaucracy and makes it more difficult for businesses to be run efficiently.

REFERENCES

Chandola, T. (2010) *Stress at Work*. British Academy, October.
CIPD (2003) Stress Factsheet. CIPD.

— (2004) *Calling Time on Working Time.* CIPD.

— (2008) *Building the Business Case for Managing Stress.* CIPD.

Corbridge, M. and Pilbeam, S. (1998) *Employee Resourcing.* Financial Times Management.

Daily Telegraph (2011) First Conviction under Corporate Manslaughter Legislation, 17 February, 23.

Fowler, A. (1995) How to Make the Workplace Safer. *People Management,* 26 January, 38–39.

Health and Safety (1999) Dead Hand Ex-miners Set for Biggest Compensation Package. March, 8.

Health and Safety Practitioner (2004a) Farm Contractor Jailed for Manslaughter. February, 8.

— (2004b) 'Recipe for Disaster' Costs Firm £132,000. April, 8.

Higginbottom, K. (2008) Do or Die: Net Closes on Negligent Employers. *People Management,* 3 April, 16.

HSE (1988) *COSHH: A Brief Guide for Employers – The Requirements of the Control of Substances Hazardous to Health (COSHH) Regulations.* HMSO.

— (1996) *Good Health is Good Business.* Health and Safety Executive.

— (2008) *Tackling Work-related Stress: A Manager's Guide to Improving and Maintaining Employee Health and Well-Being.* Health and Safety Executive.

— (2011a) *Annual Report.* Health and Safety Executive.

— (2011b) Case Studies in Stress Reduction. Health and Safety Executive, accessed at www.hse.gov.uk/stress/casestudies.

— (2012a) *Costs to Britain of Workplace Injuries and Work-related Ill-health 2010/11.* Health and Safety Executive, accessed at http://www.hse.gov.uk/statistics/pdf/cost-to-britain.pdf.

— (2012b) *Steel Company Fined £500,000 After Worker Died from Fall into Liquid Waste.* Health and Safety Executive. November, accessed at www.hse.gov.uk/press/2012/rnn-w-tatasteel.htm.

— (2012c) *Stress and Psychological Disorders.* Health and Safety Executive.

IDS (1994) *IDS Brief 511,* February, 17.

— (1998) Duties of a Health and Safety Practitioner. *Brief 622,* October, 5–6.

— (2011) Managing Stress. *HR Study 945,* July, 30–34.

IRS (2002) Court of Appeal Guidelines for Stress at Work Cases. *Employment Law Review 748,* 25 March.

NICE (2009) *Promoting Well-Being at Work.* National Institute for Health and Clinical Excellence. November.

People Management (1996) 8 February, 9.

— (2011a) Health and Well-Being. October, 12.

— (2011b) Wellbeing Training Reduces Legal & General Sickness Absence. 15 September, accessed at www.bit.ly/wellbeingpilot.

Spurgeon, P., Mazelan, P., Barwell, F. and Flanaghan, H. (2007) *New Directions in Managing Employee Absence.* CIPD.

Stevens, M. (2010) Well-being Schemes Boost the Bottom Line. *People Management,* 20 May, 9.

Taylor, P., Baldry, C., Bain, P. and Ellis, V. (2003) 'A Unique Working Environment': Health, Sickness and Absence Management in UK Call Centres. *Work, Employment and Society,* 17(3): 435–456.

Trevelyan, G. (1942) *Illustrated English Social History.* Vol 4. Longmans, Green.

Watkins, J. (2003) Wellness Beats Output Slump. *People Management,* 18 December, 12.

Whitfield, M. (1995) Negligent Employers Face Charges of Manslaughter. *People Management,* 10 August, 7–8.

Willmott, B. (2009) Tension Seeking Behaviour. *People Management,* 12 February, 22–25.

ADDITIONAL FEATURES

 Please visit the companion website at: www.routledge.com/cw/stredwick where you will find additional case studies and reading material together with short self-tests and other resources for both students and lecturers.

11 AN INTERNATIONAL PERSPECTIVE

CHAPTER OBJECTIVES

When you have completed this chapter, you should be able to understand and explain:

- The nature and importance of the global marketplace.

- The models used to analyse different national cultures.

- How the cultural differences are reflected in varying approaches to human resources.

- The role of human resources in providing services to support internationalisation.

- The debate over convergence and divergence in human resource applications internationally.

- The nature of the issues associated with expatriate employment.

INTRODUCTION

One of the major features of the late twentieth-century and early twenty-first-century economic and social environment has been the growing spread of the global marketplace where the international system, aided by the amazing speed and development of information technology and communications (ICT), allows 24-hour trading around the globe. Few organisations are now exempt from the power and influence of the competitive marketplace or can afford to ignore it. This has been true from around 1900 in manufactured goods, although the post-war re-emergence of the fallen axis powers (Germany and Japan) as major international industrial powers has caused the remaining developed countries, especially the USA, to make substantial improvements to their operating practices in response to the challenge of high-quality goods, made efficiently at competitive prices. Since the early 1990s, the West has been faced by a huge expansion in low-cost output from China where it has proved impossible to compete on price for low-value goods.

Manufacturing is collaborative as never before. The existence of Airbus as a major airframe competitor to the dominant Boeing is only due to the co-operation between four European companies, supported by their governments and a host of smaller suppliers. Books published in England are now routinely typeset in India and printed in Italy. It is said that Volvos have more British components than any other nationality, while Rolls-Royce motors is owned by a German company.

In the last 20 years, the provision of services has become equally international. UK electricity and water companies are owned and managed by French, German and American companies. The Dubai metro is being run by Serco, a UK company. In finance and banking, in communications, in music, art and architecture, there is now a truly global marketplace. With the arrival of 'offshoring', due to the developments in ICT, services can often be carried out in foreign countries where labour costs are far less, such as call centres in India. Customers have a wider choice than ever before. As countries and their inhabitants become richer, they spend a greater proportion of their wealth on services and, at the same time, on goods and services from abroad. Countries that have attempted to subvert open trading have suffered accordingly. The communist bloc found it impossible to contain the aspirations of their inhabitants once *glasnost* became more widespread, and their system collapsed almost overnight at the end of the 1980s. The Japanese have suffered since the early 1990s through their failure to open up their markets, especially in the service sector and by closing all doors to labour that would like to move into their country. Even in Europe, there are certain countries that have failed to allow the warm blast of competition into their public areas and have had to put up with a poorer, more expensive service until fairly recently. French airline services and telecommunication systems are examples here.

In the UK, the average company in the FTSE 100 (the top 100 UK companies quoted on the Stock Exchange) earn at least half of their revenues abroad and the proportion is growing. This figure rises to over 90 per cent in the mining, pharmaceutical and oil sectors. Joint enterprises and alliances are now quite frequent occurrences in order to build the bridge between local domestic capability and relevant business opportunity identification.

There are inevitable human resource implications to globalisation and this chapter will deal with identifying and analysing some of the issues involved. It is people who make and execute decisions, people who innovate, people who operate across boundaries of geography, structure and culture, and this chapter will examine some of the most important issues where people are involved. It will commence with a summary of the identification of national cultures, using the research carried out by Hofstede in the 1960s and 1970s, with a debate over its continuing validity. A second set of national cultural characteristics and leadership style, under the GLOBE research, will then be examined. Using both these areas of research, consideration will be given to the degree to which national cultures (including the national formats of human resource activities) are converging or diverging. Then follows some practical examples of differing human resource practices applying in a selection of countries around the globe. Finally, the issues involved in expatriate employment in multinational companies (MNCs) are discussed, together with a consideration of the degree of international regulation that is appropriate.

NATIONAL CULTURE – HOFSTEDE'S STUDIES

When considering the nature of human resource practices internationally, one of the biggest questions is whether they should be adapted to reflect any specific national culture. In particular, if you were head of human resources in a large MNC, would you set out policies and practices that were completely consistent across the world or would you make local adaptions to better reflect the national character and culture of that country?

Before you could answer this question, you would need to know if national cultures actually varied across the globe. IBM, the first ICT multinational company, wanted answers to this question and, starting in 1968, commissioned an ambitious young Dutch social scientist, Geert Hofstede, to carry out extensive and, as it proved, highly influential research. Using its numerous international branches and subsidiaries as his sample, he and his team surveyed over 116,000 employees in 50 different occupations in 66 countries with a questionnaire of approximately 150 questions about attitudes and values. The responses from these questionnaires were used to devise four indices that Hofstede believed were integral to the illustration of differences in national culture (Hofstede 1980). The four resulting indices were as follows:

Power distance index (PDI)

This index (see Table 11.1) measures the extent to which people in a country tend to accept the fact that power is distributed unevenly. For instance, people in a country scoring highly on the PDI might feel less inclined to question the decisions of a

Table 11.1 Power distance index

High PDI	Low PDI	Selected others
Philippines (94)	Austria (11)	UK (35)
Mexico (81)	Israel (13)	USA (35)
India (77)	Denmark (18)	Germany (35)
Singapore (74)	New Zealand (22)	France (68)

manager. Countries in South-East Asia tend to score high, whereas European countries tend to have lower scores.

Uncertainty avoidance index (UAI)

This index (see Table 11.2) measures the extent to which people tend to be challenged by ambiguity. For example, people might be less inclined to take risks or they might develop beliefs and institutions that help counter these challenges, for example, uniformity and formalised processes and structures in the workplace. The countries with the highest scores tend to be on mainland Europe. Interestingly, France has a high score and is renowned for its rigid bureaucratic structures and formalised work processes. Singapore has by far the lowest score followed at some distance by a clutch of northern European states.

Individualism index (IDV)

This index (see Table 11.3) measures the extent to which people in a particular country are more inclined to take care of themselves and their immediate families only. The opposite is 'collectivism', where people might have more pronounced mutual obligations with and to the wider community. Three 'Anglo-Saxon' societies top the table; the lowest positions tend to be held by South American countries where a more collectivist ethos prevails.

Table 11.2 Uncertainty avoidance index

High UAI	Low UAI	Selected others
Greece (112)	Singapore (8)	USA (46)
Portugal (104)	Denmark (23)	Germany (65)
Belgium (94)	Sweden (29)	Australia (51)
France (92)	UK (35)	Italy (75)

Table 11.3 Individuality index

High IDV	Low IDV	Selected others
USA (91)	Venezuela (12)	France (71)
Australia (90)	Colombia (13)	Italy (76)
UK (89)	Pakistan (13)	India (48)
Netherlands (80)	Taiwan (17)	Singapore (20)

Masculinity index (MAS)

This index (see Table 11.4) is the most controversial of the four and considers the dichotomy between 'masculine' and 'feminine' values. Hofstede maintains that masculine values tend to be more assertive, whereas feminine values are nurturing and caring. In addition, people in countries scoring highly on this index would be more prone to overt materialistic displays of wealth and status. Japan ranks the highest, whereas the lowest positions are held by Scandinavian countries.

GLOBE STUDY – CULTURE AND LEADERSHIP EFFECTIVENESS

A second major study of varying international cultures was carried out from the 1990s onwards by House *et al.* (2004), based on results from interviews and questionnaires from 17,300 middle managers from 951 organisations in the food processing, financial services and telecommunication industries. Using 9 cultural dimensions (see Table 11.5), a number of which are similar to those used by Hofstede, the GLOBE study placed 60 countries into 10 clusters where there was a cultural similarity, which can be seen to be mostly geographical clusters.

Further analysis allowed the researchers to identify the position of these clusters in a leadership grid consisting of six leadership styles (see Table 11.6) with the placement of each societal cluster within a leadership style indicating the relative importance of that style

Table 11.4 Masculinity index

High MAS	Low MAS	Selected others
Japan (95)	Sweden (5)	UK (66)
Austria (79)	Norway (8)	USA (62)
Switzerland (70)	Netherlands (14)	France (43)
Mexico (69)	Denmark (16)	Australia (61)

Table 11.5 GLOBE cultural dimensions and country clusters

Cultural dimensions	Country clusters identified
■ Power distance ■ Uncertainty avoidance ■ Humane orientation (encouraging fairness, altruism and kindness to others) ■ Institutional collectivism (encouraging and rewarding collective distribution of resources and collective action) ■ In-group collectivism (extent to which individuals express pride and loyalty to their organisation) ■ Assertiveness ■ Gender egalitarianism ■ Future orientation ■ Performance orientation	■ Anglo – England, Canada, USA, Australia, Ireland, South Africa, New Zealand ■ Germanic – Germany, Austria, Holland, Switzerland ■ Nordic – Denmark, Finland, Sweden ■ Latin European – France, Spain, Portugal, Italy, Israel ■ Eastern European – Greece, Hungary, Albania, Slovenia, Poland, Russia, Georgia, Kazakhstan ■ Middle Eastern – Turkey, Kuwait, Egypt, Morocco, Qatar ■ Confucian – Singapore, Hong Kong, Taiwan, China, South Korea, Japan ■ South-East Asian – Philippines, Indonesia, Malaysia, India, Thailand, Iran ■ Latin American – 10 countries ■ African – Nigeria, Zambia, Namibia, Zimbabwe

Source: Adapted from House *et al.* (2004) *Culture, Leadership, and Organizations: The GLOBE Study of 62 Societies.* Sage.

Table 11.6 GLOBE societal clusters and leader styles

Performance oriented	Team oriented	Participative	Humane	Autonomous	Self or group protective*
HIGH Anglo Germanic Nordic SE Asian L. European L. American	All clusters	Germanic Anglo Nordic	SE Asian Anglo African Confucian	All clusters	Middle Eastern Confucian SE Asian L. American E. European
MEDIUM Confucian African E. European		L. European L. American African	Germanic M. Eastern L. American E. European		African L. European
LOW M. Eastern		E. European SE Asian Confucian M. Eastern	L. European Nordic		Anglo Germanic Nordic

*This style emphasises procedural, status-conscious and face-saving behaviours and focuses on the safety and security of the individual and the group.

Source: Adapted from House *et al.* (2004) *Culture, Leadership, and Organizations: The GLOBE Study of 62 Societies.* Sage.

compared with other styles for that cluster. For example, the performance-oriented leader style is the highest ranked for the Anglo cluster whereas the self or group protective cluster is the lowest.

These two long-term research projects were carried out over differing time periods, had differing sample groups and measured different aspects of cultural variations. There were, however, many areas of complementary findings. The Anglo grouping (England, USA, Australia), for example, scored highly in the individuality index (Hofstede) and also performance-oriented ratings (GLOBE). This identifies the grouping as strong on decisiveness and innovation (GLOBE) and with more emphasis on looking after themselves and their immediate families (Hofstede). On the other hand, the Confucian group (China, Taiwan, Japan) pays less attention to performance-oriented values (GLOBE) and scores much lower in individuality (Hofstede), coming close to the top of the team-oriented leadership style (GLOBE). The GLOBE study finds substantial differences in leadership styles with high levels of participation in the Anglo, Germanic and Nordic clusters but surprisingly low levels in Confucian, East European and Middle Eastern clusters.

Relevance of Hofstede and GLOBE research

Why is this analysis important in practice? Although the findings from both research projects are generalisations on a nation's cultural values, they need to be taken into account when human resource practices are established in foreign subsidiaries. For example, Japanese culture regards long-term planning as vital, so trusting relationships need to be built up with employees with the expectations that relationships will last for a long time – the 'job for life' mentality. The establishment and development of these long-term relationships with Japanese employees have, traditionally, been surrounded by protocol and ceremony. According to Perkins (1999), British or American managers may feel uncomfortable having to sit through many hours of 'getting to know you' formalities with no mention of the practical business issues to be discussed. However, once that relationship is established, it may become more important than the detailed contractual elements, which may be quite vague and may include a 'sincere negotiation clause'. Although this may appear to be participative in an employer–employee relationship, the leadership style in these cultures is far less participative, with managers toeing the line and not prepared to question overall decisions by senior management. The context of what is said, and particularly who says it, may be more important than what is actually said. There is a noticeable reluctance to enter into litigation, which contrasts highly with the Anglo-American culture.

So the lesson here is that an attempt to transport the American policy of short-term, contractually based human resource relationships may well struggle in the traditional Japanese context. In Singapore, however, there is a greater willingness to take risks, so employees are prepared for fast-moving decisions, a broad job description and forms of payment for performance, as long as it is carried out through a group orientation.

Limitations and cross-cultural analysis – Hofstede and GLOBE

The first point to note about Hofstede's research was that China was excluded from the sample, as the research was mostly carried out in the period prior to the opening up of markets with the West in the early 1990s.

Secondly, the findings have been subject to a considerable degree of criticism on a number of grounds that the research is based on quantitative data derived from an attitudinal questionnaire, which is not necessarily the best way of studying something as abstract as culture (Tayeb 1999). In addition, the sample is rather narrow – are IBM employees typical of the entire working population of any country? As Tayeb explains:

> Given the complexity and dynamism of culture, it is arguable that Hofstede's findings reflect the values and attitudes of a large sample of employees in relation to their specific work environment at the time the study was conducted: nothing more, nothing less.

> (1999: 323)

The study takes little account of regional differences that can occur within a country (e.g. England, Scotland, Wales and Northern Ireland in the UK). However, perhaps one of the most profound criticisms of the study is that, as Hofstede concedes himself, the indices are derived from Western value sets and any attempt to measure countries in Asia, South America, Africa, etc. may distort the picture. This trait is known as *ethnocentrism* (Tayeb 1999), which is an assumption that the values into which you have been socialised are veritable and superior to those held by those in other countries.

More critical was the research by Gerhart and Fang (2005), which posited that the majority of the differences in national culture identified by Hofstede were due to organisational differences with far less due to the respondents' values. In other words, the way the business was structured and organised explained the different approaches, rather than the innate culture.

In general, despite the engaging picture it paints of the differences between countries, cross-cultural analysis should be viewed with certain caveats in mind. Although behavioural differences between countries are undoubtedly evident, it is far from certain whether culture matters as much as some scholars maintain. However, there are strong forces preventing the homogenisation of national systems and perhaps some explanations for this can be found in the behavioural attributes of people in the workplace in each national context.

The GLOBE research, though praised for its broader sampling methods, has been criticised for its lack of originality (for example, the utilisation of Hofstede's cultural dimensions with only minor changes), the rather mundane societal clusters based almost solely on geography (Hoppe 2007) and the mix of organisational phenomena (performance-oriented style) and the true national cultural values (Yeganeh and Su 2009).

FOCUS ON RESEARCH 11.1 INTRODUCTION OF FLEXIBLE BENEFITS IN CHINA

Based on Hofstede's cultural dimensions, it can be estimated that flexible benefits are more likely to be introduced in low power distance societies (which allows decisions to be made locally) and in low masculinity societies (because flexible benefits are seen to favour women with the flexibility they allow, such as to choose child-friendly benefits). China is characterised, like Hong Kong and Japan, by high power distance and high masculinity, so flexible benefits would appear to be unlikely to be much in evidence.

The researchers found that, indeed, flex plans were found in a minority of the companies researched, just 57 out of 324, although there was some evidence that they were spreading. The main reasons given by firms that had adopted the practice were the enhancement of job satisfaction and the improvement of recruitment and retention. Reasons given for not introducing flex schemes were the high costs over the expected benefits and the administrative burden (Barford and Stredwick 1998).

Despite these findings, the researchers found that 'some Chinese employers have begun to breach the constraints of old managerial concepts and provide flex plans, suggesting a limited degree of convergence towards western managerial practices' (ibid.: 1139).

(Source: Lin *et al.* 2011)

Despite these criticisms and the potential dating of the underpinning research, both Hofstede and the GLOBE work are still being utilised in research. This is demonstrated in focus on research 11.1 concerning the introduction of flexible benefits in China and you will find other examples in later examples of research.

CONVERGENCE AND DIVERGENCE

Given that national cultures may vary, is it possible that the spread of globalisation will mean that these national cultural values will decline and fade away? There is considerable debate on this issue with three main viewpoints.

Proposition 1: That globalisation is producing a clear convergence in human resource practices.

This proposition is based on the belief that, as the USA has emerged from the 1990s as the dominant world economy (especially in the light of the relative decline in the fortunes of Japan), and the doors have been opened by globalisation for the spread of capital, products, services and knowledge, the national cultures would converge to the extent that human resource practices would be identical in each marketplace. This belief is associated with the way that government policy on business and market decisions (such as reducing state ownership, freeing up labour markets, etc.) have spread from America (and, to a lesser extent, Japan) to Europe and world bodies such as the IMF and World Bank are making loans and financial support dependent on adopting these essentially Anglo-American values.

This view believes that 'best practice' exists which can be replicated throughout the world. In his controversial book *The McDonaldization of Society*, Ritzer (1996) proposes that work routines and consumer experiences are becoming more standardised, routinised and degraded and that the spread of the McDonald's fast food chain is an illustration of this.

Research by Stiles (2007), set out in focus on research 11.2, gave support to this proposition.

Stiles concluded that there was a great deal of similarity in how these firms manage their human relations. There were local adaptations of global standards but these were often to do with a particular country's regulatory practices, labour market issues and stages of economic development, rather than its cultural values.

For many providers of human resource services, there is a need to balance the company's overall strategy with the reality on the ground. For example, KPMG market globally HR advisory services and, in theory, each national partnership could take its own approach to assessment. However, this does not happen because KPMG have found a

---

FOCUS ON RESEARCH

FOCUS ON RESEARCH 11.2 GLOBAL CONVERGENCE IN HR PRACTICES

A study by Cambridge University in collaboration with Cornell, Insead, Erasmus and Tilburg universities, examined the HR practices of 30 MNCs, including BT, Ikea, Matsushita and Samsung. Over 350 interviews of senior managers and HR professionals were held regarding the way HR practices were organised in international contexts.

In most of the HR practices studied, very little divergence took place. They expected the approach in areas such as pay for performance or merit-based promotion to vary but they all appeared to be very similar. There was a concerted effort by group HR departments to maintain global performance standards supported by global competencies, common evaluation processes and common approaches to rewards. It was difficult to find many distinctive local practices. The only major area where divergence existed was in wage determination and the management prerogative where some cultures allowed real union negotiation and others did not or it was, in practice, a sham. In Japan, they found small differences, such as early-morning exercises and evening karaoke sessions for management but little other difference.

(Source: Stiles 2007)

collective recognition that the world is now more globally connected. So they try to ensure that their staff are working to the same set of values and have similar sets of skills and abilities. Therefore, they ensure that psychometric tests used for selection are free of cultural bias and do not indirectly discriminate against particular groups (Arkin 2009).

Proposition 2: That organisations are so locked into their respective national institutional settings that no common model of HRM practices is likely to emerge.

The convergence thesis has been criticised vigorously from a number of quarters. Much of the research into international HRM has sought to demonstrate that, although much change has taken place in national systems, their distinctiveness is still very durable and thus there are many continuities in the diversity of systems, and that the fact that industrial and technological structures are becoming more similar in developed countries does not necessarily mean that management and HRM practices, nor employment laws and labour markets, will necessarily converge with them (Muller 1997). One explanation for these enduring differences is the behaviour of people in the workplace in respect of their collectively held values, expectations and attitudes – in other words, the culture. Neither institutions nor cultures change quickly and rarely in ways that are identical to other countries, so it follows that managers within one country behave in a way that is noticeably different from managers in other countries (Brewster 2007).

Harry (2007) has pointed out that cultural differences in Asian and Gulf communities are an inescapable fact of business life and are strongly reflected in HR practices. Based on 30 years of working in these regions, he has pointed out a number of such differences:

■ The ties of family and community are much stronger than in the West, so individuals have less expectation of being supported by the employer or the state. This leads to strong cohesion, even uniformity in the workplace with employees ready to work hard, put in long hours and educate and train themselves.

■ HR is not seen as a strategic function in many Asian countries and senior HR posts are often occupied by former military officers or political appointees, responsible for dealing with government and keeping trade unions from causing problems.

■ There is a strong element of influence and connections in the recruitment and selection process ('*guanxi*' in Chinese, '*wasta*' in Arabic', '*kon*' in Japanese). Although this means that talent can be excluded, it helps to build and maintain cohesion and community spirit. Referrals from existing employees are often standard and the sponsor will be challenged if the recruit turns out to be not up to the mark and expected to put pressure on their friend to improve.

■ The hierarchy is less pyramid-shaped in Asia, with strong links across the hierarchy levels that depend on relationships outside work – family or political connections, shared membership of a group, such as a club or clan. Pay can reflect this, with older employees with connections being paid more than younger, more capable employees.

Harry reports on the head of HR at a Saudi company receiving less pay than his secretary, who was 20 years older. This was accepted as reasonable because of the greater expenses incurred by an older person.

■ Performance management systems are resisted, both because of regulatory impediments and cultural barriers, with people disliking having to make frank judgements on a colleague's performance. 'Annual appraisals, usually instituted by foreign managers, are not taken seriously and few subordinates would risk giving a negative report as part of a 360-degree appraisal system' (Harry 2007: 38).

The variation in viewpoints arising from research and experience between Stiles and Harry can be explained in a number of ways. Stiles's research was based on multinationals where it may be in the interests of employees to stress convergence to show identification with the company's culture. Much of Harry's experience has been based on locally controlled organisations who would want to retain much of their local culture, although they are willing to adopt new technology and sample Western ideas and concepts, discarding those that do not match with entrenched local culture. The adoption of Western HR processes, such as performance pay and performance management, may be acknowledged in the field but not wholly embraced. But neither concept, in reality, has a hugely successful record.

Proposition 3: Different regional models of HRM may be created.

This proposition posits that convergence is taking place, but on a regional basis, rather than a global basis. The main example of this is the convergence within the European Union where a unified legislative framework covers employment practices. Of equal importance is the adoption of the Social Charter and Social Action programme, which underpins much of current law and direction of future regulation. Regional convergence may also occur within areas, such as Asia, although little evidence is currently showing of any overall development there of a specific Asian convergence. Even in Europe, the expected convergence is not completely watertight, as Brewster *et al.* found that, although trends in HR practices (called directional convergence) were observed, there was 'very little evidence of countries becoming more alike in the way that they manage their human resources' (2006: 20).

Overall, then, there is no clear-cut evidence of a clear path towards convergence. In fact, a tension still exists between the reality of the three propositions as shown in focus on research 11.3.

GLOBAL COMPARISONS

Contextual issues

There are a number of contextual factors that can help to determine the nature of human resource practices in different countries:

Patterns of ownership vary considerably. In America, despite apparent concentration of power into large corporations, actual ownership and access to capital is far less concentrated than in most other countries. In Korea, for example, six conglomerates control a significant portion of the Korean economy, giving them significant power in the marketplace. Employment conditions therefore tend to be widely standardised. In Germany, most major companies are closely allied and owned by either a small number of national banks or a collection of regional banks (or a combination). Unwelcome takeovers can be easily resisted so share values never carry a takeover premium. Linking pay to shareholder value makes some sense in Britain and the US but little sense in Germany or Korea.

FOCUS ON RESEARCH 11.3 COMMUNICATION AND CONSULTATION – A CROSS-NATIONAL SURVEY

Researchers from Oxford University investigated employee views on communications and consultation within very different institutional practices in France, Germany, Italy and the UK, contacting over 3,500 employees. There was a general belief across the countries that employees felt they had little influence over important work decisions, despite the growing 'empowerment' initiatives over the last 20 years. In addition, a perceived belief was widespread that representative channels of communications (mostly through unions) was not very useful. However, there was general satisfaction over the amount of information provided by management.

Where the views differed across countries was in the degree of expectation over the consultation process. In the UK, employees expected few results from such exercises and they were not disappointed. They reported general disenchantment over communication initiatives and remained disengaged with the whole process. This is explained by the tradition that 'British managers have traditionally sought to assert their prerogative at all levels of the organisation and, in the absence of any statutory or joint agreed obligation to communicate or consult, they have simply not done so' (p. 530).

The views of the French are almost the reverse. They believe that upward communication should be useful, supported by strong statutory underpinning, such as at workplace level with the *groupes d'expression*. However, the vast array of practices has led French employees to expect more and to foster disappointment when they do not receive it. For German employees, the position is even more extreme due to the degree of institutional power by employee groups, such as the *betriebsrat*, and the role of worker directors. There has been all the more disappointment, therefore, in recent years when this power failed to restrict the growing round of redundancies and closures.

(Source: Kessler *et al.* 2004)

Table 11.7 International comparison of women on boards

High		Medium		Low	
Norway	35.9%	USA	11.4%	South America (average)	4.7%
Sweden	23.0%	Germany	9.0%	India	4.1%
South Africa	14.6%	Switzerland	8.4%	Italy	3.6%
		UK	7.8%	Japan	0.9%
		China	6.6%	Portugal	0.4%
		Russia	5.8%	Morocco	0.0%
		Singapore	5.7%		

Source: Adapted from Davies, M. (2011) *Independent Review of Women on Boards*. Department of Business Innovation and Skills.

Employment law frameworks also vary. Laws relating to equal opportunities are far more developed in law (and, just as important, in practice) in the developed nations as opposed to Asia and especially Muslim countries. In the European Union, despite a raft of pan-European legislation, the rules over dispensing with labour vary from country to country. Hiring and firing is comparatively straightforward in the UK but remains out of the question in France and most Mediterranean nations. Few countries outside the West have a developed form of protection against dismissal or any form of protection for agency employees.

Thirdly, major differences are evident in the *role of women in society*. There are huge differences in cultural attitudes to the position of women in society around the world. One interesting indicator in this area is the proportion of women on boards of private companies and Table 11.7 shows examples of the degree of variation.

Scandinavian countries lead the vanguard in driving through measures to raise female representation. Norway instituted a legally enforceable quota system in 2002, which resulted in all boards having 40 per cent women by 2009. Spain, France and Italy have similar systems in process, although compliance so far is weak in Spain. The European Union have set an objective of 40 per cent by 2020 but have been unable to agree a system of legally enforcing this across the 27 countries. The UK, who were one of the countries successfully opposing the EU proposal, have no objective in place, except that of a vague aim to achieve 25 per cent by 2015.

A fourth major difference relates to the *organisation of labour*, although, to a degree, this is becoming less important as trade unions are fading in the West and growth in developing countries remains uncertain. Where unions are powerful, such as in Scandinavia, France and Germany and in pockets in the UK (see Chapter 4), the speed of change and flexibility generally is constrained. On the other hand, longer-term planning for employment conditions (such as multi-year pay contracts and substantive changes to working patterns) gives a greater degree of stability in labour relations.

Specific regions

JAPAN

Although Japanese business methods and their associated human resources policies proved successful in an extraordinary way in the 1970s and 1980s, the 1990s and 2000s have proved difficult years, as other nations have copied those approaches and adjusted them equally successfully to their local environment. At the same time, the strength of the yen has made exporting increasingly difficult. To meet these challenges, Japanese employment systems are showing changes in five areas (Kyotani 1999).

The first of these is the erosion of the *Nenko Wage system*. This was established in the 1920s and has given guarantees on regular pay increases for those 80 per cent or more employees considered core employees. Since the 1970s, there has been a gradual erosion of this guarantee, because it began to be appreciated that the system, although working well in periods of economic growth and stability, ultimately produced high labour costs, a lack of flexibility and a productivity lag that became untenable. It was held to be unfair to pay more money to unproductive senior workers rather than to the younger and more productive employees (Morris *et al.* 2006). By the late 1990s, over 80 per cent of companies had abandoned the guarantee, adjusted it or planned to do so shortly. The main adjustment is to make a proportion of the wage subject to the workings of a performance management process. For example, in NEC, over half of the wage is determined by the outcome of an annual appraisal.

So bad was the state of some industrial companies by the early 2000s that unions agreed to a complete abolition of the guaranteed increase in the Mitsui Metal company. In administrative jobs, this movement has occurred at a faster pace, with many organisations now ignoring service as a determinant of pay. With inflation at nil, this is tantamount to a perpetual pay freeze for all but the above-average performer. An interesting side effect of this changed policy is the widening of the pay differentials not just between good and poor performers but also in the chain of command. An example of employee attitudes towards the replacement of the *Nenko* system to one essentially based on performance-related pay is shown in focus on research 11.4.

Associated with the *Nenko* system was the practice of *promotions based chiefly on service*. In recent years, however, the system of formal appraisal has taken over in most organisations, although some still keep a minimum service requirement, such as five years, before a promotion can be made. Within Japanese subsidiaries in other countries, career advancement for local managers is generally very limited indeed. The process of centralised decision-making requires Japanese expatriates to be in place to interpret correctly the decisions made at head office.

Shushin koyo – lifelong employment – is another tradition that is on the wane. Core workers in large organisations continue to have this guarantee (Schaede 2008) but over 90 per cent of companies in a recent survey indicated their intention to start removing this guarantee. It is estimated that only 30 per cent of new employees have received a lifetime

FOCUS ON RESEARCH 11.4 PERFORMANCE PAY AT A JAPANESE ELECTRICAL APPLIANCE COMPANY

At the time of this research, this company was about to reduce basic pay by 20 per cent and to add more individual performance components to a pay scheme where performance pay had previously played only a small part (about 5 per cent of wages). The researchers questioned 155 employees who were mostly involved in sales and support services.

It was found, not unexpectedly, that employees under the age of 35 showed a much stronger preference for performance pay, showing a much more sceptical view of the traditional pay system. At the time of the research, unions around Japan reported that there were strong views against performance pay from their senior members. A second finding was that those employees who were more committed to their occupation rather than the company also had a stronger preference for performance pay.

It was expected that employees favourable to performance pay would be less favourably inclined to 'organisational citizenship', a Japanese expression indicating discretionary extra-role behaviour such as helping co-workers and enhancing the reputation of the work unit unrelated to any reward. However, they found no connection between the two. In other words, employees can prefer performance pay without negative consequences for organisational citizenship. This latter finding supported the concept that, although there was evidence of convergence on the use of Anglo-American HR practices, there was also evidence of a separate path that managed to combine the best practice of both worlds (Keizer 2010) – in this research, a commitment to individual reward-based performance pay and a commitment to discretionary unpaid behaviour towards the unit and the company in general. Another way to explain this is in respect of the psychological contract 'where deep-rooted collectivist cultural values would continue to support a relational psychological contract, at the same time, newer, individualistic systems and the values that they engender would support a transactional psychological contract. The two may not necessarily be in conflict' (ibid.: 2105).

(Source: Lee *et al.* 2011)

guarantee from as early as the 1990s. Due to the decline in internal demand, there is also a growing policy of encouraging early retirement and voluntary redundancy, and 41 per cent of companies have programmes for transferring employees to related firms, sometimes losing their major benefits in the transfer, or reducing their hours or schemes to encourage employees to set up their own businesses. These processes (and the associated reduction of new hirings) have added to the growing unemployment rate which reached over 4.5 per cent in 2011. A prime example of this policy was the announcement in October 1999 by Nissan car company that it would close five plants in Japan as part of a major rescue plan to prevent further escalation in losses, but at the expense of more than 15,000 job losses (Bannister 1999).

However, redundancies are still regarded as culturally unacceptable compared with Anglo-American management contexts (Abegglen 2006). The evidence is that Japanese companies prefer to use attrition to reduce staff and to hire an increasing number of temporary employees. Keizer (2010) found that the percentage of employees on permanent contracts reduced from 79.2 to 67.4 per cent between 1993 and 2005.

There is also an interesting policy change in terms of *gender issues*. The overt policy stated by government, management and unions is to employ more female employees but this is not a general indication of equal opportunities. Since the establishment of the Equal Job Rights Law in 1996, many organisations have implemented the 'Job Career Path Programme' (*Kosubetsu Koyo Seido*). This divides employees into two groups. These are the 'general staff group', who are engaged in unskilled or repetitive jobs and who will never be promoted, and the 'executive candidates group', who are expected to achieve managerial or professional status after experiencing various jobs in the organisation. In practice, this policy is working as a means of segregating male and female workers. Females go into the general staff group, while the executive candidates group is made up almost entirely of men. Furthermore, the general staff group is increasingly being filled with temporary or agency staff, often provided by an associated company and at lower pay than for permanent employees. The position of women still continues to be seen as the helpers of men, making tea and doing typing. This helps to explain the recent high-profile legal suits against Japanese companies in America for sexual harassment and discrimination where multimillion-pound settlements have been reached.

The fifth area is in the *loosening of regulations*. For example, the employment of agency staff used to be restricted to only a handful of job categories, such as catering and administration. This has now been extended and complete restrictions are likely to be lifted within the next few years. The restrictions on the employment of women for health and safety reasons, such as in night work, have also been lifted. Government regulations on the length of the working week are also in the process of being weakened. The overall outcome is that there is an increase in the flexibility of the workforce but one that appears to be achieved through the elimination of longer-term benefits and rights of the employees. This has drawn the country's working patterns closer to those of the West but it may also lead to a hardening of relations with the unions who have been largely subservient to date.

There are other areas of Japanese culture that continue to be successful with little change. *Kaisen*, the process of encouraging staff to contribute ideas on incremental improvements, has been copied throughout the world. Similarly, the emphasis on quality, just-in-time and team-working have been replicated in all industrial countries.

CHINA

China's accession to the World Trade Organization in 2003 confirmed the almost unbelievable changes in the country's political and economic structure and strategy over the previous

20 years. With a GDP growing at over 8 per cent a year, it has been estimated that it will account for 25 per cent of the total world economy by 2025. Western investment has surged (Motorola's investment has reached over £6 billion) and the Chinese government has responded by introducing initiatives to level out the playing field so foreign firms will enjoy similar benefits to locals (Sappal 2003).

Traditional cultural values, however, are very different and slow to change. Many originated from Mao Tse-tung's 'iron rice bowl' regime and they provide a powerful influence on the working environment, such as:

- *Fie fan wan* – job for life
- *Da you fan* – rewards unrelated to individual performance
- *Dan wei* – cradle to grave welfare
- *Guanxi* – the importance of relationships
- *Renquing* – doing favours, which help to build relationships
- *Mianzi* – saving face, often through reciprocating favours
- *Chang dei* – respect for elders and seniority.

Confucianism (low trust in outsiders, strong sense of family and importance of 'networking') has also had a considerable traditional influence, especially in family firms. Structures tend to be more informal and paternalistic to engender a collectivist sense of teamwork with strong personal relationships of great importance. These relationships are backed up with values of mutual trust, reciprocity, loyalty and harmony together with reliable business exchanges. Strong nepotism, family control and patronage are highly manifest in HR practices (Marlow and Patton 2002; Chen 2007). Operating many of these values in the workplace has led to inefficiencies and corruption. Many managers are simply used to following orders so find it difficult to use their own initiative, while major change programmes, especially those including redundancies, face severe obstacles in acceptance and implementation. Changing to Western-style employment relationships, therefore, remains a major step, although evidence is growing that Western practices, such as psychological testing and using references, are growing, especially in joint ventures. As Armstrong explains:

> When I was first there (in the early 1990s) . . . the Chinese were content to just have good economic growth and improve their education system. Now they want to reduce dependency on low-cost labour by raising added value and building human and intellectual capital. . . . More than 70 per cent of people under 30 now speak English and Chinese firms have started to explore the HR agenda so they can compete head on with foreigners.
>
> (Sappal 2003: 37)

The adoption of Western HR practices varies according to a number of variables. The fastest movement has been implemented in subsidiaries of large Western-owned MNCs,

FOCUS ON RESEARCH 11.5 KEY FACTORS INFLUENCING HRM PRACTICES IN CHINA

Researchers examined the HRM practices in 286 Chinese subsidiaries of US, German and Japanese companies and identified a series of influences which they divided into 'push' factors from the parent firm and 'pull' factors from the 'host country'.

The strongest 'push' factor was from financial control in subsidiary investment decision and joint venture structure where such decisions led to changing existing local practices to those closer to Western HRM practices. Little difference was identified in industry sector or the country of origin. In addition, many HRM practices may be converging to a more common universal form across different types of subsidiaries. Where the subsidiary was minority-owned, the degree of HRM practices was more limited.

Interestingly, there is good evidence that parent firms start in China with global strategic imperatives for HRM practices but they become constrained by local environment and cultural conditions and make major modifications.

The largest direction of 'push' is towards a performance-oriented culture, including value systems that strive for efficiency and quality, employee appraisals focusing on financial performance and encouraging skills development. Where there is a greater pull factor from the local environment (measured by longer time period of establishment in that locality), the practices tend to show a traditional flavour, such as provision for employee housing, consideration of the educational background for hiring managers and referrals. This is not to say that Western-style practices are absent, it is more a more hybrid system that has developed.

'As the competition in the Chinese market for skilled labour becomes stronger, many multinational firms are expected to adopt more "best" HRM practices that are not only results oriented but also fit local cultural and social environments. ... Those managers adapting to the dual forces of "push" and "pull", linking global management policies and practices to the specific Chinese environments, sensitive to Chinese local culture and practices and willing to be flexible while maintaining professional standards may be most likely to succeed in the Chinese market' (p. 702).

(Source: Farley *et al.* 2004)

---

but, even here, the speed of adoption is not predictable, being shaped by political and social realities, as explained in focus on research 11.5.

While there has existed small-scale commercial and industrial activity outside the centrally planned economy, it was not until the 1970s that private firms including family firms were allowed to operate. They gained considerable momentum after 1997 when the 15th Party Congress finally recognised their legal existence. They have since become an

FOCUS ON RESEARCH 11.6 HRM IN CHINESE FAMILY-OWNED BUSINESSES

In this research, 205 family-owned firms with an average age of 9 years were questioned about the structure and formality of their HR department and their methods of operating recruitment, selection, training, performance management, reward and job specifications. Not surprisingly, they found that the larger firms were more likely to have formalised HR departments and to operate formal HR systems. The larger firms have recognised that recruiting external managers through rigorous selection processes extends family firms' limited networks, thus enhancing their social capital. The larger firms undertake formal appraisal and feedback and offer formal variable pay schemes, which, though challenging against Confucianist values of harmony and egalitarianism, proved necessary in a competitive environment. There did not appear to be resistance to such measures.

(Source: Kim and Gao 2011)

increasingly significant driver of China's remarkable economic growth, contributing 50 per cent of the country's GDP. Despite little institutional support, family businesses have significantly contributed to the marketisation of the Chinese economy. Despite their size and importance in the economy, developments in HRM have not matched those of MNCs, especially Western-owned ones. It is interesting to find that, despite some adoptions and adaptation of Western human resource practices, Confucian traditions of familism and distrust of outsiders, coupled with the country's poor legal infrastructure and underdeveloped market-oriented institutions, are a critical impediment to the professionalisation and formalisation of HRM, as shown in focus on research 11.6.

AFRICA

Africa presents a complex picture both in the economic and political context, which varies from the dire, such as the complete failure of the Somali nation state and the continuing tribal-riven conflicts in DR Congo, to the more advanced developments in Nigeria and Kenya, where economic growth in 2010, at 8 per cent and 5 per cent, respectively, were close to matching the best developing nations' rates. Northern African nations, predominantly Muslim, have a substantially different set of cultural values to sub-Saharan nations where Christian influences are much stronger, although Nigeria and Kenya straddle the ethnic divide.

Although difficult to generalise, it has been posited that there is a central tenet of African tradition of 'humanness' that stresses that a 'person is a person through other people' (Nussbaum 2003), as well as placing the collective need of the tribe or society above that of the individual. Interpersonal relationships are of great importance, as well as the desire to be treated with dignity. There is also great respect for authority, especially parents and elders. These values have been embraced in the African concept of '*ubuntu*', which stresses humanism and communalism in the workplace (Newenham-Kahindi 2009).

The recent experiences of MNCs have often reflected an inappropriate understanding of local cultures in the workplace where Western-based organisations have attempted unsuccessfully to export home-based HRM systems to African countries with widely different cultural loci. Examples are of contract-focused HRM programmes based on merit and individualism, which have clashed with the collectivist-humanist culture of African employees (Azolukwam and Perkins 2009). It should not be forgotten that many African countries have been forced into accepting Western-style HRM (sophisticated recruitment and selection, performance management, for example) as a condition of foreign aid and investment with inevitable clashes in culture. Interestingly, equal opportunities initiatives have faced comparatively little opposition, especially as the growing middle class has large numbers of well-educated, ambitious and well-respected females in the political and economic fields.

An example of the clashes that can occur with the direct transfer of Western HR practices into an African country is shown in focus on research 11.7.

FOCUS ON RESEARCH 11.7 HRM AND CULTURAL DIVERSITY – A MOZAMBIQUE CASE STUDY

Using a multinational aluminium smelting operation employing 1,100 people, the researchers investigated the cultural dimensions in an African context (again using Hofstede's measures) and added questions that related to a range of socioeconomic data and went on to identify how Western-based HRM practices could be successfully modified, if at all, in an African context.

Although the research was carried out some years after the plant was set up in 2000, many of the employees remembered vividly the initial harshness of the environment, the plethora of rules and the unresponsiveness and unawareness of the management to their culture and sensitivities. This took the form of insisting on English as the official language, a lack of regular communication, lack of welfare facilities (health and education) and the high pay of the foreign staff employed. These disputes led to an illegal strike as early as 2001, which collapsed after 26 days, after some violent activities from both sides. The company, however, did respond over the next few years by introducing far-reaching changes to communication and training. Help was given to the union to understand their function better and to negotiate more thoughtfully and effectively, employee forums were set up and more interest

FOCUS ON RESEARCH

was taken in employees' families and welfare benefits, such as medical aid and an improved pension scheme.

As far as African culture was concerned, a high level of collectivism, feminism and power distance were found, together with a moderate to high level of uncertainty avoidance. These values vary considerably from the Anglo-American set of measures where a high level of individualism and uncertainty avoidance is found. Additional societal-economic questions yielded high scores for family and health values (influenced by the fear of Aids), the maintenance of social harmony in the community and living an uncomplicated life with recourse available to the legal system.

Clashes of this culture with HRM practices were apparent. Evidence indicated that collectivist workforces prefer to influence the process of employee recruitment, such as to ensure the appointment of in-group relatives above other non-connected recruits and to rely on word of mouth. Western HR practices would regard this as nepotism, discriminatory and even corrupt at times and not necessarily the way to find the person for the job. The African culture indicated a preference for group rather than individual appraisal and for a strong link between pay and age rather than linking pay with performance.

Some of the results were contradictory. Despite high levels of power distance, the workforce preferred a more consultative type of management, although most operatives expected to work with autocratic management.

The researchers concluded that the actions by the organisation after the strike had underlined the importance of recognising the culture in the workplace as well as challenging the assumption that all aspects of Western-based HRM were irrelevant in an African context.

(Source: Sartorious *et al.* 2011)

HRM MODELS AND INTERNATIONAL STRATEGIES FOR OVERSEAS SUBSIDIARIES

In terms of formulating strategies for foreign subsidiary units, the key consideration for HR practitioners is striking a balance between the control necessary to ensure that corporate objectives are complied with consistently and the flexibility required to respond to often dynamic and volatile local circumstances where cultural mores may be substantially different from those of the home country. As we have seen in the research above, this balance is often difficult to achieve.

Dowling and Schuller (1991) have developed a useful typology of strategies for the management of people in international subsidiaries based on four broad approaches: *ethnocentric, polycentric, regiocentric* and *geocentric*. These are explained below:

- *Ethnocentric*. In this approach, subsidiaries have little autonomy with strategic decisions being made at head office. HRM practices are likely to be prescribed in accordance with those that are customary in the home country. Expatriate managers are given little language or cross-cultural training. Japanese MNCs have often been characterised in this way (e.g. single union 'no-strike' agreements, team-working, commitment-based organisational culture).

- *Polycentric*. Here, the MNC regards subsidiaries as distinct entities with some autonomy. Recruitment of staff will be conducted locally and the head office is less interested in imposing control and organisational culture on the subsidiary. Expatriate managers will be given some cross-cultural and language training.

- *Regiocentric*. This approach focuses on regional values and ways of operating, drawing specialist employees and managers from a wider pool with a specific geographical zone (e.g. Europe, North America, the Pacific Rim).

- *Geocentric* (or *Global*). According to expert opinion, this type is the one that contemporary MNCs should seek to emulate. The geocentric organisation is decentralised and flexible in its operations, but maintains an integrated set of values and mission. Managers are developed to be interchangeable between national contexts and promoted on the basis of merit. Networks are established to spread knowledge and best practice through the global operation.

Although Dowling and Schuler's typology is engaging, it should be stressed that each strategy is an ideal type and it is unlikely that any one multinational organisation would conform completely with their criteria. Neither is it the case that senior managers can simply wake up one morning and decide to pursue a particular route. An HRM strategy will emerge from a combination of evolution, management intervention and the interplay of a complex set of environmental forces.

Talent management – international staffing

Where positions need to be filled in overseas subsidiaries, there are three choices, as set out by Hendry (1994):

1 *Parent-country nationals (PCNs) where staff come from the home country.* Staff in this category would be known as expatriates, such as British oil workers working for BP in the Gulf states. More generally, PCNs will be managerial and/or specialised technical staff.

2 *Host-country nationals (HCNs) where staff are recruited locally from the country in which a subsidiary is based.* The level and status of employee will depend greatly upon the quality of the local labour market; in many developing countries, those recruited will often be semi-skilled workers assigned to low-status, low-paid work, thus taking advantage of lower labour costs.

3   *Third-country nationals (TCNs) where staff are brought in to work in a foreign subsid-iary, but are not originally from the country in which the subsidiary is located.* Again, examples are to be found in the Gulf states where workers from India, Pakistan and Sri Lanka go to work in manual and semi-skilled capacities for much higher wages than they could earn in their country of origin – by doing so, they are able to send money home to their families.

Expatriates may just have one assignment before returning to their home country to develop their career or they can work on a set of serial assignments in different locations around the world, lasting around three years for each assignment, expanding their knowledge and experience on each assignment. Alternatively, they may stay in one place, gradually rising through the local hierarchy. They are recognised as having specific and valuable skills that are not available locally. As managerial and technical/specialist employees, they are consid-ered to add value to the organisation and it is these expatriate employees who tend to receive the most investment in terms of cross-cultural training and support. However they are used, expatriates are regarded as a valuable investment and possessing talent that needs to be carefully managed. They tend to receive the highest pay and benefits in a loca-tion, including flights home, accommodation and financial assistance with schooling, either locally or in the home country. The difference in pay and benefits can cause difficulties in local offices, especially if some form of equal pay legislation is in place. Where required, the usual solution is some form of complex bonus scheme, especially a substantial bonus at the end of the contract. The relocation of not only the employees but also their families may be necessary, and, if the employee's family experiences difficulties in settling in their new envi-ronment, this may affect the quality of the employee's work. Some international companies go to great lengths to ensure that the transition from one culture to another is a smooth one as shown in focus on research 11.8.

One drawback to employing expatriates is the cost involved. The benefits alone on an average assignment for a senior manager can exceed £100,000 per annum and the cost of failure can be very high. Due to the increasing levels of management education in many developing nations and in response to local legislation on the 'nationalisation' of jobs (in other words, the insistence that a growing percentage of jobs are awarded to locals), the number of long-term expatriate appointments is tending to drop and the development of talent is transferred to local employees who can be groomed for advancement.

Strategic alliances and 'offshoring'

For multinationals to operate effectively and flexibly, they often enter into partnerships with other organisations in other countries. There can be several reasons for doing this, such as to reduce risk, to gain entry to restricted markets, and to share and enhance knowledge and expertise (Tayeb 1999). A famous example of this in the UK was the partnership of Rover

FOCUS ON RESEARCH 11.8 PROVIDING FOR EXPATRIATES' SPOUSES

Around two-thirds of international expatriates are accompanied by spouses and many also bring their children with them. Where failure in the assignment occurs, it is often due to the inability of the spouse to settle in the new location. Such failures can be very costly (up to $1 million per failure, according to Abbott *et al.* (2006)) and this does not take into account indirect costs such as damaged customer relationships and lower morale at the location. Little attention was previously given to spouses as it was assumed they were merely in the location to support their husbands and look after any children, however, half of expatriate families are dual-career couples and the number is rising (Cartus 2007), which presents a different set of difficulties as assignments can cause a disruption of family income level and repatriation issues for both the expatriate and the spouse. Research has indicated that, although around 60 per cent of spouses worked before the assignment, only around 15–20 per cent obtain equivalent work when relocated with their spouse. This is no longer a problem just with female spouses, as the proportion of female expatriates is rapidly growing and many bring their husbands along.

The researchers contacted 238 spouses, mostly taking part in assignments to China from the UK, USA, Australia, Canada and New Zealand. Most of them rated the relocation package highly as a whole. The main area of research, however, was the degree to which the organisation helped the spouse to obtain appropriate work: 25 per cent of spouses had obtained employment-related assistance but only 40 per cent rated this help as effective and 20 per cent considered that it gave no value. The success rate for obtaining employment was only around 50 per cent. The best help came in providing inside knowledge on networking, including the best employment agencies, information on job fairs, creating a 'spouses' self-help group' and having an internal spouses liaison officer who spoke the language. A small minority of companies provided short courses for the spouses in adjustment, transfer of skill sets and identity issues (especially in Muslim countries), which included providing appropriate books, cases and websites.

Many found little help from the organisation in obtaining work visas, language training and professional qualification registration or in helping the spouse set up a small business.

(Source: Cole 2011)

---

and Honda, which contributed greatly to Rover's survival during very challenging times in the 1980s. However, the number of partnerships or 'strategic alliances' in world trade has grown considerably in the last decade. In particular, Chinese businesses have been involved in a number of strategic alliances with Western firms such as Mercedes-Benz and Dell Computers (Balaam and Veseth 2005). The Chinese government expected this to be short-term as Chinese car companies reached international levels of quality, but this has failed to happen as they remain 'hooked on joint ventures like opium' (*Economist* 2013).

The HRM implications of strategic alliances depend on the extent of the partnership. It could be that the arrangement exists merely to outsource a peripheral aspect of production, in which case the senior partner will be quite content to devolve HRM responsibility to the contractor. However, often strategic alliances are used as an opportunity to exchange and enhance HRM practices. This was particularly the case with the example of Rover and Honda, where the British firm learned a great deal from their Japanese counterparts.

The sorts of arrangements referred to above can also court controversy. At the time of writing, there has been a string of features in the UK media about the increasingly common tendency of employers to move production (either in a manufacturing or service context) to other countries where wages are lower and employment rights seemingly less constraining. This trend can be seen as responsible to a considerable extent for the decline in manufacturing in developed countries (Balaam and Veseth 2005). Often these jobs are low-skill, low-discretion jobs and are outsourced to a sub-contractor. Some continental European nations such as France and Germany have introduced labour laws to prevent multinationals from taking jobs abroad. However, concerns have been raised recently in the UK about the fact that it is not merely manufacturing jobs that are moving abroad, but also service jobs, most notably call-centre customer service work which certain economically depressed regions of the UK had come to depend on. In particular, financial institutions have moved jobs to India where there is a large potential labour market of English-speaking university graduates who see call-centre jobs as having prestige. Case study 11.1 explains how this has become a highly politicised issue in the UK. However, others, such as Riddell (2004), argue that the loss of call-centre jobs offshore is not necessarily so bad as this means that the imperative is created in the British labour market for the generation of higher-skilled 'knowledge' jobs that create more wealth.

LABOUR STANDARDS AND SOCIAL RESPONSIBILITY

Although MNCs and governments are perceived as being all powerful and often portrayed as being reckless in the face of green and social issues in the pursuit of revenue, there has been something of a political and consumer backlash in recent years that has challenged some of the more unsavoury practices, such as exploiting the populations in developing countries. Stories exist of how many MNCs – often household names such as Nike (Eaton 2000) – have been making large profits while using poorly paid labour, often working in terrible conditions. These problems are compounded further with reports of the use of child and forced prison labour, and the persecution of workers because of their membership of unions and opposition political parties.

In the face of these issues, the governments of developed nations, charitable agencies and non-governmental organisations and MNCs themselves have sought to develop frameworks that seek to address these concerns and oblige bad employers in developing – and some developed! – countries to improve the conditions of their workers.

CASE STUDY 11.1 INSURER PACKS 7,000 JOBS OFF TO INDIA

In 2004, Finance union Amicus condemned insurance giant Norwich Union over its 'devastating' decision to offshore 7,000 British jobs to India. The massive jobs export came from a company that had already exported 3,700 jobs to India since December 2005 and planned to reduce its British workforce by 25 per cent by 2007. Amicus national officer David Fleming said, 'Today's announcement of 950 jobs being offshored is not only devastating to the workforce, but the double whammy is the further 2,350 to go by 2007. In the first stage, 950 jobs will go to India and Sri Lanka next year, hitting workers, their families and communities in Norwich, York and Perth.' Mr Fleming said that it pointed to a 'bleak future' for Britain's financial services industry.

'We will not accept compulsory redundancies as a consequence of offshoring in any company and that will be fundamental to our negotiations with Norwich Union. Amicus will take whatever action our members request of us. All our options are open.'

Mr Fleming said that, in talks with the company, the union hoped to ensure maximum opportunities for retraining, job mobility and skills development for all staff affected. Looking across the financial services sector, he added that employees would now be 'bracing themselves' for 'thousands more' redundancies as companies 'show their offshoring hand'.

Defending the announcement, Norwich Union chief Gary Withers insisted that it was a response to 'customers continually seeking better value for money and quality of service.'

The blow confirmed a recent opinion survey carried out by Amicus among Norwich Union staff in which 99.9 per cent of them feared further job cuts under the company's offshoring programme.

Tens of thousands of British jobs were moved to India by banks, airlines, telecommunications firms and even national rail enquiries service, chasing wage cuts of up to 40 per cent. But, aside from the devastation caused by the loss of jobs, there was also growing opposition from customers. Lloyds TSB customers, backed by the bank's in-house staff association, challenged its decision to shift jobs to India under the terms of the Data Protection Act.

Amicus was at the forefront of campaigning to highlight the fundamental problems associated with offshoring – the lack of long-term business benefits and overall benefits to the customer. The union also urged companies that exported jobs to reinvest the cost savings made into developing their British workforce and generating numbers of skilled jobs.

However, according to Amicus, not a single company had been able to demonstrate a focus on reinvestment and corporate social responsibility.

(Source: Stewart 2004)

The frameworks tend to concern low wages, human rights and worker rights abuses, child labour and poor working conditions.

These frameworks tend to operate on three distinct levels:

- Unilateral national agreements, where countries enforce conditions on other countries and MNCs that they import from.
- Multilateral national agreements where countries agree trading conditions with other countries and MNCs in return for preferential tariff rates.
- Corporate codes of conduct where individual MNCs (or groups of MNCs) impose standards within their own organisations and on their suppliers and trading partners.

It is rather unfortunate that, in the issue of labour standards, the righteous rhetoric of governments and MNCs is often not matched by reality. Standards are often not enforced as rigorously as they should be and major abuses of worker rights by MNCs continue to be a problem (Tsogas 1999).

METEOR CASE STUDY

SETTING UP A NEW UNIT IN BELGIUM

Three years later, in line with the business strategy, Meteor was set to open a unit in mainland Europe and a site near Brussels had been chosen. Sarah was successful in her application to become the HR manager for the site, her good knowledge of French being a crucial advantage. In setting out her human resource plan, she was aware that the system of pay determination and other HR practices in Belgium was highly centralised and regulated. The consensual nature of industrial relations was pivotal with the social partners in constant contact with each other through bipartite national and industry bodies, such as the Central Economic Council. Belgium's very open competitive stance was reflected in the exchange of information between the partners, which has led to reasonably harmonious agreements to protect jobs and guarantee incomes.

Sarah knew that she would have to work within national agreements reached in areas such as the average monthly minimum guaranteed income, introduced in 1975, which is linked to the national monthly consumer price index, and wage rates for employees under 21, both of which applied to the whole of Belgium. As a new employer, she needed to discover which, if any, national agreement had been reached in her industry over minimum rates, as she learned that such agreements, unlike the UK, were legally binding, and which were also indexed. Her research found the appropriate national agreement and she was relieved to see that the indexation only applied to those employees on the national minimum wage.

These agreements were reached through sub-committees of the National Labour Council that dealt separately with agreements for blue- and white-collar employees. For

Sarah, this distinction provided difficulties as, in the UK, terms and conditions were harmonised without such a distinction. The national agreement produced considerable financial implications for the company for the transfer of blue-collar employees to white-collar status, due to higher payments for sickness and redundancy. Another issue she needed to carefully consider was the traditional nature of pay increments where some industries had as many as 20 automatic increments for white-collar employees from age 21 to 55. She found that it was a standard convention for most employees to receive a Christmas bonus equivalent to an additional month's pay. In fact, some senior employees in her industry were entitled to a 14th month's pay as well! There was also a minimum notice period of 28 days for blue-collar workers.

Holiday entitlement was, she found, around the same as the UK in general but the payment surprised her, in that most of the holiday had to be paid at double the wage rate. The outcome was that blue-collar employees received a minimum of a total of seven weeks and two days' pay for four weeks' leave. Sickness payments were also more generous for the employees, in that minimum entitlement for all employees was one month, mostly paid by the employer, followed by the state sickness benefit, which paid around 60 per cent of former earnings, although this figure was capped. The statutory working week was 39 hours. There were complicated rules that restricted Sunday working. Considerably fewer employees had company cars, however, which relieved Sarah of a potential head-ache in terms of allocation and expensing. She was relieved that payment for managers and senior technologists remained outside of the scope of such agreements.

Also in her plan was the establishment of the works council, which was obligatory where there were more than 100 employees. She spent some time arranging visits to see councils in operation in the UK and Belgium, made through personal networking and the CIPD International Forum.

Overall, she was aware that the costs of employment were high, as the employers' social security contributions were in the order of 25 per cent, almost double the equivalent costs in the UK.

KEY CHAPTER SUMMARY POINTS

■ The workplace has become increasingly more exposed to international forces and knowledge of issues in international HRM is useful for practitioners.

■ There is considerable variety in the way business operates within national contexts and, therefore, the environment of HRM tends to differ also.

■ National culture can be a major determinant on the nature of workplace behaviour in different national contexts; when dealing in HRM matters with other countries, practitioners must be aware of these.

■ MNCs are a very influential phenomenon in global trade. HRM practitioners should be aware of different strategies that can be deployed to manage people and what the key issues are, e.g. managing expatriate workers.

■ Western-style HRM practices are being adopted in Far East countries but the speed of adoption and the degree of adaptation to local conditions varies greatly depending on differing factors.

■ The internationalisation of business has had some unsavoury consequences, such as exploitation, and practitioners should be aware of their ethical and social responsibilities.

STUDENT ACTIVITIES

1 Consider a country where you may want to work. Research the cultural differences you may encounter and work out how this would affect the management of people in organisations in that country.

2 If you have fellow students from a number of countries, choose five of them and discuss with them their working experience of how recruitment, performance management and reward operate in practice.

3 Debate the difficulties that could emerge with the direct transfer of Western HRM methods into a Gulf country. What approaches should you adopt to avoid these difficulties?

4 Read the article summarised in focus on research 11.7 and suggest other HRM actions that the organisation could have taken after the strike to meet the employees' aims.

5 In focus on research 11.4, what evidence is there for the *convergence* of Western and Japanese cultures? Discuss what implications any convergence may have for other HRM practices in Japan.

6 Set out the arguments for and against instituting a legal requirement for a quota of women on boards of private companies.

REFERENCES

Abbott, G., Stening, B., Atkins, P. and Grant, A. (2006) Coaching Expatriate Managers for Success. *Asia Pacific Journal of Human Resources*, 44: 295–317.

Abegglen, J. (2006) *21st Century Japanese Management – New Systems, Lasting Values*. Palgrave Macmillan.

Arkin, A. (2009) Cut from Different Cloth. *People Management Guide to Assessment*, 8 October, 13–14.

Azolukwam, V. and Perkins, S. (2009) Managerial Perspectives on HRM in Nigeria: Evolving Hybridization? *Cross-Cultural Management: an International Journal*, 16: 62–82.

Baalam, D. and Veseth, M. (2005) *Introduction to International Political Economy*, 3rd ed. Pearson.

Bannister, N. (1999) 21,000 Go in Nissan Rescue. *Guardian*, 19 October, 22.

Barford, K. and Stredwick, J. (1998) A Café Society? The Future of Flexible Working. *Journal of Flexible Working*, June, 23–26.

Brewster, C. (2007) HRM: The Comparative Dimension, in J. Storey (ed.) *Human Resource Management: A Critical Text*. Thomson.

Brewster, C., Wood, G., Brookes, M. and Van Ommered, J. (2006) What Determines the Size of the Learning HR Function? A Cross-national Analysis. *Human Resource Management*, 45(1): 3–21.

Cartus (2007) The CARTUS Survey: Emerging Trends in Global Mobility, sponsored by US National Foreign Trade Council, Danbury, CT.

Chen, W. (2007) Does the Colour of the Cat Matter? The Red Hat Strategy in China's Private Enterprises. *Management and Organisation Review*, 3: 63–80.

Cole, N. (2011) Managing Global Talent; Solving the Spousal Adjustment Problem. *International Journal of Human Resource Management*, 22(7): 1504–1530.

Davies, M. (2011) *Independent Review of Women on Boards*. Department of Business, Innovation and Skills.

Dowling, P. and Schuller, R. (1991) *International Dimensions of Human Resource Management*. Boston: PWS-Kent.

Eaton, J. (2000) *Comparative Employment Relations: An Introduction*. Polity.

Economist (2013) Voting with their Wallets, Special Report: Cars. 20 April, 7–8.

Farley, J., Hoenig, S. and Yang, J. (2004) Key Factors Influencing HRM Practices of Overseas Subsidiaries in China's Transition Economy. *International Journal of Human Resource Management*, June and August, 15(4 and 5): 688–704.

Gerhart, B. and Fang, M. (2005) National Culture and Human Resource Management. *International Journal of Human Resource Management*, 16, 6 June.

Harry, W. (2007) East is East. *People Management*, 29 November, 36–38.

Hendry, C. (1994) *Human Resource Strategies for International Growth*. Routledge.

Hofstede, G. (1980) *Culture's Consequences*. Sage.

Hoppe, M. (2007) *Culture and Leadership Effectiveness: The GLOBE Study*, accessed at www.inspireimagineinnovate.com/PDF/GLOBEsummary-by-Michael-H-Hoppe.pdf.

House, R., Hanges, P.J., Javidan, M., Dorfman, P.W. and Gupta, V. (eds) (2004) *Culture, Leadership, and Organizations: The GLOBE Study of 62 Societies*. Sage.

Keizer, A. (2010) *Changes in Japanese Employment Practices*. Routledge.

Kessler, I., Undy, R. and Heron, P. (2004) Employee Perspectives on Communication and Consultation: Findings from a Cross-national Survey. *International Journal of Human Resource Management*, May, 15(3): 512–532.

Kim, Y. and Gao, F. (2011) An Empirical Study of Human Resource Management Practices in Family Firms in China. *International Journal of Human Resource Management*, 21(10): 2095–2119.

Kyotani, E. (1999) New Managerial Strategies of Japanese Corporations, in A. Felstead and N. Jewson (eds) *Global Trends in Flexible Labour*. Macmillan Business.

Lee, H., Iilima, Y. and Reade, C. (2011) Employee Preference for Performance-related Pay: Predictors and Consequences for Organisational Citizenship Behaviour in a Japanese Firm. *International Journal of Human Resource Management*, June, 22(10): 2086–2109.

Lin, Z., Kelly, J. and Trenberth, L. (2011) Antecedents and Consequences of the Introduction of Flexible Benefit Plans in China. *International Journal of Human Resource Management*, March, 22(5): 1128–1145.

Marlow, S. and Patton, D. (2002) Minding the Gap Between Employers and Employees: The Challenge for Owner-managers of Smaller Manufacturing Firms. *Employee Relations*, 24(5): 523–539.

Morris, J., Hassard, J. and McCann, L. (2006) New Organisational Forms, Human Resource Management and Structural Convergence? A Study of Japanese Organisations. *Organisation Studies*, 27: 1485–1511.

Muller, G. (1997) Institutional Resilience in a Changing World Economy? The Case of the German Banking and Chemical Industries. *British Journal of Industrial Relations*, 35(4): 954–985.

Newenham-Kahindi, A. (2009) The Transfer of Ubuntu and Indiba Business Models Abroad: A Case of South African Multinational Banks and Telecommunication Services in Tanzania. *International Journal of Cross-Cultural Management*, 9: 87–108.

Nussbaum, B. (2003) African Culture and Ubuntu: Reflections of a South African in America. *World Business Academy*, 10: 363–382.

Perkins, S. (1999) *Globalisation – The People Dimension*. Kogan Page.

Riddell, P. (2004) The Left is Wrong to Start a Tug-of-war on Call Centres. *The Times*, 26 February.

Ritzer, G. (1996) *The McDonaldization of Society*. Pine Forge.

Sappal, P. (2003) Cultural Evolution. *People Management*, 17 April, 33–38.

Sartorious, K., Merino, A. and Carmichael, T. (2011) Human Resource Management and Cultural Diversity: A Case Study in Mozambique. *International Journal of Human Resource Management*, 22(9): 1963–1985.

Schaede, U. (2008) *Choose and Focus: Japanese Business Strategies for the 21st Century*. Cornell Press.

Stewart, K. (2004) Insurer Packs 7000 Jobs off to India. *Morning Star*, 23 September, 1.

Stiles, P. (2007) A World of Difference? *People Management*, 15 November, 36–41.

Tayeb, M. (1999) Understanding and Managing the Multicultural Workforce, in M. Tayeb (ed.) *International Business: Theories, Policies and Practices*. Financial Times/Prentice Hall.

Tsogas, G. (1999) Labour Standards, Corporate Codes of Conduct and Labour Regulation in International Trade, in M. Tayeb (ed.) *International Business: Theories, Policies and Practices*. Financial Times/Prentice Hall.

Yeganeh, H. and Su, Z. (2009) Applicability of Widely Employed Frameworks in Cross-cultural Management Research. *Journal of Academic Research in Economics*, 1(1): 1–24, accessed at http://www.jare-sh.com/volume1-issue1/applicability.pdf.

ADDITIONAL FEATURES

 Please visit the companion website at: www.routledge.com/cw/stredwick where you will find additional case studies and reading material together with short self-tests and other resources for both students and lectures.

12 HUMAN RESOURCE PLANNING

CHAPTER OBJECTIVES

When you have read this chapter and carried out the activities, you will be able to:

- Understand the purpose and importance of human resource planning (HRP) in an uncertain world.

- Draw up an outline plan by following the three-stage planning approach.

- Conduct simple mathematical calculations to identify demand and supply data.

- Implement an analysis of retention measures, including wastage, stability and half-life indexes.

- Identify approaches to improving retention rates.

- Understand and analyse the main causes of absence and how absence rates can be reduced.

- Identify the necessary implementation strategies and practices to achieve success.

INTRODUCTION

The first 11 chapters of this book have dealt with fundamental subject areas involved in human resources. This last chapter looks at ways of taking business strategies and converting them into practice through forms of human resource planning (HRP). The structure of the chapter covers:

■ Explaining why HRP operates at a far lower level than 30 years ago
■ Identifying and analysing the various purposes of HRP
■ Assessing the components of future demand
■ Assessing the components of future supply, including absence and retention policy and practice
■ Putting the plan together.

Manpower planning in large UK companies was once the centre of influence for human resource professionals. A period of two to three years in the department that collected and processed vast amounts of internal and external staffing and market data, identified the labour needs for five years ahead and then produced a master plan of recruitment, training and career development to meet all those needs was considered an essential milestone on the road to high office. The influence of the staffing master plan, just as in the Soviet equivalent, could not be underestimated, as it guided the majority of human resource activities in a predictable world.

Today, as set out in Chapter 1, we are no longer sure of what the future will hold even two or three years down the line. Large organisations still have strategic plans, but these are set out in more general terms of shareholder returns and competitive stance. They provide for flexibility to take advantage of opportunities that arise and to cope with unexpected dangers that may befall them. They are rarely written down in a formal document precisely because the world's competitive environment is no longer precise.

That is not to say that planning should not take place. On the contrary, in uncertain times, those organisations that know where they are and have a good idea of their general direction will, like the sailors who learned to calculate latitude, be more likely to be survivors than those who never learned those required skills. There is less emphasis on the single-scenario plan and more on the development of trained and competent staff that will thrive in a number of scenarios. The main thrust, according to Sparrow, written over 20 years ago in 1992, is that:

Human Resource Planning picks up the issues that are at the heart of the business, such as acquisition, decentralisation, empowerment, internationalisation or technology, and investigates their human resource management implications. HRP therefore requires a strategic approach to the recruitment, development, management and motivation of the people in the organisation, in the context of a pressing business issue. It is a systematic process of linking human resource practices with business demands in order to improve an organisation's abilities. It establishes the plans, courses of action and targets for the range of policies needed to enable the organisation to influence the management of its human resources.

(1992: 253)

The reduction in planning activities took place since the 1980s because, in the major recession and restructuring of the period, companies became more volatile. Industries, such as coal, steel and shipbuilding, declined into a shadow of their former selves, while services, especially financial and business services, expanded substantially. So the emphasis has turned away from the rigidity of detailed long-term planning towards greater flexibility and towards viewing planning as a continuous process of diagnosis and action planning (Iles 2001).

Having said this, it is strongly argued that planning remains critically important during turbulent times to ensure that staff of the right quality and with the appropriate skills and competencies are available at the right times. It is also possible to identify some major sectors where old-style planning remains absolutely essential. For example, the National Health Service, with its one million plus employees, operates in a largely predictable, non-competitive environment. It can plan its staffing in the light of longevity and other demographic forecasts matched with likely technological advances and macro-employment conditions. Even here, as Frank Dobson, Health Minister at the time, commented, 'decisions we take today to increase the number of consultants will take around 15 years to come to fruition – you must plan for improved staffing in highly skilled professions many years in advance' (*Today* programme, 2 August 1999). Even for the NHS, however, planning is not always straightforward. In 2007, the organisation was severely criticised by the House of Commons Health Select Committee for the lack of proper HR planning. It found that, between 1999 and 2004, the number of nurses increased by more than 67,000, a 340 per cent excess on original targets, and the number of GPs went up by 4,098, 105 per cent over target. The Committee found the expansion to be 'reckless and uncontrolled, often seen as a blank cheque for recruiting new staff' (Brockett 2007).

REASONS FOR LACK OF PLANNING

Rothwell (1995) distinguishes four main reasons why many organisations put few resources into the HRP process. Firstly, the belief that planning is so problematical as to be useless due to the rapidly changing technology, new forms of government policies or regulation, or competitive environment. The need for planning may, in fact, be in inverse proportion to its feasibility.

Secondly, within the organisation, there are a 'shifting kaleidoscope of policy priorities and strategies which depend on the policies of the powerful interest groups involved'

(Rothwell 1995: 178). Taken together with the weak power base of the human resources function, especially at times of economic recession, the planning process will be skimped with merely a 'spin' applied to justify political requirements.

A third reason is that UK management in general does not have the best record with long-term plans, preferring a pragmatic adaptation over conceptualisation and a distrust for theory or planning. This viewpoint very much reflects the attitude of the City of London, where short-term profits often take preference over long-term investments – the so-called City 'short-termism'. This is contrasted with German and Japanese approaches, which, while lacking a degree of flexibility, have a clear view of the future longer-term direction and the need for detailed planning to get there.

Rothwell adds a fourth explanation that human resource planning is often difficult to identify, although it may take place at an operational level and then be rationalised *post hoc* as successful strategy.

To these can be added a further reason, which is the change in nature of organisational structures. Traditional bureaucratic structures have presented a series of stepping stones for career progression, allowing individuals' careers to be mapped out. With the downsizing and de-layering that took place in the 1990s, opportunities for traditional promotion routes have been much reduced and planning far more uncertain. For example, many human resources managers spent much of the early 1990s making redundant senior staff who arrived at their current positions over 20 or 30 years through such a process. They repeated the process at the end of the 2000s in the recession that followed the financial crisis. Having gone through such an unpleasant experience, enthusiasm to continue such career planning processes has naturally waned among human resources staff. When the organisation operates in a rapidly changing international environment, it becomes impossible to centrally plan all the training, development and potential career moves for large numbers of management.

PURPOSE OF HUMAN RESOURCE PLANNING

The main purpose of human resource planning is to support the organisation's objective of securing a competitive advantage. Donald Burr, founder of People Express, set out a long-term human resource plan at an early stage of his company's development to stay non-union, pay lower salaries, have broad job categories and work within teams. This has led the organisation to compete successfully through lower people costs and given it a sustained competitive advantage (Ulrich 1987).

There are four main general objectives in developing a human resource plan:

■ *Continuity flow*: To get the right people in the right place at the right time with the necessary skills. This involves policies in respect of recruitment, succession planning and training.

- *Maintenance*: To retain the stability in the workforce through pay and benefits and individual career planning.
- *Response to change*: To put into effect changes that come about from major operational strategies. These can involve relocation, retraining or redeployment.
- *Control*: To ensure that staff move in the right direction through the establishment of standards, performance control systems and building long-term employee relationships.

The detail and direction of each of these will be fashioned by the organisation's overall strategic plan. If the strategic plan indicates a development of new products or services, the continuity plan is crucial in ensuring that staff are recruited, trained and motivated in time for the launch. If divestment of certain activities is decided, a strategy and detailed plan needs to be in place to prepare for the change, be it through redundancy or transfer of undertakings. If the strategic plan focuses on increased productivity or improved workforce relationships, the human resource plan needs to be in place to accomplish this objective.

This linkage cannot be emphasised too much. As explained by Barney and Wright:

> Sustainable competitive advantage stems from HR systems rather than a single practice. Any practice is good – until it gets copied by a competitor. . . . It requires a change in the mind-set from traditional sub-functions (selection, training, appraisal) to the view of human resources where all these independent sub-functions are viewed as inter-related components of a highly inter-dependent system.
>
> (1998: 40)

PLANNING FOR SPECIFIC PURPOSES

Taylor (2010) puts forward a number of types of planning that are aimed at achieving practical organisational objectives.

Micro-planning deals with forecasting supply and demand for specific groups, such as the example of nurses you will find later in this chapter. It is especially relevant when dealing with tight labour markets or where there are major organisational developments, such as a bank moving into hedge funds, or where there needs to be a swift change to meet a new environmental challenge, such as a new competitor or the introduction of regulation.

Contingency planning covers the situation where possible scenarios are examined and the implications assessed before major decisions are taken. An example here would be the plans for the development of a major manufacturing plant where the implications for various levels of expansion would be considered in terms of shift systems, labour availability, employee relations and payment systems. These implications would influence the decision as to whether to expand on site or elsewhere.

Succession planning is a third type where the objective is to focus human resource planning activity on the recruitment and development of individuals to fill managerial and top positions as detailed in Chapter 8. As the future leadership of the organisation is probably the most crucial aspect of its potential and continuing success, resources set aside to search out and train potential board members is a vital human resource activity. Through graduate or management trainee entry, plans can be set out for promotions every few years; organisations can plan employees' experience in a range of organisational projects and activities, ensure they have both line and staff responsibilities, and support the plan with a regular infusion of management training. Given the essential requirement of having top-quality management in today's world, it is all the more strange that the 1990s saw a sizeable reduction in this process and more concentration on 'buying in' the necessary skills and experience in the international marketplace. This was reversed in the early 2000s, according to Simms (2003), when organisations began to appreciate the statistics that 80 per cent of organisations with above-average financial performance have strong succession management systems. Moreover, regulatory institutions, such as the Financial Services Authority, have imposed the requirement on organisations to prove they have sufficiently robust succession schemes in place. An example of a successful succession planning system (GKN PLC) is set out in case study 12.1.

A further type of planning focuses on *developing skills and competencies*. This is not just identifying the volume and types of skills required but also working out ways that these can be met from both within and outside the organisations. Taylor (2010) uses an example of the skills needed in the computer software industry where the skills can be sourced from temporary or agency employees or outsourced to independent organisations.

The final type concerns the 'soft' areas of human resource planning, which deal not with numbers but with *cultural and behavioural objectives*. The most well known of these are longer-term campaigns to transform staff attitudes towards quality and customer-care issues and to raise the level of employee engagement. Planning in this area has shown a very rapid rise in recent years and has proved a necessary and crucial part in improving the competitive position of many organisations.

A different approach to the subject is taken by Armstrong (2009) who sees the practical side of HRP as a series of implementation strategies consisting of:

- Acquisition strategies, defining how the resources required to meet forecast needs will be obtained.
- Retention strategies, which indicate how the organisation intends to keep the people it wants.
- Development strategies, which deal with skills and competency requirements.
- Utilisation strategies, identifying how productivity and cost-effectiveness can be improved.

- Flexibility strategies, evaluating how various flexible working practices can lead to improved organisational effectiveness.
- Downsizing strategies, defining what needs to be done to reduce numbers to those the organisation needs.

The need to ensure that the plan is not just a collection of disjointed ideas but an integrated whole is emphasised by Mark Huselid with his concept of *'bundling' human resource practices*, as explained in Chapter 1. In his research on successful US companies who use high-performance work practices (i.e. progressive HR practices), he found that it was not the specific practices themselves that led to success. The key lies in having the right 'bundle' of practices. Because the secret to competitive success is having an advantage that is difficult to imitate, then the bundle must be specific to one organisation. If it were not, it would be easy to copy and nobody would have an advantage.

CASE STUDY 12.1 SUCCESSION PLANNING AT GKN

C
A
S
E

S
T
U
D
Y

GKN is a large engineering company with operations in 30 countries. From the mid-1990s, the organisation had adopted a more rigorous and systematic approach to management appraisal and development, arising from a major concern that too many good people were leaving the organisation. As a result, GKN was recruiting too many people from the outside to fill vacancies higher up in the organisation.

Working closely with line managers, the HR department identified 75 key roles across GKN's international spectrum, the skills needed for these roles and a talent pool of around 200 potential successors. From this point, a number of 'emerging leaders', people at the top of the talent pool, were picked out to be prepared for promotion over the longer period. Twenty-five of these went through an intense assessment and development programme with a major consultancy and were then sent to Columbia Business School in America for a week's programme called 'Emerging Leaders'.

Although the graduate intakes are tracked well, the organisation has also been concerned that non-graduates with potential have not been identified early enough. Systems to pinpoint such employees were put in place, including a 'buddy system' to encourage employees to stay in touch with others in different divisions and each of the six executive committee members actively mentor three or four younger executives – a system that is cascaded down the organisation.

While graduate retention in most organisations is 50–55 per cent after five years, GKN's is closer to 70 per cent and, among its 200-strong team of executives, the ratio between home-grown and bought-in talent is approaching 80:20.

(Source: Simms 2003)

Huselid calls the practices 'idiosyncratic contingencies', which fit with the business strategy and the organisational culture. The bundle of practices have to complement and support each other. Benchmarking, therefore, is of little value. Finding the right fit is a difficult matter and often happens by chance or experiment. So, although a plan that includes certain practices, such as linking pay to performance, a high degree of involvement, sophisticated selection processes and extensive training, may work with some companies, this is not guaranteed.

CARRYING OUT HUMAN RESOURCE PLANNING

Robinson (2010) has suggested that the main sources of an HR plan are the answers to the following organisational questions:

- What workforce problems inhibit the ability to meet organisational goals?
- What are the pressures for change that we are experiencing? What impact do they have on our workforce?
- Are there better ways of working? What is inhibiting these?
- Where will the organisation be changing in nature? What are the workforce implications?
- Are there external forces, such as legislation, which will affect the work we do and how we do it? Which employee groups will be most affected?
- What items come up repeatedly in performance management reviews or personal development plans as weaknesses or developmental needs?
- Are there roles we cannot do or jobs we cannot fill? What do internal candidates lack?

In effect, this is part of the process of understanding the strategic direction of the company and carefully considering all the implications for human resources issues.

The numerical or 'hard' aspects

In dealing with the traditional version of HRP, there are three main stages in producing a realistic plan. There is an assessment of the *future demand* for human resources, taking into account the current situation, the external environment and the organisation's business plan. This is followed by the analysis of the *likely supply* of human resources, both internal and external, taking into account the internal labour movement and the external forces. The final stage is to *draw up a plan* detailing the actions necessary to reconcile the first two parts so that organisational needs can be met. Figure 12.1 illustrates this process.

Forecasting, however, is a notoriously uncertain activity in all fields of life. There are a number of sources that can assist the process but none of them is, in itself, reliable. There is no guarantee that what has happened in the past will be repeated in the future. Information

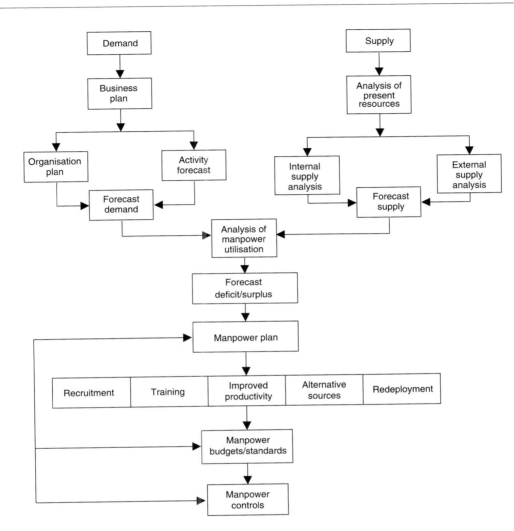

Figure 12.1
The process of human resource planning

Source: Armstrong, M. (1996) *Employee Reward.* CIPD.

on the macroeconomic front is often confused with as many different economic forecasts as there are forecasters and official figures on economic growth and employment regularly revised in retrospect. Even the information provided by employees through surveys cannot be totally relied on, as the basis for their responses (such as trust, commitment and economic well-being) may swiftly change.

Assessment of future demand

The starting point for any forecast is the organisation's *business plan*, which sets out the preferred, realistic scenario for the period ahead. This period may be a year, two years or five years, which may vary depending on for whom the plan is produced – major investors, banks or internal consumption only. The further ahead, the more difficult the planning process. The factors that will influence the direction of the plan can include:

- The driving forces behind the organisation as personified by the major shareholders, chief executive and senior management. Are they engaged in a period of rapid change, either through acquisitions or internal growth? Is a major change of direction planned, with major divestments and closures? Are they aggressively aiming for an increased market share? Are they content for a period of consolidation and stability?
- The competitive environment, both within the UK and overseas. Is the market growing or contracting? How is the competitive structure changing with new entrants or consolidation through mergers? Is there any change in the regulatory environment?
- The need to introduce new products. Product life cycles are getting shorter as customers continue to demand new and improved products and services.
- Technological developments, which lead to changes in the products or services themselves and the way that they are made or delivered.
- Legislative framework, whereby legal changes through UK or European law may lead to required changes to the products or services or, in the case of easing the regulatory environment, may lead to greater opportunities. An example of the latter is in the telecoms and airline environment in Europe.

The business plan will indicate some of the changes in the human resource requirements. New acquisitions will provide considerable activity in terms of rationalisation of terms and conditions, new appointments, possible redundancies and different working practices. The introduction of new technology may reduce the number of production or administrative employees required. A set of new products may increase the requirements. The drive for increased productivity of, say, 5 per cent, may insert into the plan a reduction by that amount in the staffing required. The introduction of legislation on HRM issues, such as the Agency Workers Directive or on health and safety may require a planned change in working practices or payments systems.

All these changes are likely to be considered first in general terms and then refined by way of more sophisticated methods. These include *computerised modelling*, where all the variables can be inserted to produce 'what if' forecasts and the most likely one is selected. The alternatives are substituted to produce a revised plan at a later date should external factors change. *Statistical techniques*, especially time-series, can be utilised to look at how the demand has varied over an extended time period. *Work study and organisation and method techniques* can also be utilised to help indicate where improvements in labour utilisation and operation can be implemented.

EXTENDED STUDENT ACTIVITY 12.1 – FORECASTING DEMAND

Here is a scenario for you to calculate the numerical demand for certain staffing groups in an NHS hospital trust in the South of England over a four-year period. The current number of employees is shown in Table 12.1.

Table 12.1 Current staff

	Permanent	Temporary
Nurses	576	24
Sisters	48	6
Admin support staff	240	16
Admin supervisors	30	2
Total	894	48

The *business plan* includes the impending reorganisation of hospital services in the entire region which will involve the transfer of a number of services to the trust and a closure of a major unit in year three. This will mean the following changes in demand:

Year 1	Year 2	Year 3	Year 4
+6%	+4%	−30%	+5%

The introduction in *new technology* affects labour requirements in two ways. A new computer system should produce an increase in staffing of six administrators in year two, but the following year a reduction of sixteen staff will occur. New medical technology planned has a higher labour content and will produce an increase in the requirement from year two onwards of sixteen nurses and one sister.

It is planned that the introduction of annual hours and other flexible working arrangements will lead to *productivity increase* of 2 per cent in year one.

The requirements arising from the *government targets* for improved customer service will lead to the need for an increase in administrative staff of 3 per cent for year one. A *flatter organisation structure* is planned which will change the ratio of sisters to nurses as follows:

	Current	Year 1	Year 2	Year 3 onwards
Sister:nurse ratio	1:12	1:14	1:14	1:16
Admin supervisor:support staff	1:8	1:10	1:10	1:14

Action required

Take each year in turn, starting with year one, and calculate the staff required in each category. You may be able to put this onto a spreadsheet to help your calculations (see Table 12.2). You may need to make certain assumptions as you go along – make

Table 12.2 Demand for nurses

	Year 1	Year 2	Year 3	Year 4
Starting point	600	624	655	
Business plan	+6% = +36	+4% = +25		
New technology		+16		
Productivity improvement	−2% = −12			
Total	= 624	= 665		

sure you keep a note of these. The first calculation for nurses in years one and two has been carried out for you.

Demand for nurses. (Existing staff = 576 + 24 temps = 600 total)

You will need to complete Table 12.2 and draw up a similar table for the other three staff categories.

Assessment of future internal supply

Staff retention (sometimes called *staff turnover*) has a critical effect upon the supply of labour to an organisation. Turnover can be put into the categories of *voluntary* or *compulsory* turnover.

Voluntary turnover includes:

- Leaving to take up a job elsewhere
- Leaving to raise a family, set up a business or enter full-time education
- Leaving due to partner's relocation
- Retirement (although the organisation may enforce a compulsory retirement age)
- Leaving due to ill-health.

Compulsory turnover includes:

- Dismissal for misconduct
- Dismissal due to ill-health
- Dismissal due to redundancy.

Staff turnover can be calculated for the organisation as a whole or by specific job or skill categories, which is more useful. This measure can be calculated in three ways:

1   *Wastage index*, which is calculated as follows:

$$\frac{\text{Number of staff leaving in a year}}{\text{Average number employed in the same period}} \times 100$$

For example, the number of staff leaving in a year may be 60, while the average number employed in that year is 200, giving a wastage index of 30 per cent. Although this is a useful comparative measure, it may hide considerable variations. In this example, the wastage rate appears very high, indicating a regular turnover of all staff. However, the reality may be that, of the 60 leaving, many have stayed only a few weeks, while the bulk of employees remain throughout the period.

2 *Stability index.* Because the wastage index does not always give a full picture of the turnover, there is an alternative calculation called a *stability index*, calculated as follows:

$$\frac{\text{Number of employees with one year's service at 31 December}}{\text{Number employed one year ago}} \times 100$$

Thus, in the above example, if the organisation employed 200 staff at the start of 2000 and, of these, 170 were still employed at the end of the year, the stability index would be 85 per cent. This gives a more positive spin on the situation than quoting a turnover rate of 30 per cent.

3 *Half-life index.* This method is to take a cohort of employees who all started either at the same time or all within the same three- or six-month period. This might be, say, a group of trainees or new employees at the start-up of a factory or office. The index is calculated by the time taken for the cohort to be cut in half through turnover. For example, if the cohort of 30 trainees started in 2006 and was reduced to 15 by 2012, the half-life is 6 years. This is a useful way of comparing the stability of different cohorts.

There are a number of possible employers' responses to labour shortages as shown in Figure 12.2. The strategic activities may take longer to put into effect but will be more likely to move towards resolving the difficulties faced.

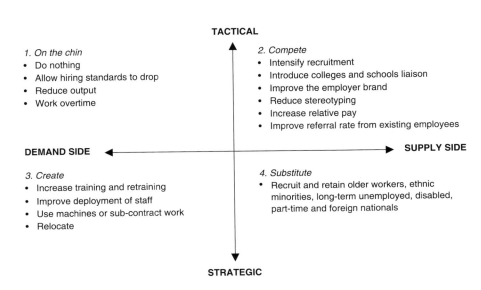

Figure 12.2 Employers' responses to labour shortages

Source: Morris, H. and Willey, B. (1996) *The Corporate Environment: A Guide for Human Resource Managers*. Financial Times/Prentice Hall.

FOCUS ON RESEARCH 12.1 LABOUR TURNOVER, 2012

The CIPD survey of labour turnover for 2012, based on information from around 500 respondents, showed that turnover was continuing to drop. A summary of the findings included the following:

- The average turnover was 12.7 per cent compared with 16 per cent in 2009 and 16 per cent in 2000.
- Voluntary turnover was 8 per cent, while involuntary turnover (redundancy, short-term contracts, death and retirement) was 4.7 per cent.
- The private sector (16 per cent) had a higher turnover rate than the public sector (10 per cent).
- In the view of the HR respondents, the biggest reasons given for voluntary turnover were promotion and changing career with pay levels coming some distance behind.
- Only 16 per cent of respondents calculated the cost of turnover.
- 66 per cent reported some difficulty over retention (down from 80 per cent in 2007) with the biggest problem areas being managers and technical staff.
- The most common methods used to address retention problems were to increase learning and development opportunities and to improve line managers' people skills. Only 28 per cent of organisations improved pay levels, compared with 53 per cent in 2007.

(Source: CIPD 2012a)

Retaining staff is one of the critical measures in human resources and much research takes place into its prevalence and causes. In focus on research 12.1, details are given of the CIPD 2012 survey.

Exit interviews

If staff turnover is high, it becomes very important to research the causes. According to Huber (2011), around 86 per cent of the larger organisations use exit interviews in one form or another. It certainly makes sense (and is only a common courtesy) to talk to employees at the point of their exit both to thank them for their contribution to the organisation and to try to elicit why they are leaving. Unfortunately, the information they provide may not be reliable, as practitioners know well. Because the leaving employee may need to rely on a reference for some years, they will be hesitant in being too critical of the organisation, be it the culture, the rewards or their own manager. Worse still, they may remain silent about disquieting events that have occurred, which may have affected them or to which they were witness, such as bullying or sexual harassment. If the information cannot be relied on, it is generally worthless. That is why it is far more sensible, if a little more expensive, to contract a third party to carry out the interview and to collate the information, while allowing the employee to remain anonymous.

Absenteeism

Another important aspect of internal supply is the *absenteeism rate*. If this deteriorates in the course of a year, the supply of labour reduces by the amount of the deterioration. The supply will increase, of course, if absenteeism improves. As much of the responsibility for sick pay schemes has been transferred to employers in recent years, the cost of absenteeism is very high, so there is a considerable incentive for employers to aim to reduce absenteeism.

The CIPD survey on Absence (CIPD 2012b) found that absenteeism rates had fallen during the recession, down from an average of 9.1 days in 2004 to 6.8 days in 2012. Absence in non-profit organisations was the highest at an average of 8.2 days, while the public sector showed a downward trend to 7.9 days. Around two-thirds of absence is short-term (less than seven days) and one-third long-term absence. One of the main reasons why absence is higher in the public and non-profit sectors is that there is a higher rate of long-term absence.

The occupations with the highest absence rate were care workers (12.2 days), health (9.4 days), education (9.3 days) and call centres (9.3 days).

Absenteeism is a more complex issue than it at first appears. It is complex because the causes are many and varied, where personal circumstances and health and organisational environment and culture both contribute. There are also a number of ways of measuring absence. The organisational responses are also complex; dealing with long-term absence due to advancing cancer will be different to dealing with short-term absence from a cold; few managers like handling return-to-work interviews; obtaining information of a person's ill-health has become more difficult due to the regulation of personal data. This section will attempt to examine these issues in turn, starting with the causes of absence, considering the ways it can be measured and, finally, the various options that organisations can take to attempt to reduce absence levels.

CAUSES OF ABSENCE

The initial response to high levels of absence is often that little can be done when employees are ill. However, Table 12.3, which shows the causes of absence, demonstrates that many aspects of absenteeism are influenced by factors that are within the control of management.

Nature of work and internal relationships

Without going too deeply into the complex field of motivational research, there is strong evidence that the line managers can make a substantial difference to employee attitudes and behaviour (Purcell and Hutchison 2007), especially in the way they conduct human resource activity, such as performance management and discipline. Employees that are unhappy with

Table 12.3 Causes of absenteeism

Causes related to the organisation	Causes related to the individual
Illness, stress and anxiety (ISA) due to the nature of the work • Excessive hours • Routine and boring job • Too much pressure with high expectations • Poor working conditions – heat, dust, etc. • Sick building syndrome (poorly designed) • Lack of control over job	*Stress and anxiety in personal life* • Inability to deal with work and caring responsibilities • Going through domestic trauma – death, divorce, etc. • Commuting too wearing • Immaturity makes it difficult to deal with work situations
ISA due to poor relationships with manager, colleagues • Poor communications • Lack of training • Lack of mutual respect or recognition of effort • Bullying or harassment	*Individual illness* • Chronic condition, such as asthma • Tendency to get routine illnesses and backache
Cultural problems • Culture of excessive absence, apparently accepted as the norm • No work–life balance processes, so sickness may be notified at times of caring responsibilities • General poor morale with little job satisfaction, no culture of achievement or values resulting in low engagement levels	*Lack of engagement* • Cannot identify with corporate culture
Problems with sick pay scheme • A scheme that is too generous, appearing to condone high absence levels • A scheme which is not followed consistently • No apparent attention given to employees with high absence levels	

the relationship with their manager are more likely to be demotivated, disengaged and to take time off through absence. This will become far more likely if there is an additional element of a manager bullying their staff. Similarly, the physical and contextual side of work can affect the level of motivation and be influential on the volume of absence in an organisation.

Cultural issues

Cultures where a high absence rate is seen as acceptable by employees and, to a lesser extent by employers, are far less prevalent than 30 years ago. While working in the shipyard in the 1970s, the writer was told by a senior supervisor (with a straight face) that he had only used up eight of his twelve days of sickness entitlement and had another four to take before Christmas, and attitudes like this can still prevail today if management do not present a coherent, fair and effective approach to handling absenteeism.

Sick pay scheme

Sick pay schemes can be very complex, with many variations. A few points of principal can be made. Firstly, although it is good practice to show that an organisation cares about the well-being of its staff, schemes which are more generous, such as those in the public sector, tend to have higher absence levels, as detailed earlier in the CIPD (2012b) report. For example, in the public sector, it is common for employees, after a service qualification, to be entitled to full pay for six months and then half pay for six months. In the private sector, the average sick pay entitlement is only ten days. At Tesco, for example, employees with one year's service are only entitled to six weeks' full pay and then three weeks' half pay. Tesco's absence rate is 3 per cent, compared with around 4.5 per cent in the public sector.

As the recession has developed, certain sections of the labour force have tightened up their criteria for paying absence. In 2012, one hospital, where staff who were absent received both their basic pay and an enhanced premium for shifts they would have worked during anti-social hours if they had not been ill, have unilaterally cut this benefit to save around £400,000 (Hookham and Mansey 2012).

Causes related to the individual

Where absence can be related more closely to the individual's own health and context, you will note that the *level of engagement* can be an important factor here. Without a commitment and liking for the workplace, employees may decide, at the margins, that they are just over the borderline of illness and call in sick. With a high level of engagement and a day to look forward to, an employee may trust that the adrenaline will carry them through and they will come in to work.

Stress is blamed for an ever-growing list of ailments and the CIPD (2012b) survey reports it as the most important constituent cause of absence. A detailed analysis of stress issues was set out in Chapter 10.

MEASURING ABSENCE

The standard measure of absence is the average number of days absent in a year. However, that does not take into account the difference between short-term and long-term absence. If a department of twelve staff has very little absence except for one member of staff off sick for the whole month with a chronic illness, the absence statistics for that department will not look good. The *Bradford formula*, used by about one in six employers (IRS 2007), has been designed to place greater emphasis on short-term absence, which most managers will see as most disruptive and avoidable.

The Bradford formula is as follows:

S x S x D

where S = nos of spells of absence and D = total days absence in 52 weeks

Examples: 12 days of absence spread over 5 spells $5 \times 5 \times 12 = 300$ points

1 day of absence followed later by 6 weeks of absence $2 \times 2 \times 31 = 124$ points

(2 spells of absence, 31 days in total)

Others measures that organisations can employ include:

- Division between long-term and short-term absence
- Breakdown into reasons given on sick notes and at return to work interview
- Breakdown into physical ailments and psychological reasons, such as stress
- Comparisons with previous years
- Comparison of organisation's absence rate with similar companies in their sector
- Measures of attitude towards absence if included in staff attitude surveys.

There have always been debates about the accuracy of records. IRS (2007) reported that only 30 per cent of respondents to their absence survey were confident that their records were fully accurate, while 10 per cent considered them to be inaccurate to a greater or lesser extent, the remainder being reasonably but not entirely sure of their veracity. The reasons given for doubt included:

- Managers failed to record short absences (such as dentist visits or half-days to look after children).
- Special arrangements were made with employees who had long-term chronic illnesses.
- Managers may want to protect employees from losing some form of incentive so did not record their absence.
- Many people rang in to say they were not well but would work at home, which was impossible to verify.
- Some staff took time off and made this up by arrangement with the manager but no records were kept.
- Staff did not always record the correct reason for their absence.
- Absence forms or return-to-work interview forms were not always completed or were not sent to HR.

SOLUTIONS TO ABSENCE PROBLEMS

Organisations often hold back from taking initiatives on absence, given some of the difficulties involved. It is not just the problems detailed above in obtaining accurate measurements of absence, but there are often difficulties faced in obtaining consistent line management support for action against individual employees and there is a general distaste for questioning employees about their health and personal problems. Some organisations do not want to encourage a rise in the level of *presenteeism*, that is, the tendency for employees to come into work, no matter how sick they are. However, it is almost inevitable that absence performance will slide unless the company, and especially the HR department, has its finger on the pulse and acts regularly to steady the ship. Practitioners know that, in almost every case, *any* action taken on absence produces improvements in the absence rate, although that improvement can often be short-lived.

The government, for its part, has attempted to encourage a more positive approach to getting employees back to work by introducing the 'fit notes' in 2010, which allowed GPs to categorise employees as 'may be fit for work', and encourage a dialogue between the employer and employee to agree some form of phased return to work with reduced hours or workload change. This initiative seems to have had only a limited success (Lalali *et al.* 2012), as employers identified reluctance among GPs to use the 'may be fit for work' option, which, in some cases, prolonged sickness absence despite the possibility of adjustments to enable a return to work. For the fit note to be effective in reducing sickness absence, employers are dependent on greater use of this option by GPs. According to the CIPD (2012b), only 10 per cent of respondents thought that the change had been of much use. A further government plan is to set up an independent assessment service to assess the health of employees signed off work for four or more weeks. This would provide a more neutral ground for assessment of the employee's needs. They have also proposed to make it easier to end the employment of long-term sick employees by paying them a statutory sum (Allison 2012).

What is required is an overall programme, applied regularly and consistently, to try to tackle all aspects of the problem. This can consist of the following elements:

A consistently applied sick pay scheme. Organisations should be cautious over the entitlements included in their sick pay scheme and ensure they balance their generosity with a degree of realism. Secondly, thought needs to be given as to how to treat the first three days of absence. A number of larger organisations, including Tesco (Ryle 2004), have experimented with non-payment of those days with mixed results.

Consistency is aided by two main vehicles. Firstly, the use of '*triggers*', which indicates that an employee has a potential absence problem. According to IRS (2007), the typical trigger is where absence in the year is over ten days, although some schemes have more complex triggers relating to short-term and long-term absence. If the Bradford system is in place, the trigger will apply where a number of points have been exceeded, the average trigger point being 200. Investigations will follow to review the absence and see if action is required, taking into account the circumstances and nature of the absence. This may involve an off-the-record discussion with the manager, or a referral to the occupational health adviser or the start of disciplinary procedure.

The second aid to consistency is the use of *return-to-work interviews*, which are used by 90 per cent of organisations (CIPD 2012b). These need to take place immediately

C
A
S
E

S
T
U
D
Y

CASE STUDY 12.2 WORK–LIFE BALANCE REDUCES ABSENCE LEVELS AT LEEDS CITY COUNCIL

Leeds City Council introduced a pilot study in 2000, which involved self-rostering teams in its benefits office. Each employee had to set a specific and achievable goal – such as leaving early on Thursday to go to the gym – then mark themselves out of five to reflect how well they had done it. Scores were aggregated for the team, so all members took responsibility for each other. Not only did the scheme lead to higher productivity but there was also a reduction in average annual absence from 16 days to 10 days over a 4-year period. It also led to an increase in female managers because flexible working was available at all levels.

(Source: Griffiths 2005)

following the return to work of the employee who has been absent. Evidence indicates that having such interviews in place actually reduces absence levels (Dunn and Wilkinson 2002), although line managers often avoid the confrontation that such an interview may bring. Because of the sensitive nature of this interview, line managers need effective training in order for them to be carried out and recorded properly.

Improve employee well-being. As set out in Chapter 10, a programme of encouraging healthy living and the provision of well-being benefits, such as employee assistance programmes, can produce a reduction in absence levels, as well as demonstrating that the employer has a serious interest in the good health of their workforce.

Improve work–life balance. Research has shown that flexible working initiatives, as set out in Chapter 7, can help reduce absence levels (Griffiths 2005). An example is shown in case study 12.2.

Improve level of engagement and change organisational culture. Details were given of the benefits of improving employee engagement and how employers can improve engagement levels in Chapter 4 and reducing absence levels is one of the best examples of the benefits obtained.

Incentives. Some organisations make payments to employees with good attendance records as a way of recognising their achievement. Pannone, a Manchester law firm, pay £100 to employees with no absence in a year and £75 to those who have taken no more than four days' absence (IDS 2011a).

Incentives to reduce absenteeism are controversial. The arguments ranged against them are:

- Employees have a duty to attend and that extra payments should not be made simply for turning up.
- Employees may come in to work when they are not fit to do so just to save their bonus, possibly spreading infection or creating a harmful incident.

- Once employees have been absent during the period and have lost the bonus, the scheme provides no further incentive.
- It discriminates against employees with chronic illnesses and therefore may be considered unlawful.

INTEGRATED APPROACH TO ABSENCE MANAGEMENT

To have a greater chance of achieving the desired results, initiatives which cover more than one of the above elements are essential. An example of an integrated approach is shown in case study 12.3.

DISMISSAL FOR ABSENCE

It is essential that a considered and consistent approach is used when action is taken against employees with a poor absence record. This is especially relevant when dealing with long-term absence and the issue of an employee's capability to carry out a job, as shown in spotlight on the law 12.1.

Other factors influencing internal supply

- *Internal transfers and promotion* also need to be considered in the equation as they affect the numbers in specific job categories.
- *Retirements.* The changes in state retirement pensions (equalising retirement dates between the sexes and extending the state retirement age to 66 by 2020 and 67 by 2028) will undoubtedly have an effect upon staffing numbers, as retirement will take place later. It is also likely to involve some employees wanting to reduce their hours as they come up to state retirement age. Some may want to take advantage of the right to request work beyond retirement age. These are all ways of analysing the current situation but may not necessarily be a reliable guide to the future. Each area needs to be assessed on what is likely to happen on current information. A sustained campaign on absenteeism may lead to a sizeable reduction. Staff leaving for domestic reasons may be persuaded to return quickly if childcare facilities or flexible hours practices are in place.
- *Voluntary turnover* needs to be analysed through an exit interview with each leaver. A number of employees may be lured to a rival organisation because of better terms, conditions or working practices so there is a need to assess what, if anything, can be changed and the costs involved, together with the costs of not doing so. Employees with high levels of skills and experience may be persuaded not to take early retirement by agreeing that they can work reduced hours. The organisation needs to examine if this is possible and beneficial in the circumstances.

CASE STUDY 12.3 ABSENCE PROGRAMME SAVES GSK £1.5 MILLION

GlaxoSmithKline (GSK) introduced a new case management model in 2004 to deal with absence. It provided support to employees so they could return to work as quickly as possible, thereby reducing sickness costs, such as replacement labour and lost or delayed production. The model is based on a collaborative and consistent approach between HR, line managers, occupational health advisers and the employee. It contains standardised trigger points that automatically initiate action. For example, occupational health advisers can contact absent employees after seven days to ascertain the situation. After 14 days' absence, they contact the employee to set a return-to-work date, explore possible modifications in the workplace to aid rehabilitation and develop an action plan with a timeline. This programme reduced absence rates by 60 per cent and saved £1.5 million at one site of 1,000 employees.

(Source: Griffiths 2005)

SPOTLIGHT ON THE LAW 12.1 DISMISSAL FOLLOWING STRESS-RELATED ILLNESS

In 2004, Doolan took six months' absence due to stress arising from his heavy workload. He recovered and was promoted in 2007 to a senior managerial position. However, within a short time, his stress condition returned and he was signed off work. In January 2008, his GP certified him as fit to return to work and a DWP doctor assessed his fitness, concluding that his incapacity benefit should cease. The company secured release of Doolan's medical records and sought advice from a health physician and an occupational psychologist. The former considered it difficult to predict whether he would fall ill again and this would depend on the strategies put in place to assist him. The psychologist reported that it was unlikely that Doolan could return to work in a demanding environment without potentially succumbing to further bouts of stress-related absence. After considering these reports, it was decided that Doolan should be dismissed on the grounds of capability and the EAT supported the company's actions.

(Source: *DB Schenker Rail (UK) Ltd v Doolan, EAT 13.04.11 (0053/09)*)

Assessment of external supply

If it is considered that internal supply factors are difficult to determine, then those for external supply present even greater problems. Here, it is the larger issues of economics and sociology that have the greatest influence in determining whether the right potential staff will present themselves at the gate, so to speak, to fill the available vacancies.

Economic factors include:

- *Local unemployment rates.* High unemployment rates should provide a greater source but this is not always the case as often the local unemployment is high because the skills level is low. Should specialist skills be wanted, then these may only be available in specific locations, especially London and other big centres.
- *The level of interest rates* can have an effect in that high rates may encourage the second earner in a family to wish to extend their hours to fund the higher mortgages.
- *The infrastructure*, which influences the ability to travel easily to the place of work.
- *The degree of competition* for labour in the area.

Sociological factors include:

- *The density of population* in the surrounding areas, their age structure and the availability of specific groups (full-time, part-time, graduates, school leavers, etc.).
- *Patterns of immigration into and emigration out of the area.* New towns have been very popular start-up sites because of the immigration of young families and skilled or semi-skilled workers into those towns. The new towns are attractive because their facilities – shopping, housing and leisure – are usually of high quality and readily available. Inner-city areas, on the contrary, are unpopular because such labour is generally moving out, being replaced by unskilled labour.
- The general *skills levels* in the area and the degree of government-backed support for improving skills generally.

General factors include:

- *The attractiveness of the company* as a place to work both in terms of its national 'brand' (IBM or Virgin carry a particular cachet and tend to attract more applicants than average) and the facilities in the workplace. A gleaming new office block with a health club, extensive car parking and haute cuisine restaurant will also tend to increase the supply of labour.
- *The links with educational establishments* and other sources of recruits.

The external factors are usually only considered in detail when organisations are considering relocating or setting up a new site. The sources of required labour are an important element in the decision process, along with land or rental cost, accessibility and any government assistance.

EXTENDED STUDENT ACTIVITY 12.2 – FORECASTING SUPPLY

Continuing with the scenario set out in activity 12.1, this exercise asks you to calculate the likely supply of labour at the hospital. Here are some of the internal factors that will influence the forecast:

Staff turnover (voluntary). The average turnovers for the last two years are as follows:

Nurses	Sisters	Admin supervisors	Support staff
20%	12%	10%	16%

In addition, three sisters and two admin supervisors have been promoted to higher positions within the organisation on average over the last four years.

Retirements. There will be two retirements each year in each of the groups for the next four years.

Promotions. When positions of sisters or admin supervisors become vacant, they are filled internally on 80 per cent of occasions.

Trainee nurses. Each year, 35 trainee nurses are recruited for a 3-year programme, 80 per cent of which usually complete the training programme.

Absenteeism has been a particular problem in respect of nurses, running at 10 per cent on average. A new agreed procedure has been introduced with the aim of reducing this to 6 per cent from year one.

In terms of *external factors*, temporary nurses can be recruited through local agencies but local sources of recruitment are becoming more difficult due to the recent opening of a private hospital in the area. Recruiting overseas, especially in the Far East, is being considered in principle.

Action required

Take each year in turn, starting with year one, and calculate the effect on the staffing in each category. You may be able to put this onto a spreadsheet to help your calculations (see Table 12.4). You may need to make certain assumptions as you go along – make sure you keep a note of these. The first calculation for nurses in years one and two has been carried out for you.

Internal supply of nurses. (Existing staff = 576 + 24 temps = 600 total)

Table 12.4 Internal supply of nurses

	Year 1	Year 2	Year 3	Year 4
Starting point for year (figure b from previous year)	600	624	665	
Voluntary turnover	−20% = −120	−20% = −125		
Retirements	= −2	= −2		
Trainees completing	= +28	= +28		
Improved absenteeism	+4% = +24	= +24		
Total (a)	= 530	= 549		
Number required (see demand) (b)	= 624	= 665		
Shortfall to be recruited in period (or surplus) (b−a)	= 94	= 116		

You will need to complete this table and draw up a similar table for the other three staff categories. So, for nurses, you will see the very high recruitment required, although you will find that this may alter by year four.

PRODUCING THE HUMAN RESOURCE PLAN

When the analysis of the right numbers and skills required (the demand for labour) and the factors that influence their supply has been carried out, the human resource plan reconciles the two and indicates how the shortfall can be met. On a few occasions, the plan indicates a surplus, so the plan will indicate how that surplus is to be shed.

The plan will consist of the traditional methods of dealing with the shortfall or surplus, which will involve a recruitment or disposal plan. However, the plan will also include ways in which recruitment or disposal can be minimised in the future through recommendations on human resource initiatives. Many of the proposals that could be included are set out in the relevant chapters on recruitment, training and other areas so the following will only be a short summary with indications of further reading.

Recruitment/selection plan. This will cover the sources and methods of recruitment/ selection including advertising campaigns, selection testing and proposals for dealing with particularly difficult recruitment areas. You will find examples of recruitment/selection issues and initiatives in Chapters 2 and 3. The system of recruitment may need to be overhauled to combat high attrition, as with O2 call centres in case study 12.4.

Retention plan. Although criticisms of exit interviews carried out by the organisation were set out earlier in the chapter, the information gleaned, especially from third parties, can often be enlightening. It may yield some of the following information:

- The payment systems can be inappropriate or not match up to that offered by the competition.
- The hours of work or shifts may not fit individuals' personal lives.
- Employees may be uncertain as to what is required of them or dissatisfied with the way they are assessed.
- The nature of the work, or the way it is organised, can be boring, undemanding or too stretching and in need of redesigning.
- The management processes may be criticised for being too controlled or too lax.
- The physical conditions may be unpleasant or unsafe.
- The opportunities for training, development and promotion may be too limited.
- Employees may have a sense of unfairness in the employment situation on the grounds of discrimination or through lack of communication or representation.

CASE STUDY

CASE STUDY 12.4 CUTTING ATTRITION AT O2 CALL CENTRES

In 2007, O2 was faced with the normal problem of high attrition at its call centres and, with the need to recruit 1,500 for its new Glasgow call centre (an area where there were already 160 call centres), and a decision was taken to revamp the recruitment and selection process. The new system used, as its heart, 'performance-based selection', which not only identified applicants who had the competence to do the job but also had the desire to do the job.

Following a sifting process involving an online application and a 20-minute telephone interview, applicants are invited to a 'Discover O2' assessment centre, involving a detailed tour of the work site and the role of call-centre staff in practice plus three assessments:

- An 'attitude and access' discussion, which assesses skills, competencies, motivation and work values by discussing in-depth four to six projects in which the candidate has been personally involved.
- An 'advice exercise', which is an improved variant of a simulation where applicants use their previous experience to think about how they will handle call-centre situations.
- Literacy, numeracy and IT testing.

After the sessions, applicants are measured against a candidate assessment profile including work values, motivation and culture. Those close to the required profile are offered a position.

The outcome has been seen to be successful in reaching its objectives, with a reduction in absenteeism and timekeeping problems, and the company won an Industry Recruiter of the Year award in 2007.

(Source: Murphy 2007)

Taking all these complaints together, it may be the case that the *level of engagement is low*. When the concept of engagement was discussed in Chapter 4, the methods of measuring engagement and the ways to try to increase the engagement outcome were explained and these need to be considered when putting together the HR plan. Included within the plan, therefore, can be change proposals on recruitment and selection, reward, effective ways of working, learning and development, performance management and the employment relationship. You will find a full discussion on all of these subject areas in the appropriate chapter, together with ideas on how initiatives can be constructed to ameliorate the problems.

Disposal plan. In the case where there is an identified surplus of labour, the plan to eliminate that surplus needs to be in place. That can include details of timings, legal consultations, and whether redundancies will be voluntary or compulsory. If compulsory, the selection procedure needs to be proposed and agreed. Alternatively, the surplus can be reduced through transfers, early retirement and natural wastage.

The 'soft' aspects. This final area concerns initiatives that may need to be introduced to meet strategic elements of the organisation's strategic plan. These deal with the need for organisational, cultural and behavioural changes and are essentially long-term processes. These include the drive to introduce a more flexible working environment, a greater concentration on quality through total quality management and quality circles, an emphasis on team-working and empowerment and encouraging employees to work more closely with the customers through customer-care campaigns. You will find more details of these subjects in earlier chapters in this book.

Introducing these initiatives is an activity not to be taken lightly. They have implications far beyond their immediate aims and have close links with other HR initiatives. In all of these areas, there need to be planned links with recruitment and selection where tests can be formulated to identify employees who are more likely to adopt flexible behaviours or those related to quality awareness, team-working or customer care. Extensive communication and training needs to be planned for all parties concerned with effective and regular evaluation. The integration of pay mechanisms to reward the desired behaviours also needs to be considered carefully and, if agreed as policy, carefully planned so that it acts effectively but does not disturb the existing (probably complex) pay system. There will also need to be a performance management scheme to support such pay mechanisms. A collection of these initiatives will aim to improve the level of employee engagement throughout the organisation.

Finally, it is now quite common for there to be the introduction of a competency framework throughout an organisation where flexibility, customer care, etc. are required competencies. Such a framework is a very long-term project, which needs highly detailed planning.

To improve the quality of HR planning, Boxall and Purcell (2008) suggest the following principles should apply:

■ *The stakeholder principle.* HR planning does not belong to the HR team and it should clearly meet the needs of all levels of line managers. In particular, it is vital to focus on those employees most affected by the outcomes of HR planning.

- *The involvement principle.* Only through dialogue with those centrally involved in managing people in the organisation can the quality of HR planning be improved. It should be driven by senior management but facilitated by the HR department who use their specialist expertise in research and communication to ensure that all sections of the workforce are involved in some way in the planned processes.
- *The rivalry principle.* Labour markets are competitive, and intelligent rivals will attempt to recruit the best people and build the best processes. So it is crucial to understand what competitors are doing in the HR area.
- *The dynamic principle.* This recognises the need for short- and long-term planning but also that constant changes and adaptations are necessary. Scenario planning is important here, looking at 'what-if' situations and moving from 'Plan A' to 'Plan B'.
- *The integration principle.* Ultimately, HR planning is only as good as its degree of constant integration with the business plan and its regular updates.

TECHNOLOGY

There are numerous software programs on the market related to human resource planning, which cover areas such as workforce demand forecasting, work scheduling and absence management. These are utilised by most large organisations as part of systems of employee data management. For example, Tameside Metropolitan Borough Council was required in 2009 to reduce its labour force by around 25 per cent and had to utilise its employee data management system to ensure that it retained all its necessary specialist skills and competencies (IDS 2011b). Involved in this process was the interrogation of absence and retention levels.

CONCLUSION

No human resource plan will be a valuable tool unless there has been *involvement and consultation* with the managers who will be implementing much of the programme. Nor should a plan be produced without the *main costs* being evaluated and a timescale placed on the constituent parts. A detailed plan involving heavy recruitment, training and a number of 'soft' initiatives will be expensive. Human resources sometimes have a reputation for inadequacy over effective costing and this is a major defect. Unless it is possible to demonstrate that a human resource plan is going to add value to the organisation and lead eventually to bottom-line improvements, the plan is unlikely to be accepted or effective when operated. It has to be delivered with conviction, even some passion, or it will carry little weight. For this reason, the rolling-out of the plan needs to take place with the overt *support of the chief executive* with the funds clearly committed.

HR planning can apply just as much to small and medium-sized organisations as to large ones (case study 12.5), as illustrated with an organisation employing just over 100 employees in case study 12.6.

CASE STUDY 12.5 PLANNING TO SOLVE SOCIAL WORKERS STAFF SHORTAGES AT ESSEX COUNTY COUNCIL

With employee numbers running beyond 40,000 and a budget of more than a billion pounds, Essex County Council was keen to ensure it had up-to-date workforce planning in place, which it achieved through a dedicated oracle system held in departmental databases. It became clear in the early 2000s that the perennial problem of shortages of qualified social workers was deteriorating, with vacancies at 25 per cent, more than twice the national average. Without a clear action plan, this problem could not be resolved.

Without a substantial increase in salaries and benefits (impossible in most cash-starved local authorities), it was unlikely to be able to make up the shortfall by recruiting from other authorities, so a more drastic solution was investigated – to focus on the capacity of existing staff. The Council carried out a survey of the time spent on 'skilled' social work activity, and how much on ancillary work, particularly administration, to identify how feasible it was to switch the administrative tasks to support staff, where recruitment was possible.

The survey also gave an opportunity for social work staff to buy into the proposal by suggesting how the service and their role could improve through changes in the way they carried out their work. A workshop took place before the survey was issued to explain the exact purpose of the survey and to dispel any fears about 'snooping'. Another workshop took place when the returns and analysis was completed to discuss the way forward. Many good ideas emerged and a number were implemented to release time for social workers to better use their skills and professional expertise, both in handling cases and in transferring skills to other staff, especially those in residential homes.

(Source: IRS 2003)

CASE STUDY 12.6 HR PLANNING AT A MEDIUM-SIZED ENTERPRISE

Harrod UK, a manufacturer of netting and sports equipment, employing 114 people, put into effect a 4-year rolling planning cycle, of which workforce planning is an integral part. The demand for labour and skills is made from the analysis of projected sales, staff turnover, absence and technological developments. Out of this analysis emerged the need to counter-balance the seasonal nature of the sports industry and move into horticultural netting and cages, so that the workforce could be fully engaged all year.

Training activities have arisen from the plan with a new programme of multi-skilling, monitored by a displayed matrix showing all the skills for each employee. This also acts as a development plan for each employee and has proved highly motivational. The HR manager has commented that: 'The formal planning process is useful – it means that I am not constantly trouble-shooting and can see more clearly what I need to do.'

(Source: Syedain 2010)

PUTTING TOGETHER A HUMAN RESOURCE PLAN

After her two-month orientation course at head office, Sarah joined the team at Forstairs, which was the new factory site in the throes of being built. The completion date was in October, five months ahead, but the management team had been appointed and all the planning was under way. Human resources at the site consisted of herself and Scott Hammond, HR manager, who was twenty-nine and had joined the organisation as a graduate five years earlier and who had experience of a similar unit, together with two years in the head office function as a training specialist.

In the first week on site, they set a day aside to start to draw up the human resource plan. Scott had already discussed the Forstairs business plan with the site director so he had a clear view of the planned culture for the site, the operations labour force, its skills and objectives. Scott suggested that they divide the day into two. The first part would be concerned with the 'number-crunching' side, working out the number of employees needed, their skills, profiles and training programmes. The second part would be concerned with the strategic elements, including the details of pay, incentives and benefits, the performance management system, the communication and involve-ment policy for the workforce and equal opportunities arrangements. From the start, Scott emphasised that the human resources policies would have to fit together into a coherent collection, or 'bundle', as was the current phrase.

The first part was dealt with smoothly with Sarah given the job of producing a Gantt chart that summarised the plan. She drew it up as shown in Table 12.5.

Employees would be phased in over the three-month period in batches of twenty. Sarah would produce a similar chart for all other groups of employees and these charts would be prominently displayed in her office and on the main notice board, and the progress to date would also be indicated. She also agreed to carry out a thorough pay survey to confirm that the original data collected 12 months earlier as a basis for the project proposal had not changed greatly. A final set of proposals would encompass the equal opportunities aspects of recruitment, selection, training and promotion which would take into account the nature of ethnic mix in the locality.

The discussions on strategy and policy took a good deal longer. They were required to work within a competency framework that had been designed by consult-ants some months earlier. This framework was divided into core competencies that all employees should develop, including problem-solving, quality focus and innovation, plus sets of specific competencies for departments and roles.

Scott considered that this framework should be the lynchpin for many of their activi-ties. For example, he wanted to test applicants to see how they matched the core compe-tencies. How close the resulting match came out would influence selection decisions. He also suggested that the performance management scheme should have a very clear focus on employees' performance in line with the competencies. Sarah was less happy with the

Table 12.5 Meteor Gantt chart

Operatives	June	July	August	Sept	Oct	Nov	Dec	Jan	Feb
Finalise job design	—								
Complete training schedules	—								
Liaise with partners (job centres, agencies, etc.)	—								
Advertise		—		—					
Interview, test		—	—	—	—				
Reference, select			—	—	—	—			
Induct and train					—	—	—		
Start prototype production									
Promote and train team leaders						—			—
First assessment at end of probationary period							—		
Start incentive scheme								—	

proposal that decisions on wages and salaries should be a direct outcome of such an assessment. She considered that a period of 'bedding in' for the framework was required before too much was weighted on it. It might crumble if it was not found to be sufficiently robust. She proposed instead a system of skills-based pay for the operatives with simple and transparent increases when individual skills modules had been achieved. Scott could see the merit in this proposal and asked her to put up a scheme in the next month, although he wanted a continuous stress on performance as part of the culture of the unit.

They needed a further meeting to discuss the system of employee representation, communication and involvement. Scott had some unhappy experiences of working with unions and wished to avoid having to recognise them. He proposed setting up an influential Employee Council from the start that had a strong role in consultation, a 'Kaizan-style' employee recognition scheme to encourage employees to join in the innovation process and briefing groups, and regular departmental meetings as an important part of the communication process. This 'bundle', he felt, would direct the employees towards positive support of the company's activities rather than the more negative aspects he associated with trade unions. Sarah agreed with the main drift but pointed out the difficulties associated with this approach that may cut across representation rights recently legislated.

They felt this was a good start and Scott agreed to arrange a meeting at the end of the month with the general management team to discuss the HR plan in detail.

EXTENDED STUDENT ACTIVITY 12.3

In activities 12.1 and 12.2, you have calculated the demand for staff and the internal supply factors which produce a deficit to be recruited or a surplus to reduce. In activity 12.3, you need to put together the human resource plan. This will set out how you plan to remedy the deficit and deal with the surplus. You will have seen in the text that the report should be in two parts. The first part will deal with the immediate policy of recruitment and disposal, in other words, the methods and sources of recruitment and the decisions to be made over disposal. Both issues are linked because you may decide to make redundancies, engage a policy of recruiting on a temporary basis or keep the surplus and reduce by natural wastage. In your report, set out which policy you adopt and why.

The second part will be your recommendations on how to avoid being faced with such large recruitment numbers in future years. In other words, the policies you would use to reduce staff turnover or the improved training you would implement to ensure a larger supply of nurses for the future. Make sure your recommendations are relevant to this case study.

KEY CHAPTER SUMMARY POINTS

- Human resource planning can be divided into the 'hard' aspects, which deal with quantitative data, such as the numbers and skills of employees required, and the 'soft' aspects that are involved with corporate culture and organisational development.
- Planning now has a much shorter timescale than in previous decades due to the unpredictable changes that organisations face and the need to respond in a flexible way.
- Aspects of planning include contingency planning, succession planning, developing skills and competencies and behavioural objectives.
- Retention and absence levels are key features in planning and reducing and both have an important effect on cost saving. Low levels will reflect the level of employee engagement.
- Planning involves identifying future demand and internal supply, identifying the gaps between the two and planning to fill them.

STUDENT ACTIVITIES

1   In the CIPD labour turnover research, the cost of replacement of employees who leave is high. Why is this?

2   In the Meteor case study, Sarah has put together a comprehensive human resource plan. Think about what could go wrong or what difficulties could be faced and work out how you could deal with these problems.

3   Read the article about the staff shortages in Essex County Council. Think of other areas where there are shortages of professional staff (accounting, legal, planning, hospitals) and suggest ideas how these shortages could be reduced through changes in job design.

4   Role-play the situation of an interview with an employee coming back to work in an engineering environment after an extended period of absence through having a bad back.

5   Using some of the ideas in case study 12.4, consider proposals to change the recruitment of one key job in your organisation that would aim to reduce the attrition rate.

REFERENCES

Allison, K. (2012) New Panel for Fitness at Work. *People Management*, January, 19.

Armstrong, M. (1996) *Employee Reward*. CIPD.

— (2009) *A Handbook of Human Resource Management Practice*. Kogan Page.

Barney, J. and Wright, P. (1998) On Becoming a Strategic Partner. The Role of Human Resources in Gaining Competitive Advantage. *Human Resource Management*, 37(1): 16–46.

Boxall, P. and Purcell, J. (2008) *Strategy and Human Resource Management*, 2nd ed. Palgrave Macmillan.

Brockett, J. (2007) MPs Condemn NHS Workforce Planning. *People Management*, 5 April, 10.

CIPD (2012a) Resourcing and Talent Planning. CIPD.

— (2012b) Absence Management. CIPD.

Dunn, C. and Wilkinson, A. (2002) Wish You Were Here: Managing Absence. *Personnel Review*, 31(2): 228–246.

Griffiths, J. (2005) Flexible Working Can Keep Your Absence Rates Healthy. *People Management*, 5 May, 14.

Hookham, M. and Mansey, K. (2012) NHS Workers Face Sack Over Double Whammy Sick Pay. *Sunday Times*, 11 November, 7.

Huber, N. (2011) Exit Interviews – Curing a Revolving Door Policy. *Professional Manager*, 11 November.

IDS (2011a) Absence Report. *HR Study 936*, February, 29–31.

— (2011b) Workforce Planning. *HR Study 944*, June.

Iles, P. (2001) Employee Resourcing, in J. Storey (ed.) *Human Resource Management: A Critical Text*, 2nd ed. Thomson Learning.

IRS (2003) Planning. *Employment Review 790*, 19 December, 43–48.

— (2007) Managing Absence: Records, Triggers and Targets. *Employment Review 876*, 2 July.

Lalali, M., Meadows, P., Metcalf, H. and Rolfe, H. (2012) *Evaluation of the Statement of Fitness for Work*. Department of Work and Pensions.

Morris, H. and Willey, B. (1996) *The Corporate Environment: A Guide for Human Resource Managers*. Financial Times/Prentice Hall.

Murphy, N. (2007) O2 Revamps Hiring to Reduce Call Centre Attrition. *IRS Employment Review 879*, 20 August.

Purcell, J. and Hutchison, S. (2007) Front-line Managers as Agents in the HRM-performance Causal Chain. *Human Resource Management Journal*, 17(1): 3–20.

Robinson, D. (2010) *Workforce Planning during Bleak Times*. Institute of Employment Studies. October.

Rothwell, S. (1995) Human Resource Planning, pp. 167–202, in J. Storey (ed.) *Human Resource Management: A Critical Text*. Routledge.

Ryle, S. (2004) Tesco Axes Sick Pay to Reduce 'Days Off' Cheats, *The Observer*, 16 May.

Simms, J. (2003) The Generation Game. *People Management*, 6 February, 26–31.

Sparrow, P. (1992) Human Resource Planning at Engindorf plc, pp. 252–259, in D. Winstanley and J. Woodall (eds) *Case Studies in Personnel*. IPD.

Syedain, H. (2010) A Force for Good. *People Management*, 3 June, 24–26.

Taylor, S. (2010) *Resourcing and Talent Management*. CIPD.

Ulrich, D. (1987) Strategic Resource Planning: Why and How? *Human Resource Planning*, 10(1): 37–56.

ADDITIONAL FEATURES

Please visit the companion website at: www.routledge.com/cw/stredwick where you will find additional case studies and reading material together with short self-tests and other resources for both students and lectures.

SUBJECT INDEX

3M PLC 291
360-degree feedback 203–211
1998 Workplace Employee Relations Survey 9

AA 170
Ability test 95
Absenteeism 481–487
    Actions to tackle absenteeism 484–487
    Causes 481–483
    Measuring absence 483
        Bradford formula 484
    Return to work interviews 485
    Sick pay scheme 483
ACAS 133–135
    Code of practice on discipline 153
    Conciliation in dismissal 157
    Conciliation in discrimination 379–380
Action learning 334
Activists 307
Adidas 45
Advertising 65–71
    Agencies 66
    Designing advertisements 68
    Mention of salary 69
AEHN Hospital 22
Africa 454–456
Age discrimination 364, 371, 393
Allen and Overy 277
Annualised hours 278–280
Application form 72
Appraisal interview 200
Apprenticeships (Modern) 338–339, 346
Aptitude tests 95
Arup 226

ASDA 388
Assessment centres 114–116, 327
AstraZeneca 265
Astrology 89
Attitude surveys 138
Automation 47
Automated telephone screening 77

B&Q 225
BBC 288
Balanced scorecard 189
Bargaining 137
Beaverbrooks 44
Belief discrimination 371–372
Benefits 263–265
Behavioural Anchored Rating Scale (BARS) 195
Behavioural observation scales 196
Best fit 29
Best practice 20, 29
Best value 288
Beyer 113
Biodata 93
Black box (opening), 23
Blended learning 326
Bloom's taxonomy 309
Bodyshop 116
BP 259
Bradford formula (absenteeism) 484
Briefing groups 139
British Airways 264
Brittania Building Society 224
Broad-banding pay structure 246–249
BT 204
Bullying 391–392

'Bundles' of HR practices 25
Business context 4
Business partners 17

Cable & Wireless PLC
California Psychological Inventory 90
Call centres 289–290
Cattell PF test 98
Career break 294
Centres of expertise 15
Centrica 143, 283, 288
CERN 78
Childcare provision 294
China 451–454
Claridges Hotel 30–31
Coaching 333, 335
Cognitive learning 306
Company council 142–5
Competency-based pay 263
Competency-based targets 190
Competency-based test 97
Competency framework 58, 188–190
    Difficulties with 194–195
Competency profile 60–62
'Complimentary' employees 277
Computerised training 323
Conciliation 134
Constructive dismissal 158
Continuous professional development 336
Contracting-out work 47
Conversational interviews 113
Corporate Manslaughter and Corporate
    Homicide Act 2007
COSHH regulations 1988 411–412
Crossrail 348–9
Culture, national 437–446
Cultural convergence and divergence
    443–445
CV 71
    Scanning 76
Cyberbullying 375
Cybernetics 309

Davies Report 2011 359
Department of Work and Pensions 340

Disability discrimination 368
    Reasonable adjustments 368–369
    Requirements 380–390
Discipline 152–156
Discrimination
    Compensation 367, 376, 378–380
    Direct 363
    Indirect 363
    and Tests 101
Dismissal 155–163
    Constructive 158–159
    Inadmissable reasons 160
    Long-term absence 161
    Unfair 155–157
Disney Corporation 257
Distance learning 324
Downshifting 277

Eircom 141
E-learning 322
Employee assistance programme (EAP)/
    well-being scheme 423, 431
Employee engagement 37, 145–150, 389
Employee involvement 25, 137–140
Employee observation 51
Employee recognition schemes 139
Employee security 26
Employee voice 26
Employer branding 43–45, 361
Empowerment 291–292
Enforcement notice 415
Engagement see employee engagement
Enrichment 22
Equality Acts 2006, 2010 363
Equality and Human Rights Commission 358,
    377–378
Equality industry: criticism 396
Equality targets 381–382
Equal opportunities 357–399
    Application to tribunals 379
    Audits 384–385
    Business case 359
    Monitoring 394
    Implications for EO practice 384–396
    Strategies 385

Equal pay 243, 369–370, 392
  and Gender gap 296
Equal Pay Act 243
Equal value regulations 1983 369–370
EU Directive on Information and Consultation of
        Employees (ICE regulations) 2005 142
European Works Council Directive 1994 142
Executive pay 256–263
  and Bankers 257
Executive search agencies 66
Exit interviews 320, 480
Expatriates 459
Expectancy theory 231

Factor-points system (job evaluation) 236–243
Family-friendly policies 292–295
Female earnings compared to men's 359
Females on boards 448
Financial involvement 139
Flexible benefits 264–265, 443
Flexible working 273–302
  Core and periphery model 274
  Geographical 282–290
  and Gender gap 296
  Numerical 281
  Occupational 290
  Outsourcing 285–287
  Policies that support 292–295
  Right to request 292
  and Talent management 296
  Temporal flexibility 276–280
  and Technology 299
Flexible firm 273–275
  Core and periphery model 274
Flexible working hours 294
Flexible working regulations 292
Flexitime 294

G4S 82
Gainsharing 250–251
Genuine Occupational Qualification 365
GKN 473
Globalisation 6
Globe study of cultural effectiveness 439–440
  Relevance of 441

Goal theory 231
Google 33–34, 53
Government initiatives in learning and
        development 342–351
Government role in employee relations 136
GrandMet PLC 361
Graphology 89
Grievance 151
Gross misconduct 156
GSK 223

Half-life index 479
Halifax bank 361
Harassment see sexual and racial
        harassment
Hay Guide Chart-Profile 240
Hay: Total Reward strategy 225
Hazard identification 418
  Hazard rating chart 419
Health and Safety Executive 411
Health and safety legislation 404
Health and Safety at Work Act 1974 405–411
Health, safety and welfare
  Costs 403
  Days lost 403
  Duty on designers 410–411
  Duty on employees 409–410
  Duty on employers 406–409
  Duty on sub-contractors 408–409
  Enforcement of law 415
  and Equal opportunities 390
  and European legislation 412–413
  Fatal accidents 402
  Health and Safety Commission 411
  and Occupational stress 420–425
  and Risk assessment 418–419
  and Role of human resources 427–431
      Welfare issues and policies 419
Hertfordshire County Council 284, 362,
        382
Hertfordshire Constabulary 80
Hewlett Packard 253–254
Hierarchy of needs (Maslow) theory 229
High performance management 23–30
  Barriers 34

Holstede's analysis of national cultures 437–439
  Relevance of 441
Homeworking 282–285
Horizontal flexibility 291
HR practitioners roles 9
HRM: policy goals 10
Human resource planning 467–498
  Future demand for labour 476–478
  Future supply of labour 478
    External 488
  'Hard' aspects 474
  Purpose 470
  Reasons for lack of 469
  'Soft' aspects 493
  Sources of HR plan 474
  Turnover of labour 478–479
Hygiene factors (Herzberg) 230

IBM 338
Ikea 116
Improvement notice 415
Induction 329–330
In-sourcing work 47
Internal candidates 63–64
International HRM 435–466
  Convergence and divergence 443–5
  Culture and HRM 437–445
  Global comparisons: Japan, China, Africa 446
  Globalisation of markets 441
  HRM in multinational corporations 456
  Models and strategies 456
  Multinationals (MNCs) and staffing 456–457
  Offshoring 458
Interviews 103–114
  Criterion-based interview 110–111
  Conversational interviews 113
  Hypothetical question 109
  Panel 105–106
  Paired 105–106
  Patterned behaviour descriptive interview 111
  Probing 108
  Problems associated 103–104

  Structured 112–113
  Techniques 107–109
  Who carries out interview 105–106
International staffing 457–8
Interns 48–49
Investors in people (IIP) 348
Involvement see employee involvement
Ipsative test format 99

Japan 449–451
Job analysis 50–51
Job Centres 67
Job description 52–54
Job evaluation 235–243
  Analytical schemes 236–243
  Difficulties with 245–246
  Non-analytical schemes 236
Job instruction 323
Job offer 120
Job profile 54
Job rotation 323
Job shares 275
John Lewis Partnership 78, 140, 224

Kaizen 345
Knowledge management 341
Kolb's Learning Cycle 306–307
KPMG 77, 327

Learning organisation 311–313
Learning and talent development 304–356
  Assessing training needs 317–320
  Assessment of learners 326
  Barriers to learning 311
  Evaluating training 328
  Government initiatives 342–351
  How people learn 306–310
  Learning across generations 317
  Learning by association 308
  Learning cycle 306
  Learning on and off job 321–322
  Legal considerations 351
  Reinforcement 310
  Styles and techniques 322
  Tailored approach to learning 313

Leitch Report 2006 350
Legal and general 144
LexisNexis 118
Lifelong learning 350
LinkedIn 80
Liverpool Victoria 17
L'Oréal 79

McDonalds 93
Macleod Report (on engagement) 2009
    145–146
Macpherson Report 1999
Managing diversity (and equal opportunities)
    383–384
Management development 340
Manpower PLC 281
Manual handling operations regulations
    412
Market tracking (pay) 241–242
Marks and Spencer 80
Mentoring 322–333
Metropolitan Housing Trust 59
Microsoft 79
Ministry of Defence 19, 110
Misdemeanour 156
Mobile learning 326
Modern Apprenticeships 338
Motivation 228–232
    Cognitive theories 231–232
    Equity theory 231
    Goal theory 231
    Instrumentality theory 228
    Needs theories 228–231
Multi-skilling 290–291

National Health Service 76, 134, 181, 331,
    341
National minimum wage 242
National Traineeships 346
National training targets 346
National Vocational Qualifications (NVQs)
    344–346
New Deal/Flexible New Deal 347
Nottingham City Hospital 48
Numerical flexibility 281

Occupational flexibility 290
Occupational stress 420–425
    Business case in respect of 427
    Causes 420–421
    Cost of 420
    Ethical case in respect of 428
    Extent of 420
    Legal issues 421–422
    Management initiatives to combat 423
    Monitoring 428
    Policies to combat stress 425
    Role of human resources 425
Offshoring 458
On target earnings (OTE) 70
Open University 210
Opportunity Now Awards 298
Optical character recognition 93
Outdoor training 332
Outsourcing 285–290
Outsourcing training 322
Overseas subsidiaries, strategies for 456–457
Owen, Robert 8

Paired interviews 105–6
Pairing for performance scheme 208
Panel interview 106
Participation, employee 137–138
Partnership agreements 143–145
Part-time employees 276–277
Patterned behavioural description interview
    111
Paying for performance 251–256
    Criticisms of 255–256
Penguin Books 388
Pepsico 297
Personal development plan 319
Performance agreements 184
    and Civil servants 212
    and Development 212
    and Discipline 212
    Interview 200
    Measuring 185–187
    Pay 28, 211
    Raising 184–185
    and Role of HR 215

Performance management 177–220
   360-degree feedback 203–211
   Balanced scorecard 189
   Competence-based systems 188–190
     Difficulties with 194–195
   and Equal opportunities 390
   Providing feedback 197–211
   Purpose 179–181
   Ratings 194–195, 252–255
   SMART 186
   Stages in 182
   Targets 186–188
     Difficulties with 191–193
   Title 182
   and Trust 181–182
Person specification 54, 58–63
Personal contracts 135
Personality tests *see* selection testing
Piecework 249
Pluralist approach to employee relations 130
Portfolio workers 277
Positive action (equal opportunities) 381–382,
   395
Pragmatists 308
Prediction market democracy 140
Pret a Manger 117
Prudential Corporation 18
Public and Commercial Services Union 290
Psychological contract 227–228, 286–287
Psychological corporation 96

Questions, interview
   Hypothetical 109
   Probing 108
   Situational 109

RAC 279
Race discrimination 365–366
Racial harassment 376–377
Rating schemes 194–195, 252–253
Reckitt Benckiser 116
Recognition schemes 139, 250–252
Recruitment 42–87
   Agencies 66

Application form 72
Attracting applicants 63–72
Cost 42
and Equal opportunities 386–387
Policy 46
Responsibility for 81
Using third parties 64–67
Using mail-shots 74
Using technology 75–80
Using word of mouth 74, 364
Redundancy 163–172
   Assisting employees in 169–170
   Causes 163–164
   Consultation 164
   Legislation concerning 164
   and Maternity leave 168
   Pay 169
   Reducing labour costs 165–166
   Rights of employees 164
   Role of human resources 170–171
   Selection for 166–168
   Special envoys in 171
References 118–120
Reflectors 307
Relationships with employees 127–176
   Discipline and grievances 151–162
   Employee engagement 145–150
   Government role 136–137
   Involvement and participation 137–145
   Workplace negotiating 128–136
   Third parties 133–136
   Trade unions 128–130
Religion or belief discrimination 371
Resource-based view of the firm 32–33
Retention and equal opportunities 389
Retention plan 479
Return to work interviews 485
Rewarding employees 221–271
   Basic pay 234–240
   Benefits 263–265
   Changing nature of 223
   Competence-based pay 263
   Component parts 233–2334
   Equal pay 243

Executive pay 256–263
Group incentive schemes 230
Job evaluation 235–243
Market tracking 241–242
National minimum wage 242
Pay for performance (PRP) 249–256
Recognition schemes 250–251
Salary structures 243–251
Skills-based pay 263
RIDDOR regulations 1995 413
Risk assessment 418–419
RMT union 129
Role-plays 323
Royal Bank of Scotland 259
Royal Mail 16

Safety committees 416
Safety officer 415
Safety representatives 416
Sainsburys PLC 189, 264
Salary structure 244–251
   Traditional 244–246
   Broad-banded structure 246–249
Sales training 336
Santander (Abbey National) 54–57, 277
Saville and Holdsworth 96
Sector Skills Councils 343
Scottish Power 424
Selection 88–126
   and Equal opportunities 387
   Evaluation 121
   Interviews 103–114
   Systems approach 90
   Validity chart 89
Selection testing 94–102
   Ability 95
   Aptitude 95–96
   Personality 97–99
Self-managed teams 27
Sexual harassment 360, 374–376, 391–392
Sexual orientation discrimination 373
Sex discrimination 365
Shared services 16, 290
Short-listing 92

Sick pay schemes 483
Simulations in selection 116
Situational judgment test 78
Skills-based pay 263
Skills funding agency 343
'SMART' targets 186
Social media
   and Dismissal 163
   and Recruitment 78
Social resumé 71
Social learning 309
Social networking
   and Recruitment 76–77
   and Discipline 163
Sony Europe 201
Strategic partnering 13
Stress see occupational stress
Strikes 130
Structured interview 112–113
Succession planning 473
Supported learning 325

Talent management 27, 35, 89–90, 296,
   313, 457
Targets for performance 186–188
Teams (building) 330, 332
Technology 5
   in Flexibility 299
   in Recruitment 75–80
   in Reward 265–266
   in Selection 116
   and Unfair dismissal 162
Telephone screening 93
Teleworking 282–285
   Difficulties with 285
Temporal flexibility 276–280
Tesco 259
Theorists 307
Total Reward 225–227
Tournament theory 258
Trade unions 128–137
   Membership 129
   Recognition 131–132
Training aims and objectives 314

Training cycle 316
Triplex Safety Glass 224
TUPE regulations 289
Turnover of labour 478–480

UK Commission for Employment and Skills
343
Unfair dismissal 157–163
Unilever 265
Union penetration 128
Unitary approach to employee relations 130
University of Bedfordshire 116
Unsupported learning 325

Vacancy analysis 46
Vertical flexibility 291
Victimisation 373

Video-conferencing 116
Virtual business game 78
V-time 277

Wachman, R. 257
Wastage index 478
Welfare Workers Association 8
Wetherspoon pubs 361, 395
Whitbread 76
Working time regulations 412
Work–life balance 264, 294–295, 297–298,
389

Xerox Corporation 47, 281

Zero-hour contracts 277–278
Zotefoams 24

AUTHOR INDEX

Adams, J. 231
Ahlstrand, B. 11
Armstrong, M. 182, 224, 239, 245, 247, 314
Ashman, I, 171
Atkinson, J. 274

Bacon, N. 143
Barney, J. 471
Becon, A. 180
Beer, M. 253
Bennett, R. 305
Bewley, H. 135
Bloom, B. 309
Boxall, P. 228, 493
Braid, M. 288
Brewster, C. 446
Brockbank, W. 13
Brophy, E. 179

Cockburn, C. 359
Corby, S. 380
Cowan, N. 118
Coyne 374

Dowling, P. 456

Edwards, P. 164
Employee Advocate 14
Evans, C. 297

Farley, J. 453
Forth, J. 135
Fowler, A. 418

France, S. 205

Gennard, J. 136
Graves, E. 103
Griffiths, J. 488
Guest, D. 10, 132, 143, 227–8

Hall, M. 164
Handy, C. 277
Hann, D. 143
Harrison, R. 312
Harry, W. 445
Hayday, S. 147
Hayes, J. 280
Herzberg, F. 230
Higgs 43
Hofstede, G. 437
Holbeche, L. 18, 150
Honey, P. 306
House, R. 440
Huselid, M. 24, 29
Huws, V. 288

Instler, D. 180

Jackson, A. 326
Judge, G. 136

Kandola, R. 383
Karren, R. 103
Kessler, I. 447
Kim, W. 34
Kim, Y. 454
Kohn, A. 255

Kolb, D. 30

Latham, G. 186
Lazear, S. 258
Legge, K. 32
Leighton, D. 275
Linman, T. 211
Locke, E. 186, 231
Lynch, R. 136

Mabey, C. 201
McCarthy, D. 141
McClelland, D. 190
Marchington, M. 30
Marrin, N. 396
Marsden, D. 251
Maslow, A. 229
Mathison, D. 200
Matthews, G. 150
Mauborgne, R. 34
Mayer, R. 182
Milkovitch, G. 248–9
Millward, N. 138
Moorby, E. 311
Mumford, A. 306
Murlis, H. 245, 261
Murphy, N. 492

Newell, S. 90

Palcic, D. 141
Patterson, M. 24, 28
Peters, T. 178
Pickard, J. 17
Purcell, J. 11, 30, 228,
   481

Ramsey, H. 23
Reid, M. 321
Reilly, P. 19, 144
Richardson, R. 251
Rice, C. 90
Roberts, G. 114

Roberts, Z. 44, 345
Robertson, I. 89
Robinson, D. 147
Rothwell 469
Rucci, A. 21

Samuel, P. 143
Sartorious, K. 456
Sedgwick, M. 116
Senge, P. 311
Sisson, K. 305
Smith, M. 89
Spears, J. 116
Speechley, N.
Spurgeon, P. 420
Stredwick, J. 281
Stiles, P. 444
Storey, J. 10, 32, 305
Suff, R. 114, 11
Swann, W. 178
Swart, J.

Tayeb, M. 442
Taylor, F. 229, 249
Taylor, S. 471
Teague, P. 143
Thompson, D. 140
Thompson, M. 24, 30, 251
Tietze, S. 286
Trompenaars, F. 99

Ulrich, D. 13, 470
Undy, R. 242

Vroom, V. 231

Waples, J. 261
Ward, K. 114
West, M. 28, 181
Wick, C. 311
Willmott, B. 422
Wolff, C. 293
Woolliams, P. 99